Blackstone's Statutes
Employment Law

Blackstone's Statutes

Employment Law

....

2006–2007

Sixteenth Edition

Edited by

Richard Kidner

MA, BCL

Professor of Law, University of Wales, Aberystwyth

OXFORD

UNIVERSITY PRESS

OXFORD
UNIVERSITY PRESS

Great Clarendon Street, Oxford OX2 6DP

Oxford University Press is a department of the University of Oxford.
It furthers the University's objective of excellence in research, scholarship,
and education by publishing worldwide in

Oxford New York

Auckland Cape Town Dar es Salaam Hong Kong Karachi
Kuala Lumpur Madrid Melbourne Mexico City Nairobi
New Delhi Shanghai Taipei Toronto

With offices in

Argentina Austria Brazil Chile Czech Republic France Greece
Guatemala Hungary Italy Japan Poland Portugal Singapore
South Korea Switzerland Thailand Turkey Ukraine Vietnam

Oxford is a registered trade mark of Oxford University Press
in the UK and in certain other countries

Published in the United States
by Oxford University Press Inc., New York

This selection © Richard Kidner 2006

First published by Blackstone Press

First edition 1988	Sixth edition 1996	Eleventh edition 2001
Second edition 1991	Seventh edition 1997	Twelfth edition 2002
Third edition 1993	Eighth edition 1998	Thirteenth edition 2003
Fourth edition 1994	Ninth edition 1999	Fourteenth edition 2004
Fifth edition 1995	Tenth edition 2000	Fifteenth edition 2005

Sixteenth edition 2006

British Library Cataloguing in Publication Data

Data available

Typeset by Newgen Imaging Systems (P) Ltd., Chennai, India
Printed in Great Britain
on acid-free paper by
CPI Bath

ISBN 0–19–928820–8   ISBN 978–0–19–928820–5

1 3 5 7 9 10 8 6 4 2

CONTENTS

PART III   Non-Statutory Materials   458

PART IV   European Community Materials   506

PART V   **International Obligations**   **540**

ALPHABETICAL CONTENTS

CHRONOLOGICAL CONTENTS

EDITOR'S PREFACE

This collection of statutes is primarily intended for students of Employment Law (whether the subject is called Employment Law or Labour Law or Industrial Law), and it includes all those statutes and parts of statutes which a student may be referred to. The subject is now mainly statutory and it is impossible to study it satisfactorily without constant reference to the statutes, for much of the case law depends to a great extent on interpretation. However, a student does not need to have access to every detail of the vast array of statutory material and accordingly the purpose of this collection is to provide at a low cost those provisions which are central to a study of employment law.

The selection has been made on the basis of what students might be referred to in their courses and the collection is necessarily not comprehensive but I hope that I have not omitted anything of relevance. Generally, I have omitted material which relates only to particular employments (such as dock workers or teachers), together with minor, regulatory or empowering provisions. Nevertheless, what has been provided covers all the law relevant for students of Employment Law, Discrimination Law, Trade Union Law and Collective Bargaining and I hope that students will find the collection useful, and a relatively inexpensive aid to the proper understanding of the subject. The statutes are not of course the whole story, but they are an essential prerequisite to appreciating the structure, nature and purpose of Employment Law.

This sixteenth edition is fully up-to-date and includes materials available to me up to June 2006. One feature of current practice is that statutes mainly take effect by amending the two principal Consolidation Acts, so that while a statute may not appear in this book under its own title, nevertheless its provisions are fully incorporated into existing legislation. This may make it more difficult to identify the changes, but it has the advantage of presenting the student with the current position as a coherent whole.

New extracts for this edition are taken from the Equality Act 2006, the Transfer of Undertakings (Protection of Employment) Regulations 2006, the Employment Equality (Age) Regulations 2006 and the Commission for Racial Equality Code of Practice on Racial Equality in Employment (2005). Amendments to existing legislation have been made by the Employment Equality (Sex Discrimination) Regulations 2005, the Working Time (Amendment) Regulations 2006 and the Information and Consultation of Employees (Amendment) Regulations 2006. All these changes have been incorporated into the text, together with other minor amendments.

There is also an Online Resource Centre which lists new material enacted since this book went to press as well as forthcoming material which is expected in the near future. This is available at www.oxfordtextbooks.co.uk/orc/statutes/.

The task of selection is becoming ever more difficult especially as regulations become even more complex and repetitive. Nevertheless, it is hoped that this book presents within a reasonable compass and at a reasonable price all the major legislation which a student will need to refer to.

Finally, I am most grateful to Oxford University Press for the remarkable efficiency and speed with which this book has been brought to press.

The statutes are arranged in chronological order (and alphabetically within years) and are printed as amended to 1 June 2006.

Richard Kidner

USEFUL WEBSITES

HMSO *www.opsi.gov.uk/legislation/about_legislation.htm*

This lists all UK Acts since 1988 and all UK statutory instruments since 1988, as well as Scottish, Welsh and Northern Irish legislation. It also lists draft statutory instruments.

The 'New Legislation' section lists all material added to the site in the previous two weeks.

Parliament *www.publications.parliament.uk/pa/pabills.htm*

This gives the text of all Bills currently before Parliament. For information on how a Bill is progressing go to the Weekly Information Bulletin at *www.publication.parliament.uk/pa/cm/cmwib.htm*. To find out how a draft statutory instrument is progressing see *www.publications.parliament.uk/pa/cm/cmsilist/cmsilist.htm*.

DTI *www.dti.gov.uk/er/hot_topics.htm*

This is the site of the Department of Trade, Employment Relations Directorate which contains consultation papers and draft regulations.

Europe *www.europa.eu.int/eur-lex/en/lif/ind/en_analytical_index_05.html*

This provides an index to Directives, most of which will be found under 'working conditions'.

ACAS *www.acas.org.uk*

This is the site of the Advisory Conciliation and Arbitration Service and under 'what's new' will list impending changes to Codes of Practice etc.

Equal Opportunities Commission *www.eoc.org.uk*

Commission for Racial Equality *www.cre.gov.uk*

Disability Rights Commission *www.drc-gb.org/*

PART I

Statutes of the UK Parliament

Equal Pay Act 1970
(1970, c. 41)

1 Requirement of equal treatment for men and women in same employment

(1) If the terms of a contract under which a woman is employed at an establishment in Great Britain do not include (directly or by reference to a collective agreement or otherwise) an equality clause they shall be deemed to include one.

(2) An equality clause is a provision which relates to terms (whether concerned with pay or not) of a contract under which a woman is employed (the 'woman's contract'), and has the effect that—

   (a) where the woman is employed on like work with a man in the same employment—

   (i) if (apart from the equality clause) any term of the woman's contract is or becomes less favourable to the woman than a term of a similar kind in the contract under which that man is employed, that term of the woman's contract shall be treated as so modified as not to be less favourable, and

   (ii) if (apart from the equality clause) at any time the woman's contract does not include a term corresponding to a term benefiting that man included in the contract under which he is employed, the woman's contract shall be treated as including such a term;

   (b) where the woman is employed on work rated as equivalent with that of a man in the same employment—

   (i) if (apart from the equality clause) any term of the woman's contract determined by the rating of the work is or becomes less favourable to the woman than a term of a similar kind in the contract under which that man is employed, that term of the woman's contract shall be treated as so modified as not to be less favourable, and

   (ii) if (apart from the equality clause) at any time the woman's contract does not include a term corresponding to a term benefiting that man included in the contract under which he is employed and determined by the rating of the work, the woman's contract shall be treated as including such a term.

   (c) where a woman is employed on work which, not being work in relation to which paragraph (a) or (b) above applies, is, in terms of the demands made on her (for instance under such headings as effort, skill and decision), of equal value to that of a man in the same employment—

   (i) if (apart from the equality clause) any term of the woman's contract is or becomes less favourable to the woman than a term of a similar kind in the contract under which that man is employed, that term of the woman's contract shall be treated as so modified as not to be less favourable, and

   (ii) if (apart from the equality clause) at any time the woman's contract does not include a term corresponding to a term benefiting that man included in the contract under which he is employed, the woman's contract shall be treated as including such a term.

(d) where—

    (i) any term of the woman's contract regulating maternity-related pay provides for any of her maternity-related pay to be calculated by reference to her pay at a particular time,

    (ii) after that time (but before the end of the statutory maternity leave period) her pay is increased, or would have increased had she not been on statutory maternity leave, and

    (iii) the maternity-related pay is neither what her pay would have been had she not been on statutory maternity leave nor the difference between what her pay would have been had she not been on statutory maternity leave and any statutory maternity pay to which she is entitled,

if (apart from the equality clause) the terms of the woman's contract do not provide for the increase to be taken into account for the purpose of calculating the maternity-related pay, the term mentioned in sub-paragraph (i) above shall be treated as so modified as to provide for the increase to be taken into account for that purpose;

(e) if (apart from the equality clause) the terms of the woman's contract as to—

    (i) pay (including pay by way of bonus) in respect of times before she begins to be on statutory maternity leave,

    (ii) pay by way of bonus in respect of times when she is absent from work in consequence of the prohibition in section 72(1) of the Employment Rights Act 1996 (compulsory maternity leave), or

    (iii) pay by way of bonus in respect of times after she returns to work following her having been on statutory maternity leave,

do not provide for such pay to be paid when it would be paid but for her having time off on statutory maternity leave, the woman's contract shall be treated as including a term providing for such pay to be paid when ordinarily it would be paid;

(f) if (apart from the equality clause) the terms of the woman's contract regulating her pay after returning to work following her having been on statutory maternity leave provide for any of that pay to be calculated without taking into account any amount by which her pay would have increased had she not been on statutory maternity leave, the woman's contract shall be treated as including a term providing for the increase to be taken into account in calculating that pay.

(3) An equality clause falling within subsection (2)(a), (b) or (c) above shall not operate in relation to a variation between the woman's contract and the man's contract if the employer proves that the variation is genuinely due to a material factor which is not the difference of sex and that factor—

(a) in the case of an equality clause falling within subsection (2)(a) or (b) above, must be a material difference between the woman's case and the man's; and

(b) in the case of an equality clause falling within subsection (2)(c) above, may be such a material difference.

(4) A woman is to be regarded as employed on like work with men if, but only if, her work and theirs is of the same or a broadly similar nature, and the differences (if any) between the things she does and the things they do are not of practical importance in relation to terms and conditions of employment; and accordingly in comparing her work with theirs regard shall be had to the frequency or otherwise with which any such differences occur in practice as well as to the nature and extent of the differences.

(5) A woman is to be regarded as employed on work rated as equivalent with that of any men if, but only if, her job and their job have been given an equal value, in terms of the demand made on a worker under various headings (for instance effort, skill, decision), on a study undertaken with a view to evaluating in those terms the jobs to be done by all or any of

the employees in an undertaking or group of undertakings, or would have been given an equal value but for the evaluation being made on a system setting different values for men and women on the same demand under any heading.

(5A) For the purposes of subsection (2)(d) to (f) above—

(a) 'maternity-related pay', in relation to a woman, means pay (including pay by way of bonus) to which she is entitled as a result of being pregnant or in respect of times when she is on statutory maternity leave, except that it does not include any statutory maternity pay to which she is entitled;

(b) 'statutory maternity leave period', in relation to a woman, means the period during which she is on statutory maternity leave;

(c) an increase in an amount is taken into account in a calculation if in the calculation the amount as increased is substituted for the unincreased amount.

(5B) For the purposes of subsections (2)(d) to (f) and (5A) above, 'on statutory maternity leave' means absent from work—

(a) in exercise of the right conferred by section 71(1) or 73(1) of the Employment Rights Act 1996 (ordinary or additional maternity leave), or

(b) in consequence of the prohibition in section 72(1) of that Act (compulsory maternity leave).

(6) Subject to the following subsections, for purposes of this section—

(a) 'employed' means employed under a contract of service or of apprenticeship or a contract personally to execute any work or labour, and related expressions shall be construed accordingly;

(b) [repealed]

(c) Two employers are to be treated as associated if one is a company of which the other (directly or indirectly) has control or if both are companies of which a third person (directly or indirectly) has control,

and men shall be treated as in the same employment with a woman if they are men employed by her employer or any associated employer at the same establishment or at establishments in Great Britain which include that one and at which common terms and conditions of employment are observed either generally or for employees of the relevant classes.

(6A) This section applies to—

(a) the holding of an office or post to which persons are appointed to discharge functions personally under the direction of another person, and in respect of which they are entitled to remuneration, or

(b) any office or post to which appointments are made by (or on the recommendation of or subject to the approval of) a Minister of the Crown, a government department, the National Assembly for Wales or any part of the Scottish Administration,

as it applies to employment by a private person, and shall so apply as if references to a contract of employment included references to the terms of appointment, and as if references to the employer included references to the person responsible for paying any remuneration that a holder of the office or post is entitled to in respect of the office or post.

(6B) For the purposes of subsection (6A), the holder of an office or post—

(a) is to be regarded as discharging her functions under the direction of another person if that other person is entitled to direct her as to when and where she discharges those functions;

(b) is not to be regarded as entitled to remuneration merely because she is entitled to payments—

(i) in respect of expenses incurred by her in carrying out the functions of the office or post, or

(ii) by way of compensation for the loss of income or benefits she would or might have received from any person had she not been carrying out the functions of the office or post.

(6C) For the purposes of subsection (6A)—

    (a) 'office or post' does not include a political office (see section 1A), and

    (b) appointment to an office or post does not include election to an office or post.

(7) [repealed]

(8) This section shall apply to—

    (a) service for purposes of a Minister of the Crown or government department, other than service of a person holding a statutory office, or

    (b) service on behalf of the Crown for purposes of a person holding a statutory office or purposes of a statutory body,

as it applies to employment by a private person, and shall so apply as if references to a contract of employment included references to the terms of service.

(9) [repealed]

(10) In this section 'statutory body' means a body set up by or in pursuance of an enactment (including an enactment comprised in, or an instrument made under, an Act of the Scottish Parliament), and 'statutory office' means an office so set up; and service 'for purposes of' a Minister of the Crown or government department does not include service in any office in Schedule 2 (Ministerial offices) to the House of Commons Disqualification Act 1975 as for the time being in force.

(10A) and (10B) [omitted]

(11) For the purposes of this Act it is immaterial whether the law which (apart from this subsection) in the law applicable to a contract is the law of any part of the United Kingdom or not.

(12) [omitted]

(13) Provisions of this section and sections 2 to 2A below framed with reference to women and their treatment relative to men are to be read as applying equally in a converse case to men and their treatment relative to women.

1A   [omitted]

2   Disputes as to, and enforcement of, requirement of equal treatment

(1) Any claim in respect of the contravention of a term modified or included by virtue of an equality clause, including a claim for arrears of remuneration or damages in respect of the contravention, may be presented by way of a complaint to an employment tribunal.

(1A) Where a dispute arises in relation to the effect of an equality clause the employer may apply to an employment tribunal for an order declaring the rights of the employer and the employee in relation to the matter in question.

(2) Where it appears to the Secretary of State that there may be a question whether the employer of any women is or has been contravening a term modified or included by virtue of their equality clauses, but that it is not reasonable to expect them to take steps to have the question determined, the question may be referred by him as respects all or any of them to an employment tribunal and shall be dealt with as if the reference were of a claim by the women or woman against the employer.

(3) Where it appears to the court in which any proceedings are pending that a claim or counterclaim in respect of the operation of an equality clause could more conveniently be disposed of separately by an employment tribunal, the court may direct that the claim or counterclaim shall be struck out; and (without prejudice to the foregoing) where in proceedings before any court a question arises as to the operation of an equality clause, the court may on the application of any party to the proceedings or otherwise refer that question, or direct it to be referred by a party to the proceedings, to an employment tribunal for determination by the tribunal, and may stay or sist the proceedings in the meantime.

(4) No determination may be made by an employment tribunal in the following proceedings—

    (a) on complaint under subsection (1) above,

    (b) on an application under subsection (1A) above, or

    (c) on a reference under subsection (2) above,

unless the proceedings are instituted on or before the qualifying date (determined in accordance with section 2ZA below).

(5) A woman shall not be entitled, in proceedings brought in respect of a contravention of a term modified or included by virtue of an equality clause (including proceedings before an employment tribunal), to be awarded any payment by way of arrears of remuneration or damages—

>>> (a) in proceedings in England and Wales, in respect of a time earlier than the arrears date (determined in accordance wtih section 2ZB below), and

>>> (b) in proceedings in Scotland, in respect of a time before the period determined in accordance with section 2ZC below.

(5A) In this section 'employer', in relation to the holder of an office or post to which section 1 above applies by virtue of subsection (6A) of that section, shall be construed in accordance with that subsection.

(6) and (7) [repealed]

2ZA 'Qualifying date' under section 2(4)

(1) This section applies for the purpose of determining the qualifying date, in relation to proceedings in respect of a woman's employment, for the purposes of section 2(4) above.

(2) In this section—

> 'concealment case' means a case where—

>> (a) the employer deliberately concealed from the woman any fact (referred to in this section as a 'qualifying fact')—

>>> (i) which is relevant to the contravention to which the proceedings relate, and

>>> (ii) without knowledge of which the woman could not reasonably have been expected to institute the proceedings, and

>> (b) the woman did not discover the qualifying fact (or could not with reasonable diligence have discovered it) until after—

>>> (i) the last day on which she was employed in the employment, or

>>> (ii) the day on which the stable employment relationship between her and the employer ended,

> (as the case may be);

> 'disability case' means a case where the woman was under a disability at any time during the six months after—

>> (a) the last day on which she was employed in the employment,

>> (b) the day on which the stable employment relationship between her and the employer ended, or

>> (c) the day on which she discovered (or could with reasonable diligence have discovered) the qualifying fact deliberately concealed from her by the employer (if that day falls after the day referred to in paragraph (a) or (b) above, as the case may be),

> (as the case may be);

> 'stable employment case' means a case where the proceedings relate to a period during which a stable employment relationship subsists between the woman and the employer, notwithstanding that the period includes any time after the ending of a contract of employment when no further contract of employment is in force;

> 'standard case' means a case which is not—

>> (a) a stable employment case,

>> (b) a concealment case,

>> (c) a disability case, or

>> (d) both a concealment and a disability case.

(3) In a standard case, the qualifying date is the date falling six months after the last day on which the woman was employed in the employment.

(4) In a case which is a stable employment case (but not also a concealment or a disability case or both), the qualifying date is the date falling six months after the day on which the stable employment relationship ended.

(5) In a case which is a concealment case (but not also a disability case), the qualifying date is the date falling six months after the day on which the woman discovered the qualifying fact in question (or could with reasonable diligence have discovered it).

(6) In a case which is a disability case (but not also a concealment case), the qualifying date is the date falling six months after the day on which the woman ceased to be under a disability.

(7) In a case which is both a concealment and a disability case, the qualifying date is the later of the dates referred to in subsections (5) and (6) above.

2ZB 'Arrears date' in proceedings in England and Wales under section 2(5)

(1) This section applies for the purpose of determining the arrears date, in relation to an award of any payment by way of arrears of remuneration or damages in proceedings in England and Wales in respect of a woman's employment, for the purposes of section 2(5)(a) above.

(2) In this section—
'concealment case" means a case where—
(a) the employer deliberately concealed from the woman any fact—
    (i)   which is relevant to the contravention to which the proceedings relate, and
    (ii) without knowledge of which the woman could not reasonably have been expected to institute the proceedings, and
(b) the woman instituted the proceedings within six years of the day on which she discovered the fact (or could with reasonable diligence have discovered it);
'disability case' means a case where—
(a) the woman was under a disability at the time of the contravention to which the proceedings relate, and
(b) the woman instituted the proceedings within six years of the day on which she ceased to be under a disability;
'standard case' means a case which is not—
(a) a concealment case,
(b) a disability case, or
(c) both.

(3) In a standard case, the arrears date is the date falling six years before the day on which the proceedings were instituted.

(4) In a case which is a concealment or a disability case or both, the arrears date is the date of the contravention.

2ZC [omitted]

2A Procedure before tribunal in certain cases

(1) Where on a complaint or reference made to an employment tribunal under section 2 above, a dispute arises as to whether any work is of equal value as mentioned in section 1(2)(c) above the tribunal may either—
(a) proceed to determine that question; or
(b) require a member of the panel of independent experts to prepare a report with respect to that question;

(1A) Subsections (1B) and (1C) below apply in a case where the tribunal has required a member of the panel of independent experts to prepare a report under paragraph (b) of subsection (1) above.

(1B) The tribunal may—
(a) withdraw the requirement, and

(b) request the member of the panel of independent experts to provide it with any documentation specified by it or make any other request to him connected with the withdrawal of the requirement.

(1C) If the requirement has not been withdrawn under paragraph (a) of subsection (1B) above, the tribunal shall not make any determination under paragraph (a) of subsection (1) above unless it has received the report.

(2) Subsection (2A) below applies in a case where—

(a) a tribunal is required to determine whether any work is of equal value as mentioned in section 1(2)(c) above, and

(b) the work of the woman and that of the man in question have been given different values on a study such as is mentioned in section 1(5) above.

(2A) The tribunal shall determine that the work of the woman and that of the man are not of equal value unless the tribunal has reasonable grounds for suspecting that the evaluation contained in the study—

(a) was (within the meaning of subsection (3) below) made on a system which discriminates on grounds of sex, or

(b) is otherwise unsuitable to be relied upon.

(3) An evaluation contained in a study such as is mentioned in section 1(5) above is made on a system which discriminates on grounds of sex where a difference, or coincidence, between values set by that system on different demands under the same or different headings is not justifiable irrespective of the sex of the person on whom those demands are made.

(4) In this section a reference to a member of the panel of independent experts is a reference to a person who is for the time being designated by the Advisory, Conciliation and Arbitration Service for the purposes of that paragraph as such a member, being neither a member of the Council of that Service nor one of its officers or servants.

3–4 [repealed]; 5 [omitted]

6 Exclusion from ss. 1 to 5 of pensions etc.

(1) An equality clause shall not operate in relation to terms—

(a) affected by compliance with the laws regulating the employment of women, or

(b) affording special treatment to women in connection with pregnancy or childbirth.

(1AA) Subsection (1)(b) does not affect the operation of an equality clause falling within section 1(2)(d), (e) or (f).

(1A) [repealed]

(1B) An equality clause shall not operate in relation to terms relating to a person's membership of, or rights under, an occupational pension scheme, being terms in relation to which, by reason only of any provision made by or under sections 62 to 64 of the Pensions Act 1995 (equal treatment), an equal treatment rule would not operate if the terms were included in the scheme.

(1C) In subsection (1B), 'occupational pension scheme' has the same meaning as in the Pension Schemes Act 1993 and 'equal treatment rule' has the meaning given by section 62 of the Pensions Act 1995.

(2) [repealed]

7 [repealed]; 7A–7B [omitted]; 8 [repealed]; 9 [omitted]; 10 [repealed]

11 Short title, interpretation and extent

(1) [omitted]

(2) In this Act the expression 'man' and 'woman' shall be read as applying to persons of whatever age.

(2A) For the purposes of this Act a woman is under a disability—

    (a) in the case of proceedings in England and Wales, if she is a minor or of unsound mind (which has the same meaning as in section 38(2) of the Limitation Act 1980); or

    (b) in the case of proceedings in Scotland, if she has not attained the age of sixteen years or is incapable within the meaning of the Adults with Incapacity (Scotland) Act 2000.

(3) [omitted]

Sex Discrimination Act 1975
(1975, c. 65)

PART I   DISCRIMINATION TO WHICH ACT APPLIES

PART II   DISCRIMINATION IN THE EMPLOYMENT FIELD

PART IV   OTHER UNLAWFUL ACTS

PART I   DISCRIMINATION TO WHICH ACT APPLIES

1   Direct and indirect discrimination against women

(1) In any circumstances relevant for the purposes of any provision of this Act, other than a provision to which subsection (2) applies, a person discriminates against a woman if—

(a) on the ground of her sex he treats her less favourably than he treats or would treat a man, or

(b) he applies to her a requirement or condition which he applies or would apply equally to a man but—

(i)   which is such that the proportion of women who can comply with it is considerably smaller than the proportion of men who can comply with it, and

(ii) which he cannot show to be justifiable irrespective of the sex of the person to whom it is applied, and

(iii) which is to her detriment because she cannot comply with it.

(2) In any circumstances relevant for the purposes of a provision to which this subsection applies, a person discriminates against a woman if—

    (a) on the ground of her sex, he treats her less favourably than he treats or would treat a man, or

    (b) he applies to her a provision, criterion or practice which he applies or would apply equally to a man, but—

        (i) which puts or would put women at a particular disadvantage when compared with men,

        (ii) which puts her at that disadvantage, and

        (iii) which he cannot show to be a proportionate means of achieving a legitimate aim.

(3) Subsection (2) applies to—

    (a) any provision of Part 2,

    (b) sections 35A and 35B, and

    (c) any other provision of Part 3, so far as it applies to vocational training.

(4) [repealed]

2 Sex discrimination against men

(1) Section 1, and the provisions of Parts II and III relating to sex discrimination against women, are to be read as applying equally to the treatment of men, and for that purpose shall have effect with such modifications as are requisite.

(2) In the application of subsection (1) no account shall be taken of special treatment afforded to women in connection with pregnancy or childbirth.

2A Discrimination on the grounds of gender reassignment

(1) A person ('A') discriminates against another person ('B') in any circum- stances relevant for the purposes of—

    (a) any provision of Part II,

    (b) section 35A or 35B, or

    (c) any other provision of Part III, so far as it applies to vocational training, if he treats B less favourably than he treats or would treat other persons, and does so on the grounds that B intends to undergo, is undergoing or has undergone gender reassignment.

(2) Subsection (3) applies to arrangements made by any person in relation to another's absence from work or from vocational training.

(3) For the purposes of subsection (1), B is treated less favourably than others under such arrangements if, in the application of the arrangements to any absence due to B undergoing gender reassignment—

    (a) he is treated less favourably than he would be if the absence was due to sickness or injury, or

    (b) he is treated less favourably than he would be if the absence was due to some other cause and, having regard to the circumstances of the case, it is reasonable for him to be treated no less favourably.

(4) In subsections (2) and (3) 'arrangements' includes terms, conditions or arrangements on which employment, a pupillage or tenancy or vocational training is offered.

(5) For the purposes of subsection (1), a provision mentioned in that subsection framed with reference to discrimination against women shall be treated as applying equally to the treatment of men with such modifications as are requisite.

3 Discrimination against married persons and civil partners in employment field

(1) In any circumstances relevant for the purposes of any provision of Part 2, a person discriminates against a person ('A') who fulfils the condition in subsection (2) if—

    (a) on the ground of the fulfilment of the condition, he treats A less favourably than he treats or would treat a person who does not fulfil the condition, or

(b) he applies to that person a provision, criterion or practice which he applies or would apply equally to an unmarried person, but—
   (i) which puts or would put married persons at a particular disadvantage when compared with unmarried persons of the same sex,
   (ii) which puts that person at that disadvantage, and
   (iii) which he cannot show to be a proportionate means of achieving a legitimate aim.

(2) The condition is that the person is—
   (a) married, or
   (b) a civil partner.

(3) For the purposes of subsection (1), a provision of Part 2 framed with reference to discrimination against women is to be treated as applying equally to the treatment of men, and for that purpose has effect with such modifications as are requisite.

3A Discrimination on the ground of pregnancy or maternity leave

(1) In any circumstances relevant for the purposes of a provision to which this subsection applies, a person discriminates against a woman if—
   (a) at a time in a protected period, and on the ground of the woman's pregnancy, the person treats her less favourably than he would treat her had she not become pregnant; or
   (b) on the ground that the woman is exercising or seeking to exercise, or has exercised or sought to exercise, a statutory right to maternity leave, the person treats her less favourably than he would treat her if she were neither exercising nor seeking to exercise, and had neither exercised nor sought to exercise, such a right.

(2) In any circumstances relevant for the purposes of a provision to which this subsection applies, a person discriminates against a woman if, on the ground that section 72(1) of the Employment Rights Act 1996 (compulsory maternity leave) has to be complied with in respect of the woman, he treats her less favourably than he would treat her if that provision did not have to be complied with in respect of her.

(3) For the purposes of subsection (1)—
   (a) in relation to a woman, a protected period begins each time she becomes pregnant, and the protected period associated with any particular pregnancy of hers ends in accordance with the following rules—
     (i) if she is entitled to ordinary but not additional maternity leave in connection with the pregnancy, the protected period ends at the end of her period of ordinary maternity leave connected with the pregnancy or, if earlier, when she returns to work after the end of her pregnancy;
     (ii) if she is entitled to ordinary and additional maternity leave in connection with the pregnancy, the protected period ends at the end of her period of additional maternity leave connected with the pregnancy or, if earlier, when she returns to work after the end of her pregnancy;
     (iii) if she is not entitled to ordinary maternity leave in respect of the pregnancy, the protected period ends at the end of the 2 weeks beginning with the end of the pregnancy;
   (b) where a person's treatment of a woman is on grounds of illness suffered by the woman as a consequence of a pregnancy of hers, that treatment is to be taken to be on the ground of the pregnancy;
   (c) a 'statutory right to maternity leave' means a right conferred by section 71(1) or 73(1) of the Employment Rights Act 1996 (ordinary and additional maternity leave).

(4) In subsection (3) 'ordinary maternity leave' and 'additional maternity leave' shall be construed in accordance with sections 71 and 73 of the Employment Rights Act 1996.

(5) Subsections (1) and (2) apply to—
  (a) any provision of Part 2,
  (b) sections 35A and 35B, and
  (c) any other provision of Part 3, so far as it applies to vocational training.

4   Discrimination by way of victimisation

(1) A person ('the discriminator') discriminates against another person ('the person victimised') in any circumstances relevant for the purposes of any provision of this Act if he treats the person victimised less favourably than in those circumstances he treats or would treat other persons, and does so by reason that the person victimised has—
  (a) brought proceedings against the discriminator or any other person under this Act or the Equal Pay Act 1970 or sections 62 to 65 of the Pensions Act 1995, or
  (b) given evidence or information in connection with proceedings brought by any person against the discriminator or any other person under this Act or the Equal Pay Act 1970 or sections 62 to 65 of the Pensions Act 1995, or
  (c) otherwise done anything under or by reference to this Act or the Equal Pay Act 1970 or sections 62 to 65 of the Pensions Act 1995 in relation to the discriminator or any other person, or
  (d) alleged that the discriminator or any other person has committed an act which (whether or not the allegation so states) would amount to a contravention of this Act or give rise to a claim under the Equal Pay Act 1970 or under sections 62 to 65 of the Pensions Act 1995,

or by reason that the discriminator knows the person victimised intends to do any of those things, or suspects the person victimised has done, or intends to do, any of them.

(2) Subsection (1) does not apply to treatment of a person by reason of any allegation made by him if the allegation was false and not made in good faith.

(3) For the purposes of subsection (1), a provision of Part II or III framed with reference to discrimination against women shall be treated as applying equally to the treatment of men and for that purpose shall have effect with such modifications as are requisite.

4A   Harassment, including sexual harassment

(1) For the purposes of this Act, a person subjects a woman to harassment if—
  (a) on the ground of her sex, he engages in unwanted conduct that has the purpose or effect—
    (i) of violating her dignity, or
    (ii) of creating an intimidating, hostile, degrading, humiliating or offensive environment for her,
  (b) he engages in any form of unwanted verbal, non-verbal or physical conduct of a sexual nature that has the purpose or effect—
    (i) of violating her dignity, or
    (ii) of creating an intimidating, hostile, degrading, humiliating or offensive environment for her, or
  (c) on the ground of her rejection of or submission to unwanted conduct of a kind mentioned in paragraph (a) or (b), he treats her less favourably than he would treat her had she not rejected, or submitted to, the conduct.

(2) Conduct shall be regarded as having the effect mentioned in sub-paragraph (i) or (ii) of subsection (1)(a) or (b) only if, having regard to all the circumstances, including in particular the perception of the woman, it should reasonably be considered as having that effect.

(3) For the purposes of this Act, a person ('A') subjects another person ('B') to harassment if—
  (a) A, on the ground that B intends to undergo, is undergoing or has undergone gender reassignment, engages in unwanted conduct that has the purpose or effect—

(i) of violating B's dignity, or

(ii) of creating an intimidating, hostile, degrading, humiliating or offensive environment for B, or

(b) A, on the ground of B's rejection of or submission to unwanted conduct of a kind mentioned in paragraph (a), treats B less favourably than A would treat B had B not rejected, or submitted to, the conduct.

(4) Conduct shall be regarded as having the effect mentioned in sub-paragraph (i) or (ii) of subsection (3)(a) only if, having regard to all the circumstances, including in particular the perception of B, it should reasonably be considered as having that effect.

(5) Subsection (1) is to be read as applying equally to the harassment of men, and for that purpose shall have effect with such modifications as are requisite.

(6) For the purposes of subsections (1) and (3), a provision of Part 2 or 3 framed with reference to harassment of women shall be treated as applying equally to the harassment of men, and for that purpose will have effect with such modifications as are requisite.

5 Interpretation

(1) In this Act—

(a) references to discrimination refer to any discrimination falling within sections 1 to 4; and

(b) references to sex discrimination refer to any discrimination falling within section 2 or 3A,

and related expressions shall be construed accordingly.

(2) In this Act—

'woman' includes a female of any age, and

'man' includes a male of any age.

(3) Each of the following comparisons, that is—

(a) a comparison of the cases of persons of different sex under section 1(1) or (2),

(b) a comparison of the cases of persons required for the purposes of section 2A, and

(c) a comparison of the cases of persons who do and who do not fulfil the condition in section 3(2),

must be such that the relevant circumstances in the one case are the same, or not materially different, in the other.

PART II   EMPLOYMENT FIELD

6 Applicants and employees

(1) It is unlawful for a person, in relation to employment by him at an establishment in Great Britain, to discriminate against a woman—

(a) in the arrangements he makes for the purpose of determining who should be offered that employment, or

(b) in the terms on which he offers her that employment, or

(c) by refusing or deliberately omitting to offer her that employment.

(2) It is unlawful for a person, in the case of a woman employed by him at an establishment in Great Britain, to discriminate against her—

(a) in the way he affords her access to opportunities for promotion, transfer or training, or to any other benefits, facilities or services, or by refusing or deliberately omitting to afford her access to them, or

(b) by dismissing her, or subjecting her to any other detriment.

(2A) It is unlawful for an employer, in relation to employment by him at an establishment in Great Britain, to subject to harassment—

(a) a woman whom he employs, or

(b) a woman who has applied to him for employment.

(3) [repealed]

(4) Subsections (1)(b) and (2) do not render it unlawful for a person to discriminate against a woman in relation to her membership of, or rights under, an occupational pension scheme in such a way that, were any term of the scheme to provide for discrimination in that way, then, by reason only of any provision made by or under sections 62 to 64 of the Pensions Act 1995 (equal treatment), an equal treatment rule would not operate in relation to that term.

(4A) In subsection (4), 'occupational pension scheme' has the same meaning as in the Pension Schemes Act 1993 and 'equal treatment rule' has the meaning given by section 62 of the Pensions Act 1995.

(5) Subject to section 8(3), subsection (1)(b) does not apply to any provision for the payment of money which, if the woman in question were given the employment, would be included (directly or otherwise) in the contract under which she was employed.

(6) Subsection (2) does not apply to benefits consisting of the payment of money when the provision of those benefits is regulated by the woman's contract of employment.

(7) Subsection (2) does not apply to benefits, facilities or services of any description if the employer is concerned with the provision (for payment or not) of benefits, facilities or services of that description to the public, or to a section of the public comprising the woman in question, unless—

    (a) that provision differs in a material respect from the provision of the benefits, facilities or services by the employer to his employees, or

    (b) the provision of the benefits, facilities or services to the woman in question is regulated by her contract of employment, or

    (c) the benefits, facilities or services relate to training.

(8) In its application to any discrimination falling within section 2A, this section shall have effect with the omission of subsections (4) to (6).

6A Exception relating to terms and conditions during maternity leave

(1) Subject to subsections (2) and (5), section 6(1)(b) and (2) does not make it unlawful to deprive a woman who is on ordinary maternity leave of any benefit from the terms and conditions of her employment relating to remuneration.

(2) Subsection (1) does not apply to benefit by way of maternity-related remuneration.

(3) Subject to subsections (4) and (5), section 6(1)(b) and (2) does not make it unlawful to deprive a woman who is on additional maternity leave of any benefit from the terms and conditions of her employment.

(4) Subsection (3) does not apply to—

    (a) benefit by way of maternity-related remuneration,

    (b) the benefit of her employer's implied obligation to her of trust and confidence, or

    (c) any benefit of terms and conditions in respect of—

        (i) notice of the termination by her employer of her contract of employment,

        (ii) compensation in the event of redundancy,

        (iii) disciplinary or grievance procedures, or

        (iv) membership of a pension scheme.

(5) Neither of subsections (1) and (3) applies to—

    (a) benefit by way of remuneration in respect of times when the woman is neither on ordinary maternity leave nor on additional maternity leave, including increase-related remuneration in respect of such times; or

    (b) benefit by way of maternity-related remuneration that is increase-related.

(6) For the purposes of subsection (5), remuneration is increase-related so far as it falls to be calculated by reference to increases in remuneration that the woman would have received had she not been on ordinary or additional maternity leave.

(7) In this section—

    'maternity-related remuneration', in relation to a woman, means remuneration to which she is entitled as a result of being pregnant or being on ordinary or additional maternity leave;

'on additional maternity leave' means absent from work in exercise of the right conferred by section 73(1) of the Employment Rights Act 1996;

'on ordinary maternity leave' means absent from work in exercise of the right conferred by section 71(1) of that Act (ordinary maternity leave) or in consequence of the prohibition in section 72(1) of that Act (compulsory maternity leave);

'remuneration' means benefits—

    (a) that consist of the payment of money to an employee by way of wages or salary, and

    (b) that are not benefits whose provision is regulated by the employee's contract of employment.

7 Exception where sex is a genuine occupational qualification

(1) In relation to sex discrimination—

    (a) section 6(1)(a) or (c) does not apply to any employment where being a man is a genuine occupational qualification for the job, and

    (b) section 6(2)(a) does not apply to opportunities for promotion or transfer to, or training for, such employment.

(2) Being a man is a genuine occupational qualification for a job only where—

    (a) the essential nature of the job calls for a man for reasons of physiology (excluding physical strength or stamina) or, in dramatic performances or other entertainment, for reasons of authenticity, so that the essential nature or the job would be materially different if carried out by a woman; or

    (b) the job needs to be held by a man to preserve decency or privacy because—

        (i) it is likely to involve physical contact with men in circumstances where they might reasonably object to its being carried out by a woman, or

        (ii) the holder of the job is likely to do his work in circumstances where men might reasonably object to the presence of a woman because they are in a state of undress or are using sanitary facilities; or

    (ba) the job is likely to involve the holder of the job doing his work, or living, in a private home and needs to be held by a man because objection might reasonably be taken to allowing to a woman—

        (i) the degree of physical or social contact with a person living in the home, or

        (ii) the knowledge of intimate details of such a person's life, which is likely, because of the nature or circumstances of the job or of the home, to be allowed to, or available to, the holder of the job; or

    (c) the nature or location of the establishment makes it impracticable for the holder of the job to live elsewhere than in premises provided by the employer, and—

        (i) the only such premises which are available for persons holding that kind of job are lived in, or normally lived in, by men and are not equipped with separate sleeping accommodation for women and sanitary facilities which could be used by women in privacy from men, and

        (ii) it is not reasonable to expect the employer either to equip those premises with such accommodation and facilities or to provide other premises for women; or

    (d) the nature of the establishment, or of the part of it within which the work is done, requires the job to be held by a man because—

        (i) it is, or is part of, a hospital, prison or other establishment for persons requiring special care, supervision or attention, and

        (ii) those persons are all men (disregarding any woman whose presence is exceptional), and

        (iii) it is reasonable, having regard to the essential character of the establishment or that part, that the job should not be held by a woman; or

(e) the holder of the job provides individuals with personal services promoting their welfare or education, or similar personal services, and those services can most effectively be provided by a man, or

(f) the job needs to be held by a man because it is likely to involve the performance of duties outside the United Kingdom in a country whose laws or customs are such that the duties could not, effectively, be performed by a woman, or

(g) the job is one of two to be held—

(i) by a married couple,

(ii) by a couple who are civil partners of each other, or

(iii) by a married couple or a couple who are civil partners of each other.

(3) Subsection (2) applies where some only of the duties of the job fall within paragraphs (a) to (g) as well as where all of them do.

(4) Paragraph (a), (b), (c), (d), (e) or (g) of subsection (2) does not apply in relation to the filling of a vacancy at a time when the employer already has male employees—

(a) who are capable of carrying out the duties falling within that paragraph, and

(b) whom it would be reasonable to employ on those duties, and

(c) whose numbers are sufficient to meet the employer's likely requirements in respect of those duties without undue inconvenience.

7A Corresponding exception relating to gender reassignment

(1) In their application to discrimination falling within section 2A, subsections (1) and (2) of section 6 do not make unlawful an employer's treatment of another person if—

(a) in relation to the employment in question—

(i) being a man is a genuine occupational qualification for the job, or

(ii) being a woman is a genuine occupational qualification for the job, and

(b) the employer can show that the treatment is reasonable in view of the circumstances described in the relevant paragraph of section 7(2) and any other relevant circumstances.

(2) In subsection (1) the reference to the employment in question is a reference—

(a) in relation to any paragraph of section 6(1), to the employment mentioned in that paragraph;

(b) in relation to section 6(2)—

(i) in its application to opportunities for promotion or transfer to any employment or for training for any employment, to that employment;

(ii) otherwise, to the employment in which the person discriminated against is employed or from which that person is dismissed.

(3) In determining for the purposes of subsection (1) whether being a man or being a woman is a genuine occupational qualification for a job, section 7(4) applies in relation to dismissal from employment as it applies in relation to the filling of a vacancy.

(4) Subsection (1) does not apply in relation to discrimination against a person whose gender has become the acquired gender under the Gender Recognition Act 2004.

7B Supplementary exceptions relating to gender reassignment

(1) In relation to discrimination falling within section 2A—

(a) section 6(1)(a) or (c) does not apply to any employment where there is a supplementary genuine occupational qualification for the job,

(b) section 6(2)(a) does not apply to a refusal or deliberate omission to afford access to opportunities for promotion or transfer to or training for such employment, and

(c) section 6(2)(b) does not apply to dismissing an employee from, or otherwise not allowing him to continue in, such employment.

(2) Subject to subsection (3), there is a supplementary genuine occupational qualification for a job only if—

(a) the job involves the holder of the job being liable to be called upon to perform intimate physical searches pursuant to statutory powers;

(b) the job is likely to involve the holder of the job doing his work, or living, in a private home and needs to be held otherwise than by a person who is undergoing or has undergone gender reassignment, because objection might reasonably be taken to allowing to such a person—
  (i) the degree of physical or social contact with a person living in the home, or
  (ii) the knowledge of intimate details of such a person's life, which is likely, because of the nature or circumstances of the job or of the home, to be allowed to, or available to, the holder of the job;
(c) the nature of location of the establishment makes it impracticable for the holder of the job to live elsewhere than in premises provided by the employer, and—
  (i) the only such premises which are available for persons holding that kind of job are such that reasonable objection could be taken, for the purpose of preserving decency and privacy, to the holder of the job sharing accommodation and facilities with either sex whilst undergoing gender reassignment, and
  (ii) it is not reasonable to except the employer either to equip those premises with suitable accommodation or to make alternative arrangements; or
(d) the holder of the job provides vulnerable individuals with personal services promoting their welfare, or similar personal services, and in the reasonable view of the employer those services cannot be effectively provided by a person whilst that person is undergoing gender reassignment.

(3) Subsection (2) does not apply in relation to discrimination against a person whose gender has become the acquired gender under the Gender Recognition Act 2004.

(4) Paragraph (a) of subsection (2) does not apply in relation to the filling of a vacancy at a time when the employer already has employees falling within subsection (5)—
(a) who are capable of carrying out the duties falling within that paragraph, and
(b) whom it would be reasonable to employ on those duties, and
(c) whose numbers are sufficient to meet the employer's likely requirements in respect of those duties without undue inconvenience.

(5) An employee falls within this subsection if the employee does not intend to undergo and is not undergoing gender reassignment and either—
(a) the employee has not undergone gender reassignment; or
(b) the employee's gender has become the acquired gender under the Gender Recognition Act 2004.

8 Equal Pay Act 1970

(1) [omitted]

(2) Section 1(1) of the Equal Pay Act 1970 does not apply in determining for the purposes of section 6(1)(b) of this Act the terms on which employment is offered.

(3) Where a person offers a woman employment on certain terms, and if she accepted the offer then, by virtue of an equality clause, any of those terms would fall to be modified, or any additional term would fall to be included, the offer shall be taken to contravene section 6(1)(b).

(4) Where a person offers a woman employment on certain terms, and subsection (3) would apply but for the fact that, on her acceptance of the offer, section 1(3) of the Equal Pay Act 1970 (as set out in subsection (1) above) would prevent the equality clause from operating, the offer shall be taken not to contravene section 6(1)(b).

(5) An act does not contravene section 6(2) if—
(a) it contravenes a term modified or included by virtue of an equality clause, or
(b) it would contravene such a term but for the fact that the equality clause is prevented from operating by section 1(3) of the Equal Pay Act 1970.

(6) [omitted]

(7) In its application to any discrimination falling within section 2A, this section shall have effect with the omission of subsections (3), (4) and (5)(b).

9   Contract workers

(1) This section applies to any work at an establishment in Great Britain, for a person ('the principal') which is available for doing by individuals ('contract workers') who are employed not by the principal himself but by another person, who supplies them under a contract made with the principal.

(2) It is unlawful for the principal, in relation to work to which this section applies, to discriminate against a woman who is a contract worker—

    (a) in the terms on which he allows her to do that work, or

    (b) by not allowing her to do it or continue to do it, or

    (c) in the way he affords her access to any benefits, facilities or services or by refusing or deliberately omitting to afford her access to them, or

    (d) by subjecting her to any other detriment.

(2A) It is unlawful for a principal, in relation to contract work at an establishment in Great Britain, to subject a contract worker to harassment.

(3) Subject to section (3A), the principal does not contravene subsection (2)(b) by doing any act in relation to a woman at a time when if the work were to be done by a person taken into his employment being a man would be a genuine occupational qualification for the job.

(3A) Subsection (3) does not apply in relation to discrimination falling within section 2A.

(3B) In relation to discrimination falling within section 2A, the principal does not contravene subsection (2)(a), (b), (c) or (d) by doing any act in relation to a woman if—

    (a) he does it at a time when, if the work were to be done by a person taken into his employment—

        (i)   being a man would be a genuine occupational qualification for the job, or

        (ii) being a woman would be a genuine occupational qualification for the job, and

    (b) he can show that the act is reasonable in view of the circumstances relevant for the purposes of paragraph (a) and any other relevant circumstances.

(3C) In relation to discrimination falling within section 2A, the principal does not contravene subsection (2)(b) by doing any act in relation to a woman at a time when, if the work were to be done by a person taken into his employment, there would be a supplementary genuine occupational qualification for the job.

(3D) Subsections (3B) and (3C) do not apply in relation to discrimination against a person whose gender has become the acquired gender under the Gender Recognition Act 2004.

(4) Subsection (2)(c) does not apply to benefits, facilities or services of any description if the principal is concerned with the provision (for payment or not) of benefits, facilities or services of that description to the public, or to a section of the public to which the woman belongs, unless that provision differs in a material respect from the provision of the benefits, facilities or services by the principal to his contract workers.

10   Meaning of employment at establishment in Great Britain

(1) For the purposes of this Part and section 1 of the Equal Pay Act 1970 ('the relevant purposes'), employment is to be regarded as being at an establishment in Great Britain if—

    (a) the employee does his work wholly or partly in Great Britain, or

    (b) the employee does his work wholly outside Great Britain and subsection (1A) applies.

(1A) This subsection applies if—

    (a) the employer has a place of business at an establishment in Great Britain,

    (b) the work is for the purposes of the business carried on at that establishment, and

    (c) the employee is ordinarily resident in Great Britain—

        (i)   at the time when he applies for or is offered the employment, or

        (ii) at any time during the course of the employment.

(2)–(3) [omitted]

(4) Where work is not done at an establishment it shall be treated for the relevant purposes as done at the establishment from which it is done or (where it is not done from any establishment) at the establishment with which it has the closest connection.

(5)–(8) [omitted]

10A Offices and posts to which section 10B applies

(1) Subject to subsections (2) and (3), section 10B applies to an office or post if—
   (a) the office or post is one—
      (i) to which persons are appointed to discharge functions personally under the direction of another person, and
      (ii) in respect of which they are entitled to remuneration,
   (b) the office or post is one to which appointments are made by a Minister of the Crown, a government department, the National Assembly for Wales or any part of the Scottish Administration, or
   (c) the office or post is one to which appointments are made on the recommendation of, or subject to the approval of, a person referred to in paragraph (b).

(2) Section 10B does not apply to an office or post if section 6 (employment), section 9 (contract work), section 11 (partnerships), section 35A (barristers) or section 35B (advocates)—
   (a) applies in relation to an appointment to the office or post, or
   (b) would apply in relation to an appointment to the office or post but for the operation of any other provision of this Act.

(3) [omitted]

(4) For the purposes of subsection (1)(a), the holder of an office or post—
   (a) is to be regarded as discharging her functions under the direction of another person if that other person is entitled to direct her as to when and where she discharges those functions;
   (b) is not to be regarded as entitled to remuneration merely because she is entitled to payments—
      (i) in respect of expenses incurred by her in carrying out the functions of the office or post, or
      (ii) by way of compensation for the loss of income or benefits she would or might have received from any person had she not been carrying out the functions of the office or post.

(5) In this section and section 10B, appointment to an office or post does not include election to an office or post.

10B Office-holders

(1) It is unlawful for a relevant person, in relation to an appointment to an office or post to which this section applies, to discriminate against a woman—
   (a) in the arrangements which he makes for the purpose of determining to whom the appointment should be offered,
   (b) in the terms on which he offers her the appointment, or
   (c) by refusing to offer her the appointment.

(2) It is unlawful, in relation to an appointment to an office or post to which this section applies and which is an office or post referred to in section 10A(1)(c), for a relevant person on whose recommendation, or subject to whose approval, appointments to the office or post are made, to discriminate against a woman—
   (a) in the arrangements which he makes for the purpose of determining who should be recommended or approved in relation to the appointment, or
   (b) in making or refusing to make a recommendation, or giving or refusing to give an approval, in relation to the appointment.

(3) It is unlawful for a relevant person, in relation to a woman who has been appointed to an office or post to which this section applies, to discriminate against her—
  (a) in the terms of the appointment,
  (b) in the opportunities which he affords her for promotion, a transfer, training or receiving any other benefit, or by refusing to afford her any such opportunity,
  (c) by terminating the appointment, or
  (d) by subjecting her to any other detriment in relation to the appointment.

(4) It is unlawful for a relevant person, in relation to an office or post to which this section applies, to subject to harassment a woman—
  (a) who has been appointed to the office or post,
  (b) who is seeking or being considered for appointment to the office or post, or
  (c) who, in relation to appointment to the office or post, is seeking or being considered for a recommendation or approval referred to in section 10A(1)(c).

(5) Subsections (1) and (3) do not apply to any act in relation to an office or post where, if holding the office or post constituted employment, that act would be lawful by virtue of section 7, 7A or 7B (exception where sex is a genuine occupational qualification etc.) or section 19 (ministers of religion etc.).

(6) Subsection (2) does not apply to any act in relation to an office or post where, if holding the office or post constituted employment, it would be lawful by virtue of section 7, 7A, 7B or 19 to refuse to offer the person such employment.

(7) Subsection (3) does not apply to benefits of any description if the relevant person is concerned with the provision (for payment or not) of benefits of that description to the public, or a section of the public to which the person appointed belongs, unless—
  (a) that provision differs in a material respect from the provision of the benefits to persons appointed to offices or posts which are the same as, or not materially different from, that which the person appointed holds,
  (b) the provision of the benefits to the person appointed is regulated by the terms and conditions of her appointment, or
  (c) the benefits relate to training.

(8) In subsection (3)(c), the reference to the termination of the appointment includes a reference—
  (a) to the termination of the appointment by the expiration of any period (including a period expiring by reference to an event or circumstance), not being a termination immediately after which the appointment is renewed on the same terms and conditions, and
  (b) to the termination of the appointment by any act of the person appointed (including the giving of notice) in circumstances such that she is entitled to terminate the appointment without notice by reason of the conduct of the relevant person.

(9) In this section 'relevant person', in relation to an office or post, means—
  (a) in a case relating to an appointment to an office or post, the person with power to make that appointment;
  (b) in a case relating to the making of a recommendation or the giving of an approval in relation to an appointment, a person or body referred to in section 10A(1)(b) with power to make that recommendation or (as the case may be) to give that approval;
  (c) in a case relating to a term of an appointment, the person with power to determine that term;
  (d) in a case relating to a working condition afforded in relation to an appointment—
    (i) the person with power to determine that working condition, or
    (ii) where there is no such person, the person with power to make the appointment;

(e) in a case relating to the termination of an appointment, the person with power to terminate the appointment;

(f) in a case relating to the subjection of a person to any other detriment or to harassment, any person or body falling within one or more of paragraphs (a) to (e) in relation to such cases as are there mentioned.

(10) In subsection (9)(d) 'working condition' includes any opportunity for promotion, a transfer, training or receiving any other benefit.

(11) In this section—

(a) references to making a recommendation include references to making a negative recommendation;

(b) references to refusal include references to deliberate omission;

(c) 'benefits' includes facilities and services.

11 [omitted]

12 Trade unions etc.

(1) This section applies to an organisation of workers, an organisation of employers, or any other organisation whose members carry on a particular profession or trade for the purposes of which the organisation exists.

(2) It is unlawful for an organisation to which this section applies, in the case of a woman who is not a member of the organisation, to discriminate against her—

(a) in the terms on which it is prepared to admit her to membership, or

(b) by refusing, or deliberately omitting to accept, her application for membership.

(3) It is unlawful for an organisation to which this section applies, in the case of a woman who is a member of the organisation, to discriminate against her—

(a) in the way it affords her access to any benefits, facilities or services, or by refusing or deliberately omitting to afford her access to them, or

(b) by depriving her of membership, or varying the terms on which she is a member, or

(c) by subjecting her to any other detriment.

(3A) It is unlawful for an organisation to which this section applies, in relation to membership of that organisation, to subject to harassment a woman who—

(a) is a member of the organisation, or

(b) has applied for membership of the organisation.

(4) [repealed]

13–20 [omitted]

20A Relationships which have come to an end

(1) This section applies where—

(a) there has been a relevant relationship between a woman and another person ('the relevant person'), and

(b) the relationship has come to an end (whether before or after the commencement of this section).

(2) In this section, a 'relevant relationship' is a relationship during the course of which an act of discrimination by one party to the relationship against the other party to it is unlawful under any proceeding provision of this Part.

(3) It is unlawful for the relevant person to discriminate against the woman by subjecting her to a detriment where the discrimination arises out of and is closely connected to the relevant relationship.

(4) It is unlawful for the relevant person to subject a woman to harassment where that treatment arises out of or is closely connected to the relevant relationship.

21–36 [omitted]

PART IV   OTHER UNLAWFUL ACTS

37   Discriminatory practices

(1) In this section 'discriminatory practice' means—

    (a) the application of a provision, criterion or practice which results in an act of discrimination which is unlawful by virtue of any provision of Part 2 or 3 taken with section 1(2)(b) or 3(1)(b) or which would be likely to result in such an act of discrimination if the persons to whom it is applied were not all of one sex, or

    (b) the application of a requirement or condition which results in an act of discrimination which is unlawful by virtue of any provision of Part 3 taken with section 1(1)(b) or which would be likely to result in such an act of discrimination if the persons to whom it is applied were not all of one sex.

(2) A person acts in contravention of this section if and so long as—

    (a) he applies a discriminatory practice, or

    (b) he operates practices or other arrangements which in any circumstances would call for the application by him of a discriminatory practice.

(3) Proceedings in respect of a contravention of this section shall be brought only by the Commission in accordance with sections 20 to 24 of the Equality Act 2006.

38   Discriminatory advertisements

(1) It is unlawful to publish or cause to be published an advertisement which indicates, or might reasonably be understood as indicating, an intention by a person to do any act which is or might be unlawful by virtue of Part II or III.

(2) Subsection (1) does not apply to an advertisement if the intended act would not in fact be unlawful.

(3) For the purposes of subsection (1), use of a job description with a sexual connotation (such as 'waiter', 'salesgirl', 'postman' or 'stewardess') shall be taken to indicate an intention to discriminate, unless the advertisement contains an indication to the contrary.

(4) The publisher of an advertisement made unlawful by subsection (1) shall not be subject to any liability under that subsection in respect of the publication of the advertisement if he proves—

    (a) that the advertisement was published in reliance on a statement made to him by the person who caused it to be published to the effect that, by reason of the operation of subsection (2), the publication would not be unlawful, and

    (b) that it was reasonable for him to rely on the statement.

(5) A person who knowingly or recklessly makes a statement such as is referred to in subsection (4) which in a material respect is false or misleading commits an offence, and shall be liable on summary conviction to a fine not exceeding level 5 on the standard scale.

(6) Proceedings in respect of a contravention of subsection (1) may be brought only—

    (a) by the Commission, and

    (b) in accordance with section 25 of the Equality Act 2006.

39   Instructions to discriminate

(1) It is unlawful for a person—

    (a) who has authority over another person, or

    (b) in accordance with whose wishes that other person is accustomed to act,

to instruct him to do any act which is unlawful by virtue of Part II or III, or procure or attempt to procure the doing by him of any such act.

(2) Proceedings in respect of a contravention of subsection (1) may be brought only—

    (a) by the Commission, and

    (b) in accordance with section 25 of the Equality Act 2006.

40 Pressure to discriminate

(1) It is unlawful to induce, or attempt to induce, a person to do any act which contravenes Part II or III by—

(a) providing or offering to provide him with any benefit, or

(b) subjecting or threatening to subject him to any detriment.

(2) An offer or threat is not prevented from falling within subsection (1) because it is not made directly to the person in question, if it is made in such a way that he is likely to hear of it.

(3) Proceedings in respect of a contravention of subsection (1) may be brought only—

(a) by the Commission, and

(b) in accordance with section 25 of the Equality Act 2006.

41 Liability of employers and principals

(1) Anything done by a person in the course of his employment shall be treated for the purposes of this Act as done by his employer as well as by him, whether or not it was done with the employer's knowledge or approval.

(2) Anything done by a person as agent for another person with the authority (whether express or implied, and whether precedent or subsequent) of that other person shall be treated for the purposes of this Act as done by that other person as well as by him.

(3) In proceedings brought under this Act against any person in respect of an act alleged to have been done by an employee of his it shall be a defence for that person to prove that he took such steps as were reasonably practicable to prevent the employee from doing that act, or from doing in the course of his employment acts of that description.

42 Aiding unlawful acts

(1) A person who knowingly aids another person to do an act made unlawful by this Act shall be treated for the purposes of this Act as himself doing an unlawful act of the like description.

(2) For the purposes of subsection (1) an employee or agent for whose act the employer or principal is liable under section 41 (or would be so liable but for section 41(3)) shall be deemed to aid the doing of the act by the employer or principal.

(3) A person does not under this section knowingly aid another to do an unlawful act if—

(a) he acts in reliance on a statement made to him by that other person that, by reason of any provision of this Act, the act which he aids would not be unlawful, and

(b) it is reasonable for him to rely on the statement.

(4) A person who knowingly or recklessly makes a statement such as is referred to in subsection (3)(a) which in a material respect is false or misleading commits an offence, and shall be liable on summary conviction to a fine not exceeding level 5 on the standard scale.

PART V   GENERAL EXCEPTIONS FROM PARTS II TO IV

42A Selection of candidates

(1) Nothing in Parts 2 to 4 shall—

(a) be construed as affecting arrangements to which this section applies, or

(b) render unlawful anything done in accordance with such arrangements.

(2) This section applies to arrangements made by a registered political party which—

(a) regulate the selection of the party's candidates in a relevant election, and

(b) are adopted for the purpose of reducing inequality in the numbers of men and women elected, as candidates of the party, to be members of the body concerned.

(3) The following elections are relevant elections for the purposes of this section—

(a) parliamentary elections;

(b) elections to the European Parliament;

(c) elections to the Scottish Parliament;

(d) elections to the National Assembly for Wales;

(e) local government elections within the meaning of sections 191, 203 or 204 of the Representation of the People Act 1983 (c. 2) (excluding any election of the Mayor of London).

(4) In this section 'registered political party' means a party registered in the Great Britain register under Part 2 of the Political Parties, Elections and Referendums Act 2000 (c. 41).

43–46   [omitted]

47   Discriminatory training by certain bodies

(1) Nothing in Parts II to IV shall render unlawful any act done in relation to particular work by any person in, or in connection with—

(a) affording women only, or men only, access to facilities for training which would help to fit them for that work, or

(b) encouraging women only, or men only, to take advantage of opportunities for doing that work,

where it reasonably appears to that person that at any time within the 12 months immediately preceding the doing of the act there were no persons of the sex in question doing that work in Great Britain, or the number of persons of that sex doing the work in Great Britain was comparatively small.

(2) Where in relation to particular work it reasonably appears to any person that although the condition for the operation of subsection (1) is not met for the whole of Great Britain it is met for an area within Great Britain, nothing in Parts II to IV shall render unlawful any act done by the training body in, or in connection with—

(a) affording persons who are of the sex in question, and who appear likely to take up that work in that area, access to facilities for training which would help to fit them for that work, or

(b) encouraging persons of that sex to take advantage of opportunities in the area for doing that work.

(3) Nothing in Parts II to IV shall render unlawful any act done by a training body in, or in connection with, affording persons access to facilities for training which would help to fit them for employment, where it reasonably appears to that person that those persons are in special need of training by reason of the period for which they have been discharging domestic or family responsibilities to the exclusion of regular full time employment.

The discrimination in relation to which this subsection applies may result from confining the training to persons who have been discharging domestic or family responsibilities, or from the way persons are selected for training, or both.

(4) The preceding provisions of this section shall not apply in relation to any discrimination which is rendered unlawful by section 6.

48   Other discriminatory training etc.

(1) Nothing in Parts II to IV shall render unlawful any act done by an employer in relation to particular work in his employment, being an act done in, or in connection with,—

(a) affording his female employees only, or his male employees only, access to facilities for training which would help to fit them for that work, or

(b) encouraging women only, or men only, to take advantage of opportunities for doing that work,

where at any time within the twelve months immediately preceding the doing of the act there were no persons of the sex in question among those doing that work or the number of persons of that sex doing the work was comparatively small.

(2) Nothing in section 12 shall render unlawful any act done by an organisation to which that section applies in, or in connection with,—

    (a) affording female members of the organisation only, or male members of the
        organisation only, access to facilities for training which would help to fit them for
        holding a post of any kind in the organisation, or

    (b) encouraging female members only, or male members only, to take advantage of
        opportunities for holding such posts in the organisation,

where at any time within the twelve months immediately preceding the doing of the act there
were no persons of the sex in question among persons holding such posts in the organisation or
the number of persons of that sex holding such posts was comparatively small.

(3) Nothing in Parts II to IV shall render unlawful any act done by an organisation to
which section 12 applies in, or in connection with, encouraging women only, or men only,
to become members of the organisation where at any time within the twelve months
immediately preceding the doing of the act there were no persons of the sex in question
among those members or the number of persons of that sex among the members was
comparatively small.

49 Trade unions etc.: elective bodies

(1) If an organisation to which section 12 applies comprises a body the membership of
which is wholly or mainly elected, nothing in section 12 shall render unlawful
provision which ensures that a minimum number of persons of one sex are members of the
body—

    (a) by reserving seats on the body for persons of that sex, or

    (b) by making extra seats on the body available (by election or co-option or other-
        wise) for persons of that sex on occasions when the number of persons of that sex
        in the other seats is below the minimum,

where in the opinion of the organisation the provision is in the circumstances needed to
secure a reasonable lower limit to the number of members of that sex serving on the body;
and nothing in Parts II to IV shall render unlawful any act done in order to give effect to such
a provision.

(2) This section shall not be taken as making lawful—

    (a) discrimination in the arrangements for determining the persons entitled to vote
        in an election of members of the body, or otherwise to choose the persons to serve
        on the body, or

    (b) discrimination in any arrangements concerning membership of the organisation
        itself.

50 Indirect access to benefits etc.

(1) References in this Act to the affording by any person of access to benefits, facilities or
services are not limited to benefits, facilities or services provided by that person himself, but
include any means by which it is in that person's power to facilitate access to benefits,
facilities or services provided by any other person (the 'actual provider').

(2) Where by any provision of this Act the affording by any person of access to benefits,
facilities or services in a discriminatory way is in certain circumstances prevented from being
unlawful, the effect of the provision shall extend also to the liability under this Act of any
actual provider.

51 Acts done for purposes of protection of women

(1) Nothing in the following provisions, namely—

    (a) Part II,

    (b) Part III so far as it applies to vocational training, or

    (c) Part IV so far as it has effect in relation to the provisions mentioned in paragraphs
        (a) and (b),

shall render unlawful any act done by a person in relation to a woman if—

        (i) it was necessary for that person to do it in order to comply with a requirement
           of an existing statutory provision concerning the protection of women, or

(ii) it was necessary for that person to do it in order to comply with a requirement of a relevant statutory provision (within the meaning of Part I of the
Health and Safety at Work etc. Act 1974) and it was done by that person for
the purpose of the protection of the woman in question (or of any class of
women that included that woman).

(2) In subsection (1)—

(a) the reference in paragraph (i) of that subsection to an existing statutory provision
concerning the protection of women is a reference to any such provision having
effect for the purpose of protecting women as regards—

(i) pregnancy or maternity, or

(ii) other circumstances giving rise to risks specifically affecting women,

whether the provision relates only to such protection or to the protection of any
other class of persons as well; and

(b) the reference in paragraph (ii) of that subsection to the protection of a particular
woman or class of women is a reference to the protection of that woman or those
women as regards any circumstances falling within paragraph (a)(i) or (ii) above.

(3) In this section 'existing statutory provision' means (subject to subsection (4)) any
provision of—

(a) an Act passed before this Act, or

(b) an instrument approved or made by or under such an Act (including one
approved or made after the passing of this Act).

(4) Where an Act passed after this Act re-enacts (with or without modification) a provision of an Act passed before this Act, that provision as re-enacted shall be treated for the
purposes of subsection (3) as if it continued to be contained in an Act passed before this Act.

51A [omitted]; 52–61 [repealed]

PART VII   ENFORCEMENT

62   Restriction of proceedings for breach of Act

(1) Except as provided by this Act no proceedings, whether civil or criminal, shall lie
against any person in respect of an act by reason that the act is unlawful by virtue of a
provision of this Act.

(2) Subsection (1) does not preclude the making of an order of certiorari, mandamus or
prohibition.

(3) [omitted]

63   Jurisdiction of employment tribunals

(1) A complaint by any person ('the complainant') that another person ('the respondent')—

(a) has committed an act of discrimination or harassment against the complainant
which is unlawful by virtue of Part II or section 35A or 35B, or

(b) is by virtue of section 41 or 42 to be treated as having committed such an act of
discrimination or harassment against the complainant,

may be presented to an employment tribunal.

(2) Subsection (1) does not apply to a complaint under section 13(1) of an act in respect
of which an appeal, or proceedings in the nature of an appeal, may be brought under any
enactment.

63A   Burden of proof: employment tribunals

(1) This section applies to any complaint presented under section 63 to an employment
tribunal.

(2) Where, on the hearing of the complaint, the complainant proves facts from which
the tribunal could, apart from this section, conclude in the absence of an adequate
explanation that the respondent—

(a) has committed an act of discrimination or harassment against the complainant which is unlawful by virtue of Part 2 or section 35A or 35B, or

(b) is by virtue of section 41 or 42 to be treated as having committed such an act of discrimination or harassment against the complainant,

the tribunal shall uphold the complaint unless the respondent proves that he did not commit, or, as the case may be, is not to be treated as having committed, that act.

64 [repealed]

65   Remedies on complaint under section 63

(1) Where an employment tribunal finds that a complaint presented to it under section 63 is well-founded the tribunal shall make such of the following as it considers just and equitable—

(a) an order declaring the rights of the complainant and the respondent in relation to the act to which the complaint relates;

(b) an order requiring the respondent to pay to the complainant compensation of an amount corresponding to any damages he could have been ordered by a county court or by a sheriff court to pay to the complainant if the complaint had fallen to be dealt with under section 66;

(c) a recommendation that the respondent take within a specified period action appearing to the tribunal to be practicable for the purpose of obviating or reducing the adverse effect on the complainant of any act of discrimination to which the complaint relates.

(1A) In applying section 66 for the purposes of subsection (1)(b), no account shall be taken of subsection (3) of that section.

(1B) As respects an unlawful act of discrimination falling within section 1(2)(b) or section 3(1)(b), if the respondent proves that the provision, criterion or practice in question was not applied with the intention of treating the complainant unfavourably on the ground of his sex or (as the case may be) fulfilment of the condition in section 3(2), an order may be made under subsection (1)(b) only if the employment tribunal—

(a) makes such order under subsection (1)(a) and such recommendation under subsection (1)(c) (if any) as it would have made if it had no power to make an order under subsection (1)(b); and

(b) (where it makes an order under subsection (1)(a) or a recommendation under subsection (1)(c) or both) considers that it is just and equitable to make an order under subsection (1)(b) as well.

(2) [repealed]

(3) If without reasonable justification the respondent to a complaint fails to comply with a recommendation made by an employment tribunal under subsection (1)(c), then, if they think it just and equitable to do so—

(a) the tribunal may increase the amount of compensation required to be paid to the complainant in respect of the complaint by an order made under subsection (1)(b), or

(b) if an order under subsection (1)(b) was not made, the tribunal may make such an order.

66–66B [omitted]; **67–73** [repealed]

74   Help for aggrieved persons in obtaining information etc.

(1) With a view to helping a person ('the person aggrieved') who considers he may have been discriminated against or subjected to harassment in contravention of this Act to decide whether to institute proceedings and, if he does so, to formulate and present his case in the most effective manner, the Secretary of State shall by order prescribe—

(a) forms by which the person aggrieved may question the respondent on his reasons for doing any relevant act, or on any other matter which is or may be relevant;

(b) forms by which the respondent may if he so wishes reply to any questions.

(2) Where the person aggrieved questions the respondent (whether in accordance with an order under subsection (1) or not)—

    (a) the question, and any reply by the respondent (whether in accordance with such an order or not) shall, subject to the following provisions of this section, be admissible as evidence in the proceedings;

    (b) if it appears to the court or tribunal that the respondent deliberately, and without reasonable excuse, omitted to reply within the period applicable under subsection (2A) or that his reply is evasive or equivocal, the court or tribunal may draw any inference from that fact that it considers it just and equitable to draw, including an inference that he committed an unlawful act.

(2A) The period applicable for the purposes of subsection (2)(b) is—

    (a) eight weeks beginning with the day when the question was served on the respondent, if the question relates to discrimination under—

        (i)   any provision of Part 2,

        (ii) section 35A or 35B, or

        (iii) any other provision of Part 3, so far as it applies to vocational training;

    (b) a reasonable period, as regards any other question.

75 [repealed]

Period within which proceedings to be brought

76 Period within which proceedings to be brought

(1) An employment tribunal shall not consider a complaint under section 63 unless it is presented to the tribunal before the end of

    (a) the period of three months beginning when the act complained of was done; or

    (b) in a case to which section 85(9A) applies, the period of six months so beginning.

(2)–(2C) [omitted]

(3) [repealed]

(4) [repealed]

(5) A court or tribunal may nevertheless consider any such complaint or claim which is out of time if, in all the circumstances of the case, it considers that it is just and equitable to do so.

(6) For the purposes of this section—

    (a) where the inclusion or any term in a contract renders the making of the contract an unlawful act that act shall be treated as extending throughout the duration of the contract, and

    (b) any act extending over a period shall be treated as done at the end of that period, and

    (c) a deliberate omission shall be treated as done when the person in question decided upon it,

and in the absence of evidence establishing the contrary a person shall be taken for the purposes of this section to decide upon an omission when he does an act inconsistent with doing the omitted act or, if he has done no such inconsistent act, when the period expires within which he might reasonably have been expected to do the omitted act if it was to be done.

PART VIII SUPPLEMENTAL

76A Public authorities: general statutory duty

(1) A public authority shall in carrying out its functions have due regard to the need—

    (a) to eliminate unlawful discrimination and harassment, and

    (b) to promote equality of opportunity between men and women.

(2) In subsection (1)—
  (a) 'public authority' includes any person who has functions of a public nature (subject to subsections (3) and (4)),
  (b) 'functions' means functions of a public nature, and
  (c) the reference to unlawful discrimination shall be treated as including a reference to contravention of terms of contracts having effect in accordance with an equality clause within the meaning of section 1 of the Equal Pay Act 1970 (c. 41).

(3)–(4) [omitted]

(5) Subsection (1)(b) is without prejudice to the effect of any exception to or limitation of the law about sex discrimination.

(6) A failure in respect of performance of the duty under subsection (1) does not confer a cause of action at private law.

76B–E [omitted]

77 Validity and revision of contracts

(1) A term of a contract is void where—
  (a) its inclusion renders the making of the contract unlawful by virtue of this Act, or
  (b) it is included in furtherance of an act rendered unlawful by this Act, or
  (c) it provides for the doing of an act which would be rendered unlawful by this Act.

(2) Subsection (1) does not apply to a term the inclusion of which constitutes, or is in furtherance of, or provides for, unlawful discrimination against a party to the contract, but the term shall be unenforceable against that party.

(3) A term in a contract which purports to exclude or limit any provision of this Act or the Equal Pay Act 1970 is unenforceable by any person in whose favour the term would operate apart from this subsection.

(4) Subsection (3) does not apply—
  (a) to a contract settling a complaint to which section 63(1) of this Act or section 2 of the Equal Pay Act 1970 applies where the contract is made with the assistance of a conciliation officer;
  (aa) to a contract settling a complaint to which section 63(1) of this Act or section 2 of the Equal Pay Act 1970 applies if the conditions regulating compromise contracts under this Act are satisfied in relation to the contract;
  (b) to a contract settling a claim to which section 66 applies.

(4A) The conditions regulating compromise contracts under this Act are that—
  (a) the contract must be in writing;
  (b) the contract must relate to the particular complaint;
  (c) the complainant must have received advice from a relevant independent adviser as to the terms and effect of the proposed contract and in particular its effect on his ability to pursue his complaint before an employment tribunal;
  (d) there must be in force, when the adviser gives the advice, a contract of insurance, or an indemnity provided for members of a profession or professional body covering the risk of a claim by the complainant in respect of loss arising in consequence of the advice;
  (e) the contract must identify the adviser; and
  (f) the contract must state that the conditions regulating compromise contracts under this Act are satisfied.

(4B) A person is a relevant independent adviser for the purposes of subsection (4A)(c)—
  (a) if he is a qualified lawyer,
  (b) if he is an officer, official, employee or member of an independent trade union who has been certified in writing by the trade union as competent to give advice and as authorised to do so on behalf of the trade union,

(c) if he works at an advice centre (whether as an employee or a volunteer) and has been certified in writing by the centre as competent to give advice and as authorised to do so on behalf of the centre, or

(d) if he is a person of a description specified in an order made by the Secretary of State.

(4BA) But a person is not a relevant independent adviser for the purposes of subsection (4A)(c) in relation to the complainant—

(a) if he is, is employed by or is acting in the matter for the other party or a person who is connected with the other party,

(b) in the case of a person within subsection (4B)(b) or (c), if the trade union or advice centre is the other party or a person who is connected with the other party,

(c) in the case of a person within subsection (4B)(c), if the complainant makes a payment for the advice received from him, or

(d) in the case of a person of a description specified in an order under subsection (4B)(d), if any condition specified in the order in relation to the giving of advice by persons of that description is not satisfied.

(4BB) In subsection (4B)(a) 'qualified lawyer' means—

(a) as respects England and Wales, a barrister (whether in practice as such or employed to give legal advice), a solicitor who holds a practising certificate, or a person other than a barrister or solicitor who is an authorised advocate or authorised litigator (within the meaning of the Courts and Legal Services Act 1990), and

(b) as respects Scotland, an advocate (whether in practice as such or employed to give legal advice), or a solicitor who holds a practising certificate.

(4BC) In subsection (4B)(b) 'independent trade union' has the same meaning as in the Trade Union and Labour Relations (Consolidation) Act 1992.

(4C) For the purposes of subsection (4BA) any two persons are to be treated as connected—

(a) if one is a company of which the other (directly or indirectly) has control, or

(b) if both are companies of which a third person (directly or indirectly) has control.

(4D) An agreement under which the parties agree to submit a dispute to arbitration—

(a) shall be regarded for the purposes of subsection (4)(a) and (aa) as being a contract settling a complaint if—

(i) the dispute is covered by a scheme having effect by virtue of an order under section 212A of the Trade Union and Labour Relations (Consolidation) Act 1992, and

(ii) the agreement is to submit it to arbitration in accordance with the scheme, but

(b) shall be regarded for those purposes as neither being nor including such a contract in any other case.

(5) On the application of any person interested in a contract to which subsection (2) applies, a county court or sheriff court may make such order as it thinks just for removing or modifying any term made unenforceable by that subsection; but such an order shall not be made unless all persons affected have been given notice of the application (except where under rules of court notice may be dispensed with) and have been afforded an opportunity to make representations to the court.

(6) An order under subsection (5) may include provision as respects any period before the making of the order.

78–81 [omitted]

82 General interpretation provisions

(1) In this Act, unless the context otherwise requires—

'access' shall be construed in accordance with section 50;

'act' includes a deliberate omission;

'advertisement' includes every form of advertisement, whether to the public or not, and whether in a newspaper or other publication, by television or radio, by display of notices, signs, labels, showcards or goods, by distribution of samples, circulars, catalogues, price lists or other material by exhibition of pictures, models or films, or in any other way, and references to the publishing of advertisements shall be construed accordingly;

'associated employer' shall be construed in accordance with subsection (2);

. . .

'designate' shall be construed in accordance with subsection (3);

references in Parts 2 and 3 to subjecting a person to a detriment do not include subjecting a person to harassment;

'discrimination' and related terms shall be construed in accordance with section 5(1);

'dispose', in relation to premises, includes granting a right to occupy the premises, and any reference to acquiring premises shall be construed accordingly;

'education' includes any form of training or instruction;

. . .

'employment' means employment under a contract of service or of apprenticeship or a contract personally to execute any work or labour, and related expressions shall be construed accordingly;

'employment agency' means a person who, for profit or not, provides services for the purpose of finding employment for workers or supplying employers with workers;

'enactment' includes an enactment comprised in, or an instrument made under, an Act of the Scottish Parliament;

'equality clause' has the meaning given in section 1(2) of the Equal Pay Act 1970 (as set out in section 8(1) of this Act);

. . .

'final' shall be construed in accordance with subsection (4);

'firm' has the meaning given by section 4 of the Partnership Act 1890;

. . .

'gender reassignment' means a process which is undertaken under medical supervision for the purpose of reassigning a person's sex by changing physiological or other characteristics of sex, and includes any part of such a process;

'general notice', in relation to any person, means a notice published by him at a time and a manner appearing to him suitable for securing that the notice is seen within a reasonable time by persons likely to be affected by it;

'genuine occupational qualification' shall be construed in accordance with section 7(2), except in the expression 'supplementary genuine occupational qualification', which shall be construed in accordance with section 7B(2);

'Great Britain' includes such of the territorial waters of the United Kingdom as are adjacent to Great Britain;

references to subjecting a person to harassment, and to acts of harassment, shall be construed in accordance with section 4A;

. . .

'man' includes a male of any age;

. . .

'near relative' shall be construed in accordance with subsection (5);

'notice' means a notice in writing;

'prescribed' means prescribed by regulations made by the Secretary of State by statutory instrument;

'profession' includes any vocation or occupation;

'provision, criterion or practice' includes 'requirement or condition';

. . .

'retirement' includes retirement (whether voluntary or not) on grounds of age, length of service or incapacity;

...

'trade' includes any business;

'training' includes any form of education or instruction;

...

'woman' includes a female of any age.

(1A) References in this Act to the dismissal of a person from employment or to the expulsion of a person from a position as partner include references—

(a) to the termination of that person's employment or partnership by the expiration of any period (including a period expiring by reference to an event or circumstances), not being a termination immediately after which the employment or partnership is renewed on the same terms; and

(b) to the termination of that person's employment or partnership by any act of his (including the giving of notice) in circumstances such that he is entitled to terminate it without notice by reason of the conduct of the employer or, as the case may be, the conduct of the other partners.

(2) For the purposes of this Act two employers are to be treated as associated if one is a company of which the other (directly or indirectly) has control or if both are companies of which a third person (directly or indirectly) has control.

(3) Any power conferred by this Act to designate establishments or persons may be exercised either by naming them or by identifying them by reference to a class or other description.

(4) For the purposes of this Act a finding by a court or tribunal becomes final when an appeal against the finding is dismissed, withdrawn or abandoned or when the time for appealing expires without an appeal having been brought;

(5) For the purposes of this Act a person is a near relative of another if that person is the wife or husband or civil partner, or parent or child, a grandparent or grandchild, or a brother or sister of the other (whether of full blood or half-blood or by marriage or civil partnership), and 'child' includes an illegitimate child and the wife or husband or civil partner of an illegitimate child.

(6)–(7) [omitted]

83–87 [omitted]

Race Relations Act 1976
(1976, c. 74)

PART I   DISCRIMINATION TO WHICH ACT APPLIES

1   Racial discrimination

(1) A person discriminates against another in any circumstances relevant for the purposes of any provision of this Act if—

(a) on racial grounds he treats that other less favourably than he treats or would treat other persons; or

(b) he applies to that other a requirement or condition which he applies or would apply equally to persons not of the same racial group as that other but—

(i)   which is such that the proportion of persons of the same racial group as that other who can comply with it is considerably smaller than the proportion of persons not of that racial group who can comply with it; and

(ii) which he cannot show to be justifiable irrespective of the colour, race, nationality or ethnic or national origins of the person to whom it is applied; and

(iii) which is to the detriment of that other because he cannot comply with it.

(1A) A person also discriminates against another if, in any circumstances relevant for the purposes of any provision referred to in subsection (1B), he applies to that other a provision, criterion or practice which he applies or would apply equally to persons not of the same race or ethnic or national origins as that other, but—

   (a) which puts or would put persons of the same race or ethnic or national origins as that other at a particular disadvantage when compared with other persons,

   (b) which puts that other at that disadvantage, and

   (c) which he cannot show to be a proportionate means of achieving a legitimate aim.

(1B) The provisions mentioned in subsection (1A) are—

   (a) Part II;

   (b)–(g) [omitted];

(1C) Where, by virtue of subsection (1A), a person discriminates against another, subsection (1)(b) does not apply to him.

(2) It is hereby declared that, for the purposes of this Act, segregating a person from other persons on racial grounds is treating him less favourably than they are treated.

2   Discrimination by way of victimisation

(1) A person ('the discriminator') discriminates against another person ('the person victimised') in any circumstances relevant for the purposes of any provision of this Act if he treats the person victimised less favourably than in those circumstances he treats or would treat other persons, and does so by reason that the person victimised has—

   (a) brought proceedings against the discriminator or any other person under this Act; or

   (b) given evidence or information in connection with proceedings brought by any person against the discriminator or any other person under this Act; or

   (c) otherwise done anything under or by reference to this Act in relation to the discriminator or any other person; or

   (d) alleged that the discriminator or any other person has committed an act which (whether or not the allegation so states) would amount to a contravention of this Act,

or by reason that the discriminator knows that the person victimised intends to do any of those things, or suspects that the person victimised has done, or intends to do, any of them.

(2) Subsection (1) does not apply to treatment of a person by reason of any allegation made by him if the allegation was false and not made in good faith.

3   Meaning of 'racial grounds', 'racial group' etc.

(1) In this Act, unless the context otherwise requires—

'racial grounds' means any of the following grounds, namely colour, race, nationality or ethnic or national origins;

'racial group' means a group of persons defined by reference to colour, race, nationality or ethnic or national origins, and references to a person's racial group refer to any racial group into which he falls.

(2) The fact that a racial group comprises two or more distinct racial groups does not prevent it from constituting a particular racial group for the purposes of this Act.

(3) In this Act—

   (a) references to discrimination refer to any discrimination falling within section 1 or 2; and

   (b) references to racial discrimination refer to any discrimination falling within section 1,

and related expressions shall be construed accordingly.

(4) A comparison of the case of a person of a particular racial group with that of a person not of that group under section 1(1) or (1A) must be such that the relevant circumstances in the one case are the same, or not materially different, in the other.

3A Harassment

(1) A person subjects another to harassment in any circumstances relevant for the purposes of any provision referred to in section 1(1B) where, on grounds of race or ethnic or national origins, he engages in unwanted conduct which has the purpose or effect of—

  (a) violating that other person's dignity, or

  (b) creating an intimidating, hostile, degrading, humiliating or offensive environment for him.

(2) Conduct shall be regarded as having the effect specified in paragraph (a) or (b) of subsection (1) only if, having regard to all the circumstances, including in particular the perception of that other person, it should reasonably be considered as having that effect.

PART II DISCRIMINATION IN THE EMPLOYMENT FIELD

4 Applicants and employees

(1) It is unlawful for a person, in relation to employment by him at an establishment in Great Britain, to discriminate against another—

  (a) in the arrangements he makes for the purpose of determining who should be offered that employment; or

  (b) in the terms on which he offers him that employment; or

  (c) by refusing or deliberately omitting to offer him that employment.

(2) It is unlawful for a person, in the case of a person employed by him at an establishment in Great Britain, to discriminate against that employee—

  (a) in the terms of employment which he affords him; or

  (b) in the way he affords him access to opportunities for promotion, transfer or training, or to any other benefits, facilities or services, or by refusing or deliberately omitting to afford him access to them; or

  (c) by dismissing him, or subjecting him to any other detriment.

(2A) It is unlawful for an employer, in relation to employment by him at an establishment in Great Britain, to subject to harassment a person whom he employs or who has applied to him for employment.

(3) Except in relation to discrimination falling within section 2 or discrimination on grounds of race or ethnic or national origins, subsections (1) and (2) do not apply to employment for the purposes of a private household.

(4) Subsection (2) does not apply to benefits, facilities or services of any description if the employer is concerned with the provision (for payment or not) of benefits, facilities or services of that description to the public, or to a section of the public comprising the employee in question, unless—

  (a) that provision differs in a material respect from the provision of the benefits, facilities or services by the employer to his employees; or

  (b) the provision of the benefits, facilities or services to the employee in question is regulated by his contract of employment; or

  (c) the benefits, facilities or services relate to training.

(4A) In subsection (2)(c) reference to the dismissal of a person from employment includes, where the discrimination is on grounds of race or ethnic or national origins, reference—

  (a) to the termination of that person's employment by the expiration of any period (including a period expiring by reference to an event or circumstance), not being a termination immediately after which the employment is renewed on the same terms; and

  (b) to the termination of that person's employment by any act of his (including the giving of notice) in circumstances such that he is entitled to terminate it without notice by reason of the conduct of the employer.'

4A Exception for genuine occupational requirement

(1) In relation to discrimination on grounds of race or ethnic or national origins—

    (a) section 4(1)(a) or (c) does not apply to any employment; and

    (b) section 4(2)(b) does not apply to promotion or transfer to, or training for, any employment; and

    (c) section 4(2)(c) does not apply to dismissal from any employment; where subsection (2) applies.

(2) This subsection applies where, having regard to the nature of the employment or the context in which it is carried out—

    (a) being of a particular race or of particular ethnic or national origins is a genuine and determining occupational requirement;

    (b) it is proportionate to apply that requirement in the particular case; and

    (c) either—

        (i) the person to whom that requirement is applied does not meet it, or

        (ii) the employer is not satisfied, and in all the circumstances it is reasonable for him not to be satisfied, that that person meets it.

5 Exceptions for genuine occupational qualifications

(1) In relation to racial discrimination in cases where section 4A does not apply—

    (a) section 4(1)(a) or (c) does not apply to any employment where being of a particular racial group is a genuine occupational qualification for the job; and

    (b) section 4(2)(b) does not apply to opportunities for promotion or transfer to, or training for, such employment.

(2) Being of a particular racial group is a genuine occupational qualification for a job only where—

    (a) the job involves participation in a dramatic performance or other entertainment in a capacity for which a person of that racial group is required for reasons of authenticity; or

    (b) the job involves participation as an artist's or photographic model in the production of a work of art, visual image or sequence of visual images for which a person of that racial group is required for reasons of authenticity; or

    (c) the job involves working in a place where food or drink is (for payment or not) provided to and consumed by members of the public or a section of the public in a particular setting for which, in that job, a person of that racial group is required for reasons of authenticity; or

    (d) the holder of the job provides persons of that racial group with personal services promoting their welfare, and those services can most effectively be provided by a person of that racial group.

(3) Subsection (2) applies where some only of the duties of the job fall within paragraph (a), (b), (c) or (d) as well as where all of them do.

(4) Paragraph (a), (b), (c) or (d) of subsection (2) does not apply in relation to the filling of a vacancy at a time when the employer already has employees of the racial group in question—

    (a) who are capable of carrying out the duties falling within that paragraph; and

    (b) whom it would be reasonable to employ on those duties; and

    (c) whose numbers are sufficient to meet the employer's likely requirements in respect of those duties without undue inconvenience

6 [omitted]

7 Contract workers

(1) This section applies to any work for a person ('the principal') which is available for doing by individuals ('contract workers') who are employed not by the principal himself but by another person, who supplies them under a contract made with the principal.

(2) It is unlawful for the principal, in relation to work to which this section applies, to discriminate against a contract worker—

    (a) in the terms on which he allows him to do that work; or

    (b) by not allowing him to do it or continue to do it; or

    (c) in the way he affords him access to any benefits, facilities or services or by refusing or deliberately omitting to afford him access to them; or

    (d) by subjecting him to any other detriment.

(3) The principal does not contravene subsection (2)(b) by doing any act in relation to a person not of a particular racial group , or not of a particular race or particular ethnic or natural origins, at a time when, if the work were to be done by a person taken into the principal's employment, being of that racial group or of that race or those origins would be a genuine occupational qualification or, as the case may be, that act would be lawful by virtue of section 4A for the job.

(3A) It is unlawful for the principal, in relation to work to which this section applies, to subject a contract worker to harassment.

(4) Nothing in this section shall render unlawful any act done by the principal on grounds other than those of race or ethnic or national origins, for the benefit of a contract worker not ordinarily resident in Great Britain in or in connection with allowing him to do work to which this section applies, where the purpose of his being allowed to do that work is to provide him with training in skills which he appears to the principal to intend to exercise wholly outside Great Britain.

(5) Subsection (2)(c) does not apply to benefits, facilities or services of any description if the principal is concerned with the provision (for payment or not) of benefits, facilities or services of that description to the public, or to a section of the public to which the contract worker in question belongs, unless that provision differs in a material respect from the provision of the benefits, facilities or services by the principal to his contract workers.

8–10   [omitted]

11   Trade unions etc.

(1) This section applies to an organisation of workers, an organisation of employers, or any other organisation whose members carry on a particular profession or trade for the purposes of which the organisation exists.

(2) It is unlawful for an organisation to which this section applies, in the case of a person who is not a member of the organisation, to discriminate against him—

    (a) in the terms on which it is prepared to admit him to membership; or

    (b) by refusing, or deliberately omitting to accept, his application for membership.

(3) It is unlawful for an organisation to which this section applies, in the case of a person who is a member of the organisation, to discriminate against him—

    (a) in the way it affords him access to any benefits, facilities or services, or by refusing or deliberately omitting to afford him access to them; or

    (b) by depriving him of membership, or varying the terms on which he is a member; or

    (c) by subjecting him to any other detriment.

(4) It is unlawful for an organisation to which this section applies, in relation to a person's membership or application for membership of that organisation, to subject him to harassment.

12–27   [omitted]

PART IV   OTHER UNLAWFUL ACTS

27A   Relationships which have come to an end

(1) In this section a 'relevant relationship' is a relationship during the course of which, by virtue of any provision referred to in section 1(1B), taken with section 1(1) or (1A), or (as the case may be) by virtue of section 3A—

(a) an act of discrimination by one party to the relationship ('the relevant party') against another party to the relationship, on grounds of race or ethnic or national origins, or

(b) harassment of another party to the relationship by the relevant party,

is unlawful.

(2) Where a relevant relationship has come to an end it is unlawful for the relevant party—

(a) to discriminate against another party, on grounds of race or ethnic or national origins, by subjecting him to a detriment, or

(b) to subject another party to harassment,

where the discrimination or harassment arises out of and is closely connected to that relationship.

(3) In subsection (1) reference to an act of discrimination or harassment which is unlawful includes, in the case of a relationship which has come to an end before 19th July 2003, reference to such an act which would, after that date, be unlawful.

(4) For the purposes of any proceedings in respect of an unlawful act under subsection (2), that act shall be treated as falling within circumstances relevant for the purposes of such of the provisions, or Parts, referred to in subsection (1) as determine most closely the nature of the relevant relationship.

28   Discrimination practices

(1) In this section 'discriminatory practice' means

(a) the application of a requirement or condition which results in an act of discrimination which is unlawful by virtue of any provision of Part II or III taken with section 1(1)(*b*), or which would be likely to result in such an act of discrimination if the persons to whom it is applied included persons of any particular racial group as regards which there has been no occasion for applying it

or

(b) the application of a provision, criterion or practice which results in an act of discrimination which is unlawful by virtue of any provision referred to in section 1(1B), taken with section 1(1A), or which would be likely to result in such an act of discrimination, if the persons to whom it is applied included persons of any particular race or of any particular ethnic or national origins, as regards which there has been no occasion for applying it.

(2) A person acts in contravention of this section if and so long as—

(a) he applies a discriminatory practice; or

(b) he operates practices or other arrangements which in any circumstances would call for the application by him of a discriminatory practice.

(3) Proceedings in respect of a contravention of this section shall be brought only by the Commission in accordance with sections 20 to 24 of the Equality Act 2006.

29   [omitted]

30   Instructions to commit unlawful acts

(1) It is unlawful for a person—

(a) who has authority over another person; or

(b) in accordance with whose wishes that other person is accustomed to act,

to instruct him to do any act which is unlawful by virtue of Part II or III, section 76ZA or, where it renders an act unlawful on grounds of race or ethnic or national origins, section 76, or procure or attempt to procure the doing by him of any such act.

(2) Proceedings in respect of a contravention of subsection (1) may be brought only—

(a) by the Commission, and

(b) in accordance with section 25 of the Equality Act 2006.

31 Pressure to commit unlawful acts

(1) It is unlawful to induce, or attempt to induce, a person to do any act which contravenes Part II or III, section 76ZA or, where it renders an act unlawful on grounds of race or ethnic or national origins, section 76.

(2) An attempted inducement is not prevented from falling within subsection (1) because it is not made directly to the person in question, if it is made in such a way that he is likely to hear of it.

(3) Proceedings in respect of a contravention of subsection (1) may be brought only—

   (a) by the Commission, and

   (b) in accordance with section 25 of the Equality Act 2006.

32 Liability of employers and principals

(1) Anything done by a person in the course of his employment shall be treated for the purposes of this Act (except as regards offences thereunder) as done by his employer as well as by him, whether or not it was done with the employer's knowledge or approval.

(2) Anything done by a person as agent for another person with the authority (whether express or implied, and whether precedent or subsequent) of that other person shall be treated for the purposes of this Act (except as regards offences there-under) as done by that other person as well as by him.

(3) In proceedings brought under this Act against any person in respect of an act alleged to have been done by an employee of his it shall be a defence for that person to prove that he took such steps as were reasonably practicable to prevent the employee from doing that act, or from doing in the course of his employment acts of that description.

33 Aiding unlawful acts

(1) A person who knowingly aids another person to do an act made unlawful by this Act shall be treated for the purposes of this Act as himself doing an unlawful act of the like description.

(2) For the purposes of subsection (1) an employee or agent for whose act the employer or principal is liable under section 32 (or would be so liable but for section 32(3)) shall be deemed to aid the doing of the act by the employer or principal.

(3) A person does not under this section knowingly aid another to do an unlawful act if—

   (a) he acts in reliance on a statement made to him by that other person that, by reason of any provision of this Act, the act which he aids would not be unlawful: and

   (b) it is reasonable for him to rely on the statement.

(4) A person who knowingly or recklessly makes a statement such as is mentioned in subsection (3)(*a*) which in a material respect is false or misleading commits an offence, and shall be liable on summary conviction to a fine not exceeding level 5 on the standard scale.

34–80 [omitted]

Sex Discrimination Act 1986
(1986, c. 59)

6 Collective agreements and rules of undertakings

(1) Without prejudice to the generality of section 77 of the 1975 Act (which makes provision with respect to the validity and revision of contracts), that section shall apply, as it applies in relation to the term of a contract, to the following, namely—

   (a) any term of a collective agreement, including an agreement which was not intended, or is presumed not to have been intended, to be a legally enforceable contract;

    (b) any rule made by an employer for application to all or any of the persons who are employed by him or who apply to be, or are, considered by him for employment;

    (c) any rule made by an organisation, authority or body to which subsection (2) below applies for application to all or any of its members or prospective members or to all or any of the persons on whom it has conferred authorisations or qualifications or who are seeking the authorisations or qualifications which it has power to confer;

and that section shall so apply whether the agreement was entered into, or the rule made, before or after the coming into force of this section.

    (2) This subsection applies to—

    (a) any organisation of workers;

    (b) any organisation of employers;

    (c) any organisation whose members carry on a particular profession or trade for the purposes of which the organisation exists;

    (d) any authority or body which can confer an authorisation or qualification which is needed for, or facilitates, engagement in a particular profession or trade.

    (3) For the purposes of the said section 77 a term or rule shall be deemed to provide for the doing of an act which would be rendered unlawful by the 1975 Act if—

    (a) it provides for the inclusion in any contract of employment of any term which by virtue of an equality clause would fall either to be modified or to be supplemented by an additional term; and

    (b) that clause would not be prevented from operating in relation to the contract by section 1(3) of the Equal Pay Act 1970 (material factors justifying discrimination).

    (4) Nothing in the said section 77 shall affect the operation of any term or rule in so far as it provides for the doing of a particular act in circumstances where the doing of that act would not be, or be deemed by virtue of subsection (3) above to be, rendered unlawful by the 1975 Act.

    (4A) A person to whom this subsection applies may present a complaint to an employment tribunal that a term or rule is void by virtue of subsection (1) of the said section 77 if he has reason to believe—

    (a) that the term or rule may at some future time have effect in relation to him, and

    (b) where he alleges that it is void by virtue of paragraph (c) of that subsection, that—

       (i) an act for the doing of which it provides may be at some such time be done in relation to him, and

       (ii) the act would be, or be deemed by virtue of subsection (3) above to be, rendered unlawful by the 1975 Act if done in relation to him in present circumstances.

    (4B) In the case of a complaint about—

    (a) a term of a collective agreement made by or on behalf of—

       (i) an employer,

       (ii) an organisation of employers of which an employer is a member, or

       (iii) an association of such organisations of one of which an employer is a member, or

    (b) a rule made by an employer,

subsection (4A) applies to any person who is, or is genuinely and actively seeking to become, one of his employees.

    (4C) In the case of a complaint about a rule made by an organisation, authority or body to which subsection (2) above applies, subsection (4A) applies to any person—

    (a) who is, or is genuinely and actively seeking to become, a member of the organisation, authority or body,

    (b) on whom the organistion, authority or body has conferred an authorisation or qualification, or

    (c) who is genuinely and actively seeking an authorisation or qualification which the organisation, authority or body has power to confer.

(4D) When an employment tribunal finds that a complaint presented to it under sub-section (4A) above is well-founded the tribunal shall make an order declaring that the term or rule is void.

(5) The avoidance by virtue of the said section 77 of any term or rule which provides for any person to be discriminated against shall be without prejudice to the following rights except in so far as they enable any person to require another person to be treated less favourably than himself, namely—

(a) such of the rights of the person to be discriminated against; and

(b) such of the rights of any person who will be treated more favourably in direct or indirect consequence of the discrimination,

as are conferred by or in respect of a contract made or modified wholly or partly in pursuance of, or by reference to, that term or rule.

(6) In this section 'collective agreement' means any agreement relating to one or more of the matters mentioned in section 178(2) of the Trade Union and Labour Relations (Consolidation) Act 1992 (meaning of trade dispute), being an agreement made by or on behalf of one or more employers or one or more organisations of employers or associations of such organisations with one or more organisations of workers or associations of such organisations.

(7) Any expression used in this section and in the 1975 Act has the same meaning in this section as in that Act, and this section shall have effect as if the terms of any service to which Parts II and IV of that Act apply by virtue of subsection (2) of section 85 of that Act (Crown application) were terms of a contract of employment and, in relation to the terms of any such service, as if service for the purposes of any person mentioned in that subsection were employment by that person.

Employment Act 1989
(1989, c. 38)

1   Overriding of statutory requirements which conflict with certain provisions of 1975 Act

(1) Any provision of—

(a) an Act passed before the Sex Discrimination Act 1975, or

(b) an instrument approved or made by or under such an Act (including one approved or made after the passing of the 1975 Act),

shall be of no effect in so far as it imposes a requirement to do an act which would be rendered unlawful by any of the provisions of that Act referred to in subsection (2).

(2) Those provisions are—

(a) Part II (discrimination as respects employment);

(b) Part III (discrimination as respects education etc.) so far as it applies to vocational training; and

(c) Part IV (other unlawful acts) so far as it has effect in relation to the provisions mentioned in paragraphs (a) and (b) above.

(3) Where in any legal proceedings (of whatever nature) there falls to be determined the question whether subsection (1) operates to negative the effect of any provision in so far as it requires the application by any person of a provision, criterion or practice falling within section 1(2)(b)(i) or 3 (1)(b)(i) of the 1975 Act (indirect discrimination on grounds of sex or marital status)—

(a) it shall be for any party to the proceedings who claims that subsection (1) does not so operate in relation to that provision to show the provision, criterion or practice in question to be justifiable as mentioned in section (1)(2)(b)(ii) or 3(1)(b)(ii) of that Act; and

(b) the said section (1)(2)(b)(ii) or 3(1)(b)(ii) shall accordingly have effect in relation to the provision, criterion or practice as if the reference to the person applying it were a reference to any such party to the proceedings.

(4) Where an Act passed after the 1975 Act, whether before or after the passing of this Act, re-enacts (with or without modification) a provision of an Act passed before the 1975 Act, the provision as re-enacted shall be treated for the purposes of subsection (1) as if it continued to be contained in an Act passed before the 1975 Act.

2–3 [omitted]

4 Exemption for discrimination under certain provisions concerned with the protection of women at work

(1) Without prejudice to the operation of section 51 of the 1975 Act nothing in—

    (a) Part II of that Act,

    (b) Part III of that Act so far as it applies to vocational training, or

    (c) Part IV of that Act so far as it has effect in relation to the provisions mentioned in paragraphs (a) and (b) above,

shall render unlawful any act done by a person in relation to a woman if it was necessary for that person to do that act in order to comply with any requirement of any of the provisions specified in Schedule 1 to this Act (which are concerned with the protection of women at work).

(3) In this section 'woman' means a female person of any age.

5–30 [omitted]

Trade Union and Labour Relations (Consolidation) Act 1992
(1992, c. 52)

PART I   TRADE UNIONS

CHAPTER I   INTRODUCTORY

Meaning of 'trade union'

Section

    1   Meaning of 'trade union'.

The list of trade unions

Certification as independent trade union

Supplementary

CHAPTER II   STATUS AND PROPERTY OF TRADE UNIONS

CHAPTER IV   ELECTIONS FOR CERTAIN POSITIONS

CHAPTER V   RIGHTS OF TRADE UNION MEMBERS

PART IV   INDUSTRIAL RELATIONS

CHAPTER I   COLLECTIVE BARGAINING

PART V   INDUSTRIAL ACTION

PART II VOLUNTARY RECOGNITION

PART IV DERECOGNITION: GENERAL

PART V DERECOGNITION WHERE RECOGNITION AUTOMATIC

PART VIII DETRIMENT

PART IX GENERAL

PART I   TRADE UNIONS

CHAPTER I INTRODUCTORY

Meaning of 'trade union'

1   Meaning of 'trade union'

In this Act a 'trade union' means an organisation (whether temporary or permanent)—

    (a) which consists wholly or mainly of workers of one or more descriptions and whose principal purposes include the regulation of relations between workers of that description or those descriptions and employers or employers' associations; or

    (b) which consists wholly or mainly of—

        (i) constituent or affiliated organisations which fulfil the conditions in paragraph (a) (or themselves consist wholly or mainly of constituent or affiliated organisations which fulfil those conditions), or

        (ii) representatives of such constituent or affiliated organisations,

and whose principal purposes include the regulation of relations between workers and employers or between workers and employers' associations, or the regulation of relations between its constituent or affiliated organisations.

The list of trade unions

2   The list of trade unions

    (1) The Certification Officer shall keep a list of trade unions containing the names of—

    (a) the organisations whose names were, immediately before the commencement of this Act, duly entered in the list of trade unions kept by him under section 8 of the Trade Union and Labour Relations Act 1974, and

    (b) the names of the organisations entitled to have their names entered in the list in accordance with this Part.

    (2) The Certification Officer shall keep copies of the list of trade unions, as for the time being in force, available for public inspection at all reasonable hours free of charge.

    (3) A copy of the list shall be included in his annual report.

    (4) The fact that the name of an organisation is included in the list of trade unions is evidence (in Scotland, sufficient evidence) that the organisation is a trade union.

    (5) On the application of an organisation whose name is included in the list, the Certification Officer shall issue it with a certificate to that effect.

    (6) A document purporting to be such a certificate is evidence (in Scotland, sufficient evidence) that the name of the organisation is entered in the list.

3   Application to have name entered in the list

    (1) An organisation of workers, whenever formed, whose name is not entered in the list of trade unions may apply to the Certification Officer to have its name entered in the list.

    (2) The application shall be made in such form and manner as the Certification Officer may require and shall be accompanied by—

    (a) a copy of the rules of the organisation,

    (b) a list of its officers,

    (c) the address of its head or main office, and

    (d) the name under which it is or is to be known, and by the prescribed fee.

    (3) If the Certification Officer is satisfied—

    (a) that the organisation is a trade union,

    (b) that subsection (2) has been complied with, and

    (c) that entry of the name in the list is not prohibited by subsection (4),

he shall enter the name of the organisation in the list of trade unions.

(4) The Certification Officer shall not enter the name of an organisation in the list of trade unions if the name is the same as that under which another organisation—

(a) was on 30 September 1971 registered as a trade union under the Trade Union Acts 1871 to 1964,

(b) was at any time registered as a trade union or employers' association under the Industrial Relations Act 1971, or

(c) is for the time being entered in the list of trade unions or in the list of employers' associations kept under Part II of this Act,

or if the name is one so nearly resembling any such name as to be likely to deceive the public.

4 Removal of name from the list

(1) If it appears to the Certification Officer, on application made to him or otherwise, that an organisation whose name is entered in the list of trade unions is not a trade union, he may remove its name from the list.

(2) He shall not do so without giving the organisation notice of his intention and considering any representations made to him by the organisation within such period (of not less than 28 days beginning with the date of the notice) as may be specified in the notice.

(3) The Certification Officer shall remove the name of an organisation from the list of trade unions if—

(a) he is requested by the organisation to do so, or

(b) he is satisfied that the organisation has ceased to exist.

Certification as independent trade union

5 Meaning of 'independent trade union'

In this Act an 'independent trade union' means a trade union which—

(a) is not under the domination or control of an employer or group of employers or of one or more employers' associations, and

(b) is not liable to interference by an employer or any such group or association (arising out of the provision of financial or material support or by any other means whatsoever) tending towards such control;

and references to 'independence', in relation to a trade union, shall be construed accordingly.

6 Application for certificate of independence

(1) A trade union whose name is entered on the list of trade unions may apply to the Certification Officer for a certificate that it is independent.

The application shall be made in such form and manner as the Certification Officer may require and shall be accompanied by the prescribed fee.

(2) The Certification Officer shall maintain a record showing details of all applications made to him under this section and shall keep it available for public inspection (free of charge) at all reasonable hours.

(3) If an application is made by a trade union whose name is not entered on the list of trade unions, the Certification Officer shall refuse a certificate of independence and shall enter that refusal on the record.

(4) In any other case, he shall not come to a decision on the application before the end of the period of one month after it has been entered on the record; and before coming to his decision he shall make such enquiries as he thinks fit and shall take into account any relevant information submitted to him by any person.

(5) He shall then decide whether the applicant trade union is independent and shall enter his decision and the date of his decision on the record.

(6) If he decides that the trade union is independent he shall issue a certificate accordingly; and if he decides that it is not, he shall give reasons for his decision.

7   Withdrawal or cancellation of certificate

(1) The Certification Officer may withdraw a trade union's certificate of independence if he is of the opinion that the union is no longer independent.

(2) Where he proposes to do so he shall notify the trade union and enter notice of the proposal in the record.

(3) He shall not come to a decision on the proposal before the end of the period of one month after notice of it was entered on the record; and before coming to his decision he shall make such enquiries as he thinks fit and shall take into account any relevant information submitted to him by any person.

(4) He shall then decide whether the trade union is independent and shall enter his decision and the date of his decision on the record.

(5) He shall confirm or withdraw the certificate accordingly; and if he decides to withdraw it, he shall give reasons for his decision.

(6) Where the name of an organisation is removed from the list of trade unions, the Certification Officer shall cancel any certificate of independence in force in respect of that organisation by entering on the record the fact that the organisation's name has been removed from that list and that the certificate is accordingly cancelled.

8   Conclusive effect of Certification Officer's decision

(1) A certificate of independence which is in force is conclusive evidence for all purposes that a trade union is independent; and a refusal, withdrawal or cancellation of a certificate of independence, entered on the record, is conclusive evidence for all purposes that a trade union is not independent.

(2) A document purporting to be a certificate of independence and to be signed by the Certification Officer, or by a person authorised to act on his behalf, shall be taken to be such a certificate unless the contrary is proved.

(3) A document purporting to be a certified copy of an entry on the record and to be signed by the Certification Officer, or by a person authorised to act on his behalf, shall be taken to be a true copy of such an entry unless the contrary is proved.

(4) If in any proceedings before a court, the Employment Appeal Tribunal, the Central Arbitration Committee, ACAS or an employment tribunal a question arises whether a trade union is independent and there is no certificate of independence in force and no refusal, withdrawal or cancellation of a certificate recorded in relation to that trade union—

   (a) that question shall not be decided in those proceedings, and

   (b) the proceedings shall instead be stayed or sisted until a certificate of independence has been issued or refused by the Certification Officer.

(5) The body before whom the proceedings are stayed or sisted may refer the question of the independence of the trade union to the Certification Officer who shall proceed in accordance with section 6 as on an application by that trade union.

Supplementary

9   Appeal against decision of Certification Officer

(1) An organisation aggrieved by the refusal of the Certification Officer to enter its name in the list of trade unions, or by a decision of his to remove its name from the list, may appeal to the Employment Appeal Tribunal on any appealable question.

(2) A trade union aggrieved by the refusal of the Certification Officer to issue it with a certificate of independence, or by a decision of his to withdraw its certificate, may appeal to the Employment Appeal Tribunal on any appealable question.

(3) [repealed]

(4) For the purposes of this section, an appealable question is any question of law arising in the proceedings before, or arising from the decision of, the Certification Officer.

CHAPTER II STATUS AND PROPERTY OF TRADE UNIONS

General

10 Quasi-corporate status of trade unions

(1) A trade union is not a body corporate but—

(a) it is capable of making contracts;

(b) it is capable of suing and being sued in its own name, whether in proceedings relating to property or founded on contract or tort or any other cause of action; and

(c) proceedings for an offence alleged to have been committed by it or on its behalf may be brought against it in its own name.

(2) A trade union shall not be treated as if it were a body corporate except to the extent authorised by the provisions of this Part.

(3) A trade union shall not be registered—

(a) as a company under the Companies Act 1985; or

(b) under the Friendly Societies Act 1974 or the Industrial and Provident Societies Act 1965;

and any such registration of a trade union (whenever effected) is void.

11 Exclusion of common law rules as to restraint of trade

(1) The purposes of a trade union are not, by reason only that they are in restraint of trade, unlawful so as—

(a) to make any member of the trade union liable to criminal proceedings for conspiracy or otherwise, or

(b) to make any agreement or trust void or voidable.

(2) No rule of a trade union is unlawful or unenforceable by reason only that it is in restraint of trade.

Property of trade union

12 Property to be vested in trustees

(1) All property belonging to a trade union shall be vested in trustees in trust for it.

(2) A judgment, order or award made in proceedings of any description brought against a trade union is enforceable, by way of execution, diligence, punishment for contempt or otherwise, against any property held in trust for it to the same extent and in the same manner as if it were a body corporate.

(3) Subsection (2) has effect subject to section 23 (restriction on enforcement of awards against certain property).

13 Vesting of property in new trustees

(1) The provisions of this section apply in relation to the appointment or discharge of trustees in whom any property is vested in trust for a trade union whose name is entered in the list of trade unions.

(2) In the following sections as they apply to such trustees references to a deed shall be construed as references to an instrument in writing—

(a) section 39 of the Trustee Act 1925 and section 38 of the Trustee Act (Northern Ireland) 1958 (retirement of trustee without a new appointment), and

(b) section 40 of the Trustee Act 1925 and section 39 of the Trustee Act (Northern Ireland) 1958 (vesting of trust property in new or continuing trustees).

(3) Where such a trustee is appointed or discharged by a resolution taken by or on behalf of the union, the written record of the resolution shall be treated for the purposes of those sections as an instrument in writing appointing or discharging the trustee.

(4) In section 40 of the Trustee Act 1925 and section 39 of the Trustee Act (Northern Ireland) 1958 as they apply to such trustees, paragraphs (a) and (c) of subsection (4) (which exclude certain property from the section) shall be omitted.

14   [omitted]

15   **Prohibition on use of funds to indemnify unlawful conduct**
(1) It is unlawful for property of a trade union to be applied in or towards—
   (a) the payment for an individual of a penalty which has been or may be imposed on him for an offence or for contempt of court,
   (b) the securing of any such payment, or
   (c) the provision of anything for indemnifying an individual in respect of such a penalty.

(2) Where any property of a trade union is so applied for the benefit of an individual on whom a penalty has been or may be imposed, then—
   (a) in the case of a payment, an amount equal to the payment is recoverable by the union from him, and
   (b) in any other case, he is liable to account to the union for the value of the property applied.

(3) If a trade union fails to bring or continue proceedings which it is entitled to bring by virtue of subsection (2), a member of the union who claims that the failure is unreasonable may apply to the court on that ground for an order authorising him to bring or continue the proceedings on the union's behalf and at the union's expense.

(4) In this section 'penalty', in relation to an offence, includes an order to pay compensation and an order for the forfeiture of any property; and references to the imposition of a penalty for an offence shall be construed accordingly.

(5) The Secretary of State may by order designate offences in relation to which the provisions of this section do not apply.
Any such order shall be made by statutory instrument which shall be subject to annulment in pursuance of a resolution of either House of Parliament.

(6) This section does not affect—
   (a) any other enactment, any rule of law or any provision of the rules of a trade union which makes it unlawful for the property of a trade union to be applied in a particular way; or
   (b) any other remedy available to a trade union, the trustees of its property or any of its members in respect of an unlawful application of the union's property.

(7) In this section 'member', in relation to a trade union consisting wholly or partly of, or of representatives of, constituent or affiliated organisations, includes a member of any of the constituent or affiliated organisations.

16   **Remedy against trustees for unlawful use of union property**
(1) A member of a trade union who claims that the trustees of the union's property—
   (a) have so carried out their functions, or are proposing so to carry out their functions, as to cause or permit an unlawful application of the union's property, or
   (b) have complied, or are proposing to comply, with an unlawful direction which has been or may be given, or purportedly given, to them under the rules of the union,
may apply to the court for an order under this section.

(2) In a case relating to property which has already been unlawfully applied, or to an unlawful direction that has already been complied with, an application under this section may be made only by a person who was a member of the union at the time when the property was applied or, as the case may be, the direction complied with.

(3) Where the court is satisfied that the claim is well-founded, it shall make such order as it considers appropriate.

The court may in particular—

    (a) require the trustees (if necessary, on behalf of the union) to take all such steps as may be specified in the order for protecting or recovering the property of the union;

    (b) appoint a receiver of, or in Scotland a judicial factor on, the property of the union;

    (c) remove one or more of the trustees.

  (4) Where the court makes an order under this section in a case in which—

    (a) property of the union has been applied in contravention of an order of any court, or in compliance with a direction given in contravention of such an order, or

    (b) the trustees were proposing to apply property in contravention of such an order or to comply with any such direction,

the court shall by its order remove all the trustees except any trustee who satisfies the court that there is a good reason for allowing him to remain a trustee.

  (5) Without prejudice to any other power of the court, the court may on an application for an order under this section grant such interlocutory relief (in Scotland, such interim order) as it considers appropriate.

  (6) This section does not affect any other remedy available in respect of a breach of trust by the trustees of a trade union's property.

  (7) In this section 'member', in relation to a trade union consisting wholly or partly of, or of representatives of, constituent or affiliated organisations, includes a member of any of the constituent or affiliated organisations.

17–19 [omitted]

Liability of trade unions in proceedings in tort

20 Liability of trade union in certain proceedings in tort

  (1) Where proceedings in tort are brought against a trade union—

    (a) on the ground that an act—

      (i) induces another person to break a contract or interferes or induces another person to interfere with its performance, or

      (ii) consists in threatening that a contract (whether one to which the union is a party or not) will be broken or its performance interfered with, or that the union will induce another person to break a contract or interfere with its performance, or

    (b) in respect of an agreement or combination by two or more persons to do or to procure the doing of an act which, if it were done without any such agreement or combination, would be actionable in tort on such a ground,

then, for the purpose of determining in those proceedings whether the union is liable in respect of the act in question, that act shall be taken to have been done by the union if, but only if, it is to be taken to have been authorised or endorsed by the trade union in accordance with the following provisions.

  (2) An act shall be taken to have been authorised or endorsed by a trade union if it was done, or was authorised or endorsed—

    (a) by any person empowered by the rules to do, authorise or endorse acts of the kind in question, or

    (b) by the principal executive committee or the president or general secretary, or

    (c) by any other committee of the union or any other official of the union (whether employed by it or not).

  (3) For the purposes of paragraph (c) of subsection (2)—

    (a) any group of persons constituted in accordance with the rules of the union is a committee of the union; and

(b) an act shall be taken to have been done, authorised or endorsed by an official if it was done, authorised or endorsed by, or by any member of, any group of persons of which he was at the material time a member, the purposes of which included organising or co-ordinating industrial action.

(4) The provisions of paragraphs (b) and (c) of subsection (2) apply notwithstanding anything in the rules of the union, or in any contract or rule of law, but subject to the provisions of section 21 (repudiation by union of certain acts).

(5) Where for the purposes of any proceedings an act is by virtue of this section taken to have been done by a trade union, nothing in this section shall affect the liability of any other person, in those or any other proceedings, in respect of that act.

(6) In proceedings arising out of an act which is by virtue of this section taken to have been done by a trade union, the power of the court to grant an injunction or interdict includes power to require the union to take such steps as the court considers appropriate for ensuring—

(a) that there is no, or no further, inducement of persons to take part or to continue to take part in industrial action, and

(b) that no person engages in any conduct after the granting of the injunction or interdict by virtue of having been induced before it was granted to take part or to continue to take part in industrial action.

The provisions of subsections (2) to (4) above apply in relation to proceedings for failure to comply with any such injunction or interdict as they apply in relation to the original proceedings.

(7) In this section 'rules', in relation to a trade union, means the written rules of the union and any other written provision forming part of the contract between a member and the other members.

21 Repudiation by union of certain acts

(1) An act shall not be taken to have been authorised or endorsed by a trade union by virtue only of paragraph (c) of section 20(2) if it was repudiated by the executive, president or general secretary as soon as reasonably practicable after coming to the knowledge of any of them.

(2) Where an act is repudiated—

(a) written notice of the repudiation must be given to the committee or official in question, without delay, and

(b) the union must do its best to give individual written notice of the fact and date of repudiation, without delay—

(i) to every member of the union who the union has reaon to believe is taking part, or might otherwise take part, in industrial action as a result of the act, and

(ii) to the employer of every such member.

(3) The notice given to members in accordance with paragraph (b)(i) of subsection (2) must contain the following statement—

'Your union has repudiated the call (or calls) for industrial action to which this notice relates and will give no support to unofficial industrial action taken in response to it (or them). If you are dismissed while taking unofficial industrial action, you will have no right to complain of unfair dismissal.'

(4) If subsection (2) or (3) is not complied with, the repudiation shall be treated as ineffective.

(5) An act shall not be treated as repudiated if at any time after the union concerned purported to repudiate it the executive, president or general secretary has behaved in a manner which is inconsistent with the purported repudiation.

(6) The executive, president or general secretary shall be treated as so behaving if, on a request made to any of them within three months of the purported repudiation by a person who—

  (a) is a party to a commercial contract whose performance has been or may be interfered with as a result of the act in question, and

  (b) has not been given written notice by the union of the repudiation, it is not forthwith confirmed in writing that the act has been repudiated.

(7) In this section 'commercial contract' means any contract other than—

  (a) a contract of employment, or

  (b) any other contract under which a person agrees personally to do work or perform services for another.

22   Limit on damages awarded against trade unions in actions in tort

(1) This section applies to any proceedings in tort brought against a trade union, except—

  (a) proceedings for personal injury as a result of negligence, nuisance or breach of duty;

  (b) proceedings for breach of duty in connection with the ownership, occupation, possession, control or use of property;

  (c) proceedings brought by virtue of Part I of the Consumer Protection Act 1987 (product liability).

(2) In any proceedings in tort to which this section applies the amount which may be awarded against the union by way of damages shall not exceed the following limit—

Number of members of union	Maximum award of damages
Less than 5,000	£10,000
5,000 or more but less than 25,000	£50,000
25,000 or more but less than 100,000	£125,000
100,000 or more	£250,000

  (3)–(4) [omitted]

  (5) In this section—

'breach of duty' means breach of a duty imposed by any rule of law or by or under any enactment;

'personal injury' includes any disease and any impairment of a person's physical or mental condition; and

'property' means any property, whether real or personal (or in Scotland, heritable or moveable).

Restriction on enforcement against certain property

23   Restriction on enforcement of awards against certain property

(1) Where in any proceedings an amount is awarded by way of damages, costs or expenses—

  (a) against a trade union,

  (b) against trustees in whom property is vested in trust for a trade union, in their capacity as such (and otherwise than in respect of a breach of trust on their part), or

  (c) against members or officials of a trade union on behalf of themselves and all of the members of the union,

no part of that amount is recoverable by enforcement against any protected property.

(2) The following is protected property—

  (a) property belonging to the trustees otherwise than in their capacity as such;

  (b) property belonging to any member of the union otherwise than jointly or in common with the other members;

  (c) property belonging to an official of the union who is neither a member nor a trustee;

(d) property comprised in the union's political fund where that fund—
   (i) is subject to rules of the union which prevent property which is or has been comprised in the fund from being used for financing strikes or other industrial action, and
   (ii) was so subject at the time when the act in respect of which the proceedings are brought was done;
(e) property comprised in a separate fund maintained in accordance with the rules of the union for the purpose only of providing provident benefits.
(3) For this purpose 'provident benefits' includes—
   (a) any payment expressly authorised by the rules of the union which is made—
      (i) to a member during sickness or incapacity from personal injury or while out of work, or
      (ii) to an aged member by way of superannuation, or
      (iii) to a member who has met with an accident or has lost his tools by fire or theft;
   (b) a payment in discharge or aid of funeral expenses on the death of a member or the spouse or civil partner of a member or as provision for the children of a deceased member.

24–45D [omitted]

CHAPTER IV   ELECTIONS FOR CERTAIN POSITIONS

Duty to hold elections

46   Duty to hold elections for certain positions
(1) A trade union shall secure—
   (a) that every person who holds a position in the union to which this Chapter applies does so by virtue of having been elected to it at an election satisfying the requirements of this Chapter, and
   (b) that no person continues to hold such a position for more than five years without being re-elected at such an election.
(2) The positions to which this Chapter applies (subject as mentioned below) are—
   (a) member of the executive,
   (b) any position by virtue of which a person is a member of the executive,
   (c) president, and
   (d) general secretary.
(3) In this Chapter 'member of the executive' includes any person who, under the rules or practice of the union, may attend and speak at some or all of the meetings of the executive, otherwise than for the purpose of providing the committee with factual information or with technical or professional advice with respect to matters taken into account by the executive in carrying out its functions.
(4) This Chapter does not apply to the position of president or general secretary if the holder of that position—
   (a) is not, in respect of that position, either a voting member of the executive or an employee of the union,
   (b) holds that position for a period which under the rules of the union cannot end more than 13 months after he took it up, and
   (c) has not held either position at any time in the period of twelve months ending with the day before he took up that position.
(4A) This Chapter also does not apply to the position of president if—
   (a) the holder of that position was elected or appointed to it in accordance with the rules of the union,

(b) at the time of his election or appointment as president he held a position mentioned in paragraph (a), (b) or (d) of subsection (2) by virtue of having been elected to it at a qualifying election,

(c) it is no more than five years since—

  (i) he was elected, or re-elected, to the position mentioned in paragraph (b) which he held at the time of his election or appointment as president, or

  (ii) he was elected to another position of a kind mentioned in that paragraph at a qualifying election held after his election or appointment as president of the union, and

(d) he has, at all times since his election or appointment as president, held a position mentioned in paragraph (a), (b) or (d) of subsection (2) by virtue of having been elected to it at a qualifying election.

(5) In subsection (4) a 'voting member of the executive' means a person entitled in his own right to attend meetings of the executive and to vote on matters on which votes are taken by the executive (whether or not he is entitled to attend all such meetings or to vote on all such matters or in all circumstances).

(5A) In subsection (4A) 'qualifying election' means an election satisfying the requirements of this Chapter.

(5B) The 'requirements of this Chapter' referred to in subsections (1) and (5A) are those set out in sections 47 to 52 below.

(6) The provisions of this Chapter apply notwithstanding anything in the rules or practice of the union; and the terms and conditions on which a person is employed by the union shall be disregarded in so far as they would prevent the union from complying with the provisions of this Chapter.

Requirements to be satisfied with respect to elections

47 Candidates

(1) No member of the trade union shall be unreasonably excluded from standing as a candidate.

(2) No candidate shall be required, directly or indirectly, to be a member of a political party.

(3) A member of a trade union shall not be taken to be unreasonably excluded from standing as a candidate if he is excluded on the ground that he belongs to a class of which all the members are excluded by the rules of the union.

But a rule which provides for such a class to be determined by reference to whom the union chooses to exclude shall be disregarded.

48–49 [omitted]

50 Entitlement to vote

(1) Subject to the provisions of this section, entitlement to vote shall be accorded equally to all members of the trade union.

(2) The rules of the union may exclude entitlement to vote in the case of all members belonging to one of the following classes, or to a class falling within one of the following—

(a) members who are not in employment;

(b) members who are in arrears in respect of any subscription or contribution due to the union;

(c) members who are apprentices, trainees or students or new members of the union.

(3) The rules of the union may restrict entitlement to vote to members who fall within—

(a) a class determined by reference to a trade or occupation,

(b) a class determined by reference to a geographical area, or

(c) a class which is by virtue of the rules of the union treated as a separate section within the union, or to members who fall within a class determined by reference to any combination of the factors mentioned in paragraphs (a), (b) and (c).

The reference in paragraph (c) to a section of a trade union includes a part of the union which is itself a trade union.

(4) Entitlement may not be restricted in accordance with subsection (3) if the effect is that any member of the union is denied entitlement to vote at all elections held for the purposes of this Chapter otherwise than by virtue of belonging to a class excluded in accordance with subsection (2).

51   Voting

(1) The method of voting must be by the marking of a voting paper by the person voting.

(2) Each voting paper must—

  (a) state the name of the independent scrutineer and clearly specify the address to which, and the date by which, it is to be returned,

  (b) be given one of a series of consecutive whole numbers every one of which is used in giving a different number in that series to each voting paper printed or otherwise produced for the purposes of the election, and

  (c) be marked with its number.

(3) Every person who is entitled to vote at the election must—

  (a) be allowed to vote without interference from, or constraint imposed by, the union or any of its members, officials or employees, and

  (b) so far as is reasonably practicable, be enabled to do so without incurring any direct cost to himself.

(4) So far as is reasonably practicable, every person who is entitled to vote at the election must—

  (a) have sent to him by post, at his home address or another address which he has requested the trade union in writing to treat as his postal address, a voting paper which either lists the candidates at the election or is accompanied by a separate list of those candidates; and

  (b) be given a convenient opportunity to vote by post.

(5) The ballot shall be conducted so as to secure that—

  (a) so far as is reasonably practicable, those voting do so in secret, and

  (b) the votes given at the election are fairly and accurately counted.

For the purposes of paragraph (b) an inaccuracy in counting shall be disregarded if it is accidental and on a scale which could not affect the result of the election.

(6) The ballot shall be so conducted as to secure that the result of the election is determined solely by counting the number of votes cast directly for each candidate.

(7) Nothing in subsection (6) shall be taken to prevent the system of voting used for the election being the single transferable vote, that is, a vote capable of being given so as to indicate the voter's order of preference for the candidates and of being transferred to the next choice—

  (a) when it is not required to give a prior choice the necessary quota of votes, or

  (b) when, owing to the deficiency in the number of votes given for a prior choice, that choice is eliminated from the list of candidates.

51A–52   [omitted]

53   Uncontested elections

Nothing in this Chapter shall be taken to require a ballot to be held at an uncontested election.

Remedy for failure to comply with requirements

54   Remedy for failure to comply with requirements: general

(1) The remedy for a failure on the part of a trade union to comply with the requirements of this Chapter is by way of application under section 55 (to the Certification Officer) or section 56 (to the court).

(2) An application under those sections may be made—
    (a) by a person who is a member of the trade union (provided, where the election has been held, he was also a member at the time when it was held), or
    (b) by a person who is or was a candidate at the election;
and the references in those sections to a person having a sufficient interest are to such a person.

(3) Where an election has been held, no application under those sections with respect to that election may be made after the end of the period of one year beginning with the day on which the union announced the result of the election.

55 Application to Certification Officer

(1) A person having a sufficient interest (see section 54(2)) who claims that a trade union has failed to comply with any of the requirements of this Chapter may apply to the Certification Officer for a declaration to that effect.

(2) On an application being made to him, the Certification Officer shall—
    (a) make such enquiries as he thinks fit, and
    (b) give the applicant and the trade union an opportunity to be heard,
and may make or refuse the declaration asked for.

(3) If he makes a declaration he shall specify in it the provisions with which the trade union has failed to comply.

(4) Where he makes a declaration and is satisfied that steps have been taken by the union with a view to remedying the declared failure, or securing that a failure of the same or any similar kind does not occur in future, or that the union has agreed to take such steps, he shall specify those steps in the declaration.

(5) Whether he makes or refuses a declaration, he shall give reasons for his decision in writing; and the reasons may be accompanied by written observations on any matter arising from, or connected with, the proceedings.

(5A) Where the Certification Officer makes a declaration he shall also, unless he considers that to do so would be inappropriate, make an enforcement order, that is, an order imposing on the union one or more of the following requirements—
    (a) to secure the holding of an election in accordance with the order;
    (b) to take such other steps to remedy the declared failure as may be specified in the order;
    (c) to abstain from such acts as may be so specified with a view to securing that a failure of the same or a similar kind does not occur in future.
The Certification Officer shall in an order imposing any such requirement as is mentioned in paragraph (a) or (b) specify the period within which the union is to comply with the requirements of the order.

(5B) Where the Certification Officer makes an order requiring the union to hold a fresh election, he shall (unless he considers that it would be inappropriate to do so in the particular circumstances of the case) require the election to be conducted in accordance with the requirements of this Chapter and such other provisions as may be made by the order.

(5C) Where an enforcement order has been made—
    (a) any person who is a member of the union and was a member at the time the order was made, or
    (b) any person who is or was a candidate in the election in question,
is entitled to enforce obedience to the order as if he had made the application on which the order was made.

(6) In exercising his functions under this section the Certification Officer shall ensure that, so far as is reasonably practicable, an application made to him is determined within six months of being made.

(7) Where he requests a person to furnish information to him in connection with enquiries made by him under this section, he shall specify the date by which that

information is to be furnished and, unless he considers that it would be inappropriate to do so, shall proceed with his determination of the application notwithstanding that the information has not been furnished to him by the specified date.

(8) A declaration made by the Certification Officer under this section may be relied on as if it were a declaration made by the court.

(9) An enforcement order made by the Certification Officer under this section may be enforced in the same way as an order of the court.

(10) the following paragraphs have effect if a person applies under section 56 in relation to an alleged failure—

    (a) that person may not apply under this section in relation to that failure;

    (b) on an application by a different person under this section in relation to that failure, the Certification Officer shall have due regard to any declaration, order, observations or reasons made or given by the court regarding that failure and brought to the Certification Officer's notice.

56   Application to court

(1) A person having a sufficient interest (see section 54(2)) who claims that a trade union has failed to comply with any of the requirements of this Chapter may apply to the court for a declaration to that effect.

(2) [repealed]

(3) If the court makes the declaration asked for, it shall specify in the declaration the provisions with which the trade union has failed to comply.

(4) Where the court makes a declaration it shall also, unless it considers that to do so would be inappropriate, make an enforcement order, that is, an order imposing on the union one or more of the following requirements—

    (a) to secure the holding of an election in accordance with the order;

    (b) to take such other steps to remedy the declared failure as may be specified in the order;

    (c) to abstain from such acts as may be so specified with a view to securing that a failure of the same or a similar kind does not occur in future.

The court shall in an order imposing any such requirement as is mentioned in paragraph (a) or (b) specify the period within which the union is to comply with the requirements of the order.

(5) where the court makes an order requiring the union to hold a fresh election, the court shall (unless it considers that it would be inappropriate to do so in the particular circumstances of the case) require the election to be conducted in accordance with the requirements of this Chapter and such other provisions as may be made by the order.

(6) Where an enforcement order has been made—

    (a) any person who is a member of the union and was a member at the time the order was made, or

    (b) any person who is or was a candidate in the election in question,

is entitled to enforce obedience to the order as if he had made the application on which the order was made.

(7) Without prejudice to any other power of the court, the court may on an application under this section grant such interlocutory relief (in Scotland, such interim order) as it considers appropriate.

(8) The following paragraphs have effect if a person applies under section 55 in relation to an alleged failure—

    (a) that person may not apply under this section in relation to that failure;

    (b) on an application by a different person under this section in relation to that failure, the court shall have due regard to any declaration, order, observations or reasons made or given by the Certification Officer regarding that failure and brought to the court's notice.

56A Appeals from Certification Officer

An appeal lies to the Employment Appeal Tribunal on any question of law arising in proceedings before or arising from any decision of the Certification Officer under section 55.

57–61 [omitted]

CHAPTER V RIGHTS OF TRADE UNION MEMBERS

Right to a ballot before industrial action

62 Right to a ballot before industrial action

(1) A member of a trade union who claims that members of the union, including himself, are likely to be or have been induced by the union to take part or to continue to take part in industrial action which does not have the support of a ballot may apply to the court for an order under this section.

In this section 'the relevant time' means the time when the application is made.

(2) For this purpose industrial action shall be regarded as having the support of a ballot only if—

(a) the union has held a ballot in respect of the action—
   (i) in relation to which the requirements of section 226B so far as applicable before and during the holding of the ballot were satisfied,
   (ii) in relation to which the requirements of sections 227 to 231 were satisfied, and
   (iii) in which the majority voting in the ballot answered 'Yes' to the question applicable in accordance with section 229(2) to industrial action of the kind which the applicant has been or is likely to be induced to take part in;

(b) such of the requirements of the following sections as have fallen to be satisfied at the relevant time have been satisfied, namely—
   (i) section 226B so far as applicable after the holding of the ballot, and
   (ii) section 231B;

(bb) section 232A does not prevent the industrial action from being regarded as having the support of the ballot; and

(c) the requirements of section 233 (calling of industrial action with support of ballot) are satisfied.

Any reference in this subsection to a requirement of a provision which is disapplied or modified by section 232 has effect subject to that section.

(3) Where on an application under this section the court is satisfied that the claim is well-founded, it shall make such order as it considers appropriate for requiring the union to take steps for ensuring—

(a) that there is no, or no further, inducement of members of the union to take part or to continue to take part in the industrial action to which the application relates, and

(b) that no member engages in conduct after the making of the order by virtue of having been induced before the making of the order to take part or continue to take part in the action.

(4) Without prejudice to any other power of the court, the court may on an application under this section grant such interlocutory relief (in Scotland, such interim order) as it considers appropriate.

(5) For the purposes of this section an act shall be taken to be done by a trade union if it is authorised or endorsed by the union; and the provisions of section 20(2) to (4) apply for the purpose of determining whether an act is to be taken to be so authorised or endorsed.

Those provisions also apply in relation to proceedings for failure to comply with an order under this section as they apply in relation to the original proceedings.

(6) In this section—

'inducement' includes an inducement which is or would be ineffective, whether because of the member's unwillingness to be influenced by it or for any other reason; and

'industrial action' means a strike or other industrial action by persons employed under contracts of employment.

(7) Where a person holds any office or employment under the Crown on terms which do not constitute a contract of employment between that person and the Crown, those terms shall nevertheless be deemed to constitute such a contract for the purposes of this section.

(8) References in this section to a contract of employment include any contract under which one person personally does work or performs services for another; and related expressions shall be construed accordingly.

(9) Nothing in this section shall be construed as requiring a trade union to hold separate ballots for the purposes of this section and sections 226 to 234 (requirement of ballot before action by trade union).

Right not to be denied access to the courts

63   Right not to be denied access to the courts

(1) This section applies where a matter is under the rules of a trade union required or allowed to be submitted for determination or conciliation in accordance with the rules of the union, but a provision of the rules purporting to provide for that to be a person's only remedy has no effect (or would have no effect if there were one).

(2) Notwithstanding anything in the rules of the union or in the practice of any court, if a member or former member of the union begins proceedings in a court with respect to a matter to which this section applies, then if—

(a) he has previously made a valid application to the union for the matter to be submitted for determination or conciliation in accordance with the union's rules, and

(b) the court proceedings are begun after the end of the period of six months beginning with the day on which the union received the application,

the rules requiring or allowing the matter to be so submitted, and the fact that any relevant steps remain to be taken under the rules, shall be regarded for all purposes as irrelevant to any question whether the court proceedings should be dismissed, stayed or sisted, or adjourned.

(3) An application shall be deemed to be valid for the purposes of subsection (2)(a) unless the union informed the applicant, before the end of the period of 28 days beginning with the date on which the union received the application, of the respects in which the application contravened the requirements of the rules.

(4) If the court is satisfied that any delay in the taking of relevant steps under the rules is attributable to unreasonable conduct of the person who commenced the proceedings, it may treat the period specified in subsection (2)(b) as extended by such further period as it considers appropriate.

(5) In this section—

(a) references to the rules of a trade union include any arbitration or other agreement entered into in pursuance of a requirement imposed by or under the rules; and

(b) references to the relevant steps under the rules, in relation to any matter, include any steps falling to be taken in accordance with the rules for the purposes of or in connection with the determination or conciliation of the matter, or any appeal, review or reconsideration of any determination or award.

(6) This section does not affect any enactment or rule of law by virtue of which a court would apart from this section disregard any such rules of a trade union or any such fact as is mentioned in subsection (2).

Right not to be unjustifiably disciplined

64   Right not to be unjustifiably disciplined

(1) An individual who is or has been a member of a trade union has the right not to be unjustifiably disciplined by the union.

(2) For this purpose an individual is 'disciplined' by a trade union if a determination is made, or purportedly made, under the rules of the union or by an official of the union or a number of persons including an official that—

(a) he should be expelled from the union or a branch or section of the union,

(b) he should pay a sum to the union, to a branch or section of the union or to any other person;

(c) sums tendered by him in respect of an obligation to pay subscriptions or other sums to the union, or to a branch or section of the union, should be treated as unpaid or paid for a different purpose,

(d) he should be deprived to any extent of, or of access to, any benefits, services or facilities which would otherwise be provided or made available to him by virtue of his membership of the union, or a branch or section of the union,

(e) another trade union, or a branch or section of it, should be encouraged or advised not to accept him as a member, or

(f) he should be subjected to some other detriment;

and whether an individual is 'unjustifiably disciplined' shall be determined in accordance with section 65.

(3) Where a determination made in infringement of an individual's right under this section requires the payment of a sum or the performance of an obligation, no person is entitled in any proceedings to rely on that determination for the purpose of recovering the sum or enforcing the obligation.

(4) Subject to that, the remedies for infringement of the right conferred by this section are as provided by sections 66 and 67, and not otherwise.

(5) The right not to be unjustifiably disciplined is in addition to (and not in substitution for) any right which exists apart from this section; and, subject to section 66(4), nothing in this section or sections 65 to 67 affects any remedy for infringement of any such right.

65   Meaning of 'unjustifiably disciplined'

(1) An individual is unjustifiably disciplined by a trade union if the actual or supposed conduct which constitutes the reason, or one of the reasons, for disciplining him is—

(a) conduct to which this section applies, or

(b) something which is believed by the union to amount to such conduct;

but subject to subsection (6) (cases of bad faith in relation to assertion of wrongdoing).

(2) This section applies to conduct which consists in—

(a) failing to participate in or support a strike or other industrial action (whether by members of the union or by others), or indicating opposition to or a lack of support for such action;

(b) failing to contravene, for a purpose connected with such a strike or other industrial action, a requirement imposed on him by or under a contract of employment;

(c) asserting (whether by bringing proceedings or otherwise) that the union, any official or representative of it or a trustee of its property has contravened, or is proposing to contravene, a requirement which is, or is thought to be, imposed by or under the rules of the union or any other agreement or by or under any enactment (whenever passed) or any rule of law;

(d) encouraging or assisting a person—

(i)   to perform an obligation imposed on him by a contract of employment, or

(ii)   to make or attempt to vindicate any such assertion as is mentioned in paragraph (c);

(e) contravening a requirement imposed by or in consequence of a determination which infringes the individual's or another individual's right not to be unjustifiably disciplined;

(f) failing to agree, or withdrawing agreement, to the making from his wages (in accordance with arrangements between his employer and the union) of deductions representing payments to the union in respect of his membership,

(g) resigning or proposing to resign from the union or from another union, becoming or proposing to become a member of another union, refusing to become a member of another union, or being a member of another union,

(h) working with, or proposing to work with, individuals who are not members of the union or who are or are not members of another union,

(i) working for, or proposing to work for, an employer who employs or who has employed individuals who are not members of the union or who are or are not members of another union, or

(j) requiring the union to do an act which the union is, by any provision of this Act, required to do on the requisition of a member.

(3) This section applies to conduct which involves the Certification Officer being consulted or asked to provide advice or assistance with respect to any matter whatever, or which involves any person being consulted or asked to provide advice or assistance with respect to a matter which forms, or might form, the subject-matter of any such assertion as is mentioned in subsection (2)(c) above.

(4) This section also applies to conduct which consists in proposing to engage in, or doing anything preparatory or incidental to, conduct falling within subsection (2) or (3).

(5) This section does not apply to an act, omission or statement comprised in conduct falling within subsection (2), (3) or (4) above if it is shown that the act, omission or statement is one in respect of which individuals would be disciplined by the union irrespective of whether their acts, omissions or statements were in connection with conduct within subsection (2) or (3) above.

(6) An individual is not unjustifiably disciplined if it is shown—

(a) that the reason for disciplining him, or one of them, is that he made such an assertion as is mentioned in subsection (2)(c), or encouraged or assisted another person to make or attempt to vindicate such an assertion,

(b) that the assertion was false, and

(c) that he made the assertion, or encouraged or assisted another person to make or attempt to vindicate it, in the belief that it was false or otherwise in bad faith,

and that there was no other reason for disciplining him or that the only other reasons were reasons in respect of which he does not fall to be treated as unjustifiably disciplined.

(7) In this section—

'conduct' includes statements, acts and omissions;

'contract of employment', in relation to an individual, includes any agreement between that individual and a person for whom he works or normally works,

'employer' includes such a person and related expressions shall be construed accordingly;

'representative', in relation to a union, means a person acting or purporting to act—

(a) in his capacity as a member of the union, or

(b) on the instructions or advice of a person acting or purporting to act in that capacity or in the capacity of an official of the union.

'require' (on the part of an individual) includes request or apply for, and 'requisition' shall be construed accordingly; and

'wages' shall be construed in accordance with the definitions of 'contract of employment', 'employer' and related expressions.

(8) Where a person holds any office or employmentunder the Crownon terms which do not constitute a contract of employment between him and the Crown, those terms shall nevertheless be deemedto constitute such a contract for the purposes of this section.

66 Complaint of infringement of right

(1) An individual who claims that he has been unjustifiably disciplined by a trade union may present a complaint against the union to an employment tribunal.

(2) The tribunal shall not entertain such a complaint unless it is presented—

(a) before the end of the period of three months beginning with the date of the making of the determination claimed to infringe the right, or

(b) where the tribunal is satisfied—

(i) that it was not reasonably practicable for the complaint to be presented before the end of that period, or

(ii) that any delay in making the complaint is wholly or partly attributable to a reasonable attempt to appeal against the determination or to have it reconsidered or reviewed,

within such further period as the tribunal considers reasonable.

(3) Where the tribunal finds the complaint well-founded, it shall make a declaration to that effect.

(4) Where a complaint relating to an expulsion which is presented under this section is declared to be well-founded, no complaint in respect of the expulsion shall be presented or proceeded with under section 174 (right not to be excluded or expelled from trade union).

67 Further remedies for infringement of right

(1) An individual whose complaint under section 66 has been declared to be well-founded may make an application to an employment tribunal for one or both of the following—

(a) an award of compensation to be paid to him by the union;

(b) an order that the union pay him an amount equal to any sum which he has paid in pursuance of any such determination as is mentioned in section 64(2)(b).

(2) [repealed]

(3) An application under this section shall not be entertained if made before the end of the period of four weeks beginning with the date of the declaration or after the end of the period of six months beginning with that date.

(4) [repealed]

(5) The amount of compensation awarded shall, subject to the following provisions, be such as the employment tribunal considers just and equitable in all the circumstances.

(6) In determining the amount of compensation to be awarded, the same rule shall be applied concerning the duty of a person to mitigate his loss as applies to damages recoverable under the common law in England and Wales or Scotland.

(7) Where the employment tribunal finds that the infringement complained of was to any extent caused or contributed to by the action of the applicant, it shall reduce the amount of the compensation by such proportion as it considers just and equitable having regard to that finding.

(8) The amount of compensation awarded calculated in accordance with subsections (5) to (7) shall not exceed the aggregate of—

(a) an amount equal to 30 times the limit for the time being imposed by section 227(1)(a) of the Employment Rights Act 1996 (maximum amount of a week's pay for basic award in unfair dismissal cases), and

(b) an amount equal to the limit for the time being imposed by section 124(1) of that Act (maximum compensatory award in such cases);

(8A) If on the date on which the application was made—

(a) the determination infringing the applicant's right not to be unjustifiably disciplined has not been revoked, or

(b) the union has failed to take all the steps necessary for securing the reversal of anything done for the purpose of giving effect to the determination, the amount of compensation shall be not less than the amount for the time being specified in section 176(6A).

(9) [repealed]

Right not to suffer deduction of unauthorised union subscriptions

68   Right not to suffer deduction of unauthorised union subscriptions

(1) Where arrangements ('subscription deduction arrangements') exist between the employer of a worker and a trade union relating to the making from workers' wages of deductions representing payments to the union in respect of the workers' membership of the union ('subscription deductions'), the employer shall ensure that no subscription deduction is made from wages payable to the worker on any day unless—

   (a) the worker has authorised in writing the making from his wages of subscription deductions; and

   (b) the worker has not withdrawn the authorisation.

(2) A worker withdraws an authorisation given for the purposes of subsection (1), in relation to a subscription deduction which falls to be made from wages payable to him on any day, if a written notice withdrawing the authorisation has been received by the employer in time for it to be reasonably practicable for the employer to secure that no such deduction is made.

(3) A worker's authorisation of the making of subscription deductions from his wages shall not give rise to any obligation on the part of the employer to the worker to maintain or continue to maintain subscription deduction arrangements.

(4) In this section and section 68A, 'employer', 'wages' and 'worker' have the same meanings as in the Employment Rights Act 1996.

68A   Complaint of infringement of rights

(1) A worker may present a complaint to an employment tribunal that his employer has made a deduction from his wages in contravention of section 68—

   (a) within the period of three months beginning with the date of the payment of the wages from which the deduction, or (if the complaint relates to more than one deduction) the last of the deductions, was made, or

   (b) where the tribunal is satisfied that it was not reasonably practicable for the complaint to be presented within that period, within such further period as the tribunal considers reasonable.

(2) Where a tribunal finds that a complaint under this section is well-founded, it shall make a declaration to that effect and shall order the employer to pay to the worker the whole amount of the deduction, less any such part of the amount as has already been paid to the worker by the employer.

(3) Where the making of a deduction from the wages of a worker both contravenes section 68(1) and invovles one or more of the contraventions specified in subsection (4) of this section, the aggregate amount which may be ordered by an employment tribunal or court (whether on the same occasion or on different occasions) to be paid in respect of the contraventions shall not exceed the amount, or (where different amounts may be ordered to be paid in respect of different contraventions) the greatest amount, which may be ordered to be paid in respect of any one of them.

(4) The contraventions referred to in subsection (3) are—

   (a) a contravention of the requirement not to make a deduction without having given the particulars required by section 8 (itemised pay statements) or 9(1) (standing statements of fixed deductions) of the Employment Rights Act 1996,

   (b) a contravention of section 13 of that Act (requirement not to make unauthorised deductions), and

   (c) a contravention of section 86(1) or 90(1) of this Act (requirements not to make deductions of political fund contributions in certain circumstances).

Right to terminate membership of union

69   Right to terminate membership of union

In every contract of membership of a trade union, whether made before or after the passing of this Act, a term conferring a right on the member, on giving reasonable notice and complying with any reasonable conditions, to terminate his membership of the union shall be implied.

Supplementary

70   Membership of constituent or affiliated organisation

In this Chapter 'member', in relation to a trade union consisting wholly or partly of, or of representatives of, constituent or affiliated organisations, includes a member of any of the constituent or affiliated organisations.

70A–70C   [omitted]

CHAPTER VI   APPLICATION OF FUNDS FOR POLITICAL OBJECTS

Restriction on use of funds for certain political objects

71   Restriction on use of funds for political objects

(1) The funds of a trade union shall not be applied in the furtherance of the political objects to which this Chapter applies unless—

(a) there is in force in accordance with this Chapter a resolution (a 'political resolution') approving the furtherance of those objects as an object of the union (see section 73 to 81), and

(b) there are in force rules of the union as to—

(i) the making of payments in furtherance of those objects out of a separate fund, and

(ii) the exemption of any member of the union objecting to contribute to that fund,

which comply with this Chapter (see sections 82, 84 and 85) and have been approved by the Certification Officer.

(2) This applies whether the funds are so applied directly, or in conjunction with another trade union, association or body, or otherwise indirectly.

72   Political objects to which restriction applies

(1) The political objects to which this Chapter applies are the expenditure of money—

(a) on any contribution to the funds of, or on the payment of expenses incurred directly or indirectly by, a political party;

(b) on the provision of any service or property for use by or on behalf of any political party;

(c) in connection with the registration of electors, the candidature of any person, the selection of any candidate or the holding of any ballot by the union in connection with any election to a political office;

(d) on the maintenance of any holder of a political office;

(e) on the holding of any conference or meeting by or on behalf of a political party or of any other meeting the main purpose of which is the transaction of business in connection with a political party;

(f) on the production, publication or distribution of any literature, document, film, sound recording or advertisement the main purpose of which is to persuade people to vote for a political party or candidate or to persuade them not to vote for a political party or candidate.

(2) Where a person attends a conference or meeting as a delegate or otherwise as a participator in the proceedings, any expenditure incurred in connection with his attendance as such shall, for the purposes of subsection (1)(e), be taken to be expenditure incurred on the holding of the conference or meeting.

(3) In determining for the purposes of subsection (1) whether a trade union has incurred expenditure of a kind mentioned in that subsection, no account shall be taken of the ordinary administrative expenses of the union.

(4) In this section—

'candidate' means a candidate for election to a political office and includes a prospective candidate;

'contribution', in relation to the funds of a political party, includes any fee payable for affiliation to, or membership of, the party and any loan made to the party;

'electors' means electors at an election to a political office;

'film' includes any record, however made, of a sequence of visual images, which is capable of being used as a means of showing that sequence as a moving picture;

'local authority' means a local authority within the meaning of section 270 of the Local Government Act 1972 or section 235 of the Local Government (Scotland) Act 1973; and

'political office' means the office of member of Parliament, member of the European Parliament or member of a local authority or any position within a political party.

72A Application of funds in breach of section 71

(1) A person who is a member of a trade union and who claims that it has applied its funds in breach of section 71 may apply to the Certification Officer for a declaration that it has done so.

(2) On an application under this section the Certification Officer—

    (a) shall make such enquiries as he thinks fit,

    (b) shall give the applicant and the union an opportunity to be heard,

    (c) shall ensure that, so far as is reasonably practicable, the application is determined within six months of being made,

    (d) may make or refuse the declaration asked for,

    (e) shall, whether he makes or refuses the declaration, give reasons for his decision in writing, and

    (f) may make written observation on any matter arising from, or connected with, the proceedings.

(3) If he makes a declaration he shall specify in it—

    (a) the provisions of section 71 breached, and

    (b) the amount of the funds applied in breach.

(4) If he makes a declaration and is satisfied that the union has taken or agreed to take steps with a view to—

    (a) remedying the declared breach, or

    (b) securing that a breach of the same or any similar kind does not occur in future,

he shall specify those steps in making the declaration.

(5) If he makes a declaration he may make such order for remedying the breach as he thinks just under the circumstances.

(6) Where the Certification Officer requests a person to furnish information to him in connection with enquiries made by him under this section, he shall specify the date by which that information is to be furnished and, unless he considers that it would be inappropriate to do so, such proceed with his determination of the application notwithstanding that the information has not been furnished to him by the specified date.

(7) A declaration made by the Certification Officer under this section may be relied on as if it were a declaration made by the court.

(8) Where an order has been made under this section, any person who is a member of the union and was a member at the time it was made is entitled to enforce obedience to the order as if he had made the application on which the order was made.

(9) An order made by the Certification Officer under this section may be enforced in the same way as an order of the court.

(10) If a person applies to the Certification Officer under this section in relation to an alleged breach he may not apply to the court in relation to the breach; but nothing in this subsection shall prevent such a person from exercising any right to appeal against or challenge the Certification Officer's decision on the application to him.

(11) If—

(a) a person applies to the court in relation to an alleged breach, and

(b) the breach is one in relation to which he could have made an application to the Certification Officer under this section,

he may not apply to the Certification Officer under this section in relation to the breach.

Political resolution

73 Passing and effect of political resolution

(1) A political resolution must be passed by a majority of those voting on a ballot of the members of the trade union held in accordance with this Chapter.

(2) A political resolution so passed shall take effect as if it were a rule of the union and may be rescinded in the same manner and subject to the same provisions as such a rule.

(3) If not previously rescinded, a political resolution shall cease to have effect at the end of the period of ten years beginning with the date of the ballot on which it was passed.

(4) Where before the end of that period a ballot is held on a new political resolution, then—

(a) if the new resolution is passed, the old resolution shall be treated as rescinded, and

(b) if it is not passed, the old resolution shall cease to have effect at the end of the period of two weeks beginning with the date of the ballot.

74 Approval of political ballot rules

(1) A ballot on a political resolution must be held in accordance with rules of the trade union (its 'political ballot rules') approved by the Certification Officer.

(2) Fresh approval is required for the purposes of each ballot which it is proposed to hold, notwithstanding that the rules have been approved for the purposes of an earlier ballot.

(3) The Certification Officer shall not approve a union's political ballot rules unless he is satisfied that the requirements set out in—

section 75 (appointment of independent scrutineer),

section 76 (entitlement to vote),

section 77 (voting),

section 77A (counting of votes etc. by independent person), and

section 78 (scrutineer's report),

would be satisfied in relation to a ballot held by the union in accordance with the rules.

75–81 [omitted]

The political fund

82 Rules as to political fund

(1) The trade union's rules must provide—

(a) that payments in the furtherance of the political objects to which this Chapter applies shall be made out of a separate fund (the 'political fund' of the union);

(b) that a member of the union who gives notice in accordance with section 84 that he objects to contributing to the political fund shall be exempt from any obligation to contribute to it;

(c) that a member shall not by reason of being so exempt—
    (i) be excluded from any benefits of the union, or
    (ii) be placed in any respect either directly or indirectly under a disability or at a disadvantage as compared with other members of the union (except in relation to the control or management of the political fund); and
(d) that contribution to the political fund shall not be made a condition for admission to the union.

(2) A member of a trade union who claims that he is aggrieved by a breach of any rule made in pursuance of this section may complain to the Certification Officer.

(2A) On a complaint being made to him the Certification Officer shall make such enquiries as he thinks fit.

(3) Where, after giving the member and a representative of the union an opportunity of being heard, the Certification Officer considers that a breach has been committed, he may make such order for remedying the breach as he thinks just under the circumstances.

(3A) Where the Certification Officer requests a person to furnish information to him in connection with enquiries made by him under this section, he shall specify the date by which that information is to be furnished and, unless he considers that it would be inappropriate to do so, shall proceed with his determination of the application notwithstanding that the information has not been furnished to him by the specified date.

(4) [repealed]

(4A) Where an order has been made under this section, any person who is a member of the union and was a member at the time it was made is entitled to enforce obedience to the order as if he had made the complaint on which it was made.

(4B) An order made by the Certification Officer under this section may be enforced—
(a) in England and Wales, in the same way as an order of the county court;
(b) in Scotland, in the same way as an order of the sheriff.

83 Assets and liabilities of political fund

(1) There may be added to a union's political fund only—
(a) sums representing contributions made to the fund by members of the union or by any person other than the union itself, and
(b) property which accrues to the fund in the course of administering the assets of the fund.

(2) The rules of the union shall not be taken to require any member to contribute to the political fund at a time when there is no political resolution in force in relation to the union.

(3) No liability of a union's political fund shall be discharged out of any other fund of the union.

This subsection applies notwithstanding any term or condition on which the liability was incurred or that an asset of the other fund has been charged in connection with the liability.

84 Notice of objection to contributing to political fund

(1) A member of a trade union may give notice in the following form, or in a form to the like effect, that he objects to contribute to the political fund:—
Name of Trade Union

POLITICAL FUND (EXEMPTION NOTICE)

I give notice that I object to contributing to the Political Fund of the Union, and am in consequence exempt, in manner provided by Chapter VI of Part I of the Trade Union and Labour Relations (Consolidation) Act 1992, from contributing to that fund.

        A.B.
        Address
    day of   19

(2) On the adoption of a political resolution, notice shall be given to members of the union acquainting them—

    (a) that each member has a right to be exempted from contributing to the union's political fund, and

    (b) that a form of exemption notice can be obtained by or on behalf of a member either by application at or by post from—

        (i) the head office or any branch office of the union, or

        (ii) the office of the Certification Officer.

(3) The notice to members shall be given in accordance with rules of the union approved for the purpose by the Certification Officer, who shall have regard in each case to the existing practice and character of the union.

(4) On giving an exemption notice in accordance with this section, a member shall be exempt from contributing to the union's political fund—

    (a) where the notice is given within one month of the giving of notice to members under subsection (2) following the passing of a political resolution on a ballot held at a time when no such resolution is in force, as from the date on which the exemption notice is given;

    (b) in any other case, as from the 1 January next after the exemption notice is given.

(5) An exemption notice continues to have effect until it is withdrawn.

85 Manner of giving effect to exemptions

(1) Effect may be given to the exemption of members from contributing to the political fund of a union either—

    (a) by a separate levy of contributions to that fund from the members who are not exempt, or

    (b) by relieving members who are exempt from the payment of the whole or part of any periodical contribution required from members towards the expenses of the union.

(2) In the latter case, the rules shall provide—

    (a) that relief shall be given as far as possible to all members who are exempt on the occasion of the same periodical payment, and

    (b) for enabling each member of the union to know what portion (if any) of any periodical contribution payable by him is a contribution to the political fund.

Duties of employer who deducts union contributions

86 Certificate of exemption or objection to contributing to political fund

(1) If a member of a trade union which has a political fund certifies in writing to his employer that, or to the effect that—

    (a) he is exempt from the obligation to contribute to the fund, or

    (b) he has, in accordance with section 84, notified the union in writing of his objection to contributing to the fund,

the employer shall ensure that no amount representing a contribution to the political fund is deducted by him from emoluments payable to the member.

(2) The employer's duty under subsection (1) applies from the first day, following the giving of the certificate, on which it is reasonably practicable for him to comply with that subsection, until the certificate is withdrawn.

(3) An employer may not refuse to deduct any union does from emoluments payable to a person who has given a certificate under this section if he continues to deduct union dues from emoluments payable to other members of the union, unless his refusal is not attributable to the giving of the certificate or otherwise connected with the duty imposed by subsection (1).

87   Complaint in respect of employer's failure

(1) A person who claims his employer has failed to comply with section 86 in deducting or refusing to deduct any amount from emoluments payable to him may present a complaint to an employment tribunal.

(2) A tribunal shall not consider a complaint under subsection (1) unless it is presented—

(a) within the period of three months beginning with the date of the payment of the emoluments or (if the complaint relates to more than one payment) the last of the payments, or

(b) where the tribunal is satisfied that it was not reasonably practicable for the complaint to be presented within that period, within such further period as the tribunal considers reasonable.

(3) Where on a complaint under subsection (1) arising out of subsection (3) (refusal to deduct union dues) of section 86 the question arises whether the employer's refusal to deduct an amount was attributable to the giving of the certificate or was otherwise connected with the duty imposed by subsection (1) of that section, it is for the employer to satisfy the tribunal that it was not.

(4) Where a tribunal finds that a complaint under subsection (1) is well-founded—

(a) it shall make a declaration to that effect and, where the complaint arises out of subsection (1) of section 86, order the employer to pay to the complainant the amount deducted in contravention of that subsection less any part of that amount already paid to him by the employer, and

(b) it may, if it considers it appropriate to do so in order to prevent a repetition of the failure, make an order requiring the employer to take, within a specified time, the steps specified in the order in relation to emoluments payable by him to the complainant.

(5) A person who claims his employer has failed to comply with an order made under subsection (4)(b) on a complaint presented by him may present a further complaint to an employment tribunal; but only one complaint may be presented under this subsection in relation to any order.

(6) A tribunal shall not consider a complaint under subsection (5) unless it is presented—

(a) after the end of the period of four weeks beginning with the date of the order, but

(b) before the end of the period of six months beginning with that date.

(7) Where on a complaint under subsection (5) a tribunal finds that an employer has, without reasonable excuse, failed to comply with an order made under subsection (4)(b), it shall order the employer to pay to the complainant an amount equal to two weeks' pay.

(8) Chapter II of Part XIV of the Employment Rights Act 1996 (calculation of a week's pay) applies for the purposes of subsection (7) with the substitution for section 225 of the following—

For the purposes of this Chapter in its application to subsection (7) of section 87 of the Trade Union and Labour Relations (Consolidation) Act 1992, the calculation date is the date of the payment, or (if more than one) the last of the payments, to which the complaint related.

88 [repealed]; 89–91 [omitted]

Supplementary

92   Manner of making union rules

If the Certification Officer is satisfied, and certifies, that rules of a trade union made for any of the purposes of this Chapter and requiring approval by him have been approved—

(a) by a majority of the members of the union voting for the purpose, or

(b) by a majority of delegates of the union at a meeting called for the purpose,

the rules shall have effect as rules of the union notwithstanding that the rules of the union as to the alteration of rules or the making of new rules have not been complied with.

93 Effect of amalgamation

(1) Where on an amalgamation of two or more trade unions—

(a) there is in force in relation to each of the amalgamating unions a political resolution and such rules as are required by this Chapter, and

(b) the rules of the amalgamated union in force immediately after the amalgamation
include such rules as are required by this Chapter,

the amalgamated union shall be treated for the purposes of this Chapter as having passed a
political resolution.

(2) That resolution shall be treated as having been passed on the date of the earliest of the
ballots on which the resolutions in force immediately before the amalgamation with respect
to the amalgamating unions were passed.

(3) Where one of the amalgamating unions is a Northern Ireland union, the references
above to the requirements of this Chapter shall be construed as references to the requirements of the corresponding provisions of the law of Northern Ireland.

94 [omitted]

95 Appeals from Certification Officer

An appeal lies to the Employment Appeal Tribunal on any question of law arising in proceedings before or arising from any decision of the Certification Officer under this Chapter.

96 Meaning of 'date of the ballot'

In this Chapter the 'date of the ballot' means, in the case of a ballot in which votes may be
cast on more than one day, the last of those days.

97–108 [omitted]

CHAPTER VIIA   BREACH OF RULES

108A   Right to apply to Certification Officer

(1) A person who claims that there has been a breach or threatened breach of the rules of
a trade union relating to any of the matters mentioned in subsection (2) may apply to the
Certification Officer for a declaration to that effect, subject to subsections (3) to (7).

(2) The matters are—

(a) the appointment or election of a person to, or the removal of a person from, any
office;

(b) disciplinary proceedings by the union (including expulsion);

(c) the balloting of members on any issue other than industrial action;

(d) the constitution or proceedings of any executive committee or of any decision-
making meeting;

(e) such other matters as may be specified in an order made by the Secretary of State.

(3) The applicant must be a member of the union, or have been one at the time of the
alleged breach or threatened breach.

(4) A person may not apply under subsection (1) in relation to a claim if he is entitled to
apply under section 80 in relation to the claim.

(5) No application may be made regarding—

(a) the dismissal of an employee of the union;

(b) disciplinary proceedings against an employee of the union.

(6) An application must be made—

(a) within the period of six months starting with the day on which the breach or
threatened breach is alleged to have taken place, or

(b) if within that period any internal complaints procedure of the union is invoked to
resolve the claim, within the period of six months starting with the earlier of the
days specified in subsection (7).

(7) Those days are—
(a) the day on which the procedure is concluded, and
(b) the last day of the period of one year beginning with the day on which the procedure is invoked.

(8) The reference in subsection (1) to the rules of a union includes references to the rules of any branch or section of the union.

(9) In subsection (2)(c) 'industrial action' means a strike or other industrial action by persons employed under contracts of employment.

(10) For the purposes of subsection (2)(d) a committee is an executive committee if—
(a) it is a committee of the union concerned and has power to make executive decisions on behalf of the union or on behalf of a constituent body,
(b) it is a committee of a major constituent body and has power to make executive decisions on behalf of that body, or
(c) It is a sub-committee of a committee falling within paragraph (a) or (b).

(11) For the purposes of subsection (2)(d) a decision-making meeting is—
(a) a meeting of members of the union concerned (or the representatives of such members) which has power to make a decision on any matter which, under the rules of the union, is final as regards the union or which, under the rules of the union or a constituent body, is final as regards that body, or
(b) a meeting of members of a major constituent body (or the representatives of such members) which has power to make a decision on any matter which, under the rules of the union or the body, is final as regards that body.

(12) For the purposes of subsections (10) and (11), in relation to the trade union concerned—
(a) a constituent body is any body which forms part of the union, including a branch, group, section or region;
(b) a major constituent body is such a body which has more than 1,000 members.

(13) Any order under subsection (2)(e) shall be made by statutory instrument; and no such order shall be made unless a draft of it has been laid before and approved by resolution of each House of Parliament.

(14) If a person applies to the Certification Officer under this section in relation to an alleged breach or threatened breach he may not apply to the court in relation to the breach or threatened breach; but nothing in this subsection shall prevent such a person from exercising any right to appeal against or challenge the Certification Officer's decision on the application to him.

(15) If—
(a) a person applies to the court in relation to an alleged breach or threatened breach, and
(b) the breach or threatened breach is one in relation to which he could have made an application to the Certification Officer under this section,
he may not apply to the Certification Officer under this section in relation to the breach or threatened breach.

108B Declarations and orders

(1) The Certification Officer may refuse to accept an application under section 108A unless he is satisfied that the applicant has taken all reasonable steps to resolve the claim by the use of any internal complaints procedure of the union.

(2) If he accepts an application under section 108A the Certification Officer—
(a) shall make such enquiries as he thinks fit,
(b) shall give the applicant and the union an opportunity to be heard,
(c) shall ensure that, so far as is reasonably practicable, the application is determined within six months of being made,
(d) may make or refuse the declaration asked for, and
(e) shall, whether he makes or refuses the declaration, give reasons for his decision in writing.

(3) Where the Certification Officer makes a declaration he shall also, unless he considers that to do so would be inappropriate, make an enforcement order, that is, an order imposing on the union one or both of the following requirements—

    (a) to take such steps to remedy the breach, or withdraw the threat of a breach, as may be specified in the order;

    (b) to abstain from such acts as may be so specified with a view to securing that a breach or threat of the same or a similar kind does not occur in future.

(4) The Certification Officer shall in an order imposing any such requirement as is mentioned in subsection (3)(a) specify the period within which the union is to comply with the requirement.

(5) Where the Certification Officer requests a person to furnish information to him in connection with enquiries made by him under this section, he shall specify the date by which that information is to be furnished and, unless he considers that it would be inappropriate to do so, shall proceed with his determination of the application notwithstanding that the information has not been furnished to him by the specified date.

(6) A declaration made by the Certification Officer under this section may be relied on as if it were a declaration made by the court.

(7) Where an enforcement order has been made, any person who is a member of the union and was a member at the time it was made is entitled to enforce obedience to the order as if he had made the application on which the order was made.

(8) An enforcement order made by the Certification Officer under this section may be enforced in the same way as an order of the court.

(9) An order under section 108A(2)(e) may provide that, in relation to an application under section 108A with regard to a prescribed matter, the preceding provisions of this section shall apply with such omissions or modifications as may be specified in the order; and a prescribed matter is such matter specified under section 108A(2)(e) as is prescribed under this subsection.

108C   Appeals from Certification Officer

An appeal lies to the Employment Appeal Tribunal on any question of law arising in proceedings before or arising from any decision of the Certification Officer under this Chapter.

109–114   [repealed]

CHAPTER IX   MISCELLANEOUS AND GENERAL PROVISIONS

115–116   [repealed]; 116A [omitted]

Exceptions and adaptations for certain bodies

117   Special register bodies

    (1) In this section a 'special register body' means an organisation whose name appeared in the special register maintained under section 84 of the Industrial Relations Act 1971 immediately before 16 September 1974, and which is a company registered under the Companies Act 1985 or is incorporated by charter or letters patent.

    (2) The provisions of this Part apply to special register bodies as to other trade unions, subject to the following exceptions and adaptations.

    (3) In Chapter II (status and property of trade unions)—

        (a) in section 10 (quasi-corporate status of trade unions)—

            (i) subsections (1) and (2) (prohibition on trade union being incorporated) do not apply, and

            (ii) subsection (3) (prohibition on registration under certain Acts) does not apply so far as it relates to registration as a company under the Companies Act 1985;

(b) section 11 (exclusion of common law rules as to restraint of trade) applies to the purposes or rules of a special register body only so far as they relate to the regulation of relations between employers or employers' associations and workers;

(c) sections 12 to 14 (vesting of property in trustees; transfer of securities) do not apply; and

(d) in section 20 (liability of trade union in certain proceedings in tort) in subsection (7) the reference to the contract between a member and the other members shall be construed as a reference to the contract between a member and the body.

(4) Sections 33 to 35 (appointment and removal of auditors) do not apply to a special register body which is registered as a company under the Companies Act 1985; and sections 36 and 37 (rights and duties of auditors) apply to the auditors appointed by such a body under Chapter V of Part XI of that Act.

(5) Sections 45B and 45C (disqualification) and Chapter IV (elections) apply only to—

(a) the position of voting member of the executive, and

(b) any position by virtue of which a person is a voting member of the executive.

In this subsection 'voting member of the executive' has the meaning given by section 46(5).

118   Federated trade unions

(1) In this section a 'federated trade union' means a trade union which consists wholly or mainly of constituent or affiliated organisations, or representatives of such organisations, as described in paragraph (b) of the definition of 'trade union' in section 1.

(2) The provisions of this Part apply to federated trade unions subject to the following exceptions and adaptations.

(3) For the purposes of section 22 (limit on amount of damages) as it applies to a federated trade union, the members of such of its constituent or affiliated organisations as have their head or main office in Great Britain shall be treated as members of the union.

(4) The following provisions of Chapter III (trade union administration) do not apply to a federated trade union which consists wholly or mainly of representatives of constituent or affiliated organisations—

(a) section 27 (duty to supply copy of rules),

(b) section 28 (duty to keep accounting records),

(c) sections 32 to 37 (annual return, statement for members, accounts and audit),

(ca) sections 37A to 37E (investigation of financial affairs), and

(d) sections 38 to 42 (Members' superannuation schemes).

(5) Sections 29 to 31 (right of member to access to accounting records) do not apply to a federated trade union which has no members other than constituent or affiliated organisations or representatives of such organisations.

(6) Sections 24 to 26 (register of Members' names and addresses) and Chapter IV (elections for certain trade union positions) do not apply to a federated trade union—

(a) if it has no individual members other than representatives of constituent or affiliated organisations, or

(b) if its individual members (other than such representatives) are all merchant seamen and a majority of them are ordinarily resident outside the United Kingdom. For this purpose 'merchant seaman' means a person whose employment, or the greater part of it, is carried out on board sea-going ships.

(7) The provisions of Chapter VI (application of funds for political objects) apply to a trade union which is in whole or part an association or combination of other unions as if the individual members of the component unions were members of that union and not of the component unions.

But nothing in that Chapter prevents a component union from collecting contributions on behalf of the association or combination from such of its members as are not exempt from the obligation to contribute to the political fund of the association or combination.

(8) [omitted]

Interpretation

119 Expressions relating to trade unions

In this Act, in relation to a trade union—

'agent' means a banker or solicitor of, or any person employed as an auditor by, the union or any branch or section of the union;

'branch or section', except where the context otherwise requires, includes a branch or section which is itself a trade union;

'executive' means the principal committee of the union exercising executive functions, by whatever name it is called;

'financial affairs' means affairs of the union relating to any fund which is applicable for the purposes of the union (including any fund of a branch or section of the union which is so applicable);

'general secretary' means the official of the union who holds the office of general secretary or, where there is no such office, holds an office which is equivalent, or (except in section 14(4)) the nearest equivalent, to that of general secretary;

'officer' includes—

    (a) any member of the governing body of the union, and

    (b) any trustee of any fund applicable for the purposes of the union;

'official' means—

    (a) an officer of the union or of a branch or section of the union, or

    (b) a person elected or appointed in accordance with the rules of the union to be a representative of its members or of some of them,

and includes a person so elected or appointed who is an employee of the same employer as the members or one or more of the members whom he is to represent;

'president' means the official of the union who holds the office of president or, where there is no such office, who holds an office which is equivalent, or (except in section 14(4) or Chapter IV) the nearest equivalent, to that of president; and

'rules', except where the context otherwise requires, includes the rules of any branch or section of the union.

120 Northern Ireland unions

In this Part a 'Northern Ireland union' means a trade union whose principal office is situated in Northern Ireland.

121 Meaning of 'the court'

In this Part 'the court' (except where the reference is expressed to be to the county court or sheriff court) means the High Court or the Court of Session.

PART II   EMPLOYERS' ASSOCIATIONS

Introductory

122 Meaning of 'employers' association'

(1) In this Act an 'employers' association' means an organisation (whether temporary or permanent)—

    (a) which consists wholly or mainly of employers or individual owners of undertakings of one or more descriptions and whose principal purposes include the regulation of relations between employers of that description or those descriptions and workers or trade unions; or

    (b) which consists wholly or mainly of—

        (i) constituent or affiliated organisations which fulfil the conditions in paragraph (a) (or themselves consist wholly or mainly of constituent or affiliated organisations which fulfil those conditions), or

(ii) representatives of such constituent or affiliated organisations,
and whose principal purposes include the regulation of relations between employers and workers or between employers and trade unions, or the regulation of relations between its constituent or affiliated organisations.

(2) References in this Act to employers' associations include combinations of employers and employers' associations.

123–136 [omitted]

PART III   RIGHTS IN RELATION TO UNION MEMBERSHIP AND ACTIVITIES

Access to employment

137   Refusal of employment on grounds related to union membership

(1) It is unlawful to refuse a person employment—
   (a) because he is, or is not, a member of a trade union, or
   (b) because he is unwilling to accept a requirement—
      (i) to take steps to become or cease to be, or to remain or not to become, a member of a trade union, or
      (ii) to make payments or suffer deductions in the event of his not being a member of a trade union.

(2) A person who is thus unlawfully refused employment has a right of complaint to an employment tribunal.

(3) Where an advertisement is published which indicates, or might reasonably be understood as indicating—
   (a) that employment to which the advertisement relates is open only to a person who is, or is not, a member of a trade union, or
   (b) that any such requirement as is mentioned in subsection (1)(b) will be imposed in relation to employment to which the advertisement relates,
a person who does not satisfy that condition or, as the case may be, is unwilling to accept that requirement, and who seeks and is refused employment to which the advertisement relates, shall be conclusively presumed to have been refused employment for that reason.

(4) Where there is an arrangement or practice under which employment is offered only to persons put forward or approved by a trade union, and the trade union puts forward or approves only persons who are members of the union, a person who is not a member of the union and who is refused employment in pursuance of the arrangement or practice shall be taken to have been refused employment because he is not a member of the trade union.

(5) A person shall be taken to be refused employment if he seeks employment of any description with a person and that person—
   (a) refuses or deliberately omits to entertain and process his application or enquiry, or
   (b) causes him to withdraw or cease to pursue his application or enquiry, or
   (c) refuses or deliberately omits to offer him employment of that description, or
   (d) makes him an offer of such employment the terms of which are such as no reasonable employer who wished to fill the post would offer and which is not accepted, or
   (e) makes him an offer of such employment but withdraws it or causes him not to accept it.

(6) Where a person is offered employment on terms which include a requirement that he is, or is not, a member of a trade union, or any such requirement as is mentioned in subsection (1)(b), and he does not accept the offer because he does not satisfy or, as the case

may be, is unwilling to accept the requirement, he shall be treated as having been refused employment for that reason.

(7) Where a person may not be considered for appointment or election to an office in a trade union unless he is a member of the union, or of a particular branch or section of the union or of one of a number of particular branches or sections of the union, nothing in this section applies to anything done for the purpose of securing compliance with that condition although as holder of the office he would be employed by the union.

For this purpose an 'office' means any position—

(a) by virtue of which the holder is an official of the union, or

(b) to which Chapter IV of Part I applies (duty to hold elections).

(8) The provisions of this section apply in relation to an employment agency acting, or purporting to act, on behalf of an employer as in relation to an employer.

138 Refusal of service of employment agency on grounds related to union membership

(1) It is unlawful for an employment agency to refuse a person any of its services—

(a) because he is, or is not, a member of a trade union, or

(b) because he is unwilling to accept a requirement to take steps to become or cease to be, or to remain or not to become, a member of a trade union.

(2) A person who is thus unlawfully refused any service of an employment agency has a right of complaint to an employment tribunal.

(3) Where an advertisement is published which indicates, or might reasonably be understood as indicating—

(a) that any service of an employment agency is available only to a person who is, or is not, a member of a trade union, or

(b) that any such requirement as is mentioned in subsection (1)(b) will be imposed in relation to a service to which the advertisement relates,

a person who does not satisfy that condition or, as the case may be, is unwilling to accept that requirement, and who seeks to avail himself of and is refused that service, shall be conclusively presumed to have been refused it for that reason.

(4) A person shall be taken to be refused a service if he seeks to avail himself of it and the agency—

(a) refuses or deliberately omits to make the service available to him, or

(b) causes him not to avail himself of the service or to cease to avail himself of it, or

(c) does not provide the same service, on the same terms, as is provided to others.

(5) Where a person is offered a service on terms which include a requirement that he is, or is not, a member of a trade union, or any such requirement as is mentioned in subsection (1)(b), and he does not accept the offer because he does not satisfy or, as the case may be, is unwilling to accept that requirement, he shall be treated as having been refused the service for that reason.

139 Time limit for proceedings

(1) An employment tribunal shall not consider a complaint under section 137 or 138 unless it is presented to the tribunal—

(a) before the end of the period of three months beginning with the date of the conduct to which the complaint relates, or

(b) where the tribunal is satisfied that it was not reasonably practicable for the complaint to be presented before the end of that period, within such further period as the tribunal considers reasonable.

(2) The date of the conduct to which a complaint under section 137 relates shall be taken to be—

(a) in the case of an actual refusal, the date of the refusal;

(b) in the case of a deliberate omission—
    (i) to entertain and process the complainant's application or enquiry, or
    (ii) to offer employment,
the end of the period within which it was reasonable to except the employer to act;
    (c) in the case of conduct causing the complainant to withdraw or cease to pursue his application or enquiry, the date of that conduct;
    (d) in a case where an offer was made but withdrawn, the date when it was withdrawn;
    (e) in any other case where an offer was made but not accepted, the date on which it was made.

(3) The date of the conduct to which a complaint under section 138 relates shall be taken to be—
    (a) in the case of an actual refusal, the date of the refusal;
    (b) in the case of a deliberate omission to make a service available, the end of the period within which it was reasonable to expect the employment agency to act;
    (c) in the case of conduct causing the complainant not to avail himself of a service or to cease to avail himself of it, the date of that conduct;
    (d) in the case of failure to provide the same service, on the same terms, as is provided to others, the date or last date on which the service in fact provided was provided.

140 Remedies

(1) Where the employment tribunal finds that a complaint under section 137 or 138 is well-founded, it shall make a declaration to that effect and may make such of the following as it considers just and equitable—
    (a) an order requiring the respondent to pay compensation to the complainant of such amount as the tribunal may determine;
    (b) a recommendation that the respondent take within a specified period action appearing to the tribunal to be practicable for the purpose of obviating or reducing the adverse effect on the complainant of any conduct to which the complaint relates.

(2) Compensation shall be assessed on the same basis as damages for breach of statutory duty and may include compensation for injury to feelings.

(3) If the respondent fails without reasonable justification to comply with a recommendation to take action, the tribunal may increase its award of compensation or, if it has not made such an award, make one.

(4) The total amount of compensation shall not exceed the limit for the time being imposed by section 124(1) of the Employment Rights Act 1996 (limit on compensation for unfair dismissal).

141 Complaint against employer and employment agency

(1) Where a person has a right of complaint against a prospective employer and against an employment agency arising out of the same facts, he may present a complaint against either of them or against them jointly.

(2) If a complaint is brought against one only, he or the complainant may request the tribunal to join or sist the other as a party to the proceedings.

The request shall be granted if it is made before the hearing of the complaint begins, but may be refused if it is made after that time; and no such request may be made after the tribunal has made its decision as to whether the complaint is well-founded.

(3) Where a complaint is brought against an employer and an employment agency jointly, or where it is brought against one and the other is joined or sisted as a party to the proceedings, and the tribunal—
    (a) finds that the complaint is well-founded as against the employer and the agency, and
    (b) makes an award of compensation,

it may order that the compensation shall be paid by the one or the other, or partly by one and partly by the other, as the tribunal may consider just and equitable in the circumstances.

142   Awards against third parties

(1) If in proceedings on a complaint under section 137 or 138 either the complainant or the respondent claims that the respondent was induced to act in the manner complained of by pressure which a trade union or other person exercised on him by calling, organising, procuring or financing a strike or other industrial action, or by threatening to do so, the complainant or the respondent may request the employment tribunal to direct that the person who he claims exercised the pressure be joined or sisted as a party to the proceedings.

(2) The request shall be granted if it is made before the hearing of the complaint begins, but may be refused if it is made after that time; and no such request may be made after the tribunal has made its decision as to whether the complaint is well-founded.

(3) Where a person has been so joined or sisted as a party to the proceedings and the tribunal—

(a) finds that the complaint is well-founded,

(b) makes an award of compensation, and

(c) also finds that the claim in subsection (1) above is well-founded,

it may order that the compensation shall be paid by the person joined instead of by the respondent, or partly by that person and partly by the respondent, as the tribunal may consider just and equitable in the circumstances.

(4) Where by virtue of section 141 (complaint against employer and employment agency) there is more than one respondent, the above provisions apply to either or both of them.

143   Interpretation and other supplementary provisions

(1) In sections 137 to 143—

'advertisement' includes every form of advertisement or notice, whether to the public or not, and references to publishing an advertisement shall be construed accordingly;

'employment' means employment under a contract of employment, and related expressions shall be construed accordingly; and

'employment agency' means a person who, for profit or not, provides services for the purpose of finding employment for workers or supplying employers with workers, but subject to subsection (2) below.

(2) For the purposes of sections 137 to 143 as they apply to employment agencies—

(a) services other than those mentioned in the definition of 'employment agency' above shall be disregarded, and

(b) a trade union shall not be regarded as an employment agency by reason of services provided by it only for, or in relation to, its members.

(3) References in sections 137 to 143 to being or not being a member of a trade union are to being or not being a member of any trade union, of a particular trade union or of one of a number of particular trade unions.

Any such reference includes a reference to being or not being a member of a particular branch or section of a trade union or of one of a number of particular branches or sections of a trade union.

(4) The remedy of a person for conduct which is unlawful by virtue of section 137 or 138 is by way of a complaint to an employment tribunal in accordance with this Part, and not otherwise.

No other legal liability arises by reason that conduct is unlawful by virtue of either of those sections.

Contracts for supply of goods or services

144 Union membership requirement in contract for goods or services void

A term or condition of a contract for the supply of goods or services is void in so far as it purports to require that the whole, or some part, of the work done for the purposes of the contract is done only by persons who are, or are not, members of trade unions or of a particular trade union.

145 Refusal to deal on union membership grounds prohibited

(1) A person shall not refuse to deal with a supplier or prospective supplier of goods or services on union membership grounds.

'Refuse to deal' and 'union membership grounds' shall be construed as follows.

(2) A person refuses to deal with a person if, where he maintains (in whatever form) a list of approved suppliers of goods or services, or of persons from whom tenders for the supply of goods or services may be invited, he fails to include the name of that person in that list.

He does so on union membership grounds if the ground, or one of the grounds, for failing to include his name is that if that person were to enter into a contract with him for the supply of goods or services, work to be done for the purposes of the contract would, or would be likely to, be done by persons who were, or who were not, members of trade unions or of a particular trade union.

(3) A person refuses to deal with a person if, in relation to a proposed contract for the supply of goods or services—

    (a) he excludes that person from the group of persons from whom tenders for the supply of the goods or services are invited, or

    (b) he fails to permit that person to submit such a tender, or

    (c) he otherwise determines not to enter into a contract with that person for the supply of the goods or services.

He does so on union membership grounds if the ground, or one of the grounds, on which he does so is that if the proposed contract were entered into with that person, work to be done for the purposes of the contract would, or would be likely to, be done by persons who were, or who were not, members of trade unions or of a particular trade union.

(4) A person refuses to deal with a person if he terminates a contract with him for the supply of goods or services.

He does so on union membership grounds if the ground, or one of the grounds, on which he does so is that work done, or to be done, for the purposes of the contract has been, or is likely to be, done by persons who are or are not members of trade unions or of a particular trade union.

(5) The obligation to comply with this section is a duty owed to the person with whom there is a refusal to deal and to any other person who may be adversely affected by its contravention; and a breach of the duty is actionable accordingly (subject to the defences and other incidents applying to actions for breach of statutory duty).

Inducements

145A Inducements relating to union membership or activities

(1) A worker has the right not to have an offer made to him by his employer for the sole or main purpose of inducing the worker—

    (a) not to be or seek to become a member of an independent trade union,

    (b) not to take part, at an appropriate time, in the activities of an independent trade union,

    (c) not to make use, at an appropriate time, of trade union services, or

    (d) to be or become a member of any trade union or of a particular trade union or of one of a number of particular trade unions.

(2) In subsection (1) 'an appropriate time' means—

(a) a time outside the worker's working hours, or

(b) a time within his working hours at which, in accordance with arrangements agreed with or consent given by his employer, it is permissible for him to take part in the activities of a trade union or (as the case may be) make use of trade union services.

(3) In subsection (2) 'working hours', in relation to a worker, means any time when, in accordance with his contract of employment (or other contract personally to do work or perform services), he is required to be at work.

(4) In subsections (1) and (2)—

(a) 'trade union services' means services made available to the worker by an independent trade union by virtue of his membership of the union, and

(b) references to a worker's 'making use' of trade union services include his consenting to the raising of a matter on his behalf by an independent trade union of which he is a member.

(5) A worker or former worker may present a complaint to an employment tribunal on the ground that his employer has made him an offer in contravention of this section.

145B   Inducements relating to collective bargaining

(1) A worker who is a member of an independent trade union which is recognised, or seeking to be recognised, by his employer has the right not to have an offer made to him by his employer if—

(a) acceptance of the offer, together with other workers' acceptance of offers which the employer also makes to them, would have the prohibited result, and

(b) the employer's sole or main purpose in making the offers is to achieve that result.

(2) The prohibited result is that the workers' terms of employment, or any of those terms, will not (or will no longer) be determined by collective agreement negotiated by or on behalf of the union.

(3) It is immaterial for the purposes of subsection (1) whether the offers are made to the workers simultaneously.

(4) Having terms of employment determined by collective agreement shall not be regarded for the purposes of section 145A (or section 146 or 152) as making use of a trade union service.

(5) A worker or former worker may present a complaint to an employment tribunal on the ground that his employer has made him an offer in contravention of this section.

145C   Time limit for proceedings

An employment tribunal shall not consider a complaint under section 145A or 145B unless it is presented—

(a) before the end of the period of three months beginning with the date when the offer was made or, where the offer is part of a series of similar offers to the complainant, the date when the last of them was made, or

(b) where the tribunal is satisfied that it was not reasonably practicable for the complaint to be presented before the end of that period, within such further period as it considers reasonable.

145D   Consideration of complaint

(1) On a complaint under section 145A it shall be for the employer to show what was his sole or main purpose in making the offer.

(2) On a complaint under section 145B it shall be for the employer to show what was his sole or main purpose in making the offers.

(3) On a complaint under section 145A or 145B, in determining any question whether the employer made the offer (or offers) or the purpose for which he did so, no account shall be taken of any pressure which was exercised on him by calling, organising, procuring or financing a strike or other industrial action, or by threatening to do so; and that question shall be determined as if no such pressure had been exercised.

(4) In determining whether an employer's sole or main purpose in making offers was the purpose mentioned in section 145B(1), the matters taken into account must include any evidence—

    (a) that when the offers were made the employer had recently changed or sought to change, or did not wish to use, arrangements agreed with the union for collective bargaining,

    (b) that when the offers were made the employer did not wish to enter into arrangements proposed by the union for collective bargaining, or

    (c) that the offers were made only to particular workers, and were made with the sole or main purpose of rewarding those particular workers for their high level of performance or of retaining them because of their special value to the employer.

145E   Remedies

(1) Subsections (2) and (3) apply where the employment tribunal finds that a complaint under section 145A or 145B is well-founded.

(2) The tribunal—

    (a) shall make a declaration to that effect, and

    (b) shall make an award to be paid by the employer to the complainant in respect of the offer complained of.

(3) The amount of the award shall be £2,600 (subject to any adjustment of the award that may fall to be made under Part 3 of the Employment Act 2002).

(4) Where an offer made in contravention of section 145A or 145B is accepted—

    (a) if the acceptance results in the worker's agreeing to vary his terms of employment, the employer cannot enforce the agreement to vary, or recover any sum paid or other asset transferred by him under the agreement to vary;

    (b) if as a result of the acceptance the worker's terms of employment are varied, nothing in section 145A or 145B makes the variation unenforceable by either party.

(5) Nothing in this section or sections 145A and 145B prejudices any right conferred by section 146 or 149.

(6) In ascertaining any amount of compensation under section 149, no reduction shall be made on the ground—

    (a) that the complainant caused or contributed to his loss, or to the act or failure complained of, by accepting or not accepting an offer made in contravention of section 145A or 145B, or

    (b) that the complainant has received or is entitled to an award under this section.

145F   Interpretation and other supplementary provisions

(1) References in sections 145A to 145E to being or becoming a member of a trade union include references—

    (a) to being or becoming a member of a particular branch or section of that union, and

    (b) to being or becoming a member of one of a number of particular branches or sections of that union.

(2) References in those sections—

    (a) to taking part in the activities of a trade union, and

    (b) to services made available by a trade union by virtue of membership of the union, shall be construed in accordance with subsection (1).

(3) In sections 145A to 145E—

'worker' means an individual who works, or normally works, as mentioned in paragraphs (a) to (c) of section 296(1), and

'employer' means—

    (a) in relation to a worker, the person for whom he works;

    (b) in relation to a former worker, the person for whom he worked.

(4) The remedy of a person for infringement of the right conferred on him by section 145A or 145B is by way of a complaint to an employment tribunal in accordance with this Part, and not otherwise.

Detriment

146   Detriment on grounds related to union membership or activities

(1) A worker has the right not to be subjected to any detriment as an individual by any act, or any deliberate failure to act, by his employer if the act or failure takes place for the sole or main purpose of—

    (a) preventing or deterring him from being or seeking to become a member of an independent trade union, or penalising him for doing so,

    (b) preventing or deterring him from taking part in the activities of an independent trade union at an appropriate time, or penalising him for doing so,

    (ba) preventing or deterring him from making use of trade union services at an appropriate time, or penalising him for doing so, or

    (c) compelling him to be or become a member of any trade union or of a particular trade union or of one of a number of particular trade unions.

(2) In subsection (1) 'an appropriate time' means—

    (a) a time outside the worker's working hours, or

    (b) a time within his working hours at which, in accordance with arrangements agreed with or consent given by his employer, it is permissible for him to take part in the activities of a trade union or (as the case may be) make use of trade union services;

and for this purpose 'working hours', in relation to a worker, means any time when, in accordance with his contract of employment (or other contract personally to do work or perform services), he is required to be at work.

(2A) In this section—

    (a) 'trade union services' means services made available to the worker by an independent trade union by virtue of his membership of the union, and

    (b) references to a worker's 'making use' of trade union services include his consenting to the raising of a matter on his behalf by an independent trade union of which he is a member.

(2B) If an independent trade union of which a worker is a member raises a matter on his behalf (with or without his consent), penalising the worker for that is to be treated as penalising him as mentioned in subsection (1)(ba).

(2C) A worker also has the right not to be subjected to any detriment as an individual by any act, or any deliberate failure to act, by his employer if the act or failure takes place because of the worker's failure to accept an offer made in contravention of section 145A or 145B.

(2D) For the purposes of subsection (2C), not conferring a benefit that, if the offer had been accepted by the worker, would have been conferred on him under the resulting agreement shall be taken to be subjecting him to a detriment as an individual (and to be a deliberate failure to act).

(3) A worker also has the right not to be subjected to any detriment as an individual by any act, or any deliberate failure to act, by his employer if the act or failure takes place for the sole or main purpose of enforcing a requirement (whether or not imposed by a contract of employment or in writing) that, in the event of his not being a member of any trade union or of a particular trade union or of one of a number of particular trade unions, he must make one or more payments.

(4) For the purposes of subsection (3) any deduction made by an employer from the remuneration payable to a worker in respect of his employment shall, if it is attributable to his not being a member of any trade union or of a particular trade union or of one of a

number of particular trade unions, be treated as a detriment to which he has been subjected as an individual by an act of his employer taking place for the sole or main purpose of enforcing a requirement of a kind mentioned in that subsection.

(5) A worker or former worker may present a complaint to an employment tribunal on the ground that he has been subjected to a detriment by his employer in contravention of this section.

(5A) This section does not apply where—
  (a) the worker is an employee; and
  (b) the detriment in question amounts to dismissal.

(6) [repealed]

147   Time limit for proceedings

(1) An employment tribunal shall not consider a complaint under section 146 unless it is presented—
  (a) before the end of the period of three months beginning with the date of the act or failure to which the complaint relates or, where that act or failure is part of a series of similar acts or failures (or both) the last of them, or
  (b) where the tribunal is satisfied that it was not reasonably practicable for the complaint to be presented before the end of that period, within such further period as it considers reasonable.

(2) For the purposes of subsection (1)—
  (a) where an act extends over a period, the reference to the date of the act is a reference to the last day of that period;
  (b) a failure to act shall be treated as done when it was decided on.

(3) For the purposes of subsection (2), in the absence of evidence establishing the contrary an employer shall be taken to decide on a failure to act—
  (a) when he does an act inconsistent with doing the failed act, or
  (b) if he has done no such inconsistent act, when the period expires within which he might reasonably have been expected to do the failed act if it was to be done.

148   Consideration of complaint

(1) On a complaint under section 146 it shall be for the employer to show what was the sole or main purpose for which he acted or failed to act.

(2) In determining any question whether the employer acted or failed to act, or the purpose for which he did so, no account shall be taken of any pressure which was exercised on him by calling, organising, procuring or financing a strike or other industrial action, or by threatening to do so; and that question shall be determined as if no such pressure had been exercised.

(3)–(5) [repealed]

149   Remedies

(1) Where the employment tribunal finds that a complaint under section 146 is well-founded, it shall make a declaration to that effect and may make an award of compensation to be paid by the employer to the complainant in respect of the act or failure complained of.

(2) The amount of the compensation awarded shall be such as the tribunal considers just and equitable in all the circumstances having regard to the infringement complained of and to any loss sustained by the complainant which is attributable to the act or failure which infringed his right.

(3) The loss shall be taken to include—
  (a) any expenses reasonably incurred by the complainant in consequence of the act or failure complained of, and
  (b) loss of any benefit which he might reasonably be expected to have had but for that act or failure.

(4) In ascertaining the loss, the tribunal shall apply the same rule concerning the duty of a person to mitigate his loss as applies to damages recoverable under the common law of England and Wales or Scotland.

(5) In determining the amount of compensation to be awarded no account shall be taken of any pressure which was exercised on the employer by calling, organising, procuring or financing a strike or other industrial action, or by threatening to do so; and that question shall be determined as if no such pressure had been exercised.

(6) Where the tribunal finds that the act or failure complained of was to any extent caused or contributed to by action of the complainant, it shall reduce the amount of the compensation by such proportion as it considers just and equitable having regard to that finding.

150 Awards against third parties

(1) If in proceedings on a complaint under section 146—

    (a) the complaint is made on the ground that the complainant has been subjected to detriment by an act or failure by his employer taking place for the sole or main purpose of compelling him to be or become a member of any trade union or of a particular trade union or of one of a number of particular trade unions, and

    (b) either the complainant or the employer claims in proceedings before the tribunal that the employer was induced to act or fail to act in the way complained of by pressure which a trade union or other person exercised on him by calling, organising, procuring or financing a strike or other industrial action, or by threatening to do so,

the complainant or the employer may request the tribunal to direct that the person who he claims exercised the pressure be joined or sisted as a party to the proceedings.

(2) The request shall be granted if it is made before the hearing of the complaint begins, but may be refused if it is made after that time; and no such request may be made after the tribunal has made a declaration that the complaint is well-founded.

(3) Where a person has been so joined or sisted as a party to proceedings and the tribunal—

    (a) makes an award of compensation, and

    (b) finds that the claim mentioned in subsection (1)(b) is well-founded,

it may order that the compensation shall be paid by the person joined instead of by the employer, or partly by that person and partly by the employer, as the tribunal may consider just and equitable in the circumstances.

151 Interpretation and other supplementary provisions

(1) References in sections 146 to 150 to being, becoming or ceasing to remain a member of a trade union include references to being, becoming or ceasing to remain a member of a particular branch or section of that union and to being, becoming or ceasing to remain a member of one of a number of particular branches or sections of that union.

(1A) References in those sections—

    (a) to taking part in the activities of a trade union, and

    (b) to services made available by a trade union by virtue of membership of the union,

shall be construed in accordance with subsection (1).

(1B) In sections 146 to 150—

'worker' means an individual who works, or normally works, as mentioned in paragraphs (a) to (c) of section 296(1), and 'employer' means—

    (a) in relation to a worker, the person for whom he works;

    (b) in relation to a former worker, the person for whom he worked.

(2) The remedy of a person for infringement of the right conferred on him by section 146 is by way of a complaint to an employment tribunal in accordance with this Part, and not otherwise.

Dismissal of an employee

152 Dismissal of an employee on grounds related to union membership or activities

(1) For purposes of Part X of the Employment Rights Act 1996 (unfair dismissal) the dismissal of an employee shall be regarded as unfair if the reason for it (or, if more than one, the principal reason) was that the employee—

  (a) was, or proposed to become, a member of an independent trade union,

  (b) had taken part, or proposed to take part, in the activities of an independent trade union at an appropriate time,

  (ba) had made use, or proposed to make use, of trade union services at an appropriate time,

  (bb) had failed to accept an offer made in contravention of section 145A or 145B, or

  (c) was not a member of any trade union, or of a particular trade union, or of one of a number of particular trade unions, or had refused, or proposed to refuse, to become or remain a member.

(2) In subsection (1) 'an appropriate time' means—

  (a) a time outside the employee's working hours, or

  (b) a time within his working hours at which, in accordance with arrangements agreed with or consent given by his employer, it is permissible for him to take part in the activities of a trade union or (as the case may be) make use of trade union services;

and for this purpose 'working hours', in relation to an employee, means any time when, in accordance with his contract of employment, he is required to be at work.

(2A) In this section—

  (a) 'trade union services' means services made available to the employee by an independent trade union by virtue of his membership of the union, and

  (b) references to an employee's 'making use' of trade union services include his consenting to the raising of a matter on his behalf by an independent trade union of which he is a member.

(2B) Where the reason or one of the reasons for the dismissal was that an independent trade union (with or without the employee's consent) raised a matter on behalf of the employee as one of its members, the reason shall be treated as falling within subsection (1)(ba).

(3) Where the reason, or one of the reasons, for the dismissal was—

  (a) the employee's refusal, or proposed refusal, to comply with a requirement (whether or not imposed by his contract of employment or in writing) that, in the event of his not being a member of any trade union, or of a particular trade union, or of one of a number of particular trade unions, he must make one or more payments, or

  (b) his objection, or proposed objection, (however expressed) to the operation of a provision (whether or not forming part of his contract of employment or in writing) under which, in the event mentioned in paragraph (a), his employer is entitled to deduct one or more sums from the remuneration payable to him in respect of his employment, the reason shall be treated as falling within subsection (1)(c).

(4) References in this section to being, becoming or ceasing to remain a member of a trade union include references to being, becoming or ceasing to remain a member of a particular branch or section of that union or of one of a number of particular branches or sections of that trade union.

(5) References in this section—

  (a) to taking part in the activities of a trade union, and

  (b) to services made available by a trade union by virtue of membership of the union,

shall be construed in accordance with subsection (4).

153 Selection for redundancy on grounds related to union membership or activities

Where the reason or principal reason for the dismissal of an employee was that he was redundant, but it is shown—

    (a) that the circumstances constituting the redundancy applied equally to one or more other employees in the same undertaking who held positions similar to that held by him and who have not been dismissed by the employer, and

    (b) that the reason (or, if more than one, the principal reason) why he was selected for dismissal was one of those specified in section 152(1),

the dismissal shall be regarded as unfair for the purposes of Part X of the Employment Rights Act 1996 (unfair dismissal).

154 Disapplication of qualifying period and upper age limit for unfair dismissal

    (1) Sections 108(1) and 109(1) of the Employment Rights Act 1996 (qualifying period and upper age limit for unfair dismissal protection) do not apply to a dismissal which by virtue of section 152 or 153 is regarded as unfair for the purposes of Part 10 of that Act.

    (2) For the purposes of this section—

'inadmissible', in relation to a reason, means that it is one of those specified in section 152(1); and

'a redundancy case' means a case where the reason or principal reason for the dismissal was that the employee was redundant but the equal application of the circumstances to non-dismissed employees required by section 153(a) is also shown.

155 Matters to be disregarded in assessing contributory fault

    (1) Where an employment tribunal makes an award of compensation for unfair dismissal in a case where the dismissal is unfair by virtue of section 152 or 153, the tribunal shall disregard, in considering whether it would be just and equitable to reduce, or further reduce, the amount of any part of the award, any such conduct or action of the complainant as is specified below.

    (2) Conduct or action of the complainant shall be disregarded in so far as it constitutes a breach or proposed breach of a requirement—

    (a) to be or become a member of any trade union or of a particular trade union or of one of a number of particular trade unions,

    (b) to cease to be, or refrain from becoming, a member of any trade union or of a particular trade union or of one of a number of particular trade unions,

    (c) not to take part in the activities of any trade union or of a particular trade union or of one of a number of particular trade unions, or

    (d) not to make use of services made available by any trade union or by a particular trade union or by one of a number of particular trade unions.

For the purposes of this subsection a requirement means a requirement imposed on the complainant by or under an arrangement or contract of employment or other agreement.

    (2A) Conduct or action of the complainant shall be disregarded in so far as it constitutes acceptance of or failure to accept an offer made in contravention of section 145A or 145B.

    (3) Conduct or action of the complainant shall be disregarded in so far as it constitutes a refusal, or proposed refusal, to comply with a requirement of a kind mentioned in section 152(3)(a) (payments in lieu of membership) or an objection, or proposed objection, (however expressed) to the operation of a provision of a kind mentioned in section 152(3)(b) (deductions in lieu of membership).

156 Minimum basic award

    (1) Where a dismissal is unfair by virtue of section 152(1) or 153, the amount of the basic award of compensation, before any reduction is made under section 122 of the Employment Rights Act 1996 shall be not less than £4,000.

(2) But where the dismissal is unfair by virtue of section 153, subsection (2) of that section (reduction for contributory fault) applies in relation to so much of the basic award as is payable because of subsection (1) above.

157–159 [repealed]

160 Awards against third parties

(1) If in proceedings before an employment tribunal on a complaint of unfair dismissal either the employer or the complainant claims—

(a) that the employer was induced to dismiss the complainant by pressure which a trade union or other person exercised on the employer by calling, organising, procuring or financing a strike or other industrial action, or by threatening to do so, and

(b) that the pressure was exercised because the complainant was not a member of any trade union or of a particular trade union or of one of a number of particular trade unions,

the employer or the complainant may request the tribunal to direct that the person who he claims exercised the pressure be joined or sisted as a party to the proceedings.

(2) The request shall be granted if it is made before the hearing of the complaint begins, but may be refused after that time; and no such request may be made after the tribunal has made an award of compensation for unfair dismissal or an order for reinstatement or re-engagement.

(3) Where a person has been so joined or sisted as a party to the proceedings and the tribunal—

(a) makes an award of compensation for unfair dismissal, and

(b) finds that the claim mentioned in subsection (1) is well-founded,

the tribunal may order that the compensation shall be paid by that person instead of the employer, or partly by that person and partly by the employer, as the tribunal may consider just and equitable.

161 Application for interim relief

(1) An employee who presents a complaint of unfair dismissal alleging that the dismissal is unfair by virtue of section 152 may apply to the tribunal for interim relief.

(2) The tribunal shall not entertain an application for interim relief unless it is presented to the tribunal before the end of the period of seven days immediately following the effective date of termination (whether before, on or after that date).

(3) In a case where the employee relies on section 152(1)(a), (b) or (ba), or on section 152(1)(bb) otherwise than in relation to an offer made in contravention of section 145A(1)(d), the tribunal shall not entertain an application for interim relief unless before the end of that period there is also so presented a certificate in writing signed by an authorised official of the independent trade union of which the employee was or proposed to become a member stating—

(a) that on the date of the dismissal the employee was or proposed to become a member of the union, and

(b) that there appear to be reasonable grounds for supposing that the reason for his dismissal (or, if more than one, the principal reason) was one alleged in the complaint.

(4) An 'authorised official' means an official of the trade union authorised by it to act for the purposes of this section.

(5) A document purporting to be an authorisation of an official by a trade union to act for the purposes of this section and to be signed on behalf of the union shall be taken to be such an authorisation unless the contrary is proved; and a document purporting to be a certificate signed by such an official shall be taken to be signed by him unless the contrary is proved.

(6) For the purposes of subsection (3) the date of dismissal shall be taken to be—

    (a) where the employee's contract of employment was terminated by notice (whether given by his employer or by him), the date on which the employer's notice was given, and

    (b) in any other case, the effective date of termination.

162 Application to be promptly determined

(1) An employment tribunal shall determine an application for interim relief as soon as practicable after receiving the application and, where appropriate, the requisite certificate.

(2) The tribunal shall give to the employer, not later than seven days before the hearing, a copy of the application and of any certificate, together with notice of the date, time and place of the hearing.

(3) If a request under section 160 (awards against third parties) is made three days or more before the date of the hearing, the tribunal shall also give to the person to whom the request relates, as soon as reasonably practicable, a copy of the application and of any certificate, together with notice of the date, time and place of the hearing.

(4) The tribunal shall not exercise any power it has of postponing the hearing of an application for interim relief except where it is satisfied that special circumstances exist which justify it in doing so.

163 Procedure on hearing of application and making of order

(1) If on hearing an application for interim relief it appears to the tribunal that it is likely that on determining the complaint to which the application relates that it will find that, by virtue of section 152, the complainant has been unfairly dismissed, the following provisions apply.

(2) The tribunal shall announce its findings and explain to both parties (if present) what powers the tribunal may exercise on the application and in what circumstances it will exercise them, and shall ask the employer (if present) whether he is willing, pending the determination or settlement of the complaint—

    (a) to reinstate the employee, that is to say, to treat him in all respects as if he had not been dismissed, or

    (b) if not, to re-engage him in another job on terms and conditions not less favourable than those which would have been applicable to him if he had not been dismissed.

(3) For this purpose 'terms and conditions not less favourable than those which would have been applicable to him if he had not been dismissed' means as regards seniority, pension rights and other similar rights that the period prior to the dismissal shall be regarded as continuous with his employment following the dismissal.

(4) If the employer states that he is willing to reinstate the employee, the tribunal shall make an order to that effect.

(5) If the employer states that he is willing to re-engage the employee in another job, and specifies the terms and conditions on which he is willing to do so, the tribunal shall ask the employee whether he is willing to accept the job on those terms and conditions; and—

    (a) if the employee is willing to accept the job on those terms and conditions, the tribunal shall make an order to that effect, and

    (b) if he is not, then, if the tribunal is of the opinion that the refusal is reasonable, the tribunal shall make an order for the continuation of his contract of employment, and otherwise the tribunal shall make no order.

(6) If on the hearing of an application for interim relief the employer fails to attend before the tribunal, or states that he is unwilling either to reinstate the employee or re-engage him as mentioned in subsection (2), the tribunal shall make an order for the continuation of the employee's contract of employment.

164   Order for continuation of contract of employment

(1) An order under section 163 for the continuation of a contract of employment is an order that the contract of employment continue in force—

(a) for the purposes of pay or any other benefit derived from the employment, seniority, pension rights and other similar matters, and

(b) for the purpose of determining for any purpose the period for which the employee has been continuously employed,

from the date of its termination (whether before or after the making of the order) until the determination or settlement of the complaint.

(2) Where the tribunal makes such an order it shall specify in the order the amount which is to be paid by the employer to the employee by way of pay in respect of each normal pay period, or part of any such period, falling between the date of dismissal and the determination or settlement of the complaint.

(3) Subject as follows, the amount so specified shall be that which the employee could reasonably have been expected to earn during that period, or part, and shall be paid—

(a) in the case of payment for any such period falling wholly or partly after the making of the order, on the normal pay day for that period, and

(b) in the case of a payment for any past period, within such time as may be specified in the order.

(4) If an amount is payable in respect only of part of a normal pay period, the amount shall be calculated by reference to the whole period and reduced proportionately.

(5) Any payment made to an employee by an employer under his contract of employment, or by way of damages for breach of that contract, in respect of a normal pay period or part of any such period shall go towards discharging the employer's liability in respect of that period under subsection (2); and conversely any payment under that subsection in respect of a period shall go towards discharging any liability of the employer under, or in respect of the breach of, the contract of employment in respect of that period.

(6) If an employee, on or after being dismissed by his employer, receives a lump sum which, or part of which, is in lieu of wages but is not referable to any normal pay period, the tribunal shall take the payment into account in determining the amount of pay to be payable in pursuance of any such order.

(7) For the purposes of this section the amount which an employee could reasonably have been expected to earn, his normal pay period and the normal pay day for each such period shall be determined as if he had not been dismissed.

165   Application for variation or revocation of order

(1) At any time between the making of an order under section 163 and the determination or settlement of the complaint, the employer or the employee may apply to an employment tribunal for the revocation or variation of the order on the ground of a relevant change of circumstances since the making of the order.

(2) Sections 161 to 163 apply in relation to such an application as in relation to an original application for interim relief, except that—

(a) no certificate need be presented to the tribunal under section 161(3), and

(b) in the case of an application by the employer, section 162(2) (service of copy of application and notice of hearing) has effect with the substitution of a reference to the employee for the reference to the employer.

166   Consequences of failure to comply with order

(1) If on the application of an employee an employment tribunal is satisfied that the employer has not complied with the terms of an order for the reinstatement or re-engagement of the employee under section 163(4) or (5), the tribunal shall—

(a) make an order for the continuation of the employee's contract of employment, and

(b) order the employer to pay the employee such compensation as the tribunal considers just and equitable in all the circumstances having regard—

(i) to the infringement of the employee's right to be reinstated or re-engaged in pursuance of the order, and

(ii) to any loss suffered by the employee in consequence of the non-compliance.

(2) Section 164 applies to an order under subsection (1)(a) as in relation to an order under section 163.

(3) If on the application of an employee an employment tribunal is satisfied that the employer has not complied with the terms of an order for the continuation of a contract of employment, the following provisions apply.

(4) If the non-compliance consists of a failure to pay an amount by way of pay specified in the order, the tribunal shall determine the amount owed by the employer on the date of the determination.

If on that date the tribunal also determines the employee's complaint that he has been unfairly dismissed, it shall specify that amount separately from any other sum awarded to the employee.

(5) In any other case, the tribunal shall order the employer to pay the employee such compensation as the tribunal considers just and equitable in all the circumstances having regard to any loss suffered by the employee in consequence of the non-compliance.

167 Interpretation and other supplementary provisions

(1) Part X of the Employment Rights Act 1996 (unfair dismissal) has effect subject to the provisions of sections 152 to 166 above.

(2) Those sections shall be construed as one with that Part; and in those sections—

'complaint of unfair dismissal' means a complaint under section 111 of the Employment Rights Act 1996;

'award of compensation for unfair dismissal' means an award of compensation for unfair dismissal under section 112(4) or 117(3)(a) of that Act; and

'order for reinstatement or re-engagement' means an order for reinstatement or re-engagement under section 113 of that Act.

(3) Nothing in those sections shall be construed as conferring a right to complain of unfair dismissal from employment of a description to which that Part does not otherwise apply.

Time off for trade union duties and activities

168 Time off for carrying out trade union duties

(1) An employer shall permit an employee of his who is an official of an independent trade union recognised by the employer to take time off during his working hours for the purpose of carrying out any duties of his, as such an official, concerned with—

(a) negotiations with the employer related to or connected with matters falling within section 178(2) (collective bargaining) in relation to which the trade union is recognised by the employer, or

(b) the performance on behalf of employees of the employer of functions related to or connected with matters falling within that provision which the employer has agreed may be so performed by the trade union, or

(c) receipt of information from the employer and consultation by the employer under section 188 (redundancies) or under the Transfer of Undertakings (Protection of Employment) Regulations 2006, or

(d) negotiations with a view to entering into an agreement under regulation 9 of the Transfer of Undertakings (Protection of Employment) Regulations 2006 that applies to employees of the employer, or

(e) the performance on behalf of employees of the employer of functions related to or connected with the making of an agreement under that regulation.

(2) He shall also permit such an employee to take time off during his working hours for the purpose of undergoing training in aspects of industrial relations—

(a) relevant to the carrying out of such duties as are mentioned in subsection (1), and

(b) approved by the Trades Union Congress or by the independent trade union of which he is an official.

(3) The amount of time off which an employee is to be permitted to take under this section and the purposes for which, the occasions on which and any conditions subject to which time off may be so taken are those that are reasonable in all the circumstances having regard to any relevant provisions of a Code of Practice issued by ACAS.

(4) An employee may present a complaint to an employment tribunal that his employer has failed to permit him to take time off as required by this section.

168A Time off for union learning representatives

(1) An employer shall permit an employee of his who is—

(a) a member of an independent trade union recognised by the employer, and

(b) a learning representative of the trade union,

to take time off during his working hours for any of the following purposes.

(2) The purposes are—

(a) carrying on any of the following activities in relation to qualifying members of the trade union—

(i)   analysing learning or training needs,

(ii) providing information and advice about learning or training matters,

(iii) arranging learning or training, and

(iv) promoting the value of learning or training,

(b) consulting the employer about carrying on any such activities in relation to such members of the trade union,

(c) preparing for any of the things mentioned in paragraphs (a) and (b).

(3)–(11) [omitted]

169 Payment for time off under section 168

(1) An employer who permits an employee to take time off under section 168 or 168A shall pay him for the time taken off pursuant to the permission.

(2) Where the employee's remuneration for the work he would ordinarily have been doing during that time does not vary with the amount of work done, he shall be paid as if he had worked at that work for the whole of that time.

(3) Where the employee's remuneration for the work he would ordinarily have been doing during that time varies with the amount of work done, he shall be paid an amount calculated by reference to the average hourly earnings for that work.

The average hourly earnings shall be those of the employee concerned or, if no fair estimate can be made of those earnings, the average hourly earnings for work of that description of persons in comparable employment with the same employer or, if there are no such persons, a figure of average hourly earnings which is reasonable in the circumstances.

(4) A right to be paid an amount under this section does not affect any right of an employee in relation to remuneration under his contract of employment, but—

(a) any contractual remuneration paid to an employee in respect of a period of time off to which this section applies shall go towards discharging any liability of the employer under this section in respect of that period, and

(b) any payment under this section in respect of a period shall go towards discharging any liability of the employer to pay contractual remuneration in respect of that period.

(5) An employee may present a complaint to an employment tribunal that his employer has failed to pay him in accordance with this section.

170 Time off for trade union activities

(1) An employer shall permit an employee of his who is a member of an independent trade union recognised by the employer in respect of that description of employee to take time off during his working hours for the purpose of taking part in—
  (a) any activities of the union, and
  (b) any activities in relation to which the employee is acting as a representative of the union.

(2) The right conferred by subsection (1) does not extend to activities which themselves consist of industrial action, whether or not in contemplation or furtherance of a trade dispute.

(2A) The right conferred by subsection (1) does not extend to time off for the purpose of acting as, or having access to services provided by, a learning representative of a trade union.

(2B) An employer shall permit an employee of his who is a member of an independent trade union recognised by the employer in respect of that description of employee to take time off during his working hours for the purpose of having access to services provided by a person in his capacity as a learning representative of the trade union.

(2C) Subsection (2B) only applies if the learning representative would be entitled to time off under subsection (1) of section 168A for the purpose of carrying on in relation to the employee activities of the kind mentioned in subsection (2) of that section.

(3) The amount of time off which an employee is to be permitted to take under this section and the purposes for which, the occasions on which and any conditions subject to which time off may be so taken are those that are reasonable in all the circumstances having regard to any relevant provisions of a Code of Practice issued by ACAS.

(4) An employee may present a complaint to an employment tribunal that his employer has failed to permit him to take time off as required by this section.

(5) For the purposes of this section—
  (a) a person is a learning representative of a trade union if he is appointed or elected as such in accordance with its rules, and
  (b) a person who is a learning representative of a trade union acts as such if he carries on the activities mentioned in section 168A(2) in that capacity.

171 Time limit for proceedings

An employment tribunal shall not consider a complaint under section 168, 168A, 169 or 170 unless it is presented to the tribunal—
  (a) within three months of the date when the failure occurred, or
  (b) where the tribunal is satisfied that it was not reasonably practicable for the complaint to be presented within that period, within such further period as the tribunal considers reasonable.

172 Remedies

(1) Where the tribunal finds a complaint under section 168, 168A or 170 is well-founded, it shall make a declaration to that effect and may make an award of compensation to be paid by the employer to the employee.

(2) The amount of the compensation shall be such as the tribunal considers just and equitable in all the circumstances having regard to the employer's default in failing to permit time off to be taken by the employee and to any loss sustained by the employee which is attributable to the matters complained of.

(3) Where on a complaint under section 169 the tribunal finds that the employer has failed to pay the employee in accordance with that section, it shall order him to pay the amount which it finds to be due.

173 Interpretation and other supplementary provisions

(1) For the purposes of sections 168, 168A, and 170 the working hours of an employee shall be taken to be any time when in accordance with his contract of employment he is required to be at work.

(2) The remedy of an employee for infringement of the rights conferred on him by section 168, 168A, 169 or 170 is by way of complaint to an employment tribunal in accordance with this Part, and not otherwise.

(3)–(4) [omitted]

Right to membership of trade union

174   Right not to be excluded or expelled from union

(1) An individual shall not be excluded or expelled from a trade union unless the exclusion or expulsion is permitted by this section.

(2) The exclusion or expulsion of an individual from a trade union is permitted by this section if (and only if)—

(a) he does not satisfy, or no longer satisfies, an enforceable membership requirement contained in the rules of the union,

(b) he does not qualify, or no longer qualifies, for membership of the union by reason of the union operating only in a particular part or particular parts of Great Britain,

(c) in the case of a union whose purpose is the regulation or relations between its members and one particular employer or a number of particular employers who are associated, he is not, or is no longer, employed by that employer or one of those employers, or

(d) the exclusion or expulsion is entirely attributable to conduct of his (other than excluded conduct) and the conduct to which it is wholly or mainly attributable is not protected conduct.

(3) A requirement in relation to membership of a union is 'enforceable' for the purposes of subsection (2)(a) if it restricts membership solely by reference to one or more of the following criteria—

(a) employment in specified trade, industry or profession,

(b) occupational description (including grade, level or category of appointment), and

(c) possession of specified trade, industrial or professional qualifications or work experience.

(4) For the purposes of subsection (2)(d) 'excluded conduct', in relation to an individual, means—

(a) conduct which consists in his being or ceasing to be, or having been or ceased to be, a member of another trade union,

(b) conduct which consists in his being or ceasing to be, or having been or ceased to be, employed by a particular employer or at a particular place, or

(c) conduct to which section 65 (conduct for which an individual may not be disciplined by a union) applies or would apply if the references in that section to the trade union which is relevant for the purposes of that section were references to any trade union.

(4A) For the purposes of subsection (2)(d) 'protected conduct' is conduct which consists in the individual's being or ceasing to be, or having been or ceased to be, a member of a political party.

(4B) Conduct which consists of activities undertaken by an individual as a member of a political party is not conduct falling within subsection (4A).

(5) An individual who claims that he has been excluded or expelled from a trade union in contravention of this section may present a complaint to an employment tribunal.

175   Time limit for proceedings

An employment tribunal shall not entertain a complaint under section 174 unless it is presented—

(a) before the end of the period of six months beginning with the date of the exclusion or explusion, or

(b) where the tribunal is satisfied that it was not reasonably practicable for the complaint to be presented before the end of that period, within such further period as the tribunal considers reasonable.

176 Remedies

(1) Where the employment tribunal finds a complaint under section 174 is well-founded, it shall make a declaration to that effect.

(1A) If a tribunal makes a declaration under subsection (1) and it appears to the tribunal that the exclusion or expulsion was mainly attributable to conduct falling within section 174(4A) it shall make a declaration to that effect.

(1B) If a tribunal makes a declaration under subsection (1A) and it appears to the tribunal that the other conduct to which the exclusion or expulsion was attributable consisted wholly or mainly of conduct of the complainant which was contrary to—

(a) a rule of the union, or

(b) an objective of the union,

it shall make a declaration to that effect.

(1C) For the purposes of subsection (1B), it is immaterial whether the complainant was a member of the union at the time of the conduct contrary to the rule or objective.

(1D) A declaration by virtue of subsection (1B)(b) shall not be made unless the union shows that, at the time of the conduct of the complainant which was contrary to the objective in question, it was reasonably practicable for that objective to be ascertained—

(a) if the complainant was not at that time a member of the union, by a member of the general public, and

(b) if he was at that time a member of the union, by a member of the union.

(2) An individual whose complaint has been declared to be well-founded may make an application to an employment tribunal for an award of compensation to be paid to him by the union.

(3) The application shall not be entertained if made—

(a) before the end of the period of four weeks beginning with the date of the declaration under subsection (1), or

(b) after the end of the period of six months beginning with that date.

(4) The amount of compensation awarded shall, subject to the following provisions, be such as the employment tribunal considers just and equitable in all the circumstances.

(5) Where the employment tribunal finds that the exclusion or expulsion complained of was to any extent caused or contributed to by the action of the applicant, it shall reduce the amount of the compensation by such proportion as it considers just and equitable having regard to that finding.

(6) The amount of compensation calculated in accordance with subsections (4) and (5) shall not exceed the aggregate of—

(a) an amount equal to thirty times the limit for the time being imposed by section 227(1)(a) of the Employment Rights Act 1996 (maximum amount of a week's pay for basic award in unfair dismissal cases), and

(b) an amount equal to the limit for the time being imposed by section 124(1) of that Act (maximum compensatory award in such cases).

(6A) If on the date on which the application was made the applicant had not been admitted or re-admitted to the union, the award shall not be less than £6,300.

(6B) Subsection (6A) does not apply in a case where the tribunal which made the declaration under subsection (1) also made declarations under subsections (1A) and (1B).

(7)–(8) [repealed]

177 Interpretation and other supplementary provisions

(1) For the purposes of section 174—

(a) 'trade union' does not include an organisation falling within paragraph (b) of section 1,

(b) 'conduct' includes statements, acts and omissions, and

(c) 'employment' includes any relationship whereby an individual personally does work or performs services for another person (related expressions being construed accordingly).

(2) For the purposes of sections 174 to 176—

(a) if an individual's application for membership of a trade union is neither granted nor rejected before the end of the period within which it might reasonably have been expected to be granted if it was to be granted, he shall be treated as having been excluded from the union on the last day of that period, and

(b) an individual who under the rules of a trade union ceases to be a member of the union on the happening of an event specified in the rules shall be treated as having been expelled from the union.

(3) The remedy of an individual for infringement of the rights conferred by section 174 is by way of a complaint to an employment tribunal in accordance with that section, sections 175 and 176 and this section, and not otherwise.

(4) Where a complaint relating to an expulsion which is presented under section 174 is declared to be well-founded, no complaint in respect of the expulsion shall be presented or proceeded with under section 66 (complaint of infringement of right not to be unjustifiably disciplined).

(5) The rights conferred by section 174 are in addition to, and not in substitution for, any right which exists apart from that section; and, subject to subsection (4), nothing in that section, section 175 or 176 or this section affects any remedy for infringement of any such right.

PART IV   INDUSTRIAL RELATIONS

CHAPTER I   COLLECTIVE BARGAINING

Introductory

178   Collective agreements and collective bargaining

(1) In this Act 'collective agreement' means any agreement or arrangement made by or on behalf of one or more trade unions and one or more employers or employers' associations and relating to one or more of the matters specified below; and 'collective bargaining' means negotiations relating to or connected with one or more of those matters.

(2) The matters referred to above are—

(a) terms and conditions of employment, or the physical conditions in which any workers are required to work;

(b) engagement or non-engagement, or termination or suspension of employment or the duties of employment, of one or more workers;

(c) allocation of work or the duties of employment between workers or groups of workers;

(d) matters of discipline;

(e) a worker's membership or non-membership of a trade union;

(f) facilities for officials of trade unions; and

(g) machinery for negotiation or consultation, and other procedures, relating to any of the above matters, including the recognition by employers or employers' associations of the right of a trade union to represent workers in such negotiation or consultation or in the carrying out of such procedures.

(3) In this Act 'recognition', in relation to a trade union, means the recognition of the union by an employer, or two or more associated employers, to any extent, for the purpose of collective bargaining; and 'recognised' and other related expressions shall be construed accordingly.

Enforceability of collective agreements

179   Whether agreement intended to be a legally enforceable contract

(1) A collective agreement shall be conclusively presumed not to have been intended by the parties to be a legally enforceable contract unless the agreement—

    (a) is in writing, and

    (b) contains a provision which (however expressed) states that the parties intend that the agreement shall be a legally enforceable contract.

(2) A collective agreement which does satisfy those conditions shall be conclusively presumed to have been intended by the parties to be a legally enforceable contract.

(3) If a collective agreement is in writing and contains a provision which (however expressed) states that the parties intend that one or more parts of the agreement specified in that provision, but not the whole of the agreement, shall be a legally enforceable contract, then—

    (a) the specified part or parts shall be conclusively presumed to have been intended by the parties to be a legally enforceable contract, and

    (b) the remainder of the agreement shall be conclusively presumed not to have been intended by the parties to be such a contract.

(4) A part of a collective agreement which by virtue of subsection (3)(b) is not a legally enforceable contract may be referred to for the purpose of interpreting a part of the agreement which is such a contract.

180   Effect of provisions restricting right to take industrial action

(1) Any terms of a collective agreement which prohibit or restrict the right of workers to engage in a strike or other industrial action, or have the effect of prohibiting or restricting that right, shall not form part of any contract between a worker and the person for whom he works unless the following conditions are met.

(2) The conditions are that the collective agreement—

    (a) is in writing,

    (b) contains a provision expressly stating that those terms shall or may be incorporated in such a contract,

    (c) is reasonably accessible at his place of work to the worker to whom it applies and is available for him to consult during working hours, and

    (d) is one where each trade union which is a party to the agreement is an independent trade union;

and that the contract with the worker expressly or impliedly incorporates those terms in the contract.

(3) The above provisions have effect notwithstanding anything in section 179 and notwithstanding any provision to the contrary in any agreement (including a collective agreement or a contract with any worker).

Disclosure of information for purposes of collective bargaining

181   General duty of employers to disclose information

(1) An employer who recognises an independent trade union shall, for the purposes of all stages of collective bargaining about matters, and in relation to descriptions of workers, in respect of which the union is recognised by him, disclose to representatives of the union, on request, the information required by this section.

In this section and sections 182 to 185 'representative', in relation to a trade union, means an official or other person authorised by the union to carry on such collective bargaining.

(2) The information to be disclosed is all information relating to the employer's undertaking which is in his possession, or that of an associated employer, and is information—

(a) without which the trade union representatives would be to a material extent impeded in carrying on collective bargaining with him, and

(b) which it would be in accordance with good industrial relations practice that he should disclose to them for the purposes of collective bargaining.

(3) A request by trade union representatives for information under this section shall, if the employer so requests, be in writing or be confirmed in writing.

(4) In determining what would be in accordance with good industrial relations practice, regard shall be had to the relevant provisions of any Code of Practice issued by ACAS, but not so as to exclude any other evidence of what that practice is.

(5) Information which an employer is required by virtue of this section to disclose to trade union representatives shall, if they so request, be disclosed or confirmed in writing.

182   Restrictions on general duty

(1) An employer is not required by section 181 to disclose information—

(a) the disclosure of which would be against the interests of national security, or

(b) which he could not disclose without contravening a prohibition imposed by or under an enactment, or

(c) which has been communicated to him in confidence, or which he has otherwise obtained in consequence of the confidence reposed in him by another person, or

(d) which relates specifically to an individual (unless that individual has consented to its being disclosed), or

(e) the disclosure of which would cause substantial injury to his undertaking for reasons other than its effect on collective bargaining, or

(f) obtained by him for the purpose of bringing, prosecuting or defending any legal proceedings.

In formulating the provisions of any Code of Practice relating to the disclosure of information, ACAS shall have regard to the provisions of this subsection.

(2) In the performance of his duty under section 181 an employer is not required—

(a) to produce, or allow inspection of, any document (other than a document prepared for the purpose of conveying or confirming the information) or to make a copy of or extracts from any document, or

(b) to compile or assemble any information where the compilation or assembly would involve an amount of work or expenditure out of reasonable proportion to the value of the information in the conduct of collective bargaining.

183   Complaint of failure to disclose information

(1) A trade union may present a complaint to the Central Arbitration Committee that an employer has failed—

(a) to disclose to representatives of the union information which he was required to disclose to them by section 181, or

(b) to confirm such information in writing in accordance with that section.

The complaint must be in writing and in such form as the Committee may require.

(2) If on receipt of a complaint the Committee is of the opinion that it is reasonably likely to be settled by conciliation, it shall refer the complaint to ACAS and shall notify the trade union and employer accordingly, whereupon ACAS shall seek to promote a settlement of the matter.

If a complaint so referred is not settled or withdrawn and ACAS is of the opinion that further attempts at conciliation are unlikely to result in a settlement, it shall inform the Committee of its opinion.

(3) If the complaint is not referred to ACAS or, if it is so referred, on ACAS informing the Committee of its opinion that further attempts at conciliation are unlikely to result in a settlement, the Committee shall proceed to hear and determine the complaint and shall make a declaration stating whether it finds the complaint well-founded, wholly or in part, and stating the reasons for its findings.

(4) On the hearing of a complaint any person who the Committee considers has a proper interest in the complaint is entitled to be heard by the Committee, but a failure to accord a hearing to a person other than the trade union and employer directly concerned does not affect the validity of any decision of the Committee in those proceedings.

(5) If the Committee finds the complaint wholly or partly well-founded, the declaration shall specify—

    (a) the information in respect of which the Committee finds that the complaint is well-founded.

    (b) the date (or, if more than one, the earliest date) on which the employer refused or failed to disclose or, as the case may be, to confirm in writing, any of the information in question, and

    (c) a period (not being less than one week from the date of the declaration) within which the employer ought to disclose that information, or, as the case may be, to confirm it in writing.

(6) On a hearing of a complaint under this section a certificate signed by or on behalf of a Minister of the Crown and certifying that a particular request for information could not be complied with except by disclosing information the disclosure of which would have been against the interests of national security shall be conclusive evidence of that fact.

A document which purports to be such a certificate shall be taken to be such a certificate unless the contrary is proved.

184 Further complaint of failure to comply with declaration

(1) After the expiration of the period specified in a declaration under section 183(5)(c) the trade union may present a further complaint to the Central Arbitration Committee that the employer has failed to disclose or, as the case may be, to confirm in writing to representatives of the union information specified in the declaration.

The complaint must be in writing and in such form as the Committee may require.

(2) On receipt of a further complaint the Committee shall proceed to hear and determine the complaint and shall make a declaration stating whether they find the complaint well-founded, wholly or in part, and stating the reasons for their finding.

(3) On the hearing of a further complaint any person who the Committee consider has a proper interest in that complaint shall be entitled to be heard by the Committee, but a failure to accord a hearing to a person other than the trade union and employer directly concerned shall not affect the validity of any decision of the Committee in those proceedings.

(4) If the Committee find the further complaint wholly or partly well-founded the declaration shall specify the information in respect of which the Committee find that that complaint is well-founded.

185 Determination of claim and award

(1) On or after presenting a further complaint under section 184 the trade union may present to the Central Arbitration Committee a claim, in writing, in respect of one or more descriptions of employees (but not workers who are not employees) specified in the claim that their contracts should include the terms and conditions specified in the claim.

(2) The right to present a claim expires if the employer discloses or, as the case may be, confirms in writing, to representatives of the trade union the information specified in the declaration under section 183(5) or 184(4); and a claim presented shall be treated as withdrawn if the employer does so before the Committee make an award on the claim.

(3) If the Committee find, or have found, the further complaint wholly or partly well-founded, they may, after hearing the parties, make an award that in respect of any description of employees specified in the claim the employer shall, from a specified date, observe either—

    (a) the terms and conditions specified in the claim; or

    (b) other terms and conditions which the Committee consider appropriate.

The date specified may be earlier than that on which the award is made but not earlier than the date specified in accordance with section 183(5)(b) in the declaration made by the Committee on the original complaint.

(4) An award shall be made only in respect of a description of employees, and shall comprise only terms and conditions relating to matters in respect of which the trade union making the claim is recognised by the employer.

(5) Terms and conditions which by an award under this section an employer is required to observe in respect of an employee have effect as part of the employee's contract of employment as from the date specified in the award, except in so far as they are superseded or varied—

(a) by a subsequent award under this section,
(b) by a collective agreement between the employer and the union for the time being representing that employee, or
(c) by express or implied agreement between the employee and the employer so far as that agreement effects an improvement in terms and conditions having effect by virtue of the award.

(6) Where—

(a) by virtue of any enactment, other than one contained in this section, providing for minimum remuneration or terms and conditions, a contract of employment is to have effect as modified by an award, order or other instrument under that enactment, and
(b) by virtue of an award under this section any terms and conditions are to have effect as part of that contract,

that contract shall have effect in accordance with that award, order or other instrument or in accordance with the award under this section, whichever is the more favourable, in respect of any terms and conditions of that contract, to the employee.

(7) No award may be made under this section in respect of terms and conditions of employment which are fixed by virtue of any enactment.

Prohibition of union recognition requirements

186 Recognition requirement in contract for goods or services void

A term or condition of a contract for the supply of goods or services is void in so far as it purports to require a party to the contract—

(a) to recognise one or more trade unions (whether or not named in the contract) for the purpose of negotiating on behalf of workers, or any class of worker, employed by him, or
(b) to negotiate or consult with, or with an official of, one or more trade unions (whether or not so named).

187 Refusal to deal on grounds of union exclusion prohibited

(1) A person shall not refuse to deal with a supplier or prospective supplier of goods or services if the ground or one of the grounds for his action is that the person against whom it is taken does not, or is not likely to—

(a) recognise one or more trade unions for the purpose of negotiating on behalf of workers, or any class of worker, employed by him, or
(b) negotiate or consult with, or with an official of, one or more trade unions.

(2) A person refuses to deal with a person if—

(a) where he maintains (in whatever form) a list of approved suppliers of goods or services, or of persons from whom tenders for the supply of goods or services may be invited, he fails to include the name of that person in that list; or
(b) in relation to a proposed contract for the supply of goods or services—
    (i) he excludes that person from the group of persons from whom tenders for the supply of the goods or services are invited, or

(ii) he fails to permit that person to submit such a tender, or

(iii) he otherwise determines not to enter into a contract with that person for the supply of the goods or services; or

(c) he terminates a contract with that person for the supply of goods or services.

(3) The obligation to comply with this section is a duty owed to the person with whom there is a refusal to deal and to any other person who may be adversely affected by its contravention; and a breach of the duty is actionable accordingly (subject to the defences and other incidents applying to actions for breach of statutory duty).

CHAPTER II   PROCEDURE FOR HANDLING REDUNDANCIES

Duty of employer to consult representatives

188   Duty of employer to consult representatives

(1) Where an employer is proposing to dismiss as redundant 20 or more employees at one establishment within a period of 90 days or less, the employer shall consult about the dismissals all the persons who are appropriate representatives of any of the employees who may be affected by the proposed dismissals or may be affected by measures taken in connection with those dismissals.

(1A) The consultation shall begin in good time and in any event—

(a) where the employer is proposing to dismiss 100 or more employees as mentioned in subsection (1), at least 90 days, and

(b) otherwise, at least 30 days,

before the first of the dismissals takes effect.

(1B) For the purposes of this section the appropriate representatives of any affected employees are—

(a) if the employees are of a description in respect of which an independent trade union is recognised by their employer, representatives of the trade union, or

(b) in any other case, whichever of the following employee representatives the employer chooses—

(i) employee representatives appointed or elected by the affected employees otherwise than for the purposes of this section, who (having regard to the purposes for and the method by which they were appointed or elected) have authority from those employees to receive information and to be consulted about the proposed dismissals on their behalf;

(ii) employee representatives elected by the affected employees, for the purposes of this section, in an election satisfying the requirements of section 188A(1).

(2) The consultation shall include consultation about ways of—

(a) avoiding the dismissals,

(b) reducing the numbers of employees to be dismissed, and

(c) mitigating the consequences of the dismissals,

and shall be undertaken by the employer with a view to reaching agreement with the appropriate representatives.

(3) In determining how many employees an employer is proposing to dismiss as redundant no account shall be taken of employees in respect of whose proposed dismissals consultation has already begun.

(4) For the purposes of the consultation the employer shall disclose in writing to the appropriate representatives—

(a) the reasons for his proposals,

(b) the numbers and descriptions of employees whom it is proposed to dismiss as redundant,

(c) the total number of employees of any such description employed by the employer at the establishment in question,

(d) the proposed method of selecting the employees who may be dismissed,

(e) the proposed method of carrying out the dismissals, with due regard to any agreed procedure, including the period over which the dismissals are to take effect.

(f) the proposed method of calculating the amount of any redundancy payments to be made (otherwise than in compliance with an obligation imposed by or by virtue of any enactment) to employees who may be dismissed.

(5) That information shall be given to each of the appropriate representatives by being delivered to them or sent by post to an address notified by them to the employer, or (in the case of representatives of a trade union) sent by post to the union at the address of its head or main office.

(5A) The employer shall allow the appropriate representatives access to the affected employees and shall afford to those representatives such accommodation and other facilities as may be appropriate.

(6) [repealed]

(7) If in any case there are special circumstances which render it not reasonably practicable for the employer to comply with a requirement of subsection (1A), (2) or (4), the employer shall take all such steps towards compliance with that requirement as are reasonably practicable in those circumstances. Where the decision leading to the proposed dismissals is that of a person controlling the employer (directly or indirectly), a failure on the part of that person to provide information to the employer shall not constitute special circumstances rendering it not reasonably practicable for the employer to comply with such a requirement.

(7A) Where—

(a) the employer has invited any of the affected employees to elect employee representatives, and

(b) the invitation was issued long enough before the time when the consultation is required by subsection (1A)(a) or (b) to begin to allow them to elect representatives by that time,

the employer shall be treated as complying with the requirements of this section in relation to those employees if he complies with those requirements as soon as is reasonably practicable after the election of the representatives.

(7B) If, after the employer has invited affected employees to elect representatives, the affected employees fail to do so within a reasonable time, he shall give to each affected employee the information set out in subsection (4).

(8) This section does not confer any rights on a trade union, a representative or an employee except as provided by sections 189 to 192 below.

188A Election of employee representatives

(1) The requirements for the election of employee representatives under section 188(1B)(b)(ii) are that—

(a) the employer shall make such arrangements as are reasonably practical to ensure that the election is fair;

(b) the employer shall determine the number of representatives to be elected so that there are sufficient representatives to represent the interests of all the affected employees having regard to the number and classes of those employees;

(c) the employer shall determine whether the affected employees should be represented either by representatives of all the affected employees or by representatives of particular classes of those employees;

(d) before the election the employer shall determine the term of office as employee representatives so that it is of sufficient length to enable information to be given and consultations under section 188 to be completed;

(e) the candidates for election as employee representatives are affected employees on the date of the election;

(f) no affected employee is unreasonably excluded from standing for election;

(g) all affected employees on the date of the election are entitled to vote for employee representatives;

(h) the employees entitled to vote may vote for as many candidates as there are representatives to be elected to represent them or, if there are to be representatives for particular classes of employees, may vote for as many candidates as there are representatives to be elected to represent their particular class of employee;

(i) the election is conducted so as to secure that—

(i)   so far as is reasonably practicable, those voting do so in secret, and

(ii) the votes given at the election are accurately counted.

(2) Where, after an election of employee representatives satisfying the requirements of subsection (1) has been held, one of those elected ceases to act as an employee representative and any of those employees are no longer represented, they shall elect another representative by an election satisfying the requirements of subsection 91)(a), (e), (f) and (i).

189 Complaint and protective award

(1) Where an employer has failed to comply with a requirement of section 188 or section 188A, a complaint may be presented to an employment tribunal on that ground—

(a) in the case of a failure relating to the election of employee representatives, by any of the affected employees or by any of the employees who have been dismissed as redundant;

(b) in the case of any other failure relating to employee representatives, by any of the employee representatives to whom the failure related;

(c) in the case of failure relating to representatives of a trade union, by the trade union; and

(d) in any other case, by any of the affected employees or by any of the employees who have been dismissed as redundant.

(1A) If on a complaint under subsection (1) a question arises as to whether or not any employee representative was an appropriate representative for the purposes of section 188, it shall be for the employer to show that the employee representative had the authority to represent the affected employees.

(1B) On a complaint under subsection (1)(a) it shall be for the employer to show that the requirements in section 188A have been satisfied.

(2) If the tribunal finds the complaint well-founded it shall make a declaration to that effect and may also make a protective award.

(3) A protective award is an award in respect of one or more descriptions of employees—

(a) who has been dismissed as redundant, or whom it is proposed to dismiss as redundant, and

(b) in respect of whose dismissal or proposed dismissal the employer has failed to comply with a requirement of section 188,

ordering the employer to pay remuneration for the protected period.

(4) The protected period—

(a) begins with the date on which the first of the dismissals to which the complaint relates takes effect, or the date of the award, whichever is the earlier, and

(b) is of such length as the tribunal determines to be just and equitable in all the circumstances having regard to the seriousness of the employer's default in complying with any requirement of section 188,

but shall not exceed 90 days.

(5) An employment tribunal shall not consider a complaint under this section unless it is presented to the tribunal—

(a) before the date on which the last of the dismissals to which the complaint relates takes effect, or

(b) during the period of three months beginning with that date, or

(c) where the tribunal is satisfied that it was not reasonably practicable for the complaint to be presented within the period of three months, within such further period as it considers reasonable.

(6) If on a complaint under this section a question arises—

(a) whether there were special circumstances which rendered it not reasonably practicable for the employer to comply with any requirement of section 188, or

(b) whether he took all such steps towards compliance with that requirement as were reasonably practicable in those circumstances,

it is for the employer to show that there were and that he did.

190   Entitlement under protective award

(1) Where an employment tribunal has made a protective award, every employee of a description to which the award relates is entitled, subject to the following provisions and to section 191, to be paid remuneration by his employer for the protected period.

(2) The rate of remuneration payable is a week's pay for each week of the period; and remuneration in respect of a period less than one week shall be calculated by reducing proportionately the amount of a week's pay.

(3) [repealed]

(4) An employee is not entitled to remuneration under a protective award in respect of a period during which he is employed by the employer unless he would be entitled to be paid by the employer in respect of that period—

(a) by virtue of his contract of employment, or

(b) by virtue of sections 87 to 91 of the Employment Rights Act 1996 (rights of employee in period of notice),

if that period fell within the period of notice required to be given by section 86(1) of that Act.

(5) Chapter II of Part XIV of the Employment Rights Act 1996 applies with respect to the calculation of a week's pay for the purposes of this section.

The calculation date for the purposes of that Chapter is the date on which the protective award was made or, in the case of an employee who was dismissed before the date on which the protective award was made, the date which by virtue of section 226(5) is the calculation date for the purpose of computing the amount of a redundancy payment in relation to that dismissal (whether or not the employee concerned is entitled to any such payment).

(6) If an employee of a description to which a protective award relates dies during the protected period, the award has effect in his case as if the protected period ended on his death.

191   Termination of employment during protected period

(1) Where the employee is employed by the employer during the protected period and—

(a) he is fairly dismissed by his employer otherwise than as redundant, or

(b) he unreasonably terminates the contract of employment, then, subject to the following provisions, he is not entitled to remuneration under the protective award in respect of any period during which but for that dismissal or termination he would have been employed.

(2) If an employer makes an employee an offer (whether in writing or not and whether before or after the ending of his employment under the previous contract) to renew his contract of employment, or to re-engage him under a new contract, so that the renewal or re-engagement would take effect before or during the protected period, and either—

(a) the provisions of the contract as renewed, or of the new contract, as to the capacity and place in which he would be employed, and as to the other terms and conditions of his employment, would not differ from the corresponding provisions of the previous contract, or

(b) the offer constitutes an offer of suitable employment in relation to the employee, the following subsections have effect.

(3) If the employee unreasonably refuses the offer, he is not entitled to remuneration under the protective award in respect of a period during which but for that refusal he would have been employed.

(4) If the employee's contract of employment is renewed, or he is re-engaged under a new contract of employment, in pursuance of such an offer as is referred to in subsection (2)(b), there shall be a trial period in relation to the contract as renewed, or the new contract (whether or not there has been a previous trial period under this section).

(5) The trial period begins with the ending of his employment under the previous contract and ends with the expiration of the period of four weeks beginning with the date on which he starts work under the contract as renewed, or the new contract, or such longer period as may be agreed in accordance with subsection (6) for the purpose of retraining the employee for employment under that contract.

(6) Any such agreement—

    (a) shall be made between the employer and the employee or his representative before the employee starts work under the contract as renewed or, as the case may be, the new contract,

    (b) shall be in writing,

    (c) shall specify the date of the end of the trial period, and

    (d) shall specify the terms and conditions of employment which will apply in the employee's case after the end of that period.

(7) If during the trial period—

    (a) the employee, for whatever reason, terminates the contract, or gives notice to terminate it and the contract is thereafter, in consequence, terminated, or

    (b) the employer, for a reason connected with or arising out of the change to the renewed, or new, employment, terminates the contract, or gives notice to terminate it and the contract is thereafter, in consequence, terminated,

the employee remains entitled under the protective award unless, in a case falling within paragraph (a), he acted unreasonably in terminating or giving notice to terminate the contract.

192 Complaint by employee to employment tribunal

(1) An employee may present a complaint to an employment tribunal on the ground that he is an employee of a description to which a protective award relates and that his employer has failed, wholly or in part, to pay him remuneration under the award.

(2) An employment tribunal shall not entertain a complaint under this section unless it is presented to the tribunal—

    (a) before the end of the period of three months beginning with the day (or, if the complaint relates to more than one day, the last of the days) in respect of which the complaint is made of failure to pay remuneration, or

    (b) where the tribunal is satisfied that it was not reasonably practicable for the complaint to be presented within the period of three months, within such further period as it may consider reasonable.

(3) Where the tribunal finds a complaint under this section well-founded it shall order the employer to pay the complainant the amount of remuneration which it finds is due to him.

(4) The remedy of an employee for infringement of his right to remuneration under a protective award is by way of complaint under this section, and not otherwise.

193–194 [omitted]

Supplementary provisions

195 Construction of references to dismissal as redundant etc.

(1) In this Chapter references to dismissal as redundant are references to dismissal for a reason not related to the individual concerned or for a number of reasons all of which are not so related.

(2) For the purposes of any proceedings under this Chapter, where an employee is or is proposed to be dismissed it shall be presumed, unless the contrary is proved, that he is or is proposed to be dismissed as redundant.

196   Construction of references to representatives
(1) For the purposes of this Chapter persons are employee representatives if—
   (a) they have been elected by employees for the specific purpose of being consulted by their employer about dismissals proposed by him, or
   (b) having been elected or appointed by employees (whether before or after dismissals have been proposed by their employer) otherwise than for that specific purpose, it is appropriate (having regard to the purposes for which they were elected) for the employer to consult them about dismissals proposed by him,

and (in either case) they are employed by the employer at the time when they are elected or appointed.

(2) References in this Chapter to representatives of a trade union, in relation to an employer, are to officials or other persons authorised by the trade union to carry on collective bargaining with the employer.

(3) References in this Chapter to affected employees are to employees who may be affected by the proposed dismissals or who may be affected by measures taken in connection with such dismissals.

197–198   [omitted]

CHAPTER III   CODES OF PRACTICE

Codes of Practice issued by ACAS

199   Issue of Codes of Practice by ACAS
(1) ACAS may issue Codes of Practice containing such practical guidance as it thinks fit for the purpose of promoting the improvement of industrial relations or for purposes connected with trade union learning representatives.

(2)–(4) [omitted]

200–202   [omitted]

Codes of Practice issued by the Secretary of State

203   Issue of Codes of Practice by the Secretary of State
(1) The Secretary of State may issue Codes of Practice containing such practical guidance as he thinks fit for the purpose—
   (a) of promoting the improvement of industrial relations, or
   (b) of promoting what appear to him to be desirable practices in relation to the conduct by trade unions of ballots and elections or for purposes connected with trade union learning representatives.

(2) [omitted]

204–206   [omitted]

Supplementary provisions

207   Effect of failure to comply with Code
(1) A failure on the part of any person to observe any provision of a Code of Practice issued under this Chapter shall not of itself render him liable to any proceedings.

(2) In any proceedings before an employment tribunal or the Central Arbitration Committee any Code of Practice issued under this Chapter by ACAS shall be admissible in

evidence, and any provision of the Code which appears to the tribunal or Committee to be relevant to any question arising in the proceedings shall be taken into account in determining that question.

(3) In any proceedings before a court or employment tribunal or the Central Arbitration Committee any Code of Practice issued under this Chapter by the Secretary of State shall be admissible in evidence, and any provision of the Code which appears to the court, tribunal or Committee to be relevant to any question arising in the proceedings shall be taken into account in determining that question.

208 [omitted]

CHAPTER IV GENERAL

Functions of ACAS

209 General duty to promote improvement of industrial relations
It is the general duty of ACAS to promote the improvement of industrial relations.

210 Conciliation
(1) Where a trade dispute exists or is apprehended ACAS may, at the request of one or more parties to the dispute or otherwise, offer the parties to the dispute its assistance with a view to bringing about a settlement.

(2) The assistance may be by way of conciliation or by other means, and may include the appointment of a person other than an officer or servant of ACAS to offer assistance to the parties to the dispute with a view to bringing about a settlement.

(3) In exercising its functions under this section ACAS shall have regard to the desirability of encouraging the parties to a dispute to use any appropriate agreed procedures for negotiation or the settlement of disputes.

211 Conciliation officers
(1) ACAS shall designate some of its officers to perform the functions of conciliation officers under any enactment (whenever passed) relating to matters which are or could be the subject to proceedings before an employment tribunal.

(2) References in any such enactment to a conciliation officer are to an officer designated under this section.

212 Arbitration
(1) Where a trade dispute exists or is apprehended ACAS may, at the request of one or more of the parties to the dispute and with the consent of all the parties to the dispute, refer all or any of the matters to which the dispute relates for settlement to the arbitration of—

(a) one or more persons appointed by ACAS for that purpose (not being officers or employees of ACAS), or
(b) the Central Arbitration Committee.

(2) In exercising its functions under this section ACAS shall consider the likelihood of the dispute being settled by conciliation.

(3) Where there exist appropriate agreed procedures for negotiation or the settlement of disputes, ACAS shall not refer a matter for settlement to arbitration under this section unless—

(a) those procedures have been used and have failed to result in a settlement, or
(b) there is, in ACAS's opinion a special reason which justifies arbitration under this section as an alternative to those procedures.

(4) Where a matter is referred to arbitration under subsection (1)(a)—

(a) if more than one arbitrator or arbiter is appointed, ACAS shall appoint one of them to act as chairman; and

(b) the award may be published if ACAS so decides and all the parties consent.

(5) Part I of the Arbitration Act 1996 (general provisions as to arbitration) does not apply to an arbitration under this section.

212A [omitted]

212B Dismissal procedures agreements

ACAS may, in accordance with any dismissal procedures agreement (within the meaning of the Employment Rights Act 1996), refer any matter to the arbitration of a person appointed by ACAS for the purpose (not being an officer or employee of ACAS).

213 Advice

(1) ACAS may, on request or otherwise, give employers, employers' associations, workers and trade unions such advice as it thinks appropriate on matters concerned with or affecting or likely to affect industrial relations.

(2) ACAS may also publish general advice on matters concerned with or affecting or likely to affect industrial relations.

214 Inquiry

(1) ACAS may, if it thinks fit, inquire into any question relating to industrial relations generally or to industrial relations in any particular industry or in any particular undertaking or part of an undertaking.

(2) The findings of an inquiry under this section, together with any advice given by ACAS in connection with those findings, may be published by ACAS if—

(a) it appears to ACAS that publication is desirable for the improvement of industrial relations, either generally or in relation to the specific question inquired into, and

(b) after sending a draft of the findings to all parties appearing to be concerned and taking account of their views, it thinks fit.

Courts of inquiry

215 Inquiry and report by court of inquiry

(1) Where a trade dispute exists or is apprehended, the Secretary of State may inquire into the causes and circumstances of the dispute, and, if he thinks fit, appoint a court of inquiry and refer to it any matters appearing to him to be connected with or relevant to the dispute.

(2) The court shall inquire into the matters referred to it and report on them to the Secretary of State; and it may make interim reports if it thinks fit.

(3) Any report of the court, and any minority report, shall be laid before both Houses of Parliament as soon as possible.

(4) The Secretary of State may, before or after the report has been laid before Parliament, publish or cause to be published from time to time, in such manner as he thinks fit, any information obtained or conclusions arrived at by the court as the result or in the course of its inquiry.

(5) No report or publication made or authorised by the court or the Secretary of State shall include any information obtained by the court of inquiry in the course of its inquiry—

(a) as to any trade union, or

(b) as to any individual business (whether carried on by a person, firm, or company), which is not available otherwise than through evidence given at the inquiry, except with the consent of the secretary of the trade union or of the person, firm, or company in question.

Nor shall any individual member of the court or any person concerned in the inquiry disclose such information without such consent.

(6) The Secretary of State shall from time to time present to Parliament a report of his proceedings under this section.

216   Constitution and proceedings of court of inquiry

(1) A court of inquiry shall consist of—

    (a) a chairman and such other persons as the Secretary of State thinks fit to appoint, or

    (b) one person appointed by the Secretary of State, as the Secretary of State thinks fit.

(2) A court may act notwithstanding any vacancy in its number.

(3) A court may conduct its inquiry in public or in private, at its discretion.

(4) The Secretary of State may make rules regulating the procedure of a court of inquiry, including rules as to summoning of witnesses, quorum, and the appointment of committees and enabling the court to call for such documents as the court may determine to be relevant to the subject-matter of the inquiry.

(5) A court of inquiry may, if and to such extent as may be authorised by rules under this section, by order require any person who appears to the court to have knowledge of the subject-matter of the inquiry—

    (a) to supply (in writing or otherwise) such particulars in relation thereto as the court may require, and

    (b) where necessary, to attend before the court and give evidence on oath;

and the court may administer or authorise any person to administer an oath for that purpose.

(6) Provision shall be made by rules under this section with respect to the cases in which persons may appear by counsel or solicitor in proceedings before a court of inquiry, and except as provided by those rules no person shall be entitled to appear in any such proceedings by counsel or solicitor.

Supplementary provisions

217   [omitted]

218   Meaning of 'trade dispute' in Part IV

(1) In this Part 'trade dispute' means a dispute between employers and workers, or between workers and workers, which is connected with one or more of the following matters—

    (a) terms and conditions of employment, or the physical conditions in which any workers are required to work;

    (b) engagement or non-engagement, or termination or suspension of employment or the duties of employment, of one or more workers;

    (c) allocation of work or the duties of employment as between workers or groups of workers;

    (d) matters of discipline;

    (e) the membership or non-membership of a trade union on the part of a worker;

    (f) facilities for officials of trade unions; and

    (g) machinery for negotiation or consultation, and other procedures, relating to any of the foregoing matters, including the recognition by employers or employers' associations of the right of a trade union to represent workers in any such negotiation or consultation or in the carrying out of such procedures.

(2) A dispute between a Minister of the Crown and any workers shall, notwithstanding that he is not the employer of those workers, be treated for the purposes of this Part as a dispute between an employer and those workers if the dispute relates—

    (a) to matters which have been referred for consideration by a joint body on which, by virtue of any provision made by or under any enactment, that minister is represented, or

    (b) to matters which cannot be settled without that Minister exercising a power conferred on him by or under an enactment.

(3) There is a trade dispute for the purpose of this Part even though it relates to matters occurring outside Great Britain.

(4) A dispute to which a trade union or employer's association is a party shall be treated for the purposes of this Part as a dispute to which workers or, as the case may be, employers are parties.

(5) In this section—

'employment' includes any relationship whereby one person personally does work or performs services for another; and

'worker', in relation to a dispute to which an employer is a party, includes any worker even if not employed by that employer.

PART V   INDUSTRIAL ACTION

Protection of acts in contemplation or furtherance of trade dispute

219   Protection from certain tort liabilities

(1) An act done by a person in contemplation or furtherance of a trade dispute is not actionable in tort on the ground only—

  (a) that it induces another person to break a contract or interferes or induces another person to interfere with its performance, or

  (b) that it consists in his threatening that a contract (whether one to which he is a party or not) will be broken or its performance interefered with, or that he will induce another person to break a contract or interfere with its performance.

(2) An agreement or combination by two or more persons to do or procure the doing of an act in contemplation or furtherance of a trade dispute is not actionable in tort if the act is one which if done without any such agreement or combination would not be actionable in tort.

(3) Nothing in subsections (1) and (2) prevents an act done in the course of picketing from being actionable in tort unless it is done in the course of attendance declared lawful by section 220 (peaceful picketing).

(4) Subsections (1) and (2) have effect subject to sections 222 to 225 (action excluded from protection) and to sections 226 (requirement of ballot before action by trade union) and 234A (requirement of notice to employer of industrial action); and in those sections 'not protected' means excluded from the protection afforded by this section or, where the expression is used with reference to a particular person, excluded from that protection as respects that person.

220   Peaceful picketing

(1) It is lawful for a person in contemplation or furtherance of a trade dispute to attend—

  (a) at or near his own place of work, or

  (b) if he is an official of a trade union, at or near the place of work of a member of the union whom he is accompanying and whom he represents,

for the purpose only of peacefully obtaining or communicating information, or peacefully persuading any person to work or abstain from working.

(2) If a person works or normally works—

  (a) otherwise than at any one place, or

  (b) at a place the location of which is such that attendance there for a purpose mentioned in subsection (1) is impracticable,

his place of work for the purposes of that subsection shall be any premises of his employer from which he works or from which his work is administered.

(3) In the case of a worker not in employment where—

  (a) his last employment was terminated in connection with a trade dispute, or

  (b) the termination of his employment was one of the circumstances giving rise to a trade dispute,

in relation to that dispute his former place of work shall be treated for the purposes of subsection (1) as being his place of work.

(4) A person who is an official of a trade union by virtue only of having been elected or appointed to be a representative of some of the members of the union shall be regarded for the purposes of subsection (1) as representing only those members; but otherwise an official of a union shall be regarded for those purposes as representing all its members.

221 Restrictions on grant of injunctions and interdicts

(1) Where—
    (a) an application for an injunction or interdict is made to a court in the absence of the party against whom it is sought or any representative of his, and
    (b) he claims, or in the opinion of the court would be likely to claim, that he acted in contemplation or furtherance of a trade dispute,

the court shall not grant the injunction or interdict unless satisfied that all steps which in the circumstances were reasonable have been taken with a view to securing that notice of the application and an opportunity of being heard with respect to the application have been given to him.

(2) Where—
    (a) an application for an interlocutory injunction is made to a court pending the trial of an action, and
    (b) the party against whom it is sought claims that he acted in contemplation or furtherance of a trade dispute,

the court shall, in exercising its discretion whether or not to grant the injunction, have regard to the likelihood of that party's succeeding at the trial of the action in establishing any matter which would afford a defence to the action under section 219 (protection from certain tort liabilities) or section 220 (peaceful picketing).

This subsection does not extend to Scotland.

Action excluded from protection

222 Action to enforce trade union membership

(1) An act is not protected if the reason, or one of the reasons, for which it is done is the fact or belief that a particular employer—
    (a) is employing, has employed or might employ a person who is not a member of a trade union, or
    (b) is failing, has failed or might fail to discriminate against such a person.

(2) For the purposes of subsection (1)(b) an employer discriminates against a person if, but only if, he ensures that his conduct in relation to—
    (a) persons, or persons of any description, employed by him, or who apply to be, or are, considered by him for employment, or
    (b) the provision of employment for such persons, is different, in some or all cases, according to whether or not they are members of a trade union, and is more favourable to those who are.

(3) An act is not protected if it constitutes, or is one of a number of acts which together constitute, an inducement or attempted inducement of a person—
    (a) to incorporate in a contract to which that person is a party, or a proposed contract to which he intends to be a party, a term or condition which is or would be void by virtue of section 144 (union membership requirement in contract for goods or services), or
    (b) to contravene section 145 (refusal to deal with person on grounds relating to union membership).

(4) References in this section to an employer employing a person are to a person acting in the capacity of the person for whom a worker works or normally works.

(5) References in this section to not being a member of a trade union are to not being a member of any trade union, of a particular trade union or of one of a number of particular trade unions.

Any such reference includes a reference to not being a member of a particular branch or section of a trade union or of one of a number of particular branches or sections of a trade union.

223   Action taken because of dismissal for taking unofficial action

An act is not protected if the reason, or one of the reasons, for doing it is the fact or belief that an employer has dismissed one or more employees in circumstances such that by virtue of section 237 (dismissal in connection with unofficial action) they have no right to complain of unfair dismissal.

224   Secondary action

(1) An act is not protected if one of the facts relied on for the purpose of establishing liability is that there has been secondary action which is not lawful picketing.

(2) There is secondary action in relation to a trade dispute when, and only when, a person—

    (a) induces another to break a contract of employment or interferes or induces another to interfere with its performance, or

    (b) threatens that a contract of employment under which he or another is employed will be broken or its performance interfered with, or that he will induce another to break a contract of employment or to interfere with its performance,

and the employer under the contract of employment is not the employer party to the dispute.

(3) Lawful picketing means acts done in the course of such attendance as is declared lawful by section 220 (peaceful picketing)—

    (a) by a worker employed (or, in the case of a worker not in employment, last employed) by the employer party to the dispute, or

    (b) by a trade union official whose attendance is lawful by virtue of subsection (1)(b) of that section.

(4) For the purposes of this section an employer shall not be treated as party to a dispute between another employer and workers of that employer; and where more than one employer is in dispute with his workers, the dispute between each employer and his workers shall be treated as a separate dispute.

In this subsection 'worker' has the same meaning as in section 244 (meaning of 'trade dispute').

(5) An act in contemplation or furtherance of a trade dispute which is primary action in relation to that dispute may not be relied on as secondary action in relation to another trade dispute.

Primary action means such action as is mentioned in paragraph (a) or (b) of subsection (2) where the employer under the contract of employment is the employer party to the dispute.

(6) In this section 'contract of employment' includes any contract under which one person personally does work or performs services for another, and related expressions shall be construed accordingly.

225   Pressure to impose union recognition requirement

(1) An act is not protected if it constitutes, or is one of a number of acts which together constitute, an inducement or attempted inducement of a person—

    (a) to incorporate in a contract to which that person is a party, or a proposed contract to which he intends to be a party, a term or condition which is or would be void by virtue of section 186 (recognition requirement in contract for goods or services), or

    (b) to contravene section 187 (refusal to deal with person on grounds of union exclusion).

(2) An act is not protected if—

    (a) it interferes with the supply (whether or not under a contract) of goods or services, or can reasonably be expected to have that effect, and

    (b) one of the facts relied upon for the purpose of establishing liability is that a person has—

        (i) induced another to brea a contract of employment or interfered or induced another to interfere with its performance, or

        (ii) threatened that a contract of employment under which he or another is employed will be broken or its performance interfered with, or that he will induce another to break a contract of employment or to interfere with its performance, and

    (c) the reason, or one of the reasons, for doing the act is the fact or belief that the supplier (not being the employer under the contract of employment mentioned in paragraph (b)) does not, or might not—

        (i) recognise one or more trade unions for the purpose of negotiating on behalf of workers, or any class of worker, employed by him, or

        (ii) negotiate or consult with, or with an official of, one or more trade unions.

Requirement of ballot before action by trade union

226 Requirement of ballot before action by trade union

(1) An act done by a trade union to induce a person to take part, or continue to take part, in industrial action

    (a) is not protected unless the industrial action has the support of a ballot, and

    (b) where section 226A falls to be complied with in relation to the person's employer, is not protected as respects the employer unless the trade union has complied with section 226A in relation to him.

In this section 'the relevant time', in relation to an act by a trade union to induce a person to take part, or continue to take part, in industrial action, means the time at which proceedings are commenced in respect of the act.

(2) Industrial action shall be regarded as having the support of a ballot only if—

    (a) the union has held a ballot in respect of the action—

        (i) in relation to which the requirements of section 226B so far as applicable before and during the holding of the ballot were satisfied,

        (ii) in relation to which the requirements of sections 227 to 231 were satisfied, and

        (iii) in which the majority voting in the ballot answered 'Yes' to the question applicable in accordance with section 229(2) to industrial action of the kind to which the act of inducement relates;

    (b) such of the requirements of the following sections as have fallen to be satisfied at the relevant time have been satisfied, namely—

        (i) section 226B so far as applicable after the holding of the ballot, and

        (ii) section 231B;

    (bb) section 232A does not prevent the industrial action from being regarded as having the support of the ballot; and

    (c) the requirements of section 233 (calling of industrial action with support of ballot) are satisfied.

Any reference in this subsection to a requirement of a provision which is disapplied or modified by section 232 has effect subject to that section.

(3) Where separate workplace ballots are held by virtue of section 228(1)—

    (a) industrial action shall be regarded as having the support of a ballot if the conditions specified in subsection (2) are satisfied, and

    (b) the trade union shall be taken to have complied with the requirements relating to a ballot imposed by section 226A if those requirements are complied with,

in relation to the ballot for the place of work of the person induced to take part, or continue to take part, in the industrial action.

(3A) If the requirements of section 231A fall to be satisfied in relation to an employer, as respects that employer industrial action shall not be regarded as having the support of a ballot unless those requirements are satisfied in relation to that employer.

(4) For the purposes of this section an inducement, in relation to a person, includes an inducement which is or would be ineffective, whether because of his unwillingness to be influenced by it or for any other reason.

226A   Notice of ballot and sample voting paper for employers

(1) The trade union must take such steps as are reasonably necessary to ensure that—

    (a) not later than the seventh day before the opening day of the ballot, the notice specified in subsection (2), and

    (b) not later than the third day before the opening day of the ballot, the sample voting paper specified in subsection (2F),

is received by every person who it is reasonable for the union to believe (at the latest time when steps could be taken to comply with paragraph (a)) will be the employer of persons who will be entitled to vote in the ballot.

(2) The notice referred to in paragraph (a) of subsection (1) is a notice in writing—

    (a) stating that the union intends to hold the ballot,

    (b) specifying the date which the union reasonably believes will be the opening day of the ballot, and

    (c) containing—

        (i) the lists mentioned in subsection (2A) and the figures mentioned in subsection (2B), together with an explanation of how those figures were arrived at, or

        (ii) where some or all of the employees concerned are employees from whose wages the employer makes deductions representing payments to the union, either those lists and figures and that explanation or the information mentioned in subsection (2C).

(2A) The lists are—

    (a) a list of the categories of employee to which the employees concerned belong, and

    (b) a list of the workplaces at which the employees concerned work.

(2B) The figures are—

    (a) the total number of employees concerned,

    (b) the number of the employees concerned in each of the categories in the list mentioned in subsection (2A)(a), and

    (c) the number of the employees concerned who work at each workplace in the list mentioned in subsection (2A)(b).

(2C) The information referred to in subsection (2)(c)(ii) is such information as will enable the employer readily to deduce—

    (a) the total number of employees concerned,

    (b) the categories of employee to which the employees concerned belong and the number of the employees concerned in each of those categories, and

    (c) the workplaces at which the employees concerned work and the number of them who work at each of those workplaces.

(2D) The lists and figures supplied under this section, or the information mentioned in subsection (2C) that is so supplied, must be as accurate as is reasonably practicable in the light of the information in the possession of the union at the time when it complies with subsection (1)(a).

(2E) For the purposes of subsection (2D) information is in the possession of the union if it is held, for union purposes—

    (a) in a document, whether in electronic form or any other form, and

    (b) in the possession or under the control of an officer or employee of the union.

(2F) The sample voting paper referred to in paragraph (b) of subsection (1) is—

    (a) a sample of the form of voting paper which is to be sent to the employees concerned, or

    (b) where the employees concerned are not all to be sent the same form of voting paper, a sample of each form of voting paper which is to be sent to any of them.

(2G) Nothing in this section requires a union to supply an employer with the names of the employees concerned.

(2H) In this section references to the 'employees concerned' are references to those employees of the employer in question who the union reasonably believes will be entitled to vote in the ballot.

(2I) For the purposes of this section, the workplace at which an employee works is—

    (a) in relation to an employee who works at or from a single set of premises, those premises, and

    (b) in relation to any other employee, the premises with which his employment has the closest connection.

(3)–(3B) [repealed]

(4) In this section references to the opening day of the ballot are references to the first day when a voting paper is sent to any person entitled to vote in the ballot.

(5) This section in its application to a ballot in which merchant seamen to whom section 230(2A) applies are entitled to vote, shall have effect with the substitution in subsection (2F), for references to the voting paper which is to be sent to the employees, of references to the voting paper which is to be sent or otherwise provided to them.

226B–226C [omitted]

227 Entitlement to vote in ballot

(1) Entitlement to vote in the ballot must be accorded equally to all the members of the trade union who it is reasonable at the time of the ballot for the union to believe will be induced by the union to take part or, as the case may be, to continue to take part in the industrial action in question, and to no others.

(2) [repealed]

228 Separate workplace ballots

(1) Subject to subsection (2), this section applies if the members entitled to vote in a ballot by virtue of section 227 do not all have the same workplace.

(2) This section does not apply if the union reasonably believes that all those members have the same workplace.

(3) Subject to section 228A, a separate ballot shall be held for each workplace; and entitlement to vote in each ballot shall be accorded equally to, and restricted to, members of the union who—

    (a) are entitled to vote by virtue of section 227, and

    (b) have that workplace.

(4) In this section and section 228A 'workplace' in relation to a person who is employed means—

    (a) if the person works at or from a single set of premises, those premises, and

    (b) in any other case, the premises with which the person's employment has the closest connection.

228A Separate workplaces: single and aggregate ballots

(1) Where section 228(3) would require separate ballots to be held for each workplace, a ballot may be held in place of some or all of the separate ballots if one of subsections (2) to (4) is satisfied in relation to it.

(2) This subsection is satisfied in relation to a ballot if the workplace of each member entitled to vote in the ballot is the workplace of at least one member of the union who is affected by the dispute.

(3) This subsection is satisfied in relation to a ballot if entitlement to vote is accorded to, and limited to, all the members of the union who—

    (a) according to the union's reasonable belief have an occupation of a particular kind or have any of a number of particular kinds of occupation, and

    (b) are employed by a particular employer, or by any of a number of particular employers, with whom the union is in dispute.

(4) This subsection is satisfied in relation to a ballot if entitlement to vote is accorded to, and limited to, all the members of the union who are employed by a particular employer, or by any of a number of particular employers, with whom the union is in dispute.

(5) For the purposes of subsection (2) the following are members of the union affected by a dispute—

    (a) if the dispute relates (wholly or partly) to a decision which the union reasonably believes the employer has made or will make concerning a matter specified in subsection (1)(a), (b) or (c) of section 244 (meaning of 'trade dispute'), members whom the decision directly affects,

    (b) if the dispute relates (wholly or partly) to a matter specified in subsection (1)(d) of that section, members whom the matter directly affects,

    (c) if the dispute relates (wholly or partly) to a matter specified in subsection (2)(e) of that section, persons whose membership or non-membership is in dispute,

    (d) if the dispute relates (wholly or partly) to a matter specified in subsection (1)(f) of that section, officials of the union who have used or would use the facilities concerned in the dispute.

229 Voting paper

(1) The method of voting in a ballot must be by the marking of a voting paper by the person voting.

(1A) Each voting paper must—

    (a) state the name of the independent scrutineer,

    (b) clearly specify the address to which, and the date by which, it is to be returned,

    (c) be given one of a series of consecutive whole numbers every one of which is used in giving a different number in that series to each voting paper printed or otherwise produced for the purposes of the ballot, and

    (d) be marked with its number.

This subsection, in its application to a ballot in which merchant seamen to whom section 230(2A) applies are entitled to vote, shall have effect with the substitution, for the reference to the address to which the voting paper is to be returned, of a reference to the ship to which the seamen belong.

(2) The voting paper must contain at least one of the following questions—

    (a) a question (however framed) which requires the person answering it to say, by answering 'Yes' or 'No', whether he is prepared to take part or, as the case may be, to continue to take part in a strike;

    (b) a question (however framed) which requires the person answering it to say, by answering 'Yes' or 'No', whether he is prepared to take part or, as the case may be, to continue to take part in industrial action short of a strike.

(2A) For the purposes of subsection (2) an overtime ban and a call-out ban constitute industrial action short of a strike.

(3) The voting paper must specify who, in the event of a vote in favour of industrial action, is authorised for the purposes of section 233 to call upon members to take part or continue to take part in the industrial action.

The person or description of persons so specified need not be authorised under the rules of the union but must be within section 20(2) (persons for whose acts the union is taken to be responsible).

(4) The following statement must (without being qualified or commented upon by anything else on the voting paper) appear on every voting paper—

'If you take part in a strike or other industrial action, you may be in breach of your contract of employment. However, if you are dismissed for taking part in strike or other industrial action which is called officially and is otherwise lawful, the dismissal will be unfair if it takes place fewer than twelve weeks after you started taking part in the action, and depending on the circumstances may be unfair if it takes place later.'

230   Conduct of ballot

(1) Every person who is entitled to vote in the ballot must—
   (a) be allowed to vote without interference from, or constraint imposed by, the union or any of its members, officials or employees, and
   (b) so far as is reasonably practicable, be enabled to do so without incurring any direct cost to himself.

(2) Except as regards persons falling within subsection (2A), so far as is reasonably practicable, every person who is entitled to vote in the ballot must—
   (a) have a young paper sent to him by post at his home address or any other address which he has requested the trade union in writing to treat as his postal address, and
   (b) be given a convenient opportunity to vote by post.

(2A) Subsection (2B) applies to a merchant seaman if the trade union reasonably believes that—
   (a) he will be employed in a ship either at sea or at a place outside Great Britain at some time in the period during which votes may be cast, and
   (b) it will be convenient for him to receive a voting paper and to vote while on the ship or while at a place where the ship is rather than in accordance with subsection (2).

(2B) Where this subsection applies to a merchant seaman he shall, if it is reasonably practicable—
   (a) have a voting paper made available to him while on the ship or while at a place where the ship is, and
   (b) be given an opportunity to vote while on the ship or while at a place where the ship is.

(2C) In subsections (2A) and (2B) 'merchant seaman' means a person whose employment, or the greater part of it, is carried out on board sea-going ships.

(3) [repealed]

(4) A ballot shall be conducted so as to secure that—
   (a) so far as is reasonably practicable, those voting do so in secret, and
   (b) the votes given in the ballot are fairly and accurately counted.

For the purposes of paragraph (b) an inaccuracy in counting shall be disregarded if it is accidental and on a scale which could not affect the result of the ballot.

231   Information as to result of ballot

As soon as is reasonably practicable after the holding of the ballot, the trade union shall take such steps as are reasonably necessary to ensure that all persons entitled to vote in the ballot are informed of the number of—
   (a) votes cast in the ballot,
   (b) individuals answering 'Yes' to the question, or as the case may be, to each question,
   (c) individuals answering 'No' to the question, or, as the case may be, to each question, and
   (d) spoiled voting papers.

231A   Employers to be informed of ballot result

(1) As soon as reasonably practicable after the holding of the ballot, the trade union shall take such steps as are reasonably necessary to ensure that every relevant employer is informed of the matters mentioned in section 231.

(2) In subsection (1) 'relevant employer' means a person who it is reasonable for the trade union to believe (at the time when the steps are taken) was at the time of the ballot the employer of any persons entitled to vote.

231B–232   [omitted]

232A   Inducement of member denied entitlement to vote
Industrial action shall not be regarded as having the support of a ballot if the following conditions apply in the case of any person—
    (a) he was a member of the trade union at the time when the ballot was held,
    (b) it was reasonable at that time for the trade union to believe he would be induced to take part or, as the case may be, to continue to take part in the industrial action,
    (c) he was not accorded entitlement to vote in the ballot, and
    (d) he was induced by the trade union to take part or, as the case may be, to continue to take part in the industrial action.

232B   Small accidental failures to be disregarded
    (1) If—
    (a) in relation to a ballot there is a failure (or there are failures) to comply with a provision mentioned in subsection (2) or with more than one of those provisions, and
    (b) the failure is accidental and on a scale which is unlikely to affect the result of the ballot or, as the case may be, the failures are accidental and taken together are on a scale which is unlikely to affect the result of the ballot,
the failure (or failures) shall be disregarded for all purposes (including, in particular, those of section 232A(c)).
    (2) The provisions are section 227(1), section 230(2) and section 230(2B).

233   Calling of industrial action with support of ballot
    (1) Industrial action shall not be regarded as having the support of a ballot unless it is called by a specified person and the conditions specified below are satisfied.
    (2) A 'specified person' means a person specified or of a description specified in the voting paper for the ballot in accordance with section 229(3).
    (3) The conditions are that—
    (a) there must have been no call by the trade union to take part or continue to take part in industrial action to which the ballot relates, or any authorisation or endorsement by the union of any such industrial action, before the date of the ballot;
    (b) there must be a call for industrial action by a specified person, and industrial action to which it relates must begin, before the ballot ceases to be effective in accordance with section 234.
    (4) For the purposes of this section a call shall be taken to have been made by a trade union if it was authorised or endorsed by the union; and the provisions of section 20(2) to (4) apply for the purpose of determining whether a call, or industrial action, is to be taken to have been so authorised or endorsed.

234   Period after which ballot ceases to be effective
    (1) Subject to the following provisions, a ballot ceases to be effective for the purposes of section 233(3)(b) in relation to industrial action by members of a trade union at the end of the period, beginning with the date of the ballot—
    (a) of four weeks, or
    (b) of such longer duration not exceeding eight weeks as is agreed between the union and the Members' employer.
    (2) Where for the whole or part of that period the calling or organising of industrial action is prohibited—

(a) by virtue of a court order which subsequently lapses or is discharged, recalled or set aside, or

(b) by virtue of an undertaking given to a court by any person from which he is subsequently released or by which he ceases to be bound,

the trade union may apply to the court for an order that the period during which the prohibition had effect shall not count towards the period referred to in subsection (1).

(3) The application must be made forthwith upon the prohibition ceasing to have effect—

(a) to the court by virtue of whose decision it ceases to have effect, or

(b) where an order lapses or an undertaking ceases to bind without any such decision, to the court by which the order was made or to which the undertaking was given;

and no application may be made after the end of the period of eight weeks beginning with the date of the ballot.

(4) The court shall not make an order if it appears to the court—

(a) that the result of the ballot no longer represents the views of the union members concerned, or

(b) that an event is likely to occur as a result of which those members would vote against industrial action if another ballot were to be held.

(5) No appeal lies from the decision of the court to make or refuse an order under this section.

(6) The period between the making of an application under this section and its determination does not count towards the period referred to in subsection (1).

But a ballot shall not by virtue of this subsection (together with any order of the court) be regarded as effective for the purposes of section 233(3)(b) after the end of the period of twelve weeks beginning with the date of the ballot.

Requirement on trade union to give notice of industrial action

234A   Notice to employers of industrial action

(1) An act done by a trade union to induce a person to take part, or continue to take part, in industrial action is not protected as respects his employer unless the union has taken or takes such steps as are reasonably necessary to ensure that the employer receives within the appropriate period a relevant notice covering the act.

(2) Subsection (1) imposes a requirement in the case of an employer only if it is reasonable for the union to believe, at the latest time when steps could be taken to ensure that he receives such a notice, that he is the employer of persons who will be or have been induced to take part, or continue to take part, in the industrial action.

(3) For the purposes of this section a relevant notice is a notice in writing which—

(a) contains—

(i) the lists mentioned in subsection (3A) and the figures mentioned in subsection (3B), together with an explanation of how those figures were arrived at, or

(ii) where some or all of the affected employees are employees from whose wages the employer makes deductions representing payments to the union, either those lists and figures and that explanation or the information mentioned in subsection (3C), and

(b) states whether industrial action is intended to be continuous or discontinuous and specifies—

(i) where it is to be continuous, the intended date for any of the affected employees to begin to take part in the action,

(ii) where it is to be discontinuous, the intended dates for any of the affected employees to take part in the action.

(3A) The lists referred to in subsection (3)(a) are—
   (a) a list of the categories of employee to which the affected employees belong, and
   (b) a list of the workplaces at which the affected employees work.

(3B) The figures referred to in subsection (3)(a) are—
   (a) the total number of the affected employees,
   (b) the number of the affected employees in each of the categories in the list mentioned in subsection (3A)(a), and
   (c) the number of the affected employees who work at each workplace in the list mentioned in subsection (3A)(b).

(3C) The information referred to in subsection (3)(a)(ii) is such information as will enable the employer readily to deduce—
   (a) the total number of the affected employees,
   (b) the categories of employee to which the affected employees belong and the number of the affected employees in each of those categories, and
   (c) the workplaces at which the affected employees work and the number of them who work at each of those workplaces.

(3D) The lists and figures supplied under this section, or the information mentioned in subsection (3C) that is so supplied, must be as accurate as is reasonably practicable in the light of the information in the possession of the union at the time when it complies with subsection (1).

(3E) For the purposes of subsection (3D) information is in the possession of the union if it is held, for union purposes—
   (a) in a document, whether in electronic form or any other form, and
   (b) in the possession or under the control of an officer or employee of the union.

(3F) Nothing in this section requires a union to supply an employer with the names of the affected employees.

(4) For the purposes of subsection (1) the appropriate period is the period—
   (a) beginning with the day when the union satisfies the requirement of section 231A in relation to the ballot in respect of the industrial action, and
   (b) ending with the seventh day before the day, or before the first of the days, specified in the relevant notice.

(5) For the purposes of subsection (1) a relevant notice covers an act done by the union if the person induced falls within a notified category of employee and the workplace at which he works is a notified workplace and—
   (a) where he is induced to take part or continue to take part in industrial action which the union intends to be continuous, if—
       (i) the notice states that the union intends the industrial action to be continuous, and
       (ii) there is no participation by him in the industrial action before the date specified in the notice in consequence of any inducement by the union not covered by a relevant notice; and
   (b) where he is induced to take part or continue to take part in industrial action which the union intends to be discontinuous, if there is no participation by him in the industrial action on a day not so specified in consequence of any inducement by the union not covered by a relevant notice.

(5A) [repealed]

(5B) In subsection (5)—
   (a) a 'notified category of employee' means—
       (i) a category of employee that is listed in the notice, or
       (ii) where the notice contains the information mentioned in subsection (3C), a category of employee that the employer (at the time he receives the notice) can readily deduce from the notice is a category of employee to which some or all of the affected employees belong, and

    (b) a 'notified workplace' means—
        (i) a workplace that is listed in the notice, or
        (ii) where the notice contains the information mentioned in subsection (3C), a workplace that the employer (at the time he receives the notice) can readily deduce from the notice is the workplace at which some or all of the affected employees work.

    (5C) In this section references to the 'affected employees' are references to those employees of the employer who the union reasonably believes will be induced by the union, or have been so induced, to take part or continue to take part in the industrial action.

    (5D) For the purposes of this section, the workplace at which an employee works is—
        (a) in relation to an employee who works at or from a single set of premises, those premises, and
        (b) in relation to any other employee, the premises with which his employment has the closest connection.

    (6) For the purposes of this section—
        (a) a union intends industrial action to be discontinuous if it intends it to take place only on some days on which there is an opportunity to take the action, and
        (b) a union intends industrial action to be continuous if it intends it to be not so restricted.

    (7) Subject to subsections (7A) and (7B) where—
        (a) continuous industrial action which has been authorised or endorsed by a union ceases to be so authorised or endorsed, and
        (b) the industrial action has at a later date again been authorised or endorsed by the union (whether as continuous or discontinuous action),
no relevant notice covering acts done to induce persons to take part in the earlier action shall operate to cover acts done to induce persons to take part in the action authorised or endorsed at the later date and this section shall apply in relation to an act to induce a person to take part, or continue to take part, in the industrial action after that date as if the references in subsection (3)(b)(i) to the industrial action were to the industrial action taking place after that date.

    (7A) Subsection (7) shall not apply where industrial action ceases to be authorised or endorsed in order to enable the union to comply with a court order or an undertaking given to a court.

    (7B) Subsection (7) shall not apply where—
        (a) a union agrees with an employer, before industrial action ceases to be authorised or endorsed, that it will cease to be authorised or endorsed with effect from a date specified in the agreement ('the suspension date') and that it may again be authorised or endorsed with effect from a date not earlier than a date specified in the agreement ('the resumption date'),
        (b) the action ceases to be authorised or endorsed with effect from the suspension date, and
        (c) the action is again authorised or endorsed with effect from a date which is not earlier than the resumption date or such later date as may be agreed between the union and the employer.

    (8) The requirement imposed on a trade union by subsection (1) shall be treated as having been complied with if the steps were taken by other relevant persons or committees whose acts were authorised or endorsed by the union and references to the belief or intention of the union in subsection (2) or as the case may be, subsections (3), (5), (5C) and (6) shall be construed as references to the belief or the intention of the person or committee taking the steps.

    (9) The provisions of section 20(2) to (4) apply for the purpose of determining for the purposes of subsection (1) who are relevant persons or committees and whether the trade union is to be taken to have authorised or endorsed the steps the person or committee took and for the purposes of subsection (7) whether the trade union is to be taken to have authorised or endorsed the industrial action.

235 Construction of references to contract of employment

In sections 226 to 234A (requirement of ballot before action by trade union) references to a contract of employment include any contract under which one person personally does work or performs services for another; and 'employer' and other related expressions shall be construed accordingly.

Industrial action affecting supply of goods or services to an individual

235A Industrial action affecting supply of goods or services to an individual

(1) Where an individual claims that—

    (a) any trade union or other person has done, or is likely to do, an unlawful act to induce any person to take part, or to continue to take part, in industrial action, and

    (b) an effect, or a likely effect, of the industrial action is or will be to—

        (i) prevent or delay the supply of goods or services, or

        (ii) reduce the quality of goods or services supplied, to the individual making the claim,

he may apply to the High Court or the Court of Session for an order under this section.

(2) For the purposes of this section an act to induce any person to take part, or to continue to take part, in industrial action is unlawful—

    (a) if it is actionable in tort by any one or more persons, or

    (b) (where it is or would be the act of a trade union) if it could form the basis of an application by a member under section 62.

(3) In determining whether an individual may make an application under this section it is immaterial whether or not the individual is entitled to be supplied with the goods or services in question.

(4) Where on an application under this section the court is satisfied that the claim is well-founded, it shall make such order as it considers appropriate for requiring the person by whom the act of inducement has been, or is likely to be, done to take steps for ensuring—

    (a) that no, or no further, act is done by him to induce any persons to take part or to continue to take part in the industrial action, and

    (b) that no person engages in conduct after the making of the order by virtue of having been induced by him before the making of the order to take part or continue to take part in the industrial action.

(5) Without prejudice to any other power of the court, the court may on an application under this section grant such interlocutory relief (in Scotland, such interim order) as it considers appropriate.

(6) For the purposes of this section an act of inducement shall be taken to be done by a trade union if it is authorised or endorsed by the union; and the provisions of section 20(2) to (4) apply for the purposes of determining whether such an act is to be taken to be so authorised or endorsed.

Those provisions also apply in relation to proceedings for failure to comply with an order under this section as they apply in relation to the original proceedings.

235B–235C [repealed]

No compulsion to work

236 No compulsion to work

No court shall, whether by way of—

    (a) an order for specific performance or specific implement of a contract of employment, or

    (b) an injunction or interdict restraining a breach or threatened breach of such a contract,

compel an employee to do any work or attend at any place for the doing of any work.

Loss of unfair dismissal protection

237   Dismissal of those taking part in unofficial industrial action

(1) An employee has no right to complain of unfair dismissal if at the time of dismissal he was taking part in an unofficial strike or other unofficial industrial action.

(1A) Subsection (1) does not apply to the dismissal of the employee if it is shown that the reason (or, if more than one, the principal reason) for the dismissal or, in a redundancy case, for selecting the employee for dismissal was one of those specified in or—

    (a) section 98B, 99, 100, 101A(d), 103, 103A or 104C of the Employment Rights Act 1996 (dismissal in jury service, family, health and safety, working time, employee representative, protected disclosure and flexible working cases),

    (b) section 104 of that Act in its application in relation to time off under section 57A of that Act (dependants).

In this subsection 'redundancy case' has the meaning given in section 105(9) of that Act, and a reference to a specified reason for dismissal includes a reference to specified circumstances of dismissal.

(2) A strike or other industrial action is unofficial in relation to an employee unless—

    (a) he is a member of a trade union and the action is authorised or endorsed by that union, or

    (b) he is not a member of a trade union but there are among those taking part in the industrial action members of a trade union by which the action has been authorised or endorsed.

Provided that, a strike or other industrial action shall not be regarded as unofficial if none of those taking part in it are members of a trade union.

(3) The provisions of section 20(2) apply for the purpose of determining whether industrial action is to be taken to have been authorised or endorsed by a trade union.

(4) The question whether industrial action is to be so taken in any case shall be determined by reference to the facts as at the time of dismissal.

Provided that, where an act is repudiated as mentioned in section 21, industrial action shall not thereby be treated as unofficial before the end of the next working day after the day on which the repudiation takes place.

(5) In this section the 'time of dismissal' means—

    (a) where the employee's contract of employment is terminated by notice, when the notice is given,

    (b) where the employee's contract of employment is terminated without notice, when the termination takes effect, and

    (c) where the employee is employed under a contract for a fixed term which expires without being renewed under the same contract, when that term expires;

and a 'working day' means any day which is not a Saturday or Sunday, Christmas Day, Good Friday or a bank holiday under the Banking and Financial Dealings Act 1971.

(6) For the purposes of this section membership of a trade union for purposes unconnected with the employment in question shall be disregarded; but an employee who was a member of a trade union when he began to take part in industrial action shall continue to be treated as a member for the purpose of determining whether that action is unofficial in relation to him or another notwithstanding that he may in fact have ceased to be a member.

238   Dismissals in connection with other industrial action

(1) This section applies in relation to an employee who has a right to complain of unfair dismissal (the 'complainant') and who claims to have been unfairly dismissed, where at the date of the dismissal—

    (a) the employer was conducting or instituting a lock-out, or

    (b) the complainant was taking part in a strike or other industrial action.

(2) In such a case an employment tribunal shall not determine whether the dismissal was fair or unfair unless it is shown—
   (a) that one or more relevant employees of the same employer have not been dismissed, or
   (b) that a relevant employee has before the expiry of the period of three months beginning with the date of his dismissal been offered re-engagement and that the complainant has not been offered re-engagement.

(2A) Subsection (2) does not apply to the dismissal of the employee if it is shown that the reason (or, if more than one, the principal reason) for the dismissal or, in a redundancy case, for selecting the employee for dismissal was one of those specified in or under—
   (a) section 99, 100, 101A(d), 103 or 104C of the Employment Rights Act 1996 (dismissal in family, health and safety, working time, employee representative and flexible working cases),
   (b) section 104 of that Act in its application in relation to time off under section 57A of that Act (dependants).

In this subsection 'redundancy case' has the meaning given in section 105(9) of that Act; and a reference to a specified reason for dismissal includes a reference to specified circumstances of dismissal.

(2B) Subsection (2) does not apply in relation to an employee who is regarded as unfairly dismissed by virtue of section 238A below.

(3) For this purpose 'relevant employees' means—
   (a) in relation to a lock-out, employees who were directly interested in the dispute in contemplation or furtherance of which the lock-out occurred, and
   (b) in relation to a strike or other industrial action, those employees at the establishment of the employer at or from which the complainant works who at the date of his dismissal were taking part in the action.

Nothing in section 237 (dismissal of those taking part in unofficial industrial action) affects the question who are relevant employees for the purposes of this section.

(4) An offer of re-engagement means an offer (made either by the original employer or by a successor of that employer or an associated employer) to re-engage an employee, either in the job which he held immediately before the date of dismissal or in a different job which would be reasonably suitable in his case.

(5) In this section 'date of dismissal' means—
   (a) where the employee's contract of employment was terminated by notice, the date on which the employer's notice was given, and
   (b) in any other case, the effective date of termination.

238A   Participation in official industrial action

(1) For the purposes of this section an employee takes protected industrial action if he commits an act which, or a series of acts each of which, he is induced to commit by an act which by virtue of section 219 is not actionable in tort.

(2) An employee who is dismissed shall be regarded for the purposes of Part X of the Employment Rights Act 1996 (unfair dismissal) as unfairly dismissed if—
   (a) the reason (or, if more than one, the principal reason) for the dismissal is that the employee took protected industrial action, and
   (b) subsection (3), (4) or (5) applies to the dismissal.

(3) This subsection applies to a dismissal if the date of the dismissal is within the protected period.

(4) This subsection applies to a dismissal if—
   (a) the date of the dismissal is after the end of that period, and
   (b) the employee had stopped taking protected industrial action before the end of that period.

(5) This subsection applies to a dismissal if—
- (a) the date of the dismissal is after the end of that period,
- (b) the employee had not stopped taking protected industrial action before the end of that period, and
- (c) the employer had not taken such procedural steps as would have been reasonable for the purposes of resolving the dispute to which the protected industrial action relates.

(6) In determining whether an employer has taken those steps regard shall be had, in particular, to—
- (a) whether the employer or a union had complied with procedures established by any applicable collective or other agreement;
- (b) whether the employer or a union offered or agreed to commence or resume negotiations after the start of the protected industrial action;
- (c) whether the employer or a union unreasonably refused, after the start of the protected industrial action, a request that conciliation services be used;
- (d) whether the employer or a union unreasonably refused, after the start of the protected industrial action, a request that mediation services be used in relation to procedures to be adopted for the purposes of resolving the dispute.
- (e) where there was agreement to use either of the services mentioned in paragraphs (c) and (d), the matters specified in section 238B.

(7) In determining whether an employer has taken those steps no regard shall be had to the merits of the dispute.

(7A) For the purposes of this section 'the protected period', in relation to the dismissal of an employee, is the sum of the basic period and any extension period in relation to that employee.

(7B) The basic period is twelve weeks beginning with the first day of protected industrial action.

(7C) An extension period in relation to an employee is a period equal to the number of days falling on or after the first day of protected industrial action (but before the protected period ends) during the whole or any part of which the employee is locked out by his employer.

(7D) In subsections (7B) and (7C), the 'first day of protected industrial action' means the day on which the employee starts to take protected industrial action (even if on that day he is locked out by his employer).

(8) For the purposes of this section no account shall be taken of the repudiation of any act by a trade union as mentioned in section 21 in relation to anything which occurs before the end of the next working day (within the meaning of section 237) after the day on which the repudiation takes place.

(9) In this section 'date of dismissal' has the meaning given by section 238(5).

238B [omitted]

239 Supplementary provisions relating to unfair dismissal

(1) Sections 237 to 238A (loss of unfair dismissal protection in connection with industrial action) shall be construed as one with Part X of the Employment Rights Act 1996 (unfair dismissal); but sections 108 and 109 of that Act (qualifying period and age limit) shall not apply in relation to section 238A of this Act.

(2) In relation to a complaint to which section 238 or 238A applies, section 111(2) of that Act (time limit for complaint) does not apply, but an employment tribunal shall not consider the complaint unless it is presented to the tribunal—
- (a) before the end of the period of six months beginning with the date of the complainant's dismissal (as defined by section 238(5)), or
- (b) where the tribunal is satisfied that it was not reasonably practicable for the complaint to be presented before the end of that period, within such further period as the tribunal considers reasonable.

(3) Where it is shown that the condition referred to in section 238(2)(b) is fulfilled (discriminatory re-engagement), the references in—

(a) sections 98 to 106 of the Employment Rights Act 1996, and

(b) sections 152 and 153 of this Act,

to the reason or principal reason for which the complainant was dismissed shall be read as references to the reason or principal reason he has not been offered re-engagement.

(4) In relation to a complaint under section 111 of the 1996 Act (unfair dismissal: complaint to employment tribunal) that a dismissal was unfair by virtue of section 238A of this Act—

(a) no order shall be made under section 113 of the 1996 Act (reinstatement or re-engagement) until after the conclusion of protected industrial action by any employee in relation to the relevant dispute,

(b) regulations under section 7 of the Employment Tribunals Act 1996 may make provision about the adjournment and renewal of applications (including provision requiring adjournment in specified circumstances), and

(c) regulations under section 9 of that Act may require a pre-hearing review to be carried out in specified circumstances.

Criminal offences

240   Breach of contract involving injury to persons or property

(1) A person commits an offence who wilfully and maliciously breaks a contract of service or hiring, knowing or having reasonable cause to believe that the probable consequences of his so doing, either alone or in combination with others, will be—

(a) to endanger human life or cause serious bodily injury, or

(b) to expose valuable property, whether real or personal, to destruction or serious injury.

(2) Subsection (1) applies equally whether the offence is committed from malice conceived against the person endangered or injured or, as the case may be, the owner of the property destroyed or injured, or otherwise.

(3) A person guilty of an offence under this section is liable on summary conviction to a fine not exceeding level 2 on the standard scale.

(4) This section does not apply to seamen.

241   Intimidation or annoyance by violence or otherwise

(1) A person commits an offence who, with a view to compelling another person to abstain from doing or to do any act which that person has a legal right to do or abstain from doing, wrongfully and without legal authority—

(a) uses violence to or intimidates that person or his spouse or civil partner or children, or injures his property,

(b) persistently follows that person about from place to place,

(c) hides any tools, clothes or other property owned or used by that person, or deprives him of or hinders him in the use thereof,

(d) watches or besets the house or other place where that person resides, works, carries on business or happens to be, or the approach to any such house or place, or

(e) follows that person with two or more other persons in a disorderly manner in or through any street or road.

(2) A person guilty of an offence under this section is liable on summary conviction to imprisonment for a term not exceeding six months or a fine not exceeding level 5 on the standard scale, or both.

(3) [repealed]

242   Restriction of offence of conspiracy: England and Wales

(1) Where in pursuance of any such agreement as is mentioned in section 1(1) of the Criminal Law Act 1977 (which provides for the offence of conspiracy) the acts in question in relation to an offence are to be done in contemplation or furtherance of a trade dispute, the offence shall be disregarded for the purposes of that subsection if it is a summary offence which is not punishable with imprisonment.

(2) This section extends to England and Wales only.

243   Restriction of offence of conspiracy: Scotland

(1) An agreement of combination by two or more persons to do or procure to be done an act in contemplation or furtherance of a trade dispute is not indictable as a conspiracy if that act committed by one person would not be punishable as a crime.

(2) A crime for this purpose means an offence punishable on indictment, or an offence punishable on summary conviction, and for the commission of which the offender is liable under the statute making the offence punishable to be imprisoned either absolutely or at the discretion of the court as an alternative for some other punishment.

(3) Where a person is convicted of any such agreement or combination as is mentioned above to do or procure to be done an act which is punishable only on summary conviction, and is sentenced to imprisonment, the imprisonment shall not exceed three months or such longer time as may be prescribed by the statute for the punishment of the act when committed by one person.

(4) Nothing in this section—

  (a) exempts from punishment a person guilty of a conspiracy for which a punishment is awarded by an Act of Parliament, or

  (b) affects the law relating to riot, unlawful assembly, breach of the peace, or sedition or any offence against the State or the Sovereign.

(5) This section extends to Scotland only.

Supplementary

244   Meaning of 'trade dispute' in Part V

(1) In this Part a 'trade dispute' means a dispute between workers and their employer which relates wholly or mainly to one or more of the following—

  (a) terms and conditions of employment, or the physical conditions in which any workers are required to work;

  (b) engagement or non-engagement, or termination or suspension of employment or the duties of employment, of one or more workers;

  (c) allocation of work or the duties of employment between workers or groups of workers;

  (d) matters of discipline;

  (e) a worker's membership or non-membership of a trade union;

  (f) facilities for officials of trade unions; and

  (g) machinery for negotiation or consultation, and other procedures, relating to any of the above matters, including the recognition by employers or employers' associations of the right of a trade union to represent workers in such negotiation or consultation or in the carrying out of such procedures.

(2) A dispute between a Minister of the Crown and any workers shall, notwithstanding that he is not the employer of those workers, be treated as a dispute between those workers and their employer if the dispute relates to matters which—

  (a) have been referred for consideration by a joint body on which, by virtue of provision made by or under any enactment, he is represented, or

  (b) cannot be settled without him exercising a power conferred on him by or under an enactment.

(3) There is a trade dispute even though it relates to matters occurring outside the United Kingdom, so long as the person or persons whose actions in the United Kingdom are said to be in contemplation or furtherance of a trade dispute relating to matters occurring outside the United Kingdom are likely to be affected in respect of one or more of the matters specified in subsection (1) by the outcome of the dispute.

(4) An act, threat or demand done or made by one person or organisation against another which, if resisted, would have led to a trade dispute with that other, shall be treated as being done or made in contemplation of a trade dispute with that other, notwithstanding that because that other submits to the act or threat or accedes to the demand no dispute arises.

(5) In this section—

'employment' includes any relationship whereby one person personally does work or performs services for another; and

'worker', in relation to a dispute with an employer, means—

    (a) a worker employed by that employer; or

    (b) a person who has ceased to be so employed if his employment was terminated in connection with the dispute or if the termination of his employment was one of the circumstances giving rise to the dispute.

245   Crown employees and contracts

Where a person holds any office or employment under the Crown on terms which do not constitute a contract of employment between that person and the Crown, those terms shall nevertheless be deemed to constitute such a contract for the purposes of—

    (a) the law relating to liability in tort of a person who commits an act which—

        (i) induces another pewrson to brea a contract, interferes with the performance of a contract or induces another person to interfere with its performance, or

        (ii) consists in a threat that a contract will be broken or its performance interfered with, or that any person will be induced to break a contract or interfere with its performance, and

    (b) the provisions of this or any other Act which refer (whether in relation to contracts generally or only in relation to contracts of employment) to such an act.

246   Minor definitions

In this Part—

'date of the ballot' means, in the case of a ballot in which votes may be cast on more than one day, the last of those days;

'strike' means any concerted stoppage of work;

'working hours', in relation to a person, means any time when under his contract of employment, or other contract personally to do work or perform services, he is required to be at work.

PART VI   ADMINISTRATIVE PROVISIONS

ACAS

247   ACAS

(1) There shall continue to be a body called the Advisory, Conciliation and Arbitration Service (referred to in this Act as 'ACAS').

(2) ACAS is a body corporate of which the corporators are the members of its Council.

(3) Its functions, and those of its officers and servants, shall be performed on behalf of the Crown, but not so as to make it subject to directions of any kind from any Minister of the Crown as to the manner in which it is to exercise its functions under any enactment.

(4) For the purposes of civil proceedings arising out of those functions the Crown Proceedings Act 1947 applies to ACAS as if it were a government department and the Crown Suits (Scotland) Act 1857 applies to it as if it were a public department.

(5)–(6) [omitted]

248 The Council of ACAS

(1) ACAS shall be directed by a Council which, subject to the following provisions, shall consist of a chairman and nine ordinary members appointed by the Secretary of State.

(2) Before appointing those ordinary members of the Council, the Secretary of State shall—

(a) as to three of them, consult such organisations representing employers as he considers appropriate, and

(b) as to three of them, consult such organisations representing workers as he considers appropriate.

(3) The Secretary of State may, if he thinks fit, appoint a further two ordinary members of the Council (who shall be appointed so as to take office at the same time); and before making those appointments he shall—

(a) as to one of them, consult such organisations representing employers as he considers appropriate, and

(b) as to one of them, consult such organisations representing workers as he considers appropriate.

(4) The Secretary of State may appoint up to three deputy chairmen who may be appointed from the ordinary members, or in addition to those members.

(5) The Council shall determine its own procedure, including the quorum necessary for its meetings.

(6) If the Secretary of State has not appointed a deputy charimen, the Council may choose a member to act as chairman in the absence or incapacity of the chairman.

(7) The validity of proceedings of the Council is not affected by any vacancy among the members of the Council or by any defect in the appointment of any of them.

249–253 [omitted]

The Certification Officer

254 The Certification Officer

(1) There shall continue to be an officer called the Certification Officer.

(2) The Certification Officer shall be appointed by the Secretary of State after consultation with ACAS.

(3) The Certification Officer may appoint one or more assistant certification officers and shall appoint an assistant certification officer for Scotland.

(4) The Certification Officer may delegate to an assistant certification officer such functions as he thinks appropriate, and in particular may delegate to the assistant certification officer for Scotland such functions as he thinks appropriate in relation to organisations whose principal office is in Scotland.

References to the Certification Officer in enactments relating to his functions shall be construed accordingly.

(5) ACAS shall provide for the Certification Officer the requisite staff (from among the officers and servants of ACAS) and the requisite accommodation, equipment and other facilities.

(5A) Subject to subsection (6), ACAS shall pay to the Certification Officer such sums as he may require for the performance of any of his functions.

(6) The Secretary of State shall pay to the Certification Officer such sums as he may require for making payments under the scheme under section 115 (payments towards expenditure in connection with secret ballots).

255–258 [omitted]

Central Arbitration Committee

259   The Central Arbitration Committee

(1) There shall continue to be a body called the Central Arbitration Committee.

(2) The functions of the Committee shall be performed on behalf of the Crown, but not so as to make it subject to directions of any kind from any Minister of the Crown as to the manner in which it is to exercise its functions.

(3) ACAS shall provide for the Committee the requisite staff (from among the officers and servants of ACAS) and the requisite accommodation, equipment and other facilities.

260   The members of the Committee

(1) The Central Arbitration Committee shall consist of members appointed by the Secretary of State.

(2) The Secretary of State shall appoint a member as chairman, and may appoint a member as deputy chairman or members as deputy chairmen.

(3) The Secretary of State may appoint as members only persons experienced in industrial relations, and they shall include some persons whose experience is as representatives of employers and some whose experience is as representatives of workers.

(3A) Before making an appointment under subsection (1) or (2) the Secretary of State shall consult ACAS and may consult other persons.

(4) At any time when the chairman of the Committee is absent or otherwise incapable of acting, or there is a vacancy in the office of chairman, and the Committee has a deputy chairman or deputy chairmen—

    (a) the deputy chairman, if there is only one, or

    (b) if there is more than one, such of the deputy chairmen as they may agree or in default of agreement as the Secretary of State may direct,

may perform any of the functions of chairman of the Committee.

(5) At any time when every person who is chairman or deputy chairman is absent or otherwise incapable of acting, or there is no such person, such member of the Committee as the Secretary of State may direct may perform any of the functions of the chairman of the Committee.

(6) The validity of any proceedings of the Committee shall not be affected by any vacancy among the members of the Committee or by any defect in the appointment of a member of the Committee.

261–265 [omitted]; **266–271** [repealed]; **272** [omitted]

PART VII   MISCELLANEOUS AND GENERAL

Crown employment, etc.

273   Crown employment

(1) The provisions of this Act have effect (except as mentioned below) in relation to Crown employment and persons in Crown employment as in relation to other employment and other workers or employees.

(2) The following provisions are excepted from subsection (1)—

    section 87(4)(b) (power of tribunal to make order in respect of employer's failure to comply with duties as to union contributions);

    sections 184 and 185 (remedy for failure to comply with declaration as to disclosure of information);

    Chapter II of Part IV (procedure for handling redundancies).

(3) In this section 'Crown employment' means employment under or for the purposes of a government department or any officer or body exercising on behalf of the Crown functions conferred by an enactment.

(4) For the purposes of the provisions of this Act as they apply in relation to Crown employment or persons in Crown employment—

    (a) 'employee' and 'contract of employment' mean a person in Crown employment and the terms of employment of such a person (but subject to subsection (5) below);

    (b) 'dismissal' means the termination of Crown employment;

    (c) [repealed]

    (d) the reference in 182(1)(e) (disclosure of information for collective bargaining: restrictions on general duty) to the employer's undertaking shall be construed as a reference to the national interest; and

    (e) any other reference to an undertaking shall be construed, in relation to a Minister of the Crown, as a reference to his functions or (as the context may require) to the department of which he is in charge, and in relation to a government department, officer or body shall be construed as a reference to the functions of the department, officer or body or (as the context may require) to the department, officer or body.

(5) Sections 137 to 143 (rights in relation to trade union membership: access to employment) apply in relation to Crown employment otherwise than under a contract only where the terms of employment correspond to those of a contract of employment.

(6) This section has effect subject to section 274 (armed forces) and section 275 (exemption on grounds of national security).

274–280 [omitted]

Excluded classes of employment

281 [repealed]

282 **Short-term employment**

(1) The provisions of Chapter II of Part IV (procedure for handling redundancies) do not apply to employment—

    (a) under a contract for a fixed term of three months or less, or

    (b) under a contract made in contemplation of the performance of a specific task which is not expected to last for more than three months,

where the employee has not been continuously employed for a period of more than three months.

(2) Chapter I of Part XIV of the Employment Rights Act 1996 (computation of period of continuous employment), and any provision modifying or supplementing that Chapter for the purposes of that Act, apply for the purposes of this section.

283 [repealed]; **284** [omitted]

285 **Employment outside Great Britain**

(1) The following provisions of this Act do not apply to employment where under his contract of employment an employee works, or in the case of a prospective employee would ordinarily work, outside Great Britain—

In Part III (rights in relation to trade union membership and activities)—

    sections 137 to 143 (access to employment),

    sections 145A to 151 (inducements and detriment), and

    sections 168 to 173 (time off for trade union duties and activities);

In Part IV, sections 193 and 194 (duty to notify Secretary of State of certain redundancies).

(1A) Sections 145A to 151 do not apply to employment where under his contract personally to do work or perform services a worker who is not an employee works outside Great Britain.

(2) For the purposes of subsections (1) and (1A) employment on board a ship registered in the United Kingdom shall be treated as employment where under his contract a person

ordinarily works in Great Britain unless—
  (a) the ship is registered at a port outside Great Britain, or
  (b) the employment is wholly outside Great Britain, or
  (c) the employee or, as the case may be, the worker or the person seeking employment or seeking to avail himself of a service of an employment agency, is not ordinarily resident in Great Britain.

286–287 [omitted]

Contracting out, etc.

288 Restriction on contracting out

(1) Any provision in an agreement (whether a contract of employment or not) is void in so far as it purports—
  (a) to exclude or limit the operation of any provision of this Act, or
  (b) to preclude a person from bringing—
    (i) proceedings before an employment tribunal or the Central Arbitration Committee under any provision of this Act.
    (ii) [repealed]

(2) Subsection (1) does not apply to an agreement to refrain from instituting or continuing proceedings where a conciliation officer has taken action under section 18 of the Employment Tribunals Act 1996 (conciliation).

(2A) Subsection (1) does not apply to an agreement to refrain from instituting or continuing any proceedings, other than excepted proceedings, specified in subsection (1)(b) of that section before an employment tribunal if the conditions regulating compromise agreements under this Act are satisfied in relation to the agreement.

(2B) The conditions regulating compromise agreements under this Act are that—
  (a) the agreement must be in writing;
  (b) the agreement must relate to the particular proceedings;
  (c) the complainant must have received advice from a relevant independent adviser as to the terms and effect of the proposed agreement and in particular its effect on his ability to pursue his rights before an employment tribunal;
  (d) there must be in force, when the adviser gives the advice, a contract of insurance, or an indemnity provided for members of a profession or professional body covering the risk of a claim by the complainant in respect of loss arising in consequence of the advice;
  (e) the agreement must identify the adviser; and
  (f) the agreement must state that the conditions regulating compromise agreements under this Act are satisfied.

(2C) The proceedings excepted from subsection (2A) are proceedings on a complaint of non-compliance with section 188.

(3) Subsection (1) does not apply—
  (a) to such an agreement as is referred to in section 185(5)(b) or (c) to the extent that it varies or supersedes an award under that section;
  (b) to any provision in a collective agreement excluding rights under Chapter II of Part IV (procedure for handling redundancies), if an order under section 198 is in force in respect of it.

(4) A person is a relevant independent adviser for the purposes of subsection (2B)(c)—
  (a) if he is a qualified lawyer,
  (b) if he is an officer, official, employee or member of an independent trade union who has been certified in writing by the trade union as competent to give advice and as authorised to do so on behalf of the trade union,
  (c) if he works at an advice centre (whether as an employee or a volunteer) and has been certified in writing by the centre as competent to give advice and as authorised to do so on behalf of the centre, or

(d) if he is a person of a description specified in an order made by the Secretary of State.

(4A) But a person is not a relevant independent adviser for the purposes of subsection (2B)(c) in relation to the complainant—

(a) if he is, is employed by or is acting in the matter for the other party or a person who is connected with the other party,

(b) in the case of a person within subsection (4)(b) or (c), if the trade union or advice centre is the other party or a person who is connected with the other party,

(c) in the case of a person within subsection (4)(c), if the complainant makes a payment for the advice received from him, or

(d) in the case of a person of a description specified in an order under sub-section(4)(d), if any condition specified in the order in relation to the giving of advice by persons of that description is not satisfied.

(4B) In subsection (4)(a) 'qualified lawyer' means—

(a) as respects England and Wales, a barrister (whether in practice as such or employed to give legal advice), a solicitor who holds a practising certificate, or a person other than a barrister or solicitor who is an authorised advocate or authorised litigator (within the meaning of the Courts and Legal Services Act 1990), and

(b) as respects Scotland, an advocate (whether in practice as such or employed to give legal advice), or a solicitor who holds a practising certificate.

(4C) An order under subsection (4)(d) shall be made by statutory instrument which shall be subject to annulment in pursuance of a resolution of either House of Parliament.

(5) For the purposes of subsection (4A) any two persons are to be treated as connected—

(a) if one is a company of which the other (directly or indirectly) has control, or

(b) if both are companies of which a third person (directly or indirectly) has control.

(6) An agreement under which the parties agree to submit a dispute to arbitration—

(a) shall be regarded for the purposes of subsections (2) and (2A) as being an agreement to refrain from instituting or continuing proceedings if—

(i) the dispute is covered by a scheme having effect by virtue of an order under section 212A, and

(ii) the agreement is to submit it to arbitration in accordance with the scheme, but

(b) shall be regarded for those purposes as neither being nor including such an agreement in any other case.

289 Employment governed by foreign law

For the purposes of this Act it is immaterial whether the law which (apart from this Act) governs any person's employment is the law of the United Kingdom, or of a part of the United Kingdom, or not.

290–291 [repealed]; 292–294 [omitted]

Interpretation

295 Meaning of 'employee' and related expressions

(1) In this Act—

'contract of employment' means a contract of service or of apprenticeship,

'employee' means an individual who has entered into or works under (or, where the employment has ceased, worked under) a contract of employment, and

'employer', in relation to an employee, means the person by whom the employee is (or, where the employment has ceased, was) employed.

(2) Subsection (1) has effect subject to section 235 and other provisions conferring a wider meaning on 'contract of employment', or related expressions.

296   Meaning of 'worker' and related expressions

(1) In this Act 'worker' means an individual who works, or normally works or seeks to work—

    (a) under a contract of employment, or

    (b) under any other contract whereby he undertakes to do or perform personally any work or services for another party to the contract who is not a professional client of his, or

    (c) in employment under or for the purposes of a government department (otherwise than as a member of the naval, military or air forces of the Crown) in so far as such employment does not fall within paragraph (a) or (b) above.

(2) In this Act 'employer', in relation to a worker, means a person for whom one or more workers work, or have worked or normally work or seek to work.

(3) This section shall have effect subject to sections 68(4), 145F(3) and 151(1B).

297   Associated employers

For the purposes of this Act any two employers shall be treated as associated if—

    (a) one is a company of which the other (directly or indirectly) has control, or

    (b) both are companies of which a third person (directly or indirectly) has control;

and 'associated employer' shall be construed accordingly.

298   Minor definitions: general

In this Act, unless the context otherwise requires—

'act' and 'action' each includes omission, and references to doing an act or taking action shall be construed accordingly;

'certificate of independence' means a certificate issued under—

    (a) section 6(6), or

    (b) section 101A(4);

'contravention' includes a failure to comply, and cognate expressions shall be construed accordingly;

'dismiss', 'dismissal' and 'effective date of termination', in relation to an employee, shall be construed in accordance with Part X of the Employment Rights Act 1996;

'tort', as respects Scotland, means delict, and cognate expressions shall be construed accordingly.

299   Index of defined expressions

In this Act the expressions listed below are defined by or otherwise fall to be construed in accordance with the provisions indicated—

ACAS	section 247(1)
act and action	section 298
advertisement (in sections 137 to 143)	section 143(1)
affected employees (in Part IV, Chapter II)	section 196(3)
agent (of trade union)	section 119
appropriately qualified actuary (in sections 38 to 41)	section 42
associated employer	section 297
branch or section (of trade union)	section 119)
certificate of independence	section 298
collective agreement and collective bargaining	section 178(1)
contract of employment	
— generally	section 295(1)
— in sections 226 to 234	section 273(4)(a)
— in relation to Crown employment	section 273(4)(a)
— in relation to House of Lords or House of Commons staff	
sections 277(4) and 278(4)(a)	
contravention	section 298
the court (in Part I)	section 121
date of the ballot (in Part V)	section 246

300–302 [omitted]

SCHEDULE A1   COLLECTIVE BARGAINING: RECOGNITION

PART I   RECOGNITION

Introduction

1. A trade union (or trade unions) seeking recognition to be entitled to conduct collective bargaining on behalf of a group or groups of workers may make a request in accordance with this Part of this Schedule.

2.—(1) This paragraph applies for the purposes of this Part of this Schedule.

(2) References to the bargaining unit are to the group of workers concerned (or the groups taken together).

(3) References to the proposed bargaining unit are to the bargaining unit proposed in the request for recognition.

(3A) References to an appropriate bargaining unit's being decided by the CAC are to a bargaining unit's being decided by the CAC to be appropriate under paragraph 19(2) or (3) or 19A(2) or (3).

(4) References to the employer are to the employer of the workers constituting the bargaining unit concerned.

(5) References to the parties are to the union (or unions) and the employer.

3.—(1) This paragraph applies for the purposes of this part of this Schedule.

(2) The meaning of collective bargaining given by section 178(1) shall not apply.

(3) References to collective bargaining are to negotiations relating to pay, hours and holidays; but this has effect subject to sub-paragraph (4).

(4) If the parties agree matters as the subject of collective bargaining, references to collective bargaining are to negotiations relating to the agreed matters; and this is the case whether the agreement is made before or after the time when the CAC issues a declaration, or the parties agree, that the union is (or unions are) entitled to conduct collective bargaining on behalf of a bargaining unit.

(5) Sub-paragraph (4) does not apply in construing paragraph 31(3).

(6) Sub-paragraphs (2) to (5) do not apply in construing paragraph 35 or 44.

Request for recognition

4.—(1) The union or unions seeking recognition must make a request for recognition to the employer.

(2) Paragraphs 5 to 9 apply to the request.

5. The request is not valid unless it is received by the employer.

6. The request is not valid unless the union (or each of the unions) has a certificate of independence.

7.—(1) The request is not valid unless the employer, taken with any associated employer or employers, employs—

(a) at least 21 workers on the day the employer receives the request, or

(b) an average of at least 21 workers in the 13 weeks ending with that day.

(2)–(8) [omitted]

8.–9. [omitted]

Parties agree

10.—(1) If before the end of the first period the parties agree a bargaining unit and that the union is (or unions are) to be recognised as entitled to conduct collective bargaining on behalf of the unit, no further steps are to be taken under this Part of this Schedule.

(2) If before the end of the first period the employer informs the union (or unions) that the employer does not accept the request but is willing to negotiate, sub-paragraph (3) applies.

(3) The parties may conduct negotiations with a view to agreeing a bargaining unit and that the union is (or unions are) to be recognised as entitled to conduct collective bargaining on behalf of the unit.

(4) If such an agreement is made before the end of the second period no further steps are to be taken under this Part of this Schedule.

(5) The employer and the union (or unions) may request ACAS to assist in conducting the negotiations.

(6) The first period is the period of 10 working days starting with the day after that on which the employer receives the request for recognition.

(7) The second period is—
> (a) the period of 20 working days starting with the day after that on which the first period ends, or
> (b) such longer period (so starting) as the parties may from time to time agree.

Employer rejects request

11.—(1) This paragraph applies if—
> (a) before the end of the first period the employer fails to respond to the request, or
> (b) before the end of the first period the employer informs the union (or unions) that the employer does not accept the request (without indicating a willingness to negotiate).

(2) The union (or unions) may apply to the CAC to decide both these questions—
> (a) whether the proposed bargaining unit is appropriate;
> (b) whether the union has (or unions have) the support of a majority of the workers constituting the appropriate bargaining unit.

Negotiations fail

12.—(1) Sub-paragraph (2) applies if—
> (a) the employer informs the union (or unions) under paragraph 10(2), and
> (b) no agreement is made before the end of the second period.

(2) The union (or unions) may apply to the CAC to decide both these questions—
> (a) whether the proposed bargaining unit is appropriate;
> (b) whether the union has (or unions have) the support of a majority of the workers constituting the appropriate bargaining unit.

(3) Sub-paragraph (4) applies if—
> (a) the employer informs the union (or unions) under paragraph 10(2), and
> (b) before the end of the second period the parties agree a bargaining unit but not that the union is (or unions are) to be recognised as entitled to conduct collective bargaining on behalf of the unit.

(4) The union (or unions) may apply to the CAC to decide the question whether the union has (or unions have) the support of a majority of the workers constituting the bargaining unit.

(5) But no application may be made under this paragraph if within the period of 10 working days starting with the day after that on which the employer informs the union (or unions) under paragraph 10(2) the employer proposes that ACAS be requested to assist in conducting the negotiations and—
> (a) the union rejects (or unions reject) the proposals, or
> (b) the union fails (or unions fail) to accept the proposal within the period of 10 working days starting with the day after that on which the employer makes the proposal.

Acceptance of applications

13. The CAC must give notice to the parties of receipt of an application under paragraph 11 or 12.

14.—(1) This paragraph applies if—
(a) two or more relevant applications are made,
(b) at least one worker falling within one of the relevant bargaining units also falls within the other relevant bargaining unit (or units), and
(c) the CAC has not accepted any of the applications.

(2) A relevant application is an application under paragraph 11 or 12.

(3) In relation to a relevant application, the relevant bargaining unit is—
(a) the proposed bargaining unit, where the application is under paragraph 11(2) or 12(2);
(b) the agreed bargaining unit, where the application is under paragraph 12(4).

(4) Within the acceptance period the CAC must decide, with regard to each relevant application, whether the 10 per cent test is satisfied.

(5) The 10 per cent test is satisfied if members of the union (or unions) constitute at least 10 per cent of the workers constituting the relevant bargaining unit.

(6) The acceptance period is—
(a) the period of 10 working days starting with the day after that on which the CAC receives the last relevant application, or
(b) such longer period (so starting) as the CAC may specify to the parties by notice containing reasons for the extension.

(7) If the CAC decides that—
(a) the 10 per cent test is satisfied with regard to more than one of the relevant applications, or
(b) the 10 per cent test is satisfied with regard to none of the relevant applications, the CAC must not accept any of the relevant applications.

(8) If the CAC decides that the 10 per cent test is satisfied with regard to one only of the relevant applications the CAC—
(a) must proceed under paragraph 15 with regard to that application, and
(b) must not accept any of the other relevant applications.

(9) The CAC must give notice of its decision to the parties.

(10) If by virtue of this paragraph the CAC does not accept an application, no further steps are to be taken under this Part of this Schedule in relation to that application.

15.–17. [omitted]

Appropriate bargaining unit

18.—(1) If the CAC accepts an application under paragraph 11(2) or 12(2) it must try to help the parties to reach within the appropriate period an agreement as to what the appropriate bargaining unit is.

(2) The appropriate period is (subject to any notice under sub-paragraph (3), (4) or (5))—
(a) the period of 20 working days starting with the day after that on which the CAC gives notice of acceptance of the application, or
(b) such longer period (so starting) as the CAC may specify to the parties by notice containing reasons for the extension.

(3) If, during the appropriate period, the CAC concludes that there is no reasonable prospect of the parties' agreeing an appropriate bargaining unit before the time when (apart from this sub-paragraph) the appropriate period would end, the CAC may, by a notice given to the parties, declare that the appropriate period ends with the date of the notice.

(4) If, during the appropriate period, the parties apply to the CAC for a declaration that the appropriate period is to end with a date (specified in the application) which is earlier than the date with which it would otherwise end, the CAC may, by a notice given to the parties, declare that the appropriate period ends with the specified date.

(5) If the CAC has declared under sub-paragraph (4) that the appropriate period ends with a specified date, it may before that date by a notice given to the parties specify a later date with which the appropriate period ends.

(6) A notice under sub-paragraph (3) must contain reasons for reaching the conclusion mentioned in that sub-paragraph.

(7) A notice under sub-paragraph (5) must contain reasons for the extension of the appropriate period.

18A.—(1) This paragraph applies if the CAC accepts an application under paragraph 11(2) or 12(2).

(2) Within 5 working days starting with the day after that on which the CAC gives the employer notice of acceptance of the application, the employer must supply the following information to the union (or unions) and the CAC—

(a) a list of the categories of worker in the proposed bargaining unit,

(b) a list of the workplaces at which the workers in the proposed bargaining unit work, and

(c) the number of workers the employer reasonably believes to be in each category at each workplace.

(3) The lists and numbers supplied under this paragraph must be as accurate as is reasonably practicable in the light of the information in the possession of the employer at the time when he complies with sub-paragraph (2).

(4) The lists and numbers supplied to the union (or unions) and to the CAC must be the same.

(5) For the purposes of this paragraph, the workplace at which a worker works is—

(a) if the person works at or from a single set of premises, those premises, and

(b) in any other case, the premises with which the worker's employment has the closest connection.

19.—(1) This paragraph applies if—

(a) the CAC accepts an application under paragraph 11(2) or 12(2),

(b) the parties have not agreed an appropriate bargaining unit at the end of the appropriate period (defined by paragraph 18), and

(c) at the end of that period either no request under paragraph 19A(1)(b) has been made or such a request has been made but the condition in paragraph 19A(1)(c) has not been met.

(2) Within the decision period, the CAC must decide whether the proposed bargaining unit is appropriate.

(3) If the CAC decides that the proposed bargaining unit is not appropriate, it must also decide within the decision period a bargaining unit which is appropriate.

(4) The decision period is—

(a) the period of 10 working days starting with the day after that with which the appropriate period ends, or

(b) such longer period (so starting) as the CAC may specify to the parties by notice containing reasons for the extension.

19A.—(1) This paragraph applies if—

(a) the CAC accepts an application under paragraph 11(2) or 12(2),

(b) during the appropriate period (defined by paragraph 18), the CAC is requested by the union (or unions) to make a decision under this paragraph, and

(c) the CAC is, either at the time the request is made or at a later time during the appropriate period, of the opinion that the employer has failed to comply with the duty imposed by paragraph 18A.

(2) Within the decision period, the CAC must decide whether the proposed bargaining unit is appropriate.

(3) If the CAC decides that the proposed bargaining unit is not appropriate, it must also decide within the decision period a bargaining unit which is appropriate.

(4) The decision period is—

(a) the period of 10 working days starting with the day after the day on which the request is made, or

(b) such longer period (so starting) as the CAC may specify to the parties by notice containing reasons for the extension.

19B.—(1) This paragraph applies if the CAC has to decide whether a bargaining unit is appropriate for the purposes of paragraph 19(2) or (3) or 19A(2) or (3).

(2) The CAC must take these matters into account—

(a) the need for the unit to be compatible with effective management;

(b) the matters listed in sub-paragraph (3), so far as they do not conflict with that need.

(3) The matters are—

(a) the views of the employer and of the union (or unions);

(b) existing national and local bargaining arrangements;

(c) the desirability of avoiding small fragmented bargaining units within an undertaking;

(d) the characteristics of workers falling within the bargaining unit under consideration and of any other employees of the employer whom the CAC considers relevant;

(e) the location of workers.

(4) In taking an employer's views into account for the purpose of deciding whether the proposed bargaining unit is appropriate, the CAC must take into account any view the employer has about any other bargaining unit that he considers would be appropriate.

(5) The CAC must give notice of its decision to the parties.

19C.–19F. [omitted]

Union recognition

20.—(1) This paragraph applies if—

(a) the CAC accepts an application under paragraph 11(2) or 12(2),

(b) the parties have agreed an appropriate bargaining unit at the end of the appropriate period (defined by paragraph 18), or the CAC has decided an appropriate bargaining unit, and

(c) that bargaining unit differs from the proposed bargaining unit.

(2) Within the decision period the CAC must decide whether the application is invalid within the terms of paragraphs 43 to 50.

(3) In deciding whether the application is invalid, the CAC must consider any evidence which it has been given by the employer or the union (or unions).

(4) If the CAC decides that the application is invalid—

(a) the CAC must give notice of its decision to the parties,

(b) the CAC must not proceed with the application, and

(c) no further steps are to be taken under this part of this Schedule.

(5) If the CAC decides that the application is not invalid it must—

(a) proceed with the application, and

(b) give notice to the parties that it is so proceeding.

(6) The decision period is—

(a) the period of 10 working days starting with the day after that on which the parties agree an appropriate bargaining unit or the CAC decides an appropriate bargaining unit, or

(b) such longer period (so starting) as the CAC may specify to the parties by notice containing reasons for the extension.

21.—(1) This paragraph applies if—

(a) the CAC accepts an application under paragraph 11(2) or 12(2),

(b) the parties have agreed an appropriate bargaining unit at the end of the appropriate period (defined by paragraph 18), or the CAC has decided an appropriate bargaining unit, and

(c) that bargaining unit is the same as the proposed bargaining unit.

(2) This paragraph also applies if the CAC accepts an application under paragraph 12(4).

(3) The CAC must proceed with the application.

22.—(1) This paragraph applies if—

    (a) the CAC proceeds with an application in accordance with paragraph 20 or 21 (and makes no declaration under paragraph 19F(5)), and

    (b) the CAC is satisfied that a majority of the workers constituting the bargaining unit are members of the union (or unions).

(2) The CAC must issue a declaration that the union is (or unions are) recognised as entitled to conduct collective bargaining on behalf of the workers constituting the bargaining unit.

(3) But if any of the three qualifying conditions is fulfilled, instead of issuing a declaration under sub-paragraph (2) the CAC must give notice to the parties that it intends to arrange for the holding of a secret ballot in which the workers constituting the bargaining unit are asked whether they want the union (or unions) to conduct collective bargaining on their behalf.

(4) These are the three qualifying conditions—

    (a) the CAC is satisfied that a ballot should be held in the interests of good industrial relations;

    (b) the CAC has evidence, which it considers to be credible, from a significant number of the union members within the bargaining unit that they do not want the union (or unions) to conduct collective bargaining on their behalf;

    (c) membership evidence is produced which leads the CAC to conclude that there are doubts whether a significant number of the union members within the bargaining unit want the union (or unions) to conduct collective bargaining on their behalf.

(5) For the purposes of sub-paragraph (4)(c) membership evidence is—

    (a) evidence about the circumstances in which union members became members;

    (b) evidence about the length of time for which union members have been members, in a case where the CAC is satisfied that such evidence should be taken into account.

23.—(1) This paragraph applies if—

    (a) the CAC proceeds with an application in accordance with paragraph 20 or 21 (and makes no declaration under paragraph 19F(5)), and

    (b) the CAC is not satisfied that a majority of the workers constituting the bargaining unit are members of the union (or unions).

(2) The CAC must give notice to the parties that it intends to arrange for the holding of a secret ballot in which the workers constituting the bargaining unit are asked whether they want the union (or unions) to conduct collective bargaining on their behalf.

24. [omitted]

25.—(1) This paragraph applies if the CAC arranges under paragraph 24 for the holding of a ballot.

(2) The ballot must be conducted by a qualified independent person appointed by the CAC.

(3) The ballot must be conducted within—

    (a) the period of 20 working days starting with the day after that on which the qualified independent person is appointed, or

    (b) such longer period (so starting) as the CAC may decide.

(4) The ballot must be conducted—

    (a) at a workplace or workplaces decided by the CAC,

    (b) by post, or

    (c) by a combination of the methods described in sub-paragraphs (a) and (b), depending on the CAC's preference.

(5) In deciding how the ballot is to be conducted the CAC must take into account—

    (a) the likelihood of the ballot being affected by unfairness or malpractice if it were conducted at a workplace or workplaces;

(b) costs and practicality;

(c) such other matters as the CAC considers appropriate.

(6) The CAC may not decide that the ballot is to be conducted as mentioned in sub--paragraph (4)(c) unless there are special factors making such a decision appropriate; and special factors include—

(a) factors arising from the location of workers or the nature of their employment;

(b) factors put to the CAC by the employer or the union (or unions).

(6A) If the CAC decides that the ballot must (in whole or in part) be conducted at a workplace (or workplaces), it may require arrangements to be made for workers—

(a) who (but for the arrangements) would be prevented by the CAC's decision from voting by post, and

(b) who are unable, for reasons relating to those workers as individuals, to cast their votes in the ballot at the workplace (or at any of them),

to be given the opportunity (if they request it far enough in advance of the ballot for this to be practicable) to vote by post; and the CAC's imposing such a requirement is not to be treated for the purposes of sub-paragraph (6) as a decision that the ballot be conducted as mentioned in sub-paragraph (4)(c).

(7) A person is a qualified independent person if—

(a) he satisfies such conditions as may be specified for the purposes of this paragraph by order of the Secretary of State or is himself so specified, and

(b) there are no grounds for believing either that he will carry out any functions conferred on him in relation to the ballot otherwise than competently or that his independence in relation to the ballot might reasonably be called into question.

(8)–(9) [omitted]

26.—(1) An employer who is informed by the CAC under paragraph 25(9) must comply with the following five duties.

(2) The first duty is to co-operate generally, in connection with the ballot, with the union (or unions) and the person appointed to conduct the ballot; and the second and third duties are not to prejudice the generality of this.

(3) The second duty is to give to the union (or unions) such access to the workers constituting the bargaining unit as is reasonable to enable the union (or unions) to inform the workers of the object of the ballot and to seek their support and their opinions on the issues involved.

(4) the third duty is to do the following (so far as it is reasonable to expect the employer to do so)—

(a) to give to the CAC, within the period of 10 working days starting with the day after that on which the employer is informed under paragraph 25(9), the names and home addresses of the workers constituting the bargaining unit;

(b) to give to the CAC, as soon as is reasonably practicable, the name and home address of any worker who joins the unit after the employer has complied with paragraph (a);

(c) to inform the CAC, as soon as is reasonably practicable, of any worker whose name has been given to the CAC under paragraph 19D or paragraph (a) or (b) of this sub- paragraph and who ceases to be within the unit.

(4A) The fourth duty is to refrain from making any offer to any or all of the workers constituting the bargaining unit which—

(a) has or is likely to have the effect of inducing any or all of them not to attend any relevant meeting between the union (or unions) and the workers constituting the bargaining unit, and

(b) is not reasonable in the circumstances.

(4B) The fifth duty is to refrain from taking or threatening to take any action against a worker solely or mainly on the grounds that he—

(a) attended or took part in any relevant meeting between the union (or unions) and the workers constituting the bargaining unit, or

(b) indicated his intention to attend or take part in such a meeting.

(4C) A meeting is a relevant meeting in relation to a worker for the purposes of sub-paragraphs (4A) and (4B) if—

(a) it is organised in accordance with any agreement reached concerning the second duty or as a result of a step ordered to be taken under paragraph 27 to remedy a failure to comply with that duty, and

(b) it is one which the employer is, by such an agreement or order as is mentioned in paragraph (a), required to permit the worker to attend.

(4D) Without prejudice to the generality of the second duty imposed by this paragraph, an employer is to be taken to have failed to comply with that duty if—

(a) he refuses a request for a meeting between the union (or unions) and any or all of the workers constituting the bargaining unit to be held in the absence of the employer or any representative of his (other than one who has been invited to attend the meeting) and it is not reasonable in the circumstances for him to do so,

(b) he or a representative of his attends such a meeting without having been invited to do so,

(c) he seeks to record or otherwise be informed of the proceedings at any such meeting and it is not reasonable in the circumstances for him to do so, or

(d) he refuses to give an undertaking that he will not seek to record or otherwise be informed of the proceedings at any such meeting unless it is reasonable in the circumstances for him to do either of those things.

(4E) The fourth and fifth duties do not confer any rights on a worker; but that does not affect any other right which a worker may have.

(4F)–(4H) [omitted]

(5) As soon as is reasonably practicable after the CAC receives any information under sub- paragraph (4) it must pass it on to the person appointed to conduct the ballot.

(6) If asked to do so by the union (or unions) the person appointed to conduct the ballot must send to any worker—

(a) whose name and home address have been given under sub-paragraph (5), and

(b) who is still within the unit (so far as the person so appointed is aware),

any information supplied by the union (or unions) to the person so appointed.

(7) The duty under sub-paragraph (6) does not apply unless the union bears (or unions bear) the cost of sending the information.

(8) [omitted]

27.—(1) If the CAC is satisfied that the employer has failed to fulfil any of the duties imposed on him by paragraph 26, and the ballot has not been held, the CAC may order the employer—

(a) to take such steps to remedy the failure as the CAC considers reasonable and specifies in the order, and

(b) to do so within such period as the CAC considers reasonable and specifies in the order.

(2) If the CAC is satisfied that the employer has failed to comply with an order under sub-paragraph (1), and the ballot has not been held, the CAC may issue a declaration that the union is (or unions are) recognised as entitled to conduct collective bargaining on behalf of the bargaining unit.

(3) If the CAC issues a declaration under sub-paragraph (2) it shall take steps to cancel the holding of the ballot; and if the ballot is held it shall have no effect.

27A.—(1) Each of the parties informed by the CAC under paragraph 25(9) must refrain from using any unfair practice.

(2) A party uses an unfair practice if, with a view to influencing the result of the ballot, the party—

(a) offers to pay money or give money's worth to a worker entitled to vote in the ballot in return for the worker's agreement to vote in a particular way or to abstain from voting,

(b) makes an outcome-specific offer to a worker entitled to vote in the ballot,

(c) coerces or attempts to coerce a worker entitled to vote in the ballot to disclose—

(i)   whether he intends to vote or to abstain from voting in the ballot, or

(ii) how he intends to vote, or how he has voted, in the ballot,

(d) dismisses or threatens to dismiss a worker,

(e) takes or threatens to take disciplinary action against a worker,

(f) subjects or threatens to subject a worker to any other detriment, or

(g) uses or attempts to use undue influence on a worker entitled to vote in the ballot.

(3) For the purposes of sub-paragraph (2)(b) an 'outcome-specific offer' is an offer to pay money or give money's worth which—

(a) is conditional on the issuing by the CAC of a declaration that—

(i)   the union is (or unions are) recognised as entitled to conduct collective bargaining on behalf of the bargaining unit, or

(ii) the union is (or unions are) not entitled to be so recognised, and

(b) is not conditional on anything which is done or occurs as a result of the declaration in question.

(4) The duty imposed by this paragraph does not confer any rights on a worker; but that does not affect any other right which a worker may have.

(5) Each of the following powers shall be taken to include power to issue Codes of Practice about unfair practices for the purposes of this paragraph—

(a) the power of ACAS under section 199(1);

(b) the power of the Secretary of State under section 203(1)(a).

27B.—(1) A party may complain to the CAC that another party has failed to comply with paragraph 27A.

(2) A complaint under sub-paragraph (1) must be made on or before the first working day after—

(a) the date of the ballot, or

(b) if votes may be cast in the ballot on more than one day, the last of those days.

(3) Within the decision period the CAC must decide whether the complaint is well-founded.

(4) A complaint is well-founded if—

(a) the CAC finds that the party complained against used an unfair practice, and

(b) the CAC is satisfied that the use of that practice changed or was likely to change, in the case of a worker entitled to vote in the ballot—

(i)   his intention to vote or to abstain from voting,

(ii) his intention to vote in a particular way, or

(iii) how he voted.

(5) The decision period is—

(a) the period of 10 working days starting with the day after that on which the complaint under sub-paragraph (1) was received by the CAC, or

(b) such longer period (so starting) as the CAC may specify to the parties by a notice containing reasons for the extension.

(6) If, at the beginning of the decision period, the ballot has not begun, the CAC may by notice to the parties and the qualified independent person postpone the date on which it is to begin until a date which falls after the end of the decision period.

27C.—(1) This paragraph applies if the CAC decides that a complaint under paragraph 27B is well-founded.

(2) The CAC must, as soon as is reasonably practicable, issue a declaration to that effect.

(3) The CAC may do either or both of the following—

(a) order the party concerned to take any action specified in the order within such period as may be so specified, or

(b) give notice to the employer and to the union (or unions) that it intends to arrange for the holding of a secret ballot in which the workers constituting the bargaining unit are asked whether they want the union (or unions) to conduct collective bargaining on their behalf.

(4) The CAC may give an order or a notice under sub-paragraph (3) either at the same time as it issues the declaration under sub-paragraph (2) or at any other time before it acts under paragraph 29.

(5) The action specified in an order under sub-paragraph (3)(a) shall be such as the CAC considers reasonable in order to mitigate the effect of the failure of the party concerned to comply with the duty imposed by paragraph 27A.

(6) The CAC may give more than one order under sub-paragraph (3)(a).

27D.—(1) This paragraph applies if the CAC issues a declaration under paragraph 27C(2) and the declaration states that the unfair practice used consisted of or included—

    (a) the use of violence, or

    (b) the dismissal of a union official.

(2) This paragraph also applies if the CAC has made an order under paragraph 27C(3)(a) and—

    (a) it is satisfied that the party subject to the order has failed to comply with it, or

    (b) it makes another declaration under paragraph 27C(2) in relation to a complaint against that party.

(3) If the party concerned is the employer, the CAC may issue a declaration that the union is (or unions are) recognised as entitled to conduct collective bargaining on behalf of the bargaining unit.

(4) If the party concerned is a union, the CAC may issue a declaration that the union is (or unions are) not entitled to be so recognised.

(5) The powers conferred by this paragraph are in addition to those conferred by paragraph 27C(3).

27E.—(1) This paragraph applies if the CAC issues a declaration that a complaint under paragraph 27B is well-founded and—

    (a) gives a notice under paragraph 27C(3)(b), or

    (b) issues a declaration under paragraph 27D.

(2) If the ballot in connection with which the complaint was made has not been held, the CAC shall take steps to cancel it.

(3) If that ballot is held, it shall have no effect.

27F.—(1) This paragraph applies if the CAC gives a notice under paragraph 27C(3)(b).

(2) Paragraphs 24 to 29 apply in relation to that notice as they apply in relation to a notice given under paragraph 22(3) or 23(2) but with the modifications specified in sub-paragraphs (3) to (6).

(3) In each of sub-paragraphs (5)(a) and (6)(a) of paragraph 24 for '10 working days' substitute '5 working days'.

(4) An employer's duty under paragraph (a) of paragraph 26(4) is limited to—

    (a) giving the CAC the names and home addresses of any workers in the bargaining unit which have not previously been given to it in accordance with that duty;

    (b) giving the CAC the names and home addresses of those workers who have joined the bargaining unit since he last gave the CAC information in accordance with that duty;

    (c) informing the CAC of any change to the name or home address of a worker whose name and home address have previously been given to the CAC in accordance with that duty; and

    (d) informing the CAC of any worker whose name had previously been given to it in accordance with that duty who has ceased to be within the bargaining unit.

(5) Any order given under paragraph 27(1) or 27C(3)(a) for the purposes of the cancelled or ineffectual ballot shall have effect (to the extent that the CAC specifies in a notice to the parties) as if it were made for the purposes of the ballot to which the notice under paragraph 27C(3)(b) relates.

(6) The gross costs of the ballot shall be borne by such of the parties and in such proportions as the CAC may determine and, accordingly, sub-paragraphs (2) and (3) of paragraph 28 shall be omitted and the reference in sub-paragraph (4) of that paragraph to the employer and the union (or each of the unions) shall be construed as a reference to the party or parties which bear the costs in accordance with the CAC's determination.

28. [omitted]

29.—(1) As soon as is reasonably practicable after the CAC is informed of the result of a ballot by the person conducting it, the CAC must act under this paragraph.

(1A) The duty in sub-paragraph (1) does not apply if the CAC gives a notice under paragraph 27C(3)(b).

(2) The CAC must inform the employer and the union (or unions) of the result of the ballot.

(3) If the result is that the union is (or unions are) supported by—

(a) a majority of the workers voting, and

(b) at least 40 per cent of the workers constituting the bargaining unit, the CAC must issue a declaration that the union is (or unions are) recognised as entitled to conduct collective bargaining on behalf of the bargaining unit.

(4) If the result is otherwise the CAC must issue a declaration that the union is (or unions are) not entitled to be so recognised.

(5)–(7) [omitted]

Consequences of recognition

30.—(1) This paragraph applies if the CAC issues a declaration under this Part of this Schedule that the union is (or unions are) recognised as entitled to conduct collective bargaining on behalf of a bargaining unit.

(2) The parties may in the negotiation period conduct negotiations with a view to agreeing a method by which they will conduct collective bargaining.

(3) If no agreement is made in the negotiation period the employer or the union (or unions) may apply to the CAC for assistance.

(4) The negotiation period is—

(a) the period of 30 working days starting with the start day, or

(b) such longer period (so starting) as the parties may from time to time agree.

(5) The start day is the day after that on which the parties are notified of the declaration.

31.—(1) This paragraph applies if an application for assistance is made to the CAC under paragraph 30.

(2) The CAC must try to help the parties to reach in the agreement period an agreement on a method by which they will conduct collective bargaining.

(3) If at the end of the agreement period the parties have not made such an agreement the CAC must specify to the parties the method by which they are to conduct collective bargaining.

(4) Any method specified under sub-paragraph (3) is to have effect as if it were contained in a legally enforceable contract made by the parties.

(5) But if the parties agree in writing—

(a) that sub-paragraph (4) shall not apply, or shall not apply to particular parts of the method specified by the CAC, or

(b) to vary or replace the method specified by the CAC, the written agreement shall have effect as a legally enforceable contract made by the parties.

(6) Specific performance shall be the only remedy available for breach of anything which is a legally enforceable contract by virtue of this paragraph.

(7) If at any time before a specification is made under sub-paragraph (3) the parties jointly apply to the CAC requesting it to stop taking steps under this paragraph, the CAC must comply with the request.

(8) The agreement period is—
  (a) the period of 20 working days starting with the day after that on which the CAC receives the application under paragraph 30, or
  (b) such longer period (so starting) as the CAC may decide with the consent of the parties.

Method not carried out

32.—(1) This paragraph applies if—
  (a) the CAC issues a declaration under this Part of this Schedule that the union is (or unions are) recognised as entitled to conduct collective bargaining on behalf of a bargaining unit,
  (b) the parties agree a method by which they will conduct collective bargaining, and
  (c) one or more of the parties fails to carry out the agreement.
(2) the employer or the union (or unions) may apply to the CAC for assistance.
(3) Paragraph 31 applies as if 'paragraph 30' (in each place) read 'paragraph 30 or paragraph 32'.

General provisions about admissibility

33.–34. [omitted]
35.—(1) An application under paragraph 11 or 12 is not admissible if the CAC is satisfied that there is already in force a collective agreement under which a union is (or unions are) recognised as entitled to conduct collective bargaining on behalf of any workers falling within the relevant bargaining unit.
(2) But sub-paragraph (1) does not apply to an application under paragraph 11 or 12 if—
  (a) the union (or unions) recognised under the collective agreement and the union (or unions) making the application under paragraph 11 or 12 are the same, and
  (b) the matters in respect of which the union is (or unions are) entitled to conduct collective bargaining do not include all of the following: pay, hours and holidays ('the core topics').
(3) A declaration of recognition which is the subject of a declaration under paragraph 83(2) must for the purposes of sub-paragraph (1) be treated as ceasing to have effect to the extent specified in paragraph 83(2) on the making of the declaration under paragraph 83(2).
(4) In applying sub-paragraph (1) an agreement for recognition (the agreement in question) must be ignored if—
  (a) the union does not have (or none of the unions has) a certificate of independence,
  (b) at sometime there was an agreement (the old agreement) between the employer and the union under which the union(whether alone or with other unions) was recognised as entitled to conduct collective bargaining on behalf of a group of workers which was the same or substantially the same as the group covered by the agreement in question, and
  (c) the old agreement ceased to have effect in the period of three years ending with the date of the agreement in question.
(5) It is for the CAC to decide whether one group of workers is the same or substantially the same as another, but in deciding the CAC may take account of the views of any person it believes has an interest in the matter.
(6) The relevant bargaining unit is—
  (a) the proposed bargaining unit, where the application is under paragraph 11(2) or 12(2);
  (b) the agreed bargaining unit, where the application is under paragraph 12(4).
36.—(1) An application under paragraph 11 or 12 is not admissible unless the CAC decides that—

    (a) members of the union (or unions) constitute at least 10 per cent of the workers constituting the relevant bargaining unit, and

    (b) a majority of the workers constituting the relevant bargaining unit would be likely to favour recognition of the union (or unions) as entitled to conduct collective bargaining on behalf of the bargaining unit.

(2) The relevant bargaining unit is—

    (a) the proposed bargaining unit, where the application is under paragraph 11(2) or 12(2);

    (b) the agreed bargaining unit, where the application is under paragraph 12(4).

(3) The CAC must give reasons for the decision.

37.—(1) This paragraph applies to an application made by more than one union under paragraph 11 or 12.

(2) The application is not admissible unless—

    (a) the unions show that they will co-operate with each other in a manner likely to secure and maintain stable and effective collective bargaining arrangements, and

    (b) the unions show that, if the employer wishes, they will enter into arrangements under which collective bargaining is conducted by the unions acting together on behalf of the workers constituting the relevant bargaining unit.

(3) The relevant bargaining unit is—

    (a) the proposed bargaining unit, where the application is under paragraph 11(2) or 12(2);

    (b) the agreed bargaining unit, where the application is under paragraph 12(4).

38. [omitted]

39.—(1) This paragraph applies if the CAC accepts a relevant application relating to a bargaining unit or proceeds under paragraph 20 with an application relating to a bargaining unit.

(2) Another relevant application is not admissible if—

    (a) the application is made within the period of 3 years starting with the day after that on which the CAC gave notice of acceptance of the application mentioned in sub-paragraph (1),

    (b) the relevant bargaining unit is the same or substantially the same as the bargaining unit mentioned in sub-paragraph (1), and

    (c) the application is made by the union (or unions) which made the application mentioned in sub-paragraph (1).

(3) A relevant application is an application under paragraph 11 or 12.

(4) The relevant bargaining unit is—

    (a) the proposed bargaining unit, where the application is under paragraph 11(2) or 12(2);

    (b) the agreed bargaining unit, where the application is under paragraph 12(4).

(5) This paragraph does not apply if paragraph 40 or 41 applies.

40.—(1) This paragraph applies if the CAC issues a declaration under paragraph 27D(4) or 29(4) that a union is (or unions are) not entitled to be recognised as entitled to conduct collective bargaining on behalf of a bargaining unit; and this is so whether the ballot concerned is arranged under this Part or Part III of this Schedule.

(2) An application under paragraph 11 or 12 is not admissible if—

    (a) the application is made within the period of 3 years starting with the day after that on which the declaration was issued,

    (b) the relevant bargaining unit is the same or substantially the same as the bargaining unit mentioned in sub-paragraph (1), and

    (c) the application is made by the union (or unions) which made the application leading to the declaration.

(3) The relevant bargaining unit is—

    (a) the proposed bargaining unit, where the application is under paragraph 11(2) or 12(2);

(b) the agreed bargaining unit, where the application is under paragraph 12(4).

41.—(1) This paragraph applies if the CAC issues a declaration under paragraph 119D(4), 119H(5) or 121(3) that bargaining arrangements are to cease to have effect; and that is so whether the ballot concerned is arranged under Part IV or Part V of this Schedule.

(2) An application under paragraph 11 or 12 is not admissible if—

    (a) the application is made within the period of 3 years starting with the day after that on which the declaration was issued,

    (b) the relevant bargaining unit is the same or substantially the same as the bargaining unit to which the bargaining arrangements mentioned in sub-paragraph (1) relate, and

    (c) the application is made by the union which was a party (or unions which were parties) to the proceedings leading to the declaration.

(3) The relevant bargaining unit is—

    (a) the proposed bargaining unit, where the application is under paragraph 11(2) or 12(2);

    (b) the agreed bargaining unit, where the application is under paragraph 12(4).

42. [omitted]

General provisions about validity

43.—(1) Paragraphs 44 to 50 apply if the CAC has to decide under paragraph 20 whether an application is valid.

(2) In those paragraphs—

    (a) references to the application in question are to that application, and

    (b) references to the relevant bargaining unit are to the bargaining unit agreed by the parties or decided by the CAC.

44.—(1) The application in question is invalid if the CAC is satisfied that there is already in force a collective agreement under which a union is (or unions are) recognised as entitled to conduct collective bargaining on behalf of any workers falling within the relevant bargaining unit.

(2) But sub-paragraph (1) does not apply to the application in question if—

    (a) the union (or unions) recognised under the collective agreement and the union (or unions) making the application in question are the same, and

    (b) the matters in respect of which the union is (or unions are) entitled to conduct collective bargaining do not include all of the following: pay, hours and holidays ('the core topics').

(3)–(5) [omitted]

45. The application in question is invalid unless the CAC decides that—

    (a) members of the union (or unions) constitute at least 10 per cent of the workers constituting the relevant bargaining unit, and

    (b) a majority of the workers constituting the relevant bargaining unit would be likely to favour recognition of the union (or unions) as entitled to conduct collective bargaining on behalf of the bargaining unit.

46. [omitted]

47.—(1) This paragraph applies if the CAC accepts an application under paragraph 11 or 12 relating to a bargaining unit or proceeds under paragraph 20 with an application relating to a bargaining unit.

(2) The application in question is invalid if—

    (a) the application is made within the period of 3 years starting with the day after that on which the CAC gave notice of acceptance of the application mentioned in sub-paragraph (1),

    (b) the relevant bargaining unit is the same or substantially the same as the bargaining unit mentioned in sub-paragraph (1), and

(c) the application is made by the union (or unions) which made the application mentioned in sub-paragraph (1).

(3) This paragraph does not apply if paragraph 48 or 49 applies.

48.—(1) This paragraph applies if the CAC issues a declaration under paragraph 27D(4) or 29(4) that a union is (or unions are) not entitled to be recognised as entitled to conduct collective bargaining on behalf of a bargaining unit; and this is so whether the ballot concerned is arranged under this Part or Part III of this Schedule.

(2) The application in question is invalid if—
   (a) the application is made within the period of 3 years starting with the date of the declaration,
   (b) the relevant bargaining unit is the same or substantially the same as the bargaining unit mentioned in sub-paragraph (1), and
   (c) the application is made by the union (or unions) which made the application leading to the declaration.

49.—(1) This paragraph applies if the CAC issues a declaration under paragraph 119D(4), 119H(5) or 121(3) that bargaining arrangements are to cease to have effect; and this is so whether the ballot concerned is arranged under Part IV or Part V of this Schedule.

(2) The application in question is invalid if—
   (a) the application is made within the period of 3 years starting with the day after that on which the declaration was issued,
   (b) the relevant bargaining unit is the same or substantially the same as the bargaining unit to which the bargaining arrangements mentioned in sub-paragraph (1) relate, and
   (c) the application is made by the union which was a party (or unions which were parties) to the proceedings leading to the declaration.

50.–51. [omitted]

PART II   VOLUNTARY RECOGNITION

Agreements for recognition

52.—(1) This paragraph applies for the purposes of this Part of this Schedule.

(2) An agreement is an agreement for recognition if the following conditions are fulfilled in relation to it—
   (a) the agreement is made in the permitted period between a union (or unions) and an employer in consequence of a request made under paragraph 4 and valid within the terms of paragraphs 5 to 9;
   (b) under the agreement the union is (or unions are) recognised as entitled to conduct collective bargaining on behalf of a group or groups of workers employed by the employer;
   (c) if sub-paragraph (5) applies to the agreement, it is satisfied.

(3) The permitted period is the period which begins with the day on which the employer receives the request and ends when the first of the following occurs—
   (a) the union withdraws (or unions withdraw) the request;
   (b) the union withdraws (or unions withdraw) any application under paragraph 11 or 12 made in consequence of the request;
   (c) the CAC gives notice of a decision under paragraph 14(7) which precludes it from accepting such an application under paragraph 11 or 12;
   (d) the CAC gives notice under paragraph 15(4)(a) or 20(4)(a) in relation to such an application under paragraph 11 or 12;
   (e) the parties give notice to the CAC under paragraph 17(2) in relation to such an application under paragraph 11 or 12;

    (f) the CAC issues a declaration under paragraph 19F(5) or 22(2) in consequence of such an application under paragraph 11 or 12;

    (g) the CAC is notified under paragraph 24(2) in relation to such an application under paragraph 11 or 12;

    (h) the last day of the notification period ends (the notification period being that defined by paragraph 24(6) and arising from such an application under paragraph 11 or 12.

(4) Sub-paragraph (5) applies to an agreement if—

    (a) at the time it is made the CAC has received an application under paragraph 11 or 12 in consequence of the request mentioned in sub-paragraph (2), and

    (b) the CAC has not decided whether the application is admissible or it has decided that it is admissible.

(5) This sub-paragraph is satisfied if, in relation to the application under paragraph 11 or 12, the parties give notice to the CAC under paragraph 17 before the final event (as defined in paragraph 17) occurs.

Other interpretation

53.—(1) This paragraph applies for the purposes of this Part of this Schedule.

(2) In relation to an agreement for recognition, references to the bargaining unit are to the group of workers (or the groups taken together) to which the agreement for recognition relates.

(3) In relation to an agreement for recognition, references to the parties are to the union (or unions) and the employer who are parties to the agreement.

54.—(1) This paragraph applies for the purposes of this Part of this Schedule.

(2) The meaning of collective bargaining given by section 178(1) shall not apply.

(3) Except in paragraph 63(2), in relation to an agreement for recognition references to collective bargaining are to negotiations relating to the matters in respect of which the union is (or unions are) recognised as entitled to conduct negotiations under the agreement for recognition.

(4) In paragraph 63(2) the reference to collective bargaining is to negotiations relating to pay, hours and holidays.

Determination of type of agreement

55.—(1) This paragraph applies if one or more of the parties to an agreement applies to the CAC for a decision whether or not the agreement is an agreement for recognition.

(2) The CAC must give notice of receipt of an application under sub-paragraph (1) to any parties to the agreement who are not parties to the application.

(3) The CAC must within the decision period decide whether the agreement is an agreement for recognition.

(4) If the CAC decides that the agreement is an agreement for recognition it must issue a declaration to that effect.

(5) If the CAC decides that the agreement is not an agreement for recognition it must issue a declaration to that effect.

(6) The decision period is—

    (a) the period of 10 working days starting with the day after that on which the CAC receives the application under sub-paragraph (1), or

    (b) such longer period (so starting) as the CAC may specify to the parties to the agreement by notice containing reasons for the extension.

Termination of agreement for recognition

56.—(1) The employer may not terminate an agreement for recognition before the relevant period ends.

(2) After that period ends the employer may terminate the agreement, with or without the consent of the union (or unions).

(3) The union (or unions) may terminate an agreement for recognition at any time, with or without the consent of the employer.

(4) Sub-paragraphs (1) to (3) have effect subject to the terms of the agreement or any other agreement of the parties.

(5) The relevant period is the period of three years starting with the day after the date of the agreement.

57.—(1) If an agreement for recognition is terminated, as from the termination the agreement and any provisions relating to the collective bargaining method shall cease to have effect.

(2) For this purpose provisions relating to the collective bargaining method are—

  (a) any agreement between the parties as to the method by which collective bargaining is to be conducted with regard to the bargaining unit, or

  (b) anything effective as, or as if contained in, a legally enforceable contract and relating to the method by which collective bargaining is to be conducted with regard to the bargaining unit.

Application to CAC to specify method

58.—(1) This paragraph applies if the parties make an agreement for recognition.

(2) The parties may in the negotiation period conduct negotiations with a view to agreeing a method by which they will conduct collective bargaining.

(3) If no agreement is made in the negotiation period the employer or the union (or unions) may apply to the CAC for assistance.

(4) The negotiation period is—

  (a) the period of 30 working days starting with the start day, or

  (b) such longer period (so starting) as the parties may from time to time agree.

(5) The start day is the day after that on which the agreement is made.

59.—(1) This paragraph applies if—

  (a) the parties to an agreement for recognition agree a method by which they will conduct collective bargaining, and

  (b) one or more of the parties fails to carry out the agreement as to a method.

(2) The employer or the union (or unions) may apply to the CAC for assistance.

60.–95. [omitted]

PART IV   DERECOGNITION: GENERAL

Introduction

96.—(1) This part of this Schedule applies if the CAC has issued a declaration that a union is (or unions are) recognised as entitled to conduct collective bargaining on behalf of a bargaining unit.

(2) In such a case references in this Part of this Schedule to the bargaining arrangements are to the declaration and to the provisions relating to the collective bargaining method.

(3) For this purpose the provisions relating to the collective bargaining method are—

  (a) the parties' agreement as to the method by which collective bargaining is to be conducted,

  (b) anything effective as, or as if contained in, a legally enforceable contract and relating to the method by which collective bargaining is to be conducted, or

  (c) any provision of Part III of this Schedule that a method of collective bargaining is to have effect.

97. For the purposes of this Part of this Schedule the relevant date is the date of the expiry of the period of 3 years starting with the date of the CAC's declaration.

98. References in this Part of this Schedule to the parties are to the employer and the union (or unions) concerned.

99.–103. [omitted]

Employer's request to end arrangements

104.—(1) This paragraph and paragraphs 105 to 111 apply if after the relevant date the employer requests the union (or each of the unions) to agree to end the bargaining arrangements.

(2) The request is not valid unless it—

(a) is in writing,

(b) is received by the union (or each of the unions),

(c) identifies the bargaining arrangements, and

(d) states that it is made under this Schedule.

105. [omitted]

106.—(1) This paragraph applies if—

(a) before the end of the first period the union fails (or unions fail) to respond to the request, or

(b) before the end of the first period the union informs the employer that it does not (or unions inform the employer that they do not) accept the request (without indicating a willingness to negotiate).

(2) The employer may apply to the CAC for the holding of a secret ballot to decide whether the bargaining arrangements should be ended.

107.—(1) This paragraph applies if—

(a) the union informs (or unions inform) the employer under paragraph 105(2), and

(b) no agreement is made before the end of the second period.

(2) The employer may apply to the CAC for the holding of a secret ballot to decide whether the bargaining arrangements should be ended.

(3) But no application may be made if within the period of 10 working days starting with the day after that on which the union informs (or unions inform) the employer under paragraph 105(2) the union proposes (or unions propose) that ACAS be requested to assist in conducting the negotiations and—

(a) the employer rejects the proposals, or

(b) the employer fails to accept the proposal within the period of 10 working days starting with the day after that on which the union makes (or unions make) the proposals.

108.–109. [omitted]

110.—(1) An application under paragraph 106 or 107 is not admissible unless the CAC decides that—

(a) at least 10 per cent of the workers constituting the bargaining unit favour an end of the bargaining arrangements, and

(b) a majority of the workers constituting the bargaining unit would be likely to favour an end of the bargaining arrangements.

(2) The CAC must give reasons for the decision.

111. [omitted]

Workers' application to end arrangements

112.—(1) A worker or workers falling within the bargaining unit may after the relevant date apply to the CAC to have the bargaining arrangements ended.

(2) An application is not admissible unless—

(a) it is made in such form as the CAC specifies, and

(b) it is supported by such documents as the CAC specifies.

(3) An application is not admissible unless the worker gives (or workers give) to the employer and to the union (or each of the unions)—
   (a) notice of the application, and
   (b) a copy of the application and any documents supporting it.
113.—(1) An application under paragraph 112 is not admissible if—
   (a) a relevant application was made, or a notice under paragraph 99(2) was given, within the period of 3 years prior to the date of the application under paragraph 112,
   (b) the relevant application, or notice under paragraph 99(2), and the application under paragraph 112 relate to the same bargaining unit, and
   (c) the CAC accepted the relevant application or (as the case may be) decided under paragraph 100 that the notice complied with paragraph 99(3).
(2) A relevant application is an application made to the CAC—
   (a) [repealed],
   (b) by the employer under paragraph 106, 107 or 128, or
   (c) by a worker (or workers) under paragraph 112.
114.—(1) An application under paragraph 112 is not admissible unless the CAC decides that—
   (a) at least 10 per cent of the workers constituting the bargaining unit favour an end of the bargaining arrangements, and
   (b) a majority of the workers constituting the bargaining unit would be likely to favour an end of the bargaining arrangements.
(2) The CAC must give reasons for the decision.
115.–116. [omitted]

Ballot on derecognition

117.—(1) This paragraph applies if the CAC accepts an application under paragraph 106 or 107.
(2) This paragraph also applies if—
   (a) the CAC accepts an application under paragraph 112, and
   (b) in the period mentioned in paragraph 116(1) there is no agreement or withdrawal as there described.
(3) The CAC must arrange for the holding of a secret ballot in which the workers constituting the bargaining unit are asked whether the bargaining arrangements should be ended.
(4) The ballot must be conducted by a qualified independent person appointed by the CAC.
(5) The ballot must be conducted within—
   (a) the period of 20 working days starting with the day after that on which the qualified independent person is appointed, or
   (b) such longer period (so starting) as the CAC may decide.
(6) The ballot must be conducted—
   (a) at a workplace or workplaces decided by the CAC,
   (b) by post, or
   (c) by a combination of the methods described in sub-paragraphs (a) and (b), depending on the CAC's preference.
(7) In deciding how the ballot is to be conducted the CAC must take into account—
   (a) the likelihood of the ballot being affected by unfairness or malpractice if it were conducted at a workplace or workplaces;
   (b) costs and practicality;
   (c) such other matters as the CAC considers appropriate.
(8) The CAC may not decide that the ballot is to be conducted as mentioned in sub-paragraph (6)(c) unless there are special factors making such a decision appropriate; and special factors include—

    (a) factors arising from the location of workers or the nature of their employment;

    (b) factors put to the CAC by the employer or the union (or unions).

(8A) If the CAC decides that the ballot must (in whole or in part) be conducted at a workplace (or workplaces), it may require arrangements to be made for workers—

    (a) who (but for the arrangements) would be prevented by the CAC's decision from voting by post, and

    (b) who are unable, for reasons relating to those workers as individuals, to cast their votes in the ballot at the workplace (or at any of them),

to be given the opportunity (if they request it far enough in advance of the ballot for this to be practicable) to vote by post; and the CAC's imposing such a requirement is not to be treated for the purposes of sub-paragraph (8) as a decision that the ballot be conducted as mentioned in sub-paragraph (6)(c).

    (9) A person is a qualified independent person if—

    (a) he satisfies such conditions as may be specified for the purposes of this paragraph by order of the Secretary of State or is himself so specified, and

    (b) there are no grounds for believing either that he will carry out any functions conferred on him in relation to the ballot otherwise than competently or that his independence in relation to the ballot might reasonably be called into question.

    (10)–(11) [omitted]

    118.—(1) An employer who is informed by the CAC under paragraph 117(11) must comply with the following five duties.

    (2) The first duty is to co-operate generally, in connection with the ballot, with the union (or unions) and the person appointed to conduct the ballot; and the second and third duties are not to prejudice the generality of this.

    (3) The second duty is to give to the union (or unions) such access to the workers constituting the bargaining unit as is reasonable to enable the union (or unions) to inform the workers of the object of the ballot and to seek their support and their opinions on the issues involved.

    (4) The third duty is to do the following (so far as it is reasonable to expect the employer to do so)—

    (a) to give to the CAC, within the period of 10 working days starting with the day after that on which the employer is informed under paragraph 117(11), the names and home addresses of the workers constituting the bargaining unit;

    (b) to give to the CAC, as soon as is reasonably practicable, the name and home address of any worker who joins the unit after the employer has complied with paragraph (a);

    (c) to inform the CAC, as soon as is reasonably practicable, of any worker whose name has been given to the CAC under paragraph (a) or (b) but who ceases to be within the unit.

    (4A) The fourth duty is to refrain from making any offer to any or all of the workers constituting the bargaining unit which—

    (a) has or is likely to have the effect of inducing any or all of them not to attend any relevant meeting between the union (or unions) and the workers constituting the bargaining unit, and

    (b) is not reasonable in the circumstances.

    (4B) The fifth duty is to refrain from taking or threatening to take any action against a worker solely or mainly on the grounds that he—

    (a) attended or took part in any relevant meeting between the union (or unions) and the workers constituting the bargaining unit, or

    (b) indicated his intention to attend or take part in such a meeting.

    (4C) A meeting is a relevant meeting in relation to a worker for the purposes of sub-paragraph (4A) and (4B) if—

    (a) it is organised in accordance with any agreement reached concerning the second duty or as a result of a step ordered to be taken under paragraph 119 to remedy a failure to comply with that duty, and

(b) it is one which the employer is, by such an agreement or order as is mentioned in paragraph (a), required to permit the worker to attend.

(4D) Without prejudice to the generality of the second duty imposed by this paragraph, an employer is to be taken to have failed to comply with that duty if—

(a) he refuses a request for a meeting between the union (or unions) and any or all of the workers constituting the bargaining unit to be held in the absence of the employer or any representative of his (other than one who has been invited to attend the meeting) and it is not reasonable in the circumstances for him to do so,

(b) he or a representative of his attends such a meeting without having been invited to do so,

(c) he seeks to record or otherwise be informed of the proceedings at any such meeting and it is not reasonable in the circumstances for him to do so, or

(d) he refuses to give an undertaking that he will not seek to record or otherwise be informed of the proceedings at any such meeting unless it is reasonable in the circumstances for him to do either of those things.

(4E) The fourth and fifth duties do not confer any rights on a worker; but that does not affect any other right which a worker may have.

(5) As soon as is reasonably practicable after the CAC receives any information under sub-paragraph (4) it must pass it on to the person appointed to conduct the ballot.

(6) If asked to do so by the union (or unions) the person appointed to conduct the ballot must send to any worker—

(a) whose name and home address have been given under sub-paragraph (5), and

(b) who is still within the unit (so far as the person so appointed is aware),

any information supplied by the union (or unions) to the person so appointed.

(7) the duty under sub-paragraph (6) does not apply unless the union bears (or unions bear) the cost of sending the information.

(8) [omitted]

119.—(1) If the CAC is satisfied that the employer has failed to fulfil any of the duties imposed on him by paragraph 118, and the ballot has not been held, the CAC may order the employer—

(a) to take such steps to remedy the failure as the CAC considers reasonable and specifies in the order, and

(b) to do so within such period as the CAC considers reasonable and specifies in the order.

(2) If—

(a) the ballot has been arranged in consequence of an application under paragraph 106 or 107,

(b) the CAC is satisfied that the employer has failed to comply with an order under sub-paragraph (1), and

(c) the ballot has not been held, the CAC may refuse the application.

(3) [repealed]

(4) If the CAC refuses an application under sub-paragraph (2) it shall take steps to cancel the holding of the ballot; and if the ballot is held it shall have no effect.

119A.—(1) Each of the parties informed by the CAC under paragraph 117(11) must refrain from using any unfair practice.

(2) A party uses an unfair practice if, with a view to influencing the result of the ballot, the party—

(a) offers to pay money or give money's worth to a worker entitled to vote in the ballot in return for the worker's agreement to vote in a particular way or to abstain from voting,

(b) makes an outcome-specific offer to a worker entitled to vote in the ballot,

(c) coerces or attempts to coerce a worker entitled to vote in the ballot to disclose—

(i) whether he intends to vote or to abstain from voting in the ballot, or

(ii) how he intends to vote, or how he has voted, in the ballot,

(d) dismisses or threatens to dismiss a worker,

(e) takes or threatens to take disciplinary action against a worker,

(f) subjects or threatens to subject a worker to any other detriment, or

(g) uses or attempts to use undue influence on a worker entitled to vote in the ballot.

(3) For the purposes of sub-paragraph (2)(b) an 'outcome-specific offer' is an offer to pay money or give money's worth which—

(a) is conditional on—

    (i) the issuing by the CAC of a declaration that the bargaining arrangements are to cease to have effect, or

    (ii) the refusal by the CAC of an application under paragraph 106, 107 or 112, and

(b) is not conditional on anything which is done or occurs as a result of that declaration or, as the case may be, of that refusal.

(4) The duty imposed by this paragraph does not confer any rights on a worker; but that does not affect any other right which a worker may have.

(5) Each of the following powers shall be taken to include power to issue Codes of Practice about unfair practices for the purposes of this paragraph—

(a) the power of ACAS under section 199(1);

(b) the power of the Secretary of State under section 203(1)(a).

119B.—(1) A party may complain to the CAC that another party has failed to comply with paragraph 119A.

(2) A complaint under sub-paragraph (1) must be made on or before the first working day after—

(a) the date of the ballot, or

(b) if votes may be cast in the ballot on more than one day, the last of those days.

(3) Within the decision period the CAC must decide whether the complaint is well-founded.

(4) A complaint is well-founded if—

(a) the CAC finds that the party complained against used an unfair practice, and

(b) the CAC is satisfied that the use of that practice changed or was likely to change, in the case of a worker entitled to vote in the ballot—

    (i) his intention to vote or to abstain from voting,

    (ii) his intention to vote in a particular way, or

    (iii) how he voted.

(5) The decision period is—

(a) the period of 10 working days starting with the day after that on which the complaint under sub-paragraph (1) was received by the CAC, or

(b) such longer period (so starting) as the CAC may specify to the parties by a notice containing reasons for the extension.

(6) If, at the beginning of the decision period, the ballot has not begun, the CAC may by notice to the parties and the qualified independent person postpone the date on which it is to begin until a date which falls after the end of the decision period.

119C.—(1) This paragraph applies if the CAC decides that a complaint under paragraph 119B is well-founded.

(2) The CAC must, as soon as is reasonably practicable, issue a declaration to that effect.

(3) The CAC may do either or both of the following—

(a) order the party concerned to take any action specified in the order within such period as may be so specified, or

(b) make arrangements for the holding of a secret ballot in which the workers constituting the bargaining unit are asked whether the bargaining arrangements should be ended.

(4) The CAC may give an order or make arrangements under sub-paragraph (3) either at the same time as it issues the declaration under sub-paragraph (2) or at any other time before it acts under paragraph 121.

(5) The action specified in an order under sub-paragraph (3)(a) shall be such as the CAC considers reasonable in order to mitigate the effect of the failure of the party complained against to comply with the duty imposed by paragraph 119A.

(6) The CAC may give more than one order under sub-paragraph (3)(a).

119D.—(1) This paragraph applies if the CAC issues a declaration under paragraph 119C(2) and the declaration states that the unfair practice used consisted of or included—

    (a) the use of violence, or

    (b) the dismissal of a union official.

(2) This paragraph also applies if the CAC has made an order under paragraph 119C(3)(a) and—

    (a) it is satisfied that the party subject to the order has failed to comply with it, or

    (b) it makes another declaration under paragraph 119C(2) in relation to a complaint against that party.

(3) If the party concerned is the employer, the CAC may refuse the employer's application under paragraph 106 or 107.

(4) If the party concerned is a union, the CAC may issue a declaration that the bargaining arrangements are to cease to have effect on a date specified by the CAC in the declaration.

(5) If a declaration is issued under sub-paragraph (4) the bargaining arrangements shall cease to have effect accordingly.

(6) The powers conferred by this paragraph are in addition to those conferred by paragraph 119C(3).

119E.—(1) This paragraph applies if the CAC issues a declaration that a complaint under paragraph 119B is well-founded and—

    (a) makes arrangements under paragraph 119C(3)(b),

    (b) refuses under paragraph 119D(3) or 119H(6) an application under paragraph 106, 107 or 112, or

    (c) issues a declaration under paragraph 119D(4) or 119H(5).

(2) If the ballot in connection with which the complaint was made has not been held, the CAC shall take steps to cancel it.

(3) If that ballot is held, it shall have no effect.

119F.—(1) This paragraph applies if the CAC makes arrangements under paragraph 119C(3)(b).

(2) Paragraphs 117(4) to (11) and 118 to 121 apply in relation to those arrangements as they apply in relation to arrangements made under paragraph 117(3) but with the modifications specified in sub-paragraphs (3) to (5).

(3) An employer's duty under paragraph (a) of paragraph 118(4) is limited to—

    (a) giving the CAC the names and home addresses of any workers in the bargaining unit which have not previously been given to it in accordance with that duty;

    (b) giving the CAC the names and home addresses of those workers who have joined the bargaining unit since he last gave the CAC information in accordance with that duty;

    (c) informing the CAC of any change to the name or home address of a worker whose name and home address have previously been given to the CAC in accordance with that duty; and

    (d) informing the CAC of any worker whose name had previously been given to it in accordance with that duty who has ceased to be within the bargaining unit.

(4) Any order given under paragraph 119(1) or 119C(3)(a) for the purposes of the cancelled or ineffectual ballot shall have effect (to the extent that the CAC specifies in a notice to the parties) as if it were made for the purposes of the ballot for which arrangements are made under paragraph 119C(3)(b).

(5) The gross costs of the ballot shall be borne by such of the parties and in such proportions as the CAC may determine and, accordingly, sub-paragraphs (2) and (3) of paragraph 120 shall be omitted and the reference in sub-paragraph (4) of that paragraph to

the employer and the union (or each of the unions) shall be construed as a reference to the party or parties which bear the costs in accordance with the CAC's determination.

119G.—(1) Paragraphs 119A to 119C, 119E and 119F apply in relation to an application under paragraph 112 as they apply in relation to an application under paragraph 106 or 107 but with the modifications specified in this paragraph.

(2) References in those paragraphs (and, accordingly, in paragraph 119H(3)) to a party shall be read as including references to the applicant worker or workers; but this is subject to sub-paragraph (3).

(3) The reference in paragraph 119A(1) to a party informed under paragraph 117(11) shall be read as including a reference to the applicant worker or workers.

119H.—(1) This paragraph applies in relation to an application under paragraph 112 in the cases specified in sub-paragraphs (2) and (3).

(2) The first case is where the CAC issues a declaration under paragraph 119C(2) and the declaration states that the unfair practice used consisted of or included—

(a) the use of violence, or

(b) the dismissal of a union official.

(3) The second case is where the CAC has made an order under paragraph 119C(3)(a) and—

(a) it is satisfied that the party subject to the order has failed to comply with it, or

(b) it makes another declaration under paragraph 119C(2) in relation to a complaint against that party.

(4) If the party concerned is the employer, the CAC may order him to refrain from further campaigning in relation to the ballot.

(5) If the party concerned is a union, the CAC may issue a declaration that the bargaining arrangements are to cease to have effect on a date specified by the CAC in the declaration.

(6) If the party concerned is the applicant worker (or any of the applicant workers), the CAC may refuse the application under paragraph 112.

(7) If a declaration is issued under sub-paragraph (5) the bargaining arrangements shall cease to have effect accordingly.

(8) The powers conferred by this paragraph are in addition to those conferred by paragraph 119C(3).

119I.—(1) This paragraph applies if—

(a) a ballot has been arranged in consequence of an application under paragraph 112,

(b) the CAC has given the employer an order under paragraph 119(1), 119C(3) or 119H(4), and

(c) the ballot for the purposes of which the order was made (or any other ballot for the purposes of which it has effect) has not been held.

(2) The applicant worker (or each of the applicant workers) and the union (or each of the unions) is entitled to enforce obedience to the order.

(3) The order may be enforced—

(a) in England and Wales, in the same way as an order of the county court;

(b) in Scotland, in the same way as an order of the sheriff.

120. [omitted]

121.—(1) As soon as is reasonably practicable after the CAC is informed of the result of a ballot by the person conducting it, the CAC must act under this paragraph.

(1A) The duty in sub-paragraph (1) does not apply if the CAC makes arrangements under paragraph 119C(3)(b).

(2) The CAC must inform the employer and the union (or unions) of the result of the ballot.

(3) If the result is that the proposition that the bargaining arrangements should be ended is supported by—

(a) a majority of the workers voting, and

(b) at least 40 per cent of the workers constituting the bargaining unit, the CAC must issue a declaration that the bargaining arrangements are to cease to have effect on a date specified by the CAC in the declaration.

(4) If the result is otherwise the CAC must refuse the application under paragraph 106, 107 or 112.

(5) If a declaration is issued under sub-paragraph (3) the bargaining arrangements shall cease to have effect accordingly.

(6) The Secretary of State may by order amend sub-paragraph (3) so as to specify a different degree of support; and different provision may be made for different circumstances.

(7) An order under sub-paragraph (6) shall be made by statutory instrument.

(8) No such order shall be made unless a draft of it has been laid before Parliament and approved by a resolution of each House of Parliament.

PART V   DERECOGNITION WHERE RECOGNITION AUTOMATIC

Introduction

122.—(1) This Part of this Schedule applies if—
  (a) the CAC has issued a declaration under paragraph 19F(5), 22(2), 27(2) or 27D(3) that a union is (or unions are) recognised as entitled to conduct collective bargaining on behalf of a bargaining unit, and
  (b) the parties have agreed under paragraph 30 or 31 a method by which they will conduct collective bargaining.

(2) In such a case references in this Part of this Schedule to the bargaining arrangements are to—
  (a) the declaration, and
  (b) the parties' agreement.

123.—(1) This Part of this Schedule also applies if—
  (a) the CAC has issued a declaration under paragraph 19F(5), 22(2), 27(2) or 27D(3) that a union is (or unions are) recognised as entitled to conduct collective bargaining on behalf of a bargaining unit, and
  (b) the CAC has specified to the parties under paragraph 31(3) the method by which they are to conduct collective bargaining.

(2) In such a case references in this Part of this Schedule to the bargaining arrangements are to—
  (a) the declaration, and
  (b) anything effective as, or as if contained in, a legally enforceable contract by virtue of paragraph 31.

124.—(1) This part of this Schedule also applies if the CAC has issued a declaration under paragraph 87(2) that a union is (or unions are) recognised as entitled to conduct collective bargaining on behalf of a bargaining unit.

(2) In such a case references in this Part of this Schedule to the bargaining arrangements are to—
  (a) the declaration, and
  (b) paragraph 87(6)(b).

125. For the purposes of this Part of this Schedule the relevant date is the date of the expiry of the period of 3 years starting with the date of the CAC's declaration.

126. References in this Part of this Schedule to the parties are to the employer and the union (or unions) concerned.

Employer's request to end arrangements

127.—(1) The employer may after the relevant date request the union (or each of the unions) to agree to end the bargaining arrangements.

(2) The request is not valid unless it—

    (a) is in writing,

    (b) is received by the union (or each of the unions),

    (c) identifies the bargaining arrangements,

    (d) states that it is made under this Schedule, and

    (e) states that fewer than half of the workers constituting the bargaining unit are members of the union (or unions).

128.—(1) If before the end of the negotiation period the parties agree to end the bargaining arrangements no further steps are to be taken under this Part of this Schedule.

(2) If no such agreement is made before the end of the negotiation period, the employer may apply to the CAC for the holding of a secret ballot to decide whether the bargaining arrangements should be ended.

(3) The negotiation period is the period of 10 working days starting with the day after—

    (a) the day on which the union receives the request, or

    (b) the last day on which any of the unions receives the request;

or such longer period (so starting) as the parties may from time to time agree.

129.–130. [omitted]

131.—(1) An application under paragraph 128 is not admissible unless the CAC is satisfied that fewer than half of the workers constituting the bargaining unit are members of the union (or unions).

(2) The CAC must give reasons for the decision.

132. [omitted]

Ballot on derecognition

133.—(1) Paragraph 117 applies if the CAC accepts an application under paragraph 128 (as well as in the cases mentioned in paragraph 117(1) and (2)).

(2) Paragraphs 118 to 121 apply accordingly, but as if—

    (a) the references in paragraphs 119(2)(a) and 119D(3) to paragraph 106 or 107 were to paragraph 106, 107 or 128;

    (b) the references in paragraphs 119A(3)(a)(ii), 119E(1)(b) and 121(4) to paragraph 106, 107 or 112 were to paragraph 106, 107, 112 or 128.

134.–155. [omitted]

PART VIII   DETRIMENT

Detriment

156.—(1) A worker has a right not to be subjected to any detriment by any act, or any deliberate failure to act, by his employer if the act or failure takes place on any of the grounds set out in sub-paragraph (2).

(2) The grounds are that—

    (a) the worker acted with a view to obtaining or preventing recognition of a union (or unions) by the employer under this Schedule;

    (b) the worker indicated that he supported or did not support recognition of a union (or unions) by the employer under this Schedule;

    (c) the worker acted with a view to securing or preventing the ending under this Schedule of bargaining arrangements;

    (d) the worker indicated that he supported or did not support the ending under this Schedule of bargaining arrangements;

    (e) the worker influenced or sought to influence the way in which votes were to be cast by other workers in a ballot arranged under this Schedule;

    (f) the worker influenced or sought to influence other workers to vote or to abstain from voting in such a ballot;

    (g) the worker voted in such a ballot;

(h) the worker proposed to do, failed to do, or proposed to decline to do, any of the things referred to in paragraphs (a) to (g).

(3) A ground does not fall within sub-paragraph (2) if it constitutes an unreasonable act or omission by the worker.

(4) This paragraph does not apply if the worker is an employee and the detriment amounts to dismissal within the meaning of the Employment Rights Act 1996.

(5) A worker may present a complaint to an employment tribunal on the ground that he has been subjected to a detriment in contravention of this paragraph.

(6) Apart from the remedy by way of complaint as mentioned in sub-paragraph (5), a worker has no remedy for infringement of the right conferred on him by this paragraph.

157.—(1) An employment tribunal shall not consider a complaint under paragraph 156 unless it is presented—

(a) before the end of the period of 3 months starting with the date of the act or failure to which the complaint relates or, if that act or failure is part of a series of similar acts or failures (or both), the last of them, or

(b) where the tribunal is satisfied that it was not reasonably practicable for the complaint to be presented before the end of that period, within such further period as it considers reasonable.

(2) For the purposes of sub-paragraph (1)—

(a) where an act extends over a period, the reference to the date of the act is a reference to the last day of that period;

(b) a failure to act shall be treated as done when it was decided on.

(3) For the purposes of sub-paragraph (2), in the absence of evidence establishing the contrary an employer must be taken to decide on a failure to act—

(a) when he does an act inconsistent with doing the failed act, or

(b) if he has done no such inconsistent act, when the period expires within which he might reasonably have been expected to do the failed act if it was to be done.

158. On a complaint under paragraph 156 it shall be for the employer to show the ground on which he acted or failed to act.

159.—(1) If the employment tribunal finds that a complaint under paragraph 156 is well-founded it shall make a declaration to that effect and may make an award of compensation to be paid by the employer to the complainant in respect of the act or failure complained of.

(2) The amount of the compensation awarded shall be such as the tribunal considers just and equitable in all the circumstances having regard to the infringement complained of and to any loss sustained by the complainant which is attributable to the act or failure which infringed his right.

(3) The loss shall be taken to include—

(a) any expenses reasonably incurred by the complainant in consequence of the act or failure complained of, and

(b) loss of any benefit which he might reasonably be expected to have had but for that act or failure.

(4) In ascertaining the loss, the tribunal shall apply the same rule concerning the duty of a person to mitigate his loss as applies to damages recoverable under the common law of England and Wales or Scotland.

(5) If the tribunal finds that the act or failure complained of was to any extent caused or contributed to by action of the complainant, it shall reduce the amount of the compensation by such proportion as it considers just and equitable having regard to the finding.

160.—(1) If the employment tribunal finds that a complaint under paragraph 156 is well-founded and—

(a) the detriment of which the worker has complained is the termination of his worker's contract, but

(b) that contract was not a contract of employment,

any compensation awarded under paragraph 159 must not exceed the limit specified in sub-paragraph (2).

(2) The limit is the total of—

(a) the sum which would be the basic award for unfair dismissal, calculated in accordance with section 119 of the Employment Rights Act 1996, if the worker had been an employee and the contract terminated had been a contract of employment, and

(b) the sum for the time being specified in section 124(1) of that Act which is the limit for a compensatory award to a person calculated in accordance with section 123 of that Act.

Dismissal

161.—(1) For the purposes of Part X of the Employment Rights Act 1996 (unfair dismissal) the dismissal of an employee shall be regarded as unfair if the dismissal was made—

(a) for a reason set out in sub-paragraph (2), or

(b) for reasons the main one of which is one of those set out in sub-paragraph (2).

(2) The reasons are that—

(a) the employee acted with a view to obtaining or preventing recognition of a union (or unions) by the employer under this Schedule;

(b) the employee indicated that he supported or did not support recognition of a union (or unions) by the employer under this Schedule;

(c) the employee acted with a view to securing or preventing the ending under this Schedule of bargaining arrangements;

(d) the employee indicated that he supported or did not support the ending under this Schedule of bargaining arrangements;

(e) the employee influenced or sought to influence the way in which votes were to be cast by other workers in a ballot arranged under this Schedule;

(f) the employee influenced or sought to influence other workers to vote or to abstain from voting in such a ballot;

(g) the employee voted in such a ballot;

(h) the employee proposed to do, failed to do, or proposed to decline to do, any of the things referred to in paragraphs (a) to (g).

(3) A reason does not fall within sub-paragraph (2) if it constitutes an unreasonable act or omission by the employee.

Selection for redundancy

162. For the purposes of Part X of the Employment Rights Act 1996 (unfair dismissal) the dismissal of an employee shall be regarded as unfair if the reason or principal reason for the dismissal was that he was redundant but it is shown—

(a) that the circumstances constituting the redundancy applied equally to one or more other employees in the same undertaking who held positions similar to that held by him and who have not been dismissed by the employer, and

(b) that the reason (or, if more than one, the principal reason) why he was selected for dismissal was one falling within paragraph 161(2).

163. [repealed]

Exclusion of requirement as to qualifying period

164. Sections 108 and 109 of the Employment Rights Act 1996 (qualifying period and upper age limit for unfair dismissal protection) do not apply to a dismissal which by virtue of paragraph 161 or 162 is regarded as unfair for the purposes of Part X of that Act.

Meaning of worker's contract

165. References in this Part of this Schedule to a worker's contract are to the contract mentioned in paragraph (a) or (b) of section 296(1) or the arrangements for the employment mentioned in paragraph (c) of section 296(1).

PART IX   GENERAL

165A.–170. [omitted]

Supply of information to CAC

170A.—(1) The CAC may, if it considers it necessary to do so to enable or assist it to exercise any of its functions under this Schedule, exercise any or all of the powers conferred in sub-paragraphs (2) to (4).

(2) The CAC may require an employer to supply the CAC case manager, within such period as the CAC may specify, with specified information concerning either or both of the following—

(a) the workers in a specified bargaining unit who work for the employer;

(b) the likelihood of a majority of those workers being in favour of the conduct by a specified union (or specified unions) of collective bargaining on their behalf.

(3) The CAC may require a union to supply the CAC case manager, within such period as the CAC may specify, with specified information concerning either or both of the following—

(a) the workers in a specified bargaining unit who are members of the union;

(b) the likelihood of a majority of the workers in a specified bargaining unit being in favour of the conduct by the union (or by it and other specified unions) of collective bargaining on their behalf.

(4) The CAC may require an applicant worker to supply the CAC case manager, within such period as the CAC may specify, with specified information concerning the likelihood of a majority of the workers in his bargaining unit being in favour of having bargaining arrangements ended.

(5) The recipient of a requirement under this paragraph must, within the specified period, supply the CAC case manager with such of the specified information as is in the recipient's possession.

(6) From the information supplied to him under this paragraph, the CAC case manager must prepare a report and submit it to the CAC.

(7) If an employer, a union or a worker fails to comply with sub-paragraph (5), the report under sub-paragraph (6) must mention that failure; and the CAC may draw an inference against the party concerned.

(8) The CAC must give a copy of the report under sub-paragraph (6) to the employer, to the union (or unions) and, in the case of an application under paragraph 112 or 137, to the applicant worker (or applicant workers).

(9) In this paragraph—

'applicant worker' means a worker who—

(a) falls within a bargaining unit ('his bargaining unit') and

(b) has made an application under paragraph 112 or 137 to have bargaining arrangements ended;

'the CAC case manager' means the member of the staff provided to the CAC by ACAS who is named in the requirement (but the CAC may, by notice given to the recipient of a requirement under this paragraph, change the member of that staff who is to be the CAC case manager for the purposes of that requirement);

'collective bargaining' is to be construed in accordance with paragraph 3; and

'specified' means specified in a requirement under this paragraph.

CAC's general duty

171. In exercising functions under this Schedule in any particular case the CAC must have regard to the object of encouraging and promoting fair and efficient practices and arrangements in the workplace, so far as having regard to that object is consistent with applying other provisions of this Schedule in the case concerned.

'Pay' and other matters subject to collective bargaining

171A.—(1) In this Schedule 'pay' does not include terms relating to a person's membership of or rights under, or his employer's contributions to—
    (a) an occupational pension scheme (as defined by section 1 of the Pension Schemes Act 1993), or
    (b) a personal pension scheme (as so defined).
  (2)–(7) [omitted]
  172. [omitted]

Disability Discrimination Act 1995
(1995, c. 50)

PART I   DISABILITY

PART II   THE EMPLOYMENT FIELD

Meaning of 'discrimination' and 'harassment'

Employment

Trade and professional bodies

Other unlawful acts

Enforcement etc.

Supplementary and general

PART I   DISABILITY

1   Meaning of 'disability' and 'disabled person'
   (1) Subject to the provisions of Schedule 1, a person has a disability for the purposes of this Act if he has a physical or mental impairment which has a substantial and long-term adverse effect on his ability to carry out normal day-to-day activities.
   (2) In this Act 'disabled person' means a person who has a disability.

2   Past disabilities
   (1) The provisions of this Part and Parts 2 to 4 and 5A apply in relation to a person who has had a disability as they apply in relation to a person who has that disability.
   (2) Those provisions are subject to the modifications made by Schedule 2.
   (3) Any regulations or order made under this Act by the Secretary of State, the Scottish Ministers or the National Assembly for Wales may include provision with respect to persons who have had a disability.
   (4) In any proceedings under Part 2, 3, 4 or 5A of this Act, the question whether a person had a disability at a particular time ('the relevant time') shall be determined, for the purposes of this section, as if the provisions of, or made under, this Act in force when the act complained of was done had been in force at the relevant time.
   (5) The relevant time may be a time before the passing of this Act.

3   [omitted]

PART II   THE EMPLOYMENT FIELD AND MEMBERS
OF LOCALLY-ELECTABLE AUTHORITIES

3A   Meaning of 'discrimination'
   (1) For the purposes of this Part, a person discriminates against a disabled person if—
      (a) for a reason which relates to the disabled person's disability, he treats him less favourably than he treats or would treat others to whom that reason does not or would not apply, and
      (b) he cannot show that the treatment in question is justified.

(2) For the purposes of this Part, a person also discriminates against a disabled person if he fails to comply with a duty to make reasonable adjustments imposed on him in relation to the disabled person.

(3) Treatment is justified for the purposes of subsection (1)(b) if, but only if, the reason for it is both material to the circumstances of the particular case and substantial.

(4) But treatment of a disabled person cannot be justified under subsection (3) if it amounts to direct discrimination falling within subsection (5).

(5) A person directly discriminates against a disabled person if, on the ground of the disabled person's disability, he treats the disabled person less favourably than he treats or would treat a person not having that particular disability whose relevant circumstances, including his abilities, are the same as, or not materially different from, those of the disabled person.

(6) If, in a case falling within subsection (1), a person is under a duty to make reasonable adjustments in relation to a disabled person but fails to comply with that duty, his treatment of that person cannot be justified under subsection (3) unless it would have been justified even if he had complied with that duty.

3B Meaning of 'harassment'

(1) For the purposes of this Part, a person subjects a disabled person to harassment where, for a reason which relates to the disabled person's disability, he engages in unwanted conduct which has the purpose or effect of—

(a) violating the disabled person's dignity, or

(b) creating an intimidating, hostile, degrading, humiliating or offensive environment for him.

(2) Conduct shall be regarded as having the effect referred to in paragraph (a) or (b) of subsection (1) only if, having regard to all the circumstances, including in particular the perception of the disabled person, it should reasonably be considered as having that effect.

Employment

4 Employers: discrimination and harassment

(1) It is unlawful for an employer to discriminate against a disabled person—

(a) in the arrangements which he makes for the purpose of determining to whom he should offer employment;

(b) in the terms on which he offers that person employment; or

(c) by refusing to offer, or deliberately not offering, him employment.

(2) It is unlawful for an employer to discriminate against a disabled person whom he employs—

(a) in the terms of employment which he affords him;

(b) in the opportunities which he affords him for promotion, a transfer, training or receiving any other benefit;

(c) by refusing to afford him, or deliberately not affording him, any such opportunity; or

(d) by dismissing him, or subjecting him to any other detriment.

(3) It is also unlawful for an employer, in relation to employment by him, to subject to harassment—

(a) a disabled person whom he employs; or

(b) a disabled person who has applied to him for employment.

(4) Subsection (2) does not apply to benefits of any description if the employer is concerned with the provision (whether or not for payment) of benefits of that description to the public, or to a section of the public which includes the employee in question, unless—

(a) that provision differs in a material respect from the provision of the benefits by the employer to his employees;

(b) the provision of the benefits to the employee in question is regulated by his contract of employment; or

(c) the benefits relate to training.

(5) The reference in subsection (2)(d) to the dismissal of a person includes a reference—

(a) to the termination of that person's employment by the expiration of any period (including a period expiring by reference to an event or circumstance), not being a termination immediately after which the employment is renewed on the same terms; and

(b) to the termination of that person's employment by any act of his (including the giving of notice) in circumstances such that he is entitled to terminate it without notice by reason of the conduct of the employer.

(6) This section applies only in relation to employment at an establishment in Great Britain.

4A   Employers: duty to make adjustments

(1) Where—

(a) a provision, criterion or practice applied by or on behalf of an employer, or

(b) any physical feature of premises occupied by the employer,

places the disabled person concerned at a substantial disadvantage in comparison with persons who are not disabled, it is the duty of the employer to take such steps as it is reasonable, in all the circumstances of the case, for him to have to take in order to prevent the provision, criterion or practice, or feature, having that effect.

(2) In subsection (1), 'the disabled person concerned' means—

(a) in the case of a provision, criterion or practice for determining to whom employment should be offered, any disabled person who is, or has notified the employer that he may be, an applicant for that employment;

(b) in any other case, a disabled person who is—

(i)   an applicant for the employment concerned, or

(ii)   an employee of the employer concerned.

(3) Nothing in this section imposes any duty on an employer in relation to a disabled person if the employer does not know, and could not reasonably be expected to know—

(a) in the case of an applicant or potential applicant, that the disabled person concerned is, or may be, an applicant for the employment; or

(b) in any case, that that person has a disability and is likely to be affected in the way mentioned in subsection (1).

Contract workers

4B   Contract workers

(1) It is unlawful for a principal, in relation to contract work, to discriminate against a disabled person who is a contract worker (a 'disabled contract worker')—

(a) in the terms on which he allows him to do that work;

(b) by not allowing him to do it or continue to do it;

(c) in the way he affords him access to any benefits or by refusing or deliberately omitting to afford him access to them; or

(d) by subjecting him to any other detriment.

(2) It is also unlawful for a principal, in relation to contract work, to subject a disabled contract worker to harassment.

(3) Subsection (1) does not apply to benefits of any description if the principal is concerned with the provision (whether or not for payment) of benefits of that description to the public, or to a section of the public that provision differs in a material respect from the provision of the benefits by the principal to contract workers.

(4) This subsection applies to a disabled contract worker where, by virtue of—

    (a) a provision, criterion or practice applied by or on behalf of all or most of the principals to whom he is or might be supplied, or

    (b) a physical feature of premises occupied by such persons,

he is likely, on each occasion when he is supplied to a principal to do contract work, to be placed at a substantial disadvantage in comparison with persons who are not disabled which is the same or similar in each case.

(5) Where subsection (4) applies to a disabled contract worker, his employer must take such steps as he would have to take under section 4A if the provision, criterion or practice were applied by him or on his behalf or (as the case may be) if the premises were occupied by him.

(6) Section 4A applies to any principal, in relation to contract work, as if he were, or would be, the employer of the disabled contract worker and as if any contract worker supplied to do work for him were an employee of his.

(7) However, for the purposes of section 4A as applied by subsection (6), a principal is not required to take a step in relation to a disabled contract worker if under that section the disabled contract worker's employer is required to take the step in relation to him.

(8) This section applies only in relation to contract work done at an establishment in Great Britain (the provisions of section 68 about the meaning of 'employment at an establishment in Great Britain' applying for the purposes of this subsection with the appropriate modifications).

(9) In this section—

'principal' means a person ('A') who makes work available for doing by individuals who are employed by another person who supplies them under a contract made with A;

'contract work' means work so made available; and

'contract worker' means any individual who is supplied to the principal under such a contract.

4C–4K [omitted]; **5–6** [repealed]; **6A–6C** [omitted]; **7** [repealed]; **7A–7D** [omitted]; **8** [became s. 17A]; **9** [repealed]; **10** [became s. 18C]; **11–12** [repealed]

Trade and professional bodies

13 Trade organisations: discrimination and harassment

    (1) It is unlawful for a trade organisation to discriminate against a disabled person—

        (a) in the arrangements which it makes for the purpose of determining who should be offered membership of the organisation;

        (b) in the terms on which it is prepared to admit him to membership of the organisation; or

        (c) by refusing to accept, or deliberately not accepting, his application for membership.

(2) It is unlawful for a trade organisation, in the case of a disabled person who is a member of the organisation, to discriminate against him—

        (a) in the way it affords him access to any benefits or by refusing or deliberately omitting to afford him access to them;

        (b) by depriving him of membership, or varying the terms on which he is a member; or

        (c) by subjecting him to any other detriment.

(3) It is also unlawful for a trade organisation, in relation to membership of that organisation, to subject to harassment a disabled person who–

        (a) is a member of the organisation; or

        (b) has applied for membership of the organisation.

(4) In this section and section 14 'trade organisation' means–

        (a) an organisation of workers;

        (b) an organisation of employers; or

(c) any other organisation whose members carry on a particular profession or trade for the purposes of which the organisation exists.

14   Trade organisations: duty to make adjustments

(1) Where—
(a) a provision, criterion or practice applied by or on behalf of a trade organisation, or
(b) any physical feature of premises occupied by the organisation,

places the disabled person concerned at a substantial disadvantage in comparison with persons who are not disabled, it is the duty of the organisation to take such steps as it is reasonable, in all the circumstances of the case, for it to have to take in order to prevent the provision, criterion or practice, or feature, having that effect.

(2) In this section 'the disabled person concerned' means—
(a) in the case of a provision, criterion or practice for determining to whom membership should be offered, any disabled person who is, or has notified the organisation that he may be, an applicant for membership;
(b) in any other case, a disabled person who is—
(i)   a member of the organisation, or
(ii) an applicant for membership of the organisation.

(3) Nothing in this section imposes any duty on an organisation in relation to a disabled person if the organisation does not know, and could not reasonably be expected to know—
(a) in the case of an applicant or potential applicant, that the disabled person concerned is, or may be, an applicant for membership of the organisation; or
(b) in any case, that that person has a disability and is likely to be affected in the way mentioned in subsection (1).

14A–16   [omitted]

Other unlawful acts

16A   Relationships which have come to an end

(1) This section applies where—
(a) there has been a relevant relationship between a disabled person and another person ('the relevant person'); and
(b) the relationship has come to an end.

(2) In this section a 'relevant relationship' is—
(a) a relationship during the course of which an act of discrimination against, or harassment of, one party to the relationship by the other party to it is unlawful under any preceding provision of this Part, other than sections 15B and 15C; or
(b) a relationship between a person providing employment services and a person receiving such services.

(3) It is unlawful for the relevant person—
(a) to discriminate against the disabled person by subjecting him to a detriment, or
(b) to subject the disabled person to harassment,

where the discrimination or harassment arises out of and is closely connected to the relevant relationship.

(4) This subsection applies where—
(a) a provision, criterion or practice applied by the relevant person to the disabled person in relation to any matter arising out of the relevant relationship, or
(b) a physical feature of premises which are occupied by the relevant person,

places the disabled person at a substantial disadvantage in comparison with persons who are not disabled, but are in the same position as the disabled person in relation to the relevant person.

(5) Where subsection (4) applies, it is the duty of the relevant person to take such steps as it is reasonable, in all the circumstances of the case, for him to have to take in order to prevent the provision, practice or criterion, or feature, having that effect.

(6) Nothing in subsection (5) imposes any duty on the relevant person if he does not know, and could not reasonably be expected to know, that the disabled person has a disability and is likely to be affected in the way mentioned in that subsection.

(7) In subsection (2), reference to an act of discrimination or harassment which is unlawful includes, in the case of a relationship which has come to an end before the commencement of this section, reference to such an act which would, after the commencement of this section, be unlawful.

16B   Discriminatory advertisements

(1) It is unlawful for a person to publish or cause to be published an advertisement which—

   (a) invites applications for a relevant appointment or benefit; and
   (b) indicates, or might reasonably be understood to indicate, that an application will or may be determined to any extent by reference to—
       (i)   the applicant not having any disability, or any particular disability,
       (ii) the applicant not having had any disability, or any particular disability, or
       (iii) any reluctance of the person determining the application to comply with a duty to make reasonable adjustments or (in relation to employment services) with the duty imposed by section 21(1) as modified by section 21A(6).

(2) Subsection (1) does not apply where it would not in fact be unlawful under this Part or, to the extent that it relates to the provision of employment services, Part 3 for an application to be determined in the manner indicated (or understood to be indicated) in the advertisement.

(2A) A person who publishes an advertisement of the kind described in subsection (1) shall not be subject to any liability under subsection (1) in respect of the publication of the advertisement if he proves—

   (a) that the advertisement was published in reliance on a statement made to him by the person who caused it to be published to the effect that, by reason of the operation of subsection (2), the publication would not be unlawful; and
   (b) that it was reasonable for him to rely on the statement.

(2B) A person who knowingly or recklessly makes a statement such as is mentioned in subsection (2A)(a) which in a material respect is false or misleading commits an offence, and shall be liable on summary conviction to a fine not exceeding level 5 on the standard scale.

(2C) Subsection (1) does not apply in relation to an advertisement so far as it invites persons to apply, in their capacity as members of an authority to which sections 15B and 15C apply, for a relevant appointment or benefit which the authority is intending to make or confer.

(3) In this section, 'relevant appointment or benefit' means—

   (a) any employment, promotion or transfer of employment;
   (b) membership of, or a benefit under, an occupational pension scheme;
   (c) an appointment to any office or post to which section 4D applies;
   (d) any partnership in a firm (within the meaning of section 6A);
   (e) any tenancy or pupillage (within the meaning of section 7A or 7C);
   (f) any membership of a trade organisation (within the meaning of section 13);
   (g) any professional or trade qualification (within the meaning of section 14A);
   (h) any work placement (within the meaning of section 14C);
   (i) any employment services.

(4) In this section, 'advertisement' includes every form of advertisement or notice, whether to the public or not.

(5) Proceedings in respect of a contravention of subsection (1) may be brought only—

   (a) by the Commission for Equality and Human Rights, and
   (b) in accordance with section 25 of the Equality Act 2006.

16C   Instructions and pressure to discriminate

(1) It is unlawful for a person—

(a) who has authority over another person, or

(b) in accordance with whose wishes that other person is accustomed to act, to instruct him to do any act which is unlawful under this Part or, to the extent that it relates to the provision of employment services, Part 3, or to procure or attempt to procure the doing by him of any such act.

(2) It is also unlawful to induce, or attempt to induce, a person to do any act which contravenes this Part or, to the extent that it relates to the provision of employment services, Part 3 by—

(a) providing or offering to provide him with any benefit, or

(b) subjecting or threatening to subject him to any detriment.

(3) An attempted inducement is not prevented from falling within subsection (2) because it is not made directly to the person in question, if it is made in such a way that he is likely to hear of it.

(4) Proceedings in respect of a contravention of this section may be brought only—

(a) by the Commission for Equality and Human Rights, and

(b) in accordance with section 25 of the Equality Act 2006.

17   [repealed]

Enforcement etc.

17A   Enforcement, remedies and procedure

(1) A complaint by any person that another person—

(a) has discriminated against him or subjected him to harassment in a way which is unlawful under this Part, or

(b) is, by virtue of section 57 or 58, to be treated as having done so in such a way, may be presented to an employment tribunal.

(1A) Subsection (1) does not apply to a complaint under section 14A(1) or (2) of an act in respect of which an appeal, or proceedings in the nature of an appeal, may be brought under any enactment.

(1B) [repealed]

(1C) Where, on the hearing of a complaint under subsection (1), the complainant proves facts from which the tribunal could, apart from this subsection, conclude in the absence of an adequate explanation that the respondent has acted in a way which is unlawful under this Part, the tribunal shall uphold the complaint unless the respondent proves that he did not so act.

(2) Where an employment tribunal finds that a complaint presented to it under this section is well-founded, it shall take such of the following steps as it considers just and equitable—

(a) making a declaration as to the rights of the complainant and the respondent in relation to the matters to which the complaint relates;

(b) ordering the respondent to pay compensation to the complainant;

(c) recommending that the respondent take, within a specified period, action appearing to the tribunal to be reasonable, in all the circumstances of the case, for the purpose of obviating or reducing the adverse effect on the complainant of any matter to which the complaint relates.

(3) Where a tribunal orders compensation under subsection (2)(b), the amount of the compensation shall be calculated by applying the principles applicable to the calculation of damages in claims in tort or (in Scotland) in reparation for breach of statutory duty.

(4) For the avoidance of doubt it is hereby declared that compensation in respect of discrimination in a way which is unlawful under this Part may include compensation for injury to feelings whether or not it includes compensation under any other head.

(5) If the respondent to a complaint fails, without reasonable justification, to comply with a recommendation made by an employment tribunal under subsection (2)(c) the tribunal may, if it thinks it just and equitable to do so—

    (a) increase the amount of compensation required to be paid to the complainant in respect of the complaint, where an order was made under subsection (2)(b); or

    (b) make an order under subsection (2)(b).

  (6)–(8) [omitted]

17B   [repealed]; 17C [omitted]

Supplementary and general

18   [repealed]; 18A [omitted]

18B   Reasonable adjustments: supplementary

(1) In determining whether it is reasonable for a person to have to take a particular step in order to comply with a duty to make reasonable adjustments, regard shall be had, in particular, to—

    (a) the extent to which taking the step would prevent the effect in relation to which the duty is imposed;

    (b) the extent to which it is practicable for him to take the step;

    (c) the financial and other costs which would be incurred by him in taking the step and the extent to which taking it would disrupt any of his activities;

    (d) the extent of his financial and other resources;

    (e) the availability to him of financial or other assistance with respect to taking the step;

    (f) the nature of his activities and the size of his undertaking;

    (g) where the step would be taken in relation to a private household, the extent to which taking it would—

        (i) disrupt that household, or

        (ii) disturb any person residing there.

(2) The following are examples of steps which a person may need to take in relation to a disabled person in order to comply with a duty to make reasonable adjustments—

    (a) making adjustments to premises;

    (b) allocating some of the disabled person's duties to another person;

    (c) transferring him to fill an existing vacancy;

    (d) altering his hours of working or training;

    (e) assigning him to a different place of work or training;

    (f) allowing him to be absent during working or training hours for rehabilitation, assessment or treatment;

    (g) giving, or arranging for, training or mentoring (whether for the disabled person or any other person);

    (h) acquiring or modifying equipment;

    (i) modifying instructions or reference manuals;

    (j) modifying procedures for testing or assessment;

    (k) providing a reader or interpreter;

    (l) providing supervision or other support.

(3) For the purposes of a duty to make reasonable adjustments, where under any binding obligation a person is required to obtain the consent of another person to any alteration of the premises occupied by him—

    (a) it is always reasonable for him to have to take steps to obtain that consent; and

    (b) it is never reasonable for him to have to make that alteration before that consent is obtained.

(4) The steps referred to in subsection (3)(a) shall not be taken to include an application to a court or tribunal.

(5) In subsection (3), 'binding obligation' means a legally binding obligation (not contained in a lease (within the meaning of section 18A(3)) in relation to the premises, whether arising from an agreement or otherwise.

(6) A provision of this Part imposing a duty to make reasonable adjustments applies only for the purpose of determining whether a person has discriminated against a disabled person; and accordingly a breach of any such duty is not actionable as such.

18C   [omitted]

18D   Interpretation of Part 2

(1) Subject to any duty to make reasonable adjustments, nothing in this Part is to be taken to require a person to treat a disabled person more favourably than he treats or would treat others.

(2) In this Part—

'benefits', except in sections 4G to 4K, includes facilities and services;

'detriment', except in section 16C(2)(b), does not include conduct of the nature referred to in section 3B (harassment);

'discriminate', 'discrimination' and other related expressions are to be construed in accordance with section 3A;

'duty to make reasonable adjustments' means a duty imposed by or under section 4A, 4B(5) or (6), 4E, 4H, 6B, 7B, 7D, 14, 14B, 14D, 15C or 16A(5);

'employer' includes a person who has no employees but is seeking to employ another person;

'harassment' is to be construed in accordance with section 3B;

'physical feature', in relation to any premises, includes (subject to any provision under section 15(c)(4)(e)) any of the following (whether permanent or temporary)—

> (a) any feature arising from the design or construction of a building on the premises;
>
> (b) any feature on the premises of any approach to, exit from or access to such a building;
>
> (c) any fixtures, fittings, furnishings, furniture, equipment or material in or on the premises;
>
> (d) any other physical element or quality of any land comprised in the premises;

'provision, criterion or practice' includes any arrangements.

18E–54H   [omitted]

PART VII   SUPPLEMENTAL

55   Victimisation

(1) For the purposes of Part 2 or Part 4 or Part 3 other than sections 24A to 24L, a person ('A') discriminates against another person ('B') if—

> (a) he treats B less favourably than he treats or would treat other persons whose circumstances are the same as B's; and
>
> (b) he does so for a reason mentioned in subsection (2).

(2) The reasons are that—

> (a) B has—
>
> > (i)   brought proceedings against A or any other person under this Act; or
> >
> > (ii) given evidence or information in connection with such proceedings brought by any person; or
> >
> > (iii) otherwise done anything under or by reference to this Act in relation to A or any other person; or
> >
> > (iv) alleged that A or any other person has (whether or not the allegation so states) contravened this Act; or

(b) A believes or suspects that B has done or intends to do any of those things.

(3) Where B is a disabled person, or a person who has had a disability, the disability in question shall be disregarded in comparing his circumstances with those of any other person for the purposes of subsection (1)(a).

(3A) [omitted]

(4) Subsection (1) does not apply to treatment of a person because of an allegation made by him if the allegation was false and not made in good faith.

(5) In the case of an act which constitutes discrimination by virtue of this section, sections 4, 4B, 4D, 4G, 6A, 7A, 7C, 13, 14A, 14C, 15B and 16A also apply to discrimination against a person who is not disabled.

(6) [repealed]

56 [omitted]

57 Aiding unlawful acts

(1) A person who knowingly aids another person to do an unlawful act is to be treated for the purposes of this Act as himself doing the same kind of unlawful act.

(2) For the purposes of subsection (1), an employee or agent for whose act the employer or principal is liable under section 58 (or would be so liable but for section 58(5)) shall be taken to have aided the employer or principal to do the act.

(3) For the purposes of this section, a person does not knowingly aid another to do an unlawful act if—

(a) he acts in reliance on a statement made to him by that other person that, because of any provision of this Act, the act would not be unlawful; and

(b) it is reasonable for him to rely on the statement.

(4) A person who knowingly or recklessly makes such a statement which is false or misleading in a material respect is guilty of an offence.

(5) Any person guilty of an offence under subsection (4) shall be liable on summary conviction to a fine not exceeding level 5 on the standard scale.

(6) 'Unlawful act' means an act made unlawful by any provision of this Act other than a provision contained in Chapter 1 of Part IV.

58 Liability of employers and principals

(1) Anything done by a person in the course of his employment shall be treated for the purposes of this Act as also done by his employer, whether or not it was done with the employer's knowledge or approval.

(2) Anything done by a person as agent for another person with the authority of that other person shall be treated for the purposes of this Act as also done by that other person.

(3) Subsection (2) applies whether the authority was—

(a) express or implied; or

(b) given before or after the act in question was done.

(4) Subsections (1) and(2) do not apply in relation to an offence under section 57(4).

(5) In proceedings under this Act against any person in respect of an act alleged to have been done by an employee of his, it shall be a defence for that person to prove that he took such steps as were reasonably practicable to prevent the employee from—

(a) doing that act; or

(b) doing, in the course of his employment, acts of that description.

59 Statutory authority and national security etc.

(1) Nothing in this Act makes unlawful any act done—

(a) in pursuance of any enactment; or

(b) in pursuance of any instrument made under any enactment by—

(i)   a Minister of the Crown,

(ii) a member of the Scottish Executive, or

(iii) the National Assembly for Wales; or

(c) to comply with any condition or requirement—
    (i) imposed by a Minister of the Crown (whether before or after the passing of this Act) by virtue of any enactment,
    (ii) imposed by a member of the Scottish Executive (whether before or after the coming into force of this sub-paragraph) by virtue of any enactment, or
    (iii) imposed by the National Assembly for Wales (whether before or after the coming into force of this sub-paragraph) by virtue of any enactment.

(2) In subsection (1) 'enactment' includes one passed or made after the date on which this Act is passed and 'instrument' includes one made after that date.

(2A) Nothing in—
    (a) Part 2 of this Act, or
    (b) Part 3 of this Act to the extent that it relates to the provision of employment services,
makes unlawful any act done for the purpose of safeguarding national security if the doing of the act was justified by that purpose.

(3) Nothing in any other provision of this Act makes unlawful any act done for the purpose of safeguarding national security.

59A [omitted]

PART VIII   MISCELLANEOUS

60–65 [omitted]; **66** [repealed]; **67–67B** [omitted]

68 Interpretation
(1) In this Act—
... 'act' includes a deliberate omission;
    ...
'conciliation officer' means a person designated under section 211 of the Trade Union and Labour Relations (Consolidation) Act 1992;
'employment' means, subject to any prescribed provision, employment under a contract of service or of apprenticeship or a contract personally to do any work, and related expressions are to be construed accordingly;
'employment at an establishment in Great Britain' is to be construed in accordance with subsections (2) to (4A);
    ...
'mental impairment' does not have the same meaning as in the Mental Health Act 1983 but the fact that an impairment would be a mental impairment for the purposes of that Act does not prevent it from being a mental impairment for the purposes of this Act;
'Minister of the Crown' includes the Treasury and the Defence Council;
'occupational pension scheme' has the same meaning as in the Pension Schemes Act 1993;
'premises' includes land of any description;
'prescribed' means prescribed by regulations, except in section 28D (where it has the meaning given by section 28D(17));
'profession' includes any vocation or occupation;
    ...
(1A)–(1C) [omitted]
(2) Employment (including employment on board a ship to which subsection (2B) applies or on an aircraft or hovercraft to which subsection (2C) applies) is to be regarded as being employment at an establishment in Great Britain if the employee—
    (a) does his work wholly or partly in Great Britain; or
    (b) does his work wholly outside Great Britain and subsection (2A) applies.
(2A) This subsection applies if—
    (a) the employer has a place of business at an establishment in Great Britain;
    (b) the work is for the purposes of the business carried on at the establishment; and

(c) the employee is ordinarily resident in Great Britain—
    (i) at the time when he applies for or is offered the employment, or
    (ii) at any time during the course of the employment.
(2B)–(2D) [omitted]
(4) Employment of a prescribed kind, or in prescribed circumstances, is to be regarded as not being employment at an establishment in Great Britain.
(4A) [omitted]; (5) [repealed]

69–70 [omitted]

SCHEDULE 1 PROVISIONS SUPPLEMENTING SECTION 1

Impairment

1.—(1) [repealed]
(2) Regulations may make provision, for the purposes of this Act—
    (a) for conditions of a prescribed description to be treated as amounting to impairments;
    (b) for conditions of a prescribed description to be treated as not amounting to impairments.
(3) Regulations made under sub-paragraph (2) may make provision as to the meaning of 'condition' for the purposes of those regulations.

Long-term effects

2.—(1) The effect of an impairment is a long-term effect if—
    (a) it has lasted at least 12 months;
    (b) the period for which it lasts is likely to be at least 12 months; or
    (c) it is likely to last for the rest of the life of the person affected.
(2) Where an impairment ceases to have a substantial adverse effect on a person's ability to carry out normal day-to-day activities, it is to be treated as continuing to have that effect if that effect is likely to recur.
(3) For the purposes of sub-paragraph (2), the likelihood of an effect recurring shall be disregarded in prescribed circumstances.
(4) Regulations may prescribe circumstances in which, for the purposes of this Act—
    (a) an effect which would not otherwise be a long-term effect is to be treated as such an effect; or
    (b) an effect which would otherwise be a long-term effect is to be treated as not being such an effect.

Severe disfigurement

3.—(1) An impairment which consists of a severe disfigurement is to be treated as having a substantial adverse effect on the ability of the person concerned to carry out normal day-to-day activities.
(2) Regulations may provide that in prescribed circumstances a severe disfigurement is not to be treated as having that effect.
(3) Regulations under sub-paragraph (2) may, in particular, make provision with respect to deliberately acquired disfigurements.

Normal day-to-day activities

4.—(1) An impairment is to be taken to affect the ability of the person concerned to carry out normal day-to-day activities only if it affects one of the following—
    (a) mobility;

(b) manual dexterity;
(c) physical co-ordination;
(d) continence;
(e) ability to lift, carry or otherwise move everyday objects;
(f) speech, hearing or eyesight;
(g) memory or ability to concentrate, learn or understand; or
(h) perception of the risk of physical danger.
(2) Regulations may prescribe—
(a) circumstances in which an impairment which does not have an effect falling within sub-paragraph (1) is to be taken to affect the ability of the person concerned to carry out normal day-to-day activities;
(b) circumstances in which an impairment which has an effect falling within sub-paragraph (1) is to be taken not to affect the ability of the person concerned to carry out normal day-to-day activities.

Substantial adverse effects

5. Regulations may make provision for the purposes of this Act—
(a) for an effect of a prescribed kind on the ability of a person to carry out normal day-to-day activities to be treated as a substantial adverse effect;
(b) for an effect of a prescribed kind on the ability of a person to carry out normal day-to-day activities to be treated as not being a substantial adverse effect.

Effect of medical treatment

6.—(1) An impairment which would be likely to have a substantial adverse effect on the ability of the person concerned to carry out normal day-to-day activities, but for the fact that measures are being taken to treat or correct it, is to be treated as having that effect.
(2) In sub-paragraph (1) 'measures' includes, in particular, medical treatment and the use of a prosthesis or other aid.
(3) Sub-paragraph (1) does not apply—
(a) in relation to the impairment of a person's sight, to the extent that the impairment is, in his case, correctable by spectacles or contact lenses or in such other ways as may be prescribed; or
(b) in relation to such other impairments as may be prescribed, in such circumstances as may be prescribed.

Persons deemed to be disabled

6A.—(1) Subject to sub-paragraph (2), a person who has cancer, HIV infection or multiple sclerosis is to be deemed to have a disability, and hence to be a disabled person.
(2) Regulations may provide for sub-paragraph (1) not to apply in the case of a person who has cancer if he has cancer of a prescribed description.
(3) A description of cancer prescribed under sub-paragraph (2) may (in particular) be framed by reference to consequences for a person of his having it.
7.—(1) Sub-paragraph (2) applies to any person whose name is, both on 12th January 1995 and on the date when this paragraph comes into force, in the register of disabled persons maintained under section 6 of the Disabled Persons (Employment) Act 1944.
(2) That person is to be deemed—
(a) during the initial period, to have a disability, and hence to be a disabled person; and
(b) afterwards, to have had a disability and hence to have been a disabled person during that period.
(3) A certificate of registration shall be conclusive evidence, in relation to the person with respect to whom it was issued, of the matters certified.

(4) Unless the contrary is shown, any document purporting to be a certificate of registration shall be taken to be such a certificate and to have been validly issued.

(5) Regulations may provide for prescribed descriptions of person to be deemed to have disabilities, and hence to be disabled persons, for the purposes of this Act.

(5A) The generality of sub-paragraph (5) shall not be taken to be prejudiced by the other provisions of this Schedule.

(6) Regulations may prescribe circumstances in which a person who has been deemed to be a disabled person by the provisions of sub-paragraph (1) or regulations made under sub-paragraph (5) is to be treated as no longer being deemed to be such a person.

(7) In this paragraph—

'certificate of registration' means a certificate issued under regulations made under section 6 of the Act of 1944; and

'initial period' means the period of three years beginning with the date on which this paragraph comes into force.

Progressive conditions

8.—(1) Where—
- (a) a person has a progressive condition (such as cancer, multiple sclerosis or muscular dystrophy or HIV infection),
- (b) as a result of that condition, he has an impairment which has (or had) an effect on his ability to carry out normal day-to-day activities, but
- (c) that effect is not (or was not) a substantial adverse effect,

he shall be taken to have an impairment which has such a substantial adverse effect if the condition is likely to result in his having such an impairment.

(2) Regulations may make provision, for the purposes of this paragraph—
- (a) for conditions of a prescribed description to be treated as being progressive;
- (b) for conditions of a prescribed description to be treated as not being progressive.

Interpretation

9.—In this Schedule 'HIV infection' means infection by a virus capable of causing the Acquired Immune Deficiency Syndrome.

SCHEDULE 2   PAST DISABILITIES

1. The modifications referred to in section 2 are as follows.

2. References in Parts II to 4 and 5A to a disabled person are to be read as references to a person who has had a disability.

2A–2C [omitted]

3. In sections 4A(1), 4B(4), 4E(1), 4H(1), 6B(1), 7B(1), 7D(1), 14(1), 14B(1), 14D(1), 15C(1) and 16A(4), section 21A(4)(a) (in the words to be read as section 19(1)(aa)) and section 21A(6)(a) (in the words to be substituted in section 21(1)) and section 31AD(1)(d), (2)(c) and 3, after 'not disabled' (in each place it occurs) insert 'and who have not had a disability'.

4. In sections 4A(3)(b), 4E(3)(b), 4H(3)(b), 6B(3)(b), 7B(4)(b), 7D(3)(b), 14(3)(b), 14B(3)(b), 15C(3)(a), 14D(3)(b), 16A(6) and 31AD(4)(b), for 'has' (in each place it occurs) substitute 'has had'.

4ZA, 4ZB and 4A to 4E [omitted]

5. For paragraph 2(1) to (3) of Schedule 1, substitute—

'(1) The effect of an impairment is a long-term effect if it has lasted for at least 12 months.

(2) Where an impairment ceases to have a substantial adverse effect on a person's ability to carry out normal day-to-day activities, it is to be treated as continuing to have that effect if that effect recurs.

(3) For the purposes of sub-paragraph (2), the recurrence of an effect shall be disregarded in prescribed circumstances.'

SCHEDULE 3   ENFORCEMENT AND PROCEDURE

PART I   EMPLOYMENT

1. [repealed]

Restriction on proceedings for breach of Part II

2.—(1) Except as provided by Part 2, no civil or criminal proceedings may be brought against any person in respect of an act merely because the act is unlawful under that Part.

(2) Sub-paragraph (1) does not prevent the making of an application for judicial review or the investigation or determination of any matter in accordance with Part 10 (investigations) of the Pension Schemes Act 1993 by the Pensions Ombudsman.

(3) Sub-paragraph 1 does not prevent the bringing of proceedings in respect of an offence under section 16B(2B).

Period within which proceedings must be brought

3.—(1) An employment tribunal shall not consider a complaint under section 8 unless it is presented before the end of the period of three months beginning when the act complained of was done.

(2) A tribunal may consider any such complaint which is out of time if, in all the circumstances of the case, it considers that it is just and equitable to do so.

(3) For the purposes of sub-paragraph (1)—

    (a) where an unlawful act is attributable to a term in a contract, that act is to be treated as extending throughout the duration of the contract;

    (b) any act extending over a period shall be treated as done at the end of that period; and

    (c) a deliberate omission shall be treated as done when the person in question decided upon it.

(4) In the absence of evidence establishing the contrary, a person shall be taken for the purposes of this paragraph to decide upon an omission—

    (a) when he does an act inconsistent with doing the omitted act; or

    (b) if he has done no such inconsistent act, when the period expires within which he might reasonably have been expected to do the omitted act if it was to be done.

4.–15. [omitted]

SCHEDULE 3A

SECTION 17C   VALIDITY OF CONTRACTS, COLLECTIVE AGREEMENTS AND RULES OF UNDERTAKINGS

PART 1   VALIDITY AND REVISION OF CONTRACTS

1.—(1) A term of a contract is void where—

    (a) the making of the contract is, by reason of the inclusion of the term, unlawful by virtue of this Part of this Act;

    (b) it is included in furtherance of an act which is unlawful by virtue of this Part of this Act; or

    (c) it provides for the doing of an act which is unlawful by virtue of this Part of this Act.

(2) Sub-paragraph (1) does not apply to a term the inclusion of which constitutes, or is in furtherance of, or provides for, unlawful discrimination against, or harassment of, a party to the contract, but the term shall be unenforceable against that party.

(3) A term in a contract which purports to exclude or limit any provision of this Part of this Act is unenforceable by any person in whose favour the term would operate apart from this paragraph.

(4) Sub-paragraphs (1), (2) and (3) apply whether the contract was entered into before or after the date on which this Schedule comes into force; but in the case of a contract made before that date, those sub-paragraphs do not apply in relation to any period before that date.

2.—(1) Paragraph 1(3) does not apply—

(a) to a contract settling a complaint to which section 17A(1) or 25(8) applies where the contract is made with the assistance of a conciliation officer (within the meaning of the Trade Union and Labour Relations (Consolidation) Act 1992; or

(b) to a contract settling a complaint to which section 17A(1) or 25(8) applies if the conditions regulating compromise contracts under this Schedule are satisfied in relation to the contract.

(2) The conditions regulating compromise contracts under this Schedule are that—

(a) the contract must be in writing;

(b) the contract must relate to the particular complaint;

(c) the complainant must have received advice from a relevant independent adviser as to the terms and effect of the proposed contract and in particular its effect on his ability to pursue a complaint before an employment tribunal;

(d) there must be in force, when the adviser gives the advice, a contract of insurance, or an indemnity provided for members of a profession or professional body, covering the risk of a claim by the complainant in respect of loss arising in consequence of the advice;

(e) the contract must identify the adviser; and

(f) the contract must state that the conditions regulating compromise contracts under this Schedule are satisfied.

(3)–(8) [omitted]

3.—(1) On the application of a disabled person interested in a contract to which paragraph 1 (1) or (2) applies, a county court or a sheriff court may make such order as it thinks fit for—

(a) removing or modifying any term rendered void by paragraph 1(1), or

(b) removing or modifying any term made unenforceable by paragraph 1(2),

but such an order shall not be made unless all persons affected have been given notice in writing of the application (except where under rules of court notice may be dispensed with) and have been afforded an opportunity to make representations to the court.

(2) An order under sub-paragraph (1) may include provision as respects any period before the making of the order (but after the coming into force of this Schedule).

PART 2 COLLECTIVE AGREEMENTS AND RULES OF UNDERTAKINGS

4.—(1) This Part of this Schedule applies to—

(a) any term of a collective agreement, including an agreement which was not intended, or is presumed not to have been intended, to be a legally enforceable contract;

(b) any rule made by an employer for application to all or any of the persons who are employed by him or who apply to be, or are, considered by him for employment;

(c) any rule made by a trade organisation (within the meaning of section 13) or a qualifications body (within the meaning of section 14A) for application to—
 (i) all or any of its members or prospective members; or
 (ii) all or any of the persons on whom it has conferred authorisations or qualifications or who are seeking the authorisations or qualifications which it has power to confer.

(2) Any term or rule to which this Part of this Schedule applies is void where—
 (a) the making of the collective agreement is, by reason of the inclusion of the term, unlawful by virtue of this Part of this Act;
 (b) the term or rule is included in furtherance of an act which is unlawful by virtue of this Part of this Act; or
 (c) the term or rule provides for the doing of an act which is unlawful by virtue of this Part of this Act.

(3) Sub-paragraph (2) applies whether the agreement was entered into, or the rule made, before or after the date on which this Schedule comes into force; but in the case of an agreement entered into, or a rule made, before the date on which this Schedule comes into force, that sub-paragraph does not apply in relation to any period before that date.

5. A disabled person to whom this paragraph applies may present a complaint to an employment tribunal that a term or rule is void by virtue of paragraph 4 if he has reason to believe—
 (a) that the term or rule may at some future time have effect in relation to him; and
 (b) where he alleges that it is void by virtue of paragraph 4(2)(c), that—
  (i) an act for the doing of which it provides, may at some such time be done in relation to him, and
  (ii) the act would be unlawful by virtue of this Part of this Act if done in relation to him in present circumstances.

6. In the case of a complaint about—
 (a) a term of a collective agreement made by or on behalf of—
  (i) an employer,
  (ii) an organisation of employers of which an employer is a member, or
  (iii) an association of such organisations of one of which an employer is a member, or
 (b) a rule made by an employer within the meaning of paragraph 4(1)(b),
paragraph 5 applies to any disabled person who is, or is genuinely and actively seeking to become, one of his employees.

7. In the case of a complaint about a rule made by an organisation, authority or body to which paragraph 4(1)(c) applies, paragraph 5 applies to any disabled person—
 (a) who is, or is genuinely and actively seeking to become, a member of the organisation or body;
 (b) on whom the organisation or body has conferred an authorisation or qualification; or
 (c) who is genuinely and actively seeking an authorisation or qualification which the organisation, authority or body has power to confer.

8.—(1) When an employment tribunal finds that a complaint presented to it under paragraph 5 is well-founded the tribunal shall make an order declaring that the term or rule is void.

(2) An order under sub-paragraph (1) may include provision as respects any period before the making of the order (but after the coming into force of this Schedule).

9. The avoidance by virtue of paragraph 4 (2) of any term or rule which provides for any person to be discriminated against shall be without prejudice to the following rights (except in so far as they enable any person to require another person to be treated less favourably than himself), namely—
 (a) such of the rights of the person to be discriminated against, and
 (b) such of the rights of any person who will be treated more favourably in direct or indirect consequence of the discrimination,

as are conferred by or in respect of a contract made or modified wholly or partly in pursuance of, or by reference to, that term or rule.

PART 3   INTERPRETATION

10. In this Schedule 'collective agreement' means any agreement relating to one or more of the matters mentioned in section 178(2) of the Trade Union and Labour Relations (Consolidation) Act 1992 (meaning of trade dispute), being an agreement made by or on behalf of one or more employers or one or more organisations of employers or associations of such organisations with one or more organisations of workers or associations of such organisations.

11. Any reference in this Schedule to this Part of this Act shall be taken to include a reference to Part 3 of this Act, to the extent that it relates to—

    (a) the provision of employment services; or

    (b) the provision under a group insurance arrangement of facilities by way of insurance.

12. Where a term to which section 26(1A)(c) applies is a term in an agreement which is not a contract, Part 1 of this Schedule shall have effect as if the agreement were a contract.

Jobseekers Act 1995
(1995, c. 18)

Trade disputes

14   Trade disputes

(1) Where—

    (a) there is a stoppage of work which causes a person not to be employed on any day, and

    (b) the stoppage is due to a trade dispute at his place of work,

that person is not entitled to a jobseeker's allowance for the week which includes that day unless he proves that he is not directly interested in the dispute.

(2) A person who withdraws his labour on any day in furtherance of a trade dispute, but to whom subsection (1) does not apply, is not entitled to a jobseeker's allowance for the week which includes that day.

(3) If a person who is prevented by subsection (1) from being entitled to a jobseeker's allowance proves that during the stoppage—

    (a) he became bona fide employed elsewhere,

    (b) his employment was terminated by reason of redundancy within the meaning of section 139(1) of the Employment Rights Act 1996, or

    (c) he bona fide resumed employment with his employer but subsequently left for a reason other than the trade dispute,

subsection (1) shall be taken to have ceased to apply to him on the occurrence of the event referred to in paragraph (a) or (b) or (as the case may be) the first event referred to in paragraph (c).

(4) In this section 'place of work', in relation to any person, means the premises or place at which he was employed.

(5) Where separate branches of work which are commonly carried on as separate businesses in separate premises or at separate places are in any case carried on in separate departments on the same premises or at the same place, each of those departments shall, for the purposes of subsection (4), be deemed to be separate premises or (as the case may be) a separate place.

Denial of jobseeker's allowance

19   Circumstances in which a jobseeker's allowance is not payable

(1) Even though the conditions for entitlement to a jobseeker's allowance are satisfied with respect to a person, the allowance shall not be payable in any of the circumstances mentioned in subsection (5) or (6).

(1A) [omitted]

(2) If the circumstances are any of those mentioned in subsection (5), the period for which the allowance is not to be payable shall be such period (of at least one week but not more than 26 weeks) as may be prescribed.

(3) If the circumstances are any of those mentioned in subsection (6), the period for which the allowance is not to be payable shall be such period (of at least one week but not more than 26 weeks) as may be determined by the Secretary of State.

(4) Regulations may prescribe—

   (a) circumstances which the Secretary of State is to take into account, and

   (b) circumstances which he is not to take into account,

in determining a period under subsection (3).

(5) The circumstances referred to in subsections (1) and (2) are that the claimant—

   (a) has, without good cause, refused or failed to carry out any jobseeker's direction which was reasonable, having regard to his circumstances;

   (b) has, without good cause

     (i) neglected to avail himself of a reasonable opportunity of a place on a training scheme or employment programme;

     (ii) after a place on such a scheme or programme has been notified to him by an employment officer as vacant or about to become vacant, refused or failed to apply for it or to accept it when offered to him;

     (iii) given up a place on such a scheme or programme; or

     (iv) failed to attend such a scheme or programme on which he has been given a place; or

   (c) has lost his place on such a scheme or programme through misconduct.

(6) The circumstances referred to in subsections (1) and (3) are that the claimant—

   (a) has lost his employment as an employed earner through misconduct;

   (b) has voluntarily left such employment without just cause;

   (c) has, without good cause, after a situation in any employment has been notified to him by an employment officer as vacant or about to become vacant, refused or failed to apply for it or to accept it when offered to him; or

   (d) has, without good cause, neglected to avail himself of a reasonable opportunity of employment.

(7) In such circumstances as may be prescribed, including in particular where he has been dismissed by his employer by reason of redundancy within the meaning of section 139(1) of the Employment Rights Act 1996 after volunteering or agreeing to be so dismissed, a person who might otherwise be regarded as having left his employment voluntarily is to be treated as not having left voluntarily.

(8)–(10) [omitted]

20   Exemptions from section 19

(1) Nothing in section 19, or in regulations under that section, shall be taken to prevent payment of a jobseeker's allowance merely because the claimant refuses to seek or accept employment in a situation which is vacant in consequence of a stoppage of work due to a trade dispute.

(2)–(8) [omitted]

35   Interpretation

(1) In this Act—

   . . .

'trade dispute' means any dispute between employers and employees, or between employees and employees, which is connected with the employment or non-employment or the terms of employment or the conditions of employment of any persons, whether employees in the employment of the employer with whom the dispute arises, or not;

Employment Rights Act 1996
(1996, c. 18)

PART I   EMPLOYMENT PARTICULARS

Right to statements of employment particulars

Right to itemised pay statement

Enforcement

PART II   PROTECTION OF WAGES

Deductions by employer

Payments to employer

Cash shortages and stock deficiencies in retail employment

PART IX   TERMINATION OF EMPLOYMENT

PART X   UNFAIR DISMISSAL

CHAPTER I   RIGHT NOT TO BE UNFAIRLY DISMISSED

PART XII   INSOLVENCY OF EMPLOYERS

PART XIII   MISCELLANEOUS

CHAPTER I   PARTICULAR TYPES OF EMPLOYMENT

Crown employment etc.

Excluded classes of employment

CHAPTER II   OTHER MISCELLANEOUS MATTERS

Restrictions on disclosure of information

Contracting out etc. and remedies

PART XIV   INTERPRETATION

CHAPTER I   CONTINUOUS EMPLOYMENT

CHAPTER II   A WEEK'S PAY

Introductory

Employments with normal working hours

PART I   EMPLOYMENT PARTICULARS

Right to statements of employment particulars

1   Statement of initial employment particulars

(1) Where an employee begins employment with an employer, the employer shall give to the employee a written statement of particulars of employment.

(2) The statement may (subject to section 2(4)) be given in instalments and (whether or not given in instalments) shall be given not later than two months after the beginning of the employment.

(3) The statement shall contain particulars of—

    (a) the names of the employer and employee,

    (b) the date when the employment began, and

    (c) the date on which the employee's period of continuous employment began (taking into account any employment with a previous employer which counts towards that period).

(4) The statement shall also contain particulars, as at a specified date not more than seven days before the statement (or the instalment containing them) is given, of—

    (a) the scale or rate of remuneration or the method of calculating remuneration,

    (b) the intervals at which remuneration is paid (that is, weekly, monthly or other specified intervals),

    (c) any terms and conditions relating to hours of work (including any terms and conditions relating to normal working hours),

    (d) any terms and conditions relating to any of the following—

        (i) entitlement to holidays, including public holidays, and holiday pay (the particulars given being sufficient to enable the employee's entitlement, including any entitlement to accrued holiday pay on the termination of employment, to be precisely calculated),

(ii)   incapacity for work due to sickness or injury, including any provision for sick pay, and

(iii) pensions and pension schemes,

(e) the length of notice which the employee is obliged to give and entitled to receive to terminate his contract of employment,

(f) the title of the job which the employee is employed to do or a brief description of the work for which he is employed,

(g) where the employment is not intended to be permanent, the period for which it is expected to continue or, if it is for a fixed term, the date when it is to end,

(h) either the place of work or, where the employee is required or permitted to work at various places, an indication of that and of the address of the employer,

(j) any collective agreements which directly affect the terms and conditions of the employment including, where the employer is not a party, the persons by whom they were made, and

(k) where the employee is required to work outside the United Kingdom for a period of more than one month—

(i)   the period for which he is to work outside the United Kingdom,

(ii)   the currency in which remuneration is to be paid while he is working outside the United Kingdom,

(iii) any additional remuneration payable to him, and any benefits to be provided to or in respect of him, by reason of his being required to work outside the United Kingdom, and

(iv) any terms and conditions relating to his return to the United Kingdom.

(5) Subsection (4)(d)(iii) does not apply to an employee of a body or authority if—

(a) the employee's pension rights depend on the terms of a pension scheme established under any provision contained in or having effect under any Act, and

(b) any such provision requires the body or authority to give to a new employee information concerning the employee's pension rights or the determination of questions affecting those rights.

2 Statement of initial particulars: supplementary

(1) If, in the case of a statement under section 1, there are no particulars to be entered under any of the heads of paragraph (d) or (k) of subsection (4) of that section, or under any of the other paragraphs of subsection (3) or (4) of that section, that fact shall be stated.

(2) A statement under section 1 may refer the employee for particulars of any of the matters specified in subsection (4)(d)(ii) and (iii) of that section to the provisions of some other document which is reasonably accessible to the employee.

(3) A statement under section 1 may refer the employee for particulars of either of the matters specified in subsection (4)(e) of that section to the law or to the provisions of any collective agreement directly affecting the terms and conditions of the employment which is reasonably accessible to the employee.

(4) The particulars required by section 1(3) and (4)(a) to (c), (d)(i), (f) and (h) shall be included in a single document.

(5) Where before the end of the period of two months after the beginning of an employee's employment the employee is to begin to work outside the United Kingdom for a period of more than one month, the statement under section 1 shall be given to him not later than the time when he leaves the United Kingdom in order to begin so to work.

(6) A statement shall be given to a person under section 1 even if his employment ends before the end of the period within which the statement is required to be given.

3 Note about disciplinary procedures and pensions

(1) A statement under section 1 shall include a note—

(a) specifying any disciplinary rules applicable to the employee or referring the employee to the provisions of a document specifying such rules which is reasonably accessible to the employee,

(aa) specifying any procedure applicable to the taking of disciplinary decisions relating to the employee, or to a decision to dismiss the employee, or referring the employee to the provisions of a document specifying such a procedure which is reasonably accessible to the employee,

(b) specifying (by description or otherwise)—

(i) a person to whom the employee can apply if dissatisfied with any disciplinary decision relating to him, or any decision to dismiss him, and

(ii) a person to whom the employee can apply for the purpose of seeking redress of any grievance relating to his employment, and the manner in which any such application should be made, and

(c) where there are further steps consequent on any such application, explaining those steps or referring to the provisions of a document explaining them which is reasonably accessible to the employee.

(2) Subsection (1) does not apply to rules, disciplinary decisions, decisions to dismiss, grievances or procedures relating to health or safety at work.

(3)–(4) [repealed]

(5) The note shall also state whether there is in force a contracting-out certificate (issued in accordance with Chapter I of Part III of the Pension Schemes Act 1993) stating that the employment is contracted-out employment (for the purposes of that Part of that Act).

4 Statement of changes

(1) If, after the material date, there is a change in any of the matters particulars of which are required by sections 1 to 3 to be included or referred to in a statement under section 1, the employer shall give to the employee a written statement containing particulars of the change.

(2) For the purposes of subsection (1)—

(a) in relation to a matter particulars of which are included or referred to in a statement given under section 1 otherwise than in instalments, the material date is the date to which the statement relates,

(b) in relation to a matter particulars of which—

(i) are included or referred to in an instalment of a statement given under section 1, or

(ii) are required by section 2(4) to be included in a single document but are not included in an instalment of a statement given under section 1 which does include other particulars to which that provision applies,

the material date is the date to which the instalment relates, and

(c) in relation to any other matter, the material date is the date by which a statement under section 1 is required to be given.

(3) A statement under subsection (1) shall be given at the earliest opportunity and, in any event, not later than—

(a) one month after the change in question, or

(b) where that change results from the employee being required to work outside the United Kingdom for a period of more than one month, the time when he leaves the United Kingdom in order to begin so to work, if that is earlier.

(4) A statement under subsection (1) may refer the employee to the provisions of some other document which is reasonably accessible to the employee for a change in any of the matters specified in sections 1(4)(d)(ii) and (iii) and 3(1)(a) and (c).

(5) A statement under subsection (1) may refer the employee for a change in either of the matters specifed in section 1(4)(e) to the law or to the provisions of any collective agreement

directly affecting the terms and conditions of the employment which is reasonably accessible to the employee.

(6) Where, after an employer has given to an employee a statement under section 1, either—

 (a) the name of the employer (whether an individual or a body corporate or partnership) is changed without any change in the identity of the employer, or

 (b) the identity of the employer is changed in circumstances in which the continuity of the employee's period of employment is not broken,

and subsection (7) applies in relation to the change, the person who is the employer immediately after the change is not required to give to the employee a statement under section 1; but the change shall be treated as a change falling within subsection (1) of this section.

(7) This subsection applies in relation to a change if it does not involve any change in any of the matters (other than the names of the parties) particulars of which are required by sections 1 to 3 to be included or referred to in the statement under section 1.

(8) A statement under subsection (1) which informs an employee of a change such as is referred to in subsection (6)(b) shall specify the date on which the employee's period of continuous employment began.

5 Exclusion from rights to statements

(1) Sections 1 to 4 apply to an employee who at any time comes or ceases to come within the exceptions from those sections provided by section 199, and under section 209, as if his employment with his employer terminated or began at that time.

(2) The fact that section 1 is directed by subsection (1) to apply to an employee as if his employment began on his ceasing to come within the exceptions referred to in that subsection does not affect the obligation under section 1(3)(b) to specify the date on which his employment actually began.

6 Reasonably accessible document or collective agreement

In sections 2 to 4 references to a document or collective agreement which is reasonably accessible to an employee are references to a document or collective agreement which—

 (a) the employee has reasonable opportunities of reading in the course of his employment, or

 (b) is made reasonably accessible to the employee in some other way.

7 Power to require particulars of further matters

The Secretary of State may by order provide that section 1 shall have effect as if particulars of such further matters as may be specified in the order were included in the particulars required by that section; and, for that purpose, the order may include such provisions amending that section as appear to the Secretary of State to be expedient.

7A Use of alternative documents to give particulars

(1) Subsections (2) and (3) apply where—

 (a) an employer gives an employee a document in writing in the form of a contract of employment or letter of engagement,

 (b) the document contains information which, were the document in the form of a statement under section 1, would meet the employer's obligation under that section in relation to the matters mentioned in subsections (3) and (4)(a) to (c), (d)(i), (f) and (h) of that section, and

 (c) the document is given after the beginning of the employment and before the end of the period for giving a statement under that section.

(2) The employer's duty under section 1 in relation to any matter shall be treated as met if the document given to the employee contains information which, were the document in the form of a statement under that section, would meet the employer's obligation under that section in relation to that matter.

(3) The employer's duty under section 3 shall be treated as met if the document given to the employee contains information which, were the document in the form of a statement under section 1 and the information included in the form of a note, would meet the employer's obligation under section 3.

(4) For the purposes of this section a document to which subsection (1)(a) applies shall be treated, in relation to information in respect of any of the matters mentioned in section 1(4), as specifying the date on which the document is given to the employee as the date as at which the information applies.

(5) Where subsection (2) applies in relation to any matter, the date on which the document by virtue of which that subsection applies is given to the employee shall be the material date in relation to that matter for the purposes of section 4(1).

(6) Where subsection (3) applies, the date on which the document by virtue of which that subsection applies is given to the employee shall be the material date for the purposes of section 4(1) in relation to the matters of which particulars are required to be given under section 3.

(7) The reference in section 4(6) to an employer having given a statement under section 1 shall be treated as including his having given a document by virtue of which his duty to give such a statement is treated as met.

7B Giving of alternative documents before start of employment

A document in the form of a contract of employment or letter of engagement given by an employer to an employee before the beginning of the employee's employment with the employer shall, when the employment begins, be treated for the purposes of section 7A as having been given at that time.

Right to itemised pay statement

8 Itemised pay statement

(1) An employee has the right to be given by his employer, at or before the time at which any payment of wages or salary is made to him, a written itemised pay statement.

(2) The statement shall contain particulars of—
  (a) the gross amount of the wages or salary,
  (b) the amounts of any variable, and (subject to section 9) any fixed, deductions from that gross amount and the purposes for which they are made,
  (c) the net amount of wages or salary payable, and
  (d) where different parts of the net amount are paid in different ways, the amount and method of payment of each part-payment.

9 Standing statement of fixed deductions

(1) A pay statement given in accordance with section 8 need not contain separate particulars of a fixed deduction if—
  (a) it contains instead an aggregate amount of fixed deductions, including that deduction, and
  (b) the employer has given to the employee, at or before the time at which the pay statement is given, a standing statement of fixed deductions which satisfies subsection (2).

(2) A standing statement of fixed deductions satisfies this subsection if—
  (a) it is in writing,
  (b) it contains, in relation to each deduction comprised in the aggregate amount of deductions, particulars of—
    (i)   the amount of the deduction,
    (ii) the intervals at which the deduction is to be made, and
    (iii) the purpose for which it is made, and
  (c) it is (in accordance with subsection (5)) effective at the date on which the pay statement is given.

(3) A standing statement of fixed deductions may be amended, whether by—

(a) addition of a new deduction,

(b) a change in the particulars, or

(c) cancellation of an existing deduction, by notice in writing, containing particulars of the amendment, given by the employer to the employee.

(4) An employer who has given to an employee a standing statement of fixed deductions shall—

(a) within the period of twelve months beginning with the date on which the first standing statement was given, and

(b) at intervals of not more than twelve months afterwards,

re-issue it in a consolidated form incorporating any amendments notified in accordance with subsection (3).

(5) For the purposes of subsection (2)(c) a standing statement of fixed deductions—

(a) becomes effective on the date on which it is given to the employee, and

(b) ceases to be effective at the end of the period of twelve months beginning with that date or, where it is re-issued in accordance with subsection (4), with the end of the period of twelve months beginning with the date of the last re-issue.

10 [omitted]

Enforcement

11 References to employment tribunals

(1) Where an employer does not give an employee a statement as required by section 1, 4 or 8 (either because he gives him no statement or because the statement he gives does not comply with what is required), the employee may require a reference to be made to an employment tribunal to determine what particulars ought to have been included or referred to in a statement so as to comply with the requirements of the section concerned.

(2) Where—

(a) a statement purporting to be a statement under section 1 or 4, or a pay statement or a standing statement of fixed deductions purporting to comply with section 8 or 9, has been given to an employee, and

(b) a question arises as to the particulars which ought to have been included or referred to in the statement so as to comply with the requirements of this Part,

either the employer or the employee may require the question to be referred to and determined by an employment tribunal.

(3) For the purposes of this section—

(a) a question as to the particulars which ought to have been included in the note required by section 3 to be included in the statement under section 1 does not include any question whether the employment is, has been or will be contracted-out employment (for the purposes of Part III of the Pension Schemes Act 1993), and

(b) a question as to the particulars which ought to have been included in a pay statement or standing statement of fixed deductions does not include a question solely as to the accuracy of an amount stated in any such particulars.

(4) An employment tribunal shall not consider a reference under this section in a case where the employment to which the reference relates has ceased unless an application requiring the reference to be made was made—

(a) before the end of the period of three months beginning with the date on which the employment ceased, or

(b) within such further period as the tribunal considers reasonable in a case where it is satisfied that it was not reasonably practicable for the application to be made before the end of that period of three months.

12   Determination of references

(1) Where, on a reference under section 11(1), an employment tribunal determines particulars as being those which ought to have been included or referred to in a statement given under section 1 or 4, the employer shall be deemed to have given to the employee a statement in which those particulars were included, or referred to, as specified in the decision of the tribunal.

(2) On determining a reference under section 11(2) relating to a statement purporting to be a statement under section 1 or 4, an employment tribunal may—

   (a) confirm the particulars as included or referred to in the statement given by the employer,

   (b) amend those particulars, or

   (c) substitute other particulars for them, as the tribunal may determine to be appropriate; and the statement shall be deemed to have been given by the employer to the employee in accordance with the decision of the tribunal.

(3) Where on a reference under section 11 an employment tribunal finds—

   (a) that an employer has failed to give an employee any pay statement in accordance with section 8, or

   (b) that a pay statement or standing statement of fixed deductions does not, in relation to a deduction, contain the particulars required to be included in that statement by that section or section 9, the tribunal shall make a declaration to that effect.

(4) Where on a reference in the case of which subsection (3) applies the tribunal further finds that any unnotified deductions have been made from the pay of the employee during the period of thirteen weeks immediately preceding the date of the application for the reference (whether or not the deductions were made in breach of the contract of employment), the tribunal may order the employer to pay the employee a sum not exceeding the aggregate of the unnotified deductions so made.

(5) For the purposes of subsection (4) a deduction is an unnotified deduction if it is made without the employer giving the employee, in any pay statement or standing statement of fixed deductions, the particulars of the deduction required by section 8 or 9.

PART II   PROTECTION OF WAGES

Deductions by employer

13   Right not to suffer unauthorised deductions

(1) An employer shall not make a deduction from wages of a worker employed by him unless—

   (a) the deduction is required or authorised to be made by virtue of a statutory provision or a relevant provision of the worker's contract, or

   (b) the worker has previously signified in writing his agreement or consent to the making of the deduction.

(2) In this section 'relevant provision', in relation to a worker's contract, means a provision of the contract comprised—

   (a) in one or more written terms of the contract of which the employer has given the worker a copy on an occasion prior to the employer making the deduction in question, or

   (b) in one or more terms of the contract (whether express or implied and, if express, whether oral or in writing) the existence and effect, or combined effect, of which in relation to the worker the employer has notified to the worker in writing on such an occasion.

(3) Where the total amount of wages paid on any occasion by an employer to a worker employed by him is less than the total amount of the wages properly payable by him to the

worker on that occasion (after deductions), the amount of the deficiency shall be treated for the purposes of this Part as a deduction made by the employer from the worker's wages on that occasion.

(4) Subsection (3) does not apply in so far as the deficiency is attributable to an error of any description on the part of the employer affecting the computation by him of the gross amount of the wages properly payable by him to the worker on that occasion.

(5) For the purposes of this section a relevant provision of a worker's contract having effect by virtue of a variation of the contract does not operate to authorise the making of a deduction on account of any conduct of the worker, or any other event occurring, before the variation took effect.

(6) For the purposes of this section an agreement or consent signified by a worker does not operate to authorise the making of a deduction on account of any conduct of the worker, or any other event occurring, before the agreement or consent was signified.

(7) This section does not affect any other statutory provision by virtue of which a sum payable to a worker by his employer but not constituting 'wages' within the meaning of this Part is not to be subject to a deduction at the instance of the employer.

14 Excepted deductions

(1) Section 13 does not apply to a deduction from a worker's wages made by his employer where the purpose of the deduction is the reimbursement of the employer in respect of—

(a) an overpayment of wages, or

(b) an overpayment in respect of expenses incurred by the worker in carrying out his employment,

made (for any reason) by the employer to the worker.

(2) Section 13 does not apply to a deduction from a worker's wages made by his employer in consequence of any disciplinary proceedings if those proceedings were held by virtue of a statutory provision.

(3) Section 13 does not apply to a deduction from a worker's wages made by his employer in pursuance of a requirement imposed on the employer by a statutory provision to deduct and pay over to a public authority amounts determined by that authority as being due to it from the worker if the deduction is made in accordance with the relevant determination of that authority.

(4) Section 13 does not apply to a deduction from a worker's wages made by his employer in pursuance of any arrangements which have been established—

(a) in accordance with a relevant provision of his contract to the inclusion of which in the contract the worker has signified his agreement or consent in writing, or

(b) otherwise with the prior agreement or consent of the worker signified in writing,

and under which the employer is to deduct and pay over to a third person amounts notified to the employer by that person as being due to him from the worker, if the deduction is made in accordance with the relevant notification by that person.

(5) Section 13 does not apply to a deduction from a worker's wages made by his employer where the worker has taken part in a strike or other industrial action and the deduction is made by the employer on account of the worker's having taken part in that strike or other action.

(6) Section 13 does not apply to a deduction from a worker's wages made by his employer with his prior agreement or consent signified in writing where the purpose of the deduction is the satisfaction (whether wholly or in part) of an order of a court or tribunal requiring the payment of an amount by the worker to the employer.

Payments to employer

15 Right not to have to make payments to employer

(1) An employer shall not receive a payment from a worker employed by him unless—

(a) the payment is required or authorised to be made by virtue of a statutory provision or a relevant provision of the worker's contract, or

(b) the worker has previously signified in writing his agreement or consent to the making of the payment.

(2) In this section 'relevant provision', in relation to a worker's contract, means a provision of the contract comprised—

(a) in one or more written terms of the contract of which the employer has given the worker a copy on an occasion prior to the employer receiving the payment in question, or

(b) in one or more terms of the contract (whether express or implied and, if express, whether oral or in writing) the existence and effect, or combined effect, of which in relation to the worker the employer has notified to the worker in writing on such an occasion.

(3) For the purposes of this section a relevant provision of a worker's contract having effect by virtue of a variation of the contract does not operate to authorise the receipt of a payment on account of any conduct of the worker, or any other event occurring, before the variation took effect.

(4) For the purposes of this section an agreement or consent signified by a worker does not operate to authorise the receipt of a payment on account of any conduct of the worker, or any other event occurring, before the agreement or consent was signified.

(5) Any reference in this Part to an employer receiving a payment from a worker employed by him is a reference to his receiving such a payment in his capacity as the worker's employer.

16   Excepted payments

(1) Section 15 does not apply to a payment received from a worker by his employer where the purpose of the payment is the reimbursement of the employer in respect of—

(a) an overpayment of wages, or

(b) an overpayment in respect of expenses incurred by the worker in carrying out his employment,

made (for any reason) by the employer to the worker.

(2) Section 15 does not apply to a payment received from a worker by his employer in consequence of any disciplinary proceedings if those proceedings were held by virtue of a statutory provision.

(3) Section 15 does not apply to a payment received from a worker by his employer where the worker has taken part in a strike or other industrial action and the payment has been required by the employer on account of the worker's having taken part in that strike or other action.

(4) Section 15 does not apply to a payment received from a worker by his employer where the purpose of the payment is the satisfaction (whether wholly or in part) of an order of a court or tribunal requiring the payment of an amount by the worker to the employer.

Cash shortages and stock deficiencies in retail employment

17   Introductory

(1) In the following provisions of this Part—

'cash shortage' means a deficit arising in relation to amounts received in connection with retail transactions, and

'stock deficiency' means a stock deficiency arising in the course of retail transactions.

(2) In the following provisions of this Part 'retail employment', in relation to a worker, means employment involving (whether or not on a regular basis)—

(a) the carrying out by the worker of retail transactions directly with members of the public or with fellow workers or other individuals in their personal capacities, or

(b) the collection by the worker of amounts payable in connection with retail transactions carried out by other persons directly with members of the public or with fellow workers or other individuals in their personal capacities.

(3) References in this section to a 'retail transaction' are to the sale or supply of goods or the supply of services (including financial services).

(4) References in the following provisions of this Part to a deduction made from wages of a worker in retail employment, or to a payment received from such a worker by his employer, on account of a cash shortage or stock deficiency include references to a deduction or payment so made or received on account of—

> (a) any dishonesty or other conduct on the part of the worker which resulted in any such shortage or deficiency, or
>
> (b) any other event in respect of which he (whether or not together with any other workers) has any contractual liability and which so resulted,

in each case whether or not the amount of the deduction or payment is designed to reflect the exact amount of the shortage or deficiency.

(5) References in the following provisions of this Part to the recovery from a worker of an amount in respect of a cash shortage or stock deficiency accordingly include references to the recovery from him of an amount in respect of any such conduct or event as is mentioned in subsection (4)(a) or (b).

(6) In the following provisions of this Part 'pay day', in relation to a worker, means a day on which wages are payable to the worker.

18 Limits on amount and time of deductions

(1) Where (in accordance with section 13) the employer of a worker in retail employment makes, on account of one or more cash shortages or stock deficiencies, a deduction or deductions from wages payable to the worker on a pay day, the amount or aggregate amount of the deduction or deductions shall not exceed one-tenth of the gross amount of the wages payable to the worker on that day.

(2) Where the employer of a worker in retail employment makes a deduction from the worker's wages on account of a cash shortage or stock deficiency, the employer shall not be treated as making the deduction in accordance with section 13 unless (in addition to the requirements of that section being satisfied with respect to the deduction)—

> (a) the deduction is made, or
>
> (b) in the case of a deduction which is one of a series of deductions relating to the shortage or deficiency, the first deduction in the series was made, not later than the end of the relevant period.

(3) In subsection (2) 'the relevant period' means the period of twelve months beginning with the date when the employer established the existence of the shortage or deficiency or (if earlier) the date when he ought reasonably to have done so.

19 Wages determined by reference to shortages etc.

(1) This section applies where—

> (a) by virtue of an agreement between a worker in retail employment and his employer, the amount of the worker's wages or any part of them is or may be determined by reference to the incidence of cash shortages or stock deficiencies, and
>
> (b) the gross amount of the wages payable to the worker on any pay day is, on account of any such shortages or deficiencies, less than the gross amount of the wages that would have been payable to him on that day if there had been no such shortages or deficiencies.

(2) The amount representing the difference between the two amounts referred to in subsection (1)(b) shall be treated for the purposes of this Part as a deduction from the wages payable to the worker on that day made by the employer on account of the cash shortages or stock deficiencies in question.

(3) The second of the amounts referred to in subsection (1)(b) shall be treated for the purposes of this Part (except subsection (1)) as the gross amount of the wages payable to him on that day.

(4) Accordingly—
    (a) section 13, and
    (b) if the requirements of section 13 and subsection (2) of section 18 are satisfied,
        subsection (1) of section 18,
have effect in relation to the amount referred to in subsection (2) of this section.

20 Limits on method and timing of payments

(1) Where the employer of a worker in retail employment receives from the worker a payment on account of a cash shortage or stock deficiency, the employer shall not be treated as receiving the payment in accordance with section 15 unless (in addition to the requirements of that section being satisfied with respect to the payment) he has previously—
    (a) notified the worker in writing of the worker's total liability to him in respect of
        that shortage or deficiency, and
    (b) required the worker to make the payment by means of a demand for payment
        made in accordance with the following provisions of this section.

(2) A demand for payment made by the employer of a worker in retail employment in respect of a cash shortage or stock deficiency—
    (a) shall be made in writing, and
    (b) shall be made on one of the worker's pay days.

(3) A demand for payment in respect of a particular cash shortage or stock deficiency, or (in the case of a series of such demands) the first such demand, shall not be made—
    (a) earlier than the first pay day of the worker following the date when he is notified
        of his total liability in respect of the shortage or deficiency in pursuance of sub-
        section (1)(a) or, where he is so notified on a pay day, earlier than that day, or
    (b) later than the end of the period of twelve months beginning with the date when
        the employer established the existence of the shortage or deficiency or (if earlier)
        the date when he ought reasonably to have done so.

(4) For the purposes of this Part a demand for payment shall be treated as made by the employer on one of a worker's pay days if it is given to the worker or posted to, or left at, his last known address—
    (a) on that pay day, or
    (b) in the case of a pay day which is not a working day of the employer's business, on
        the first such working day following that pay day.

(5) Legal proceedings by the employer of a worker in retail employment for the recovery from the worker of an amount in respect of a cash shortage or stock deficiency shall not be instituted by the employer after the end of the period referred to in subsection (3)(b) unless the employer has within that period made a demand for payment in respect of that amount in accordance with this section.

21 Limit on amount of payments

(1) Where the employer of a worker in retail employment makes on any pay day one or more demands for payment in accordance with section 20, the amount or aggregate amount required to be paid by the worker in pursuance of the demand or demands shall not exceed—
    (a) one-tenth of the gross amount of the wages payable to the worker on that day, or
    (b) where one or more deductions falling within section 18(1) are made by the
        employer from those wages, such amount as represents the balance of that one-
        tenth after subtracting the amount or aggregate amount of the deduction or
        deductions.

(2) Once an amount has been required to be paid by means of a demand for payment made in accordance with section 20 on any pay day, that amount shall not be taken into account under subsection (1) as it applies to any subsequent pay day, even though the employer is obliged to make further requests for it to be paid.

(3) Where in any legal proceedings the court finds that the employer of a worker in retail employment is (in accordance with section 15 as it applies apart from section 20(1)) entitled

to recover an amount from the worker in respect of a cash shortage or stock deficiency, the court shall, in ordering the payment by the worker to the employer of that amount, make such provision as appears to the court to be necessary to ensure that it is paid by the worker at a rate not exceeding that at which it could be recovered from him by the employer in accordance with this section.

22   Final instalments of wages

(1) In this section 'final instalment of wages', in relation to a worker, means—

    (a) the amount of wages payable to the worker which consists of or includes an amount payable by way of contractual remuneration in respect of the last of the periods for which he is employed under his contract prior to its termination for any reason (but excluding any wages referable to any earlier such period), or

    (b) where an amount in lieu of notice is paid to the worker later than the amount referred to in paragraph (a), the amount so paid,

in each case whether the amount in question is paid before or after the termination of the worker's contract.

(2) Section 18(1) does not operate to restrict the amount of any deductions which may (in accordance with section 13(1)) be made by the employer of a worker in retail employment from the worker's final instalment of wages.

(3) Nothing in section 20 or 21 applies to a payment falling within section 20(1) which is made on or after the day on which any such worker's final instalment of wages is paid; but (even if the requirements of section 15 would otherwise be satisfied with respect to it) his employer shall not be treated as receiving any such payment in accordance with that section if the payment was first required to be made after the end of the period referred to in section 20(3)(b).

(4) Section 21(3) does not apply to an amount which is to be paid by a worker on or after the day on which his final instalment of wages is paid.

Enforcement

23   Complaints to employment tribunals

(1) A worker may present a complaint to an employment tribunal—

    (a) that his employer has made a deduction from his wages in contravention of section 13 (including a deduction made in contravention of that section as it applies by virtue of section 18(2)),

    (b) that his employer has received from him a payment in contravention of section 15 (including a payment received in contravention of that section as it applies by virtue of section 20(1)),

    (c) that his employer has recovered from his wages by means of one or more deductions falling within section 18(1) an amount or aggregate amount exceeding the limit applying to the deduction or deductions under that provision, or

    (d) that his employer has received from him in pursuance of one or more demands for payment made (in accordance with section 20) on a particular pay day, a payment or payments of an amount or aggregate amount exceeding the limit applying to the demand or demands under section 21(1).

(2) Subject to subsection (4), an employment tribunal shall not consider a complaint under this section unless it is presented before the end of the period of three months beginning with—

    (a) in the case of a complaint relating to a deduction by the employer, the date of payment of the wages from which the deduction was made, or

    (b) in the case of a complaint relating to a payment received by the employer, the date when the payment was received.

(3) Where a complaint is brought under this section in respect of—

    (a) a series of deductions or payments, or

(b) a number of payments falling within subsection (1)(d) and made in pursuance of demands for payment subject to the same limit under section 21(1) but received by the employer on different dates,

the references in subsection (2) to the deduction or payment are to the last deduction or payment in the series or to the last of the payments so received.

(4) Where the employment tribunal is satisfied that it was not reasonably practicable for a complaint under this section to be presented before the end of the relevant period of three months, the tribunal may consider the complaint if it is presented within such further period as the tribunal considers reasonable.

(5) No complaint shall be presented under this section in respect of any deduction made in contravention of section 86 of the Trade Union and Labour Relations (Consolidation) Act 1992 (deduction of political fund contribution where certificate of exemption or objection has been given).

24 Determination of complaints

Where a tribunal finds a complaint under section 23 well-founded, it shall make a declaration to that effect and shall order the employer—
- (a) in the case of a complaint under section 23(1)(a), to pay to the worker the amount of any deduction made in contravention of section 13,
- (b) in the case of a complaint under section 23(1)(b), to repay to the worker the amount of any payment received in contravention of section 15,
- (c) in the case of a complaint under section 23(1)(c), to pay to the worker any amount recovered from him in excess of the limit mentioned in that provision, and
- (d) in the case of a complaint under section 23(1)(d), to repay to the worker any amount received from him in excess of the limit mentioned in that provision.

25 Determinations: supplementary

(1) Where, in the case of any complaint under section 23(1)(a), a tribunal finds that, although neither of the conditions set out in section 13(1)(a) and (b) was satisfied with respect to the whole amount of the deduction, one of those conditions was satisfied with respect to any lesser amount, the amount of the deduction shall for the purposes of section 24(a) be treated as reduced by the amount with respect to which that condition was satisfied.

(2) Where, in the case of any complaint under section 23(1)(b), a tribunal finds that, although neither of the conditions set out in section 15(1)(a) and (b) was satisfied with respect to the whole amount of the payment, one of those conditions was satisfied with respect to any lesser amount, the amount of the payment shall for the purposes of section 24(b) be treated as reduced by the amount with respect to which that condition was satisfied.

(3) An employer shall not under section 24 be ordered by a tribunal to pay or repay to a worker any amount in respect of a deduction or payment, or in respect of any combination of deductions or payments, in so far as it appears to the tribunal that he has already paid or repaid any such amount to the worker.

(4) Where a tribunal has under section 24 ordered an employer to pay or repay to a worker any amount in respect of a particular deduction or payment falling within section 23(1)(a) to (d), the amount which the employer is entitled to recover (by whatever means) in respect of the matter in relation to which the deduction or payment was originally made or received shall be treated as reduced by that amount.

(5) Where a tribunal has under section 24 ordered an employer to pay or repay to a worker any amount in respect of any combination of deductions or payments falling within section 23(1)(c) or (d), the aggregate amount which the employer is entitled to recover (by whatever means) in respect of the cash shortages or stock deficiencies in relation to which the deductions or payments were originally made or required to be made shall be treated as reduced by that amount.

26 Complaints and other remedies

Section 23 does not affect the jurisdiction of an employment tribunal to consider a reference under section 11 in relation to any deduction from the wages of a worker; but the aggregate of any amounts ordered by an employment tribunal to be paid under section 12(4) and under section 24 (whether on the same or different occasions) in respect of a particular deduction shall not exceed the amount of the deduction.

Supplementary

27 Meaning of 'wages' etc.

(1) In this Part 'wages', in relation to a worker, means any sums payable to the worker in connection with his employment, including—

(a) any fee, bonus, commission, holiday pay or other emolument referable to his employment, whether payable under his contract or otherwise,

(b) statutory sick pay under Part XI of the Social Security Contributions and Benefits Act 1992,

(c) statutory maternity pay under Part XII of that Act,

(ca) statutory paternity pay under Part XIIZA of that Act,

(cb) statutory adoption pay under Part XIIZB of that Act,

(d) a guarantee payment (under section 28 of this Act),

(e) any payment for time off under Part VI of this Act or section 169 of the Trade Union and Labour Relations (Consolidation) Act 1992 (payment for time off for carrying out trade union duties etc.),

(f) remuneration on suspension on medical grounds under section 64 of this Act and remuneration on suspension on maternity grounds under section 68 of this Act,

(g) any sum payable in pursuance of an order for reinstatement or re-engagement under section 113 of this Act,

(h) any sum payable in pursuance of an order for the continuation of a contract of employment under section 130 of this Act or section 164 of the Trade Union and Labour Relations (Consolidation) Act l992, and

(j) remuneration under a protective award under section 189 of that Act, but excluding any payments within subsection (2).

(2) Those payments are—

(a) any payment by way of an advance under an agreement for a loan or by way of an advance of wages (but without prejudice to the application of section 13 to any deduction made from the worker's wages in respect of any such advance),

(b) any payment in respect of expenses incurred by the worker in carrying out his employment,

(c) any payment by way of a pension, allowance or gratuity in connection with the worker's retirement or as compensation for loss of office,

(d) any payment referable to the worker's redundancy, and

(e) any payment to the worker otherwise than in his capacity as a worker.

(3) Where any payment in the nature of a non-contractual bonus is (for any reason) made to a worker by his employer, the amount of the payment shall for the purposes of this Part—

(a) be treated as wages of the worker, and

(b) be treated as payable to him as such on the day on which the payment is made.

(4) In this Part 'gross amount', in relation to any wages payable to a worker, means the total amount of those wages before deductions of whatever nature.

(5) For the purposes of this Part any monetary value attaching to any payment or benefit in kind furnished to a worker by his employer shall not be treated as wages of the worker except in the case of any voucher, stamp or similar document which is—

(a) of a fixed value expressed in monetary terms, and

(b) capable of being exchanged (whether on its own or together with other vouchers, stamps or documents, and whether immediately or only after a time) for money, goods or services (or for any combination of two or more of those things).

28–43 [omitted]

PART IVA   PROTECTED DISCLOSURES

43A   Meaning of 'protected disclosure'

In this Act a 'protected disclosure' means a qualifying disclosure (as defined by section 43B) which is made by a worker in accordance with any of sections 43C to 43H.

43B   Disclosures qualifying for protection

(1) In this Part a 'qualifying disclosure' means any disclosure of information which, in the reasonable belief of the worker making the disclosure, tends to show one or more of the following—

(a) that a criminal offence has been committed, is being committeed or is likely to be committed,

(b) that a person has failed, is failing or is likely to fail to comply with any legal obligation to which he is subject,

(c) that a miscarriage of justice has occurred, is occurring or is likely to occur,

(d) that the health or safety of any individual has been, is being or is likely to be endangered,

(e) that the environment has been, is being or is likely to be damaged, or

(f) that information tending to show any matter falling within any one of the preceding paragraphs has been, is being or is likely to be deliberately concealed.

(2) For the purposes of subsection (1), it is immaterial whether the relevant failure occurred, occurs or would occur in the United Kingdom or elsewhere, and whether the law applying to it is that of the United Kingdom or of any other country or territory.

(3) A disclosure of information is not a qualifying disclosure if the person making the disclosure commits an offence by making it.

(4) A disclosure of information in respect of which a claim to legal professional privilege (or, in Scotland, to confidentiality as between client and professional legal adviser) could be maintained in legal proceedings is not a qualifying disclosure if it is made by a person to whom the information had been disclosed in the course of obtaining legal advice.

(5) In this Part 'the relevant failure', in relation to a qualifying disclosure, means the matter falling within paragraphs (a) to (f) of subsection (1).

43C   Disclosure to employer or other responsible person

(1) A qualifying disclosure is made in accordance with this section if the worker makes the disclosure in good faith—

(a) to his employer, or

(b) where the worker reasonably believes that the relevant failure relates solely or mainly to—

(i) the conduct of a person other than his employer, or

(ii) any other matter for which a person other than his employer has legal responsiblity,

to that other person.

(2) A worker who, in accordance with a procedure whose use by him is authorised by his employer, makes a qualifying disclosure to a person other than his employer, is to be treated for the purposes of this Part as making the qualifying disclosure to his employer.

43D   Disclosure to legal adviser

A qualifying disclosure is made in accordance with this section if it is made in the course of obtaining legal advice.

43E   Disclosure to Minister of the Crown

A qualifying disclosure is made in accordance with this section if—
  (a) the worker's employer is—
    (i) an individual appointed under any enactment (including any enactment comprised in, or in an instrument made under, an Act of the Scottish Parliament) by a Minister of the Crown or a member of the Scottish Executive, or
    (ii) a body any of whose members are so appointed, and
  (b) the disclosure is made in good faith to a Minister of the Crown or a member of the Scottish Executive.

43F   Disclosure to prescribed person

  (1) A qualifying disclosure is made in accordance with this section if the worker—
    (a) makes the disclosure in good faith to a person prescribed by an order made by the Secretary of State for the purposes of this section, and
    (b) reasonably believes—
      (i) that the relevant failure falls within any description of matters in respect of which that person is so prescribed, and
      (ii) that the information disclosed, and any allegation contained in it, are substantially true.
  (2) An order prescribing persons for the purposes of this section may specify persons or descriptions of persons and shall specify the descriptions of matters in respect of which each person, or persons of each description, is or are prescribed.

43G   Disclosure in other cases

  (1) A qualifying disclosure is made in accordance with this section if—
    (a) the worker makes the disclosure in good faith,
    (b) he reasonably believes that the information disclosed, and any allegation contained in it, are substantially true,
    (c) he does not make the disclosure for purposes of personal gain,
    (d) any of the conditions in subsection (2) is met, and
    (e) in all the circumstances of the case, it is reasonable for him to make the disclosure.
  (2) The conditions referred to in subsection (1)(d) are—
    (a) that, at the time he makes the disclosure, the worker reasonably believes that he will be subjected to a detriment by his employer if he makes a disclosure to his employer or in accordance with section 43F,
    (b) that, in a case where no person is prescribed for the purposes of section 43F in relation to the relevant failure, the worker reasonably believes that it is likely that evidence relating to the relevant failure will be concealed or destroyed if he makes a disclosure to his employer, or
    (c) that the worker has previously made a disclosure of substantially the same information—
      (i) to his employer, or
      (ii) in accordance with section 43F.
  (3) In determining for the purposes of subsection (1)(e) whether it is reasonable for the worker to make the disclosure, regard shall be had, in particular, to—
    (a) the identity of the person to whom the disclosure is made,
    (b) the seriousness of the relevant failure,
    (c) whether the relevant failure is continuing or is likely to occur in the future,
    (d) whether the disclosure is made in breach of a duty of confidentiality owed by the employer to any other person,

(e) in a case falling within subsection (2)(c)(i) or (ii), any action which the employer or the person to whom the previous disclosure in accordance with section 43F was made has taken or might reasonably be expected to have taken as a result of the previous disclosure, and

(f) in a case falling within subsection (2)(c)(i), whether in making the disclosure to the employer the worker complied with any procedure whose use by him was authorised by the employer.

(4) For the purposes of this section a subsequent disclosure may be regarded as a disclosure of substantially the same information as that disclosed by a previous disclosure as mentioned in subsection (2)(c) even though the subsequent disclosure extends to information about action taken or not taken by any person as a result of the previous disclosure.

43H   Disclosure of exceptionally serious failure

(1) A qualifying disclosure is made in accordance with this section if—
    (a) the worker makes the disclosure in good faith,
    (b) he reasonably believes that the information disclosed, and any allegation contained in it, are substantially true,
    (c) he does not make the disclosure for purposes of personal gain,
    (d) the relevant failure is of an exceptionally serious nature, and
    (e) in all the circumstances of the case, it is reasonable for him to make the disclosure.

(2) In determining for the purposes of subsection (1)(e) whether it is reasonable for the worker to make the disclosure, regard shall be had, in particular, to the identity of the person to whom the disclosure is made.

43J   Contractual duties of confidentiality

(1) Any provision in an agreement to which this section applies is void in so far as it purports to preclude the worker from making a protected disclosure.

(2) This section applies to any agreement between a worker and his employer (whether a worker's contract or not), including an agreement to refrain from instituting or continuing any proceedings under this Act or any proceedings for breach of contract.

43K   Extension of meaning of 'worker' etc. for Part IVA

(1) For the purposes of this Part 'worker' includes an individual who is not a worker as defined by section 230(3) but who—
    (a) works or worked for a person in circumstances in which—
        (i) he is or was introduced or supplied to do that work by a third person, and
        (ii) the terms on which he is or was engaged to do the work are or were in practice substantially determined not by him but by the person for whom he works or worked, by the third person or by both of them,
    (b) contracts or contracted with a person, for the purposes of that person's business, for the execution of work to be done in a place not under the control or management of that person and would fall within section 230(3)(b) if for 'personally' in that provision there were substituted '(whether personally or otherwise)',
    (ba) works or worked as a person performing services under a contract entered into by him with a Primary Care Trust or Local Health Board under section 28K or 28Q of the National Health Service Act 1977,
    (bb) works or worked as a person performing services under a contract entered into by him with a Health Board under section 17J of the National Health Service (Scotland) Act 1978,
    (c) works or worked as a person providing general dental services, general ophthalmic services or pharmaceutical services in accordance with arrangements made—
        (i) by a Primary Care Trust or Health Authority under section 38 or 41 of the National Health Service Act 1997, or

   (ii) by a Health Board under section 25, 26 or 27 of the National Health Service
        (Scotland) Act 1978, or
 (d) is or was provided with work experience provided pursuant to a training course
     or programme or with training for employment (or with both) otherwise than—
   (i) under a contract of employment, or
   (ii) by an educational establishment on a course run by that establishment; and
        any reference to a worker's contract, to employment or to a worker being
        'employed' shall be construed accordingly.
(2) For the purposes of this Part 'employer' includes—
 (a) in relation to a worker falling within paragraph (a) of subsection (1), the person
     who substantially determines or determined the terms on which he is or was
     engaged,
 (aa) in relation to a worker falling within paragraph (ba) of that subsection, the Pri-
      mary Care Trust or Local Health Board referred to in that paragraph,
 (ab) in relation to a worker falling within paragraph (bb) of that subsection, the
      Health Board referred to in that paragraph,
 (b) in relation to a worker falling within paragraph (c) of that subsection, the
     authority or board referred to in that paragraph, and
 (c) in relation to a worker falling within paragraph (d) of that subsection, the person
     providing the work experience or training.
(3) In this section 'educational establishment' includes any university, college, school or
other educational establishment.

43KA [omitted]

43L Other interpretative provisions
(1) In this Part—
'qualifying disclosure' has the meaning given by section 43B;
'the relevant failure', in relation to a qualifying disclosure, has the meaning given by
section 43B(5).
(2) In determining for the purposes of this Part whether a person makes a disclosure for
purposes of personal gain, there shall be disregarded any reward payable by or under any
enactment.
(3) Any reference in this Part to the disclosure of information shall have effect, in relation to any case where the person receiving the information is already aware of it, as a
reference to bringing the information to his attention.

PART V   PROTECTION FROM SUFFERING
DETRIMENT IN EMPLOYMENT

Rights not to suffer detriment

43M [omitted]

44 Health and safety cases
(1) An employee has the right not to be subjected to any detriment by any act, or any
deliberate failure to act, by his employer done on the ground that—
 (a) having been designated by the employer to carry out activities in connection
     with preventing or reducing risks to health and safety at work, the employee
     carried out (or proposed to carry out) any such activities,
 (b) being a representative of workers on matters of health and safety at work or
     member of a safety committee—

      (i) in accordance with arrangements established under or by virtue of any enactment, or

     (ii) by reason of being acknowledged as such by the employer, the employee performed (or proposed to perform) any functions as such a representative or a member of such a committee,

  (ba) the employee took part (or proposed to take part) in consultation with the employer pursuant to the Health and Safety (Consultation with Employees) Regulations 1996 or in an election of representatives of employee safety within the meaning of those Regulations (whether as a candidate or otherwise),

   (c) being an employee at a place where—

      (i) there was no such representative or safety committee, or

     (ii) there was such a representative or safety committee but it was not reasonably practicable for the employee to raise the matter by those means, he brought to his employer's attention, by reasonable means, circumstances connected with his work which he reasonably believed were harmful or potentially harmful to health or safety,

   (d) in circumstances of danger which the employee reasonably believed to be serious and imminent and which he could not reasonably have been expected to avert, he left (or proposed to leave) or (while the danger persisted) refused to return to his place of work or any dangerous part of his place of work, or

   (e) in circumstances of danger which the employee reasonably believed to be serious and imminent, he took (or proposed to take) appropriate steps to protect himself or other persons from the danger.

(2) For the purposes of subsection (1)(e) whether steps which an employee took (or proposed to take) were appropriate is to be judged by reference to all the circumstances including, in particular, his knowledge and the facilities and advice available to him at the time.

(3) An employee is not to be regarded as having been subjected to any detriment on the ground specified in subsection (1)(e) if the employer shows that it was (or would have been) so negligent for the employee to take the steps which he took (or proposed to take) that a reasonable employer might have treated him as the employer did.

(4) This section does not apply where the detriment in question amounts to dismissal (within the meaning of Part X).

45 [omitted]

45A Working time cases

(1) A worker has the right not to be subjected to any detriment by any act, or any deliberate failure to act, by his employer done on the ground that the worker—

   (a) refused (or proposed to refuse) to comply with a requirement which the employer imposed(or proposed to impose) incontravention of the Working Time Regulations 1998,

   (b) refused (or proposed to refuse) to forgo a right conferred on him by those Regulations,

   (c) failed to sign a workforce agreement for the purposes of those Regulations, or to enter into, or agree to vary or extend, any other agreement with his employer which is provided for in those Regulations,

   (d) being—

      (i) a representative of members of the workforce for the purposes of Schedule 1 to those Regulations, or

     (ii) a candidate in an election in which any person elected will, on being elected, be such a representative,

  performed (or proposed to perform) any functions or activities as such a representative or candidate,

(e) brought proceedings against the employer to enforce a right conferred on him by those Regulations, or

(f) alleged that the employer had infringed such a right.

(2) It is immaterial for the purposes of subsection (1)(e) or (f)—

(a) whether or not the worker has the right, or

(b) whether or not the right has been infringed, but, for those provisions to apply, the claim to the right and that it has been infringed must be made in good faith.

(3) It is sufficient for subsection (1)(f) to apply that the worker, without specifying the right, made it reasonably clear to the employer what the right claimed to have been infringed was.

(4) This section does not apply where a worker is an employee and the detriment in question amounts to dismissal within the meaning of Part X.

(5) [omitted]

46 [omitted]

47 Employee representatives

(1) An employee has the right not to be subjected to any detriment by any act, or any deliberate failure to act, by his employer done on the ground that, being—

(a) an employee representative for the purposes of Chapter II of Part IV of the Trade Union and Labour Relations (Consolidation) Act 1992 (redundancies) or Regulations 9, 13 and 15 of the Transfer of Undertakings (Protection of Employment) Regulations 2006, or

(b) a candidate in an election in which any person elected will, on being elected, be such an employee representative,

he performed (or proposed to perform) any functions or activities as such an employee representative or candidate.

(1A) An employee has the right not to be subjected to any detriment by any act, or by any deliberate failure to act, by his employer done on the ground of his participation in an election of employee representatives for the purposes of Chapter II of Part IV of the Trade Union and Labour Relations (Consolidation) Act 1992 (redundancies) or Regulations 9, 13 and 15 of the Transfer of Undertakings (Protection of Employment) Regulations 2006.

(2) This section does not apply where the detriment in question amounts to a dismissal (within the meaning of Part X).

47A Employees exercising right to time off work for study or training

(1) An employee has the right not to be subjected to any detriment by any act, or any deliberate failure to act, by his employer or the principal (within the meaning of section 63A(3)) done on the ground that, being a person entitled to—

(a) time off under section 63A(1) or (3), and

(b) remuneration under section 63B(1) in respect of that time taken off, the employee exercised (or proposed to exercise) that right or received (or sought to receive) such remuneration.

(2) This section does not apply where the detriment in question amounts to dismissal (within the meaning of Part X).

47B Protected disclosures

(1) A worker has the right not to be subjected to any detriment by any act, or any deliberate failure to act, by his employer done on the ground that the worker has made a protected disclosure.

(2) This section does not apply where—

(a) the worker is an employee, and

(b) the detriment in question amounts to dismissal (within the meaning of Part X).

(3) For the purposes of this section, and of sections 48 and 49 so far as relating to this section, 'worker', 'worker's contract', 'employment' and 'employer' have the extended meaning given by section 43K.

47C   Leave for family and domestic reasons

(1) An employee has the right not to be subjected to any detriment by any act, or any deliberate failure to act, by his employer done for a prescribed reason.

(2) A prescribed reason is one which is prescribed by regulations made by the Secretary of State and which relates to—

    (a)   pregnancy, childbirth or maternity,

    (b)   ordinary, compulsory or additional maternity leave,

    (ba) ordinary or additional adoption leave

    (c)   parental leave,

    (ca) paternity leave, or

    (d)   time off under section 57A.

(3) A reason prescribed under this section in relation to parental leave may relate to action which an employee takes, agrees to take or refuses to take under or in respect of a collective or workforce agreement.

(4) Regulations under this section may make different provision for different cases or circumstances.

47D   Tax credits

(1) An employee has the right not to be subjected to any detriment by any act, or any deliberate failure to act, by his employer, done on the ground that—

    (a)   any action was taken, or was proposed to be taken, by or on behalf of the employee with a view to enforcing, or otherwise securing the benefit of, a right conferred on the employee by regulations under section 25 of the Tax Credits Act 2002,

    (b)   a penalty was imposed on the employer, or proceedings for a penalty were brought against him, under that Act, as a result of action taken by or on behalf of the employee for the purpose of enforcing, or otherwise securing the benefit of, such a right, or

    (c)   the employee is entitled, or will or may be entitled, to working tax credit.

(2) It is immaterial for the purposes of subsection (1)(a) or (b)—

    (a)   whether or not the employee has the right, or

    (b)   whether or not the right has been infringed,

but, for those provisions to apply, the claim to the right and (if applicable) the claim that it has been infringed must be made in good faith.

(3) Subsections (1) and (2) apply to a person who is not an employee within the meaning of this Act but who is an employee within the meaning of section 25 of the Tax Credits Act 2002, with references to his employer in those subsections (and sections 48(2) and (4) and 49(1)) being construed in accordance with that section.

(4) Subsections (1) and (2) do not apply to an employee if the detriment in question amounts to dismissal (within the meaning of Part 10).

47E   Flexible working

(1) An employee has the right not to be subjected to any detriment by any act, or any deliberate failure to act, by his employer done on the ground that the employee—

    (a)   made (or proposed to make) an application under section 80F,

    (b)   exercised (or proposed to exercise) a right conferred on him under section 80G,

    (c)   brought proceedings against the employer under section 80H, or

    (d)   alleged the existence of any circumstance which would constitute a ground for bringing such proceedings.

(2) This section does not apply where the detriment in question amounts to dismissal within the meaning of Part 10.

Enforcement

48 Complaints to employment tribunals

(1) An employee may present a complaint to an employment tribunal that he has been subjected to a detriment in contravention of section 43M, 44, 45, 46, 47, 47A, 47C or 47E.

(1ZA) A worker may present a complaint to an employment tribunal that he has been subjected to a detriment in contravention of section 45A.

(1A) A worker may present a complaint to an employment tribunal that he has been subjected to a detriment in contravention of section 47B.

(1B) A person may present a complaint to an employment tribunal that he has been subjected to a detriment in contravention of section 47D.

(2) On such a complaint it is for the employer to show the ground on which any act, or deliberate failure to act, was done.

(3) An employment tribunal shall not consider a complaint under this section unless it is presented—

   (a) before the end of the period of three months beginning with the date of the act or failure to act to which the complaint relates or, where that act or failure is part of a series of similar acts or failures, the last of them, or

   (b) within such further period as the tribunal considers reasonable in a case where it is satisfied that it was not reasonably practicable for the complaint to be presented before the end of that period of three months.

(4) For the purposes of subsection (3)—

   (a) where an act extends over a period, the 'date of the act' means the last day of hat period, and

   (b) a deliberate failure to act shall be treated as done when it was decided on;

and, in the absence of evidence establishing the contrary, an employer shall be taken to decide on a failure to act when he does an act inconsistent with doing the failed act or, if he has done no such inconsistent act, when the period expires within which he might reasonably have been expected to do the failed act if it was to be done.

(5) In this section and section 49 any reference to the employer includes, where a person complains that he has been subjected to a detriment in contravention of section 47A, the principal (within the meaning of section 63A(3)).

49 Remedies

(1) Where an employment tribunal finds a complaint under section 48 well-founded, the tribunal—

   (a) shall make a declaration to that effect, and

   (b) may make an award of compensation to be paid by the employer to the complainant in respect of the act or failure to act to which the complaint relates.

(2) Subject to subsections (5A) and (6) the amount of the compensation awarded shall be such as the tribunal considers just and equitable in all the circumstances having regard to—

   (a) the infringement to which the complaint relates, and

   (b) any loss which is attributable to the act, or failure to act, which infringed the complainant's right.

(3) The loss shall be taken to include—

   (a) any expenses reasonably incurred by the complainant in consequence of the act, or failure to act, to which the complaint relates, and

   (b) loss of any benefit which he might reasonably be expected to have had but for that act or failure to act.

(4) In ascertaining the loss the tribunal shall apply the same rule concerning the duty of a person to mitigate his loss as applies to damages recoverable under the common law of England and Wales or (as the case may be) Scotland.

(5) Where the tribunal finds that the act, or failure to act, to which the complaint relates was to any extent caused or contributed to by action of the complainant, it shall reduce the amount of the compensation by such proportion as it considers just and equitable having regard to that finding.

(5A) Where—

    (a) the complaint is made under section 48(1ZA),

    (b) the detriment to which the worker is subjected is the termination of his worker's contract, and

    (c) that contract is not a contract of employment,

any compensation must not exceed the compensation that would be payable under Chapter II of Part X if the worker had been an employee and had been dismissed for the reason specified in section 101A.

(6) Where—

    (a) the complaint is made under section 48(1A),

    (b) the detriment to which the worker is subjected is the termination of his worker's contract, and

    (c) that contract is not a contract of employment,

any compensation must not exceed the compensation that would be payable under Chapter II of Part X if the worker had been an employee and had been dismissed for the reason specified in section 103A.

(7) Where—

    (a) the complaint is made under section 48(1B) by a person who is not an employee, and

    (b) the detriment to which he is subjected is the termination of his contract with the person who is his employer for the purposes of section 25 of the Tax Credits Act 2002,

any compensation must not exceed the compensation that would be payable under Chapter 2 of Part 10 if the complainant had been an employee and had been dismissed for the reason specified in section 104B.

49A   [omitted]

PART VI   TIME OFF WORK

Public duties

50   Right to time off for public duties

(1) An employer shall permit an employee of his who is a justice of the peace to take time off during the employee's working hours for the purpose of performing any of the duties of his office.

(2) An employer shall permit an employee of his who is a member of—

    (a) a local authority,

    (b) a statutory tribunal,

    (c) a police authority,

    (ca) [repealed]

    (d) a board of prison visitors or a prison visiting committee,

    (e) a relevant health body,

    (f) a relevant education body,

    (g) the Environment Agency or the Scottish Environment Protection Agency, or

    (h) Scottish Water or a Water Customer Consultation Panel,

to take time off during the employee's working hours for the purposes specified in subsection (3).

(3) The purposes referred to in subsection (2) are—

    (a) attendance at a meeting of the body or any of its committees or subcommittees, and

(b) the doing of any other thing approved by the body, or anything of a class so approved, for the purpose of the discharge of the functions of the body or of any of its committees or sub-committees, and

(c) in the case of a local authority which are operating executive arrangements—

    (i) attendance at a meeting of the executive of that local authority or committee of that executive; and

    (ii) the doing of any other thing, by an individual member of that executive, for the purposes of the discharge of any function which is to any extent the responsibility of that executive.

(4) The amount of time off which an employee is to be permitted to take under this section, and the occasions on which and any conditions subject to which time off maybe so taken, are those that are reasonable in all the circumstances having regard, in particular, to—

(a) how much time off is required for the performance of the duties of the office or as a member of the body in question, and how much time off is required for the performance of the particular duty,

(b) how much time off the employee has already been permitted under this section or sections 168 and 170 of the Trade Union and Labour Relations (Consolidation) Act 1992 (time off for trade union duties and activities), and

(c) the circumstances of the employer's business and the effect of the employee's absence on the running of that business.

(5) In subsection (2)(a) 'a local authority' means—

(a) a local authority within the meaning of the Local Government Act 1972,

(b) a council constituted under section 2 of the Local Government etc. (Scotland) Act 1994,

(c) the Common Council of the City of London,

(d) a National Park authority, or

(e) the Broads Authority.

(6) The reference in subsection (2) to a member of a police authority is to a person appointed as such a member under Schedule 2 to the Police Act 1996.

(7) In subsection (2)(d)—

(a) 'a board of prison visitors' means a board of visitors appointed under section 6(2) of the Prison Act 1952, and

(b) 'a prison visiting committee' means a visiting committee appointed under section 19(3) of the Prisons (Scotland) Act 1989 or constituted by virtue of rules made under section 39 (as read with section 8(1)) of that Act.

(8) In subsection (2)(e) 'a relevant health body' means—

(a) a National Health Service trust established under Part I of the National Health Service and Community Care Act 1990 or the National Health Service (Scotland) Act 1978,

(ab) an NHS foundation trust,

(b) a Strategic Health Authority or Health Authority established under section 8 of the National Health Service Act 1977, a Special Health Authority established under section 11 of that Act, or a Primary Care Trust established under section 16A of that Act, or

(c) a Health Board constituted under section 2 of the National Health Service (Scotland) Act 1978.

(9) In subsection (2)(f) 'a relevant education body' means—

(a) a managing or governing body of an educational establishment maintained by a local education authority,

(b) a governing body of a further education corporation or higher education corporation,

(c) a school council appointed under section 125(1) of the Local Government (Scotland) Act 1973,

(d) a school board within the meaning of section 1(1) of the School Boards (Scotland) Act 1988,

(e) a board of management of a self-governing school within the meaning of section 135(1) of the Education (Scotland) Act 1980,

(f) a board of management of a college of further education within the meaning of section 36(1) of the Further and Higher Education (Scotland) Act 1992,

(g) a governing body of a central institution within the meaning of section 135(1) of the Education (Scotland) Act 1980,

(h) a governing body of a designated institution within the meaning of Part II of the Further and Higher Education (Scotland) Act 1992,

(i) the General Teaching Council for England, or

(j) the General Teaching Council for Wales.

(9A) In subsection (3)(c) of this section 'executive' and 'executive arrangements' have the same meaning as in Part II of the Local Government Act 2000.

(10) [omitted]

(11) For the purposes of this section the working hours of an employee shall be taken to be any time when, in accordance with his contract of employment, the employee is required to be at work.

51 Complaints to employment tribunals

(1) An employee may present a complaint to an employment tribunal that his employer has failed to permit him to take time off as required by section 50.

(2) An employment tribunal shall not consider a complaint under this section that an employer has failed to permit an employee to take time off unless it is presented—

(a) before the end of the period of three months beginning with the date on which the failure occurred, or

(b) within such further period as the tribunal considers reasonable in a case where it is satisfied that it was not reasonably practicable for the complaint to be presented before the end of that period of three months.

(3) Where an employment tribunal finds a complaint under this section well-founded, the tribunal—

(a) shall make a declaration to that effect, and

(b) may make an award of compensation to be paid by the employer to the employee.

(4) The amount of the compensation shall be such as the tribunal considers just and equitable in all the circumstances having regard to—

(a) the employer's default in failing to permit time off to be taken by the employee, and

(b) any loss sustained by the employee which is attributable to the matters to which the complaint relates.

Looking for work and making arrangements for training

52 Right to time off to look for work or arrange training

(1) An employee who is given notice of dismissal by reason of redundancy is entitled to be permitted by his employer to take reasonable time off during the employee's working hours before the end of his notice in order to—

(a) look for new employment, or

(b) make arrangements for training for future employment.

(2) An employee is not entitled to take time off under this section unless, on whichever is the later of—

(a) the date on which the notice is due to expire, and

(b) the date on which it would expire were it the notice required to be given by section 86(1),

he will have been (or would have been) continuously employed for a period of two years or more.

(3) For the purposes of this section the working hours of an employee shall be taken to be any time when, in accordance with his contract of employment, the employee is required to be at work.

53 Right to remuneration for time off under section 52

(1) An employee who is permitted to take time off under section 52 is entitled to be paid remuneration by his employer for the period of absence at the appropriate hourly rate.

(2) The appropriate hourly rate, in relation to an employee, is the amount of one week's pay divided by the number of normal working hours in a week for that employee when employed under the contract of employment in force on the day when the notice of dismissal was given.

(3) But where the number of normal working hours differs from week to week or over a longer period, the amount of one week's pay shall be divided instead by the average number of normal working hours calculated by dividing by twelve the total number of the employee's normal working hours during the period of twelve weeks ending with the last complete week before the day on which the notice was given.

(4) If an employer unreasonably refuses to permit an employee to take time off from work as required by section 52, the employee is entitled to be paid an amount equal to the remuneration to which he would have been entitled under subsection (1) if he had been permitted to take the time off.

(5) The amount of an employer's liability to pay remuneration under subsection (1) shall not exceed, in respect of the notice period of any employee, forty per cent. of a week's pay of that employee.

(6) A right to any amount under subsection (1) or (4) does not affect any right of an employee in relation to remuneration under his contract of employment ('contractual remuneration').

(7) Any contractual remuneration paid to an employee in respect of a period of time off under section 52 goes towards discharging any liability of the employer to pay remuneration under subsection (1) in respect of that period; and, conversely, any payment of remuneration under subsection (1) in respect of a period goes towards discharging any liability of the employer to pay contractual remuneration in respect of that period.

54 Complaints to employment tribunals

(1) An employee may present a complaint to an employment tribunal that his employer—

(a) has unreasonably refused to permit him to take time off as required by section 52, or

(b) has failed to pay the whole or any part of any amount to which the employee is entitled under section 53(1) or (4).

(2) An employment tribunal shall not consider a complaint under this section unless it is presented—

(a) before the end of the period of three months beginning with the date on which it is alleged that the time off should have been permitted, or

(b) within such further period as the tribunal considers reasonable in a case where it is satisfied that it was not reasonably practicable for the complaint to be presented before the end of that period of three months.

(3) Where an employment tribunal finds a complaint under this section well-founded, the tribunal shall—

(a) make a declaration to that effect, and

(b) order the employer to pay to the employee the amount which it finds due to him.

(4) The amount which may be ordered by a tribunal to be paid by an employer under subsection (3) (or, where the employer is liable to pay remuneration under section 53, the aggregate of that amount and the amount of that liability) shall not exceed, in respect of the notice period of any employee, forty per cent. of a week's pay of that employee.

Ante-natal care

55 Right to time off for ante-natal care

(1) An employee who—

(a) is pregnant, and

(b) has, on the advice of a registered medical practitioner, registered midwife or registered nurse, made an appointment to attend at any place for the purpose of receiving ante-natal care,

is entitled to be permitted by her employer to take time off during the employee's working hours in order to enable her to keep the appointment.

(2) An employee is not entitled to take time off under this section to keep an appointment unless, if her employer requests her to do so, she produces for his inspection—

(a) a certificate from a registered medical practitioner, registered midwife or registered nurse stating that the employee is pregnant, and

(b) an appointment card or some other document showing that the appointment has been made.

(3) Subsection (2) does not apply where the employee's appointment is the first appointment during her pregnancy for which she seeks permission to take time off in accordance with subsection (1).

(4) For the purposes of this section the working hours of an employee shall be taken to be any time when, in accordance with her contract of employment, the employee is required to be at work.

(5) References in this section to a registered nurse are to such a nurse—

(a) who is also registered in the Specialist Community Public Health Nurses' Part of the register maintained under article 5 of the Nursing and Midwifery Order 2001, and

(b) whose entry in that Part of the register is annotated to show that he holds a qualification in health visiting.

56 Right to remuneration for time off under section 55

(1) An employee who is permitted to take time off under section 55 is entitled to be paid remuneration by her employer for the period of absence at the appropriate hourly rate.

(2) The appropriate hourly rate, in relation to an employee, is the amount of one week's pay divided by the number of normal working hours in a week for that employee when employed under the contract of employment in force on the day when the time off is taken.

(3) But where the number of normal working hours differs from week to week or over a longer period, the amount of one week's pay shall be divided instead by—

(a) the average number of normal working hours calculated by dividing by twelve the total number of the employee's normal working hours during the period of twelve weeks ending with the last complete week before the day on which the time off is taken, or

(b) where the employee has not been employed for a sufficient period to enable the calculation to be made under paragraph (a), a number which fairly represents the number of normal working hours in a week having regard to such of the considerations specified in subsection (4) as are appropriate in the circumstances.

(4) The considerations referred to in subsection (3)(b) are—

(a) the average number of normal working hours in a week which the employee could expect in accordance with the terms of her contract, and

(b) the average number of normal working hours of other employees engaged in relevant comparable employment with the same employer.

(5) A right to any amount under subsection (1) does not affect any right of an employee in relation to remuneration under her contract of employment ('contractual remuneration').

(6) Any contractual remuneration paid to an employee in respect of a period of time off under section 55 goes towards discharging any liability of the employer to pay remuneration under subsection (1) in respect of that period; and, conversely, any payment of remuneration under subsection (1) in respect of a period goes towards discharging any liability of the employer to pay contractual remuneration in respect of that period.

57 Complaints to employment tribunals

(1) An employee may present a complaint to an employment tribunal that her employer—

(a) has unreasonably refused to permit her to take time off as required by section 55, or

(b) has failed to pay the whole or any part of any amount to which the employee is entitled under section 56.

(2) An employment tribunal shall not consider a complaint under this section unless it is presented—

(a) before the end of the period of three months beginning with the date of the appointment concerned, or

(b) within such further period as the tribunal considers reasonable in a case where it is satisfied that it was not reasonably practicable for the complaint to be presented before the end of that period of three months.

(3) Where an employment tribunal finds a complaint under this section well-founded, the tribunal shall make a declaration to that effect.

(4) If the complaint is that the employer has unreasonably refused to permit the employee to take time off, the tribunal shall also order the employer to pay to the employee an amount equal to the remuneration to which she would have been entitled under section 56 if the employer had not refused.

(5) If the complaint is that the employer has failed to pay the employee the whole or part of any amount to which she is entitled under section 56, the tribunal shall also order the employer to pay to the employee the amount which it finds due to her.

Dependants

57A Time off for dependants

(1) An employee is entitled to be permitted by his employer to take a reasonable amount of time off during the employee's working hours in order to take action which is necessary—

(a) to provide assistance on an occasion when a dependant falls ill, gives birth or is injured or assaulted,

(b) to make arrangements for the provision of care for a dependant who is ill or injured,

(c) in consequence of the death of a dependant,

(d) because of the unexpected disruption or termination of arrangements for the care of a dependant, or

(e) to deal with an incident which involves a child of the employee and which occurs unexpectedly in a period during which an educational establishment which the child attends is responsible for him.

(2) Subsection (1) does not apply unless the employee—

  (a) tells his employer the reason for his absence as soon as reasonably practicable, and

  (b) except where paragraph (a) cannot be complied with until after the employee has returned to work, tells his employer for how long he expects to be absent.

(3) Subject to subsections (4) and (5), for the purposes of this section 'dependant' means, in relation to an employee—

  (a) a spouse or civil partner,

  (b) a child,

  (c) a parent,

  (d) a person who lives in the same household as the employee, otherwise than by reason of being his employee, tenant, lodger or boarder.

(4) For the purposes of subsection (1)(a) or (b) 'dependant' includes, in addition to the persons mentioned in subsection (3), any person who reasonably relies on the employee—

  (a) for assistance on an occasion when the person falls ill or is injured or assaulted, or

  (b) to make arrangements for the provision of care in the event of illness or injury.

(5) For the purposes of subsection (1)(d) 'dependant' includes, in addition to the persons mentioned in subsection (3), any person who reasonably relies on the employee to make arrangements for the provision of care.

(6) A reference in this section to illness or injury includes a reference to mental illness or injury.

57B Complaint to employment tribunal

(1) An employee may present a complaint to an employment tribunal that his employer has unreasonably refused to permit him to take time off as required by section 57A.

(2) An employment tribunal shall not consider a complaint under this section unless it is presented—

  (a) before the end of the period of three months beginning with the date when the refusal occurred, or

  (b) within such further period as the tribunal considers reasonable in a case where it is satisfied that it was not reasonably practicable for the complaint to be presented before the end of that period of three months.

(3) Where an employment tribunal finds a complaint under subsection (1) well-founded, it—

  (a) shall make a declaration to that effect, and

  (b) may make an award of compensation to be paid by the employer to the employee.

(4) the amount of compensation shall be such as the tribunal considers just and equitable in all the circumstances having regard to—

  (a) the employer's default in refusing to permit time off to be taken by the employee, and

  (b) any loss sustained by the employee which is attributable to the matters complained of.

58–60 [omitted]

Employee representatives

61 Right to time off for employee representatives

(1) An employee who is—

  (a) an employee representative for the purposes of Chapter II of Part IV of the Trade Union and Labour Relations (Consolidation) Act 1992 (redundancies) or Regulations 9, 13 and 15 of the Transfer of Undertakings (Protection of Employment) Regulations 2006, or

  (b) a candidate in an election in which any person elected will, on being elected, be such an employee representative,

is entitled to be permitted by his employer to take reasonable time off during the employee's working hours in order to perform his functions as such an employee representative or candidate or in order to undergo training to perform such functions.

(2) For the purposes of this section the working hours of an employee shall be taken to be any time when, in accordance with his contract of employment, the employee is required to be at work.

62 Right to remuneration for time off under section 61

(1) An employee who is permitted to take time off under section 61 is entitled to be paid remuneration by his employer for the time taken off at the appropriate hourly rate.

(2) The appropriate hourly rate, in relation to an employee, is the amount of one week's pay divided by the number of normal working hours in a week for that employee when employed under the contract of employment in force on the day when the time off is taken.

(3) But where the number of normal working hours differs from week to week or over a longer period, the amount of one week's pay shall be divided instead by—

> (a) the average number of normal working hours calculated by dividing by twelve the total number of the employee's normal working hours during the period of twelve weeks ending with the last complete week before the day on which the time off is taken, or
>
> (b) where the employee has not been employed for a sufficient period to enable the calculation to be made under paragraph (a), a number which fairly represents the number of normal working hours in a week having regard to such of the considerations specified in subsection (4) as are appropriate in the circumstances.

(4) The considerations referred to in subsection (3)(b) are—

> (a) the average number of normal working hours in a week which the employee could expect in accordance with the terms of his contract, and
>
> (b) the average number of normal working hours of other employees engaged in relevant comparable employment with the same employer.

(5) A right to any amount under subsection (1) does not affect any right of an employee in relation to remuneration under his contract of employment ('contractual remuneration').

(6) Any contractual remuneration paid to an employee in respect of a period of time off under section 61 goes towards discharging any liability of the employer to pay remuneration under subsection (1) in respect of that period; and, conversely, any payment of remuneration under subsection (1) in respect of a period goes towards discharging any liability of the employer to pay contractual remuneration in respect of that period.

63 Complaints to employment tribunals

(1) An employee may present a complaint to an employment tribunal that his employer—

> (a) has unreasonably refused to permit him to take time off as required by section 61, or
>
> (b) has failed to pay the whole or any part of any amount to which the employee is entitled under section 62.

(2) An employment tribunal shall not consider a complaint under this section unless it is presented—

> (a) before the end of the period of three months beginning with the day on which the time off was taken or on which it is alleged the time off should have been permitted, or
>
> (b) within such further period as the tribunal considers reasonable in a case where it is satisfied that it was not reasonably practicable for the complaint to be presented before the end of that period of three months.

(3) Where an employment tribunal finds a complaint under this section well-founded, the tribunal shall make a declaration to that effect.

(4) If the complaint is that the employer has unreasonably refused to permit the employee to take time off, the tribunal shall also order the employer to pay to the employee an amount equal to the remuneration to which he would have been entitled under section 62 if the employer had not refused.

(5) If the complaint is that the employer has failed to pay the employee the whole or part of any amount to which he is entitled under section 62, the tribunal shall also order the employer to pay to the employee the amount which it finds due to him.

63A–C [omitted]

PART VII   SUSPENSION FROM WORK

Suspension on medical grounds

64 Right to remuneration on suspension on medical grounds

(1) An employee who is suspended from work by his employer on medical grounds is entitled to be paid by his employer remuneration while he is so suspended for a period not exceeding twenty-six weeks.

(2) For the purposes of this Part an employee is suspended from work on medical grounds if he is suspended from work in consequence of—

(a) a requirement imposed by or under a provision of an enactment or of an instrument made under an enactment, or

(b) a recommendation in a provision of a code of practice issued or approved under section 16 of the Health and Safety at Work etc. Act 1974,

and the provision is for the time being specified in subsection (3).

(3) The provisions referred to in subsection (2) are—

Regulation 16 of the Control of Lead at Work Regulations 1980,

Regulation 24 of the Ionising Radiations Regulations 1999 [SI 1999/3232], and

Regulation 11 of the Control of Substances Hazardous to Health Regulations 1988.

(4) The Secretary of State may by order add provisions to or remove provisions from the list of provisions specified in subsection (3).

(5) For the purposes of this Part an employee shall be regarded as suspended from work on medical grounds only if and for so long as he—

(a) continues to be employed by his employer, but

(b) is not provided with work or does not perform the work he normally performed before the suspension.

65 Exclusions from right to remuneration

(1) An employee is not entitled to remuneration under section 64 unless he has been continuously employed for a period of not less than one month ending with the day before that on which the suspension begins.

(2) [repealed]

(3) An employee is not entitled to remuneration under section 64 in respect of any period during which he is incapable of work by reason of disease or bodily or mental disablement.

(4) An employee is not entitled to remuneration under section 64 in respect of any period if—

(a) his employer has offered to provide him with suitable alternative work during the period (whether or not it is work which the employee is under his contract, or was under the contract in force before the suspension, employed to perform) and the employee has unreasonably refused to perform that work, or

(b) he does not comply with reasonable requirements imposed by his employer with a view to ensuring that his services are available.

Suspension on maternity grounds

66 Meaning of suspension on maternity grounds

(1) For the purposes of this Part an employee is suspended from work on maternity grounds if, in consequence of any relevant requirement or relevant recommendation, she is

suspended from work by her employer on the ground that she is pregnant, has recently given birth or is breastfeeding a child.

(2) In subsection (1)—

'relevant requirement' means a requirement imposed by or under a specified provision of an enactment or of an instrument made under an enactment, and

'relevant recommendation' means a recommendation in a specified provision of a code of practice issued or approved under section 16 of the Health and Safety at Work etc. Act 1974;

and in this subsection 'specified provision' means a provision for the time being specified in an order made by the Secretary of State under this subsection.

(3) For the purposes of this Part an employee shall be regarded as suspended from work on maternity grounds only if and for so long as she—

(a) continues to be employed by her employer, but

(b) is not provided with work or (disregarding alternative work for the purposes of section 67) does not perform the work she normally performed before the suspension.

67 Right to offer of alternative work

(1) Where an employer has available suitable alternative work for an employee, the employee has a right to be offered to be provided with the alternative work before being suspended from work on maternity grounds.

(2) For alternative work to be suitable for an employee for the purposes of this section—

(a) the work must be of a kind which is both suitable in relation to her and appropriate for her to do in the circumstances, and

(b) the terms and conditions applicable to her for performing the work, if they differ from the corresponding terms and conditions applicable to her for performing the work she normally performs under her contract of employment, must not be substantially less favourable to her than those corresponding terms and conditions.

68 Right to remuneration

(1) An employee who is suspended from work on maternity grounds is entitled to be paid remuneration by her employer while she is so suspended.

(2) An employee is not entitled to remuneration under this section in respect of any period if—

(a) her employer has offered to provide her during the period with work which is suitable alternative work for her for the purposes of section 67, and

(b) the employee has unreasonably refused to perform that work.

General

69 Calculation of remuneration

(1) The amount of remuneration payable by an employer to an employee under section 64 or 68 is a week's pay in respect of each week of the period of suspension; and if in any week remuneration is payable in respect of only part of that week the amount of a week's pay shall be reduced proportionately.

(2) A right to remuneration under section 64 or 68 does not affect any right of an employee in relation to remuneration under the employee's contract of employment ('contractual remuneration').

(3) Any contractual remuneration paid by an employer to an employee in respect of any period goes towards discharging the employer's liability under section 64 or 68 in respect of that period; and, conversely, any payment of remuneration in discharge of an employer's liability under section 64 or 68 in respect of any period goes towards discharging any obligation of the employer to pay contractual remuneration in respect of that period.

70 Complaints to employment tribunals

(1) An employee may present a complaint to an employment tribunal that his or her employer has failed to pay the whole or any part of remuneration to which the employee is entitled under section 64 or 68.

(2) An employment tribunal shall not consider a complaint under subsection (1) relating to remuneration in respect of any day unless it is presented—

(a) before the end of the period of three months beginning with that day, or

(b) within such further period as the tribunal considers reasonable in a case where it is satisfied that it was not reasonably practicable for the complaint to be presented within that period of three months.

(3) Where an employment tribunal finds a complaint under subsection (1) well-founded, the tribunal shall order the employer to pay the employee the amount of remuneration which it finds is due to him or her.

(4) An employee may present a complaint to an employment tribunal that in contravention of section 67 her employer has failed to offer to provide her with work.

(5) An employment tribunal shall not consider a complaint under subsection (4) unless it is presented—

(a) before the end of the period of three months beginning with the first day of the suspension, or

(b) within such further period as the tribunal considers reasonable in a case where it is satisfied that it was not reasonably practicable for the complaint to be presented within that period of three months.

(6) Where an employment tribunal finds a complaint under subsection (4) well-founded, the tribunal may make an award of compensation to be paid by the employer to the employee.

(7) The amount of the compensation shall be such as the tribunal considers just and equitable in all the circumstances having regard to—

(a) the infringement of the employee's right under section 67 by the failure on the part of the employer to which the complaint relates, and

(b) any loss sustained by the employee which is attributable to that failure.

PART VIII

CHAPTER I   MATERNITY LEAVE

71 Ordinary maternity leave

(1) An employee may, provided that she satisfies any conditions which may be prescribed, be absent from work at any time during an ordinary maternity leave period.

(2) An ordinary maternity leave period is a period calculated in accordance with regulations made by the Secretary of State.

(3) Regulations under subsection (2)—

(a) shall secure that no ordinary maternity leave period is less than 18 weeks;

(b) may allow an employee to choose, subject to any prescribed restrictions, the date on which an ordinary maternity leave period starts.

(4) Subject to section 74, an employee who exercises her right under subsection (1)—

(a) is entitled for such purposes and to such extent as may be prescribed to the benefit of the terms and conditions of employment which would have applied if she had not been absent,

(b) is bound for such purposes and to such extent as may be prescribed by any obligations arising under those terms and conditions (except in so far as they are inconsistent with subsection (1)), and

(c) is entitled to return from leave to a job of a prescribed kind.

(5) In subsection (4)(a) 'terms and conditions of employment'—

(a) includes matters connected with an employee's employment whether or not they arise under her contract of employment, but

(b) does not include terms and conditions about remuneration.

(6)–(7) [omitted]

72   Compulsory maternity leave

(1) An employer shall not permit an employee who satisfies prescribed conditions to work during a compulsory maternity leave period.

(2) A compulsory maternity leave period is a period calculated in accordance with regulations made by the Secretary of State.

(3) Regulations under subsection (2) shall secure—

(a) that no compulsory leave period is less than two weeks, and

(b) that every compulsory maternity leave period falls within an ordinary maternity leave period.

(4) Subject to subsection (5), any provision of or made under the Health and Safety at Work etc. Act 1974 shall apply in relation to the prohibition under subsection (1) as if it were imposed by regulations under section 15 of that Act.

(5) Section 33(1)(c) of the 1974 Act shall not apply in relation to the prohibition under subsection (1); and an employer who contravenes that subsection shall be—

(a) guilty of an offence, and

(b) liable on summary conviction to a fine not exceeding level 2 on the standard scale.

73   Additional maternity leave

(1) An employee who satisfies prescribed conditions may be absent from work at any time during an additional maternity leave period.

(2) An additional maternity leave period is a period calculated in accordance with regulations made by the Secretary of State.

(3) Regulations under subsection (2) may allow an employee to choose, subject to prescribed restrictions, the date on which an additional maternity leave period ends.

(4) Subject to section 74, an employee who exercises her right under subsection (1)—

(a) is entitled, for such purposes and to such extent as may be prescribed, to the benefit of the terms and conditions of employment which would have applied if she had not been absent,

(b) is bound, for such purposes and to such extent as may be prescribed, by obligations arising under those terms and conditions (except in so far as they are inconsistent with subsection (1), and

(c) is entitled to return from leave to a job of a prescribed kind.

(5) In subsection (4)(a) 'terms and conditions of employment'—

(a) includes matters connected with an employee's employment whether or not they arise under her contract of employment, but

(b) does not include terms and conditions about remuneration.

(5A) In subsection (4)(c), the reference to return from leave includes, where appropriate, a reference to a continuous period of absence attributable partly to additional maternity leave and partly to ordinary maternity leave.

(6)–(7) [omitted]

74–75   [omitted]

CHAPTER 1A   ADOPTION LEAVE

75A   Ordinary adoption leave

(1) An employee who satisfies prescribed conditions may be absent from work at any time during an ordinary adoption leave period.

(2) An ordinary adoption leave period is a period calculated in accordance with regulations made by the Secretary of State.

(3) Subject to section 75C, an employee who exercises his right under subsection (1)—

    (a) is entitled, for such purposes and to such extent as may be prescribed, to the benefit of the terms and conditions of employment which would have applied if he had not been absent,

    (b) is bound, for such purposes and to such extent as may be prescribed, by any obligations arising under those terms and conditions (except in so far as they are inconsistent with subsection (1)), and

    (c) is entitled to return from leave to a job of a prescribed kind.

(4) In subsection (3)(a) 'terms and conditions of employment'—

    (a) includes matters connected with an employee's employment whether or not they arise under his contract of employment, but

    (b) does not include terms and conditions about remuneration.

(5) In subsection (3)(c), the reference to return from leave includes, where appropriate, a reference to a continuous period of absence attributable partly to ordinary adoption leave and partly to maternity leave.

(6)–(7) [omitted]

75B Additional adoption leave

(1) An employee who satisfies prescribed conditions may be absent from work at any time during an additional adoption leave period.

(2) An additional adoption leave period is a period calculated in accordance with regulations made by the Secretary of State.

(3) Regulations under subsection (2) may allow an employee to choose, subject to prescribed restrictions, the date on which an additional adoption leave period ends.

(4) Subject to section 75C, an employee who exercises his right under subsection (1)—

    (a) is entitled, for such purposes and to such extent as may be prescribed, to the benefit of the terms and conditions of employment which would have applied if he had not been absent,

    (b) is bound, for such purposes and to such extent as may be prescribed, by obligations arising under those terms and conditions (except in so far as they are inconsistent with subsection (1)), and

    (c) is entitled to return from leave to a job of a prescribed kind.

(5) In subsection (4)(a) 'terms and conditions of employment'—

    (a) includes matters connected with an employee's employment whether or not they arise under his contract of employment, but

    (b) does not include terms and conditions about remuneration.

(6) In subsection (4)(c), the reference to return from leave includes, where appropriate, a reference to a continuous period of absence attributable partly to additional adoption leave and partly to—

    (a) maternity leave, or

    (b) ordinary adoption leave,

or to both.

(7)–(8) [omitted]

75C–E and 76–79 [omitted]

CHAPTER II   PARENTAL LEAVE

80 Complaint to employment tribunal

(1) An employee may present a complaint to an employment tribunal that his employer—

    (a) has unreasonably postponed a period of parental leave requested by the employee, or

(b) has prevented or attempted to prevent the employee from taking parental leave.

(2) An employment tribunal shall not consider a complaint under this section unless it is presented—

(a) before the end of the period of three months beginning with the date (or last date) of the matters complained of, or

(b) within such further period as the tribunal considers reasonable in a case where it is satisfied that it was not reasonably practicable for the complaint to be presented before the end of that period of three months.

(3) Where an employment tribunal finds a complaint under this section well-founded it—

(a) shall make a declaration to that effect, and

(b) may make an award of compensation to be paid by the employer to the employee.

(4) The amount of compensation shall be such as the tribunal considers just and equitable in all the circumstances having regard to—

(a) the employer's behaviour, and

(b) any loss sustained by the employee which is attributable to the matters complained of.

80A–80E [omitted]

PART VIIIA   FLEXIBLE WORKING

80F Statutory right to request contract variation

(1) A qualifying employee may apply to his employer for a change in his terms and conditions of employment if—

(a) the change relates to—

(i)   the hours he is required to work,

(ii) the times when he is required to work,

(iii) where, as between his home and a place of business of his employer, he is required to work, or

(iv) such other aspect of his terms and conditions of employment as the Secretary of State may specify by regulations, and

(b) his purpose in applying for the change is to enable him to care for someone who, at the time of application, is a child in respect of whom he satisfies such conditions as to relationship as the Secretary of State may specify by regulations.

(2) An application under this section must—

(a) state that it is such an application,

(b) specify the change applied for and the date on which it is proposed the change should become effective,

(c) explain what effect, if any, the employee thinks making the change applied for would have on his employer and how, in his opinion, any such effect might be dealt with, and

(d) explain how the employee meets, in respect of the child concerned, the conditions as to relationship mentioned in subsection (1)(b).

(3) An application under this section must be made before the fourteenth day before the day on which the child concerned reaches the age of six or, if disabled, eighteen.

(4) If an employee has made an application under this section, he may not make a further application under this section to the same employer before the end of the period of twelve months beginning with the date on which the previous application was made.

(5)–(6) [omitted]

80G Employer's duties in relation to application under section 80F

(1) An employer to whom an application under section 80F is made—

(a) shall deal with the application in accordance with regulations made by the Secretary of State, and

(b) shall only refuse the application because he considers that one or more of the following grounds applies—

    (i)   the burden of additional costs,

    (ii) detrimental effect on ability to meet customer demand,

    (iii) inability to re-organise work among existing staff,

    (iv) inability to recruit additional staff,

    (v) detrimental impact on quality,

    (vi) detrimental impact on performance,

    (vii) insufficiency of work during the periods the employee proposes to work,

    (viii) planned structural changes, and

    (ix) such other grounds as the Secretary of State may specify by regulations.

(2)–(4) [omitted]

80H   Complaints to employment tribunals

(1) An employee who makes an application under section 80F may present a complaint to an employment tribunal—

(a) that his employer has failed in relation to the application to comply with section 80G(1), or

(b) that a decision by his employer to reject the application was based on incorrect facts.

(2) No complaint under this section may be made in respect of an application which has been disposed of by agreement or withdrawn.

(3) In the case of an application which has not been disposed of by agreement or withdrawn, no complaint under this section may be made until the employer—

(a) notifies the employee of a decision to reject the application on appeal, or

(b) commits a breach of regulations under section 80G(1)(a) of such description as the Secretary of State may specify by regulations.

(4) No complaint under this section may be made in respect of failure to comply with provision included in regulations under subsection (1)(a) of section 80G because of subsection (2)(k), (1) or (m) of that section.

(5) An employment tribunal shall not consider a complaint under this section unless it is presented—

(a) before the end of the period of three months beginning with the relevant date, or

(b) within such further period as the tribunal considers reasonable in a case where it is satisfied that it was not reasonably practicable for the complaint to be presented before the end of that period of three months.

(6) In subsection (5)(a), the reference to the relevant date is—

(a) in the case of a complaint permitted by subsection (3)(a), the date on which the employee is notified of the decision on the appeal, and

(b) in the case of a complaint permitted by subsection (3)(b), the date on which the breach concerned was committed.

80I   Remedies

(1) Where an employment tribunal finds a complaint under section 80H well-founded it shall make a declaration to that effect and may—

(a) make an order for reconsideration of the application, and

(b) make an award of compensation to be paid by the employer to the employee.

(2) The amount of compensation shall be such amount, not exceeding the permitted maximum, as the tribunal considers just and equitable in all the circumstances.

(3) For the purposes of subsection (2), the permitted maximum is such number of weeks' pay as the Secretary of State may specify by regulations.

(4) Where an employment tribunal makes an order under subsection (1)(a), section 80G, and the regulations under that section, shall apply as if the application had been made on the date of the order.

81–85 [repealed]

PART IX   TERMINATION OF EMPLOYMENT

Minimum period of notice

86 Rights of employer and employee to minimum notice

(1) The notice required to be given by an employer to terminate the contract of employment of a person who has been continuously employed for one month or more—

    (a) is not less than one week's notice if his period of continuous employment is less than two years,

    (b) is not less than one week's notice for each year of continuous employment if his period of continuous employment is two years or more but less than twelve years, and

    (c) is not less than twelve weeks' notice if his period of continuous employment is twelve years or more.

(2) The notice required to be given by an employee who has been continuously employed for one month or more to terminate his contract of employment is not less than one week.

(3) Any provision for shorter notice in any contract of employment with a person who has been continuously employed for one month or more has effect subject to subsections (1) and (2); but this section does not prevent either party from waiving his right to notice on any occasion or from accepting a payment in lieu of notice.

(4) Any contract of employment of a person who has been continuously employed for three months or more which is a contract for a term certain of one month or less shall have effect as if it were for an indefinite period; and, accordingly, subsections (1) and (2) apply to the contract.

(5) [repealed]

(6) This section does not affect any right of either party to a contract of employment to treat the contract as terminable without notice by reason of the conduct of the other party.

87 Rights of employee in period of notice

(1) If an employer gives notice to terminate the contract of employment of a person who has been continuously employed for one month or more, the provisions of sections 88 to 91 have effect as respects the liability of the employer for the period of notice required by section 86(1).

(2) If an employee who has been continuously employed for one month or more gives notice to terminate his contract of employment, the provisions of sections 88 to 91 have effect as respects the liability of the employer for the period of notice required by section 86(2).

(3) In sections 88 to 91 'period of notice' means—

    (a) where notice is given by an employer, the period of notice required by section 86(1), and

    (b) where notice is given by an employee, the period of notice required by section 86(2).

(4) This section does not apply in relation to a notice given by the employer or the employee if the notice to be given by the employer to terminate the contract must be at least one week more than the notice required by section 86(1).

88 Employments with normal working hours

(1) If an employee has normal working hours under the contract of employment in force during the period of notice and during any part of those normal working hours—

(a) the employee is ready and willing to work but no work is provided for him by his employer,

(b) the employee is incapable of work because of sickness or injury,

(c) the employee is absent from work wholly or partly because of pregnancy or childbirth or on adoption leave, parental leave or paternity leave or

(d) the employee is absent from work in accordance with the terms of his employment relating to holidays,

the employer is liable to pay the employee for the part of normal working hours covered by any of paragraphs (a), (b), (c) and (d) a sum not less than the amount of remuneration for that part of normal working hours calculated at the average hourly rate of remuneration produced by dividing a week's pay by the number of normal working hours.

(2) Any payments made to the employee by his employer in respect of the relevant part of the period of notice (whether by way of sick pay, statutory sick pay, maternity pay, statutory maternity pay, paternity pay, statutory paternity pay, adoption pay, statutory adoption pay, holiday pay or otherwise) go towards meeting the employer's liability under this section.

(3) Where notice was given by the employee, the employer's liability under this section does not arise unless and until the employee leaves the service of the employer in pursuance of the notice.

89 Employments without normal working hours

(1) If an employee does not have normal working hours under the contract of employment in force in the period of notice, the employer is liable to pay the employee for each week of the period of notice a sum not less than a week's pay.

(2) The employer's liability under this section is conditional on the employee being ready and willing to do work of a reasonable nature and amount to earn a week's pay.

(3) Subsection (2) does not apply—

(a) in respect of any period during which the employee is incapable of work because of sickness or injury,

(b) in respect of any period during which the employee is absent from work wholly or partly because of pregnancy or childbirth or on adoption leave, parental leave or paternity leave, or

(c) in respect of any period during which the employee is absent from work in accordance with the terms of his employment relating to holidays.

(4) Any payment made to an employee by his employer in respect of a period within subsection (3) (whether by way of sick pay, statutory sick pay, maternity pay, statutory maternity pay, paternity pay, statutory paternity pay, adoption pay, statutory adoption pay, holiday pay or otherwise) shall be taken into account for the purposes of this section as if it were remuneration paid by the employer in respect of that period.

(5) Where notice was given by the employee, the employer's liability under this section does not arise unless and until the employee leaves the service of the employer in pursuance of the notice.

90 Short-term incapacity benefit and industrial injury benefit

(1) This section has effect where the arrangements in force relating to the employment are such that—

(a) payments by way of sick pay are made by the employer to employees to whom the arrangements apply, in cases where any such employees are incapable of work because of sickness or injury, and

(b) in calculating any payment so made to any such employee an amount representing, or treated as representing, short-term incapacity benefit or industrial injury benefit is taken into account, whether by way of deduction or by way of calculating the payment as a supplement to that amount.

(2) If—

(a) during any part of the period of notice the employee is incapable of work because of sickness or injury,

(b) one or more payments by way of sick pay are made to him by the employer in respect of that part of the period of notice, and

(c) in calculating any such payment such an amount as is referred to in paragraph (b) of subsection (1) is taken into account as mentioned in that paragraph,

for the purposes of section 88 or 89 the amount so taken into account shall be treated as having been paid by the employer to the employee by way of sick pay in respect of that part of that period, and shall go towards meeting the liability of the employer under that section accordingly.

91 Supplementary

(1) An employer is not liable under section 88 or 89 to make any payment in respect of a period during which an employee is absent from work with the leave of the employer granted at the request of the employee, including any period of time off taken in accordance with—

(a) Part VI of this Act, or

(b) section 168 or 170 of the Trade Union and Labour Relations (Consolidation) Act 1992 (trade union duties and activities).

(2) No payment is due under section 88 or 89 in consequence of a notice to terminate a contract given by an employee if, after the notice is given and on or before the termination of the contract, the employee takes part in a strike of employees of the employer.

(3) If, during the period of notice, the employer breaks the contract of employment, payments received under section 88 or 89 in respect of the part of the period after the breach go towards mitigating the damages recoverable by the employee for loss of earnings in that part of the period of notice.

(4) If, during the period of notice, the employee breaks the contract and the employer rightfully treats the breach as terminating the contract, no payment is due to the employee under section 88 or 89 in respect of the part of the period falling after the termination of the contract.

(5) If an employer fails to give the notice required by section 86, the rights conferred by sections 87 to 90 and this section shall be taken into account in assessing his liability for breach of the contract.

(6) Sections 86 to 90 and this section apply in relation to a contract all or any of the terms of which are terms which take effect by virtue of any provision contained in or having effect under an Act (whether public or local) as in relation to any other contract; and the reference in this subsection to an Act includes, subject to any express provision to the contrary, an Act passed after this Act.

Written statement of reasons for dismissal

92 Right to written statement of reasons for dismissal

(1) An employee is entitled to be provided by his employer with a written statement giving particulars of the reasons for the employee's dismissal—

(a) if the employee is given by the employer notice of termination of his contract of employment,

(b) if the employee's contract of employment is terminated by the employer without notice, or

(c) if the employee is employed under a limited-term contract and the contract terminates by virtue of the limiting event without being renewed under the same contract.

(2) Subject to subsections (4) and (4A), an employee is entitled to a written statement under this section only if he makes a request for one; and a statement shall be provided within fourteen days of such a request.

(3) Subject to subsection (4), an employee is not entitled to a written statement under this section unless on the effective date of termination he has been, or will have been, continuously employed for a period of not less than one year ending with that date.

(4) An employee is entitled to a written statement under this section without having to request it and irrespective of whether she has been continuously employed for any period if she is dismissed—

(a) at any time while she is pregnant, or

(b) after childbirth in circumstances in which her ordinary or additional maternity leave period ends by reason of the dismissal.

(4A) An employee who is dismissed while absent from work during an ordinary or additional adoption leave period is entitled to a written statement under this section without having to request it and irrespective of whether he has been continuously employed for any period if he is dismissed in circumstances in which that period ends by reason of the dismissal.

(5) A written statement under this section is admissible in evidence in any proceedings.

(6) Subject to subsection (7), in this section 'the effective date of termination'—

(a) in relation to an employee whose contract of employment is terminated by notice, means the date on which the notice expires,

(b) in relation to an employee whose contract of employment is terminated without notice, means the date on which the termination takes effect, and

(c) in relation to an employee who is employed under a limited-term contract which terminates by virtue of the limiting event without being renewed under the same contract, means the date on which the termination takes effect.

(7) Where—

(a) the contract of employment is terminated by the employer, and

(b) the notice required by section 86 to be given by an employer would, if duly given on the material date, expire on a date later than the effective date of termination (as defined by subsection (6)),

the later date is the effective date of termination.

(8) In subsection (7)(b) 'the material date' means—

(a) the date when notice of termination was given by the employer, or

(b) where no notice was given, the date when the contract of employment was terminated by the employer.

93 Complaints to employment tribunal

(1) A complaint may be presented to an employment tribunal by an employee on the ground that—

(a) the employer unreasonably failed to provide a written statement under section 92, or

(b) the particulars of reasons given in purported compliance with that section are inadequate or untrue.

(2) Where an employment tribunal finds a complaint under this section well-founded, the tribunal—

(a) may make a declaration as to what it finds the employer's reasons were for dismissing the employee, and

(b) shall make an award that the employer pay to the employee a sum equal to the amount of two weeks' pay.

(3) An employment tribunal shall not consider a complaint under this section relating to the reasons for a dismissal unless it is presented to the tribunal at such a time that the tribunal

would, in accordance with section 111, consider a complaint of unfair dismissal in respect of that dismissal presented at the same time.

PART X UNFAIR DISMISSAL

CHAPTER I RIGHT NOT TO BE UNFAIRLY DISMISSED

The right

94 The right

(1) An employee has the right not to be unfairly dismissed by his employer.

(2) Subsection (1) has effect subject to the following provisions of this Part (in particular sections 108 to 110) and to the provisions of the Trade Union and Labour Relations (Consolidation) Act 1992 (in particular sections 237 to 239).

Dismissal

95 Circumstances in which an employee is dismissed

(1) For the purposes of this Part an employee is dismissed by his employer if (and, subject to subsection (2), only if)—

    (a) the contract under which he is employed is terminated by the employer (whether with or without notice),

    (b) he is employed under a limited-term contract and that contract terminates by virtue of the limiting event without being renewed under the same contract, or

    (c) the employee terminates the contract under which he is employed (with or without notice) in circumstances in which he is entitled to terminate it without notice by reason of the employer's conduct.

(2) An employee shall be taken to be dismissed by his employer for the purposes of this Part if—

    (a) the employer gives notice to the employee to terminate his contract of employment, and

    (b) at a time within the period of that notice the employee gives notice to the employer to terminate the contract of employment on a date earlier than the date on which the employer's notice is due to expire;

and the reason for the dismissal is to be taken to be the reason for which the employer's notice is given.

96 [repealed]

97 Effective date of termination

(1) Subject to the following provisions of this section, in this Part 'the effective date of termination'—

    (a) in relation to an employee whose contract of employment is terminated by notice, whether given by his employer or by the employee, means the date on which the notice expires,

    (b) in relation to an employee whose contract of employment is terminated without notice, means the date on which the termination takes effect, and

    (c) in relation to an employee who is employed under a limited-term contract which terminates by virtue of the limiting event without being renewed under the same contract, means the date on which the termination takes effect.

(2) Where—

    (a) the contract of employment is terminated by the employer, and

    (b) the notice required by section 86 to be given by an employer would, if duly given on the material date, expire on a date later than the effective date of termination (as defined by subsection (1)), for the purposes of sections 108(1), 119(1) and 227(3) the later date is the effective date of termination.

(3) In subsection (2)(b) 'the material date' means—

    (a) the date when notice of termination was given by the employer, or

    (b) where no notice was given, the date when the contract of employment was terminated by the employer.

(4) Where—

    (a) the contract of employment is terminated by the employee,

    (b) the material date does not fall during a period of notice given by the employer to terminate that contract, and

    (c) had the contract been terminated not by the employee but by notice given on the material date by the employer, that notice would have been required by section 86 to expire on a date later than the effective date of termination (as defined by subsection (1)),

for the purposes of sections 108(1), 119(1) and 227(3) the later date is the effective date of termination.

(5) In subsection (4) 'the material date' means—

    (a) the date when notice of termination was given by the employee, or

    (b) where no notice was given, the date when the contract of employment was terminated by the employee.

(6) [repealed]

Fairness

98   General

(1) In determining for the purposes of this Part whether the dismissal of an employee is fair or unfair, it is for the employer to show—

    (a) the reason (or, if more than one, the principal reason) for the dismissal, and

    (b) that it is either a reason falling within subsection (2) or some other substantial reason of a kind such as to justify the dismissal of an employee holding the position which the employee held.

(2) A reason falls within this subsection if it—

    (a) relates to the capability or qualifications of the employee for performing work of the kind which he was employed by the employer to do,

    (b) relates to the conduct of the employee,

    (ba) is retirement of the employee,

    (c) is that the employee was redundant, or

    (d) is that the employee could not continue to work in the position which he held without contravention (either on his part or on that of his employer) of a duty or restriction imposed by or under an enactment.

(2A) Subsections (1) and (2) are subject to sections 98ZA to 98ZF.

(3) In subsection (2)(a)—

    (a) 'capability', in relation to an employee, means his capability assessed by reference to skill, aptitude, health or any other physical or mental quality, and

    (b) 'qualifications', in relation to an employee, means any degree, diploma or other academic, technical or professional qualification relevant to the position which he held.

(3A) In any case where the employer has fulfilled the requirements of subsection (1) by showing that the reason (or the principal reason) for the dismissal is retirement of the employee, the question whether the dismissal is fair or unfair shall be determined in accordance with section 98ZG.

(4) In any other case where the employer has fulfilled the requirements of subsection (1), the determination of the question whether the dismissal is fair or unfair (having regard to the reason shown by the employer)—

(a) depends on whether in the circumstances (including the size and administrative resources of the employer's undertaking) the employer acted reasonably or unreasonably in treating it as a sufficient reason for dismissing the employee, and

(b) shall be determined in accordance with equity and the substantial merits of the case.

(5) [repealed]

(6) Subsection (4) is subject to—

(a) sections 98A to 107 of this Act, and

(b) sections 152, 153, 238 and 238A of the Trade Union and Labour Relations (Consolidation) Act 1992 (dismissal on ground of trade union membership or activities or in connection with industrial action).

Retirement

98ZA   No normal retirement age: dismissal before 65

(1) This section applies to the dismissal of an employee if—

(a) the employee has no normal retirement age, and

(b) the operative date of termination falls before the date when the employee reaches the age of 65.

(2) Retirement of the employee shall not be taken to be the reason (or a reason) for the dismissal.

98ZB   No normal retirement age: dismissal at or after 65

(1) This section applies to the dismissal of an employee if—

(a) the employee has no normal retirement age, and

(b) the operative date of termination falls on or after the date when the employee reaches the age of 65.

(2) In a case where—

(a) the employer has notified the employee in accordance with paragraph 2 of Schedule 6 to the 2006 Regulations, and

(b) the contract of employment terminates on the intended date of retirement,

retirement of the employee shall be taken to be the only reason for the dismissal by the employer and any other reason shall be disregarded.

(3) In a case where—

(a) the employer has notified the employee in accordance with paragraph 2 of Schedule 6 to the 2006 Regulations, but

(b) the contract of employment terminates before the intended date of retirement,

retirement of the employee shall not be taken to be the reason (or a reason) for dismissal.

(4) In a case where—

(a) the employer has not notified the employee in accordance with paragraph 2 of Schedule 6 to the 2006 Regulations, and

(b) there is an intended date of retirement in relation to the dismissal, but

(c) the contract of employment terminates before the intended date of retirement,

retirement of the employee shall not be taken to be the reason (or a reason) for dismissal.

(5) In all other cases where the employer has not notified the employee in accordance with paragraph 2 of Schedule 6 to the 2006 Regulations, particular regard shall be had to the matters in section 98ZF when determining the reason (or principal reason) for dismissal.

98ZC   Normal retirement age: dismissal before retirement age

(1) This section applies to the dismissal of an employee if—

(a) the employee has a normal retirement age, and

(b) the operative date of termination falls before the date when the employee reaches the normal retirement age.

(2) Retirement of the employee shall not be taken to be the reason (or a reason) for the dismissal.

98ZD   Normal retirement age 65 or higher: dismissal at or after retirement age

(1) This section applies to the dismissal of an employee if—

    (a) the employee has a normal retirement age,

    (b) the normal retirement age is 65 or higher, and

    (c) the operative date of termination falls on or after the date when the employee reaches the normal retirement age.

(2) In a case where—

    (a) the employer has notified the employee in accordance with paragraph 2 of Schedule 6 to the 2006 Regulations, and

    (b) the contract of employment terminates on the intended date of retirement,

retirement of the employee shall be taken to be the only reason for the dismissal by the employer and any other reason shall be disregarded.

(3) In a case where—

    (a) the employer has notified the employee in accordance with paragraph 2 of Schedule 6 to the 2006 Regulations, but

    (b) the contract of employment terminates before the intended date of retirement,

retirement of the employee shall not be taken to be the reason (or a reason) for dismissal.

(4) In a case where—

    (a) the employer has not notified the employee in accordance with paragraph 2 of Schedule 6 to the 2006 Regulations, and

    (b) there is an intended date of retirement in relation to the dismissal, but

    (c) the contract of employment terminates before the intended date of retirement,

retirement of the employee shall not be taken to be the reason (or a reason) for dismissal.

(5) In all other cases where the employer has not notified the employee in accordance with paragraph 2 of Schedule 6 to the 2006 Regulations, particular regard shall be had to the matters in section 98ZF when determining the reason (or principal reason) for dismissal.

98ZE   Normal retirement age below 65: dismissal at or after retirement age

(1) This section applies to the dismissal of an employee if—

    (a) the employee has a normal retirement age,

    (b) the normal retirement age is below 65, and

    (c) the operative date of termination falls on or after the date when the employee reaches the normal retirement age.

(2) If it is unlawful discrimination under the 2006 Regulations for the employee to have that normal retirement age, retirement of the employee shall not be taken to be the reason (or a reason) for dismissal.

(3) Subsections (4) to (7) apply if it is not unlawful discrimination under the 2006 Regulations for the employee to have that normal retirement age.

(4) In a case where—

    (a) the employer has notified the employee in accordance with paragraph 2 of Schedule 6 to the 2006 Regulations, and

    (b) the contract of employment terminates on the intended date of retirement,

retirement of the employee shall be taken to be the only reason for dismissal by the employer and any other reason shall be disregarded.

(5) In a case where—

    (a) the employer has notified the employee in accordance with paragraph 2 of Schedule 6 to the 2006 Regulations, but

    (b) the contract of employment terminates before the intended date of retirement,

retirement of the employee shall not be taken to be the reason (or a reason) for dismissal.

(6) In a case where—

    (a) the employer has not notified the employee in accordance with paragraph 2 of Schedule 6 to the 2006 Regulations, and

    (b) there is an intended date of retirement in relation to the dismissal, but

(c) the contract of employment terminates before the intended date of retirement, retirement of the employee shall not be taken to be the reason (or a reason) for dismissal.

(7) In all other cases where the employer has not notified the employee in accordance with paragraph 2 of Schedule 6 to the 2006 Regulations, particular regard shall be had to the matters in section 98ZF when determining the reason (or principal reason) for dismissal

98ZF Reason for dismissal: particular matters

(1) These are the matters to which particular regard is to be had in accordance with section 98ZB(5), 98ZD(5) or 98ZE(7)—

(a) whether or not the employer has notified the employee in accordance with paragraph 4 of Schedule 6 to the 2006 Regulations;

(b) if the employer has notified the employee in accordance with that paragraph, how long before the notified retirement date the notification was given;

(c) whether or not the employer has followed, or sought to follow, the procedures in paragraph 7 of Schedule 6 to the 2006 Regulations.

(2) In subsection (1)(b) 'notified retirement date' means the date notified to the employee in accordance with paragraph 4 of Schedule 6 to the 2006 Regulations as the date on which the employer intends to retire the employee.

98ZG Retirement dismissals: fairness

(1) This section applies if the reason (or principal reason) for a dismissal is retirement of the employee.

(2) The employee shall be regarded as unfairly dismissed if, and only if, there has been a failure on the part of the employer to comply with an obligation imposed on him by any of the following provisions of Schedule 6 to the 2006 Regulations—

(a) paragraph 4 (notification of retirement, if not already given under paragraph 2),

(b) paragraphs 6 and 7 (duty to consider employee's request not to be retired),

(c) paragraph 8 (duty to consider appeal against decision to refuse request not to be retired).

98ZG Interpretation

In sections 98ZA to 98ZG—

'2006 Regulations' means the Employment Equality (Age) Regulations 2006;

'intended date of retirement' means the date which, by virtue of paragraph 1(2) of Schedule 6 to the 2006 Regulations, is the intended date of retirement in relation to a particular dismissal;

'normal retirement age', in relation to an employee, means the age at which employees in the employer's undertaking who hold, or have held, the same kind of position as the employee are normally required to retire;

'operative date of termination' means—

(a) where the employer terminates the employee's contract of employment by notice, the date on which the notice expires, or

(b) where the employer terminates the contract of employment without notice, the date on which the termination takes effect.

Other dismissals

98A Procedural fairness

(1) An employee who is dismissed shall be regarded for the purposes of this Part as unfairly dismissed if—

(a) one of the procedures set out in Part 1 of Schedule 2 to the Employment Act 2002 (dismissal and disciplinary procedures) applies in relation to the dismissal,

(b) the procedure has not been completed, and

(c) the non-completion of the procedure is wholly or mainly attributable to failure by the employer to comply with its requirements.

(2) Subject to subsection (1), failure by an employer to follow a procedure in relation to the dismissal of an employee shall not be regarded for the purposes of section 98(4)(a) as by itself making the employer's action unreasonable if he shows that he would have decided to dismiss the employee if he had followed the procedure.

(3) For the purposes of this section, any question as to the application of a procedure set out in Part 1 of Schedule 2 to the Employment Act 2002, completion of such a procedure or failure to comply with the requirements of such a procedure shall be determined by reference to regulations under section 31 of that Act.

98B   [omitted]

99   Leave for family reasons

(1) An employee who is dismissed shall be regarded for the purposes of this Part as unfairly dismissed if—

(a) the reason or principal reason for the dismissal is of a prescribed kind, or

(b) the dismissal takes place in prescribed circumstances.

(2) In this section 'prescribed' means prescribed by regulations made by the Secretary of State.

(3) A reason or set of circumstances prescribed under this section must relate to—

(a) pregnancy, childbirth or maternity,

(b) ordinary, compulsory or additional maternity leave,

(ba) ordinary or additional adoption leave,

(c) parental leave,

(ca) paternity leave, or

(d) time off under section 57A;

and it may also relate to redundancy or other factors.

(4) A reason or set of circumstances prescribed under subsection (1) satisfies subsection (3)(c) or (d) if it relates to action which an employee—

(a) takes,

(b) agrees to take, or

(c) refuses to take,

under or in respect of a collective or workforce agreement which deals with parental leave.

(5) [omitted]

100   Health and safety cases

(1) An employee who is dismissed shall be regarded for the purposes of this Part as unfairly dismissed if the reason (or, if more than one, the principal reason) for the dismissal is that—

(a) having been designated by the employer to carry out activities in connection with preventing or reducing risks to health and safety at work, the employee carried out (or proposed to carry out) any such activities,

(b) being a representative of workers on matters of health and safety at work or member of a safety committee—

   (i)   in accordance with arrangements established under or by virtue of any enactment, or

   (ii) by reason of being acknowledged as such by the employer, the employee performed (or proposed to perform) any functions as such a representative or a member of such a committee,

(ba) the employee took part (or proposed to take part) in consultation with the employer pursuant to the Health and Safety (Consultation with Employees) Regulations 1996 or in an election of representatives of employee safety within the meaning of those Regulations (whether as a candidate or otherwise),

(c) being an employee at a place where—

   (i)   there was no such representative or safety committee, or

(ii) there was such a representative or safety committee but it was not reasonably practicable for the employee to raise the matter by those means,

he brought to his employer's attention, by reasonable means, circumstances connected with his work which he reasonably believed were harmful or potentially harmful to health or safety,

(d) in circumstances of danger which the employee reasonably believed to be serious and imminent and which he could not reasonably have been expected to avert, he left (or proposed to leave) or (while the danger persisted) refused to return to his place of work or any dangerous part of his place of work, or

(e) in circumstances of danger which the employee reasonably believed to be serious and imminent, he took (or proposed to take) appropriate steps to protect himself or other persons from the danger.

(2) For the purposes of subsection (1)(e) whether steps which an employee took (or proposed to take) were appropriate is to be judged by reference to all the circumstances including, in particular, his knowledge and the facilities and advice available to him at the time.

(3) Where the reason (or, if more than one, the principal reason) for the dismissal of an employee is that specified in subsection (1)(e), he shall not be regarded as unfairly dismissed if the employer shows that it was (or would have been) so negligent for the employee to take the steps which he took (or proposed to take) that a reasonable employer might have dismissed him for taking (or proposing to take) them.

101 [omitted]

101A Working time cases

(1) An employee who is dismissed shall be regarded for the purposes of this Part as unfairly dismissed if the reason (or, if more than one, the principal reason) for the dismissal is that the employee—

(a) refused (or proposed to refuse) to comply with a requirement which the employer imposed (or proposed to impose) in contravention of the Working Time Regulations 1998,

(b) refused (or proposed to refuse) to forgo a right conferred on him by those Regulations,

(c) failed to sign a workforce agreement for the purposes of those Regulations, or to enter into, or agree to vary or extend, any other agreement with his employer which is provided for in those Regulations, or

(d) being—

(i) a representative of members of the workforce for the purposes of Schedule 1 to those Regulations, or

(ii) a candidate in an election in which any person elected will, on being elected, be such a representative,

performed (or proposed to perform) any functions or activities as such a representative or candidate.

(2) [omitted]

102 Trustees of occupational pension schemes

(1) An employee who is dismissed shall be regarded for the purposes of this Part as unfairly dismissed if the reason (or, if more than one, the principal reason) for the dismissal is that, being a trustee of a relevant occupational pension scheme which relates to his employment, the employee performed (or proposed to perform) any functions as such a trustee.

(1A) This section applies to an employee who is a director of a company which is a trustee of a relevant occupational pension scheme as it applies to an employee who is a trustee of such a scheme (references to such a trustee being read for this purpose as references to such a director).

(2) In this section 'relevant occupational pension scheme' means an occupational pension scheme (as defined in section 1 of the Pension Schemes Act 1993) established under a trust.

103 Employee representatives

(1) An employee who is dismissed shall be regarded for the purposes of this Part as unfairly dismissed if the reason (or, if more than one, the principal reason) for the dismissal is that the employee, being—

    (a) an employee representative for the purposes of Chapter II of Part IV of the Trade Union and Labour Relations (Consolidation) Act 1992 (redundancies) or Regulations 9, 13 and 15 of the Transfer of Undertakings (Protection of Employment) Regulations 2006, or

    (b) a candidate in an election in which any person elected will, on being elected, be such an employee representative,

    performed (or proposed to perform) any functions or activities as such an employee representative or candidate.

(2) An employee who is dismissed shall be regarded for the purposes of this Part as unfairly dismissed if the reason (or, if more than one, the principal reason) for the dismissal is that the employee took part in an election of employee representatives for the purposes of Chapter II of Part IV of the Trade Union and Labour Relations (Consolidation) Act 1992 (redundancies) or Regulations 9, 13 and 15 of the Transfer of Undertakings (Protection of Employment) Regulations 2006.

103A Protected disclosure

An employee who is dismissed shall be regarded for the purposes of this Part as unfairly dismissed if the reason (or, if more than one, the principal reason) for the dismissal is that the employee made a protected disclosure.

104 Assertion of statutory right

(1) An employee who is dismissed shall be regarded for the purposes of this Part as unfairly dismissed if the reason (or, if more than one, the principal reason) for the dismissal is that the employee—

    (a) brought proceedings against the employer to enforce a right of his which is a relevant statutory right, or

    (b) alleged that the employer had infringed a right of his which is a relevant statutory right.

(2) It is immaterial for the purposes of subsection (1)—

    (a) whether or not the employee has the right, or

    (b) whether or not the right has been infringed;

but, for that subsection to apply, the claim to the right and that it has been infringed must be made in good faith.

(3) It is sufficient for subsection (1) to apply that the employee, without specifying the right, made it reasonably clear to the employer what the right claimed to have been infringed was.

(4) The following are relevant statutory rights for the purposes of this section—

    (a) any right conferred by this Act for which the remedy for its infringement is by way of a complaint or reference to an employment tribunal,

    (b) the right conferred by section 86 of this Act,

    (c) the rights conferred by sections 68, 86, 145A, 145B, 146, 168, 168A, 169 and 170 of the Trade Union and Labour Relations (Consolidation) Act 1992 (deductions from pay, union activities and time off),

    (d) the rights conferred by the Working Time Regulations 1998, the Merchant Shipping (Working Time: Inland Waterways) Regulations 2003 or the Fishing Vessels (Working Time: Sea-fishermen) Regulations 2004, and

    (e) the rights conferred by the Transfer of Undertakings (Protection of Employment) Regulations 2006.

(5) In this section any reference to an employer includes, where the right in question is conferred by section 63A, the principal (within the meaning of section 63A(3)).

104A The national minimum wage

(1) An employee who is dismissed shall be regarded for the purposes of this Part as unfairly dismissed if the reason (or, if more than one, the principal reason) for the dismissal is that—

    (a) any action was taken, or was proposed to be taken, by or on behalf of the employee with a view to enforcing, or otherwise securing the benefit of, a right of the employee's to which this section applies, or

    (b) the employer was prosecuted for an offence under section 31 of the National Minimum Wage Act 1998 as a result of action taken by or on behalf of the employee for the purpose of enforcing, or otherwise securing the benefit of, a right of the employee's to which this section applies, or

    (c) the employee qualifies, or will or might qualify, for the national minimum wage or for a particular rate of national minimum wage.

(2) It is immaterial for the purposes of paragraph (a) or (b) of subsection (1) above—

    (a) whether or not the employee has the right, or

    (b) whether or not the right has been infringed, but, for that subsection to apply, the claim to the right and, if applicable, the claim that it has been infringed must be made in good faith.

(3) The following are the rights to which this section applies—

    (a) any right conferred by, or by virtue of, any provision of the National Minimum Wage Act 1998 for which the remedy for its infringement is by way of a complaint to an employment tribunal, and

    (b) any right conferred by section 17 of the National Minimum Wage Act 1998 (worker receiving less than national minimum wage entitled to additional remuneration).

104B Tax credit

(1) An employee who is dismissed shall be regarded for the purposes of this Part as unfairly dismissed if the reason (or, if more than one, the principal reason) for the dismissal is that—

    (a) any action was taken, or was proposed to be taken, by or on behalf of the employee with a view to enforcing, or otherwise securing the benefit of, a right conferred on the employee by regulations under section 25 of the Tax Credits Act 2002,

    (b) a penalty was imposed on the employer, or proceedings for a penalty were brought against him, under that Act, as a result of action taken by or on behalf of the employee for the purpose of enforcing, or otherwise securing the benefit of, such a right, or

    (c) the employee is entitled, or will or may be entitled, to working families' tax credit or disabled person's tax credit.

(2) It is immaterial for the purposes of subsection 1(a) or (b)—

    (a) whether or not the employee has the right, or

    (b) whether or not the right has been infringed,

but, for those provision to apply, the claim to the right and, (if applicable) the claim that it has been infringed must be made in good faith.

104C Flexible working

An employee who is dismissed shall be regarded for the purposes of this Part as unfairly dismissed if the reason (or, if more than one, the principal reason) for the dismissal is that the employee—

    (a) made (or proposed to make) an application under section 80F,

    (b) exercised (or proposed to exercise) a right conferred on him under section 80G,

    (c) brought proceedings against the employer under section 80H, or

    (d) alleged the existence of any circumstance which would constitute a ground for bringing such proceedings.

105 Redundancy

(1) An employee who is dismissed shall be regarded for the purposes of this Part as unfairly dismissed if—

    (a) the reason (or, if more than-one, the principal reason) for the dismissal is that the employee was redundant,

    (b) it is shown that the circumstances constituting the redundancy applied equally to one or more other employees in the same undertaking who held positions similar to that held by the employee and who have not been dismissed by the employer, and

    (c) it is shown that any of subsections (2A) to (7I) apply.

(2) [repealed]

(2A) [omitted]

(3) This subsection applies if the reason (or, if more than one, the principal reason) for which the employee was selected for dismissal was one of those specified in subsection (1) of section 100 (read with subsections (2) and (3) of that section).

(4) This subsection applies if either—

    (a) the employee was a protected shop worker or an opted-out shop worker, or a protected betting worker or an opted-out betting worker, and the reason (or, if more than one, the principal reason) for which the employee was selected for dismissal was that specified in subsection (1) of section 101 (read with subsection (2) of that section), or

    (b) the employee was a shop worker or a betting worker and the reason (or, if more than one, the principal reason) for which the employee was selected for dismissal was that specified in subsection (3) of that section.

(4A) This subsection applies if the reason (or, if more than one, the principal reason) for which the employee was selected for dismissal was one of those specified in section 101A.

(5) This subsection applies if the reason (or, if more than one, the principal reason) for which the employee was selected for dismissal was that specified in section 102(1).

(6) This subsection applies if the reason (or, if more than one, the principal reason) for which the employee was selected for dismissal was that specified in section 103.

(6A) This subsection applies if the reason (or, if more than one, the principal reason) for which the employee was selected for dismissal was that specified in section 103A.

(7) This subsection applies if the reason (or, if more than one, the principal reason) for which the employee was selected for dismissal was one of those specified in subsection (1) of section 104 (read with subsections (2) and (3) of that section).

(7A) This subsection applies if the reason (or, if more than one, the principal reason) for which the employee was selected for dismissal was one of those specified in subsection (1) of section 104A (read with subsection (2) of that section).

(7B) This subsection applies if the reason (or, if more than one, the principal reason) for which the employee has selected for dismissal was one of those specified in subsection (1) of section 104B (read with subsection (2) of that section).

(7BA) This subsection applies if the reason (or, if more than one, the principal reason) for which the employee was selected for dismissal was one of those specified in section 104C.

(7C) This subsection applies if—

    (a) the reason (or, if more than one, the principal reason) for which the employee was selected for dismissal was the reason mentioned in section 238A(2) of the Trade Union and Labour Relations (Consolidation) Act 1992 (participation in official industrial action), and

    (b) subsection (3), (4) or (5) of that section applies to the dismissal.

(7D) This subsection applies if the reason (or, if more than one, the principal reason) for which the employee was selected for dismissal was one specified in paragraph (3) or (6) of regulation 28 of the Transnational Information and Consultation of Employees Regulations 1999 (read with paragraphs (4) and (7) of that regulation).

(7E) This subsection applies if the reason (or, if more than one, the principal reason) for which the employee was selected for dismissal was one specified in paragraph (3) of regulation 7 of the Part-time Workers (Prevention of Less Favourable Treatment) Regulations 2000 (unless the case is one to which paragraph (4) of that regulation applies).

(7F) This subsection applies if the reason (or, if more than one, the principal reason) for which the employee was selected for dismissal was one specified in paragraph (3) of regulation 6 of the Fixed-term Employees (Prevention of Less Favourable Treatment) Regulations 2002 (unless the case is one to which paragraph (4) of that regulation applies).

(7G) [omitted]

(7H) This subsection applies if the reason (or, if more than one, the principal reason) for which the employee was selected for dismissal was one specified in paragraph (3) or (6) of regulation 30 of the Information and Consultation of Employees Regulations 2004 (read with paragraphs (4) and (7) of that regulation).

(7I) This subsection applies if the reason (or, if more than one, the principal reason) for which the employee was selected for dismissal was one specified in paragraph 5(3) or (5) of the Schedule to the Occupational and Personal Pension Schemes (Consultation by Employers and Miscellaneous Amendment) Regulations 2006 (read with paragraph 5(6) of that Schedule).

(8) For the purposes of section 36(2)(b) or 41(1)(b), the appropriate date in relation to this section is the effective date of termination.

(9) In this Part 'redundancy case' means a case where paragraphs (a) and (b) of subsection (1) of this section are satisfied.

106 Replacements

(1) Where this section applies to an employee he shall be regarded for the purposes of section 98(1)(b) as having been dismissed for a substantial reason of a kind such as to justify the dismissal of an employee holding the position which the employee held.

(2) This section applies to an employee where—
   (a) on engaging him the employer informs him in writing that his employment will be terminated on the resumption of work by another employee who is, or will be, absent wholly or partly because of pregnancy or childbirth, or on adoption leave and
   (b) the employer dismisses him in order to make it possible to give work to the other employee.

(3) This section also applies to an employee where—
   (a) on engaging him the employer informs him in writing that his employment will be terminated on the end of a suspension of another employee from work on medical grounds or maternity grounds (within the meaning of Part VII), and
   (b) the employer dismisses him in order to make it possible to allow the resumption of work by the other employee.

(4) Subsection (1) does not affect the operation of section 98(4) in a case to which this section applies.

107 Pressure on employer to dismiss unfairly

(1) This section applies where there falls to be determined for the purposes of this Part a question—
   (a) as to the reason, or principal reason, for which an employee was dismissed,
   (b) whether the reason or principal reason for which an employee was dismissed was a reason fulfilling the requirement of section 98(1)(b), or
   (c) whether an employer acted reasonably in treating the reason or principal reason for which an employee was dismissed as a sufficient reason for dismissing him.

(2) In determining the question no account shall be taken of any pressure which by calling, organising, procuring or financing a strike or other industrial action, or threatening to do so, was exercised on the employer to dismiss the employee; and the question shall be determined as if no such pressure had been exercised.

Exclusion of right

108   Qualifying period of employment

(1) Section 94 does not apply to the dismissal of an employee unless he has been continuously employed for a period of not less than one year ending with the effective date of termination.

(2) If an employee is dismissed by reason of any such requirement or recommendation as is referred to in section 64(2), subsection (1) has effect in relation to that dismissal as if for the words 'one year' there were substituted the words 'one month'.

(3) Subsection (1) does not apply if—

    (a)   [repealed]

    (aa) [omitted]

    (b)   subsection (1) of section 99 (read with any regulation made under that section) applies,

    (c)   subsection (1) of section 100 (read with subsections (2) and (3) of that section) applies,

    (d)   subsection (1) of section 101 (read with subsection (2) of that section) or subsection (3) of that section applies,

    (dd) section 101A applies,

    (e)   section 102 applies,

    (f)   section 103 applies,

    (ff)   section 103A applies,

    (g)   subsection (1) of section 104 (read with subsections (2) and (3) of that section) applies,

    (gg) subsection (1) of section 104A (read with subsection (2) of that section) applies,

    (gh) subsection (1) of section 104B (read with subsection (2) of that section) applies,

    (gi) section 104C applies,

    (h)   section 105 applies,

    (hh) paragraph (3) or (6) of regulation 28 of the Transnational Information and Consultation of Employees Regulations 1999 (read with paragraphs (4) and (7) of that regulation) applies,

    (i)   paragraph (1) of regulation 7 of the Part-time Workers (Prevention of Less Favourable Treatment) Regulations 2000 applies,

    (j)   paragraph (1) of regulation 6 of the Fixed-term Employees (Prevention of Less Favourable Treatment) Regulations 2002 applies,

    (k)   paragraph (3) or (6) of regulation 42 of the European Public Limited-Liability Company Regulations 2004,

    (l)   paragraph (3) or (6) of regulation 30 of the Information and Consultation of Employees Regulations 2004 (read with paragraphs (4) and (7) of that regulation) applies,

    (m)   paragraph 5(3) or (5) of the Schedule to the Occupational and Personal Pension Schemes (Consultation by Employers and Miscellaneous Amendment) Regulations 2006 (read with paragraph 5(6) of that Schedule) applies, or

    (n)   paragraph (a) or (b) of paragraph 13(5) of Schedule 6 to the Employment Equality (Age) Regulations 2006 applies.

109   [repealed]; 110 [omitted]

CHAPTER II   REMEDIES FOR UNFAIR DISMISSAL

Introductory

111   Complaints to employment tribunal

(1) A complaint may be presented to an employment tribunal against an employer by any person that he was unfairly dismissed by the employer.

(2) Subject to subsection (3), an employment tribunal shall not consider a complaint under this section unless it is presented to the tribunal—

    (a) before the end of the period of three months beginning with the effective date of termination, or

    (b) within such further period as the tribunal considers reasonable in a case where it is satisfied that it was not reasonably practicable for the complaint to be presented before the end of that period of three months.

(3) Where a dismissal is with notice, an employment tribunal shall consider a complaint under this section if it is presented after the notice is given but before the effective date of termination.

(4) In relation to a complaint which is presented as mentioned in subsection (3), the provisions of this Act, so far as they relate to unfair dismissal, have effect as if—

    (a) references to a complaint by a person that he was unfairly dismissed by his employer included references to a complaint by a person that his employer has given him notice in such circumstances that he will be unfairly dismissed when the notice expires,

    (b) references to reinstatement included references to the withdrawal of the notice by the employer,

    (c) references to the effective date of termination included references to the date which would be the effective date of termination on the expiry of the notice, and

    (d) references to an employee ceasing to be employed included references to an employee having been given notice of dismissal.

112   The remedies: orders and compensation

(1) This section applies where, on a complaint under section 111, an employment tribunal finds that the grounds of the complaint are well-founded.

(2) The tribunal shall—

    (a) explain to the complainant what orders may be made under section 113 and in what circumstances they may be made, and

    (b) ask him whether he wishes the tribunal to make such an order.

(3) If the complainant expresses such a wish, the tribunal may make an order under section 113.

(4) If no order is made under section 113, the tribunal shall make an award of compensation for unfair dismissal (calculated in accordance with sections 118 to 126) to be paid by the employer to the employee.

(5) Where—

    (a) an employee is regarded as unfairly dismissed by virtue of section 98ZG or 98A(1) (whether or not his dismissal is unfair or regarded as unfair for any other reason), and

    (b) an order is made in respect of the employee under section 113,

the employment tribunal shall, subject to subsection (6), also make an award of four weeks' pay to be paid by the employer to the employee.

(6) An employment tribunal shall not be required to make an award under subsection (5) if it considers that such an award would result in injustice to the employer.

Orders for reinstatement or re-engagement

113   The orders

An order under this section may be—

    (a) an order for reinstatement (in accordance with section 114), or

    (b) an order for re-engagement (in accordance with section 115), as the tribunal may decide.

114   Order for reinstatement

(1) An order for reinstatement is an order that the employer shall treat the complainant in all respects as if he had not been dismissed.

(2) On making an order for reinstatement the tribunal shall specify—

  (a) any amount payable by the employer in respect of any benefit which the complainant might reasonably be expected to have had but for the dismissal (including arrears of pay) for the period between the date of termination of employment and the date of reinstatement,

  (b) any rights and privileges (including seniority and pension rights) which must be restored to the employee, and

  (c) the date by which the order must be complied with.

(3) If the complainant would have benefited from an improvement in his terms and conditions of employment had he not been dismissed, an order for reinstatement shall require him to be treated as if he had benefited from that improvement from the date on which he would have done so but for being dismissed.

(4) In calculating for the purposes of subsection (2)(a) any amount payable by the employer, the tribunal shall take into account, so as to reduce the employer's liability, any sums received by the complainant in respect of the period between the date of termination of employment and the date of reinstatement by way of—

  (a) wages in lieu of notice or ex gratia payments paid by the employer, or

  (b) remuneration paid in respect of employment with another employer, and such other benefits as the tribunal thinks appropriate in the circumstances.

(5) [repealed]

115 Order for re-engagement

(1) An order for re-engagement is an order, on such terms as the tribunal may decide, that the complainant be engaged by the employer, or by a successor of the employer or by an associated employer, in employment comparable to that from which he was dismissed or other suitable employment.

(2) On making an order for re-engagement the tribunal shall specify the terms on which re-engagement is to take place, including—

  (a) the identity of the employer,

  (b) the nature of the employment,

  (c) the remuneration for the employment,

  (d) any amount payable by the employer in respect of any benefit which the complainant might reasonably be expected to have had but for the dismissal (including arrears of pay) for the period between the date of termination of employment and the date of re-engagement,

  (e) any rights and privileges (including seniority and pension rights) which must be restored to the employee, and

  (f) the date by which the order must be complied with.

(3) In calculating for the purposes of subsection (2)(d) any amount payable by the employer, the tribunal shall take into account, so as to reduce the employer's liability, any sums received by the complainant in respect of the period between the date of termination of employment and the date of re-engagement by way of—

  (a) wages in lieu of notice or ex gratia payments paid by the employer, or

  (b) remuneration paid in respect of employment with another employer, and such other benefits as the tribunal thinks appropriate in the circumstances.

(4) [repealed]

116 Choice of order and its terms

(1) In exercising its discretion under section 113 the tribunal shall first consider whether to make an order for reinstatement and in so doing shall take into account—

  (a) whether the complainant wishes to be reinstated,

  (b) whether it is practicable for the employer to comply with an order for reinstatement, and

(c) where the complainant caused or contributed to some extent to the dismissal, whether it would be just to order his reinstatement.

(2) If the tribunal decides not to make an order for reinstatement it shall then consider whether to make an order for re-engagement and, if so, on what terms.

(3) In so doing the tribunal shall take into account—

(a) any wish expressed by the complainant as to the nature of the order to be made,

(b) whether it is practicable for the employer (or a successor or an associated employer) to comply with an order for re-engagement, and

(c) where the complainant caused or contributed to some extent to the dismissal, whether it would be just to order his re-engagement and (if so) on what terms.

(4) Except in a case where the tribunal takes into account contributory fault under subsection (3)(c) it shall, if it orders re-engagement, do so on terms which are, so far as is reasonably practicable, as favourable as an order for reinstatement.

(5) Where in any case an employer has engaged a permanent replacement for a dismissed employee, the tribunal shall not take that fact into account in determining, for the purposes of subsection (1)(b) or (3)(b), whether it is practicable to comply with an order for reinstatement or re-engagement.

(6) Subsection (5) does not apply where the employer shows—

(a) that it was not practicable for him to arrange for the dismissed employee's work to be done without engaging a permanent replacement, or

(b) that—

(i) he engaged the replacement after the lapse of a reasonable period, without having heard from the dismissed employee that he wished to be reinstated or re-engaged, and

(ii) when the employer engaged the replacement it was no longer reasonable for him to arrange for the dismissed employee's work to be done except by a permanent replacement.

117   Enforcement of order and compensation

(1) An employment tribunal shall make an award of compensation, to be paid by the employer to the employee, if—

(a) (a) an order under section 113 is made and the complainant is reinstated or re-engaged, but

(b) the terms of the order are not fully complied with.

(2) Subject to section 124, the amount of the compensation shall be such as the tribunal thinks fit having regard to the loss sustained by the complainant in consequence of the failure to comply fully with the terms of the order.

(2A) There shall be deducted from any award under subsection (1) the amount of any award made under section 112(5) at the time of the order under section 113.

(3) Subject to subsections (1) and (2), if an order under section 113 is made but the complainant is not reinstated or re-engaged in accordance with the order, the tribunal shall make—

(a) an award of compensation for unfair dismissal (calculated in accordance with sections 118 to 126), and

(b) except where this paragraph does not apply, an additional award of compensation of an amount not less than twenty-six nor more than fifty-two weeks' pay, to be paid by the employer to the employee.

(4) Subsection (3)(b) does not apply where—

(a) the employer satisfies the tribunal that it was not practicable to comply with the order,

(b) [repealed]

(5)–(6) [repealed]

(7) Where in any case an employer has engaged a permanent replacement for a dismissed employee, the tribunal shall not take that fact into account in determining for the purposes

of subsection (4)(a) whether it was practicable to comply with the order for reinstatement or re-engagement unless the employer shows that it was not practicable for him to arrange for the dismissed employee's work to be done without engaging a permanent replacement.

(8) Where in any case an employment tribunal finds that the complainant has unreasonably prevented an order under section 113 from being complied with, in making an award of compensation for unfair dismissal it shall take that conduct into account as a failure on the part of the complainant to mitigate his loss.

Compensation

118   General

(1) Where a tribunal makes an award of compensation for unfair dismissal under section 112(4) or 117(3)(a) the award shall consist of—

   (a) a basic award (calculated in accordance with sections 119 to 122 and 126), and
   (b) a compensatory award (calculated in accordance with sections 123, 124, 124A and 126).

(2)–(4) [repealed]

119   Basic award

(1) Subject to the provisions of this section, sections 120 to 122 and section 126, the amount of the basic award shall be calculated by—

   (a) determining the period, ending with the effective date of termination, during which the employee has been continuously employed,
   (b) reckoning backwards from the end of that period the number of years of employment falling within that period, and
   (c) allowing the appropriate amount for each of those years of employment.

(2) In subsection (1)(c) 'the appropriate amount' means—

   (a) one and a half weeks' pay for a year of employment in which the employee was not below the age of forty-one,
   (b) one week's pay for a year of employment (not within paragraph (a)) in which he was not below the age of twenty-two, and
   (c) half a week's pay for a year of employment not within paragraph (a) or (b).

(3) Where twenty years of employment have been reckoned under subsection (1), no account shall be taken under that subsection of any year of employment earlier than those twenty years.

(4)–(6) [repealed]

120   Basic award: minimum in certain cases

(1) The amount of the basic award (before any reduction under section 122) shall not be less than £4,000 where the reason (or, if more than one, the principal reason)—

   (a) in a redundancy case, for selecting the employee for dismissal, or
   (b) otherwise, for the dismissal,

is one of those specified in section 100(1)(a) and (b), 101A(d), 102(1) or 103.

(1A) Where—

   (a) an employee is regarded as unfairly dismissed by virtue of section 98ZG or 98A(1) (whether or not his dismissal is unfair or regarded as unfair for any other reason),
   (b) an award of compensation falls to be made under section 112(4), and
   (c) the amount of the award under section 118(1)(a), before any reduction under section 122(3A) or (4), is less than the amount of four weeks' pay,

the employment tribunal shall, subject to subsection (1B), increase the award under section 118(1)(a) to the amount of four weeks' pay.

(1B) An employment tribunal shall not be required by subsection (1A) to increase the amount of an award if it considers that the increase would result in injustice to the employer.

(2) [repealed]

121 Basic award of two weeks' pay in certain cases

The amount of the basic award shall be two weeks' pay where the tribunal finds that the reason (or, where there is more than one, the principal reason) for the dismissal of the employee is that he was redundant and the employee—

(a) by virtue of section 138 is not regarded as dismissed for the purposes of Part XI, or

(b) by virtue of section 141 is not, or (if he were otherwise entitled) would not be, entitled to a redundancy payment.

122 Basic award: reductions

(1) Where the tribunal finds that the complainant has unreasonably refused an offer by the employer which (if accepted) would have the effect of reinstating the complainant in his employment in all respects as if he had not been dismissed, the tribunal shall reduce or further reduce the amount of the basic award to such extent as it considers just and equitable having regard to that finding.

(2) Where the tribunal considers that any conduct of the complainant before the dismissal (or, where the dismissal was with notice, before the notice was given) was such that it would be just and equitable to reduce or further reduce the amount of the basic award to any extent, the tribunal shall reduce or further reduce that amount accordingly.

(3) Subsection (2) does not apply in a redundancy case unless the reason for selecting the employee for dismissal was one of those specified in section 100(1)(a) and (b), 101A(d), 102(1) or 103; and in such a case subsection (2) applies only to so much of the basic award as is payable because of section 120.

(3A) Where the complainant has been awarded any amount in respect of the dismissal under a designated dismissal procedures agreement, the tribunal shall reduce or further reduce the amount of the basic award to such extent as it considers just and equitable having regard to that award.

(4) The amount of the basic award shall be reduced or further reduced by the amount of—

(a) any redundancy payment awarded by the tribunal under Part XI in respect of the same dismissal, or

(b) any payment made by the employer to the employee on the ground that the dismissal was by reason of redundancy (whether in pursuance of Part XI or otherwise).

123 Compensatory award

(1) Subject to the provisions of this section and sections 124, 124A and 126, the amount of the compensatory award shall be such amount as the tribunal considers just and equitable in all the circumstances having regard to the loss sustained by the complainant in consequence of the dismissal in so far as that loss is attributable to action taken by the employer.

(2) The loss referred to in subsection (1) shall be taken to include—

(a) any expenses reasonably incurred by the complainant in consequence of the dismissal, and

(b) subject to subsection (3), loss of any benefit which he might reasonably be expected to have had but for the dismissal.

(3) The loss referred to in subsection (1) shall be taken to include in respect of any loss of—

(a) any entitlement or potential entitlement to a payment on account of dismissal by reason of redundancy (whether in pursuance of Part XI or otherwise), or

(b) any expectation of such a payment, only the loss referable to the amount (if any) by which the amount of that payment would have exceeded the amount of a basic award (apart from any reduction under section 122) in respect of the same dismissal.

(4) In ascertaining the loss referred to in subsection (1) the tribunal shall apply the same rule concerning the duty of a person to mitigate his loss as applies to damages recoverable under the common law of England and Wales or (as the case may be) Scotland.

(5) In determining, for the purposes of subsection (1), how far any loss sustained by the complainant was attributable to action taken by the employer, no account shall be taken of any pressure which by—

(a) calling, organising, procuring or financing a strike or other industrial action, or

(b) threatening to do so,

was exercised on the employer to dismiss the employee; and that question shall be determined as if no such pressure had been exercised.

(6) Where the tribunal finds that the dismissal was to any extent caused or contributed to by any action of the complainant, it shall reduce the amount of the compensatory award by such proportion as it considers just and equitable having regard to that finding.

(7) If the amount of any payment made by the employer to the employee on the ground that the dismissal was by reason of redundancy (whether in pursuance of Part XI or otherwise) exceeds the amount of the basic award which would be payable but for section 122(4), that excess goes to reduce the amount of the compensatory award.

(8) Where the amount of the compensatory award falls to be calculated for the purposes of an award under section 117(3)(a), there shall be deducted from the compensatory award any award made under section 112(5) at the time of the order under section 113.

124   Limit of compensatory award etc.

(1) The amount of—

(a) any compensation awarded to a person under section 117(1) and (2), or

(b) a compensatory award to a person calculated in accordance with section 123, shall not exceed £58,400.

(1A) Subsection (1) shall not apply to compensation awarded, or a compensatory award made, to a person in a case where he is regarded as unfairly dismissed by virtue of section 100, 103A, 105(3) or 105(6A).

(2) [repealed]

(3) In the case of compensation awarded to a person under section 117(1) and (2), the limit imposed by this section may be exceeded to the extent necessary to enable the award fully to reflect the amount specified as payable under section 114(2)(a) or section 115(2)(d).

(4) Where—

(a) a compensatory award is an award under paragraph (a) of subsection (3) of section 117, and

(b) an additional award falls to be made under paragraph (b) of that subsection, the limit imposed by this section on the compensatory award may be exceeded to the extent necessary to enable the aggregate of the compensatory and additional awards fully to reflect the amount specified as payable under section 114(2)(a) or section 115(2)(d).

(5) The limit imposed by this section applies to the amount which the employment tribunal would, apart from this section, award in respect of the subject matter of the complaint after taking into account—

(a) any payment made by the respondent to the complainant in respect of that matter, and

(b) any reduction in the amount of the award required by any enactment or rule of law.

124A   Adjustments under the Employment Act 2002

Where an award of compensation for unfair dismissal falls to be—

(a) reduced or increased under section 31 of the Employment Act 2002 (non- completion of statutory procedures), or

(b) increased under section 38 of that Act (failure to give statement of employment particulars),

the adjustment shall be in the amount awarded under section 118(1)(b) and shall be applied immediately before any reduction under section 123(6) or (7).

125 [repealed]

126 Acts which are both unfair dismissal and discrimination

(1) This section applies where compensation falls to be awarded in respect of any act both under—

    (a) the provisions of this Act relating to unfair dismissal, and

    (b) any one or more of the following—

        (i)   the Sex Discrimination Act 1975;

        (ii) the Race Relations Act 1976;

        (iii) the Disability Discrimination Act 1995;

        (iv) the Employment Equality (Sexual Orientation) Regulation 2003;

        (v)   the Employment Equality (Religion or Belief) Regulations 2003;

        (vi) the Employment Equality (Age) Regulations 2006.

(2) An employment tribunal shall not award compensation under any one of those Acts or Regulations in respect of any loss or other matter which is or has been taken into account under any other of them, by the tribunal (or another employment tribunal) in awarding compensation on the same or another complaint in respect of that act.

127 and 127A–B [repealed]

Interim relief

128 Interim relief pending determination of complaint

(1) An employee who presents a complaint to an employment tribunal—

    (a) that he has been unfairly dismissed by his employer, and

    (b) that the reason (or, if more than one, the principal reason) for the dismissal is one of those specified in section 100(1)(a) and (b), 101A(d), 102(1), 103 or 103A, or in paragraph 161(2) Schedule A1 to the Trade Union and Labour Relations Consolidation Act 1992,

may apply to the tribunal for interim relief.

(2) The tribunal shall not entertain an application for interim relief unless it is presented to the tribunal before the end of the period of seven days immediately following the effective date of termination (whether before, on or after that date).

(3) The tribunal shall determine the application for interim relief as soon as practicable after receiving the application.

(4) The tribunal shall give to the employer not later than seven days before the date of the hearing a copy of the application together with notice of the date, time and place of the hearing.

(5) The tribunal shall not exercise any power it has of postponing the hearing of an application for interim relief except where it is satisfied that special circumstances exist which justify it in doing so.

129 Procedure on hearing of application and making of order

(1) This section applies where, on hearing an employee's application for interim relief, it appears to the tribunal that it is likely that on determining the complaint to which the application relates the tribunal will find that the reason (or, if more than one, the principal reason) for his dismissal is one of those specified in section 100(1)(a) and (b), 101A(d), 102(1), 103 or 103A or in paragraph 161(2) Schedule A1 to the Trade Union and Labour Relations Consolidation Act 1992.

(2) The tribunal shall announce its findings and explain to both parties (if present)—

    (a) what powers the tribunal may exercise on the application, and

    (b) in what circumstances it will exercise them.

(3) The tribunal shall ask the employer (if present) whether he is willing, pending the determination or settlement of the complaint—

    (a) to reinstate the employee (that is, to treat him in all respects as if he had not been dismissed), or

(b) if not, to re-engage him in another job on terms and conditions not less favourable than those which would have been applicable to him if he had not been dismissed.

(4) For the purposes of subsection (3)(b) 'terms and conditions not less favourable than those which would have been applicable to him if he had not been dismissed' means, as regards seniority, pension rights and other similar rights, that the period prior to the dismissal should be regarded as continuous with his employment following the dismissal.

(5) If the employer states that he is willing to reinstate the employee, the tribunal shall make an order to that effect.

(6) If the employer—

(a) states that he is willing to re-engage the employee in another job, and

(b) specifies the terms and conditions on which he is willing to do so,

the tribunal shall ask the employee whether he is willing to accept the job on those terms and conditions.

(7) If the employee is willing to accept the job on those terms and conditions, the tribunal shall make an order to that effect.

(8) If the employee is not willing to accept the job on those terms and conditions—

(a) where the tribunal is of the opinion that the refusal is reasonable, the tribunal shall make an order for the continuation of his contract of employment, and

(b) otherwise, the tribunal shall make no order.

(9) If on the hearing of an application for interim relief the employer—

(a) fails to attend before the tribunal, or

(b) states that he is unwilling either to reinstate or re-engage the employee as mentioned in subsection (3),

the tribunal shall make an order for the continuation of the employee's contract of employment.

130   Order for continuation of contract of employment

(1) An order under section 129 for the continuation of a contract of employment is an order that the contract of employment continue in force—

(a) for the purposes of pay or any other benefit derived from the employment, seniority, pension rights and other similar matters, and

(b) for the purposes of determining for any purpose the period for which the employee has been continuously employed,

from the date of its termination (whether before or after the making of the order) until the determination or settlement of the complaint.

(2) Where the tribunal makes such an order it shall specify in the order the amount which is to be paid by the employer to the employee by way of pay in respect of each normal pay period, or part of any such period, falling between the date of dismissal and the determination or settlement of the complaint.

(3) Subject to the following provisions, the amount so specified shall be that which the employee could reasonably have been expected to earn during that period, or part, and shall be paid—

(a) in the case of a payment for any such period falling wholly or partly after the making of the order, on the normal pay day for that period, and

(b) in the case of a payment for any past period, within such time as may be specified in the order.

(4) If an amount is payable in respect only of part of a normal pay period, the amount shall be calculated by reference to the whole period and reduced proportionately.

(5) Any payment made to an employee by an employer under his contract of employment, or by way of damages for breach of that contract, in respect of a normal pay period, or part of any such period, goes towards discharging the employer's liability in respect of that period under subsection (2); and, conversely, any payment under that subsection in respect of a period goes towards discharging any liability of the employer under, or in respect of breach of, the contract of employment in respect of that period.

(6) If an employee, on or after being dismissed by his employer, receives a lump sum which, or part of which, is in lieu of wages but is not referable to any normal pay period, the tribunal shall take the payment into account in determining the amount of pay to be payable in pursuance of any such order.

(7) For the purposes of this section, the amount which an employee could reasonably have been expected to earn, his normal pay period and the normal pay day for each such period shall be determined as if he had not been dismissed.

131 Application for variation or revocation of order

(1) At any time between—
   (a) the making of an order under section 129, and
   (b) the determination or settlement of the complaint,
the employer or the employee may apply to an employment tribunal for the revocation or variation of the order on the ground of a relevant change of circumstances since the making of the order.

(2) Sections 128 and 129 apply in relation to such an application as in relation to an original application for interim relief except that, in the case of an application by the employer, section 128(4) has effect with the substitution of a reference to the employee for the reference to the employer.

132 Consequence of failure to comply with order

(1) If, on the application of an employee, an employment tribunal is satisfied that the employer has not complied with the terms of an order for the reinstatement or re-engagement of the employee under section 129(5) or (7), the tribunal shall—
   (a) make an order for the continuation of the employee's contract of employment, and
   (b) order the employer to pay compensation to the employee.

(2) Compensation under subsection (1)(b) shall be of such amount as the tribunal considers just and equitable in all the circumstances having regard—
   (a) to the infringement of the employee's right to be reinstated or re-engaged in pursuance of the order, and
   (b) to any loss suffered by the employee in consequence of the non-compliance.

(3) Section 130 applies to an order under subsection (1)(a) as in relation to an order under section 129.

(4) If on the application of an employee an employment tribunal is satisfied that the employer has not complied with the terms of an order for the continuation of a contract of employment subsection (5) or (6) applies.

(5) Where the non-compliance consists of a failure to pay an amount by way of pay specified in the order—
   (a) the tribunal shall determine the amount owed by the employer on the date of the determination, and
   (b) if on that date the tribunal also determines the employee's complaint that he has been unfairly dismissed, it shall specify that amount separately from any other sum awarded to the employee.

(6) In any other case, the tribunal shall order the employer to pay the employee such compensation as the tribunal considers just and equitable in all the circumstances having regard to any loss suffered by the employee in consequence of the non-compliance.

CHAPTER III   SUPPLEMENTARY

133 Death of employer or employee

(1) Where—
   (a) an employer has given notice to an employee to terminate his contract of employment, and
   (b) before that termination the employee or the employer dies,

this Part applies as if the contract had been duly terminated by the employer by notice expiring on the date of the death.

(2) Where—

    (a) an employee's contract of employment has been terminated,

    (b) by virtue of subsection (2) or (4) of section 97 a date later than the effective date of termination as defined in subsection (1) of that section is to be treated for certain purposes as the effective date of termination, and

    (c) the employer or the employee dies before that date,

subsection (2) or (4) of section 97 applies as if the notice referred to in that subsection as required by section 86 expired on the date of the death.

(3) Where an employee has died, sections 113 to 116 do not apply; and, accordingly, if the employment tribunal finds that the grounds of the complaint are well-founded, the case shall be treated as falling within section 112(4) as a case in which no order is made under section 113.

(4) Subsection (3) does not prejudice an order for reinstatement or re-engagement made before the employee's death.

(5) Where an order for reinstatement or re-engagement has been made and the employee dies before the order is complied with—

    (a) if the employer has before the death refused to reinstate or re-engage the employee in accordance with the order, subsections (3) to (6) of section 117 apply, and an award shall be made under subsection (3)(b) of that section, unless the employer satisfies the tribunal that it was not practicable at the time of the refusal to comply with the order, and

    (b) if there has been no such refusal, subsections (1) and (2) of that section apply if the employer fails to comply with any ancillary terms of the order which remain capable of fulfilment after the employee's death as they would apply to such a failure to comply fully with the terms of an order where the employee had been reinstated or re-engaged.

134–134A [omitted]

PART XI REDUNDANCY PAYMENTS ETC.

CHAPTER I RIGHT TO REDUNDANCY PAYMENT

135 The right

(1) An employer shall pay a redundancy payment to any employee of his if the employee—

    (a) is dismissed by the employer by reason of redundancy, or

    (b) is eligible for a redundancy payment by reason of being laid off or kept on short-time.

(2) Subsection (1) has effect subject to the following provisions of this Part (including, in particular, sections 140 to 144, 149 to 152, 155 to 161 and 164).

CHAPTER II RIGHT ON DISMISSAL BY REASON OF REDUNDANCY

Dismissal by reason of redundancy

136 Circumstances in which an employee is dismissed

(1) Subject to the provisions of this section and sections 137 and 138, for the purposes of this Part an employee is dismissed by his employer if (and only if)—

    (a) the contract under which he is employed by the employer is terminated by the employer (whether with or without notice),

    (b) he is employed under a limited-term contract which terminates by virtue of the limiting event without being renewed under the same contract, or

(c) the employee terminates the contract under which he is employed (with or without notice) in circumstances in which he is entitled to terminate it without notice by reason of the employer's conduct.

(2) Subsection (1)(c) does not apply if the employee terminates the contract without notice in circumstances in which he is entitled to do so by reason of a lock-out by the employer.

(3) An employee shall be taken to be dismissed by his employer for the purposes of this Part if—

    (a) the employer gives notice to the employee to terminate his contract of employment, and

    (b) at a time within the obligatory period of notice the employee gives notice in writing to the employer to terminate the contract of employment on a date earlier than the date on which the employer's notice is due to expire.

(4) In this Part the 'obligatory period of notice', in relation to notice given by an employer to terminate an employee's contract of employment, means—

    (a) the actual period of the notice in a case where the period beginning at the time when the notice is given and ending at the time when it expires is equal to the minimum period which (by virtue of any enactment or otherwise) is required to be given by the employer to terminate the contract of employment, and

    (b) the period which—

        (i) is equal to the minimum period referred to in paragraph (a), and

        (ii) ends at the time when the notice expires, in any other case.

(5) Where in accordance with any enactment or rule of law—

    (a) an act on the part of an employer, or

    (b) an event affecting an employer (including, in the case of an individual, his death),

operates to terminate a contract under which an employee is employed by him, the act or event shall be taken for the purposes of this Part to be a termination of the contract by the employer.

137 [repealed]

138 No dismissal in cases of renewal of contract or re-engagement

(1) Where—

    (a) an employee's contract of employment is renewed, or he is re-engaged under a new contract of employment in pursuance of an offer (whether in writing or not) made before the end of his employment under the previous contract, and

    (b) the renewal or re-engagement takes effect either immediately on, or after an interval of not more than four weeks after, the end of that employment, the employee shall not be regarded for the purposes of this Part as dismissed by his employer by reason of the ending of his employment under the previous contract.

(2) Subsection (1) does not apply if—

    (a) the provisions of the contract as renewed, or of the new contract, as to—

        (i) the capacity and place in which the employee is employed, and

        (ii) the other terms and conditions of his employment, differ (wholly or in part) from the corresponding provisions of the previous contract, and

    (b) during the period specified in subsection (3)—

        (i) the employee (for whatever reason) terminates the renewed or new contract, or gives notice to terminate it and it is in consequence terminated, or

        (ii) the employer, for a reason connected with or arising out of any difference between the renewed or new contract and the previous contract, terminates the renewed or new contract, or gives notice to terminate it and it is in consequence terminated.

(3) The period referred to in subsection (2)(b) is the period—

    (a) beginning at the end of the employee's employment under the previous contract, and

   (b) ending with—
      (i) the period of four weeks beginning with the date on which the employee starts work under the renewed or new contract, or
      (ii) such longer period as may be agreed in accordance with subsection (6) for the purpose of retraining the employee for employment under that contract;
and is in this Part referred to as the 'trial period'.

   (4) Where subsection (2) applies, for the purposes of this Part—
      (a) the employee shall be regarded as dismissed on the date on which his employment under the previous contract (or, if there has been more than one trial period, the original contract) ended, and
      (b) the reason for the dismissal shall be taken to be the reason for which the employee was then dismissed, or would have been dismissed had the offer (or original offer) of renewed or new employment not been made, or the reason which resulted in that offer being made.

   (5) Subsection (2) does not apply if the employee's contract of employment is again renewed, or he is again re-engaged under a new contract of employment, in circumstances such that subsection (1) again applies.

   (6) For the purposes of subsection (3)(b)(ii) a period of retraining is agreed in accordance with this subsection only if the agreement—
      (a) is made between the employer and the employee or his representative before the employee starts work under the contract as renewed, or the new contract,
      (b) is in writing,
      (c) specifies the date on which the period of retraining ends, and
      (d) specifies the terms and conditions of employment which will apply in the employee's case after the end of that period.

139 Redundancy

   (1) For the purposes of this Act an employee who is dismissed shall be taken to be dismissed by reason of redundancy if the dismissal is wholly or mainly attributable to—
      (a) the fact that his employer has ceased or intends to cease—
         (i) to carry on the business for the purposes of which the employee was employed by him, or
         (ii) to carry on that business in the place where the employee was so employed, or
      (b) the fact that the requirements of that business—
         (i) for employees to carry out work of a particular kind, or
         (ii) for employees to carry out work of a particular kind in the place where the employee was employed by the employer,
      have ceased or diminished or are expected to cease or diminish.

   (2) For the purposes of subsection (1) the business of the employer together with the business or businesses of his associated employers shall be treated as one (unless either of the conditions specified in paragraphs (a) and (b) of that subsection would be satisfied without so treating them).

   (3) For the purposes of subsection (1) the activities carried on by a local education authority with respect to the schools maintained by it, and the activities carried on by the governing bodies of those schools, shall be treated as one business (unless either of the conditions specified in paragraphs (a) and (b) of that subsection would be satisfied without so treating them).

   (4) Where—
      (a) the contract under which a person is employed is treated by section 136(5) as terminated by his employer by reason of an act or event, and
      (b) the employee's contract is not renewed and he is not re-engaged under a new contract of employment,

he shall be taken for the purposes of this Act to be dismissed by reason of redundancy if the circumstances in which his contract is not renewed, and he is not re-engaged, are wholly or mainly attributable to either of the facts stated in paragraphs (a) and (b) of subsection (1).

(5) In its application to a case within subsection (4), paragraph (a)(i) of subsection (1) has effect as if the reference in that subsection to the employer included a reference to any person to whom, in consequence of the act or event, power to dispose of the business has passed.

(6) In subsection (1) 'cease' and 'diminish' mean cease and diminish either permanently or temporarily and for whatever reason.

Exclusions

140   Summary dismissal

(1) Subject to subsections (2) and (3), an employee is not entitled to a redundancy payment by reason of dismissal where his employer, being entitled to terminate his contract of employment without notice by reason of the employee's conduct, terminates it either—
  (a) without notice,
  (b) by giving shorter notice than that which, in the absence of conduct entitling the employer to terminate the contract without notice, the employer would be required to give to terminate the contract, or
  (c) by giving notice which includes, or is accompanied by, a statement in writing that the employer would, by reason of the employee's conduct, be entitled to terminate the contract without notice.

(2) Where an employee who—
  (a) has been given notice by his employer to terminate his contract of employment, or
  (b) has given notice to his employer under section 148(1) indicating his intention to claim a redundancy payment in respect of lay-off or short-time,
takes part in a strike at any relevant time in circumstances which entitle the employer to treat the contract of employment as terminable without notice, subsection (1) does not apply if the employer terminates the contract by reason of his taking part in the strike.

(3) Where the contract of employment of an employee who—
  (a) has been given notice by his employer to terminate his contract of employment, or
  (b) has given notice to his employer under section 148(1) indicating his intention to claim a redundancy payment in respect of lay-off or short-time,
is terminated as mentioned in subsection (1) at any relevant time otherwise than by reason of his taking part in a strike, an employment tribunal may determine that the employer is liable to make an appropriate payment to the employee if on a reference to the tribunal it appears to the tribunal, in the circumstances of the case, to be just and equitable that the employee should receive it.

(4) In subsection (3) 'appropriate payment' means—
  (a) the whole of the redundancy payment to which the employee would have been entitled apart from subsection (1), or
  (b) such part of that redundancy payment as the tribunal thinks fit.

(5) In this section 'relevant time'—
  (a) in the case of an employee who has been given notice by his employer to terminate his contract of employment, means any time within the obligatory period of notice, and
  (b) in the case of an employee who has given notice to his employer under section 148(1), means any time after the service of the notice.

141   Renewal of contract or re-engagement

(1) This section applies where an offer (whether in writing or not) is made to an employee before the end of his employment—

(a) to renew his contract of employment, or

(b) to re-engage him under a new contract of employment,

with renewal or re-engagement to take effect either immediately on, or after an interval of not more than four weeks after, the end of his employment.

(2) Where subsection (3) is satisfied, the employee is not entitled to a redundancy payment if he unreasonably refuses the offer.

(3) This subsection is satisfied where—

(a) the provisions of the contract as renewed, or of the new contract, as to—

    (i) the capacity and place in which the employee would be employed, and

    (ii) the other terms and conditions of his employment, would not differ from the corresponding provisions of the previous contract, or

(b) those provisions of the contract as renewed, or of the new contract, would differ from the corresponding provisions of the previous contract but the offer constitutes an offer of suitable employment in relation to the employee.

(4) The employee is not entitled to a redundancy payment if—

(a) his contract of employment is renewed, or he is re-engaged under a new contract of employment, in pursuance of the offer,

(b) the provisions of the contract as renewed or new contract as to the capacity or place in which he is employed or the other terms and conditions of his employment differ (wholly or in part) from the corresponding provisions of the previous contract,

(c) the employment is suitable in relation to him, and

(d) during the trial period he unreasonably terminates the contract, or unreasonably gives notice to terminate it and it is in consequence terminated.

142 Employee anticipating expiry of employer's notice

(1) Subject to subsection (3), an employee is not entitled to a redundancy payment where—

(a) he is taken to be dismissed by virtue of section 136(3) by reason of giving to his employer notice terminating his contract of employment on a date earlier than the date on which notice by the employer terminating the contract is due to expire,

(b) before the employee's notice is due to expire, the employer gives him a notice such as is specified in subsection (2), and

(c) the employee does not comply with the requirements of that notice.

(2) The employer's notice referred to in subsection (1)(b) is a notice in writing—

(a) requiring the employee to withdraw his notice terminating the contract of employment and to continue in employment until the date on which the employer's notice terminating the contract expires, and

(b) stating that, unless he does so, the employer will contest any liability to pay to him a redundancy payment in respect of the termination of his contract of employment.

(3) An employment tribunal may determine that the employer is liable to make an appropriate payment to the employee if on a reference to the tribunal it appears to the tribunal, having regard to—

(a) the reasons for which the employee seeks to leave the employment, and

(b) the reasons for which the employer requires him to continue in it,

to be just and equitable that the employee should receive the payment.

(4) In subsection (3) 'appropriate payment' means—

(a) the whole of the redundancy payment to which the employee would have been entitled apart from subsection (1), or

(b) such part of that redundancy payment as the tribunal thinks fit.

143 Strike during currency of employer's notice
(1) This section applies where—
- (a) an employer has given notice to an employee to terminate his contract of employment ('notice of termination'),
- (b) after the notice is given the employee begins to take part in a strike of employees of the employer, and
- (c) the employer serves on the employee a notice of extension.

(2) A notice of extension is a notice in writing which—
- (a) requests the employee to agree to extend the contract of employment beyond the time of expiry by a period comprising as many available days as the number of working days lost by striking ('the proposed period of extension'),
- (b) indicates the reasons for which the employer makes that request, and
- (c) states that the employer will contest any liability to pay the employee a redundancy payment in respect of the dismissal effected by the notice of termination unless either—
  - (i) the employee complies with the request, or
  - (ii) the employer is satisfied that, in consequence of sickness or injury or otherwise, the employee is unable to comply with it or that (even though he is able to comply with it) it is reasonable in the circumstances for him not to do so.

(3) Subject to subsections (4) and (5), if the employee does not comply with the request contained in the notice of extension, he is not entitled to a redundancy payment by reason of the dismissal effected by the notice of termination.

(4) Subsection (3) does not apply if the employer agrees to pay a redundancy payment to the employee in respect of the dismissal effected by the notice of termination even though he has not complied with the request contained in the notice of extension.

(5) An employment tribunal may determine that the employer is liable to make an appropriate payment to the employee if on a reference to the tribunal it appears to the tribunal that—
- (a) the employee has not complied with the request contained in the notice of extension and the employer has not agreed to pay a redundancy payment in respect of the dismissal effected by the notice of termination, but
- (b) either the employee was unable to comply with the request or it was reasonable in the circumstances for him not to comply with it.

(6) In subsection (5) 'appropriate payment' means—
- (a) the whole of the redundancy payment to which the employee would have been entitled apart from subsection (3), or
- (b) such part of that redundancy payment as the tribunal thinks fit.

(7) If the employee—
- (a) complies with the request contained in the notice of extension, or
- (b) does not comply with it but attends at his proper or usual place of work and is ready and willing to work on one or more (but not all) of the available days within the proposed period of extension,

the notice of termination has effect, and shall be deemed at all material times to have had effect, as if the period specified in it had been appropriately extended; and sections 87 to 91 accordingly apply as if the period of notice required by section 86 were extended to a corresponding extent.

(8) In subsection (7) 'appropriately extended' means—
- (a) in a case within paragraph (a) of that subsection, extended beyond the time of expiry by an additional period equal to the proposed period of extension, and
- (b) in a case within paragraph (b) of that subsection, extended beyond the time of expiry up to the end of the day (or last of the days) on which he attends at his proper or usual place of work and is ready and willing to work.

144 Provisions supplementary to section 143

(1) For the purposes of section 143 an employee complies with the request contained in a notice of extension if, but only if, on each available day within the proposed period of extension, he—

(a) attends at his proper or usual place of work, and

(b) is ready and willing to work,

whether or not he has signified his agreement to the request in any other way.

(2) The reference in section 143(2) to the number of working days lost by striking is a reference to the number of working days in the period—

(a) beginning with the date of service of the notice of termination, and

(b) ending with the time of expiry,

which are days on which the employee in question takes part in a strike of employees of his employer.

(3) In section 143 and this section—

'available day', in relation to an employee, means a working day beginning at or after the time of expiry which is a day on which he is not taking part in a strike of employees of the employer,

'available day within the proposed period of extension' means an available day which begins before the end of the proposed period of extension,

'time of expiry', in relation to a notice of termination, means the time at which the notice would expire apart from section 143, and

'working day', in relation to an employee, means a day on which, in accordance with his contract of employment, he is normally required to work.

(4) Neither the service of a notice of extension nor any extension by virtue of section 143(7) of the period specified in a notice of termination affects—

(a) any right either of the employer or of the employee to terminate the contract of employment (whether before, at or after the time of expiry) by a further notice or without notice, or

(b) the operation of this Part in relation to any such termination of the contract of employment.

Supplementary

145 The relevant date

(1) For the purposes of the provisions of this Act relating to redundancy payments 'the relevant date' in relation to the dismissal of an employee has the meaning given by this section.

(2) Subject to the following provisions of this section, 'the relevant date'—

(a) in relation to an employee whose contract of employment is terminated by notice, whether given by his employer or by the employee, means the date on which the notice expires,

(b) in relation to an employee whose contract of employment is terminated without notice, means the date on which the termination takes effect, and

(c) in relation to an employee who is employed under a limited-term contract which terminates by virtue of the limiting event without being renewed under the same contract, means the date on which the termination takes effect.

(3) Where the employee is taken to be dismissed by virtue of section 136(3) the 'relevant date' means the date on which the employee's notice to terminate his contract of employment expires.

(4) Where the employee is regarded by virtue of section 138(4) as having been dismissed on the date on which his employment under an earlier contract ended, 'the relevant date' means—

(a) for the purposes of section 164(1), the date which is the relevant date as defined by subsection (2) in relation to the renewed or new contract or, where there has been more than one trial period, the last such contract, and

(b) for the purposes of any other provision, the date which is the relevant date as defined by subsection (2) in relation to the previous contract or, where there has been more than one such trial period, the original contract.

(5) Where—

(a) the contract of employment is terminated by the employer, and

(b) the notice required by section 86 to be given by an employer would, if duly given on the material date, expire on a date later than the relevant date (as defined by the previous provisions of this section),

for the purposes of sections 155, 162(1) and 227(3) the later date is the relevant date.

(6) In subsection (5)(b) 'the material date' means—

(a) the date when notice of termination was given by the employer, or

(b) where no notice was given, the date when the contract of employment was terminated by the employer.

(7) [repealed]

146 Provisions supplementing sections 138 and 141

(1) In sections 138 and 141—

(a) references to re-engagement are to re-engagement by the employer or an associated employer, and

(b) references to an offer are to an offer made by the employer or an associated employer.

(2) For the purposes of the application of section 138(1) or 141(1) to a contract under which the employment ends on a Friday, Saturday or Sunday—

(a) the renewal or re-engagement shall be treated as taking effect immediately on the ending of the employment under the previous contract if it takes effect on or before the next Monday after that Friday, Saturday or Sunday, and

(b) the interval of four weeks to which those provisions refer shall be calculated as if the employment had ended on that next Monday.

(3) [repealed]

CHAPTER III   RIGHT BY REASON OF LAY-OFF OR SHORT-TIME

Lay-off and short-time

147 Meaning of 'lay-off' and 'short-time'

(1) For the purposes of this Part an employee shall be taken to be laid off for a week if—

(a) he is employed under a contract on terms and conditions such that his remuneration under the contract depends on his being provided by the employer with work of the kind which he is employed to do, but

(b) he is not entitled to any remuneration under the contract in respect of the week because the employer does not provide such work for him.

(2) For the purposes of this Part an employee shall be taken to be kept on short-time for a week if by reason of a diminution in the work provided for the employee by his employer (being work of a kind which under his contract the employee is employed to do) the employee's remuneration for the week is less than half a week's pay.

148 Eligibility by reason of lay-off or short-time

(1) Subject to the following provisions of this Part, for the purposes of this Part an employee is eligible for a redundancy payment by reason of being laid off or kept on short-time if—

(a) he gives notice in writing to his employer indicating (in whatever terms) his intention to claim a redundancy payment in respect of lay-off or short-time (referred to in this Part as 'notice of intention to claim'), and

(b) before the service of the notice he has been laid off or kept on short-time in circumstances in which subsection (2) applies.

(2) This subsection applies if the employee has been laid off or kept on short-time—

    (a) for four or more consecutive weeks of which the last before the service of the notice ended on, or not more than four weeks before, the date of service of the notice, or

    (b) for a series of six or more weeks (of which not more than three were consecutive) within a period of thirteen weeks, where the last week of the series before the service of the notice ended on, or not more than four weeks before, the date of service of the notice.

Exclusions

149 Counter-notices

Where an employee gives to his employer notice of intention to claim but—

    (a) the employer gives to the employee, within seven days after the service of that notice, notice in writing (referred to in this Part as a 'counter-notice') that he will contest any liability to pay to the employee a redundancy payment in pursuance of the employee's notice, and

    (b) the employer does not withdraw the counter-notice by a subsequent notice in writing,

the employee is not entitled to a redundancy payment in pursuance of his notice of intention to claim except in accordance with a decision of an employment tribunal.

150 Resignation

(1) An employee is not entitled to a redundancy payment by reason of being laid off or kept on short-time unless he terminates his contract of employment by giving such period of notice as is required for the purposes of this section before the end of the relevant period.

(2) The period of notice required for the purposes of this section—

    (a) where the employee is required by his contract of employment to give more than one week's notice to terminate the contract, is the minimum period which he is required to give, and

    (b) otherwise, is one week.

(3) In subsection (1) 'the relevant period'—

    (a) if the employer does not give a counter-notice within seven days after the service of the notice of intention to claim, is three weeks after the end of those seven days,

    (b) if the employer gives a counter-notice within that period of seven days but withdraws it by a subsequent notice in writing, is three weeks after the service of the notice of withdrawal, and

    (c) if—

        (i) the employer gives a counter-notice within that period of seven days, and does not so withdraw it, and

        (ii) a question as to the right of the employee to a redundancy payment in pursuance of the notice of intention to claim is referred to an employment tribunal,

    is three weeks after the tribunal has notified to the employee its decision on that reference.

(4) For the purposes of subsection (3)(c) no account shall be taken of—

    (a) any appeal against the decision of the tribunal, or

    (b) any proceedings or decision in consequence of any such appeal.

151 Dismissal

(1) An employee is not entitled to a redundancy payment by reason of being laid off or kept on short-time if he is dismissed by his employer.

(2) Subsection (1) does not prejudice any right of the employee to a redundancy payment in respect of the dismissal.

152 Likelihood of full employment

(1) An employee is not entitled to a redundancy payment in pursuance of a notice of intention to claim if—

(a) on the date of service of the notice it was reasonably to be expected that the employee (if he continued to be employed by the same employer) would, not later than four weeks after that date, enter on a period of employment of not less than thirteen weeks during which he would not be laid off or kept on short-time for any week, and

(b) the employer gives a counter-notice to the employee within seven days after the service of the notice of intention to claim.

(2) Subsection (1) does not apply where the employee—

(a) continues or has continued, during the next four weeks after the date of service of the notice of intention to claim, to be employed by the same employer, and

(b) is or has been laid off or kept on short-time for each of those weeks.

Supplementary

153 The relevant date

For the purposes of the provisions of this Act relating to redundancy payments 'the relevant date' in relation to a notice of intention to claim or a right to a redundancy payment in pursuance of such a notice—

(a) in a case falling within paragraph (a) of subsection (2) of section 148, means the date on which the last of the four or more consecutive weeks before the service of the notice came to an end, and

(b) in a case falling within paragraph (b) of that subsection, means the date on which the last of the series of six or more weeks before the service of the notice came to an end.

154 Provisions supplementing sections 148 and 152

For the purposes of sections 148(2) and 152(2)—

(a) it is immaterial whether a series of weeks consists wholly of weeks for which the employee is laid off or wholly of weeks for which he is kept on short-time or partly of the one and partly of the other, and

(b) no account shall be taken of any week for which an employee is laid off or kept on short-time where the lay-off or short-time is wholly or mainly attributable to a strike or a lock-out (whether or not in the trade or industry in which the employee is employed and whether in Great Britain or elsewhere).

CHAPTER IV GENERAL EXCLUSIONS FROM RIGHT

155 Qualifying period of employment

An employee does not have any right to a redundancy payment unless he has been continuously employed for a period of not less than two years ending with the relevant date.

156 [repealed]; **157** [omitted]; **158** [repealed]; **159–161** [omitted]

CHAPTER V OTHER PROVISIONS ABOUT REDUNDANCY PAYMENTS

162 Amount of a redundancy payment

(1) The amount of a redundancy payment shall be calculated by—

(a) determining the period, ending with the relevant date, during which the employee has been continuously employed,

(b) reckoning backwards from the end of that period the number of years of employment falling within that period, and

(c) allowing the appropriate amount for each of those years of employment.

(2) In subsection (1)(c) 'the appropriate amount' means—
   (a) one and a half weeks' pay for a year of employment in which the employee was not below the age of forty-one,
   (b) one week's pay for a year of employment (not within paragraph (a)) in which he was not below the age of twenty-two, and
   (c) half a week's pay for each year of employment not within paragraph (a) or (b).

(3) Where twenty years of employment have been reckoned under subsection (1), no account shall be taken under that subsection of any year of employment earlier than those twenty years.

(4)–(5) [repealed]

(6) Subsections (1) to (3) apply for the purposes of any provision of this Part by virtue of which an employment tribunal may determine that an employer is liable to pay to an employee—
   (a) the whole of the redundancy payment to which the employee would have had a right apart from some other provision, or
   (b) such part of the redundancy payment to which the employee would have had a right apart from some other provision as the tribunal thinks fit,
as if any reference to the amount of a redundancy payment were to the amount of the redundancy payment to which the employee would have been entitled apart from that other provision.

(7)–(8) [repealed]

163   References to employment tribunals

(1) Any question arising under this Part as to—
   (a) the right of an employee to a redundancy payment, or
   (b) the amount of a redundancy payment, shall be referred to and determined by an employment tribunal.

(2) For the purposes of any such reference, an employee who has been dismissed by his employer shall, unless the contrary is proved, be presumed to have been so dismissed by reason of redundancy.

(3) Any question whether an employee will become entitled to a redundancy payment if he is not dismissed by his employer and he terminates his contract of employment as mentioned in section 150(1) shall for the purposes of this Part be taken to be a question as to the right of the employee to a redundancy payment.

(4) Where an order under section 157 is in force in respect of an agreement, this section has effect in relation to any question arising under the agreement as to the right of an employee to a payment on the termination of his employment, or as to the amount of such a payment, as if the payment were a redundancy payment and the question arose under this Part.

164   Claims for redundancy payment

(1) An employee does not have any right to a redundancy payment unless, before the end of the period of six months beginning with the relevant date—
   (a) the payment has been agreed and paid,
   (b) the employee has made a claim for the payment by notice in writing given to the employer,
   (c) a question as to the employee's right to, or the amount of, the payment has been referred to an employment tribunal, or
   (d) a complaint relating to his dismissal has been presented by the employee under section 111.

(2) An employee is not deprived of his right to a redundancy payment by subsection (1) if, during the period of six months immediately following the period mentioned in that subsection, the employee—
   (a) makes a claim for the payment by notice in writing given to the employer,

    (b) refers to an employment tribunal a question as to his right to, or the amount of,
        the payment, or
    (c) presents a complaint relating to his dismissal under section 111,
and it appears to the tribunal to be just and equitable that the employee should receive a
redundancy payment.

    (3) In determining under subsection (2) whether it is just and equitable that an employee
should receive a redundancy payment an employment tribunal shall have regard to—
    (a) the reason shown by the employee for his failure to take any such step as is
        referred to in subsection (2) within the period mentioned in subsection (1), and
    (b) all the other relevant circumstances.

165 Written particulars of redundancy payment

    (1) On making any redundancy payment, otherwise than in pursuance of a decision of a
tribunal which specifies the amount of the payment to be made, the employer shall give to
the employee a written statement indicating how the amount of the payment has been
calculated.

    (2) An employer who without reasonable excuse fails to comply with subsection (1) is
guilty of an offence and liable on summary conviction to a fine not exceeding level 1 on the
standard scale.

    (3) If an employer fails to comply with the requirements of subsection (1), the employee
may by notice in writing to the employer require him to give to the employee a written
statement complying with those requirements within such period (not being less than one
week beginning with the day on which the notice is given) as may be specified in the notice.

    (4) An employer who without reasonable excuse fails to comply with a notice under
subsection (3) is guilty of an offence and liable on summary conviction to a fine not
exceeding level 3 on the standard scale.

166–170 [omitted]

CHAPTER VII SUPPLEMENTARY

Application of Part to particular cases

171–172 [omitted]

173 Employees paid by person other than employer

    (1) For the purposes of the operation of the provisions of this Part (and Chapter I of Part
XIV) in relation to any employee whose remuneration is, by virtue of any statutory provision,
payable to him by a person other than his employer, each of the references to the employer
specified in subsection (2) shall be construed as a reference to the person by whom the
remuneration is payable.

    (2) The references referred to in subsection (1) are the first reference in section 135(1), the
third reference in section 140(3), the first reference in section 142(3) and the first reference in
section 143(2)(c) and the references in sections 142(2)(b), 143(4) and (5), 149(a) and (b),
150(3), 152(1)(b), 158(4), 162(6), 164 to 169, 170(1) and 214(5).

Death of employer or employee

174 Death of employer: dismissal

    (1) Where the contract of employment of an employee is taken for the purposes of this
Part to be terminated by his employer by reason of the employer's death, this Part has effect
in accordance with the following provisions of this section.

    (2) Section 138 applies as if—
    (a) in subsection (1)(a), for the words 'in pursuance' onwards there were substituted
        'by a personal representative of the deceased employer',

    (b) in subsection (1)(b), for the words 'either immediately' onwards there were sub-
stituted 'not later than eight weeks after the death of the deceased employer', and

    (c) in subsections (2)(b) and (6)(a), for the word 'employer' there were substituted
'personal representative of the deceased employer'.

  (3) Section 141(1) applies as if—

    (a) for the words 'before the end of his employment' there were substituted 'by a
personal representative of the deceased employer', and

    (b) for the words 'either immediately' onwards there were substituted 'not later than
eight weeks after the death of the deceased employer.'

  (4) For the purposes of section 141—

    (a) provisions of the contract as renewed, or of the new contract, do not differ from
the corresponding provisions of the contract in force immediately before the
death of the deceased employer by reason only that the personal representative
would be substituted for the deceased employer as the employer, and

    (b) no account shall be taken of that substitution in determining whether refusal of
the offer was unreasonable or whether the employee acted reasonably in terminating or giving notice to terminate the new or renewed employment.

  (5) Section 146 has effect as if—

    (a) subsection (1) were omitted, and

    (b) in subsection (2), paragraph (a) were omitted and, in paragraph (b), for the word
'four' there were substituted 'eight'.

  (6) For the purposes of the application of this Part (in accordance with section 161(2)) in
relation to an employee who was employed as a domestic servant in a private household,
references in this section and sections 175 and 218(4) and (5) to a personal representative
include a person to whom the management of the household has passed, otherwise than in
pursuance of a sale or other disposition for valuable consideration, in consequence of the
death of the employer.

175 Death of employer: lay-off and short-time

  (1) Where an employee is laid off or kept on short-time and his employer dies, this Part
has effect in accordance with the following provisions of this section.

  (2) Where the employee—

    (a) has been laid off or kept on short-time for one or more weeks before the death of
the employer,

    (b) has not given the deceased employer notice of intention to claim before the
employer's death,

    (c) after the employer's death has his contract of employment renewed, or is re-
engaged under a new contract, by a personal representative of the deceased
employer, and

    (d) after renewal or re-engagement is laid off or kept on short-time for one or more
weeks by the personal representative,

the week in which the employer died and the first week of the employee's employment by
the personal representative shall be treated for the purposes of Chapter III as consecutive
weeks (and references to four weeks or thirteen weeks shall be construed accordingly).

  (3) The following provisions of this section apply where—

    (a) the employee has given the deceased employer notice of intention to claim before
the employer's death,

    (b) the employer's death occurred before the end of the period of four weeks after the
service of the notice, and

    (c) the employee has not terminated his contract of employment by notice expiring
before the employer's death.

  (4) If the contract of employment is not renewed, and the employee is not re-engaged
under a new contract, by a personal representative of the deceased employer before the end
of the period of four weeks after the service of the notice of intention to claim—

(a) sections 149 and 152 do not apply, but

(b) (subject to that) Chapter III applies as if the employer had not died and the employee had terminated the contract of employment by a week's notice, or by the minimum notice which he is required to give to terminate the contract (if longer than a week), expiring at the end of that period.

(5) If—

(a) the contract of employment is renewed, or the employee is re-engaged under a new contract, by a personal representative of the deceased employer before the end of the period of four weeks after the service of the notice of intention to claim, and

(b) the employee was laid off or kept on short-time by the deceased employer for one or more of those weeks and is laid off or kept on short-time by the personal representative for the week, or for the next two or more weeks, following the renewal or re-engagement,

subsection (6) has effect.

(6) Where this subsection has effect Chapter III applies as if—

(a) all the weeks mentioned in subsection (5) were consecutive weeks during which the employee was employed (but laid off or kept on short-time) by the same employer, and

(b) the periods specified by section 150(3)(a) and (b) as the relevant period were extended by any week or weeks any part of which was after the death of the employer and before the date on which the renewal or re-engagement took effect.

176 Death of employee

(1) Where an employee whose employer has given him notice to terminate his contract of employment dies before the notice expires, this Part applies as if the contract had been duly terminated by the employer by notice expiring on the date of the employee's death.

(2) Where—

(a) an employee's contract of employment has been terminated by the employer,

(b) (by virtue of subsection (5) of section 145) a date later than the relevant date as defined by the previous provisions of that section is the relevant date for the purposes of certain provisions of this Act, and

(c) the employee dies before that date,

that subsection applies as if the notice to which it refers would have expired on the employee's death.

(3) Where—

(a) an employer has given notice to an employee to terminate his contract of employment and has offered to renew his contract of employment or to re-engage him under a new contract, and

(b) the employee dies without having accepted or refused the offer and without the offer having been withdrawn,

section 141(2) applies as if for the words 'he unreasonably refuses' there were substituted 'it would have been unreasonable on his part to refuse'.

(4) Where an employee's contract of employment has been renewed or he has been re-engaged under a new contract—

(a) if he dies during the trial period without having terminated, or given notice to terminate, the contract, section 141(4) applies as if for paragraph (d) there were substituted—

'(d) it would have been unreasonable for the employee during the trial period to terminate or give notice to terminate the contract.', and

(b) if during that trial period he gives notice to terminate the contract but dies before the notice expires, sections 138(2) and 141(4) apply as if the notice had expired (and the contract had been terminated by its expiry) on the date of the employee's death.

(5) Where in the circumstances specified in paragraphs (a) and (b) of subsection (3) of section 136 the employee dies before the notice given by him under paragraph (b) of that subsection expires—

> (a) if he dies before his employer has given him a notice such as is specified in subsection (2) of section 142, subsections (3) and (4) of that section apply as if the employer had given him such a notice and he had not complied with it, and
>
> (b) if he dies after his employer has given him such a notice, that section applies as if the employee had not died but did not comply with the notice.

(6) Where an employee has given notice of intention to claim—

> (a) if he dies before he has given notice to terminate his contract of employment and before the relevant period (as defined in subsection (3) of section 150) has expired, that section does not apply, and
>
> (b) if he dies within the period of seven days after the service of the notice of intention to claim, and before the employer has given a counter-notice, Chapter III applies as if the employer had given a counter-notice within that period of seven days.

(7) Where a claim for a redundancy payment is made by a personal representative of a deceased employee—

> (a) if the employee died before the end of the period of six months beginning with the relevant date, subsection (1) of section 164, and
>
> (b) if the employee died after the end of the period of six months beginning with the relevant date but before the end of the following period of six months, subsection (2) of that section,

applies as if for the words 'six months' there were substituted 'one year'.

177   [omitted]

Other supplementary provisions

178–179   [omitted]

180   Offences

(1) Where an offence under this Part committed by a body corporate is proved—

> (a) to have been committed with the consent or connivance of, or
>
> (b) to be attributable to any neglect on the part of,

any director, manager, secretary or other similar officer of the body corporate, or any person who was purporting to act in any such capacity, he (as well as the body corporate) is guilty of the offence and liable to be proceeded against and punished accordingly.

(2) In this section 'director', in relation to a body corporate established by or under any enactment for the purpose of carrying on under national ownership any industry or part of an industry or undertaking, being a body corporate whose affairs are managed by its members, means a member of that body corporate.

181   Interpretation

(1) In this Part—

'counter-notice' shall be construed in accordance with section 149(a),

'dismissal' and 'dismissed' shall be construed in accordance with sections 136 to 138

'employer's payment' has the meaning given by section 166,

'notice of intention to claim' shall be construed in accordance with section 148(1),

'obligatory period of notice' has the meaning given by section 136(4), and

'trial period' shall be construed in accordance with section 138(3).

(2) In this Part—

> (a) references to an employee being laid off or being eligible for a redundancy payment by reason of being laid off, and

(b) references to an employee being kept on short-time or being eligible for a
   redundancy payment by reason of being kept on short-time,
shall be construed in accordance with sections 147 and 148.

PART XII   INSOLVENCY OF EMPLOYERS

182   Employee's rights on insolvency of employer

If, on an application made to him in writing by an employee, the Secretary of State is satisfied
that—
   (a) the employee's employer has become insolvent,
   (b) the employee's employment has been terminated, and
   (c) on the appropriate date the employee was entitled to be paid the whole or part of
       any debt to which this Part applies,
the Secretary of State shall, subject to section 186, pay the employee out of the National
Insurance Fund the amount to which, in the opinion of the Secretary of State, the employee
is entitled in respect of the debt.

183   [omitted]

184   Debts to which Part applies

(1) This Part applies to the following debts—
   (a) any arrears of pay in respect of one or more (but not more than eight) weeks,
   (b) any amount which the employer is liable to pay the employee for the period of
       notice required by section 86(1) or (2) or for any failure of the employer to give
       the period of notice required by section 86(1),
   (c) any holiday pay—
       (i) in respect of a period or periods of holiday not exceeding six weeks in all, and
       (ii) to which the employee became entitled during the twelve months ending
            with the appropriate date,
   (d) any basic award of compensation for unfair dismissal or so much of an award
       under a designated dismissal procedures agreement as does not exceed any basic
       award of compensation for unfair dismissal to which the employee would be
       entitled but for the agreement, and
   (e) any reasonable sum by way of reimbursement of the whole or part of any fee or
       premium paid by an apprentice or articled clerk.

(2) For the purposes of subsection (1)(a) the following amounts shall be treated as arrears
of pay—
   (a) a guarantee payment,
   (b) any payment for time off under Part VI of this Act or section 169 of the Trade
       Union and Labour Relations (Consolidation) Act 1992 (payment for time off for
       carrying out trade union duties etc.),
   (c) remuneration on suspension on medical grounds under section 64 of this Act and
       remuneration on suspension on maternity grounds under section 68 of this Act, and
   (d) remuneration under a protective award under section 189 of the Trade Union and
       Labour Relations (Consolidation) Act 1992.

(3) In subsection (1)(c) 'holiday pay', in relation to an employee, means—
   (a) pay in respect of a holiday actually taken by the employee, or
   (b) any accrued holiday pay which, under the employee's contract of employment,
       would in the ordinary course have become payable to him in respect of the period
       of a holiday if his employment with the employer had continued until he became
       entitled to a holiday.

(4) A sum shall be taken to be reasonable for the purposes of subsection (1)(e) in a case
where a trustee in bankruptcy, or (in Scotland) a permanent or interim trustee (within the

meaning of the Bankruptcy (Scotland) Act 1985), or liquidator has been or is required to be appointed—

> (a) as respects England and Wales, if it is admitted to be reasonable by the trustee in bankruptcy or liquidator under section 348 of the Insolvency Act 1986 (effect of bankruptcy on apprenticeships etc.), whether as originally enacted or as applied to the winding up of a company by rules under section 411 of that Act, and
> (b) as respects Scotland, if it is accepted by the permanent or interim trustee or liquidator for the purposes of the sequestration or winding up.

185   The appropriate date

In this Part 'the appropriate date'—

> (a) in relation to arrears of pay (not being remuneration under a protective award made under section 189 of the Trade Union and Labour Relations (Consolidation) Act 1992 and to holiday pay, means the date on which the employer became insolvent,
> (b) in relation to a basic award of compensation for unfair dismissal and to remuneration under a protective award so made, means whichever is the latest of—
> > (i)   the date on which the employer became insolvent,
> > (ii) the date of the termination of the employee's employment, and
> > (iii) the date on which the award was made, and
> (c) in relation to any other debt to which this Part applies, means whichever is the latter of—
> > (i) the date on which the employer became insolvent, and
> > (ii) the date of the termination of the employee's employment.

186   Limit on amount payable under section 182

(1) The total amount payable to an employee in respect of any debt to which this Part applies, where the amount of the debt is referable to a period of time, shall not exceed—

> (a) £290 in respect of any one week, or
> (b) in respect of a shorter period, an amount bearing the same proportion to £290 as that shorter period bears to a week.

(2) [repealed]

187–190   [omitted]

PART XIII   MISCELLANEOUS

CHAPTER I   PARTICULAR TYPES OF EMPLOYMENT

Crown employment etc.

191   Crown employment

(1) Subject to sections 192 and 193, the provisions of this Act to which this section applies have effect in relation to Crown employment and persons in Crown employment as they have effect in relation to other employment and other employees or workers.

(2) This section applies to—

> (a) Parts I to III,
> (aa) Part IVA,
> (b) Part V, apart from section 45,
> (c) Parts 6 to 8A
> (d) in Part IX, sections 92 and 93,
> (e) Part X, apart from section 101, and
> (f) this Part and Parts XIV and XV.

(3) In this Act 'Crown employment' means employment under or for the purposes of a government department or any officer or body exercising on behalf of the Crown functions conferred by a statutory provision.

(4) For the purposes of the application of provisions of this Act in relation to Crown employment in accordance with subsection (1)—

    (a) references to an employee or a worker shall be construed as references to a person in Crown employment,

    (b) references to a contract of employment, or a workers contract, shall be construed as references to the terms of employment of a person in Crown employment,

    (c) references to dismissal, or to the termination of a worker's contract, shall be construed as references to the termination of Crown employment,

    (d) references to redundancy shall be construed as references to the existence of such circumstances as are treated, in accordance with any arrangements falling within section 177(3) for the time being in force, as equivalent to redundancy in relation to Crown employment,

    (da) the reference in section 98B(2)(a) to the employer's undertaking shall be construed as a reference to the national interest, and

    (e) any other reference to an undertaking shall be construed—

        (i) in relation to a Minister of the Crown, as references to his functions or (as the context may require) to the department of which he is in charge, and

        (ii) in relation to a government department, officer or body, as references to the functions of the department, officer or body or (as the context may require) to the department, officer or body.

(5) Where the terms of employment of a person in Crown employment restrict his right to take part in—

    (a) certain political activities, or

    (b) activities which may conflict with his official functions,

nothing in section 50 requires him to be allowed time off work for public duties connected with any such activities.

(6) Sections 159 and 160 are without prejudice to any exemption or immunity of the Crown.

192 Armed forces

(1) Section 191—

    (a) applies to service as a member of the naval, military or air forces of the Crown but subject to the following provisions of this section, and

    (b) applies to employment by an association established for the purposes of Part XI of the Reserve Forces Act 1996.

(2) The provisions of this Act which have effect by virtue of section 191 in relation to service as a member of the naval, military or air forces of the Crown are—

    (a) Part I,

    (aa) in Part V, sections 45A, 43M, 47C and 47D, and sections 48 and 49 so far as relating to those sections,

    (ab) [repealed]

    (b) in Part VI, sections 55 to 57B,

    (c) Parts VII and VIII,

    (d) in Part IX, sections 92 and 93,

    (e) Part X, apart from sections 98B(2) and (3), 100 to 103, 104C and 134, and

    (f) this Part and Parts XIV and XV.

(3)–(8) [omitted]

193 National security

(1) Part IVA and section 47B of this Act do not apply in relation to employment for the purposes of—

    (a) the Security Service,

    (b) the Secret Intelligence Service, or

    (c) the Government Communications Headquarters.

194–195 [omitted]; **196–197** [repealed]

198   Short-term employment
Sections 1 to 7 do not apply to an employee if his employment continues for less than one month.

199–201   [omitted]

CHAPTER II   OTHER MISCELLANEOUS MATTERS

Restrictions on disclosure of information

202   National security
   (1) Where in the opinion of any Minister of the Crown the disclosure of any information would be contrary to the interests of national security—
     (a) nothing in any of the provisions to which this section applies requires any person to disclose the information, and
     (b) no person shall disclose the information in any proceedings in any court or tribunal relating to any of those provisions.
   (2) This section applies to—
     (a) Part I, so far as it relates to employment particulars,
     (b) in Part V, sections 43M, 44, 45A, 47 and 47C, and sections 48 and 49 so far as relating to those sections,
     (c) in Part VI, sections 55 to 57B and 61 to 63,
     (d) in Part VII, sections 66 to 68, and sections 69 and 70 so far as relating to those sections,
     (e) Part VIII,
     (f) in Part IX, sections 92 and 93 where they apply by virtue of section 92(4),
     (g) Part X so far as relating to a dismissal which is treated as unfair—
       (i)   by section 98B, 99, 100, 101A(d) or 103, or by section 104 in its application in relation to time off under section 57A,
       (ii) by subsection (1) of section 105 by reason of the application of subsection (2A), (3) or (6) of that section or by reason of the application of subsection (4A) in so far as it applies where the reason (or, if more than one, the principal reason) for which an employee was selected for dismissal was that specified in section 101A(d), and
     (h) this Part and Parts XIV and XV (so far as relating to any of the provisions in paragraphs (a) to (g)).

Contracting out etc. and remedies

203   Restrictions on contracting out
   (1) Any provision in an agreement (whether a contract of employment or not) is void in so far as it purports—
     (a) to exclude or limit the operation of any provision of this Act, or
     (b) to preclude a person from bringing any proceedings under this Act before an employment tribunal.
   (2) Subsection (1)—
     (a) does not apply to any provision in a collective agreement excluding rights under section 28 if an order under section 35 is for the time being in force in respect of it,
     (b) does not apply to any provision in a dismissal procedures agreement excluding the right under section 94 if that provision is not to have effect unless an order under section 110 is for the time being in force in respect of it,
     (c) does not apply to any provision in an agreement if an order under section 157 is for the time being in force in respect of it,

(d) [repealed]

(e) does not apply to any agreement to refrain from instituting or continuing proceedings where a conciliation officer has taken action under section 18 of the Employment Tribunals Act 1996, and

(f) does not apply to any agreement to refrain from instituting or continuing any proceedings within the following provisions of section 18(1) of the Employment Tribunals Act 1996 (cases where conciliation available)—

(i) paragraph (d) (proceedings under this Act),

(ii) paragraph (h) (proceedings arising out of the Part-time Workers (Prevention of Less Favourable Treatment) Regulations 2000),

(iii) paragraph (i) (proceedings arising out of the Fixed-term Employees (Prevention of Less Favourable Treatment) Regulations 2002),

(iv) paragraph (j) (proceedings under those Regulations),

if the conditions regulating compromise agreements under this Act are satisfied in relation to the agreement.

(3) For the purposes of subsection (2)(f) the conditions regulating compromise agreements under this Act are that—

(a) the agreement must be in writing,

(b) the agreement must relate to the particular proceedings,

(c) the employee or worker must have received advice from a relevant independent adviser as to the terms and effect of the proposed agreement and, in particular, its effect on his ability to pursue his rights before an employment tribunal,

(d) there must be in force, when the adviser gives the advice, a contract of insurance, or an indemnity provided for members of a profession or professional body covering the risk of a claim by the employee or worker in respect of loss arising in consequence of the advice,

(e) the agreement must identify the adviser, and

(f) the agreement must state that the conditions regulating compromise agreements under this Act are satisfied.

(3A) A person is a relevant independent adviser for the purposes of subsection (3)(c)—

(a) if he is a qualified lawyer,

(b) if he is an officer, official, employee or member of an independent trade union who has been certified in writing by the trade union as competent to give advice and as authorised to do so on behalf of the trade union,

(c) if he works at an advice centre (whether as an employee or a volunteer) and has been certified in writing by the centre as competent to give advice and as authorised to do so on behalf of the centre, or

(d) if he is a person of a description specified in an order made by the Secretary of State.

(3B) But a person is not a relevant independent adviser for the purposes of subsection (3)(c) in relation to the employee or worker—

(a) if he is, is employed by or is acting in the matter for the employer or an associated employer,

(b) in the case of a person within subsection (3A)(b) or (c), if the trade union or advice centre is the employer or an associated employer,

(c) in the case of a person within subsection (3A)(c), if the employee or worker makes a payment for the advice received from him, or

(d) in the case of a person of a description specified in an order under subsection (3A)(d), if any condition specified in the order in relation to the giving of advice by persons of that description is not satisfied.

(4) In subsection (3A)(a) 'qualified lawyer' means—

(a) as respects England and Wales, a barrister (whether in practice as such or employed to give legal advice), a solicitor who holds a practising certificate, or a person other than a barrister or solicitor who is an authorised advocate or authorised litigator (within the meaning of the Courts and Legal Services Act 1990), and

(b) as respects Scotland, an advocate (whether in practice as such or employed to give legal advice), or a solicitor who holds a practising certificate.

(5) An agreement under which the parties agree to submit a dispute to arbitration—

(a) shall be regarded for the purposes of subsection (2)(e) and (f) as being an agreement to refrain from instituting or continuing proceedings if—

    (i) the dispute is covered by a scheme having effect by virtue of an order under section 212A of the Trade Union and Labour Relations (Consolidation) Act 1992, and

    (ii) the agreement is to submit it to arbitration in accordance with the scheme, but

(b) shall be regarded as neither being nor including such an agreement in any other case.

204   Law governing employment

(1) For the purposes of this Act it is immaterial whether the law which (apart from this Act) governs any person's employment is the law of the United Kingdom, or of a part of the United Kingdom, or not.

(2) [repealed]

205   Remedy for infringement of certain rights

(1) The remedy of an employee for infringement of any of the rights conferred by section 8, Part III, Parts V to VIII, section 92, Part X and Part XII is, where provision is made for a complaint or the reference of a question to an employment tribunal, by way of such a complaint or reference and not otherwise.

(1ZA) In relation to the right conferred by section 45A, the reference in subsection to an employee has effect as a reference to a worker.

(1A) In relation to the right conferred by section 47B, the reference in subsection (1) to an employee has effect as a reference to a worker.

(2) The remedy of a worker in respect of any contravention of section 13, 15, 18(1) or 21(1) is by way of a complaint under section 23 and not otherwise.

206–207 [omitted]; 208 [repealed]; 209 [omitted]

PART XIV   INTERPRETATION

CHAPTER I   CONTINUOUS EMPLOYMENT

210   Introductory

(1) References in any provision of this Act to a period of continuous employment are (unless provision is expressly made to the contrary) to a period computed in accordance with this Chapter.

(2) In any provision of this Act which refers to a period of continuous employment expressed in months or years—

(a) a month means a calendar month, and

(b) a year means a year of twelve calendar months.

(3) In computing an employee's period of continuous employment for the purposes of any provision of this Act, any question—

(a) whether the employee's employment is of a kind counting towards a period of continuous employment, or

(b) whether periods (consecutive or otherwise) are to be treated as forming a single period of continuous employment, shall be determined week by week; but where it is necessary to compute the length of an employee's period of employment it shall be computed in months and years of twelve months in accordance with section 211.

(4) Subject to sections 215 to 217, a week which does not count in computing the length of a period of continuous employment breaks continuity of employment.

(5) A person's employment during any period shall, unless the contrary is shown, be presumed to have been continuous.

211 Period of continuous employment

(1) An employee's period of continuous employment for the purposes of any provision of this Act—

(a) (subject to subsection (3)) begins with the day on which the employee starts work, and

(b) ends with the day by reference to which the length of the employee's period of continuous employment is to be ascertained for the purposes of the provision.

(2) [repealed]

(3) If an employee's period of continuous employment includes one or more periods which (by virtue of section 215, 216 or 217) while not counting in computing the length of the period do not break continuity of employment, the beginning of the period shall be treated as postponed by the number of days falling within that intervening period, or the aggregate number of days falling within those periods, calculated in accordance with the section in question.

212 Weeks counting in computing period

(1) Any week during the whole or part of which an employee's relations with his employer are governed by a contract of employment counts in computing the employee's period of employment.

(2) [repealed]

(3) Subject to subsection (4), any week (not within subsection (1)) during the whole or part of which an employee is—

(a) incapable of work in consequence of sickness or injury,

(b) absent from work on account of a temporary cessation of work, or

(c) absent from work in circumstances such that, by arrangement or custom, he is regarded as continuing in the employment of his employer for any purpose,

(d) [repealed]

(4) Not more than twenty-six weeks count under subsection (3)(a) between any periods falling under subsection (1).

213 Intervals in employment

(1) Where in the case of an employee a date later than the date which would be the effective date of termination by virtue of subsection (1) of section 97 is treated for certain purposes as the effective date of termination by virtue of subsection (2) or (4) of that section, the period of the interval between the two dates counts as a period of employment in ascertaining for the purposes of section 108(1) or 119(1) the period for which the employee has been continuously employed.

(2) Where an employee is by virtue of section 138(1) regarded for the purposes of Part XI as not having been dismissed by reason of a renewal or re-engagement taking effect after an interval, the period of the interval counts as a period of employment in ascertaining for the purposes of section 155 or 162(1) the period for which the employee has been continuously employed (except so far as it is to be disregarded under section 214 or 215).

(3) Where in the case of an employee a date later than the date which would be the relevant date by virtue of subsections (2) to (4) of section 145 is treated for certain purposes as the relevant date by virtue of subsection (5) of that section, the period of the interval between the two dates counts as a period of employment in ascertaining for the purposes of section

155 or 162(1) the period for which the employee has been continuously employed (except so far as it is to be disregarded under section 214 or 215).

214 Special provisions for redundancy payments

(1) This section applies where a period of continuous employment has to be determined in relation to an employee for the purposes of the application of section 155 or 162(1).

(2) The continuity of a period of employment is broken where—

(a) a redundancy payment has previously been paid to the employee (whether in respect of dismissal or in respect of lay-off or short-time), and

(b) the contract of employment under which the employee was employed was renewed (whether by the same or another employer) or the employee was re-engaged under a new contract of employment (whether by the same or another employer).

(3) The continuity of a period of employment is also broken where—

(a) a payment has been made to the employee (whether in respect of the termination of his employment or lay-off or short-time) in accordance with a scheme under section 1 of the Superannuation Act 1972 or arrangements falling within section 177(3), and

(b) he commenced new, or renewed, employment.

(4) The date on which the person's continuity of employment is broken by virtue of this section—

(a) if the employment was under a contract of employment, is the date which was the relevant date in relation to the payment mentioned in subsection (2)(a) or (3)(a), and

(b) if the employment was otherwise than under a contract of employment, is the date which would have been the relevant date in relation to the payment mentioned in subsection (2)(a) or (3)(a) had the employment been under a contract of employment.

(5) For the purposes of this section a redundancy payment shall be treated as having been paid if—

(a) the whole of the payment has been paid to the employee by the employer,

(b) a tribunal has determined liability and found that the employer must pay part (but not all) of the redundancy payment and the employer has paid that part, or

(c) the Secretary of State has paid a sum to the employee in respect of the redundancy payment under section 167.

215 Employment abroad etc.

(1) This Chapter applies to a period of employment—

(a) (subject to the following provisions of this section) even where during the period the employee was engaged in work wholly or mainly outside Great Britain, and

(b) even where the employee was excluded by or under this Act from any right conferred by this Act.

(2) For the purposes of sections 155 and 162(1) a week of employment does not count in computing a period of employment if the employee—

(a) was employed outside Great Britain during the whole or part of the week, and

(b) was not during that week an employed earner for the purposes of the Social Security Contributions and Benefits Act 1992 in respect of whom a secondary Class 1 contribution was payable under that Act (whether or not the contribution was in fact paid).

(3) Where by virtue of subsection (2) a week of employment does not count in computing a period of employment, the continuity of the period is not broken by reason only that the week does not count in computing the period; and the number of days which, for the purposes of section 211(3), fall within the intervening period is seven for each week within this subsection.

(4) Any question arising under subsection (2) whether—

(a) a person was an employed earner for the purposes of the Social Security Contributions and Benefits Act 1992, or

(b) if so, whether a secondary Class 1 contribution was payable in respect of him under that Act,

shall be determined by an officer of the Commissioners of the Inland Revenue.

(5) Part II of the Social Security Contributions (Transfer of Functions, etc.) Act 1999 (decisions and appeals) shall apply in relation to the determination of any issue by the Inland Revenue under subsection (4) as if it were a decision falling within section 8(1) of that Act.

(6) Subsection (2) does not apply in relation to a person who is—

(a) employed as a master or seaman in a British ship, and

(b) ordinarily resident in Great Britain.

216 Industrial disputes

(1) A week does not count under section 212 if during the week, or any part of the week, the employee takes part in a strike.

(2) The continuity of an employee's period of employment is not broken by a week which does not count under this Chapter (whether or not by virtue only of subsection (1)) if during the week, or any part of the week, the employee takes part in a strike; and the number of days which, for the purposes of section 211(3), fall within the intervening period is the number of days between the last working day before the strike and the day on which work was resumed.

(3) The continuity of an employee's period of employment is not broken by a week if during the week, or any part of the week, the employee is absent from work because of a lockout by the employer; and the number of days which, for the purposes of section 211(3), fall within the intervening period is the number of days between the last working day before the lock-out and the day on which work was resumed.

217 [omitted]

218 Change of employer

(1) Subject to the provisions of this section, this Chapter relates only to employment by the one employer.

(2) If a trade or business, or an undertaking (whether or not established by or under an Act), is transferred from one person to another—

(a) the period of employment of an employee in the trade or business or undertaking at the time of the transfer counts as a period of employment with the transferee, and

(b) the transfer does not break the continuity of the period of employment.

(3) If by or under an Act (whether public or local and whether passed before or after this Act) a contract of employment between any body corporate and an employee is modified and some other body corporate is substituted as the employer—

(a) the employee's period of employment at the time when the modification takes effect counts as a period of employment with the second body corporate, and

(b) the change of employer does not break the continuity of the period of employment.

(4) If on the death of an employer the employee is taken into the employment of the personal representatives or trustees of the deceased—

(a) the employee's period of employment at the time of the death counts as a period of employment with the employer's personal representatives or trustees, and

(b) the death does not break the continuity of the period of employment.

(5) If there is a change in the partners, personal representatives or trustees who employ any person—

(a) the employee's period of employment at the timeof the change counts as a period of employment with the partners, personal representatives or trustees after the change, and

(b) the change does not break the continuity of the period of employment.

(6) If an employee of an employer is taken into the employment of another employer who, at the time when the employee enters the second employer's employment, is an associated employer of the first employer—

(a) the employee's period of employment at that time counts as a period of employment with the second employer, and

(b) the change of employer does not break the continuity of the period of employment.

(7)–(10) [omitted]

219   [omitted]

CHAPTER II   A WEEK'S PAY

Introductory

220   Introductory

The amount of a week's pay of an employee shall be calculated for the purposes of this Act in accordance with this Chapter.

Employments with normal working hours

221   General

(1) This section and sections 222 and 223 apply where there are normal working hours for the employee when employed under the contract of employment in force on the calculation date.

(2) Subject to section 222, if the employee's remuneration for employment in normal working hours (whether by the hour or week or other period) does not vary with the amount of work done in the period, the amount of a week's pay is the amount which is payable by the employer under the contract of employment in force on the calculation date if the employee works throughout his normal working hours in a week.

(3) Subject to section 222, if the employee's remuneration for employment in normal working hours (whether by the hour or week or other period) does vary with the amount of work done in the period, the amount of a week's pay is the amount of remuneration for the number of normal working hours in a week calculated at the average hourly rate of remuneration payable by the employer to the employee in respect of the period of twelve weeks ending—

(a) where the calculation date is the last day of a week, with that week, and

(b) otherwise, with the last complete week before the calculation date.

(4) In this section references to remuneration varying with the amount of work done includes remuneration which may include any commission or similar payment which varies in amount.

(5) This section is subject to sections 227 and 228.

222   Remuneration varying according to time of work

(1) This section applies if the employee is required under the contract of employment in force on the calculation date to work during normal working hours on days of the week, or at times of the day, which differ from week to week or over a longer period so that the remuneration payable for, or apportionable to, any week varies according to the incidence of those days or times.

(2) The amount of a week's pay is the amount of remuneration for the average number of weekly normal working hours at the average hourly rate of remuneration.

(3) For the purposes of subsection (2)—

    (a) the average number of weekly hours is calculated by dividing by twelve the total number of the employee's normal working hours during the relevant period of twelve weeks, and

    (b) the average hourly rate of remuneration is the average hourly rate of remuneration payable by the employer to the employee in respect of the relevant period of twelve weeks.

(4) In subsection (3) 'the relevant period of twelve weeks' means the period of twelve weeks ending—

    (a) where the calculation date is the last day of a week, with that week, and

    (b) otherwise, with the last complete week before the calculation date.

(5) This section is subject to sections 227 and 228.

223 Supplementary

(1) For the purposes of sections 221 and 222, in arriving at the average hourly rate of remuneration, only—

    (a) the hours when the employee was working, and

    (b) the remuneration payable for, or apportionable to, those hours,

shall be brought in.

(2) If for any of the twelve weeks mentioned in sections 221 and 222 no remuneration within subsection (1)(b) was payable by the employer to the employee, account shall be taken of remuneration in earlier weeks so as to bring up to twelve the number of weeks of which account is taken.

(3) Where—

    (a) in arriving at the average hourly rate of remuneration, account has to be taken of remuneration payable for, or apportionable to, work done in hours other than normal working hours, and

    (b) the amount of that remuneration was greater than it would have been if the work had been done in normal working hours (or, in a case within section 234(3), in normal working hours falling within the number of hours without overtime),

account shall be taken of that remuneration as if the work had been done in such hours and the amount of that remuneration had been reduced accordingly.

Employments with no normal working hours

224 Employment with no normal working hours

(1) This section applies where there are no normal working hours for the employee when employed under the contract of employment in force on the calculation date.

(2) The amount of a week's pay is the amount of the employee's average weekly remuneration in the period of twelve weeks ending—

    (a) where the calculation date is the last day of a week, with that week, and

    (b) otherwise, with the last complete week before the calculation date.

(3) In arriving at the average weekly remuneration no account shall be taken of a week in which no remuneration was payable by the employer to the employee and remuneration in earlier weeks shall be brought in so as to bring up to twelve the number of weeks of which account is taken.

(4) This section is subject to sections 227 and 228.

The calculation date

225 Rights during employment

(1) Where the calculation is for the purposes of section 30, the calculation date is—

    (a) where the employee's contract has been varied, or a new contract entered into, in connection with a period of short-time working, the last day on which the original contract was in force, and

    (b) otherwise, the day in respect of which the guarantee payment is payable.

(2) Where the calculation is for the purposes of section 53 or 54, the calculation date is the day on which the employer's notice was given.

(3) Where the calculation is for the purposes of section 56, the calculation date is the day of the appointment.

(4) Where the calculation is for the purposes of section 62, the calculation date is the day on which the time off was taken or on which it is alleged the time off should have been permitted.

(4A) Where the calculation is for the purposes of section 63B, the calculation date is the day on which the time off was taken or on which it is alleged the time off should have been permitted.

(5) Where the calculation is for the purposes of section 69—

    (a) in the case of an employee suspended on medical grounds, the calculation date is the day before that on which the suspension begins, and

    (b) in the case of an employee suspended on maternity grounds, the calculation date is—

        (i) where the day before that on which the suspension begins falls during a period of ordinary or additional maternity leave, the day before the beginning of that period,

        (ii) otherwise, the day before that on which the suspension begins.

(6) Where the calculation is for the purposes of section 80I, the calculation date is the day on which the application under section 80F was made.

226   Rights on termination

(1) Where the calculation is for the purposes of section 88 or 89, the calculation date is the day immediately preceding the first day of the period of notice required by section 86(1) or (2).

(2) Where the calculation is for the purposes of section 93, 117 or 125, the calculation date is—

    (a) if the dismissal was with notice, the date on which the employer's notice was given, and

    (b) otherwise, the effective date of termination.

(3) Where the calculation is for the purposes of section 112, 119, 120 or 121, the calculation date is—

    (a) [repealed]

    (b) if by virtue of subsection (2) or (4) of section 97 a date later than the effective date of termination as defined in subsection (1) of that section is to be treated for certain purposes as the effective date of termination, the effective date of termination as so defined, and

    (c) otherwise, the date specified in subsection (6).

(4) Where the calculation is for the purposes of section 147(2), the calculation date is the day immediately preceding the first of the four, or six, weeks referred to in section 148(2).

(5) Where the calculation is for the purposes of section 162, the calculation date is—

    (a) [repealed]

    (b) if by virtue of subsection (5) of section 145 a date is to be treated for certain purposes as the relevant date which is later than the relevant date as defined by the previous provisions of that section, the relevant date as so defined, and

    (c) otherwise, the date specified in subsection (6).

(6) The date referred to in subsections (3)(c) and (5)(c) is the date on which notice would have been given had—

    (a) the contract been terminable by notice and been terminated by the employer giving such notice as is required by section 86 to terminate the contract, and

    (b) the notice expired on the effective date of termination, or the relevant date, (whether or not those conditions were in fact fulfilled).

Maximum amount of week's pay

227 Maximum amount

    (1) For the purpose of calculating—

        (za) an award of compensation under section 80I(1)(b),

        (a) an award of compensation ua basic award of compensation for unfair dismissal,

        (b) an additional award of compensation for unfair dismissal,

        (ba) an award under section 112(5), or

        (c) a redundancy payment, the amount of a week's pay shall not exceed £290.

    (2)–(4) [repealed]

Miscellaneous

228 New employments and other special cases

    (1) In any case in which the employee has not been employed for a sufficient period to enable a calculation to be made under the preceding provisions of this Chapter, the amount of a week's pay is the amount which fairly represents a week's pay.

    (2) In determining that amount the employment tribunal—

        (a) shall apply as nearly as may be such of the preceding provisions of this Chapter as it considers appropriate, and

        (b) may have regard to such of the considerations specified in subsection (3) as it thinks fit.

    (3) The considerations referred to in subsection (2)(b) are—

        (a) any remuneration received by the employee in respect of the employment in question,

        (b) the amount offered to the employee as remuneration in respect of the employment in question,

        (c) the remuneration received by other persons engaged in relevant comparable employment with the same employer, and

        (d) the remuneration received by other persons engaged in relevant comparable employment with other employers.

    (4) The Secretary of State may by regulations provide that in cases prescribed by the regulations the amount of a week's pay shall be calculated in such manner as may be so prescribed.

229 Supplementary

    (1) In arriving at—

        (a) an average hourly rate of remuneration, or

        (b) average weekly remuneration,

under this Chapter, account shall be taken of work for a former employer within the period for which the average is to be taken if, by virtue of Chapter I of this Part, a period of employment with the former employer counts as part of the employee's continuous period of employment.

    (2) Where under this Chapter account is to be taken of remuneration or other payments for a period which does not coincide with the periods for which the remuneration or other payments are calculated, the remuneration or other payments shall be apportioned in such manner as may be just.

CHAPTER III   OTHER INTERPRETATION PROVISIONS

230 Employees, workers etc.

    (1) In this Act 'employee' means an individual who has entered into or works under (or, where the employment has ceased, worked under) a contract of employment.

    (2) In this Act 'contract of employment' means a contract of service or apprenticeship, whether express or implied, and (if it is express) whether oral or in writing.

(3) In this Act 'worker' (except in the phrases 'shop worker' and 'betting worker') means an individual who has entered into or works under (or, where the employment has ceased, worked under)—

 (a) a contract of employment, or

 (b) any other contract, whether express or implied and (if it is express) whether oral or in writing, whereby the individual undertakes to do or perform personally any work or services for another party to the contract whose status is not by virtue of the contract that of a client or customer of any profession or business undertaking carried on by the individual;

and any reference to a worker's contract shall be construed accordingly.

(4) In this Act 'employer', in relation to an employee or a worker, means the person by whom the employee or worker is (or, where the employment has ceased, was) employed.

(5) In this Act 'employment'—

 (a) in relation to an employee, means (except for the purposes of section 171) employment under a contract of employment, and

 (b) in relation to a worker, means employment under his contract; and 'employed' shall be construed accordingly.

(6) This section has effect subject to sections 43K and 47B(3); and for the purposes of Part XIII so far as relating to Part IVA or section 47B, 'worker', 'worker's contract' and, in relation to a worker, 'employer', 'employment' and 'employed' have the extended meaning given by section 43K.

231 Associated employer

For the purposes of this Act any two employers shall be treated as associated if—

 (a) one is a company of which the other (directly or indirectly) has control, or

 (b) both are companies of which a third person (directly or indirectly) has control; and 'associated employer' shall be construed accordingly.

232–233 [omitted]

234 Normal working hours

(1) Where an employee is entitled to overtime pay when employed for more than a fixed number of hours in a week or other period, there are for the purposes of this Act normal working hours in his case.

(2) Subject to subsection (3), the normal working hours in such a case are the fixed number of hours.

(3) Where in such a case—

 (a) the contract of employment fixes the number, or minimum number, of hours of employment in a week or other period (whether or not it also provides for the reduction of that number or minimum in certain circumstances), and

 (b) that number or minimum number of hours exceeds the number of hours without overtime,

the normal working hours are that number or minimum number of hours (and not the number of hours without overtime).

235 Other definitions

(1) In this Act, except in so far as the context otherwise requires—

'act' and 'action' each includes omission and references to doing an act or taking action shall be construed accordingly,

'basic award of compensation for unfair dismissal' shall be construed in accordance with section 118,

'business' includes a trade or profession and includes any activity carried on by a body of persons (whether corporate or unincorporated),

'childbirth' means the birth of a living child or the birth of a child whether living or dead after twenty-four weeks of pregnancy, 'collective agreement' has the meaning given by section 178(1) and (2) of the Trade Union and Labour Relations (Consolidation) Act 1992,

'conciliation officer' means an officer designated by the Advisory, Conciliation and Arbitration Service under section 211 of that Act,

'dismissal procedures agreement' means an agreement in writing with respect to procedures relating to dismissal made by or on behalf of one or more independent trade unions and one or more employers or employers' associations,

'employers' association' has the same meaning as in the Trade Union and Labour Relations (Consolidation) Act 1992,

'expected week of childbirth' means the week, beginning with midnight between Saturday and Sunday, in which it is expected that childbirth will occur,

'guarantee payment' has the meaning given by section 28, 'independent trade union' means a trade union which—

(a) is not under the domination or control of an employer or a group of employers or of one or more employers' associations, and

(b) is not liable to interference by an employer or any such group or association (arising out of the provision of financial or material support or by any other means whatever) tending towards such control,

'job', in relation to an employee, means the nature of the work which he is employed to do in accordance with his contract and the capacity and place in which he is so employed,

'paternity leave' means leave under section 80A or 80B,

'position', in relation to an employee, means the following matters taken as a whole—

(a) his status as an employee,

(b) the nature of his work, and

(c) his terms and conditions of employment,

'protected disclosure' has the meaning given by section 43A,

'redundancy payment' has the meaning given by Part XI,

'relevant date' has the meaning given by sections 145 and 153,

'renewal' includes extension, and any reference to renewing a contract or a fixed term shall be construed accordingly,

'statutory provision' means a provision, whether of a general or a special nature, contained in, or in any document made or issued under, any Act, whether of a general or special nature,

'successor', in relation to the employer of an employee, means (subject to subsection (2)) a person who in consequence of a change occurring (whether by virtue of a sale or other disposition or by operation of law) in the ownership of the undertaking, or of the part of the undertaking, for the purposes of which the employee was employed, has become the owner of the undertaking or part,

'trade union' has the meaning given by section 1 of the Trade Union and Labour Relations (Consolidation) Act 1992,

'week'—

(a) in Chapter I of this Part means a week ending with Saturday, and

(b) otherwise, except in sections 80A, 80B and 86, means, in relation to an employee whose remuneration is calculated weekly by a week ending with a day other than Saturday, a week ending with that other day and, in relation to any other employee, a week ending with Saturday.

(2) The definition of 'successor' in subsection (1) has effect (subject to the necessary modifications) in relation to a case where—

(a) the person by whom an undertaking or part of an undertaking is owned immediately before a change is one of the persons by whom (whether as partners, trustees or otherwise) it is owned immediately after the change, or

(b) the persons by whom an undertaking or part of an undertaking is owned immediately before a change (whether as partners, trustees or otherwise) include the persons by whom, or include one or more of the persons by whom, it is owned immediately after the change,

as it has effect where the previous owner and the new owner are wholly different persons.

(2A) For the purposes of this Act a contract of employment is a 'limited-term contract' if—

(a) the employment under the contract is not intended to be permanent, and

(b) provision is accordingly made in the contract for it to terminate by virtue of a limiting event.

(2B) In this Act, 'limiting event', in relation to a contract of employment means—

(a) in the case of a contract for a fixed-term, the expiry of the term,

(b) in the case of a contract made in contemplation of the performance of a specific task, the performance of the task, and

(c) in the case of a contract which provides for its termination on the occurrence of an event (or the failure of an event to occur), the occurrence of the event (or the failure of the event to occur).

(3) References in this Act to redundancy, dismissal by reason of redundancy and similar expressions shall be construed in accordance with section 139.

(4) In sections 136(2), 154 and 216(3) and paragraph 14 of Schedule 2 'lock-out' means—

(a) the closing of a place of employment,

(b) the suspension of work, or

(c) the refusal by an employer to continue to employ any number of persons employed by him in consequence of a dispute,

done with a view to compelling persons employed by the employer, or to aid another employer in compelling persons employed by him, to accept terms or conditions of or affecting employment.

(5) In sections 91(2), 140(2) and (3), 143(1), 144(2) and (3), 154 and 216(1) and (2) and paragraph 14 of Schedule 2 'strike' means—

(a) the cessation of work by a body of employed persons acting in combination, or

(b) a concerted refusal, or a refusal under a common understanding, of any number of employed persons to continue to work for an employer in consequence of a dispute,

done as a means of compelling their employer or any employed person or body of employed persons, or to aid other employees in compelling their employer or any employed person or body of employed persons, to accept or not to accept terms or conditions of or affecting employment.

236–245 [omitted]

Employment Tribunals Act 1996
(1996, c. 17)

PART I   EMPLOYMENT TRIBUNALS

Membership etc.

Section

Procedure

Conciliation

PART II   THE EMPLOYMENT APPEAL TRIBUNAL

Introductory

Jurisdiction

Membership etc.

Procedure

PART I   EMPLOYMENT TRIBUNALS

1–3   [omitted]

Membership etc.

4   Composition of a tribunal

(1) Subject to the following provisions of this section and to section 7(3)(A), proceedings before an employment tribunal shall be heard by—

(a) the person who, in accordance with regulations made under section 1(1), is the chairman, and

(b) two other members selected as the other members in accordance with regulations so made or, with appropriate consent, one other member selected as the other member in accordance with regulations so made,

and in paragraph (b) 'appropriate consent' means either consent given at the beginning of the hearing by such of the parties as are then present in person or represented, or consent given by each of the parties.

(2) Subject to subsection (5), the proceedings specified in subsection (3) shall be heard by the person mentioned in subsection (1)(a) alone.

(3) The proceedings referred to in subsection (2) are—

(a) proceedings on a complaint under section 68A, 87 or 192 of the Trade Union and Labour Relations (Consolidation) Act 1992 or on an application under section 161, 165 or 166 of that Act,

(b) proceedings on a complaint under section 126 of the Pension Schemes Act 1993,

(c) proceedings on a reference under section 11, 163 or 170 of the Employment Rights Act 1996, on a complaint under section 23, 34 or 188 of that Act, on a complaint under section 70(1) of that Act relating to section 64 of that Act, on an application under section128, 131or 132 of that Act or for an appointment under section 206(4) of that Act,

(ca) proceedings on a complaint under regulation 15(10) of the Transfer of Undertakings (Protection of Employment) Regulations 2006,

(cc) proceedings on a complaint under section 11 of the National Minimum Wage Act 1998,

(cd) proceedings on an appeal under section 19 or 22 of the National Minimum Wage Act 1998,

(d) proceedings in respect of which an employment tribunal has jurisdiction by virtue of section 3 of this Act,

(e) proceedings in which the parties have given their written consent to the proceedings being heard in accordance with subsection (2) (whether or not they
have subsequently withdrawn it),

(f) ...

(g) proceedings in which the person (or, where more than one, each of the persons)
against whom the proceedings are brought does not, or has ceased to, contest the
case.

(4) The Secretary of State may by order amend the provisions of subsection (3).

(5) Proceedings specified in subsection (3) shall be heard in accordance with subsection
(1) if a person who, in accordance with regulations made under section 1(1), may be the
chairman of an employment tribunal, having regard to—

(a) whether there is a likelihood of a dispute arising on the facts which makes it
desirable for the proceedings to be heard in accordance with subsection (1),

(b) whether there is a likelihood of an issue of law arising which would make it
desirable for the proceedings to be heard in accordance with subsection (2),

(c) any views of any of the parties as to whether or not the proceedings ought to be
heard in accordance with either of those subsections, and

(d) whether there are other proceedings which might be heard concurrently but
which are not proceedings specified in subsection (3),

decides at any stage of the proceedings that the proceedings are to be heard in accordance
with subsection (1).

(6)–(6C) [omitted]; (7) [repealed]

5   [omitted]

Procedure

6   Conduct of hearings

(1) A person may appear before an employment tribunal in person or be represented by—

(a) counsel or a solicitor,

(b) a representative of a trade union or an employers' association, or

(c) any other person whom he desires to represent him.

(2) Part I of the Arbitration Act 1996 does not apply to any proceedings before an
employment tribunal.

7   [omitted]

8   Procedure in contract cases

(1) Where in proceedings brought by virtue of section 3 an employment tribunal finds
that the whole or part of a sum claimed in the proceedings is due, the tribunal shall order the
respondent to the proceedings to pay the amount which it finds due.

(2) An order under section 3 may provide that an employment tribunal shall not in
proceedings in respect of a claim, or a number of claims relating to the same contract, order
the payment of an amount exceeding such sum as may be specified in the order as the
maximum amount which an employment tribunal may order to be paid in relation to a claim
or in relation to a contract.

(3) An order under section 3 may include provisions—

(a) as to the manner in which and time within which proceedings are to be brought
by virtue of that section, and

(b) modifying any other enactment.

(4) An order under that section may make different provision in relation to proceedings
in respect of different descriptions of claims.

9–14   [omitted]

15 Enforcement

(1) Any sum payable in pursuance of a decision of an employment tribunal in England and Wales which has been registered in accordance with employment tribunal procedure regulations shall, if a county court so orders, be recoverable by execution issued from the county court or otherwise as if it were payable under an order of that court.

(2) Any order for the payment of any sum made by an employment tribunal in Scotland (or any copy of such an order certified by the Secretary of the Tribunals) may be enforced as if it were an extract registered decree arbitral bearing a warrant for execution issued by the sheriff court of any sheriffdom in Scotland.

(3) In this section a reference to a decision or order of an employment tribunal—

> (a) does not include a decision or order which, on being reviewed, has been revoked by the tribunal, and
>
> (b) in relation to a decision or order which on being reviewed, has been varied by the tribunal shall be construed as a reference to the decision or order as so varied.

16–17 [omitted]

Conciliation

18 Conciliation

(1) This section applies in the case of employment tribunal proceedings and claims which could be the subject of employment tribunal proceedings—

> (a) under—
>> (i)   section 2(1) of the Equal Pay Act 1970,
>>
>> (ii) section 63 of the Sex Discrimination Act 1975, or
>>
>> (iii) section 54 of the Race Relations Act 1976,
>
> (b) arising out of a contravention, or alleged contravention, of section 64, 68, 86, 137, 138, 145A, 145B, 146, 168, 168A, 169, 170, 174, 188 or 190 of the Trade Union and Labour Relations (Consolidation) Act 1992,
>
> (c) under section 8 of the Disability Discrimination Act 1995,
>
> (d) under or arising out of a contravention, or alleged contravention, of section 8, 13, 15, 18(1), 21(1), 28, 80G(1), 80H(1)(b), 80(1), 92 or 135, or of Part V, VI, VII or X, of the Employment Rights Act 1996,
>
> (dd) under or by virtue of section 11, 18, 20(1)(a) or 24 of the National Minimum Wage Act 1998,
>
> (e) which are proceedings in respect of which an employment tribunal has jurisdiction by virtue of section 3 of this Act,
>
> (f) under or arising out of a contravention, or alleged contravention, of a provision specified by an order under subsection (8)(b) as a provision to which this paragraph applies,
>
> (ff) under regulation 30 of the Working Time Regulations 1998,
>
> (g) under regulation 27 or 32 of the Transnational Information and Consultation Regulations 1999,
>
> (h) arising out of a contravention, or alleged contravention, of regulation 5(1) or 7(2) of the Part-time Workers (Prevention of Less Favourable Treatment) Regulations 2000,
>
> (i) arising out of a contravention, or alleged contravention of regulation 3 or 6(2) of the Fixed-term Employees (Prevention of Less Favourable Treatment) Regulations 2002,
>
> (j) under regulation 9 of those Regulations,
>
> (k) under regulation 28 of the Employment Equality (Sexual Orientation) Regulations 2003, or
>
> (l) under regulation 28 of the Employment Equality (Religion or Belief) Regulations 2003,

(m) under regulation 18 of the Merchant Shipping (Working Time: Inland Water-ways) Regulations 2003,

(n) under regulation 41 or 45 of the European Public Limited-Liability Company Regulations 2004,

(o) under regulation 19 of the Fishing Vessels (Working Time: Sea-fishermen) Regulations 2004,

(p) under regulation 29 or 33 of the Information and Consultation of Employees Regulations 2004,

(q) under paragraph 4 or 8 of the Schedule to the Occupational and Personal Pension Schemes (Consultation by Employers and Miscellaneous Amendment) Regulations 2006, or

(r) under regulation 36 of the Employment Equality (Age) Regulations 2006.

(2) Where an application has been presented to an employment tribunal and a copy of it has been sent to a conciliation officer, it is the duty of the conciliation officer—

(a) if he is requested to do so by the person by whom and the person against whom the proceedings are brought, or

(b) if, in the absence of any such request, the conciliation officer considers that he could act under this subsection with a reasonable prospect of success,

to endeavour to promote a settlement of the proceedings without their being determined by an employment tribunal.

(2A) Where employment tribunal procedure regulations include provision postponing the fixing of a time and place for a hearing for the purpose of giving an opportunity for the proceedings to be settled by way of conciliation and withdrawn, subsection (2) shall have effect from the end of the postponement to confer a power on the conciliation officer, instead of imposing a duty.

(3) Where at any time—

(a) a person claims that action has been taken in respect of which proceedings could be brought by him before an employment tribunal, but

(b) before any application relating to that action has been presented by him a request is made to a conciliation officer (whether by that person or by the person against whom the proceedings could be instituted) to make his services available to them,

the conciliation officer shall act in accordance with subsection (2) as if an application had been presented to an employment tribunal.

(4) Where a person who has presented a complaint to an employment tribunal under section 111 of the Employment Rights Act 1996 has ceased to be employed by the employer against whom the complaint was made, the conciliation officer shall (for the purpose of promoting a settlement of the complaint in accordance with subsection (2)) in particular—

(a) seek to promote the reinstatement or re-engagement of the complainant by the employer, or by a successor of the employer or by an associated employer, on terms appearing to the conciliation officer to be equitable, or

(b) where the complainant does not wish to be reinstated or re-engaged, or where reinstatement or re-engagement is not practicable, and the parties desire the concili- ation officer to act, seek to promote agreement between them as to a sum by way of compensation to be paid by the employer to the complainant.

(5) Where at any time—

(a) a person claims that action has been taken in respect of which a complaint could be presented by him to an employment tribunal under section 111 of the Employment Rights Act 1996, but

(b) before any complaint relating to that action has been presented by him a request is made to a conciliation officer (whether by that person or by the employer) to make his services available to them,

the conciliation officer shall act in accordance with subsection (4) as if a complaint had been presented to an employment tribunal under section 111.

(6) In proceeding under this section a conciliation officer shall, where appropriate, have regard to the desirability of encouraging the use of other procedures available for the settlement of grievances.

(7) Anything communicated to a conciliation officer in connection with the performance of his functions under this section shall not be admissible in evidence in any proceedings before an employment tribunal, except with the consent of the person who communicated it to that officer.

(8) [omitted]

19   [omitted]

PART II   THE EMPLOYMENT APPEAL TRIBUNAL

Introductory

20   The Appeal Tribunal

(1) The Employment Appeal Tribunal ('the Appeal Tribunal') shall continue in existence.

(2) The Appeal Tribunal shall have a central office in London but may sit at any time and in any place in Great Britain.

(3) The Appeal Tribunal shall be a superior court of record and shall have an official seal which shall be judicially noticed.

(4) Subsection (2) is subject to regulation 34 of the Transnational Information and Consultation of Employees Regulations 1999 and regulation 46(1) of the European Public Limited-Liability Company Regulations 2004.

Jurisdiction

21   Jurisdiction of Appeal Tribunal

(1) An appeal lies to the Appeal Tribunal on any question of law arising from any decision of, or arising in any proceedings before, an employment tribunal under or by virtue of—

    (a) the Equal Pay Act 1970,

    (b) the Sex Discrimination Act 1975,

    (c) the Race Relations Act 1976,

    (d) the Trade Union and Labour Relations (Consolidation) Act 1992,

    (e) the Disability Discrimination Act 1995,

    (f) the Employment Rights Act 1996,

    (g) this Act,

    (ga) the National Minimum Wage Act 1998,

    (gb) the Employment Relations Act 1999,

    (gc) the Equality Act 2006,

    (h) the Working Time Regulations,

    (i) the Transnational Information and Consultation of Employees Regulations 1999,

    (j) the Part-time Workers (Prevention of Less Favourable Treatment) Regulations 2000,

    (k) the Fixed-term Employees (Prevention of Less Favourable Treatment) Regulations 2002,

    (l) the Employment Equality (Sexual Orientation) Regulations 2003,

    (m) the Employment Equality (Religion or Belief) Regulations 2003,

    (n) the Merchant Shipping (Working Time: Inland Waterways) Regulations 2003,

    (o) the European Public Limited-Liability Company Regulations 2004,

    (p) the Fishing Vessels (Working Time: Sea Fishermen) Regulations 2004,

(q) the Information and Consultation of Employees Regulations 2004,

(r) under paragraph 4 or 8 of the Schedule to the Occupational and Personal Pension Schemes (Consultation by Employers and Miscellaneous Amendment) Regulations 2006, or

(s) under regulation 36 of the Employment Equality (Age) Regulations 2006.

(2) No appeal shall lie except to the Appeal Tribunal from any decision of an employment tribunal under or by virtue of the Acts listed or the Regulations referred to in subsection (1).

(3) Subsection (1) does not affect any provision contained in, or made under, any Act which provides for an appeal to lie to the Appeal Tribunal (whether from an employment tribunal, the Certification Officer or any other person or body) otherwise than on a question to which that subsection applies.

(4) The Appeal Tribunal also has any jurisdiction in respect of matters other than appeals which is conferred on it by or under—

(a) the Trade Union and Labour Relations (Consolidation) Act 1992,

(b) this Act, or

(c) any other Act.

Membership etc.

22   Membership of Appeal Tribunal

(1) The Appeal Tribunal shall consist of—

(a) such number of judges as may be nominated from time to time by the Lord Chief Justice, after consulting the Lord Chancellor, from the judges of the High Court and the Court of Appeal,

(b) at least one judge of the Court of Session nominated from time to time by the Lord President of the Court of Session, and

(c) such number of other members as may be appointed from time to time by Her Majesty on the joint recommendation of the Lord Chancellor and the Secretary of State ('appointed Members').

(2) The appointed members shall be persons who appear to the Lord Chancellor and the Secretary of State to have special knowledge or experience of industrial relations either—

(a) as representatives of employers, or

(b) as representatives of workers (within the meaning of the Trade Union and Labour Relations (Consolidation) Act 1992).

(3) The Lord Chief Justice shall appoint one of the judges nominated under subsection (1) to be the President of the Appeal Tribunal.

(3A)–(6) [omitted]

23–27   [omitted]

28   Composition of Appeal Tribunal

(1) The Appeal Tribunal may sit, in accordance with directions given by the President of the Appeal Tribunal, either as a single tribunal or in two or more divisions concurrently.

(2) Subject to subsections (3) to (5), proceedings before the Appeal Tribunal shall be heard by a judge and either two or four appointed members, so that in either case there is an equal number—

(a) of persons whose knowledge or experience of industrial relations is as representatives of employers, and

(b) of persons whose knowledge or experience of industrial relations is as representatives of workers.

(3) With the consent of the parties, proceedings before the Appeal Tribunal may be heard by a judge and one appointed member or by a judge and three appointed members.

(4) Proceedings on an appeal on a question arising from any decision of, or arising in any proceedings before, an employment tribunal consisting of the person mentioned in section

4(1)(a) alone shall be heard by a judge alone unless a judge directs that the proceedings shall be heard in accordance with subsections (2) and (3).

(5) [repealed]

Procedure

29 Conduct of hearings

(1) A person may appear before the Appeal Tribunal in person or be represented by—
(a) counsel or a solicitor,
(b) a representative of a trade union or an employers' association, or
(c) any other person whom he desires to represent him.
(2) The Appeal Tribunal has in relation to—
(a) the attendance and examination of witnesses,
(b) the production and inspection of documents, and
(c) all other matters incidental to its jurisdiction,
the same powers, rights, privileges and authority (in England and Wales) as the High Court and (in Scotland) as the Court of Session.

30–32 [omitted]

33 Restriction of vexatious proceedings

(1) If, on an application made by the Attorney General or the Lord Advocate under this section, the Appeal Tribunal is satisfied that a person has habitually and persistently and without any reasonable ground—
(a) instituted vexatious proceedings, whether before the Certification Officer, in an employment tribunal or before the Appeal Tribunal, and whether against the same person or against different persons, or
(b) made vexatious applications in any proceedings, whether before the Certification Officer, in an employment tribunal or before the Appeal Tribunal,
the Appeal Tribunal may, after hearing the person or giving him an opportunity of being heard, make a restriction of proceedings order.
(2) A 'restriction of proceedings order' is an order that—
(a) no proceedings shall without the leave of the Appeal Tribunal be instituted before the Certification Officer, in any employment tribunal or before the Appeal Tribunal by the person against whom the order is made,
(b) any proceedings instituted by him before the Certification Officer, in any employment tribunal or before the Appeal Tribunal before the making of the order shall not be continued by him without the leave of the Appeal Tribunal, and
(c) no application (other than one for leave under this section) is to be made by him in any proceedings before the Certification Officer, in any employment tribunal or before the Appeal Tribunal without the leave of the Appeal Tribunal.
(3) A restriction of proceedings order may provide that it is to cease to have effect at the end of a specified period, but otherwise it remains in force indefinitely.
(4) Leave for the institution or continuance of, or for the making of an application in, any proceedings before the Certification Officer, in an employment tribunal or before the Appeal Tribunal by a person who is the subject of a restriction of proceedings order shall not be given unless the Appeal Tribunal is satisfied—
(a) that the proceedings or application are not an abuse of process, and
(b) that there are reasonable grounds for the proceedings or application.
(5) A copy of a restriction of proceedings order shall be published in the London Gazette and the Edinburgh Gazette.

34–48 [omitted]

National Minimum Wage Act 1998
(1998, c. 39)

Entitlement to the national minimum wage

1 Workers to be paid at least the national minimum wage

(1) A person who qualifies for the national minimum wage shall be remunerated by his employer in respect of his work in any pay reference period at a rate which is not less than the national minimum wage.

(2) A person qualifies for the national minimum wage if he is an individual who—

(a) is a worker;

(b) is working, or ordinarily works, in the United Kingdom under his contract;

(c) has ceased to be of compulsory school age.

(3) The national minimum wage shall be such single hourly rate as the Secretary of State may from time to time prescribe.

(4) For the purposes of this Act a 'pay reference period' is such period as the Secretary of State may prescribe for the purpose.

(5) Subsections (1) to (4) above are subject to the following provisions of this Act.

Regulations relating to the national minimum wage

2 Determination of hourly rate of remuneration

(1) The Secretary of State may by regulations make provision for determining what is the hourly rate at which a person is to be regarded for the purposes of this Act as remunerated by his employer in respect of his work in any pay reference period.

(2)–(7) [omitted]

(8) No provision shall be made under this section which treats the same circumstances differently in relation to—

(a) different areas;

(b) different sectors of employment;

(c) undertakings of different sizes;

(d) persons of different ages; or

(e) persons of different occupations.

3 Exclusion of, and modifications for, certain classes of person

(1) This section applies to persons who have not attained the age of 26.

(1A) This section also applies to persons who have attained the age of 26 who are—

(a) within the first six months after the commencement of their employment with an employer by whom they have not previously been employed;

(b) participating in a scheme under which shelter is provided in return for work;

(c) participating in a scheme designed to provide training, work experience or temporary work;

(d) participating in a scheme to assist in the seeking or obtaining of work; or

(e) attending a course of higher education requiring attendance for a period of work experience.

(2) The Secretary of State may by regulations make provision in relation to any of the persons to whom this section applies—

(a) preventing them being persons who qualify for the national minimum wage; or

(b) prescribing an hourly rate for the national minimum wage other than the single hourly rate for the time being prescribed under section 1(3) above.

(3) No provision shall be made under subsection (2) above which treats persons differently in relation to—

(a) different areas;

(b) different sectors of employment;

(c) undertakings of different sizes; or

(d) different occupations.

(4) If any description of persons who have attained the age of 26 is added by regulations under section 4 below to the descriptions of person to whom this section applies, no

provision shall be made under subsection (2) above which treats persons of that description differently in relation to different ages over 26.

4 Power to add to the persons to whom section 3 applies

(1) The Secretary of State may by regulations amend section 3 above by adding descriptions of persons who have attained the age of 26 to the descriptions of person to whom that section applies.

(2) No amendment shall be made under subsection (1) above which treats persons differently in relation to—

(a) different areas;

(b) different sectors of employment;

(c) undertakings of different sizes;

(d) different ages over 26; or

(f) different occupations.

The Low Pay Commission

5–16A [omitted]

Enforcement

17 Non-compliance: worker entitled to additional remuneration

(1) If a worker who qualifies for the national minimum wage is remunerated for any pay reference period by his employer at a rate which is less than the national minimum wage, the worker shall be taken to be entitled under his contract to be paid, as additional remuneration in respect of that period, the amount described in subsection (2) below.

(2) That amount is the difference between—

(a) the relevant remuneration received by the worker for the pay reference period;

(b) the relevant remuneration which the worker would have received for that period had he been remunerated by the employer at a rate equal to the national minimum wage.

(3) In subsection (2) above, 'relevant remuneration' means remuneration which falls to be brought into account for the purposes of regulations under section 2 above.

18 Enforcement in the case of special classes of worker

(1) If the persons who are the worker and the employer for the purposes of section 17 above would not (apart from this section) fall to be regarded as the worker and the employer for the purposes of—

(a) Part II of the Employment Rights Act 1996 (protection of wages); or

(b) in relation to Northern Ireland, Part IV of the Employment Rights (Northern Ireland) Order 1996;

they shall be so regarded for the purposes of the application of that Part in relation to the entitlement conferred by that section.

(2) In the application by virtue of subsection (1) above of—

(a) Part II of the Employment Rights Act 1996, or

(b) Part IV of the Employment Rights (Northern Ireland) Order 1996,

in a case where there is or was, for the purposes of that Part, no worker's contract between the persons who are the worker and the employer for the purposes of section 17 above, it shall be assumed that there is or, as the case may be, was such a contract.

(3) For the purpose of enabling the amount described as additional remuneration in subsection (1) of section 17 above to be recovered in civil proceedings on a claim in contract in a case where in fact there is or was no worker's contract between the persons who are the worker and the employer for the purposes of that section, it shall be assumed for the purpose of any civil proceedings, so far as relating to that amount, that there is or, as the case may be, was such a contract.

19   Power of officer to issue enforcement notice

(1) If an officer acting for the purposes of this Act is of the opinion that a worker who qualifies for the national minimum wage has not been remunerated for any pay reference period by his employer at a rate at least equal to the national minimum wage, the officer may serve a notice (an 'enforcement notice') on the employer requiring the employer to remunerate the worker for pay reference periods ending on or after the date of the notice at a rate equal to the national minimum wage.

(2) An enforcement notice may also require the employer to pay to the worker within such time as may be specified in the notice the sum due to the worker under section 17 above in respect of the employer's previous failure to remunerate the worker at a rate at least equal to the national minimum wage.

(2A) If an officer acting for the purposes of this Act is of the opinion that a worker who has at any time qualified for the national minimum wage has not been remunerated for any pay reference period (whether ending before or after the coming into force of this subsection) by his employer at a rate at least equal to the national minimum wage, the officer may serve on the employer an enforcement notice which imposes a requirement under subsection (2) above in relation to the worker, whether or not a requirement under subsection (1) above is, or may be, imposed in relation to that worker (or any other worker to whom the notice relates).

(2B) An enforcement notice may not impose a requirement under subsection (2) above in respect of any pay reference period ending more than 6 years before the date on which the notice is served.

(2C) Where an enforcement notice imposes a requirement under subsection (2) above, the amount specified in the notice as the sum due to the worker under section 17 above need not include any sum so due to him in respect of any very recent pay reference period (although the amount so specified may include any such sum).

(2D) In subsection (2C) above a 'very recent' pay reference period means a pay reference period ending less than 3 months before the date on which the notice is served.

(3) An enforcement notice may relate to more than one worker (and, where it does so, may be so framed as to relate to workers specified in the notice or to workers of a description so specified).

(4) A person on whom an enforcement notice is served may appeal against the notice before the end of the period of four weeks following the date of service of the notice.

(5) An appeal under subsection (4) above lies to an employment tribunal.

(6) On an appeal under subsection (4) above, the employment tribunal shall dismiss the appeal unless it is established—

    (a) that, in the case of the worker or workers to whom the enforcement notice relates, the facts are such that an officer who was aware of them would have had no reason to serve any enforcement notice on the appellant; or

    (b) where the enforcement notice relates to two or more workers, that the facts are such that an officer who was aware of them would have had no reason to include some of the workers in any enforcement notice served on the appellant; or

    (c) where the enforcement notice imposes a requirement under subsection (2) above in relation to a worker—

        (i) that no sum was due to the worker under section 17 above; or

        (ii) that the amount specified in the notice as the sum due to the worker under that section is too great; or

        (iii) that the notice contravenes section (2B) above;

and in this subsection any reference to a worker includes a reference to a person whom the enforcement notice purports to treat as a worker.

(7) Where an appeal is allowed by virtue of paragraph (a) of subsection (6) above, the employment tribunal shall rescind the enforcement notice.

(8) If, in a case where subsection (7) above does not apply, an appeal is allowed by virtue of paragraph (b) or (c) of subsection (6) above—

    (a) the employment tribunal shall rectify the enforcement notice; and

    (b) the enforcement notice shall have effect as if it had originally been served as so rectified.

(9) The powers of an employment tribunal in allowing an appeal in a case where subsection (8) above applies shall include power to rectify, as the tribunal may consider appropriate in consequence of its decision on the appeal, any penalty notice which has been served under section 21 below in respect of the enforcement notice.

(10) Where a penalty notice is rectified under subsection (9) above, it shall have effect as if it had originally been served as so rectified.

20   Non-compliance: power of officer to sue on behalf of worker

(1) If an enforcement notice is not complied with in whole or in part, an officer acting for the purposes of this Act may, on behalf of any worker to whom the notice relates,—

    (a) present a complaint under section 23(1)(a) of the Employment Rights Act 1996 (deductions from worker's wages in contravention of section 13 of that Act) to an employment tribunal in respect of any sums due to the worker by virtue of section 17 above; or

    (b) in relation to Northern Ireland, present a complaint under Article 55(1)(a) of the Employment Rights (Northern Ireland) Order 1996 (deductions from worker's wages in contravention of Article 45 of that Order) to an industrial tribunal in respect of any sums due to the worker by virtue of section 17 above; or

    (c) commence other civil proceedings for the recovery, on a claim in contract, of any sums due to the worker by virtue of section 17 above.

(2) The powers conferred by subsection (1) above for the recovery of sums due from an employer to a worker shall not be in derogation of any right which the worker may have to recover such sums by civil proceedings.

21   Financial penalty for non-compliance

(1) If an officer acting for the purposes of this Act is satisfied that a person on whom an enforcement notice has been served has failed, in whole or in part, to comply with the notice, the officer may serve on that person a notice (a 'penalty notice') requiring the person to pay a financial penalty to the Secretary of State.

(2) A penalty notice must state—

    (a) the amount of the financial penalty;

    (b) the time within which the financial penalty is to be paid (which must not be less than four weeks from the date of service of the notice);

    (c) the period to which the financial penalty relates;

    (d) the respects in which the officer is of the opinion that the enforcement notice has not been complied with; and

    (e) the calculation of the amount of the financial penalty.

(3) The amount of the financial penalty shall be calculated at a rate equal to twice the hourly amount of the national minimum wage (as in force at the date of the penalty notice) in respect of each worker to whom the failure to comply relates for each day during which the failure to comply has continued in respect of the worker.

(4) The Secretary of State may by regulations from time to time amend the multiplier for the time being specified in subsection (3) above in relation to the hourly amount of the national minimum wage.

(5) A financial penalty under this section—

    (a) in England and Wales, shall be recoverable, if a county court so orders, by execution issued from the county court or otherwise as if it were payable under an order of that court;

(b) in Scotland, may be enforced in the same manner as an extract registered decree arbitral bearing a warrant for execution issued by the sheriff court of any sheriffdom in Scotland;

(c) in Northern Ireland, shall be recoverable, if the county court so orders, as if it were payable under an order of that court.

(6) Where a person has appealed under subsection (4) of section 19 above against an enforcement notice and the appeal has not been withdrawn or finally determined, then, notwithstanding the appeal,—

(a) the enforcement notice shall have effect; and

(b) an officer may serve a penalty notice in respect of the enforcement notice.

(7) If, in a case falling within subsection (6) above, an officer serves a penalty notice in respect of the enforcement notice, the penalty notice—

(a) shall not be enforceable until the appeal has been withdrawn or finally determined; and

(b) shall be of no effect if the enforcement notice is rescinded as a result of the appeal; but

(c) subject to paragraph (b) above and section 22(4) and (6)(a) below, as from the withdrawal or final determination of the appeal shall be enforceable as if paragraph (a) above had not had effect.

(8) Any sums received by the Secretary of State by virtue of this section shall be paid into the Consolidated Fund.

22   Appeals against penalty notices

(1) A person on whom a penalty notice is served may appeal against the notice before the end of the period of four weeks following the date of service of the notice.

(2) An appeal under subsection (1) above lies to an employment tribunal.

(3) On an appeal under subsection (1) above, the employment tribunal shall dismiss the appeal unless it is shown—

(a) that, in the case of each of the allegations of failure to comply with the enforcement notice, the facts are such that an officer who was aware of them would have had no reason to serve any penalty notice on the appellant; or

(b) that the amount of the financial penalty is too great because the penalty notice is incorrect in some of the particulars which affect that amount; or

(c) that the amount of the financial penalty is too great because its calculation is incorrect;

and for the purposes of any appeal relating to a penalty notice, the enforcement notice in question shall (subject to rescission or rectification on any appeal brought under section 19 above) be taken to be correct.

(4) Where an appeal is allowed by virtue of paragraph (a) of subsection (3) above, the employment tribunal shall rescind the penalty notice.

(5) If, in a case where subsection (4) above does not apply, an appeal is allowed by virtue of paragraph (b) or (c) of subsection (3) above—

(a) the employment tribunal shall rectify the penalty notice; and

(b) the penalty notice shall have effect as if it had originally been served as so rectified.

(6) Where a person has appealed under subsection (1) above against a penalty notice and the appeal has not been withdrawn or finally determined, the penalty notice—

(a) shall not be enforceable until the appeal has been withdrawn or finally determined; but

(b) subject to subsection (4) above and section 21(7)(a) and (b) above, as from the withdrawal or final determination of the appeal shall be enforceable as if paragraph (a) above had not had effect.

22A–F [omitted]

Rights not to suffer unfair dismissal or other detriment

23 The right not to suffer detriment

(1) A worker has the right not to be subjected to any detriment by any act, or any deliberate failure to act, by his employer, done on the ground that—

    (a) any action was taken, or was proposed to be taken, by or on behalf of the worker with a view to enforcing, or otherwise securing the benefit of, a right of the worker's to which this section applies; or

    (b) the employer was prosecuted for an offence under section 31 below as a result of action taken by or on behalf of the worker for the purpose of enforcing, or otherwise securing the benefit of, a right of the worker's to which this section applies; or

    (c) the worker qualifies, or will or might qualify, for the national minimum wage or for a particular rate of national minimum wage.

(2) It is immaterial for the purposes of paragraph (a) or (b) of subsection (1) above—

    (a) whether or not the worker has the right; or

    (b) whether or not the right has been infringed;

but, for that subsection to apply, the claim to the right and, if applicable, the claim that it has been infringed must be made in good faith.

(3) The following are the rights to which this section applies—

    (a) any right conferred by, or by virtue of, any provision of this Act for which the remedy for its infringement is by way of a complaint to an employment tribunal; and

    (b) any right conferred by section 17 above.

(4) This section does not apply where the detriment in question amounts to dismissal within the meaning of—

    (a) Part X of the Employment Rights Act 1996 (unfair dismissal); or

    (b) Part XI, of the Employment Rights (Northern Ireland) Order 1996 (corresponding provision for Northern Ireland);

except wherein relation to Northern Ireland the person in question is dismissed in circumstances in which by virtue of Article 240 of that Order (fixed term contracts), Part XI does not apply to the dismissal.

24 Enforcement of the right

(1) A worker may present a complaint to an employment tribunal that he has been subjected to a detriment in contravention of section 23 above.

(2) Subject to the following provisions of this section, the provisions of—

    (a) sections 48(2) to (4) and 49 of the Employment Rights Act 1996 (complaints to employment tribunals and remedies), or

    (b) in relation to Northern Ireland, Articles 71(2) to (4) and 72 of the Employment Rights (Northern Ireland) Order 1996 (complaints to industrial tribunals and remedies),

shall apply in relation to a complaint under this section as they apply in relation to a complaint under section 48 of that Act or Article 71 of that Order (as the case may be), but taking references in those provisions to the employer as references to the employer within the meaning of section 23(1) above.

(3) Where—

    (a) the detriment to which the worker is subjected is the termination of his worker's contract, but

    (b) that contract is not a contract of employment,

any compensation awarded under section 49 of the Employment Rights Act 1996 or Article 72 of the Employment Rights (Northern Ireland) Order 1996 by virtue of subsection (2) above must not exceed the limit specified in subsection (4) below.

(4) The limit mentioned in subsection (3) above is the total of—

(a) the sum which would be the basic award for unfair dismissal, calculated in accordance with section 119 of the Employment Rights Act 1996 or Article 153 of the Employment Rights (Northern Ireland) Order 1996 (as the case may be), if the worker had been an employee and the contract terminated had been a contract of employment; and

(b) the sum for the time being specified in section 124(1) of that Act or Article 158(1) of that Order (as the case may be) which is the limit for a compensatory award to a person calculated in accordance with section 123 of that Act or Article 157 of that Order (as the case may be).

(5) Where the worker has been working under arrangements which do not fall to be regarded as a worker's contract for the purposes of—

(a) the Employment Rights Act 1996, or

(b) in relation to Northern Ireland, the Employment Rights (Northern Ireland) Order 1996,

he shall be treated for the purposes of subsections (3) and (4) above as if any arrangements under which he has been working constituted a worker's contract falling within section 230(3)(b) of that Act or Article 3(3)(b) of that Order (as the case may be).

25–27   [omitted]

28   Reversal of burden of proof

(1) Where in any civil proceedings any question arises as to whether an individual qualifies or qualified at any time for the national minimum wage, it shall be presumed that the individual qualifies or, as the case may be, qualified at that time for the national minimum wage unless the contrary is established.

(2) Where—

(a) a complaint is made—

(i)   to an employment tribunal under section 23(1)(a) of the Employment Rights Act 1996 (unauthorised deductions from wages), or

(ii) to an industrial tribunal under Article 55(1)(a) of the Employment Rights (Northern Ireland) Order 1996, and

(b) the complaint relates in whole or in part to the deduction of the amount described as additional remuneration in section 17(1) above,

it shall be presumed for the purposes of the complaint, so far as relating to the deduction of that amount, that the worker in question was remunerated at a rate less than the national minimum wage unless the contrary is established.

(3) Where in any civil proceedings a person seeks to recover on a claim in contract the amount described as additional remuneration in section 17(1) above, it shall be presumed for the purposes of the proceedings, so far as relating to that amount, that the worker in question was remunerated at a rate less than the national minimum wage unless the contrary is established.

29–30   [omitted]

Offences

31   Offences

(1) If the employer of a worker who qualifies for the national minimum wage refuses or wilfully neglects to remunerate the worker for any pay reference period at a rate which is at least equal to the national minimum wage, that employer is guilty of an offence.

(2) If a person who is required to keep or preserve any record in accordance with regulations under section 9 above fails to do so, that person is guilty of an offence.

(3) If a person makes, or knowingly causes or allows to be made, in a record required to be kept in accordance with regulations under section 9 above any entry which he knows to be false in a material particular, that person is guilty of an offence.

(4) If a person, for purposes connected with the provisions of this Act, produces or furnishes, or knowingly causes or allows to be produced or furnished, any record or information which he knows to be false in a material particular, that person is guilty of an offence.

(5) If a person—

(a) intentionally delays or obstructs an officer acting for the purposes of this Act in the exercise of any power conferred by this Act, or

(b) refuses or neglects to answer any question, furnish any information or produce any document when required to do so under section 14(1) above,

that person is guilty of an offence.

(6) Where the commission by any person of an offence under subsection (1) or (2) above is due to the act or default of some other person, that other person is also guilty of the offence.

(7) A person may be charged with and convicted of an offence by virtue of subsection (6) above whether or not proceedings are taken against any other person.

(8) In any proceedings for an offence under subsection (1) or (2) above it shall be a defence for the person charged to prove that he exercised all due diligence and took all reasonable precautions to secure that the provisions of this Act, and of any relevant regulations made under it, were complied with by himself and by any person under his control.

(9) A person guilty of an offence under this section shall be liable on summary conviction to a fine not exceeding level 5 on the standard scale.

32   Offences by bodies corporate etc.

(1) This section applies to any offence under this Act.

(2) If an offence committed by a body corporate is proved—

(a) to have been committed with the consent or connivance of an officer of the body, or

(b) to be attributable to any neglect on the part of such an officer,

the officer as well as the body corporate is guilty of the offence and liable to be proceeded against and punished accordingly.

(3) In subsection (2) above 'officer', in relation to a body corporate, means a director, manager, secretary or other similar officer of the body, or a person purporting to act in any such capacity.

(4) If the affairs of a body corporate are managed by its members, subsection (2) above applies in relation to the acts and defaults of a member in connection with his functions of management as if he were a director of the body corporate.

(5) If an offence committed by a partnership in Scotland is proved—

(a) to have been committed with the consent or connivance of a partner, or

(b) to be attributable to any neglect on the part of a partner,

the partner as well as the partnership is guilty of the offence and liable to be proceeded against and punished accordingly.

(6) In subsection (5) above, 'partner' includes a person purporting to act as a partner.

33   [omitted]

Special classes of person

34   Agency workers who are not otherwise 'workers'

(1) This section applies in any case where an individual ('the agency worker')—

(a) is supplied by a person ('the agent') to do work for another ('the principal') under a contract or other arrangements made between the agent and the principal; but

(b) is not, as respects that work, a worker, beause of the absence of a worker's contract between the individual and the agent or the principal; and

(c) is not a party to a contract under which he undertakes to do the work for another party to the contract whose status is, by virtue of the contract, that of a client or customer of any profession or business undertaking carried on by the individual.

(2) In a case where this section applies, the other provisions of this Act shall have effect as if there were a worker's contract for the doing of the work by the agency worker made between the agency worker and—

    (a) whichever of the agent and the principal is responsible for paying the agency worker in respect of the work; or

    (b) if neither the agent nor the principal is so responsible, whichever of them pays the agency worker in respect of the work.

35 Home workers who are not otherwise 'workers'

(1) In determining for the purposes of this Act whether a home worker is or is not a worker, section 54(3)(b) below shall have effect as if for the word 'personally' there were substituted '(whether personally or otherwise)'.

(2) In this section 'home worker' means an individual who contracts with a person, for the purposes of that person's business, for the execution of work to be done in a place not under the control or management of that person.

36 Crown employment

(1) Subject to section 37 below, the provisions of this Act have effect in relation to Crown employment and persons in Crown employment as they have effect in relation to other employment and other workers.

(2) In this Act, subject to section 37 below, 'Crown employment' means employment under or for the purposes of a government department or any officer or body exercising on behalf of the Crown functions conferred by statutory provision.

(3) For the purposes of the application of the other provisions of this Act in relation to Crown employment in accordance with subsection (1) above—

    (a) references to an employee or a worker shall be construed as references to a person in Crown employment;

    (b) references to a contract of employment or a worker's contract shall be construed as references to the terms of employment of a person in Crown employment; and

    (c) references to dismissal, or to the termination of a worker's contract, shall be construed as references to the termination of Crown employment.

37 Armed forces

(1) A person serving as a member of the naval, military or air forces of the Crown does not qualify for the national minimum wage in respect of that service.

(2) Section 36 above applies to employment by an association established for the purposes of Part XI of the Reserve Forces Act 1996, notwithstanding anything in subsection (1) above.

38–43 [omitted]

Exclusions

44 Voluntary workers

(1) A worker employed by a charity, a voluntary organisation, an associated fund-raising body or a statutory body does not qualify for the national minimum wage in respect of that employment if he receives, and under the terms of his employment (apart from this Act) is entitled to,—

    (a) no monetary payments of any description, or no monetary payments except in respect of expenses—

        (i) actually incurred in the performance of his duties; or

        (ii) reasonably estimated as likely to be or to have been so incurred; and

        (iii) no benefits in kind of any description, or no benefits in kind other than the provision of some or all of his subsistence or of such accommodation as is reasonable in the circumstances of the employment.

(2) A person who would satisfy the conditions in subsection (1) above but for receiving monetary payments made solely for the purpose of providing him with means of subsistence shall be taken to satisfy those conditions if—

(a) he is employed to do the work in question as a result of arrangements made between a charity acting in pursuance of its charitable purposes and the body for which the work is done; and

(b) the work is done for a charity, a voluntary organisation, an associated fund-raising body or a statutory body.

(3) For the purposes of subsection (1)(b) above—

(a) any training (other than that which a person necessarily acquires in the course of doing his work) shall be taken to be a benefit in kind; but

(b) there shall be left out of account any training provided for the sole or main purpose of improving the worker's ability to perform the work which he has agreed to do.

(4) In this section—

'associated fund-raising body' means a body of persons the profits of which are applied wholly for the purposes of a charity or voluntary organisation;

'charity' means a body of persons, or the trustees of a trust, established for charitable purposes only;

'receive', in relation to a monetary payment or a benefit in kind, means receive in respect of, or otherwise in connection with, the employment in question (whether or not under the terms of the employment);

'statutory body' means a body established by or under an enactment (including an enactment comprised in Northern Ireland legislation);

'subsistence' means such subsistence as is reasonable in the circumstances of the employment in question, and does not include accommodation;

'voluntary organisation' means a body of persons, or the trustees of a trust, which is established only for charitable purposes (whether or not those purposes are charitable within the meaning of any rule of law), benevolent purposes or philanthropic purposes, but which is not a charity.

44A Religious and other communities: resident workers

(1) A residential member of a community to which this section applies does not qualify for the national minimum wage in respect of employment by the community.

(2) Subject to subsection (3), this section applies to a community if—

(a) it is a charity or is established by a charity,

(b) a purpose of the community is to practise or advance a belief of a religious or similar nature, and

(c) all or some of its members live together for that purpose.

(3) This section does not apply to a community which—

(a) is an independent school, or

(b) provides a course of further or higher education.

(4) The residential members of a community are those who live together as mentioned in subsection (2)(c).

(5)–(6) [omitted]

45 Prisoners

(1) A prisoner does not qualify for the national minimum wage in respect of any work which he does in pursuance of prison rules.

(2) In this section—

'prisoner' means a person detained in, or on temporary release from, a prison;

'prison' includes any other institution to which prison rules apply;

'prison rules' means—

(a) in relation to England and Wales, rules made under section 47 of the Prison Act 1952;

(b) in relation to Scotland, rules made under section 39 of the Prisons (Scotland) Act 1989; and

(c) in relation to Northern Ireland, rules made under section 13 of the Prison Act (Northern Ireland) 1953.

45A   Persons discharging fines by unpaid work

A person does not qualify for the national minimum wage in respect of any work that he does in pursuance of a work order under Schedule 6 to the Courts Act 2003 (discharge of fines by unpaid work).

46–47   [omitted]

Miscellaneous

48   Application of Act to superior employers

Where—

(a) the immediate employer of a worker is himself in the employment of some other person, and

(b) the worker is employed on the premises of that other person,

that other person shall be deemed for the purposes of this Act to be the employer of the worker jointly with the immediate employer.

49   Restrictions on contracting out

(1) Any provision in any agreement (whether a worker's contract or not) is void in so far as it purports—

(a) to exclude or limit the operation of any provision of this Act; or

(b) to preclude a person from bringing proceedings under this Act before an employment tribunal.

(2) Subsection (1) above does not apply to any agreement to refrain from instituting or continuing proceedings where a conciliation officer has taken action under—

(a) section 18 of the Employment Tribunals Act 1996 (conciliation), or

(b) in relation to Northern Ireland, Article 20 of the Industrial Tribunals (Northern Ireland) Order 1996.

(3) Subsection (1) above does not apply to any agreement to refrain from instituting or continuing before an employment tribunal any proceedings within—

(a) section 18(1)(dd) of the Employment Tribunals Act 1996 (proceedings under or by virtue of this Act where conciliation is available), or

(b) in relation to Northern Ireland, Article 20(1)(cc) of the Industrial Tribunals (Northern Ireland) Order 1996,

if the conditions regulating compromise agreements under this Act are satisfied in relation to the agreement.

(4) For the purposes of subsection (3) above the conditions regulating compromise agreements under this Act are that—

(a) the agreement must be in writing,

(b) the agreement must relate to the particular proceedings,

(c) the employee or worker must have received advice from a relevant independent adviser as to the terms and effect of the proposed agreement and, in particular, its effect on his ability to pursue his rights before an employment tribunal,

(d) there must be in force, when the adviser gives the advice, a contract of insurance, or an indemnity provided for members of a profession or a professional body, covering the risk of a claim by the employee or worker in respect of loss arising in consequence of the advice,

(e) the agreement must identify the adviser, and

(f) the agreement must state that the conditions regulating compromise agreements under this Act are satisfied.

(5) A person is a relevant independent adviser for the purposes of subsection (4)(c) above—

(a) if he is a qualified lawyer,

(b) if he is an officer, official, employee or member of an independent trade union who has been certified in writing by the trade union as competent to give advice and as authorised to do so on behalf of the trade union,

(c) if he works at an advice centre (whether as an employee or a volunteer) and has been certified in writing by the centre as competent to give advice and as authorised to do so on behalf of the centre, or

(d) if he is a person of a description specified in an order made by the Secretary of State.

(6) But a person is not a relevant independent adviser for the purposes of subsection (4)(c) above in relation to the employee or worker—

(a) if he is employed by, or is acting in the matter for, the employer or an associated employer,

(b) in the case of a person within subsection (5)(b) or (c) above, if the trade union or advice centre is the employer or an associated employer,

(c) in the case of a person within subsection (5)(c) above, if the employee or worker makes a payment for the advice received from him, or

(d) in the case of a person of a description specified in an order under subsection (5)(d) above, if any condition specified in the order in relation to the giving of advice by persons of that description is not satisfied.

(7) [omitted]

(8) For the purposes of this section any two employers shall be treated as associated if—

(a) one is a company of which the other (directly or indirectly) has control; or

(b) both are companies of which a third person (directly or indirectly) has control;

and 'associated employer' shall be construed accordingly.

(9)–(11) [omitted]

50–53 [omitted]

Supplementary

54 Meaning of 'worker', 'employee' etc.

(1) In this Act 'employee' means an individual who has entered into or works under (or, where the employment has ceased, worked under) a contract of employment.

(2) In this Act 'contract of employment' means a contract of service or apprenticeship, whether express or implied, and (if it is express) whether oral or in writing.

(3) In this Act 'worker' (except in the phrases 'agency worker' and 'home worker') means an individual who has entered into or works under (or, where the employment has ceased, worked under)—

(a) a contract of employment; or

(b) any other contract, whether express or implied and (if it is express) whether oral or in writing, whereby the individual undertakes to do or perform personally any work or services for another party to the contract whose status is not by virtue of the contract that of a client or customer of any profession or business undertaking carried on by the individual;

and any reference to a worker's contract shall be construed accordingly.

(4) In this Act 'employer', in relation to an employee or a worker, means the person by whom the employee or worker is (or, where the employment has ceased, was) employed.

(5) In this Act 'employment'—

(a) in relation to an employee, means employment under a contract of employment; and

(b) in relation to a worker, means employment under his contract; and 'employed' shall be construed accordingly.

55 Interpretation

(1) In this Act, unless the context otherwise requires,—

'civil proceedings' means proceedings before an employment tribunal or civil proceedings before any other court;

'enforcement notice' shall be construed in accordance with section 19 above;

'government department' includes a Northern Ireland department, except in section 52(a) above;

'industrial tribunal' means a tribunal established under Article 3 of the Industrial Tribunals (Northern Ireland) Order 1996;

'notice' means notice in writing;

'pay reference period' shall be construed in accordance with section 1(4) above;

'penalty notice' shall be construed in accordance with section 21 above;

'person who qualifies for the national minimum wage' shall be construed in accordance with section 1(2) above; and related expressions shall be construed accordingly;

'prescribe' means prescribe by regulations;

'regulations' means regulations made by the Secretary of State, except in the case of regulations under section 47(2) or (4) above made by the Secretary of State and the Minister of Agriculture, Fisheries and Food acting jointly or by the Department of Agriculture for Northern Ireland.

(2) Any reference in this Act to a person being remunerated for a pay reference period is a reference to the person being remunerated by his employer in respect of his work in that pay reference period.

(3) Any reference in this Act to doing work includes a reference to performing services; and 'work' and other related expressions shall be construed accordingly.

(4) For the purposes of this Act, a person ceases to be of compulsory school age in Scotland when he ceases to be of school age in accordance with sections 31 and 33 of the Education (Scotland) Act 1980.

(5) Any reference in this Act to a person ceasing to be of compulsory school age shall, in relation to Northern Ireland, be construed in accordance with Article 46 of the Education and Libraries (Northern Ireland) Order 1986.

(6) Any reference in this Act to an employment tribunal shall, in relation to Northern Ireland, be construed as a reference to an industrial tribunal.

56 [omitted]

Employment Relations Act 1999
(1999, c. 26)

ARRANGEMENT OF SECTIONS

Trade unions

Disciplinary and grievance hearings

Other rights of individuals

23. Power to confer rights on individuals.

Miscellaneous

34. Indexation of amounts, etc.

Trade unions

1–2 [omitted]

3 Detriment related to trade union membership. Blacklists

(1) The Secretary of State may make regulations prohibiting the compilation of lists which—

  (a) contain details of members of trade unions or persons who have taken part in the activities of trade unions, and

  (b) are compiled with a view to being used by employers or employment agencies for the purposes of discrimination in relation to recruitment or in relation to the treatment of workers.

(2) The Secretary of State may make regulations prohibiting—

  (a) the use of lists to which subsection (1) applies;

  (b) the sale or supply of lists to which subsection (1) applies.

(3) Regulations under this section may, in particular—

  (a) confer jurisdiction (including exclusive jurisdiction) on employment tribunals and on the Employment Appeal Tribunal;

  (b) include provision for or about the grant and enforcement of specified remedies by courts and tribunals;

  (c) include provision for the making of awards of compensation calculated in accordance with the regulations;

  (d) include provision permitting proceedings to be brought by trade unions on behalf of members in specified circumstances;

  (e) include provision about cases where an employee is dismissed by his employer and the reason or principal reason for the dismissal, or why the employee was selected for dismissal, relates to a list to which subsection (1) applies;

  (f) create criminal offences;

  (g) in specified cases or circumstances, extend liability for a criminal offence created under paragraph (f) to a person who aids the commission of the offence or to a person who is an agent, principal, employee, employer or officer of a person who commits the offence;

  (h) provide for specified obligations or offences not to apply in specified circumstances;

  (i) include supplemental, incidental, consequential and transitional provision, including provision amending an enactment;

  (j) make different provision for different cases or circumstances.

(4) Regulations under this section creating an offence may not provide for it to be punishable—

(a) by imprisonment,

(b) by a fine in excess of level 5 on the standard scale in the case of an offence triable only summarily, or

(c) by a fine in excess of the statutory maximum in the case of summary conviction for an offence triable either way.

(5) In this section—

'list' includes any index or other set of items whether recorded electronically or by any other means, and

'worker' has the meaning given by section 13.

(6) Subject to subsection (5), expressions used in this section and in the Trade Union and Labour Relations (Consolidation) Act 1992 have the same meaning in this section as in that Act.

4–9 [omitted]

Disciplinary and grievance hearings

10 Right to be accompanied

(1) This section applies where a worker—

(a) is required or invited by his employer to attend a disciplinary or grievance hearing, and

(b) reasonably requests to be accompanied at the hearing.

(2) [repealed]

(2A) Where this section applies, the employer must permit the worker to be accompanied at the hearing by one companion who—

(a) is chosen by the worker; and

(b) is within subsection (3).

(2B) The employer must permit the worker's companion to—

(a) address the hearing in order to do any or all of the following—

(i) put the worker's case;

(ii) sum up that case;

(iii) respond on the worker's behalf to any view expressed at the hearing;

(b) confer with the worker during the hearing.

(2C) Subsection (2B) does not require the employer to permit the worker's companion to—

(a) answer questions on behalf of the worker;

(b) address the hearing if the worker indicates at it that he does not wish his companion to do so; or

(c) use the powers conferred by that subsection in a way that prevents the employer from explaining his case or prevents any other person at the hearing from making his contribution to it.

(3) A person is within this subsection if he is—

(a) employed by a trade union of which he is an official within the meaning of section 1 and 119 of the Trade Union and Labour Relations (Consolidation) Act 1992,

(b) an official of a trade union (within that meaning) whom the union has reasonably certified in writing as having experience of, or as having received training in, acting as a worker's companion at disciplinary or grievance hearings, or

(c) another of the employer's workers.

(4) If—

(a) a worker has a right under this section to be accompanied at a hearing,

(b) his chosen companion will not be available at the time proposed for the hearing by the employer, and

(c) the worker proposes an alternative time which satisfies subsection (5), the employer must postpone the hearing to the time proposed by the worker.

(5) An alternative time must—

(a) be reasonable, and

(b) fall before the end of the period of five working days beginning with the first working day after the day proposed by the employer.

(6) An employer shall permit a worker to take time off during working hours for the purpose of accompanying another of the employer's workers in accordance with a request under subsection (1)(b).

(7) Sections 168(3) and (4), 169 and 171 to 173 of the Trade Union and Labour Relations (Consolidation) Act 1992 (time off for carrying out trade union duties) shall apply in relation to subsection (6) above as they apply in relation to section 168(1) of that Act.

11 Complaint to employment tribunal

(1) A worker may present a complaint to an employment tribunal that his employer has failed, or threatened to fail, to comply with section 10(2A), (2B) or (4).

(2) A tribunal shall not consider a complaint under this section in relation to a failure or threat unless the complaint is presented—

(a) before the end of the period of three months beginning with the date of the failure or threat, or

(b) within such further period as the tribunal considers reasonable in a case where it is satisfied that it was not reasonably practicable for the complaint to be presented before the end of that period of three months.

(3) Where a tribunal finds that a complaint under this section is well-founded it shall order the employer to pay compensation to the worker of an amount not exceeding two weeks' pay.

(4) Chapter II of Part XIV of the Employment Rights Act 1996 (calculation of a week's pay) shall apply for the purposes of subsection (3); and in applying that Chapter the calculation date shall be taken to be—

(a) in the case of a claim which is made in the course of a claim for unfair dismissal, the date on which the employer's notice of dismissal was given or, if there was no notice, the effective date of termination, and

(b) in any other case, the date on which the relevant hearing took place (or was to have taken place).

(5) The limit in section 227(1) of the Employment Rights Act 1996 (maximum amount of week's pay) shall apply for the purposes of subsection (3) above.

(6) [repealed]

12 Detriment and dismissal

(1) A worker has the right not to be subjected to any detriment by any act, or any deliberate failure to act, by his employer done on the ground that he—

(a) exercised or sought to exercise the right under section 10(2A), (2B) or (4), or

(b) accompanied or sought to accompany another worker (whether of the same employer or not) pursuant to a request under that section.

(2) Section 48 of the Employment Rights Act 1996 shall apply in relation to contraventions of subsection (1) above as it applies in relation to contraventions of certain sections of that Act.

(3) A worker who is dismissed shall be regarded for the purposes of Part X of the Employment Rights Act 1996 as unfairly dismissed if the reason (or, if more than one, the principal reason) for the dismissal is that he—

(a) exercised or sought to exercise the right under section 10(2A), (2B) or (4), or

(b) accompanied or sought to accompany another worker (whether of the same employer or not) pursuant to a request under that section.

(4) Sections 108 and 109 of that Act (qualifying period of employment and upper age limit) shall not apply in relation to subsection (3) above.

(5) Sections 128 to 132 of that Act (interim relief) shall apply in relation to dismissal for the reason specified in subsection (3)(a) or (b) above as they apply in relation to dismissal for a reason specified in section 128(1)(b) of that Act.

(6) In the application of Chapter II of Part X of that Act in relation to subsection (3) above, a reference to an employee shall be taken as a reference to a worker.

(7) References in this section to a worker having accompanied or sought to accompany another worker include references to his having exercised or sought to exercise any of the powers conferred by section 10(2A) or (2B).

13 Interpretation

(1) In sections 10 to 12 and this section 'worker' means an individual who is—

(a) a worker within the meaning of section 230(3) of the Employment Rights Act 1996,

(b) an agency worker,

(c) a home worker,

(d) a person in Crown employment within the meaning of section 191 of that Act, other than a member of the naval, military, air or reserve forces of the Crown, or

(e) employed as a relevant member of the House of Lords staff or the House of Commons staff within the meaning of section 194(6) or 195(5) of that Act.

(2) In subsection (1) 'agency worker' means an individual who—

(a) is supplied by a person ('the agent') to do work for another ('the principal') by arrangement between the agent and the principal,

(b) is not a party to a worker's contract, within the meaning of section 230(3) of that Act, relating to that work, and

(c) is not a party to a contract relating to that work under which he undertakes to do the work for another party to the contract whose status is, by virtue of the contract, that of a client or customer of any professional or business undertaking carried on by the individual;

and, for the purposes of sections 10 to 12, both the agent and the principal are employers of an agency worker.

(3) In subsection (1) 'home worker' means an individual who—

(a) contracts with a person, for the purposes of the person's business, for the execution of work to be done in a place not under the person's control or management, and

(b) is not a party to a contract relating to that work under which the work is to be executed for another party to the contract whose status is, by virtue of the contract, that of a client or customer of any professional or business undertaking carried on by the individual;

and, for the purposes of sections 10 to 12, the person mentioned in paragraph (a) is the home worker's employer.

(4) For the purposes of section 10 a disciplinary hearing is a hearing which could result in—

(a) the administration of a formal warning to a worker by his employer,

(b) the taking of some other action in respect of a worker by his employer, or

(c) the confirmation of a warning issued or some other action taken.

(5) For the purposes of section 10 a grievance hearing is a hearing which concerns the performance of a duty by an employer in relation to a worker.

(6) For the purposes of section 10(5)(b) in its application to a part of Great Britain a working day is a day other than—

(a) a Saturday or a Sunday,

(b) Christmas Day or Good Friday, or

(c) a day which is a bank holiday under the Banking and Financial Dealings Act 1971 in that part of Great Britain.

14 Contracting out and conciliation

Sections 10 to 13 of this Act shall be treated as provisions of Part V of the Employment Rights act 1996 for the purposes of—

(a) section 203(1), (2)(e) and (f), (3) and (4) of that Act (restrictions on contracting out), and

(b) section 18(1)(d) of the Employment Tribunals Act 1996 (conciliation).

15 National security employees

Sections 10 to 13 of this Act shall not apply in relation to a person employed for the purposes of—

(a) the Security Service,

(b) the Secret Intelligence Service, or

(c) the Government Communications Headquarters.

Other rights of individuals

16 [omitted]; **17** [repealed]; **18–22** [omitted]
23 Power to confer rights on individuals
    (1) This section applies to any right conferred on an individual against an employer (however defined) under or by virtue of any of the following—
        (a) the Trade Union and Labour Relations (Consolidation) Act 1992;
        (b) the Employment Rights Act 1996;
        (ba) the Employment Act 2002;
        (c) this Act;
        (d) any instrument made under section 2(2) of the European Communities Act 1972.
    (2) The Secretary of State may by order make provision which has the effect of conferring any such right on individuals who are of a specified description.
    (3) the reference in subsection (2) to individuals includes a reference to individuals expressly excluded from exercising the right.
    (4) An order under this section may—
        (a) provide that individuals are to be treated as parties to workers' contracts or contracts of employment;
        (b) make provision as to who are to be regarded as the employers of individuals;
        (c) make provision which has the effect of modifying the operation of any right as conferred on individuals by the order;
        (d) include such consequential, incidental or supplementary provisions as the Secretary of State thinks fit.
    (5)–(7) [omitted]

24–29 [omitted]

Miscellaneous

30–33 [omitted]

34 Indexation of amounts, etc.
    (1) This section applies to the sums specified in the following provisions—
        (a) section 31(1) of the Employment Rights Act 1996 (guarantee payments: limits);
        (b) section 120(1) of that Act (unfair dismissal: minimum amount of basic award);
        (c) section 124(1) of that Act (unfair dismissal: limit of compensatory award);
        (d) section 186(1)(a) and (b) of that Act (employee's rights on insolvency of employer: maximum amount payable);
        (e) section 227(1) of that Act (maximum amount of a week's pay for purposes of certain calculations);
        (ea) section 145E(3) of the Trade Union and Labour Relations (Consolidation) Act 1992 (unlawful inducements: amount of award);
        (f) section 156(1) of that Act (unfair dismissal: minimum basic award);
        (g) section 176(6A) of that Act (right to membership of trade union: remedies).
    (2) If the retail prices index for September of a year is higher or lower than the index for the previous September, the Secretary of State shall as soon as practicable make an order in relation to each sum mentioned in subsection (1)—
        (a) increasing each sum, if the new index is higher, or
        (b) decreasing each sum, if the new index is lower,
by the same percentage as the amount of the increase or decrease of the index.
    (3) In making the calculation required by subsection (2) the Secretary of State shall—
        (a) in the case of the sum mentioned in subsection (1)(a), round the result up to the nearest 10 pence,
        (b) in the case of the sums mentioned in subsection (1)(b), (c), (ea), (f) and (g), round the result up to the nearest £100, and

    (c) in the case of the sums mentioned in subsection (1)(d) and (e), round the result up to the nearest £10.

(4) [omitted]

(5) In this section 'retail prices index' means—

    (a) the general index of retail prices (for all items) published by the Office for National Statistics, or

    (b) where that index is not published for a month, any substituted index or figures published by that Office.

(6) [omitted]

35–47   [omitted]

Employment Act 2002
(2002, c. 22)

30 Contracts of employment

(1) Every contract of employment shall have effect to require the employer and employee to comply, in relation to any matter to which a statutory procedure applies, with the requirements of the procedure.

(2) Subsection (1) shall have effect notwithstanding any agreement to the contrary, but does not affect so much of an agreement to follow a particular procedure as requires the employer or employee to comply with a requirement which is additional to, and not inconsistent with, the requirements of the statutory procedure.

(3) The Secretary of State may for the purpose of this section by regulations make provision about the application of the statutory procedures.

(4) In this section, 'contract of employment' has the same meaning as in the Employment Rights Act 1996 (c. 18).

31 Non-completion of statutory procedure: adjustment of awards

(1) This section applies to proceedings before an employment tribunal relating to a claim under any of the jurisdictions listed in Schedule 3 by an employee.

(2) If, in the case of proceedings to which this section applies, it appears to the employment tribunal that—

    (a) the claim to which the proceedings relate concerns a matter to which one of the statutory procedures applies,

    (b) the statutory procedure was not completed before the proceedings were begun, and

    (c) the non-completion of the statutory procedure was wholly or mainly attributable to failure by the employee—

        (i)   to comply with a requirement of the procedure, or

        (ii) to exercise a right of appeal under it,

it must, subject to subsection (4), reduce any award which it makes to the employee by 10 per cent, and may, if it considers it just and equitable in all the circumstances to do so, reduce it by a further amount, but not so as to make a total reduction of more than 50 per cent.

(3) If, in the case of proceedings to which this section applies, it appears to the employment tribunal that—

    (a) the claim to which the proceedings relate concerns a matter to which one of the statutory procedures applies,

    (b) the statutory procedure was not completed before the proceedings were begun, and

    (c) the non-completion of the statutory procedure was wholly or mainly attributable to failure by the employer to comply with a requirement of the procedure, it must, subject to subsection (4), increase any award which it makes to the employee by 10 per cent and may, if it considers it just and equitable in all the circumstances to do so, increase it by a further amount, but not so as to make a total increase of more than 50 per cent.

(4) The duty under subsection (2) or (3) to make a reduction or increase of 10 per cent does not apply if there are exceptional circumstances which would make a reduction or increase of that percentage unjust or inequitable, in which case the tribunal may make no reduction or increase or a reduction or increase of such lesser percentage as it considers just and equitable in all the circumstances.

(5) Where an award falls to be adjusted under this section and under section 38, the adjustment under this section shall be made before the adjustment under that section.

(6)–(7) [omitted]

32   Complaints about grievances

(1) This section applies to the jurisdictions listed in Schedule 4.

(2) An employee shall not present a complaint to an employment tribunal under a jurisdiction to which this section applies if—

(a) it concerns a matter in relation to which the requirement in paragraph 6 or 9 of Schedule 2 applies, and

(b) the requirement has not been complied with.

(3) An employee shall not present a complaint to an employment tribunal under a jurisdiction to which this section applies if—

(a) it concerns a matter in relation to which the requirement in paragraph 6 or 9 of Schedule 2 has been complied with, and

(b) less than 28 days have passed since the day on which the requirement was complied with.

(4) An employee shall not present a complaint to an employment tribunal under a jurisdiction to which this section applies if—

(a) it concerns a matter in relation to which the requirement in paragraph 6 or 9 of Schedule 2 has been complied with, and

(b) the day on which the requirement was complied with was more than one month after the end of the original time limit for making the complaint.

(5) In such circumstances as the Secretary of State may specify by regulations, an employment tribunal may direct that subsection (4) shall not apply in relation to a particular matter.

(6) An employment tribunal shall be prevented from considering a complaint presented in breach of subsections (2) to (4), but only if—

(a) the breach is apparent to the tribunal from the information supplied to it by the employee in connection with the bringing of the proceedings, or

(b) the tribunal is satisfied of the breach as a result of his employer raising the issue of compliance with those provisions in accordance with regulations under section 7 of the Employment Tribunals Act 1996 (c. 17) (employment tribunal procedure regulations).

(7)–(10) [omitted]

38   Failure to give statement of employment particulars, etc.

(1) This section applies to proceedings before an employment tribunal relating to a claim by an employee under any of the jurisdictions listed in Schedule 5.

(2) If in the case of proceedings to which this section applies—

(a) the employment tribunal finds in favour of the employee, but makes no award to him in respect of the claim to which the proceedings relate, and

(b) when the proceedings were begun the employer was in breach of his duty to the employee under section 1(1) or 4(1) of the Employment Rights Act 1996 (c. 18) (duty to give a written statement of initial employment particulars or of particulars of change),

the tribunal must, subject to subsection (5), make an award of the minimum amount to be paid by the employer to the employee and may, if it considers it just and equitable in all the circumstances, award the higher amount instead.

(3) If in the case of proceedings to which this section applies—

    (a) the employment tribunal makes an award to the employee in respect of the claim to which the proceedings relate, and

    (b) when the proceedings were begun the employer was in breach of his duty to the employee under section 1(1) or 4(1) of the Employment Rights Act 1996,

the tribunal must, subject to subsection (5), increase the award by the minimum amount and may, if it considers it just and equitable in all the circumstances, increase the award by the higher amount instead.

(4) In subsections (2) and (3)—

    (a) references to the minimum amount are to an amount equal to two weeks' pay, and

    (b) references to the higher amount are to an amount equal to four weeks' pay.

(5) The duty under subsection (2) or (3) does not apply if there are exceptional circumstances which would make an award or increase under that subsection unjust or inequitable.

(6) The amount of a week's pay of an employee shall—

    (a) be calculated for the purposes of this section in accordance with Chapter 2 of Part 14 of the Employment Rights Act 1996, and

    (b) not exceed the amount for the time being specified in section 227 of that Act (maximum amount of week's pay).

(7) For the purposes of Chapter 2 of Part 14 of the Employment Rights Act 1996 as applied by subsection (8), the calculation date shall be taken to be—

    (a) if the employee was employed by the employer on the date the proceedings were begun, that date, and

    (b) if he was not, the effective date of termination as defined by section 97 of that Act.

(8) [omitted]

SCHEDULE 2   STATUTORY DISPUTE RESOLUTION PROCEDURES

PART 1   DISMISSAL AND DISCIPLINARY PROCEDURES

Chapter 1   Standard procedure

1   Step 1: statement of grounds for action and invitation to meeting

(1) The employer must set out in writing the employee's alleged conduct or characteristics, or other circumstances, which lead him to contemplate dismissing or taking disciplinary action against the employee.

(2) The employer must send the statement or a copy of it to the employee and invite the employee to attend a meeting to discuss the matter.

2   Step 2: meeting

(1) The meeting must take place before action is taken, except in the case where the disciplinary action consists of suspension.

(2) The meeting must not take place unless—

    (a) the employer has informed the employee what the basis was for including in the statement under paragraph 1(1) the ground or grounds given in it, and

    (b) the employee has had a reasonable opportunity to consider his response to that information.

(3) The employee must take all reasonable steps to attend the meeting.

(4) After the meeting, the employer must inform the employee of his decision and notify him of the right to appeal against the decision if he is not satisfied with it.

3 Step 3: appeal

(1) If the employee does wish to appeal, he must inform the employer.

(2) If the employee informs the employer of his wish to appeal, the employer must invite him to attend a further meeting.

(3) The employee must take all reasonable steps to attend the meeting.

(4) The appeal meeting need not take place before the dismissal or disciplinary action takes effect.

(5) After the appeal meeting, the employer must inform the employee of his final decision.

Chapter 2 Modified procedure

4 Step 1: statement of grounds for action

The employer must—

  (a) set out in writing—
    (i) the employee's alleged misconduct which has led to the dismissal,
    (ii) what the basis was for thinking at the time of the dismissal that the employee was guilty of the alleged misconduct, and
    (iii) the employee's right to appeal against dismissal, and
  (b) send the statement, or a copy of it, to the employee.

5 Step 2: appeal

(1) If the employee does wish to appeal, he must inform the employer.

(2) If the employee informs the employer of his wish to appeal, the employer must invite him to attend a meeting.

(3) The employee must take all reasonable steps to attend the meeting.

(4) After the appeal meeting, the employer must inform the employee of his final decision.

PART 2   GRIEVANCE PROCEDURES

Chapter 1 Standard procedure

6 Step 1: statement of grievance

The employee must set out the grievance in writing and send the statement or a copy of it to the employer.

7 Step 2: meeting

(1) The employer must invite the employee to attend a meeting to discuss the grievance.

(2) The meeting must not take place unless—

  (a) the employee has informed the employer what the basis for the grievance was when he made the statement under paragraph 6, and
  (b) the employer has had a reasonable opportunity to consider his response to that information.

(3) The employee must take all reasonable steps to attend the meeting.

(4) After the meeting, the employer must inform the employee of his decision as to his response to the grievance and notify him of the right to appeal against the decision if he is not satisfied with it.

8 Step 3: appeal

(1) If the employee does wish to appeal, he must inform the employer.

(2) If the employee informs the employer of his wish to appeal, the employer must invite him to attend a further meeting.

(3) The employee must take all reasonable steps to attend the meeting.

(4) After the appeal meeting, the employer must inform the employee of his final decision.

Chapter 2   Modified procedure

9   Step 1: statement of grievance

The employee must—
- (a) set out in writing—
    - (i)   the grievance, and
    - (ii) the basis for it, and
- (b) send the statement, or a copy of it, to the employer.

10   Step 2: response

The employer must set out his response in writing and send the statement or a copy of it to the employee.

PART 3   GENERAL REQUIREMENTS

11   Introductory

The following requirements apply to each of the procedures set out above (so far as applicable).

12   Timetable

Each step and action under the procedure must be taken without unreasonable delay.

13   Meetings

(1) Timing and location of meetings must be reasonable.

(2) Meetings must be conducted in a manner that enables both employer and employee to explain their cases.

(3) In the case of appeal meetings which are not the first meeting, the employer should, as far as is reasonably practicable, be represented by a more senior manager than attended the first meeting (unless the most senior manager attended that meeting).

PART 4   SUPPLEMENTARY

14   Status of meetings

A meeting held for the purposes of this Schedule is a hearing for the purposes of section 13(4) and (5) of the Employment Relations Act 1999 (c. 26) (definition of 'disciplinary hearing' and 'grievance hearing' in relation to the right to be accompanied under section 10 of that Act).

15   Scope of grievance procedures

(1) The procedures set out in Part 2 are only applicable to matters raised by an employee with his employer as a grievance.

(2) Accordingly, those procedures are only applicable to the kind of disclosure dealt with in Part 4A of the Employment Rights Act 1996 (c. 18) (protected disclosures of information) if information is disclosed by an employee to his employer in circumstances where—
- (a) the information relates to a matter which the employee could raise as a grievance with his employer, and
- (b) it is the intention of the employee that the disclosure should constitute the raising of the matter with his employer as a grievance.

SCHEDULE 3   TRIBUNAL JURISDICTIONS TO WHICH SECTION 31 APPLIES

Section 2 of the Equal Pay Act 1970 (c. 41) (equality clauses)

Section 63 of the Sex Discrimination Act 1975 (c. 65) (discrimination in the employment field)

Section 54 of the Race Relations Act 1976 (c. 74) (discrimination in the employment field)

Section 145A of the Trade Union and Labour Relations (Consolidation) Act 1992 (inducements relating to union membership or activities)

Section 145B of that Act (inducements relating to collective bargaining)

Section 146 of that Act (detriment in relation to union membership and activities)

Paragraph 156 of Schedule A1 to that Act (detriment in relation to union recognition rights)

Section 17A of the Disability Discrimination Act 1995 (c. 50) (discrimination in the employment field)

Section 23 of the Employment Rights Act 1996 (c. 18) (unauthorised deductions and payments)

Section 48 of that Act (detriment in employment)

Section 111 of that Act (unfair dismissal)

Section 163 of that Act (redundancy payments)

Section 24 of the National Minimum Wage Act 1998 (c. 39) (detriment in relation to national minimum wage)

The Employment Tribunal Extension of Jurisdiction (England and Wales) Order 1994 (SI 1994/1623) (breach of employment contract and termination)

The Employment Tribunal Extension of Jurisdiction (Scotland) Order 1994 (SI 1994/1624) (corresponding provision for Scotland)

Regulation 30 of the Working Time Regulations 1998 (SI 1998/1833) (breach of regulations)

Regulation 32 of the Transnational Information and Consultation of Employees Regulations 1999 (SI 1999/3323) (detriment relating to European Works Councils)

Regulation 28 of the Employment Equality (Sexual Orientation) Regulations 2003 (discrimination in the employment field)

Regulation 28 of the Employment Equality (Religion or Belief) Regulations (discrimination in the employment field)

Regulation 36 of the Employment Equality (Age) Regulations 2006 (discrimination in the employment field)

SCHEDULE 4   TRIBUNAL JURISDICTIONS TO WHICH SECTION 32 APPLIES

Section 2 of the Equal Pay Act 1970 (c. 41) (equality clauses)

Section 63 of the Sex Discrimination Act 1975 (c. 65) (discrimination in the employment field)

Section 54 of the Race Relations Act 1976 (c. 74) (discrimination in the employment field)

Section 145A of the Trade Union and Labour Relations (Consolidation) Act 1992 (inducements relating to union membership or activities)

Section 145B of that Act (inducements relating to collective bargaining)

Section 146 of that Act (detriment in relation to union membership and activities)

Paragraph 156 of Schedule A1 to that Act (detriment in relation to union recognition rights)

Section 17A of the Disability Discrimination Act 1995 (c. 50) (discrimination in the employment field)

Section 23 of the Employment Rights Act 1996 (c. 18) (unauthorised deductions and payments)

Section 48 of that Act (detriment in employment)

Section 111 of that Act (unfair dismissal)

Section 163 of that Act (redundancy payments)

Section 24 of the National Minimum Wage Act 1998 (c. 39) (detriment in relation to national minimum wage)

Regulation 30 of the Working Time Regulations 1998 (SI 1998/1833) (breach of regulations)

Regulation 32 of the Transnational Information and Consultation of Employees Regulations 1999 (SI 1999/3323) (detriment relating to European Works Councils).

Regulation 28 of the Employment Equality (Sexual Orientation) Regulations 2003 (discrimination in the employment field)

Regulation 28 of the Employment Equality (Religion or Belief) Regulations (discrimination in the employment field)

Regulation 36 of the Employment Equality (Age) Regulations 2006 (discrimination in the employment field)

SCHEDULE 5   SECTION 38

TRIBUNAL JURISDICTIONS TO WHICH SECTION 38 APPLIES

Section 2 of the Equal Pay Act 1970 (c. 41) (equality clauses)

Section 63 of the Sex Discrimination Act 1975 (c. 65) (discrimination in the employment field)

Section 54 of the Race Relations Act 1976 (c. 74) (discrimination in the employment field)

Section 145A of the Trade Union and Labour Relations (Consolidation) Act 1992 (inducements relating to union membership or activities)

Section 145B of that Act (inducements relating to collective bargaining)

Section 146 of that Act (detriment in relation to union membership and activities)

Paragraph 156 of Schedule A1 to that Act (detriment in relation to union recognition rights)

Section 17A of the Disability Discrimination Act 1995 (c. 50) (discrimination in the employment field)

Section 23 of the Employment Rights Act 1996 (c. 18) (unauthorised deductions and payments)

Section 48 of that Act (detriment in employment)

Section 111 of that Act (unfair dismissal)

Section 163 of that Act (redundancy payments)

Section 24 of the National Minimum Wage Act 1998 (c. 39) (detriment in relation to national minimum wage)

The Employment Tribunal Extension of Jurisdiction (England and Wales) Order 1994 (SI 1994/1623) (breach of employment contract and termination)

The Employment Tribunal Extension of Jurisdiction (Scotland) Order 1994 (SI 1994/1624) (corresponding provision for Scotland)

Regulation 30 of the Working Time Regulations 1998 (SI 1998/1833) (breach of regulations)

Regulation 32 of the Transnational Information and Consultation of Employees Regulations 1999 (SI 1999/3323) (detriment relating to European Works Councils)

Regulation 28 of the Employment Equality (Sexual Orientation) Regulations 2003 (discrimination in the employment field)

Regulation 28 of the Employment Equality (Religion or Belief) Regulations (discrimination in the employment field)

Regulation 36 of the Employment Equality (Age) Regulations 2006 (discrimination in the employment field)

Equality Act 2006
(2006, c. 3)

PART 1   THE COMMISSION FOR EQUALITY AND HUMAN RIGHTS

The Commission

1 Establishment
There shall be a body corporate known as the Commission for Equality and Human Rights.

2 [omitted]

3 General duty
The Commission shall exercise its functions under this Part with a view to encouraging and supporting the development of a society in which—
  (a) people's ability to achieve their potential is not limited by prejudice or discrimination,
  (b) there is respect for and protection of each individual's human rights,
  (c) there is respect for the dignity and worth of each individual,
  (d) each individual has an equal opportunity to participate in society, and
  (e) there is mutual respect between groups based on understanding and valuing of diversity and on shared respect for equality and human rights.

4–7 [omitted]

Duties

8 Equality and diversity
  (1) The Commission shall, by exercising the powers conferred by this Part—
  (a) promote understanding of the importance of equality and diversity,
  (b) encourage good practice in relation to equality and diversity,
  (c) promote equality of opportunity,
  (d) promote awareness and understanding of rights under the equality enactments,
  (e) enforce the equality enactments,
  (f) work towards the elimination of unlawful discrimination, and
  (g) work towards the elimination of unlawful harassment.

(2) In subsection (1)—

'diversity' means the fact that individuals are different,

'equality' means equality between individuals, and

'unlawful' is to be construed in accordance with section 34.

(3) In promoting equality of opportunity between disabled persons and others, the Commission may, in particular, promote the favourable treatment of disabled persons.

(4) In this Part 'disabled person' means a person who—

    (a) is a disabled person within the meaning of the Disability Discrimination Act 1995 (c. 50), or

    (b) has been a disabled person within that meaning (whether or not at a time when that Act had effect).

9 Human rights

(1) The Commission shall, by exercising the powers conferred by this Part—

    (a) promote understanding of the importance of human rights,

    (b) encourage good practice in relation to human rights,

    (c) promote awareness, understanding and protection of human rights, and

    (d) encourage public authorities to comply with section 6 of the Human Rights Act 1998 (c. 42) (compliance with Convention rights).

(2) In this Part 'human rights' means—

    (a) the Convention rights within the meaning given by section 1 of the Human Rights Act 1998, and

    (b) other human rights.

(3) In determining what action to take in pursuance of this section the Commission shall have particular regard to the importance of exercising the powers conferred by this Part in relation to the Convention rights.

(4) In fulfilling a duty under section 8 or 10 the Commission shall take account of any relevant human rights.

(5) A reference in this Part (including this section) to human rights does not exclude any matter by reason only of its being a matter to which section 8 or 10 relates.

10 Groups

(1) The Commission shall, by exercising the powers conferred by this Part—

    (a) promote understanding of the importance of good relations—

        (i) between members of different groups, and

        (ii) between members of groups and others,

    (b) encourage good practice in relation to relations—

        (i) between members of different groups, and

        (ii) between members of groups and others,

    (c) work towards the elimination of prejudice against, hatred of and hostility towards members of groups, and

    (d) work towards enabling members of groups to participate in society.

(2) In this Part 'group' means a group or class of persons who share a common attribute in respect of any of the following matters—

    (a) age,

    (b) disability,

    (c) gender,

    (d) proposed, commenced or completed reassignment of gender (within the meaning given by section 82(1) of the Sex Discrimination Act 1975 (c. 65)),

    (e) race,

    (f) religion or belief, and

    (g) sexual orientation.

(3) For the purposes of this Part a reference to a group (as defined in subsection (2)) includes a reference to a smaller group or smaller class, within a group, of persons who share a

common attribute (in addition to the attribute by reference to which the group is defined) in respect of any of the matters specified in subsection (2)(a) to (g).

(4) In determining what action to take in pursuance of this section the Commission shall have particular regard to the importance of exercising the powers conferred by this Part in relation to groups defined by reference to race, religion or belief.

(5) The Commission may, in taking action in pursuance of subsection (1) in respect of groups defined by reference to disability and others, promote or encourage the favourable treatment of disabled persons.

(6) [omitted]

(7) This section is without prejudice to the generality of section 8.

11–15 [omitted]

16 Inquiries

(1) The Commission may conduct an inquiry into a matter relating to any of the Commission's duties under sections 8, 9 and 10.

(2) If in the course of an inquiry the Commission begins to suspect that a person may have committed an unlawful act—

    (a) in continuing the inquiry the Commission shall, so far as possible, avoid further consideration of whether or not the person has committed an unlawful act,

    (b) the Commission may commence an investigation into that question under section 20,

    (c) the Commission may use information or evidence acquired in the course of the inquiry for the purpose of the investigation, and

    (d) the Commission shall so far as possible ensure (whether by aborting or suspending the inquiry or otherwise) that any aspects of the inquiry which concern the person investigated, or may require his involvement, are not pursued while the investigation is in progress.

(3) The report of an inquiry—

    (a) may not state (whether expressly or by necessary implication) that a specified or identifiable person has committed an unlawful act, and

    (b) shall not otherwise refer to the activities of a specified or identifiable person unless the Commission thinks that the reference—

        (i) will not harm the person, or

        (ii) is necessary in order for the report adequately to reflect the results of the inquiry.

(4) Subsections (2) and (3) shall not prevent an inquiry from considering or reporting a matter relating to human rights (whether or not a necessary implication arises in relation to the equality enactments).

(5) Before settling a report of an inquiry which records findings which in the Commission's opinion are of an adverse nature and relate (whether expressly or by necessary implication) to a specified or identifiable person the Commission shall—

    (a) send a draft of the report to the person,

    (b) specify a period of at least 28 days during which he may make written representations about the draft, and

    (c) consider any representations made.

(6) Schedule 2 makes supplemental provision about inquiries.

17–19 [omitted]

Enforcement powers

20 Investigations

(1) The Commission may investigate whether or not a person—

    (a) has committed an unlawful act,

(b) has complied with a requirement imposed by an unlawful act notice under section 21, or

(c) has complied with an undertaking given under section 23.

(2) The Commission may conduct an investigation under subsection (1)(a) only if it suspects that the person concerned may have committed an unlawful act.

(3) A suspicion for the purposes of subsection (2) may (but need not) be based on the results of, or a matter arising during the course of, an inquiry under section 16.

(4) Before settling a report of an investigation recording a finding that a person has committed an unlawful act or has failed to comply with a requirement or undertaking the Commission shall—

(a) send a draft of the report to the person,

(b) specify a period of at least 28 days during which he may make written representations about the draft, and

(c) consider any representations made.

(5) Schedule 2 makes supplemental provision about investigations.

21 Unlawful act notice

(1) The Commission may give a person a notice under this section (an 'unlawful act notice') if—

(a) he is or has been the subject of an investigation under section 20(1)(a), and

(b) the Commission is satisfied that he has committed an unlawful act.

(2) A notice must specify—

(a) the unlawful act, and

(b) the provision of the equality enactments by virtue of which the act is unlawful.

(3) A notice must inform the recipient of the effect of—

(a) subsections (5) to (7),

(b) section 20(1)(b), and

(c) section 24(1).

(4) A notice may—

(a) require the person to whom the notice is given to prepare an action plan for the purpose of avoiding repetition or continuation of the unlawful act;

(b) recommend action to be taken by the person for that purpose.

(5) A person who is given a notice may, within the period of six weeks beginning with the day on which the notice is given, appeal to the appropriate court or tribunal on the grounds—

(a) that he has not committed the unlawful act specified in the notice, or

(b) that a requirement for the preparation of an action plan imposed under subsection (4)(a) is unreasonable.

(6) On an appeal under subsection (5) the court or tribunal may—

(a) affirm a notice;

(b) annul a notice;

(c) vary a notice;

(d) affirm a requirement;

(e) annul a requirement;

(f) vary a requirement;

(g) make an order for costs or expenses.

(7) In subsection (5) 'the appropriate court or tribunal' means—

(a) an employment tribunal, if a claim in respect of the alleged unlawful act could be made to it, or

(b) a county court (in England and Wales) or the sheriff (in Scotland), if a claim in respect of the alleged unlawful act could be made to it or to him.

22 Action plans

(1) This section applies where a person has been given a notice under section 21 which requires him (under section 21(4)(a)) to prepare an action plan.

(2) The notice must specify a time by which the person must give the Commission a first draft plan.

(3) After receiving a first draft plan from a person the Commission shall—

(a) approve it, or

(b) give the person a notice which—

(i) states that the draft is not adequate,

(ii) requires the person to give the Commission a revised draft by a specified time, and

(iii) may make recommendations about the content of the revised draft.

(4) Subsection (3) shall apply in relation to a revised draft plan as it applies in relation to a first draft plan.

(5) An action plan comes into force—

(a) if the period of six weeks beginning with the date on which a first draft or revised draft is given to the Commission expires without the Commission—

(i) giving a notice under subsection (3)(b), or

(ii) applying for an order under subsection (6)(b), or

(b) upon a court's declining to make an order under subsection (6)(b) in relation to a revised draft of the plan.

(6) The Commission may apply to a county court (in England and Wales) or to the sheriff (in Scotland)—

(a) for an order requiring a person to give the Commission a first draft plan by a time specified in the order,

(b) for an order requiring a person who has given the Commission a revised draft plan to prepare and give to the Commission a further revised draft plan—

(i) by a time specified in the order, and

(ii) in accordance with any directions about the plan's content specified in the order, or

(c) during the period of five years beginning with the date on which an action plan prepared by a person comes into force, for an order requiring the person—

(i) to act in accordance with the action plan, or

(ii) to take specified action for a similar purpose.

(7) An action plan may be varied by agreement between the Commission and the person who prepared it.

(8) Paragraphs 10 to 14 of Schedule 2 apply (but omitting references to oral evidence) in relation to consideration by the Commission of the adequacy of a draft action plan as they apply in relation to the conduct of an inquiry.

(9) A person commits an offence if without reasonable excuse he fails to comply with an order under subsection (6); and a person guilty of an offence under this subsection shall be liable on summary conviction to a fine not exceeding level 5 on the standard scale.

23 Agreements

(1) The Commission may enter into an agreement with a person under which—

(a) the person undertakes—

(i) not to commit an unlawful act of a specified kind, and

(ii) to take, or refrain from taking, other specified action (which may include the preparation of a plan for the purpose of avoiding an unlawful act), and

(b) the Commission undertakes not to proceed against the person under section 20 or 21 in respect of any unlawful act of the kind specified under paragraph (a)(i).

(2) The Commission may enter into an agreement with a person under this section only if it thinks that the person has committed an unlawful act.

(3) But a person shall not be taken to admit to the commission of an unlawful act by reason only of entering into an agreement under this section.

(4) An agreement under this section—

(a) may be entered into whether or not the person is or has been the subject of an investigation under section 20,

(b) may include incidental or supplemental provision (which may include provision for termination in specified circumstances), and

(c) may be varied or terminated by agreement of the parties.

(5) This section shall apply in relation to the breach of a duty specified in section 34(2) as it applies in relation to the commission of an unlawful act; and for that purpose the reference in subsection (1)(b) above to section 20 or 21 shall be taken as a reference to section 32.

24 Applications to court

(1) If the Commission thinks that a person is likely to commit an unlawful act, it may apply—

(a) in England and Wales, to a county court for an injunction restraining the person from committing the act, or

(b) in Scotland, to the sheriff for an interdict prohibiting the person from committing the act.

(2) Subsection (3) applies if the Commission thinks that a party to an agreement under section 23 has failed to comply, or is likely not to comply, with an undertaking under the agreement.

(3) The Commission may apply to a county court (in England and Wales) or to the sheriff (in Scotland) for an order requiring the person—

(a) to comply with his undertaking, and

(b) to take such other action as the court or the sheriff may specify.

25 Application to restrain unlawful advertising, pressure, &c.

(1) This section applies to an act which is unlawful under any of the following—

(a) sections 38 to 40 of the Sex Discrimination Act 1975 (c. 65) (advertising; and instructions or pressure to discriminate),

(b) sections 29 to 31 of the Race Relations Act 1976 (c. 74) (advertising; and instructions or pressure to discriminate),

(c) sections 16B and 16C of the Disability Discrimination Act 1995 (c. 50) (advertising; and instructions or pressure to discriminate), and

(d) sections 54 and 55 below (religious discrimination: advertising; and instructions or pressure to discriminate).

(2) Legal proceedings in relation to action to which this section applies—

(a) may be brought by the Commission in accordance with this section, and

(b) may not be brought by anyone else.

(3) Where the Commission thinks that a person has done an act to which this section applies the Commission may—

(a) present a complaint to an employment tribunal, where the act is alleged to be unlawful by reference to—

(i) Part 2 of the Sex Discrimination Act 1975,

(ii) Part 2 of the Race Relations Act 1976,

(iii) Part 2 of the Disability Discrimination Act 1995,

(iv) Part 3 of that Act in so far as it relates to employment services, or

(v) Part 2 of this Act, or

(b) in any other case, apply to a county court (in England and Wales) or the sheriff (in Scotland).

(4) On a complaint or application under subsection (3) in respect of an alleged act to which this section applies, the tribunal, court or sheriff shall determine whether the allegation is correct.

(5) The Commission may apply to a county court (in England and Wales) for an injunction restraining a person from doing an act to which this section applies where—

    (a) either—
        (i) a tribunal or court has determined under subsection (4) that the person has done an act to which this section applies, or
        (ii) the Commission thinks that the person has done an act to which this section applies, and
    (b) the Commission thinks that if unrestrained the person is likely to do another act to which this section applies.

(6) The Commission may apply to the sheriff (in Scotland) for an interdict prohibiting a person from doing an act to which this section applies where—
    (a) either—
        (i) a tribunal or the sheriff has determined under subsection (4) that the person has done an act to which this section applies, or
        (ii) the Commission thinks that the person has done an act to which this section applies, and
    (b) the Commission thinks that without an interdict the person is likely to do another act to which this section applies.

(7) Subsection (1) does not apply to an act which constitutes an offence.

26 Section 25: supplemental

(1) A complaint or application under section 25(3) may be presented or made only—
    (a) within the period of six months beginning with the date (or last date) on which the alleged unlawful act occurred, or
    (b) with the permission of the tribunal, court or sheriff.

(2) A determination under section 25(4) shall not be relied upon by a county court or the sheriff in proceedings under section 25(5) or (6) while an appeal against the determination—
    (a) is pending, or
    (b) may be brought (disregarding the possibility of an appeal out of time with permission).

(3) An application under section 25(5) or (6) may be made only—
    (a) within the period of five years beginning with the date (or last date) on which the unlawful act referred to in that subsection occurred, or
    (b) with the permission of the court or sheriff.

27 [omitted]

28 Legal assistance

(1) The Commission may assist an individual who is or may become party to legal proceedings if—
    (a) the proceedings relate or may relate (wholly or partly) to a provision of the equality enactments, and
    (b) the individual alleges that he has been the victim of behaviour contrary to a provision of the equality enactments.

(2)–(3) [omitted]

(4) In giving assistance under this section the Commission may provide or arrange for the provision of—
    (a) legal advice;
    (b) legal representation;
    (c) facilities for the settlement of a dispute;
    (d) any other form of assistance.

(5)–(11) [omitted]

(12) A reference in this section to a provision of the equality enactments includes a reference to a provision of Community law which—
    (a) relates to discrimination on grounds of sex (including reassignment of gender), racial origin, ethnic origin, religion, belief, disability, age or sexual orientation, and
    (b) confers rights on individuals.

(13) In its application by virtue of subsection (12), subsection (1)(b) shall have effect as if it referred to an allegation by an individual that he is disadvantaged by—

(a) an enactment (including an enactment in or under an Act of the Scottish Parliament) which is contrary to a provision of Community law, or

(b) a failure by the United Kingdom to implement a right as required by Community law.

29–32 [omitted]

Interpretation

33 Equality and human rights enactments

(1) In this Part 'the equality enactments' means—

(a) the Equal Pay Act 1970 (c. 41),

(b) the Sex Discrimination Act 1975,

(c) the Race Relations Act 1976,

(d) the Disability Discrimination Act 1995,

(e) Part 2 of this Act,

(f) regulations under Part 3 of this Act,

(g) the Employment Equality (Sexual Orientation) Regulations 2003 (S.I. 2003/1661),

(h) the Employment Equality (Religion or Belief) Regulations 2003 (S.I. 2003/1660),

(i) the Employment Equality (Age) Regulations 2006.

(2) In this Part 'the equality and human rights enactments' means the equality enactments and the Human Rights Act 1998 (c. 42).

(3) [omitted]

34 Unlawful

(1) In this Part (except section 30(3)) 'unlawful' means contrary to a provision of the equality enactments.

(2) But action is not unlawful for the purposes of this Part by reason only of the fact that it contravenes a duty under or by virtue of—

(a) section 76A, 76B or 76C of the Sex Discrimination Act 1975 (c. 65) (public authorities: duty to eliminate discrimination, &c.),

(b) section 71 of the Race Relations Act 1976 (c. 74) (public authorities: duty to eliminate discrimination, &c.), or

(c) any of the following provisions of the Disability Discrimination Act 1995 (c. 50)—

(i) Part 5 (public transport),

(ii) sections 49A and 49D (public authorities), and

(iii) section 49G (consent to tenant's improvements).

35 General

In this Part—

'act' includes deliberate omission,

'groups' has the meaning given by section 10,

'the Commission' means the Commission for Equality and Human Rights,

'disabled person' has the meaning given by section 8,

'human rights' has the meaning given by section 9,

'race' includes colour, nationality, ethnic origin and national origin,

'religion or belief' has the same meaning as in Part 2 (as defined by section 44), and

'sexual orientation' means an individual's sexual orientation towards—

(a) persons of the same sex as him or her,

(b) persons of the opposite sex, or

(c) both.

36–95 [omitted]

....

Statutory Instruments

The Employment Tribunals Extension of Jurisdiction (England and Wales) Order 1994
(SI 1994 No. 1623)

1.–2. [omitted]

Extension of jurisdiction

3. Proceedings may be brought before an employment tribunal in respect of a claim of an employee for the recovery of damages or any other sum (other than a claim for damages, or for a sum due, in respect of personal injuries) if—

    (a) the claim is one to which section 131(2) of the 1978 Act applies and which a court in England and Wales would under the law for the time being in force have jurisdiction to hear and determine;

    (b) the claim is not one to which article 5 applies; and

    (c) the claim arises or is outstanding on the termination of the employee's employment.

4. Proceedings may be brought before an employment tribunal in respect of a claim of an employer for the recovery of damages or any other sum (other than a claim for damages, or for a sum due, in respect of personal injuries) if—

    (a) the claim is one to which section 131(2) of the 1978 Act applies and which a court in England and Wales would under the law for the time being in force have jurisdiction to hear and determine;

    (b) the claim is not one to which article 5 applies;

    (c) the claim arises or is outstanding on the termination of the employment of the employee against whom it is made; and

    (d) proceedings in respect of a claim of that employee have been brought before an employment tribunal by virtue of this Order.

5. This article applies to a claim for breach of a contractual term of any of the following descriptions—

    (a) a term requiring the employer to provide living accommodation for the employee;

    (b) a term imposing an obligation on the employer or the employee in connection with the provision of living accommodation;

    (c) a term relating to intellectual property;

    (d) a term imposing an obligation of confidence;

    (e) a term which is a covenant in restraint of trade.

In this article, 'intellectual property' includes copyright, rights in performances, moral rights, design right, registered designs, patents and trade marks.

6. [omitted]

Time within which proceedings may be brought

7. An employment tribunal shall not entertain a complaint in respect of an employee's contract claim unless it is presented—
  (a) within the period of three months beginning with the effective date of termination of the contract giving rise to the claim, or
  (b) where there is no effective date of termination, within the period of three months beginning with the last day upon which the employee worked in the employment which has terminated, or
  (ba) where the period within which a complaint must be presented in accordance with paragraph (a) or (b) is extended by regulation 15 of the Employment Act 2002 (Dispute Resolution) Regulations 2004, the period within which the complaint must be presented shall be the extended period rather than the period in paragraph (a) or (b), or
  (c) where the tribunal is satisfied that it was not reasonably practicable for the complaint to be presented within whichever of those periods is applicable, within such further period as the tribunal considers reasonable.

8. An employment tribunal shall not entertain a complaint in respect of an employer's contract claim unless—
  (a) it is presented at a time when there is before the tribunal a complaint in respect of a contract claim of a particular employee which has not been settled or withdrawn;
  (b) it arises out of a contract with that employee; and
  (c) it is presented—
    (i) within the period of six weeks beginning with the day, or if more than one the last of the days, on which the employer (or other person who is the respondent party to the employee's contract claim) received from the tribunal a copy of an originating application in respect of a contract claim of that employee; or
    (ii) where the tribunal is satisfied that it was not reasonably practicable for the complaint to be presented within that period, within such further period as the tribunal considers reasonable.

9. [omitted]

Limit on payment to be ordered

10. An employment tribunal shall not in proceedings in respect of a contract claim, or in respect of a number of contract claims relating to the same contract, order the payment of an amount exceeding £25,000.

The Employment Protection (Continuity of Employment) Regulations 1996
(SI 1996 No. 3147)

Application

2. These Regulations apply to any action taken in relation to the dismissal of an employee which consists of—
  (a) his making a claim in accordance with a dismissal procedures agreement designated by an order under section 110 of the Employment Rights Act 1996,
  (b) the presentation by him of a relevant complaint of dismissal,
  (c) any action taken by a conciliation officer under section 18 of the Employment Tribunals Act 1996,

    (d) the making of a relevant compromise contract,

    (e) the making of an agreement to submit a dispute to arbitration in accordance with a scheme having effect by virtue of an order under section 212A of the Trade Union and Labour Relations (Consolidation) Act 1992,

    (f) a decision taken arising out of the use of a statutory dispute resolution procedure contained in Schedule 2 to the Employment Act 2002 in a case where, in accordance with the Employment Act 2002 (Dispute Resolution) Regulations 2004, such a procedure applies, or

    (g) a decision taken arising out of the use of the statutory duty to consider procedure contained in Schedule 6 to the Employment Equality (Age) Regulations 2006.

Continuity of employment where employee re-engaged

3.—(1) The provisions of this regulation shall have effect to preserve the continuity of a person's period of employment for the purposes of—

    (a) Chapter I of Part XIV of the Employment Rights Act 1996 (continuous employment), and

    (b) that Chapter as applied by subsection (2) of section 282 of the Trade Union and Labour Relations (Consolidation) Act 1992 for the purposes of that section.

(2) If in consequence of any action to which these Regulations apply a dismissed employee is reinstated or re-employed by his employer or by a successor or associated employer of the employer—

    (a) the continuity of that employee's period of employment shall be preserved,

    (b) the period beginning with the date on which the dismissal takes effect and ending with the date of reinstatement or re-engagement shall count in the computation of the employee's period of continuous employment.

Exclusion of operation of section 214 of the Employment Rights Act 1996 where redundancy or equivalent payment repaid

4.—(1) Section 214 of the Employment Rights Act 1996 (continuity broken where employee re-employed after the making of a redundancy payment or equivalent payment) shall not apply where—

    (a) in consequence of any action to which these Regulations apply a dismissed employee is reinstated or re-employed by his employer or by a successor or associated employer of the employer,

    (b) the terms upon which he is so reinstated or re-engaged include provision for him to repay the amount of a redundancy payment or an equivalent payment paid in respect of the relevant dismissal, and

    (c) that provision is complied with.

(2) For the purposes of this regulation the cases in which a redundancy payment shall be treated as having been paid are the cases mentioned in section 214(5) of the Employment Rights Act 1996.

The Working Time Regulations 1998
(SI 1998 No. 1833)

ARRANGEMENT OF REGULATIONS
PART I   GENERAL

Regulation
  2. Interpretation

PART II   RIGHTS AND OBLIGATIONS CONCERNING
WORKING TIME

PART III   EXCEPTIONS

PART IV   MISCELLANEOUS

PART V   SPECIAL CLASSES OF PERSON

SCHEDULE 1

Workforce agreements

PART I   GENERAL

1 **[omitted]**
2 **Interpretation**
(1) In these Regulations—
'the 1996 Act' means the Employment Rights Act 1996;
   'adult worker' means a worker who has attained the age of 18;
   'the armed forces' means any of the naval, military and air forces of the Crown;
   'calendar year' means the period of twelve months beginning with 1 January in any year;
   'the civil protection services' includes the police, fire brigades and ambulance services, the security and intelligence services, customs and immigration officers, the prison service, the coastguard, and lifeboat crew and other voluntary rescue services;
   'collective agreement' means a collective agreement within the meaning of section 178 of the Trade Union and Labour Relations (Consolidation) Act 1992, the trade union parties to which are independent trade unions within the meaning of section 5 of that Act;
   'day' means a period of 24 hours beginning at midnight;
   'employer', in relation to a worker, means the person by whom the worker is (or, where the employment has ceased, was) employed;
   'employment', in relation to a worker, means employment under his contract, and 'employed' shall be construed accordingly;
   'fishing vessel' has the same meaning as in section 313 of the Merchant Shipping Act 1995;
   'mobile worker' means any worker employed as a member of travelling or flying personnel by an undertaking which operates transport services for passengers or goods by road or air;
   'night time', in relation to a worker, means a period—
      (a) the duration of which is not less than seven hours, and
      (b) which includes the period between midnight and 5 a.m.,
which is determined for the purposes of these Regulations by a relevant agreement, or, in default of such a determination, the period between 11 p.m. and 6 a.m.;
   'night work' means work during night time;
   'night worker' means a worker—
      (a) who, as a normal course, works at least three hours of his daily working time during night time, or
      (b) who is likely, during night time, to work at least such proportion of his annual working time as may be specified for the purposes of these Regulations in a collective agreement or a workforce agreement,
and, for the purpose of paragraph (a) of this definition, a person works hours as a normal course (without prejudice to the generality of that expression) if he works such hours on the majority of days on which he works;
   'offshore work' means work performed mainly on or from offshore installations (including drilling rigs), directly or indirectly in connection with the exploration, extraction or exploitation of mineral resources, including hydrocarbons, and diving in connection with such activities, whether performed from an offshore installation or a vessel;
   'relevant agreement', in relation to a worker, means a workforce agreement which applies to him, any provision of a collective agreement which forms part of a contract between him and his employer, or any other agreement in writing which is legally enforceable as between the worker and his employer;
   'relevant training' means work experience provided pursuant to a training course or programme, training for employment, or both, other than work experience or training—

(a) the immediate provider of which is an educational institution or a person whose main business is the provision of training, and

(b) which is provided on a course run by that institution or person;

'rest period', in relation to a worker, means a period which is not working time, other than a rest break or leave to which the worker is entitled under these Regulations;

'the restricted period', in relation to a worker, means the period between 10 p.m. and 6 a.m. or, where the worker's contract provides for him to work after 10 p.m., the period between 11 p.m. and 7 a.m.;

'ship' has the same meaning as in section 313 of the Merchant Shipping Act 1995;

'worker' means an individual who has entered into or works under (or, where the employment has ceased, worked under)—

(a) a contract of employment, or

(b) any other contract, whether express or implied and (if it is express) whether oral or in writing, whereby the individual undertakes to do or perform personally any work or services for another party to the contract whose status is not by virtue of the contract that of a client or customer of any profession or business undertaking carried on by the individual,

and any reference to a worker's contract shall be construed accordingly;

'worker employed in agriculture' has the same meaning as in the Agricultural Wages Act 1948 or the Agricultural Wages (Scotland) Act 1949, and a reference to a worker partly employed in agriculture is to a worker employed in agriculture whose employer also employs him for non-agricultural purposes;

'workforce agreement' means an agreement between an employer and worker employed by him or their representatives in respect of which the conditions set out in Schedule 1 to these Regulations are satisfied;

'working time', in relation to a worker, means—

(a) any period during which he is working, at his employer's disposal and carrying out his activity or duties,

(b) any period during which he is receiving relevant training, and

(c) any additional period which is to be treated as working time for the purpose of these Regulations under a relevant agreement,

and 'work' shall be construed accordingly;

'Working Time Directive' means Council Directive 93/104/EC of 23 November 1993 concerning certain aspects of the organisation of working time;

'young worker' means a worker who has attained the age of 15 but not the age of 18 and who, as respects England and Wales, is over compulsory school age (construed in accordance with section 8 of the Education Act 1996) and, as respects Scotland, is over school age (construed in accordance with section 31 of the Education (Scotland) Act 1980); and

'Young Workers Directive' means Council Directive 94/33/EC of 22 June 1994 on the protection of young people at work.

(2) In the absence of a definition in these Regulations, words and expressions used in particular provisions which are also used in corresponding provisions of the Working Time Directive or the Young Workers Directive have the same meaning as they have in those corresponding provisions.

(3) [omitted]

PART II   RIGHTS AND OBLIGATIONS CONCERNING WORKING TIME

3   General

(1) The provisions of this Part have effect subject to the exceptions provided for in Part III of these Regulations.

(2) Where, in this Part, separate provision is made as respects the same matter in relation to workers generally and to young workers, the provision relating to workers generally applies only to adult workers and those young workers to whom, by virtue of any exception in Part 3, the provision relating to young workers does not apply.

4   Maximum weekly working time

(1) Unless his employer has first obtained the worker's agreement in writing to perform such work a worker's working time, including overtime, in any reference period which is applicable in his case shall not exceed an average of 48 hours for each seven days.

(2) An employer shall take all reasonable steps, in keeping with the need to protect the health and safety of workers, to ensure that the limit specified in paragraph (1) is complied with in the case of each worker employed by him in relation to whom it applies and shall keep up-to-date records of all workers who carry out work to which it does not apply by reason of the fact that the employer has obtained the worker's agreement as mentioned in paragraph (1).

(3) Subject to paragraphs (4) and (5) and any agreement under regulation 23(b), the reference periods which apply in the case of a worker are—

(a) where a relevant agreement provides for the application of this regulation in relation to successive periods of 17 weeks, each such period, or

(b) in any other case, any period of 17 weeks in the course of his employment.

(4) Where a worker has worked for his employer for less than 17 weeks, the reference period applicable in his case is the period that has elapsed since he started work for his employer.

(5) Paragraphs (3) and (4) shall apply to a worker who is excluded from the scope of certain provisions of these Regulations by regulation 21 as if for each reference to 17 weeks there were substituted a reference to 26 weeks.

(6) For the purposes of this regulation, a worker's average working time for each seven days during a reference period shall be determined according to the formula—

$$\frac{A + B}{C}$$

where—

A is the aggregate number of hours comprised in the worker's working time during the course of the reference period;

B is the aggregate number of hours comprised in his working time during the course of the period beginning immediately after the end of the reference period and ending when the number of days in that subsequent period on which he has worked equals the number of excluded days during the reference period; and

C is the number of weeks in the reference period.

(7) In paragraph (6), 'excluded days' means days comprised in—

(a) any period of annual leave taken by the worker in exercise of his entitlement under regulation 13;

(b) any period of sick leave taken by the worker;

(c) any period of maternity, paternity, adoption or parental leave taken by the worker; and

(d) any period in respect of which the limit specified in paragraph (1) did not apply in relation to the worker by reason of the fact that the employer has obtained the worker's agreement as mentioned in paragraph (1).

5   Agreement to exclude the maximum

(1) [revoked]

(2) An agreement for the purposes of regulation 4—

(a) may either relate to a specified period or apply indefinitely; and

    (b) subject to any provision in the agreement for a different period of notice, shall be terminable by the worker by giving not less than seven days' notice to his employer in writing.

(3) Where an agreement for the purposes of regulation 4 makes provision for the termination of the agreement after a period of notice, the notice period provided for shall not exceed three months.

(4) [revoked]

5A   Maximum working time for young workers

(1) A young worker's working time shall not exceed—

    (a) eight hours a day, or

    (b) 40 hours a week.

(2) If, on any day, or, as the case may be, during any week, a young worker is employed by more than one employer, his working time shall be determined for the purpose of paragraph (1) by aggregating the number of hours worked by him for each employer.

(3) For the purposes of paragraphs (1) and (2), a week starts at midnight between Sunday and Monday.

(4) An employer shall take all reasonable steps, in keeping with the need to protect the health and safety of workers, to ensure that the limits specified in paragraph (1) are complied with in the case of each worker employed by him in relation to whom they apply.

6   Length of night work

(1) A night worker's normal hours of work in any reference period which is applicable in his case shall not exceed an average of eight hours for each 24 hours.

(2) An employer shall take all reasonable steps, in keeping with the need to protect the health and safety of workers, to ensure that the limit specified in paragraph (1) is complied with in the case of each night worker employed by him.

(3) The reference periods which apply in the case of a night worker are—

    (a) where a relevant agreement provides for the application of this regulation in relation to successive periods of 17 weeks, each such period, or

    (b) in any other case, any period of 17 weeks in the course of his employment.

(4) Where a worker has worked for his employer for less than 17 weeks, the reference period applicable in his case is the period that has elapsed since he started work for his employer.

(5) For the purposes of this regulation, a night worker's average normal hours of work for each 24 hours during a reference period shall be determined according to the formula—

$$\frac{A}{B-C}$$

where—

A is the number of hours during the reference period which are normal working hours for that worker;

B is the number of days during the reference period; and

C is the total number of hours during the reference period comprised in rest periods spent by the worker in pursuance of his entitlement under regulation 11, divided by 24.

(6) A night worker's normal hours of work for the purposes of this regulation are his normal working hours for the purposes of the 1996 Act in a case where section 234 of that Act (which provides for the interpretation of normal working hours in the case of certain employees) applies to him.

(7) An employer shall ensure that no night worker employed by him whose work involves special hazards or heavy physical or mental strain works for more than eight hours in any 24-hour period during which the night worker performs night work.

(8) For the purposes of paragraph (7), the work of a night worker shall be regarded as involving special hazards or heavy physical or mental strain if—

    (a) it is identified as such in—
      (i) a collective agreement, or
      (ii) a workforce agreement, which takes account of the specific effects and hazards of night work, or
    (b) it is recognised in a risk assessment made by the employer under regulation 3 of the Management of Health and Safety at Work Regulations 1992 as involving a significant risk to the health or safety of workers employed by him.

6A   Night work by young workers

An employer shall ensure that no young worker employed by him works during the restricted period.

7   Health assessment and transfer of night workers to day work

(1) An employer—
    (a) shall not assign an adult worker to work which is to be undertaken during periods such that the worker will become a night worker unless—
      (i) the employer has ensured that the worker will have the opportunity of a free health assessment before he takes up the assignment; or
      (ii) the worker had a health assessment before being assigned to work to be undertaken during such periods on an earlier occasion, and the employer has no reason to believe that that assessment is no longer valid, and
    (b) shall ensure that each night worker employed by him has the opportunity of a free health assessment at regular intervals of whatever duration maybe appropriate in his case

(2) Subject to paragraph (4), an employer—
    (a) shall not assign a young worker to work during 'the restricted period' unless—
      (i) the employer has ensured that the young worker will have the opportunity of a free assessment of his health and capacities before he takes up the assignment; or
      (ii) the young worker had an assessment of his health and capacities before being assigned to work during the restricted period on an earlier occasion, and the employer has no reason to believe that that assessment is no longer valid; and
    (b) shall ensure that each young worker employed by him and assigned to work during the restricted period has the opportunity of a free assessment of his health and capacities at regular intervals of whatever duration may be appropriate in his case.

(3) For the purposes of paragraphs (1) and (2), an assessment is free if it is at no cost to the worker to whom it relates.

(4) The requirements in paragraph (2) do not apply in a case where the work a young worker is assigned to do is of an exceptional nature.

(5) No person shall disclose an assessment made for the purposes of this regulation to any person other than the worker to whom it relates, unless—
    (a) the worker has given his consent in writing to the disclosure, or
    (b) the disclosure is confined to a statement that the assessment shows the worker to be fit—
      (i) in a case where paragraph (1)(a)(i) or (2)(a)(i) applies, to take up an assignment, or
      (ii) in a case where paragraph (1)(b) or (2)(b) applies, to continue to undertake an assignment.

(6) Where—
    (a) a registered medical practitioner has advised an employer that a worker employed by the employer is suffering from health problems which the practitioner considers to be connected with the fact that the worker performs night work, and

(b) it is possible for the employer to transfer the worker to work—
(i) to which the worker is suited, and
(ii) which is to be undertaken during periods such that the worker will cease to be a night worker,

the employer shall transfer the worker accordingly.

8 Pattern of work

Where the pattern according to which an employer organises work is such as to put the health and safety of a worker employed by him at risk, in particular because the work is monotonous or the work-rate is predetermined, the employer shall ensure that the worker is given adequate rest breaks.

9 Records

An employer shall—
(a) keep records which are adequate to show whether the limits specified in regulations 4(1), 5A(1) and 6(1) and 6A and (7) and the requirements in regulations 7(1) and (2) are being complied with in the case of each worker employed by him in relation to whom they apply; and
(b) retain such records for two years from the date on which they were made.

10 Daily rest

(1) A worker is entitled to a rest period of not less than eleven consecutive hours in each 24-hour period during which he works for his employer.

(2) Subject to paragraph (3), a young worker is entitled to a rest period of not less than twelve consecutive hours in each 24-hour period during which he works for his employer.

(3) The minimum rest period provided for in paragraph (2) may be interrupted in the case of activities involving periods of work that are split up over the day or of short duration.

11 Weekly rest period

(1) Subject to paragraph (2), a worker is entitled to an uninterrupted rest period of not less than 24 hours in each seven-day period during which he works for his employer.

(2) If his employer so determines, a worker shall be entitled to either—
(a) two uninterrupted rest periods each of not less than 24 hours in each 14 day period during which he works for his employer; or
(b) one uninterrupted rest period of not less than 48 hours in each such 14-day period,

in place of the entitlement provided for in paragraph (1).

(3) Subject to paragraph (8), a young worker is entitled to a rest period of not less than 48 hours in each seven-day period during which he works for his employer.

(4) For the purpose of paragraphs (1) to (3), a seven-day period or (as the case may be) 14-day period shall be taken to begin—
(a) at such times on such days as may be provided for for the purposes of this regulation in a relevant agreement; or
(b) where there are no provisions of a relevant agreement which apply, at the start of each week or (as the case may be) every other week.

(5) In a case where, in accordance with paragraph (4), 14-day periods are to be taken to begin at the start of every other week, the first such period applicable in the case of a particular worker shall be taken to begin—
(a) if the worker's employment began on or before the date on which these Regulations come into force, on 5 October 1998; or
(b) if the worker's employment begins after the date on which these Regulations come into force, at the start of the week in which that employment begins.

(6) For the purposes of paragraphs (4) and (5), a week starts at midnight between Sunday and Monday.

(7) The minimum rest period to which a worker is entitled under paragraph (1) or (2) shall not include any part of a rest period to which the worker is entitled under regulation 10(1), except where this is justified by objective or technical reasons or reasons concerning the organisation of work.

(8) The minimum rest period to which a young worker is entitled under paragraph (3)—

    (a) may be interrupted in the case of activities involving periods of work that are split up over the day or are of short duration; and

    (b) may be reduced where this is justified by technical or organisation reasons, but not to less than 36 consecutive hours.

12   Rest breaks

(1) Where a worker's daily working time is more than six hours, he is entitled to a rest break.

(2) The details of the rest break to which a worker is entitled under paragraph (1), including its duration and the terms on which it is granted, shall be in accordance with any provisions for the purposes of this regulation which are contained in a collective agreement or a workforce agreement.

(3) Subject to the provisions of any applicable collective agreement or workforce agreement, the rest break provided for in paragraph (1) is an uninterrupted period of not less than 20 minutes, and the worker is entitled to spend it away from his workstation if he has one.

(4) Where a young worker's daily working time is more than four and a half hours, he is entitled to a rest break of at least 30 minutes, which shall be consecutive if possible, and he is entitled to spend it away from his workstation if he has one.

(5) If, on any day, a young worker is employed by more than one employer, his daily working time shall be determined for the purpose of paragraph (4) by aggregating the number of hours worked by him for each employer.

13   Entitlement to annual leave

(1) Subject to paragraph (5), a worker is entitled to four weeks' annual leave in each leave year.

(2) [revoked]

(3) A worker's leave year, for the purposes of this regulation, begins—

    (a) on such date during the calendar year as may be provided for in a relevant agreement; or

    (b) where there are no provisions of a relevant agreement which apply—

        (i) if the worker's employment began on or before 1 October 1998, on that date and each subsequent anniversary of that date; or

        (ii) if the worker's employment begins after 1 October 1998, on the date on which that employment begins and each subsequent anniversary of that date.

(4) Paragraph (3) does not apply to a worker to whom Schedule 2 applies (workers employed in agriculture) except where, in the case of a worker partly employed in agriculture, a relevant agreement so provides.

(5) Where the date on which a worker's employment begins is later than the date on which (by virtue of a relevant agreement) his first leave year begins, the leave to which he is entitled in that leave year is a proportion of the period applicable under paragraph (1) equal to the proportion of that leave year remaining on the date on which his employment begins.

(6) Where by virtue of paragraph (5) the period of leave to which a worker is entitled is or includes a proportion of a week, the proportion shall be determined in days and any fraction of a day shall be treated as a whole day.

(7)—(8) [revoked]

(9) Leave to which a worker is entitled under this regulation may be taken in instalments, but—

(a) it may only be taken in the leave year in respect of which it is due, and

(b) it may not be replaced by a payment in lieu except where the worker's employment is terminated.

14   Compensation related to entitlement to leave

(1) This regulation applies where—

(a) a worker's employment is terminated during the course of his leave year, and

(b) on the date on which the termination takes effect ('the termination date'), the proportion he has taken of the leave to which he is entitled in the leave year under regulation 13 differs from the proportion of the leave year which has expired.

(2) Where the proportion of leave taken by the worker is less than the proportion of the leave year which has expired, his employer shall make him a payment in lieu of leave in accordance with paragraph (3).

(3) The payment due under paragraph (2) shall be—

(a) such sum as may be provided for for the purposes of this regulation in a relevant agreement, or

(b) where there are no provisions of a relevant agreement which apply, a sum equal to the amount that would be due to the worker under regulation 16 in respect of a period of leave determined according to the formula—

$$(A \times B) - C$$

where—

A is the period of leave to which the worker is entitled under regulation 13;

B is the proportion of the worker's leave year which expired before the termination date; and

C is the period of leave taken by the worker between the start of the leave year and the termination date.

(4) A relevant agreement may provide that, where the proportion of leave taken by the worker exceeds the proportion of the leave year which has expired, he shall compensate his employer, whether by a payment, by undertaking additional work or otherwise.

15   Dates on which leave is taken

(1) A worker may take leave to which he is entitled under regulation 13 on such days as he may elect by giving notice to his employer in accordance with paragraph (3), subject to any requirement imposed on him by his employer under paragraph (2).

(2) A worker's employer may require the worker—

(a) to take leave to which the worker is entitled under regulation 13, or

(b) not to take such leave,

on particular days, by giving notice to the worker in accordance with paragraph (3).

(3) A notice under paragraph (1) or (2)—

(a) may relate to all or part of the leave to which a worker is entitled in a leave year;

(b) shall specify the days on which leave is or (as the case may be) is not to be taken and, where the leave on a particular day is to be in respect of only part of the day, its duration; and

(c) shall be given to the employer or, as the case may be, the worker before the relevant date.

(4) The relevant date, for the purposes of paragraph (3), is the date—

(a) in the case of a notice under paragraph (1) or (2)(a), twice as many days in advance of the earliest day specified in the notice as the number of days or part-days to which the notice relates, and

(b) in the case of a notice under paragraph (2)(b), as many days in advance of the earliest day so specified as the number of days or part-days to which the notice relates.

(5) Any right or obligation under paragraphs (1) to (4) may be varied or excluded by a relevant agreement.

(6) This regulation does not apply to a worker to whom Schedule 2 applies (workers employed in agriculture) except where, in the case of a worker partly employed in agriculture, a relevant agreement so provides.

15A   Leave during the first year of employment

(1) During the first year of his employment, the amount of leave a worker may take at any time in exercise of his entitlement under regulation 13 is limited to the amount which is deemed to have accrued in his case at that time under paragraph (2), as modified under paragraph (3) in a case where that paragraph applies, less the amount of leave (if any) that he has already taken during that year.

(2) For the purposes of paragraph (1), leave is deemed to accrue over the course of the worker's first year of employment, at the rate of one-twelfth of the amount specified in regulation 13(1) on the first day of each month of that year.

(3) Where the amount of leave that has accrued in a particular case includes a fraction of a day other than a half-day, the fraction shall be treated as a half-day if it is less than a half-day and as a whole day if it is more than a half-day.

(4) This regulation does not apply to a worker whose employment began on or before 25th October 2001.

16   Payment in respect of periods of leave

(1) A worker is entitled to be paid in respect of any period of annual leave to which he is entitled under regulation 13, at the rate of a week's pay in respect of each week of leave.

(2) Sections 221 to 224 of the 1996 Act shall apply for the purpose of determining the amount of a week's pay for the purposes of this regulation, subject to the modifications set out in paragraph (3).

(3) The provisions referred to in paragraph (2) shall apply—

(a) as if references to the employee were references to the worker;

(b) as if references to the employee's contract of employment were references to the worker's contract;

(c) as if the calculation date were the first day of the period of leave in question; and

(d) as if the references to sections 227 and 228 did not apply.

(4) A right to payment under paragraph (1) does not affect any right of a worker to remuneration under his contract ('contractual remuneration').

(5) Any contractual remuneration paid to a worker in respect of a period of leave goes towards discharging any liability of the employer to make payments under this regulation in respect of that period; and, conversely, any payment of remuneration under this regulation in respect of a period goes towards discharging any liability of the employer to pay contractual remuneration in respect of that period.

17   Entitlements under other provisions

Where during any period a worker is entitled to a rest period, rest break or annual leave both under a provision of these Regulations and under a separate provision (including a provision of his contract), he may not exercise the two rights separately, but may, in taking a rest period, break or leave during that period, take advantage of whichever right is, in any particular respect, the more favourable.

PART III   EXCEPTIONS

18   [omitted]

19   Domestic service

Regulations 4(1) and (2), 5A(1) and (4), 6(1), (2) and (7), 6A, 7(1), (2) and (6) and 8 do not apply in relation to a worker employed as a domestic servant in a private household.

20 Unmeasured working time

(1) Regulations 4(1) and (2), 6(1), (2) and (7), 10(1), 11(1) and (2) and 12(1) do not apply in relation to a worker where, on account of the specific characteristics of the activity in which he is engaged, the duration of his working time is not measured or predetermined or can be determined by the worker himself, as may be the case for—

(a) managing executives or other persons with autonomous decision-taking powers;

(b) family workers; or

(c) workers officiating at religious ceremonies in churches and religious communities.

(2) [revoked]

21 Other special cases

Subject to regulation 24, regulations 6(1), (2) and (7), 10(1), 11(1) and (2) and 12(1) do not apply in relation to a worker—

(a) where the worker's activities are such that his place of work and place of residence are distant from one another, including cases where the worker is employed in offshore work, or his different places of work are distant from one another;

(b) where the worker is engaged in security and surveillance activities requiring a permanent presence in order to protect property and persons, as may be the case for security guards and caretakers or security firms;

(c) where the worker's activities involve the need for continuity of service or production, as may be the case in relation to—

   (i)   services relating to the reception, treatment or care provided by hospitals or similar establishments (including the activities of doctors in training), residential institutions and prisons;

   (ii) work at docks or airports;

   (iii) press, radio, television, cinematographic production, postal and telecommunications services and civil protection services;

   (iv) gas, water and electricity production, transmission and distribution, household refuse collection and incineration;

   (v)   industries in which work cannot be interrupted on technical grounds;

   (vi) research and development activities;

   (vii) agriculture;

   (viii) the carriage of passengers on regular urban transport services;

(d) where there is a foreseeable surge of activity, as may be the case in relation to—

   (i)   agriculture;

   (ii) tourism; and

   (iii) postal services;

(e) where the worker's activities are affected by—

   (i)   an occurrence due to unusual and unforeseeable circumstances, beyond the control of the worker's employer;

   (ii) exceptional events, the consequences of which could not have been avoided despite the exercise of all due care by the employer; or

   (iii) an accident or the imminent risk of an accident;

(f) where the worker works in railway transport and—

   (i)   his activities are intermittent;

   (ii) he spends his working time on board trains; or

   (iii) his activities are linked to transport timetables and to ensuring the continuity and regularity of traffic.

22 Shift workers

(1) Subject to regulation 24—

(a) regulation 10(1) does not apply in relation to a shift worker when he changes shift and cannot take a daily rest period between the end of one shift and the start of the next one;

(b) paragraphs (1) and (2) of regulation 11 do not apply in relation to a shift worker when he changes shift and cannot take a weekly rest period between the end of one shift and the start of the next one; and

(c) neither regulation 10(1) nor paragraphs (1) and (2) of regulation 11 apply to workers engaged in activities involving periods of work split up over the day, as may be the case for cleaning staff.

(2) For the purposes of this regulation—

'shift worker' means any worker whose work schedule is part of shift work; and

'shift work' means any method of organising work in shifts whereby workers succeed each other at the same workstations according to a certain pattern, including a rotating pattern, and which may be continuous or discontinuous, entailing the need for workers to work at different times over a given period of days or weeks.

23   Collective and workforce agreements

A collective agreement or a workforce agreement may—

(a) modify or exclude the application of regulations 6(1) to (3) and (7), 10(1), 11(1) and (2) and 12(1), and

(b) for objective or technical reasons or reasons concerning the organisation of work, modify the application of regulation 4(3) and (4) by the substitution, for each reference to 17 weeks, of a different period, being a period not exceeding 52 weeks,

in relation to particular workers or groups of workers.

24   Compensatory rest

Where the application of any provision of these Regulations is excluded by regulation 21 or 22, or is modified or excluded by means of a collective agreement or a workforce agreement under regulation 23(a), and a worker is accordingly required by his employer to work during a period which would otherwise be a rest period or rest break—

(a) his employer shall wherever possible allow him to take an equivalent period of compensatory rest, and

(b) in exceptional cases in which it is not possible, for objective reasons, to grant such a period of rest, his employer shall afford him such protection as may be appropriate in order to safeguard the worker's health and safety.

24A   Mobile workers

(1) Regulations 6(1), (2) and (7), 10(1), 11(1) and (2) and 12(1) do not apply to a mobile worker in relation to whom the application of those regulations is not excluded by any provision of regulation 18.

(2) A mobile worker, to whom paragraph (1) applies, is entitled to adequate rest, except where the worker's activities are affected by any of the matters referred to in regulation 21(e).

(3) For the purposes of this regulation, 'adequate rest' means that a worker has regular rest periods, the duration of which are expressed in units of time and which are sufficiently long and continuous to ensure that, as a result of fatigue or other irregular working patterns, he does not cause injury to himself, to fellow workers or to others and that he does not damage his health, either in the short term or in the longer term.

25–25B [omitted]; 26 [revoked]
27   Young workers: *force majeure*

(1) Regulations 5A, 6A, 10(2) and 12(4) do not apply in relation to a young worker where his employer requires him to undertake work which no adult worker is available to perform and which—

(a) is occasioned by either—

(i)   an occurrence due to unusual and unforseeable circumstances, beyond the employer's control, or

     (ii) exceptional events, the consequences of which could not have been avoided despite the exercise of all due care by the employer;

   (b) is of a temporary nature; and

   (c) must be performed immediately.

(2) Where the application of regulation 5A, 6A, 10(2) or 12(4) is excluded by paragraph(1), and a young worker is accordingly required to work during a period which would otherwise be a rest period or rest break, his employer shall allow him to take an equivalent period of compensatory rest within the following three weeks.

27A   Other exceptions relating to young workers

(1) Regulation 5A does not apply in relation to a young worker where—

   (a) the young worker's employer requires him to undertake work which is necessary either to maintain continuity of service or production or to respond to a surge in demand for a service or product;

   (b) no adult worker is available to perform the work; and

   (c) performing the work would not adversely affect the young worker's education or training.

(2) Regulation 6A does not apply in relation to a young worker employed—

   (a) in a hospital or similar establishment, or

   (b) in connection with cultural, artistic, sporting or advertising activities,

in the circumstances referred to in paragraph (1).

(3) Regulation 6A does not apply, except in so far as it prohibits work between midnight and 4 a.m., in relation to a young worker employed in—

   (a) agriculture;

   (b) retail trading;

   (c) postal or newspaper deliveries;

   (d) a catering business;

   (e) a hotel, public house, restaurant, bar or similar establishment; or

   (f) a bakery;

in the circumstances referred to in paragraph (1).

(4) Where the application of regulation 6A is excluded by paragraph (2) or (3), and a young worker is accordingly required to work during a period which would otherwise be a rest period or rest break—

   (a) he shall be supervised by an adult worker where such supervision is necessary for the young worker's protection; and

   (b) he shall be allowed an equivalent period of compensatory rest.

PART IV   MISCELLANEOUS

28   Enforcement

(1) In this regulation, regulations 29–29E and Schedule 3—

. . .

'the relevant requirements' means the following provisions—

   (a) regulations 4(2), 5A(4), 6(2) and (7), 6A, 7(1), (2) and (6), 8, 9 and 27A(4)(a);

   (b) regulation 24, in so far as it applies where regulation 6(1), (2) or (7) is modified or excluded; and

   (c) regulation 24A(2), in so far as it applies where regulations 6(1), (2) or (7) is excluded;

. . .

29   Offences

(1) An employer who fails to comply with any of the relevant requirements shall be guilty of an offence.

(2) The provisions of paragraph (3) shall apply where an inspector is exercising or has exercised any power conferred by Schedule 3.

(3) It is an offence for a person—

(a) to contravene any requirement imposed by the inspector under paragraph 2 of Schedule 3;

(b) to prevent or attempt to prevent any other person from appearing before the inspector or from answering any question to which the inspector may by virtue of paragraph 2(2)(e) of Schedule 3 require an answer;

(c) to contravene any requirement or prohibition imposed by an improvement notice or a prohibition notice (including any such notice as is modified on appeal);

(d) intentionally to obstruct the inspector in the exercise or performance of his powers or duties;

(e) to use or disclose any information in contravention of paragraph 8 of Schedule 3;

(f) to make a statement which he knows to be false or recklessly to make a statement which is false, where the statement is made in purported compliance with a requirement to furnish any information imposed by or under these Regulations.

(4) An employer guilty of an offence under paragraph (1) shall be liable—

(a) on summary conviction, to a fine not exceeding the statutory maximum;

(b) on conviction on indictment, to a fine.

(5) A person guilty of an offence under paragraph (3) shall be liable to the penalty prescribed in relation to that provision by paragraphs (6), (7) or (8) as the case may be.

(6) A person guilty of an offence under sub-paragraph (3)(a),(b) or (d) shall be liable on summary conviction to a fine not exceeding level 5 on the standard scale.

(7) A person guilty of an offence under sub-paragraph (3)(c) shall be liable—

(a) on summary conviction, to imprisonment for a term not exceeding three months, or a fine not exceeding the statutory maximum;

(b) on conviction on indictment, to imprisonment for a term not exceeding two years, or a fine, or both.

(8) A person guilty of an offence under any of the sub-paragraphs of paragraph (3) not falling within paragraphs (6) or (7) above, shall be liable—

(a) on summary conviction, to a fine not exceeding the statutory maximum;

(b) on conviction on indictment—

(i) if the offence is under sub-paragraph (3)(e), to imprisonment for a term not exceeding two years or a fine or both;

(ii) if the offence is not one to which the preceding sub-paragraph applies, to a fine.

(9) The provisions set out in regulations 29A–29E below shall apply in relation to the offences provided for in paragraphs (1) and (3).

29A   Offences due to fault of other person

Where the commission by any person of an offence is due to the act or default of some other person, that other person shall be guilty of the offence, and a person may be charged with and convicted of the offence by virtue of this paragraph whether or not proceedings are taken against the first-mentioned person.

29B   Offences by bodies corporate

(1) Where an offence committed by a body corporate is proved to have been committed with the consent or connivance of, or to have been attributable to any neglect on the part of, any director, manager, secretary or other similar officer of the body corporate or a person who was purporting to act in any such capacity, he as well as the body corporate shall be guilty of that offence and shall be liable to be proceeded against and punished accordingly.

(2) Where the affairs of a body corporate are managed by its members, the preceding paragraph shall apply in relation to the acts and defaults of a member in connection with his functions of management as if he were a director of the body corporate.

29C   Restriction on institution of proceedings in England and Wales

Proceedings for an offence shall not, in England and Wales, be instituted except by an inspector or by or with the consent of the Director of Public Prosecutions.

29D   Prosecutions by inspectors

(1) An inspector, if authorised in that behalf by an enforcement authority, may, although not of counsel or a solicitor, prosecute before a magistrate's court proceedings for an offence under these Regulations.

(2) This regulation shall not apply to Scotland.

29E   Power of court to order cause of offence to be remedied

(1) Where a person is convicted of an offence in respect of any matters which appear to the court to be matters which it is in his power to remedy, the court may, in addition to or instead of imposing any punishment, order him, within such time as may be fixed by the order, to take such steps as may be specified in the order for remedying the said matters.

(2) The time fixed by an order under paragraph (1) may be extended or further extended by order of the court on an application made before the end of that time as originally fixed or as extended under this paragraph, as the case may be.

(3) Where a person is ordered under paragraph (1) to remedy any matters, that person shall not be liable under these Regulations in respect of those matters in so far as they continue during the time fixed by the order or any further time allowed under paragraph (2).

30   Remedies

(1) A worker may present a complaint to an employment tribunal that his employer—
  (a) has refused to permit him to exercise any right he has under—
      (i) regulation 10(1) or (2), 11(1), (2) or (3), 12(1) or (4) or 13;
      (ii) regulation 24, in so far as it applies where regulation 10(1), 11(1) or (2) or 12(1) is modified or excluded;
      (iii) regulation 24A, in so far as it applies where regulation 10(1), 11(1) or (2) or 12(1) is excluded; or
      (iv) regulation 25(3), 27A(4)(b) or 27(2); or
  (b) has failed to pay him the whole or any part of any amount due to him under regulation 14(2) or 16(1).

(2) An employment tribunal shall not consider a complaint under this regulation unless it is presented—
  (a) before the end of the period of three months (or, in a case to which regulation 38(2) applies, six months) beginning with the date on which it is alleged that the exercise of the right should have been permitted (or in the case of a rest period or leave extending over more than one day, the date on which it should have been permitted to begin) or, as the case may be, the payment should have been made;
  (b) within such further period as the tribunal considers reasonable in a case where it is satisfied that it was not reasonably practicable for the complaint to be presented before the end of that period of three or, as the case may be, six months.

(2A) Where the period within which a complaint must be presented in accordance with paragraph (2) is extended by regulation 15 of the Employment Act 2002 (Dispute Resolution) Regulations 2004, the period within which the complaint must be presented shall be the extended period rather than the period in paragraph (2).

(3) Where an employment tribunal finds a complaint under paragraph (1)(a) well-founded, the tribunal—

    (a) shall make a declaration to that effect, and

    (b) may make an award of compensation to be paid by the employer to the worker.

(4) The amount of the compensation shall be such as the tribunal considers just and equitable in all the circumstances having regard to—

    (a) the employer's default in refusing to permit the worker to exercise his right, and

    (b) any loss sustained by the worker which is attributable to the matters complained of.

(5) Where on a complaint under paragraph (1)(b) an employment tribunal finds that an employer has failed to pay a worker in accordance with regulation 14(2) or 16(1), it shall order the employer to pay to the worker the amount which it finds to be due to him.

31–34 [omitted]

35 Restrictions on contracting out

(1) Any provision in an agreement (whether a contract of employment or not) is void in so far as it purports—

    (a) to exclude or limit the operation of any provision of these Regulations, save in so far as these Regulations provide for an agreement to have that effect, or

    (b) to preclude a person from bringing proceedings under these Regulations before an employment tribunal.

(2) Paragraph (1) does not apply to—

    (a) any agreement to refrain from instituting or continuing proceedings where a conciliation officer has taken action under section 18 of the Employment Tribunals Act 1996 (conciliation); or

    (b) any agreement to refrain from instituting or continuing proceedings within section 18(1)(ff) of the Employment Tribunals Act 1996 (proceedings under these Regulations where conciliation is available), if the conditions regulating compromise agreements under these Regulations are satisfied in relation to the agreement.

(3) For the purposes of paragraph (2)(b) the conditions regulating compromise agreements under these Regulations are that—

    (a) the agreement must be in writing,

    (b) the agreement must relate to the particular complaint,

    (c) the worker must have received advice from a relevant independent adviser as to the terms and effect of the proposed agreement and, in particular, its effect on his ability to pursue his rights before an employment tribunal,

    (d) there must be in force, when the adviser gives the advice, a contract of insurance, or an indemnity provided for members of a profession or professional body, covering the risk of a claim by the worker in respect of loss arising in consequence of the advice,

    (e) the agreement must identify the adviser, and (f) the agreement must state that the conditions regulating compromise agreements under these Regulations are satisfied.

(4)–(7) [omitted].

35A [omitted]

PART V   SPECIAL CLASSES OF PERSON

36 Agency workers not otherwise 'workers'

(1) This regulation applies in any case where an individual ('the agency worker')—

    (a) is supplied by a person ('the agent') to do work for another ('the principal') under a contract or other arrangements made between the agent and the principal; but

(b) is not, as respects that work, a worker, because of the absence of a worker's contract between the individual and the agent or the principal; and

(c) is not a party to a contract under which he undertakes to do the work for another party to the contract whose status is, by virtue of the contract, that of a client or customer of any profession or business undertaking carried on by the individual.

(2) In a case where this regulation applies, the other provisions of these Regulations shall have effect as if there were a worker's contract for the doing of the work by the agency worker made between the agency worker and—

(a) whichever of the agent and the principal is responsible for paying the agency worker in respect of the work; or

(b) if neither the agent nor the principal is so responsible, whichever of them pays the agency worker in respect of the work,

and as if that person were the agency worker's employer.

37 Crown employment

(1) Subject to paragraph (4) and regulation 38, these Regulations have effect in relation to Crown employment and persons in Crown employment as they have effect in relation to other employment and other workers.

(2) In paragraph (1) 'Crown employment' means employment under or for the purposes of a government department or any officer or body exercising on behalf of the Crown functions conferred by a statutory provision.

(3) For the purposes of the application of the provisions of these Regulations in relation to Crown employment in accordance with paragraph (1)—

(a) references to a worker shall be construed as references to a person in Crown employment; and

(b) references to a worker's contract shall be construed as references to the terms of employment of a person in Crown employment.

(4) No act or omission by the Crown which is an offence under regulation 29 shall make the Crown criminally liable, but the High Court or, in Scotland, the Court of Session may, on the application of a person appearing to the Court to have an interest, declare any such act or omission unlawful.

38–41 [omitted]

42 Non-employed trainees

For the purposes of these Regulations, a person receiving relevant training, otherwise than under a contract of employment, shall be regarded as a worker, and the person whose undertaking is providing the training shall be regarded as his employer.

43 [omitted]

SCHEDULE 1   WORKFORCE AGREEMENTS

1. An agreement is a workforce agreement for the purposes of these Regulations if the following conditions are satisfied—

(a) the agreement is in writing;

(b) it has effect for a specified period not exceeding five years;

(c) it applies either—

(i) to all of the relevant members of the workforce, or

(ii) to all of the relevant members of the workforce who belong to a particular group;

(d) the agreement is signed—

(i) in the case of an agreement of the kind referred to in sub-paragraph(c)(i), by the representatives of the workforce, and in the case of an agreement of the kind referred to in sub-paragraph(c) (ii) by the representatives of the group to which the agreement applies (excluding, in either case, any representative not a relevant member of the workforce on the date on which the agreement was first made available for signature), or

    (ii) if the employer employed 20 or fewer workers on the date referred to in sub-paragraph (d)(i), either by the appropriate representatives in accordance with that sub-paragraph or by the majority of the workers employed by him;

  (e) before the agreement was made available for signature, the employer provided all the workers to whom it was intended to apply on the date on which it came into effect with copies of the text of the agreement and such guidance as those workers might reasonably require in order to understand it fully.

2. For the purposes of this Schedule—

'a particular group' is a group of the relevant members of a workforce who undertake a particular function, work at a particular workplace or belong to a particular department or unit within their employer's business;

'relevant members of the workforce' are all of the workers employed by a particular employer, excluding any worker whose terms and conditions of employment are provided for, wholly or in part, in a collective agreement;

'representatives of the workforce' are workers duly elected to represent the relevant members of the workforce, 'representatives of the group' are workers duly elected to represent the members of a particular group, and representatives are 'duly elected' if the election at which they were elected satisfied the requirements of paragraph 3 of this Schedule.

3. The requirements concerning elections referred to in paragraph 2 are that—

  (a) the number of representatives to be elected is determined by the employer;

  (b) the candidates for election as representatives of the workforce are relevant members of the workforce, and the candidates for election as representatives of a group arc members of the group;

  (c) no worker who is eligible to be a candidate is unreasonably excluded from standing for election;

  (d) all the relevant members of the workforce are entitled to vote for representatives of the workforce, and all the members of a particular group are entitled to vote for representatives of the group;

  (e) the workers entitled to vote may vote for as many candidates as there are representatives to be elected;

  (f) the election is conducted so as to secure that—

    (i) so far as is reasonably practicable, those voting do so in secret, and

    (ii) the votes given at the election are fairly and accurately counted.

The Maternity and Parental Leave etc. Regulations 1999
(SI 1999 No. 3312)

PART I   GENERAL

1 [omitted]

2 Interpretation

(1) In these Regulations—

'the 1996; Act' means the Employment Rights Act 1996;

'additional adoption leave' means leave under section 75B of the 1996 Act;

'additional maternity leave' means leave under section 73 of the 1996 Act;

'business' includes a trade or profession and includes any activity carried on by a body of persons (whether corporate or unincorporated);

'child' means a person under the age of eighteen;

'childbirth' means the birth of a living child or the birth of a child whether living or dead after 24 weeks of pregnancy;

'collective agreement' means a collective agreement within the meaning of section 178 of the Trade Union and Labour Relations (Consolidation) Act 1992, the trade union parties to which are independent trade unions within the meaning of section 5 of that Act;

'contract of employment' means a contract of service or apprenticeship, whether express or implied, and (if it is express) whether oral or in writing;

'disability living allowance' means the disability living allowance provided for in Part III of the Social Security Contributions and Benefits Act 1992;

'employee' means an individual who has entered into or works under (or, where the employment has ceased, worked under) a contract of employment;

'employer' means the person by whom an employee is (or, where the employment has ceased, was) employed;

'expected week of childbirth' means the week, beginning with midnight between Saturday and Sunday, in which it is expected that childbirth will occur, and 'week of childbirth' means the week, beginning with midnight between Saturday and Sunday, in which childbirth occurs;

'job', in relation to an employee returning after maternity leave or parental leave, means the nature of the work which she is employed to do in accordance with her contract and the capacity and place in which she is so employed;

'ordinary maternity leave' means leave under section 71 of the 1996 Act; 'parental leave' means leave under regulation 13(1);

'parental responsibility' has the meaning given by section 3 of the Children Act 1989, and 'parental responsibilities' has the meaning given by section 1(3) of the Children (Scotland) Act 1995;

'statutory leave' means leave provided for in Part 8 of the 1996 Act;

'workforce agreement' means an agreement between an employer and his employees or their representatives in respect of which the conditions set out in Schedule 1 to these Regulations are satisfied.

(2) A reference in any provision of these Regulations to a period of continuous employment is to a period computed in accordance with Chapter I of Part XIV of the 1996 Act, as if that provision were a provision of that Act.

(3) For the purposes of these Regulations any two employers shall be treated as associated if—

    (a) one is a company of which the other (directly or indirectly) has control; or

    (b) both are companies of which a third person (directly or indirectly) has control;
        and 'associated employer' shall be construed accordingly.

(4) [omitted]

3 [omitted]

PART II   MATERNITY LEAVE

4 Entitlement to ordinary maternity leave

(1) An employee is entitled to ordinary maternity leave provided that she satisfies the following conditions—

    (a) no later than the end of the fifteenth week before her expected week of childbirth, or, if that is not reasonably practicable, as soon as is reasonably practicable, she notifies her employer of—

        (i) her pregnancy,

        (ii) the expected week of childbirth, and

        (iii) the date on which she intends her ordinary maternity leave period to start, and

(b) if requested to do so by her employer, she produces for his inspection a certificate from—

    (i)   a registered medical practitioner, or

    (ii) a registered midwife, stating the expected week of childbirth.

(1A) An employee who has notified her employer under paragraph (1)(a)(iii) of the date on which she intends her ordinary maternity leave period to start may subsequently vary that date, provided that she notifies her employer of the variation at least—

(a) 28 days before the date varied, or

(b) 28 days before the new date,

whichever is the earlier, or, if that is not reasonably practicable, as soon as is reasonably practicable.

(2) Notification under paragraph (1)(a)(iii) or (1A)—

(a) shall be given in writing, if the employer so requests, and

(b) shall not specify a date earlier than the beginning of the eleventh week before the expected week of childbirth.

(3) Where, by virtue of regulation 6(1)(b), an employee's ordinary maternity leave period commences with the day which follows the day which follows the first day after the beginning of the fourth week before the expected week of childbirth on which she is absent from work wholly or partly because of pregnancy—

(a) paragraph (1) does not require her to notify her employer of the date specified in that paragraph, but

(b) (whether or not she has notified him of that date) she is not entitled to ordinary maternity leave unless she notifies him as soon as is reasonably practicable that she is absent from work wholly or partly because of pregnancy and of the date on which the birth occurred and of the date on which her absence on that account began.

(4) Where, by virtue of regulation 6(2), an employee's ordinary maternity leave period commences on the day which follows the day on which childbirth occurs—

(a) paragraph (1) does not require her to notify her employer of the date specified in that paragraph, but

(b) (whether or not she has notified him of that date) she is not entitled to ordinary maternity leave unless she notifies him as soon as is reasonably practicable after the birth that she has given birth and of the date on which the birth occurred.

(5) The notification provided for in paragraphs (3)(b) and (4)(b) shall be given in writing, if the employer so requests.

5   Entitlement to additional maternity leave

An employee who satisfies the following conditions is entitled to additional maternity leave—

(a) she is entitled to ordinary maternity leave, and

(b) she has, at the beginning of the fourteenth week before the expected week of childbirth, been continuously employed for a period of not less than 26 weeks.

6   Commencement of maternity leave periods

(1) Subject to paragraph (2), an employee's ordinary maternity leave period commences with the earlier of—

(a) the date which she notifies to her employer in accordance with regulation 4, as the date on which she intends her ordinary maternity leave period to start or, if by virtue of the provision for variation in that regulation she has notified more than one such date, the last date she notifies, and

(b) the day which follows the first day after the beginning of the fourth week before the expected week of childbirth on which she is absent from work wholly or partly because of pregnancy.

(2) Where the employee's ordinary maternity leave period has not commenced by virtue of paragraph (1) when childbirth occurs, her ordinary maternity leave period commences on the day which follows the day on which childbirth occurs.

(3) An employee's additional maternity leave period commences on the day after the last day of her ordinary maternity leave period.

7 Duration of maternity leave periods

(1) Subject to paragraphs (2) and (5), an employee's ordinary maternity leave period continues for the period of 26 weeks from its commencement, or until the end of the compulsory maternity leave period provided for in regulation 8 if later.

(2) Subject to paragraph (5), where any requirement imposed by or under any relevant statutory provision prohibits the employee from working for any period after the end of the period determined under paragraph (1) by reason of her having recently given birth, her ordinary maternity leave period continues until the end of that later period.

(3) In paragraph (2), 'relevant statutory provision' means a provision of—
>   (a) an enactment, or
>   (b) an instrument under an enactment, other than a provision for the time being specified in an order under section 66(2) of the 1996 Act.

(4) Subject to paragraph (5), where an employee is entitled to additional maternity leave her additional maternity leave period continues until the end of the period of 26 weeks from the day on which it commenced.

(5) Where the employee is dismissed after the commencement of an ordinary or additional maternity leave period but before the time when (apart from this paragraph) that period would end, the period ends at the time of the dismissal.

(6) An employer who is notified under any provision of regulation 4 of the date on which, by virtue of any provision of regulation 6, an employee's ordinary maternity leave period will commence or has commenced shall notify the employee of the date on which—
>   (a) if the employee is entitled only to ordinary maternity leave, her ordinary maternity leave period will end, or
>   (b) if the employee is entitled to both ordinary and additional maternity leave, her additional maternity leave period will end.

(7) The notification provided for in paragraph (6) shall be given to the employee—
>   (a) where the employer is notified under regulation 4(1)(a)(iii), (3)(b) or (4)(b), within 28 days of the date on which he received the notification;
>   (b) where the employer is notified under regulation 4(1A), within 28 days of the date on which the employee's ordinary maternity leave period commenced.

8 Compulsory maternity leave

The prohibition in section 72 of the 1996 Act, against permitting an employee who satisfies prescribed conditions to work during a particular period (referred to as a 'compulsory maternity leave period'), applies—
>   (a) in relation to an employee who is entitled to ordinary maternity leave, and
>   (b) in respect of the period of two weeks which commences with the day on which childbirth occurs.

9 Application of terms and conditions during ordinary maternity leave

(1) An employee who takes ordinary maternity leave—
>   (a) is entitled, during the period of leave, to the benefit of all of the terms and conditions of employment which would have applied if she had not been absent, and
>   (b) is bound, during that period, by any obligations arising under those terms and conditions, subject only to the exception in section 71(4)(b) of the 1996 Act.

(2) In paragraph (1)(a), 'terms and conditions' has the meaning given by section 71(5) of the 1996 Act, and accordingly does not include terms and conditions about remuneration.

(3) For the purposes of section 71 of the 1996 Act, only sums payable to an employee by way of wages or salary are to be treated as remuneration.

10 Redundancy during maternity leave

(1) This regulation applies where, during an employee's ordinary or additional maternity leave period, it is not practicable by reason of redundancy for her employer to continue to employ her under her existing contract of employment.

(2) Where there is a suitable available vacancy, the employee is entitled to be offered (before the end of her employment under her existing contract) alternative employment with her employer or his successor, or an associated employer, under a new contract of employment which complies with paragraph (3) (and takes effect immediately on the ending of her employment under the previous contract).

(3) The new contract of employment must be such that—

(a) the work to be done under it is of a kind which is both suitable in relation to the employee and appropriate for her to do in the circumstances, and

(b) its provisions as to the capacity and place in which she is to be employed, and as to the other terms and conditions of her employment, are not substantially less favourable to her than if she had continued to be employed under the previous contract.

11 Requirement to notify intention to return during a maternity leave period

(1) An employee who intends to return to work earlier than the end of her ordinary maternity leave period or, where she is entitled to both ordinary and additional maternity leave, the end of her additional maternity leave period, shall give to her employer not less than 28 days' notice of the date on which she intends to return.

(2) If an employee attempts to return to work earlier than the end of a maternity leave period without complying with paragraph (1), her employer is entitled to postpone her return to a date such as will secure, subject to paragraph (3), that he has 28 days' notice of her return.

(3) An employer is not entitled under paragraph (2) to postpone an employee's return to work to a date after the end of the relevant maternity leave period.

(4) If an employee whose return to work has been postponed under paragraph (2) has been notified that she is not to return to work before the date to which her return was postponed, the employer is under no contractual obligation to pay her remuner- ation until the date to which her return was postponed if she returns to work before that date.

(5) This regulation does not apply in a case where the employer did not notify the employee in accordance with regulation 7(6) and (7) of the date on which the relevant maternity leave period would end.

12 [revoked]

PART III   PARENTAL LEAVE

13 Entitlement to parental leave

(1) An employee who—

(a) has been continuously employed for a period of not less than a year or is to be treated as having been so employed by virtue of paragraph (1A); and

(b) has, or expects to have, responsibility for a child,

is entitled, in accordance with these Regulations, to be absent from work on parental leave for the purpose of caring for that child.

(1A) If, in a case where regulation 15(2) or (3) applies—

(a) the employee was employed, during the period between 15th December 1998 and 9th January 2002, by a person other than the person who was his employer on 9th January 2002, and

(b) the period of his employment by that person (or, if he was employed by more than one person during that period, any such person) was not less than a year, then, for the purpose of paragraph (1), he shall be treated as having been continuously employed for a period of not less than a year.

(2) An employee has responsibility for a child, for the purposes of paragraph (1), if—

(a) he has parental responsibility or, in Scotland, parental responsibilities for the child; or

(b) he has been registered as the child's father under any provision of section 10(1) or 10A(1) of the Births and Deaths Registration Act 1953 or of section 18(1) or (2) of the Registration of Births, Deaths and Marriages (Scotland) Act 1965.

(3) [revoked].

14   Extent of entitlement

(1) Except in the case referred to in paragraph (1A) an employee is entitled to thirteen weeks' leave in respect of any individual child.

(1A) An employee is entitled to eighteen weeks' leave in respect of a child who is entitled to a disability living allowance.

(2) Where the period for which an employee is normally required, under his contract of employment, to work in the course of a week does not vary, a week's leave for the employee is a period of absence from work which is equal in duration to the period for which he is normally required to work.

(3) Where the period for which an employee is normally required, under his contract of employment, to work in the course of a week varies from week to week or over a longer period, or where he is normally required under his contract to work in some weeks but not in others a week's leave for the employee is a period of absence from work which is equal in duration to the period calculated by dividing the total of the periods for which he is normally required to work in a year by 52.

(4) Where an employee takes leave in periods shorter than the period which constitutes, for him, a week's leave under whichever of paragraphs (2) and (3) is applicable in his case, he completes a week's leave when the aggregate of the periods of leave he has taken equals the period constituting a week's leave for him under the applicable paragraph.

15   When parental leave may be taken

(1) Except in the cases referred to in paragraphs (2)–(4), an employee may not exercise any entitlement to parental leave in respect of a child after the date of the child's fifth birthday or, in the case of a child placed with the employee for adoption by him, on or after—

(a) the fifth anniversary of the date on which the placement began, or

(b) the date of the child's eighteenth birthday,

whichever is the earlier.

(2) In the case of child—

(a) born before 15th December 1999, whose fifth birthday was or is on or after that date, or

(b) placed with the employee for adoption by him before 15th December 1999, the fifth anniversary of whose placement was or is on or after that date,

not being a case to which paragraph (3) or (4) applies, any entitlement to parental leave may not be exercised after 31st March 2005.

(3) In the case of a child who is entitled to a disability living allowance, any entitlement to parental leave may not be exercised on or after the date of the child's eighteenth birthday.

(4) In a case where—

(a) the provisions set out in Schedule 2 apply, and

(b) the employee was unable to take leave in respect of a child within the time permitted in the case of that child under paragraphs (1) or (2) because the employer postponed the period of leave under paragraph 6 of that Schedule, the entitlement to leave is exercisable until the end of the period to which the leave was postponed.

16   Default provisions in respect of parental leave

The provisions set out in Schedule 2 apply in relation to parental leave in the case of an employee whose contract of employment does not include a provision which—

> (a) confers an entitlement to absence from work for the purpose of caring for a child, and
>
> (b) incorporates or operates by reference to all or part of a collective agreement or workforce agreement.

PART IV   PROVISIONS APPLICABLE IN RELATION TO MORE THAN ONE KIND OF ABSENCE

17   Application of terms and conditions during periods of leave

An employee who takes additional maternity leave or parental leave—

> (a) is entitled, during the period of leave, to the benefit of her employer's implied obligation to her of trust and confidence and any terms and conditions of her employment relating to—
>
> > (i)   notice of the termination of the employment contract by her employer;
> >
> > (ii) compensation in the event of redundancy, or
> >
> > (iii) disciplinary or grievance procedures;
>
> (b) is bound, during that period, by her implied obligation to her employer of good faith and any terms and conditions of her employment relating to—
>
> > (i)   notice of the termination of the employment contract by her;
> >
> > (ii) the disclosure of confidential information;
> >
> > (iii) the acceptance of gifts or other benefits, or
> >
> > (iv) the employee's participation in any other business.

18   Right to return after maternity or parental leave

(1) An employee who returns to work after a period of ordinary maternity leave, or a period of parental leave of four weeks or less, which was—

> (a) an isolated period of leave, or
>
> (b) the last of two or more consecutive periods of statutory leave which did not include any period of additional maternity leave or additional adoption leave, or a period of parental leave of more than four weeks,

is entitled to return to the job in which she was employed before her absence.

(2) An employee who returns to work after—

> (a) a period of additional maternity leave, or a period of parental leave of more than four weeks, whether or not preceded by another period of statutory leave, or
>
> (b) a period of ordinary maternity leave, or a period of parental leave of four weeks or less, not falling within the description in paragraph (1)(a) or (b) above,

is entitled to return from leave to the job in which she was employed before her absence or, if it is not reasonably practicable for the employer to permit her to return to that job, to another job which is both suitable for her and appropriate for her to do in the circumstances.

(3) The reference in paragraphs (1) and (2) to the job in which an employee was employed before her absence is a reference to the job in which she was employed—

> (a) if her return is from an isolated period of statutory leave, immediately before that period began;
>
> (b) if her return is from consecutive periods of statutory leave, immediately before the first such period.

(4) This regulation does not apply where regulation 10 applies.

18A   Incidents of the right to return

(1) An employee's right to return under regulation 18(1) or (2) is a right to return—

    (a) with her seniority, pension rights and similar rights—

        (i) in a case where the employee is returning from additional maternity leave, or consecutive periods of statutory leave which included a period of additional maternity leave or additional adoption leave, as they would have been if the period or periods of her employment prior to her additional maternity leave or (as the case may be) additional adoption leave were continuous with the period of employment following it;

        (ii) in any other case, as they would have been if she had not been absent, and

    (b) on terms and conditions not less favourable than those which would have applied if she had not been absent.

(2) The provision in paragraph (1)(a)(i) concerning the treatment of periods of additional maternity leave or additional adoption leave is subject to the requirements of paragraph 5 and 6 of Schedule 5 to the Social Security Act 1989 (equal treatment under pension schemes: maternity absence and family leave).

(3) The provisions in paragraph (1)(a)(ii) and (b)for an employee to be treated as if she had not been absent refer to her absence—

    (a) if her return is from an isolated period of statutory leave, since the beginning of that period;

    (b) if her return is from consecutive periods of statutory leave, since the beginning of the first such period.

19   Protection from detriment

(1) An employee is entitled under section 47C of the 1996 Act not to be subjected to any detriment by any act, or any deliberate failure to act, by her employer done for any of the reasons specified in paragraph (2).

(2) The reasons referred to in paragraph (1) are that the employee—

    (a)   is pregnant;

    (b)   has given birth to a child;

    (c)   is the subject of a relevant requirement, or a relevant recommendation, as defined by section 66(2) of the 1996 Act;

    (d)   took, sought to take or availed herself of the benefits of, ordinary maternity leave;

    (e)   took or sought to take—

        (i)   additional maternity leave,

        (ii)   parental leave, or

        (iii) time off under section 57A of the 1996 Act;

    (ee)   failed to return after a period of ordinary or additional maternity leave in a case where—

        (i)   the employer did not notify her, in accordance with regulation 7(6) and (7) or otherwise, of the date on which the period in question would end, and she reasonably believed that that period had not ended, or

        (ii)   the employer gave her less than 28 days' notice of the date on which the period in question would end, and it was not reasonably practicable for her to return on that date;

    (f)   declined to sign a workforce agreement for the purpose of these Regulations, or

    (g)   being—

        (i)   a representative of members of the workforce for the purposes of Schedule 1, or

        (ii)   a candidate in an election in which any person elected will, on being elected, become such a representative;

performed (or proposed to perform) any functions or activities as such a representative or candidate.

(3) For the purposes of paragraph (2)(d), a woman avails herself of the benefits of ordinary maternity leave if, during her ordinary maternity leave period, she avails herself of the benefit of any of the terms and conditions of her employment preserved by section 71 of the 1996 Act and regulation 9 during that period.

(4) Paragraph (1) does not apply in a case where the detriment in question amounts to dismissal within the meaning of Part X of the 1996 Act.

(5) Paragraph (2)(b) only applies where the act or failure to act takes place during the employee's ordinary or additional maternity leave period.

(6) For the purposes of paragraph (5)—

    (a) where an act extends over a period, the reference to the date of the act is a reference to the last day of that period, and

    (b) a failure to act is to be treated as done when it was decided on.

(7) For the purposes of paragraph (6), in the absence of evidence establishing the contrary an employer shall be taken to decide on a failure to act—

    (a) when he does an act inconsistent with doing the failed act, or

    (b) if he has done no such inconsistent act, when the period expires within which he might reasonably have been expected to do the failed act if it were to be done.

20   Unfair dismissal

(1) An employee who is dismissed is entitled under section 99 of the 1996 Act to be regarded for the purposes of Part X of that Act as unfairly dismissed if—

    (a) the reason or principal reason for the dismissal is of a kind specified in paragraph (3), or

    (b) the reason or principal reason for the dismissal is that the employee is redundant, and regulation 10 has not been complied with.

(2) An employee who is dismissed shall also be regarded for the purposes of Part X of the 1996 Act as unfairly dismissed if—

    (a) the reason (or, if more than one, the principal reason) for the dismissal is that the employee was redundant;

    (b) it is shown that the circumstances constituting the redundancy applied equally to one or more employees in the same undertaking who held positions similar to that held by the employee and who have not been dismissed by the employer, and

    (c) it is shown that the reason (or, if more than one, the principal reason) for which the employee was selected for dismissal was a reason of a kind specified in paragraph (3).

(3) The kinds of reason referred to in paragraphs (1) and (2) are reasons connected with—

    (a) the pregnancy of the employee;

    (b) the fact that the employee has given birth to a child;

    (c) the application of a relevant requirement, or a relevant recommendation, as defined by section 66(2) of the 1996 Act;

    (d) the fact that she took, sought to take or availed herself of the benefits of, ordinary maternity leave;

    (e) the fact that she took or sought to take—

        (i)   additional maternity leave;

        (ii) parental leave, or

        (iii) time off under section 57A of the 1996 Act;

    (ee) the fact that she failed to return after a period of ordinary or additional maternity leave in a case where—

        (i)   the employer did not notify her, in accordance with regulation 7(6) and (7) or otherwise, of the date on which the period in question would end, and she reasonably believed that that period had not ended, or

(ii) the employer gave her less than 28 days' notice of the date on which the period in question would end, and it was not reasonably practicable for her to return on that date;

(f) the fact that she declined to sign a workforce agreement for the purposes of these Regulations, or

(g) the fact that the employee, being—

(i) a representative of members of the workforce for the purposes of Schedule 1, or

(ii) a candidate in an election in which any person elected will, on being elected, become such a representative,

performed (or proposed to perform) any functions or activities as such a representative or candidate.

(4) Paragraphs (1)(b) and (3)(b) only apply where the dismissal ends the employee's ordinary or additional maternity leave period.

(5) Paragraph (3) of regulation 19 applies for the purposes of paragraph (3)(d) as it applies for the purpose of paragraph (2)(d) of that regulation.

(6) Paragraph (1) does not apply in relation to an employee if—

(a) immediately before the end of her additional maternity leave period (or, if it ends by reason of dismissal, immediately before the dismissal) the number of employees employed by her employer, added to the number employed by any associated employer of his, did not exceed five, and

(b) it is not reasonably practicable for the employer (who may be the same employer or a successor of his) to permit her to return to a job which is both suitable for her and appropriate for her to do in the circumstances or for an associated employer to offer her a job of that kind.

(7) Paragraph (1) does not apply in relation to an employee if—

(a) it is not reasonably practicable for a reason other than redundancy for the employer (who may be the same employer or a successor of his) to permit her to return to a job which is both suitable for her and appropriate for her to do in the circumstances;

(b) an associated employer offers her a job of that kind, and

(c) she accepts or unreasonably refuses that offer.

(8) Where on a complaint of unfair dismissal any question arises as to whether the operation of paragraph (1) is excluded by the provisions of paragraph (6) or (7), it is for the employer to show that the provisions in question were satisfied in relation to the complainant.

21 Contractual rights to maternity or parental leave

(1) This regulation applies where an employee is entitled to—

(a) ordinary maternity leave;

(b) additional maternity leave, or

(c) parental leave,

(referred to in paragraph (2) as a 'statutory right') and also to a right which corresponds to that right and which arises under the employee's contract of employment or otherwise.

(2) In a case where this regulation applies—

(a) the employee may not exercise the statutory right and the corresponding right separately but may, in taking the leave for which the two rights provide, take advantage of whichever right is, in any particular respect, the more favourable, and

(b) the provisions of the 1996 Act and of these Regulations relating to the statutory right apply, subject to any modifications necessary to give effect to any more favourable contractual terms, to the exercise of the composite right described in sub-paragraph (a) as they apply to the exercise of the statutory right.

22 [omitted]

SCHEDULE 1

WORKFORCE AGREEMENTS

1. An agreement is a workforce agreement for the purposes of these Regulations if the following conditions are satisfied—

    (a) the agreement is in writing;

    (b) it has effect for a specified period not exceeding five years;

    (c) it applies either—

        (i) to all of the relevant members of the workforce, or

        (ii) to all of the relevant members of the workforce who belong to a particular group;

    (d) the agreement is signed—

        (i) in the case of an agreement of the kind referred to in sub-paragraph (c)(i), by the representatives of the workforce, and in the case of an agreement of the kind referred to in sub-paragraph (c)(ii), by the representatives of the group to which the agreement applies (excluding, in either case, any representative not a relevant member of the workforce on the date on which the agreement was first made available for signature), or

        (ii) if the employer employed 20 or fewer employees on the date referred to in sub-paragraph (d)(i), either by the appropriate representatives in accordance with that sub-paragraph or by the majority of the employees employed by him; and

    (e) before the agreement was made available for signature, the employer provided all the employees to whom it was intended to apply on the date on which it came into effect with copies of the text of the agreement and such guidance as those employees might reasonably require in order to understand it in full.

2. For the purposes of this Schedule—

'a particular group' is a group of the relevant members of a workforce who undertake a particular function, work at a particular workplace or belong to a particular department or unit within their employer's business;

'relevant members of the workforce' are all of the employees employed by a particular employer, excluding any employee whose terms and conditions of employment are provided for, wholly or in part, in a collective agreement;

'representatives of the workforce' are employees duly elected to represent the relevant members of the workforce, 'representatives of the group' are employees duly elected to represent the members of a particular group, and representatives are 'duly elected' if the election at which they were elected satisfied the requirements of paragraph 3 of this Schedule.

3. The requirements concerning elections referred to in paragraph 2 are that—

    (a) the number of representatives to be elected is determined by the employer;

    (b) the candidates for election as representatives of the workforce are relevant members of the workforce, and the candidates for election as representatives of a group are members of the group;

    (c) no employee who is eligible to be a candidate is unreasonably excluded from standing for election;

    (d) all the relevant members of the workforce are entitled to vote for representatives of the workforce, and all the members of a particular group are entitled to vote for representatives of the group;

    (e) the employees entitled to vote may vote for as many candidates as there are representatives to be elected, and

(f) the election is conducted so as to secure that—
  (i) so far as is reasonably practicable, those voting do so in secret, and
  (ii) the votes given at the election are fairly and accurately counted.

Regulation 16   SCHEDULE 2

DEFAULT PROVISIONS INRESPECT OF PARENTAL LEAVE

Conditions of entitlement

1. An employee may not exercise any entitlement to parental leave unless—
  (a) he has complied with any request made by his employer to produce for the employer's inspection evidence of his entitlement, of the kind described in paragraph 2;
  (b) he has given his employer notice, in accordance with whichever of paragraphs 3 to 5 is applicable, of the period of leave he proposes to take, and
  (c) in a case where paragraph 6 applies, his employer has not postponed the period of leave in accordance with that paragraph.

2. The evidence to be produced for the purpose of paragraph 1(a) is such evidence as may reasonably be required of—
  (a) the employee's responsibility or expected responsibility for the child in respect of whom the employee proposes to take parental leave;
  (b) the child's date of birth or, in the case of a child who was placed with the employee for adoption, the date on which the placement began, and
  (c) in a case where the employee's right to exercise an entitlement to parental leave under regulation 15, or to take a particular period of leave under paragraph 7, depends upon whether the child is entitled to a disability living allowance, the child's entitlement to that allowance.

2A. Where regulation 13(1A) applies, and the employee's entitlement to parental leave arises out of a period of employment by a person other than the person who was his employer on 9th January 2002, the employee may not exercise the entitlement unless he has given his employer notice of that period of employment, and provided him with such evidence of it as the employer may reasonably require.

Notice to be given to employer

3. Except in a case where paragraph 4 or 5 applies, the notice required for the purpose of paragraph 1(b) is notice which—
  (a) specifies the dates on which the period of leave is to begin and end, and
  (b) is given to the employer at least 21 days before the date on which that period is to begin.

4. Where the employee is the father of the child in respect of whom the leave is to be taken, and the period of leave is to begin on the date on which the child is born, the notice required for the purpose of paragraph 1(b) is notice which—
  (a) specifies the expected week of childbirth and the duration of the period of leave, and
  (b) is given to the employer at least 21 days before the beginning of the expected week of childbirth.

5. Where the child in respect of whom the leave is to be taken is to be placed with the employee for adoption by him and the leave is to begin on the date of the placement, the notice required for the purpose of paragraph 1(b) is notice which—
  (a) specifies the week in which the placement is expected to occur and the duration of the period of leave, and

(b) is given to the employer at least 21 days before the beginning of that week, or, if that is not reasonably practicable, as soon as is reasonably practicable.

Postponement of leave

6. An employer may postpone a period of parental leave where—
   (a) neither paragraph 4 nor paragraph 5 applies, and the employee has accordingly given the employer notice in accordance with paragraph 3;
   (b) the employer considers that the operation of his business would be unduly disrupted if the employee took leave during the period identified in his notice;
   (c) the employer agrees to permit the employee to take a period of leave—
      (i) of the same duration as the period identified in the employee's notice,
      (ii) beginning on a date determined by the employer after consulting the employee, which is no later than six months after the commencement of that period, and
      (iii) ending before the date of the child's eighteenth birthday.
   (d) the employer gives the employee notice in writing of the postponement which—
      (i) states the reason for it, and
      (ii) specifies the dates on which the period of leave the employer agrees to permit the employee to take will begin and end, and
   (e) that notice is given to the employee not more than seven days after the employee's notice was given to the employer.

Minimum periods of leave

7. An employee may not take parental leave in a period other than the period which constitutes a week's leave for him under regulation 14 or a multiple of that period, except in a case where the child in respect of whom leave is taken is entitled to a disability living allowance.

Maximum annual leave allowance

8. An employee may not take more than four weeks' leave in respect of any individual child during a particular year.

9. For the purposes of paragraph 8, a year is the period of twelve months beginning—
   (a) except where sub-paragraph (b) applies, on the date on which the employee first became entitled to take parental leave in respect of the child in question, or
   (b) in a case where the employee's entitlement has been interrupted at the end of a period of continuous employment, on the date on which the employee most recently became entitled to take parental leave in respect of that child,
and each successive period of twelve months beginning on the anniversary of that date.

The Public Interest Disclosure (Compensation) Regulations 1999
(SI 1999 No. 1548)

3 Compensation

Sections 117 to 127A of the 1996 Act shall apply to compensation awarded, or a compensatory award made, to a person in a case where he is regarded as unfairly dismissed by virtue of section 103A or 105(6A) of the 1996 Act, with the following modifications—
   (a) as if, after section 124(1), there was inserted the following subsection—
      '(1A) Subsection (1) shall not apply to compensation awarded, or a compensatory award made, to a person in a case where he is regarded as unfairly dismissed by virtue of section 103A or 105(6A)'; and

(b) as if, in section 117(6)—
    (i) after paragraph (b), the word 'and' was omitted; and
    (ii) after paragraph (c), there was inserted 'and
(d) a dismissal where the reason (or, if more than one, the principal reason)—
    (i) in a redundancy case, for selecting the employee for dismissal, or
    (ii) otherwise, for the dismissal,
is that specified in section 103A'.

The Part-Time Workers (Prevention of Less Favourable Treatment) Regulations 2000
(SI 2000 No. 1551)

ARRANGEMENT OF REGULATIONS

PART I   GENERAL AND INTERPRETATION

PART II   RIGHTS AND REMEDIES

PART III   MISCELLANEOUS

PART IV   SPECIAL CLASSES OF PERSON

PART I   GENERAL AND INTERPRETATION

1 Citation, commencement and interpretation
(1) [omitted]
(2) In these Regulations—
'the 1996 Act' means the Employment Rights Act 1996;
'contract of employment' means a contract of service or of apprenticeship, whether express or implied, and (if it is express) whether oral or in writing;
'employee' means an individual who has entered into or works under or (except where a provision of these Regulations otherwise requires) where the employment has ceased, worked under a contract of employment;

'employer', in relation to any employee or worker, means the person by whom the employee or worker is or (except where a provision of these Regulations otherwise requires) where the employment has ceased, was employed;

'pro rata principle' means that where a comparable full-time worker receives or is entitled to receive pay or any other benefit, a part-time worker is to receive or be entitled to receive not less than the proportion of that pay or other benefit that the number of his weekly hours bears to the number of weekly hours of the comparable full-time worker;

'worker' means an individual who has entered into or works under or (except where a provision of these Regulations otherwise requires) where the employment has ceased, worked under—

(a) a contract of employment; or

(b) any other contract, whether express or implied and (if it is express) whether oral or in writing, whereby the individual undertakes to do or perform personally any work or services for another party to the contract whose status is not by virtue of the contract that of a client or customer of any profession or business undertaking carried on by the individual.

(3) In the definition of the pro rata principle and in regulations 3 and 4 'weekly hours' means the number of hours a worker is required to work under his contract of employment in a week in which he has no absences from work and does not work any overtime or, where the number of such hours varies according to a cycle, the average number of such hours.

2 Meaning of full-time worker, part-time worker and comparable full-time worker

(1) A worker is a full-time worker for the purpose of these Regulations if he is paid wholly or in part by reference to the time he works and, having regard to the custom and practice of the employer in relation to workers employed by the worker's employer under the same type of contract, is identifiable as a full-time worker.

(2) A worker is a part-time worker for the purpose of these Regulations if he is paid wholly or in part by reference to the time he works and, having regard to the custom and practice of the employer in relation to workers employed by the worker's employer under the same type of contract, is not identifiable as a full-time worker.

(3) For the purposes of paragraphs (1), (2) and (4), the following shall be regarded as being employed under different types of contract—

(a) employees employed under a contract that is not a contract of apprenticeship;

(b) employees employed under a contract of apprenticeship;

(c) workers who are not employees;

(d) any other description of worker that it is reasonable for the employer to treat differently from other workers on the ground that workers of that description have a different type of contract.

(4) A full-time worker is a comparable full-time worker in relation to a part-time worker if, at the time when the treatment that is alleged to be less favourable to the part-time worker takes place—

(a) both workers are—

    (i) employed by the same employer under the same type of contract, and

    (ii) engaged in the same or broadly similar work having regard, where relevant, to whether they have a similar level of qualification, skills and experience; and

(b) the full-time worker works or is based at the same establishment as the part-time worker or, where there is no full-time worker working or based at that establishment who satisfies the requirements of sub-paragraph (a), works or is based at a different establishment and satisfies those requirements.

3 Workers becoming part-time

(1) This regulation applies to a worker who—

(a) was identifiable as a full-time worker in accordance with regulation 2(1); and

(b) following a termination or variation of his contract, continues to work under a new or varied contract, whether of the same type or not, that requires him to work for a number of weekly hours that is lower than the number he was required to work immediately before the termination or variation.

(2) Notwithstanding regulation 2(4), regulation 5 shall apply to a worker to whom this regulation applies as if he were a part-time worker and as if there were a comparable full-time worker employed under the terms that applied to him immediately before the variation or termination.

(3) The fact that this regulation applies to a worker does not affect any right he may have under these Regulations by virtue of regulation 2(4).

4 Workers returning part-time after absence

(1) This regulation applies to a worker who—

(a) was identifiable as a full-time worker in accordance with regulation 2(1) immediately before a period of absence (whether the absence followed a termination of the worker's contract or not);

(b) returns to work for the same employer within a period of less than twelve months beginning with the day on which the period of absence started;

(c) returns to the same job or to a job at the same level under a contract, whether it is a different contract or a varied contract and regardless of whether it is of the same type, under which he is required to work for a number of weekly hours that is lower than the number he was required to work immediately before the period of absence.

(2) Notwithstanding regulation 2(4), regulation 5 shall apply to a worker to whom this regulation applies ('the returning worker') as if he were a part-time worker and as if there were a comparable full-time worker employed under—

(a) the contract under which the returning worker was employed immediately before the period of absence; or

(b) where it is shown that, had the returning worker continued to work under the contract mentioned in sub-paragraph (a) a variation would have been made to its term during the period of absence, the contract mentioned in that sub-paragraph including that variation.

(3) The fact that this regulation applies to a worker does not affect any right he may have under these Regulations by virtue of regulation 2(4).

PART II   RIGHTS AND REMEDIES

5 Less favourable treatment of part-time workers

(1) A part-time worker has the right not to be treated by his employer less favourably than the employer treats a comparable full-time worker—

(a) as regards the terms of his contract; or

(b) by being subjected to any other detriment by any act, or deliberate failure to act, of his employer.

(2) The right conferred by paragraph (1) applies only if—

(a) the treatment is on the ground that the worker is a part-time worker, and

(b) the treatment is not justified on objective grounds.

(3) In determining whether a part-time worker has been treated less favourably than a comparable full-time worker the pro rata principle shall be applied unless it is inappropriate.

(4) A part-time worker paid at a lower rate for overtime worked by him in a period than a comparable full-time worker is or would be paid for overtime worked by him in the same

period shall not, for that reason, be regarded as treated less favourably than the comparable full-time worker where, or to the extent that, the total number of hours worked by the part-time worker in the period, including overtime, does not exceed the number of hours the comparable full-time worker is required to work in the period, disregarding absences from work and overtime.

6 Right to receive a written statement of reasons for less favourable treatment

(1) If a worker who considers that his employer may have treated him in a manner which infringes a right conferred on him by regulation 5 requests in writing from his employer a written statement giving particulars of the reasons for the treatment, the worker is entitled to be provided with such a statement within twenty-one days of his request.

(2) A written statement under this regulation is admissible as evidence in any proceedings under these Regulations.

(3) If it appears to the tribunal in any proceedings under these Regulations—

    (a) that the employer deliberately, and without reasonable excuse, omitted to provide a written statement, or

    (b) that the written statement is evasive or equivocal,

it may draw any inference which it considers it just and equitable to draw, including an inference that the employer has infringed the right in question.

(4) This regulation does not apply where the treatment in question consists of the dismissal of an employee, and the employee is entitled to a written statement of reasons for his dismissal under section 92 of the 1996 Act.

7 Unfair dismissal and the right not to be subjected to detriment

(1) An employee who is dismissed shall be regarded as unfairly dismissed for the purposes of Part X of the 1996 Act if the reason (or, if more than one, the principal reason) for the dismissal is a reason specified in paragraph (3).

(2) A worker has the right not to be subjected to any detriment by any act, or any deliberate failure to act, by his employer done on a ground specified in paragraph (3).

(3) The reasons or, as the case may be, grounds are—

    (a) that the worker has—

        (i)   brought proceedings against the employer under these Regulations;

        (ii) requested from his employer a written statement of reasons under regulation 6;

        (iii) given evidence or information in connection with such proceedings brought by any worker;

        (iv) otherwise done anything under these Regulations in relation to the employer or any other person;

        (v) alleged that the employer had infringed these Regulations; or

        (vi) refused (or proposed to refuse) to forgo a right conferred on him by these Regulations; or

    (b) that the employer believes or suspects that the worker has done or intends to do any of the things mentioned in sub-paragraph (a).

(4) Where the reason or principal reason for dismissal or, as the case may be, ground for subjection to any act or deliberate failure to act, is that mentioned in paragraph (3)(a)(v), or (b) so far as it relates thereto, neither paragraph (1) nor paragraph (2) applies if the allegation made by the worker is false and not made in good faith.

(5) Paragraph (2) does not apply where the detriment in question amounts to the dismissal of an employee within the meaning of Part X of the 1996 Act.

8 Complaints to employment tribunals etc.

(1) Subject to regulation 7(5), a worker may present a complaint to an employment tribunal that his employer has infringed a right conferred on him by regulation 5 or 7(2).

(2) Subject to paragraph (3), an employment tribunal shall not consider a complaint under this regulation unless it is presented before the end of the period of three months (or, in a case to which regulation 13 applies, six months) beginning with the date of the less favourable treatment or detriment to which the complaint relates or, where an act or failure to act is part of a series of similar acts or failures comprising the less favourable treatment or detriment, the last of them.

(3) A tribunal may consider any such complaint which is out of time if, in all the circumstances of the case, it considers that it is just and equitable to do so.

(4) For the purposes of calculating the date of the less favourable treatment or detriment under paragraph (2)—

> (a) where a term in a contract is less favourable, that treatment shall be treated, subject to paragraph (b), as taking place on each day of the period during which the term is less favourable;
>
> (b) where an application relies on regulation 3 or 4 the less favourable treatment shall be treated as occurring on, and only on, in the case of regulation 3, the first day on which the applicant worked under the new or varied contract and, in the case of regulation 4, the day on which the applicant returned; and
>
> (c) a deliberate failure to act contrary to regulation 5 or 7(2) shall be treated as done when it was decided on.

(5) In the absence of evidence establishing the contrary, a person shall be taken for the purposes of paragraph (4)(c) to decide not to act—

> (a) when he does an act inconsistent with doing the failed act; or
>
> (b) if he has done no such inconsistent act, when the period expires within which he might reasonably have been expected to have done the failed act if it was to be done.

(6) Where a worker presents a complaint under this regulation it is for the employer to identify the ground for the less favourable treatment or detriment.

(7) Where an employment tribunal finds that a complaint presented to it under this regulation is well founded, it shall take such of the following steps as it considers just and equitable—

> (a) making a declaration as to the rights of the complainant and the employer in relation to the matters to which the complaint relates;
>
> (b) ordering the employer to pay compensation to the complainant;
>
> (c) recommending that the employer take, within a specified period, action appearing to the tribunal to be reasonable, in all the circumstances of the case, for the purpose of obviating or reducing the adverse effect on the complainant of any matter to which the complaint relates.

(8) [revoked]

(9) Where a tribunal orders compensation under paragraph (7)(b), the amount of the compensation awarded shall be such as the tribunal considers just and equitable in all the circumstances having regard to—

> (a) the infringement to which the complaint relates; and
>
> (b) any loss which is attributable to the infringement having regard, in the case of an infringement of the right conferred by regulation 5, to the pro rata principle except where it is inappropriate to do so.

(10) The loss shall be taken to include—

> (a) any expenses reasonably incurred by the complainant in consequence of the infringement; and
>
> (b) loss of any benefit which he might reasonably be expected to have had but for the infringement.

(11) Compensation in respect of treating a worker in a manner which infringes the right conferred on him by regulation 5 shall not include compensation for injury to feelings.

(12) In ascertaining the loss the tribunal shall apply the same rule concerning the duty of a person to mitigate his loss as applies to damages recoverable under the common law of England and Wales or (as the case may be) Scotland.

(13) Where the tribunal finds that the act, or failure to act, to which the complaint relates was to any extent caused or contributed to by action of the complainant, it shall reduce the amount of the compensation by such proportion as it considers just and equitable having regard to that finding.

(14) If the employer fails, without reasonable justification, to comply with a recommendation made by an employment tribunal under paragraph (7)(c) the tribunal may, if it thinks it just and equitable to do so—

(a) increase the amount of compensation required to be paid to the complainant in respect of the complaint, where an order was made under paragraph (7)(b); or

(b) make an order under paragraph (7)(b).

9 Restrictions on contracting out

Section 203 of the 1996 Act (restrictions on contracting out) shall apply in relation to these Regulations as if they were contained in that Act.

PART III   MISCELLANEOUS

10 [omitted]

11 Liability of employers and principals

(1) Anything done by a person in the course of his employment shall be treated for the purposes of these Regulations as also done by his employer, whether or not it was done with the employer's knowledge or approval.

(2) Anything done by a person as agent for the employer with the authority of the employer shall be treated for the purposes of these Regulations as also done by the employer.

(3) In proceedings under these Regulations against any person in respect of an act alleged to have been done by a worker of his, it shall be a defence for that person to prove that he took such steps as were reasonably practicable to prevent the worker from—

(a) doing that act; or

(b) doing, in the course of his employment, acts of that discription.

PART IV   SPECIAL CLASSES OF PERSON

12 Crown employment

(1) Subject to regulation 13, these Regulations have effect in relation to Crown employment and persons in Crown employment as they have effect in relation to other employment and other employees and workers.

(2) In paragraph (1) 'Crown employment' means employment under or for the purposes of a government department or any officer or body exercising on behalf of the Crown functions conferred by a statutory provision.

(3) For the purposes of the application of the provisions of these Regulations in relation to Crown employment in accordance with paragraph (1)—

(a) references to an employee and references to a worker shall be construed as references to a person in Crown employment to whom the definition of employee or, as the case may be, worker is appropriate; and

(b) references to a contract in relation to an employee and references to a contract in relation to a worker shall be construed as references to the terms of employment of a person in Crown employment to whom the definition of employee or, as the case may be, worker is appropriate.

13–17 [omitted]

The Trade Union Recognition
(Method of Collective Bargaining) Order 2000
(SI 2000 No. 1300)

2 Specification of method

The method specified for the purposes of paragraphs 31(3) and 63(2) of Schedule A1 to the Trade Union and Labour Relations (Consolidation) Act 1992 is the method set out under the heading 'the specified method' in the Schedule to this Order.

Article 2   THE SCHEDULE

PREAMBLE

The method specified below ('the specified method') is one by which collective bargaining might be conducted in the particular, and possibly rare, circumstances discussed in the following paragraph. The specified method is not designed to be applied as a model for voluntary procedural agreements between employers and unions. Because most voluntary agreements are not legally binding and are usually concluded in a climate of trust and co-operation, they do not need to be as prescriptive as the specified method. However, the Central Arbitration Committee ('CAC') must take the specified method into account when exercising its powers to impose a method of collective bargaining under paragraphs 31(3) and 63(2) of Schedule A1 to the Trade Union and Labour Relations (Consolidation) Act 1992. In exercising those powers the CAC may depart from the specified method to such extent as it thinks appropriate in the circumstances of individual cases.

Paragraph 31(3) provides for the CAC to impose a method of collective bargaining in cases where a union (or unions, where two or more unions act jointly) has been recognised by an employer by means of an award of the CAC under Part 1 of Schedule A1, but the employer and union(s) have been unable to agree a method of bargaining between themselves, or have failed to follow an agreed method. Paragraph 63(2) provides for the CAC to impose a bargaining method in cases where an employer and a union (or unions) have entered an agreement for recognition, as defined by paragraph 52 of Part II of Schedule A1, but cannot agree a method of bargaining, or have failed to follow the agreed method.

The bargaining method imposed by the CAC has effect as if it were a legally binding contract between the employer and the union(s). If one party believes the other is failing to respect the method, the first party may apply to the court for an order of specific performance, ordering the other party to comply with the method. Failure to comply with such an order could constitute contempt of court.

Once the CAC has imposed a bargaining method, the parties can vary it, including the fact that it is legally binding, by agreement provided that they do so in writing.

The fact that the CAC has imposed a method does not affect the rights of individual workers under either statute or their contracts of employment. For example, it does not prevent or limit the rights of individual workers to discuss, negotiate or agree with their employer terms of their contract of employment, which differ from the terms of any collective agreement into which the employer and the union may enter as a result of collective bargaining conducted by this method. Nor does the imposed method affect an individual's statutory entitlement to time off for trade union activities or duties.

In cases where the CAC imposes a bargaining method on the parties, the employer is separately obliged, in accordance with Section 70B of the Trade Union and Labour Relations (Consolidation) Act 1992 (as inserted by section 5 of the Employment Relations Act 1999), to consult union representatives periodically on his policy, actions and plans on training. The specified method does not discuss how such consultations should be organised.

The law confers certain entitlements on independent trade unions which are recognised for collective bargaining purposes. For example, employers must disclose, on request, certain types of information to the representatives of the recognised unions. The fact that the CAC has imposed a bargaining method does not affect these existing statutory entitlements.

THE SPECIFIED METHOD

The Parties

1. The method shall apply in each case to two parties, who are referred to here as the 'employer' and the 'union'. Unless the text specifies otherwise, the term 'union' should be read to mean 'unions' in cases where two or more unions are jointly recognised.

The Purpose

2. The purpose is to specify a method by which the employer and the union conduct collective bargaining concerning the pay, hours and holidays of the workers comprising the bargaining unit.

3. The employer shall not grant the right to negotiate pay, hours and holidays to any other union in respect of the workers covered by this method.

The Joint Negotiating Body

4. The employer and the union shall establish a Joint Negotiating Body (JNB) to discuss and negotiate the pay, hours and holidays of the workers comprising the bargaining unit. No other body or group shall undertake collective bargaining on the pay, hours and holidays of these workers, unless the employer and the union so agree.

JNB Membership

5. The membership of the JNB shall usually comprise three employer representatives (who together shall constitute the Employer Side of the JNB) and three union representatives (who together shall constitute the Union Side of the JNB). Each union recognised by the employer in respect of the bargaining unit shall be entitled to one seat at least. To meet this requirement, the Union Side may need to be larger than three and in this eventuality the employer shall be entitled to increase his representation on the JNB by the same number, if he wishes.

6. The employer shall select those individuals who comprise the Employer Side. The individuals must either be those who take the final decisions within the employer's organisation in respect of the pay, hours and holidays of the workers in the bargaining unit or who are expressly authorised by the employer to make recommendations directly to those who take such final decisions. Unless it would be unreasonable to do so, the employer shall select as a representative the most senior person responsible for employment relations in the bargaining unit.

7. The union shall select those individuals who comprise the Union Side in accordance with its own rules and procedures. The representatives must either be individuals employed by the employer or individuals employed by the union who are officials of the union within the meaning of sections 1 and 119 of the Trade Union and Labour Relations (Consolidation) Act 1992 ('the 1992 Act').

8. The JNB shall determine their own rules in respect of the attendance at JNB meetings of observers and substitutes who deputise for JNB members.

Officers

9. The Employer Side shall select one of its members to act as its Chairman and one to act as its Secretary. The Union Side shall select one of its members to act as its Chairman and one

to act as its Secretary. The same person may perform the roles of Chairman and Secretary of a Side.

10. For the twelve months from the date of the JNB's first meeting, meetings of the JNB shall be chaired by the Chairman of the Employer Side. The Chairman of the Union Side shall chair the JNB's meetings for the following twelve months. The chairmanship of JNB meetings will alternate in the same way thereafter at intervals of twelve months. In the absence of the person who should chair JNB meetings, a JNB meeting shall be chaired by another member of that person's Side.

11. The Secretary of the Employer Side shall act as Secretary to the JNB. He shall circulate documentation and agendas in advance of JNB meetings, arrange suitable accommodation for meetings, notify members of meetings and draft the written record of JNB meetings. The Secretary of the Employer Side shall work closely with the Secretary of the Union Side in the discharge of these duties, disclosing full information about his performance of these tasks.

JNB Organisation

12. Draft agendas shall be circulated at least three working days in advance of JNB meetings. The draft record of JNB meetings shall be circulated within ten working days of the holding of meetings for approval at the next JNB meeting. The record does not need to be a verbatim account, but should fully describe the conclusions reached and the actions to be taken.

13. Subject to the timetable of meetings stipulated in paragraphs 15, 17, 20 and 28 below, the date, timing and location of meetings shall be arranged by the JNB's Secretary, in full consultation with the Secretary of the Union Side, to ensure maximum attendance at meetings. A meeting of the JNB shall be quorate if 50% or more of each Side's members (or, where applicable, their substitutes) are in attendance.

Bargaining Procedure

14. The union's proposals for adjustments to pay, hours and holidays shall be dealt with on an annual basis, unless the two Sides agree a different bargaining period.

15. The JNB shall conduct these negotiations for each bargaining round according to the following staged procedure.

Step 1—The union shall set out in writing, and send to the employer, its proposals (the 'claim') to vary the pay, hours and holidays, specifying which aspects it wants to change. In its claim, the union shall set out the reasons for its proposals, together with the main supporting evidence at its disposal at the time. In cases where there is no established annual date when the employer reviews the pay, hours and holidays of all the workers in the bargaining unit, the union shall put forward its first claim within three months of this method being imposed (and by the same date in subsequent rounds). Where such a common review date is established, the union shall submit its first claim at least a month in advance of that date (and by the same date in subsequent rounds). In either case, the employer and the union may agree a different date by which the claim should be submitted each year. If the union fails to submit its claim by this date, then the procedure shall be ended for the bargaining round in question. Exceptionally, the union may submit a late claim without this penalty if its work on the claim was delayed while the Central Arbitration Committee considered a relevant complaint by the union of failure by the employer to disclose information for collective bargaining purposes.

Step 2—Within ten working days of the Employer Side's receipt of the union's letter, a quorate meeting of the JNB shall be held to discuss the claim. At this meeting, the Union Side shall explain its claim and answer any reasonable questions arising to the best of its ability.

Step 3—

    (a) Within fifteen working days immediately following the Step 2 meeting, the employer shall either accept the claim in full or write to the union responding to its claim. If the Employer Side requests it, a quorate meeting of the JNB shall be held within the fifteen day period to enable the employer to present this written response directly to the Union Side. In explaining the basis of his response, the employer shall set out in this written communication all relevant information in his possession. In particular, the written communication shall contain information costing each element of the claim and describing the business consequences, particularly any staffing implications, unless the employer is not required to disclose such information for any of the reasons specified in section 182(1) of the 1992 Act. The basis of these estimated costs and effects, including the main assumptions that the employer has used, shall be set out in the communication. In determining what information is disclosed as relevant, the employer shall be under no greater obligation that he is under the general duty imposed on him by sections 181 and 182 of the 1992 Act to disclose information for the purposes of collective bargaining.

    (b) If the response contains any counter-proposals, the written communication shall set out the reasons for making them, together with the supporting evidence. The letter shall provide information estimating the costs and staffing consequences of implementing each element of the counter proposals, unless the employer is not required to disclose such information for any of the reasons specified in section 182(1) of the 1992 Act.

Step 4—Within ten working days of the Union Side's receipt of the employer's written communication, a further quorate meeting of the JNB shall be held to discuss the employer's response. At this meeting, the Employer Side shall explain its response and answer any reasonable questions arising to the best of its ability.

Step 5—If no agreement is reached at the Step 4 meeting (or the last of such meetings if more than one is held at that stage in the procedure), another quorate meeting of the JNB shall be held within ten working days. The union may bring to this meeting a maximum of two other individuals employed by the union who are officials within the meaning of the sections 1 and 119 of the 1992 Act. The employer may bring to the meeting a maximum of two other individuals who are employees or officials of an employer's organisation to which the employer belongs. These additional persons shall be allowed to contribute to the meeting, as if they were JNB members.

Step 6—If no agreement is reached at the Step 5 meeting (or the last of such meetings if more than one meeting is held at that stage in the procedure), within five working days the employer and the union shall consider, separately or jointly, consulting ACAS about the prospect of ACAS helping them to find a settlement of their differences through conciliation. In the event that both parties agree to invite ACAS to conciliate, both parties shall give such assistance to ACAS as is necessary to enable it to carry out the conciliation efficiently and effectively.

16. The parties shall set aside half a working day for each JNB meeting, unless the Employer Side Chairman and the Union Side Chairman agree a different length of time for the meeting. Unless it is essential to do otherwise, meetings shall be held during the normal working time of most union members of the JNB. Meetings may be adjourned, if both Sides agree. Additional meetings at any point in the procedure may be arranged, if both Sides agree. In addition, if the Employer Side requests it, a meeting of the JNB shall be held before the union has submitted its claim or before the employer is required to respond, enabling the Employer Side to explain the business context within which the employer shall assess the claim.

17. The employer shall not vary the contractual terms affecting the pay, hours or holidays of workers in the bargaining unit, unless he has first discussed his proposals with the

union. Such proposals shall normally be made by the employer in the context of his consideration of the union's claim at Steps 3 or 4. If, however, the employer has not tabled his proposals during that process and he wishes to make proposals before the next bargaining round commences, he must write to the union setting out his proposals and the reasons for making them, together with the supporting evidence. The letter shall provide information estimating the costs and staffing consequences of implementing each element of the proposals, unless the employer is not required to disclose such information for any of the reasons specified in section 182(1) of the 1992 Act. A quorate meeting of the JNB shall be held within five working days of the Union Side's receipt of the letter. If there is a failure to resolve the issue at that meeting, then meetings shall be arranged, and steps shall be taken, in accordance with Steps 5 and 6 of the above procedure.

18. Paragraph 17 does not apply to terms in the contract of an individual worker where that worker has agreed that the terms may be altered only by direct negotiation between the worker and the employer.

Collective Agreements

19. Any agreements affecting the pay, hours and holidays of workers in the bargaining unit, which the employer and the union enter following negotiations, shall be set down in writing and signed by the Chairman of the Employer Side and by the Chairman of the Union Side or, in their absence, by another JNB member on their respective Sides.

20. If either the employer or union consider that there has been a failure to implement the agreement, then that party can request in writing a meeting of the JNB to discuss the alleged failure. A quorate meeting shall be held within five working days of the receipt of the request by the JNB Secretary. If there is a failure to resolve the issue at that meeting, then meetings shall be arranged, and steps shall be taken, in accordance with Steps 5 and 6 of the above procedure.

Facilities and Time Off

21. If they are employed by the employer, union members of the JNB:
   —shall be given paid time off by the employer to attend JNB meetings;
   —shall be given paid time off by the employer to attend a two hour pre-meeting of the Union Side before each JNB meeting; and shall be given paid time off by the employer to hold a day-long meeting to prepare the claim at Step 1 in the bargaining procedure.
The union members of the JNB shall schedule such meetings at times which minimise the effect on production and services. In arranging these meetings, the union members of the JNB shall provide the employer and their line management with as much notice as possible and give details of the purpose of the time off, the intended location of the meeting and the timing and duration of the time off. The employer shall provide adequate heating and lighting for these meetings, and ensure that they are held in private.

22. If they are not employed by the employer, union members of the JNB or other union officials attending JNB meetings shall be given sufficient access to the employer's premises to allow them to attend Union Side pre-meetings, JNB meetings and meetings of the bargaining unit as specified in paragraph 23.

23. The employer shall agree to the union's reasonable request to hold meetings with members of the bargaining unit on company premises to discuss the Step 1 claim, the employer's offer or revisions to either. The request shall be made at least three working days in advance of the proposed meeting. However, the employer is not required to provide such facilities, if the employer does not possess available premises which can be used for meetings on the scale suggested by the union. The employer shall provide adequate heating and lighting for meetings, and ensure that the meeting is held in private. Where such meetings are held in working time, the employer is under no obligation to pay individuals for the time

off. Where meetings take place outside normal working hours, they should be arranged at a time which is otherwise convenient for the workers.

24. Where resources permit, the employer shall make available to the Union Side of the JNB such typing, copying and word-processing facilities as it needs to conduct its business in private.

25. Where resources permit, the employer shall set aside a room for the exclusive use of the Union Side of the JNB. The room shall possess a secure cabinet and a telephone.

26. In respect of issues which are not otherwise specified in this method, the employer and the union shall have regard to the guidance issued in the ACAS Code of Practice on Time Off for Trade Union Duties and Activities and ensure that there is no unwarranted or unjustified failure to abide by it.

Disclosure of Information

27. The employer and the union shall have regard to the ACAS Code of Practice on the Disclosure of Information to Trade Unions for Collective Bargaining Purposes and ensure that there is no unwarranted or unjustified failure to abide by it in relation to the bargaining arrangements specified by this method.

Revision of the Method

28. The employer or the union may request in writing a meeting of the JNB to discuss revising any element of this method, including its status as a legally binding contract. A quorate meeting of the JNB shall be held within ten working days of the receipt of the request by the JNB Secretary. This meeting shall be held in accordance with the same arrangements for the holding of other JNB meetings.

General

29. The employer and the union shall take all reasonable steps to ensure that this method to conduct collective bargaining is applied efficiently and effectively.

30. The definition of a 'working day' used in this method is any day other than a Saturday or a Sunday, Christmas Day or Good Friday, or a day which is a bank holiday.

31. All time limits mentioned in this method may be varied on any occasion, if both the employer and the union agree.

The Fixed-term Employees (Prevention of Less Favourable Treatment) Regulations 2002
(SI 2002 No. 2034)

ARRANGEMENT OF REGULATIONS

PART I   GENERAL AND INTERPRETATION

PART II RIGHTS AND REMEDIES

PART III   MISCELLANEOUS

PART V   EXCLUSIONS

SCHEDULE I   WORKFORCE AGREEMENTS

PART I   GENERAL AND INTERPRETATION

Citation, commencement and interpretation

1.—(1) [omitted]

(2) In these Regulations—

'the 1996 Act' means the Employment Rights Act 1996; 'collective agreement' means a collective agreement within the meaning of section 178 of the Trade Union and Labour Relations (Consolidation) Act 1992; the trade union parties to which are independent trade unions within the meaning of section 5 of that Act;

'employer', in relation to any employee, means the person by whom the employee is (or, where the employment has ceased, was) employed;

'fixed-term contract' means a contract of employment that, under its provisions determining how it will terminate in the normal course, will terminate—

    (a) on the expiry of a specific term,

    (b) on the completion of a particular task, or

    (c) on the occurrence or non-occurrence of any other specific event other than the attainment by the employee of any normal and bona fide retiring age in the establishment for an employee holding the position held by him,

and any reference to 'fixed-term' shall be construed accordingly;

'fixed-term employee' means an employee who is employed under a fixed-term contract;

'permanent employee' means an employee who is not employed under a fixed-term contract, and any reference to 'permanent employment' shall be construed accordingly;

'pro rata principle' means that where a comparable permanent employee receives or is entitled to pay or any other benefit, a fixed-term employee is to receive or be entitled to such proportion of that pay or other benefit as is reasonable in the circumstances having regard to the length of his contract of employment and to the terms on which the pay or other benefit is offered;

'renewal' includes extension and references to renewing a contract shall be construed accordingly;

'workforce agreement' means an agreement between an employer and his employees or their representatives in respect of which the conditions set out in Schedule 1 to these Regulations are satisfied.

Comparable employees

2.—(1) For the purposes of these Regulations, an employee is a comparable permanent employee in relation to a fixed-term employee if, at the time when the treatment that is alleged to be less favourable to the fixed-term employee takes place,

    (a) both employees are—
       (i) employed by the same employer, and
       (ii) engaged in the same or broadly similar work having regard, where relevant, to whether they have a similar level of qualification and skills; and
    (b) the permanent employee works or is based at the same establishment as the fixed-term employee or, where there is no comparable permanent employee working or based at that establishment who satisfies the requirements of sub-paragraph (a), works or is based at a different establishment and satisfies those requirements.

(2) For the purposes of paragraph (1), an employee is not a comparable permanent employee if his employment has ceased.

PART II   RIGHTS AND REMEDIES

Less favourable treatment of fixed-term employees

3.—(1) A fixed-term employee has the right not to be treated by his employer less favourably than the employer treats a comparable permanent employee—
    (a) as regards the terms of his contract; or
    (b) by being subjected to any other detriment by any act, or deliberate failure to act, of his employer.

(2) Subject to paragraphs (3) and (4), the right conferred by paragraph (1) includes in particular the right of the fixed-term employee in question not to be treated less favourably than the employer treats a comparable permanent employee in relation to—
    (a) any period of service qualification relating to any particular condition of service,
    (b) the opportunity to receive training, or
    (c) the opportunity to secure any permanent position in the establishment.

(3) The right conferred by paragraph (1) applies only if—
    (a) the treatment is on the ground that the employee is a fixed-term employee, and
    (b) the treatment is not justified on objective grounds.

(4) Paragraph (3)(b) is subject to regulation 4.

(5) In determining whether a fixed-term employee has been treated less favourably than a comparable permanent employee, the pro rata principle shall be applied unless it is inappropriate.

(6) In order to ensure that an employee is able to exercise the right conferred by paragraph (1) as described in paragraph (2)(c) the employee has the right to be informed by his employer of available vacancies in the establishment.

(7) For the purposes of paragraph (6) an employee is 'informed by his employer' only if the vacancy is contained in an advertisement which the employee has a reasonable opportunity of reading in the course of his employment or the employee is given reasonable notification of the vacancy in some other way.

Objective justification

4.—(1) Where a fixed-term employee is treated by his employer less favourably than the employer treats a comparable permanent employee as regards any term of his contract, the treatment in question shall be regarded for the purposes of regulation 3(3)(b) as justified on objective grounds if the terms of the fixed-term employee's contract of employment, taken as a whole, are at least as favourable as the terms of the comparable permanent employee's contract of employment.

(2) Paragraph (1) is without prejudice to the generality of regulation 3(3)(b).

Right to receive a written statement of reasons for less favourable treatment

5.—(1) If an employee who considers that his employer may have treated him in a manner which infringes a right conferred on him by regulation 3 requests in writing from his employer a written statement giving particulars of the reasons for the treatment, the employee is entitled to be provided with such a statement within twenty-one days of his request.

(2) A written statement under this regulation is admissible as evidence in any proceedings under these Regulations.

(3) If it appears to the tribunal in any proceedings under these Regulations—

(a) that the employer deliberately, and without reasonable excuse, omitted to provide a written statement, or

(b) that the written statement is evasive or equivocal,

it may draw any inference which it considers it just and equitable to draw, including an inference that the employer has infringed the right in question.

(4) This regulation does not apply where the treatment in question consists of the dismissal of an employee, and the employee is entitled to a written statement of reasons for his dismissal under section 92 of the 1996 Act.

Unfair dismissal and the right not to be subjected to detriment

6.—(1) An employee who is dismissed shall be regarded as unfairly dismissed for the purposes of Part 10 of the 1996 Act if the reason (or, if more than one, the principal reason) for the dismissal is a reason specified in paragraph (3).

(2) An employee has the right not to be subjected to any detriment by any act, or any deliberate failure to act, of his employer done on a ground specified in paragraph (3).

(3) The reasons or, as the case may be, grounds are—

(a) that the employee—

(i) brought proceedings against the employer under these Regulations;

(ii) requested from his employer a written statement under regulation 5 or regulation 9;

(iii) gave evidence or information in connection with such proceedings brought by any employee;

(iv) otherwise did anything under these Regulations in relation to the employer or any other person;

(v) alleged that the employer had infringed these Regulations;

(vi) refused (or proposed to refuse) to forgo a right conferred on him by these Regulations;

(vii) declined to sign a workforce agreement for the purposes of these Regulations, or

(viii) being—

(aa) a representative of members of the workforce for the purposes of Schedule 1, or

(bb) a candidate in an election in which any person elected will, on being elected, become such a representative,

performed (or proposed to perform) any functions or activities as such a representative or candidate, or

(b) that the employer believes or suspects that the employee has done or intends to do any of the things mentioned in sub-paragraph (a).

(4) Where the reason or principal reason for dismissal or, as the case may be, ground for subjection to any act or deliberate failure to act, is that mentioned in paragraph (3)(a)(v), or (b) so far as it relates thereto, neither paragraph (1) nor paragraph (2) applies if the allegation made by the employee is false and not made in good faith.

(5) Paragraph (2) does not apply where the detriment in question amounts to dismissal within the meaning of Part 10 of the 1996 Act.

Complaints to employment tribunals etc.

7.—(1) An employee may present a complaint to an employment tribunal that his employer has infringed a right conferred on him by regulation 3, or (subject to regulation 6(5)), regulation 6(2).

(2)–(5) [omitted]

(6) Where an employee presents a complaint under this regulation in relation to a right conferred on him by regulation 3 or 6(2) it is for the employer to identify the ground for the less favourable treatment or detriment.

(7) Where an employment tribunal finds that a complaint presented to it under this regulation is well founded, it shall take such of the following steps as it considers just and equitable—

(a) making a declaration as to the rights of the complaint and the employer in relation to the matters to which the complaint relates;

(b) ordering the employer to pay compensation to the complainant;

(c) recommending that the employer take, within a specified period, action appearing to the tribunal to be reasonable, in all the circumstances of the case, for the purpose of obviating or reducing the adverse effect on the complainant of any matter to which the complaint relates.

(8) Where a tribunal orders compensation under paragraph (7)(b), the amount of the compensation awarded shall be such as the tribunal considers just and equitable in all the circumstances having regard to—

(a) the infringement to which the complaint relates, and

(b) any loss which is attributable to the infringement.

(9) The loss shall be taken to include—

(a) any expenses reasonably incurred by the complainant in consequence of the infringement, and

(b) loss of any benefit which he might reasonably be expected to have had but for the infringement.

(10) Compensation in respect of treating an employee in a manner which infringes the right conferred on him by regulation 3 shall not include compensation for injury to feelings.

(11) In ascertaining the loss the tribunal shall apply the same rule concerning the duty of a person to mitigate his loss as applies to damages recoverable under the common law of England and Wales or (as the case may be) the law of Scotland.

(12) Where the tribunal finds that the act, or failure to act, to which the complaint relates was to any extent caused or contributed to by action of the complainant, it shall reduce the amount of the compensation by such proportion as it considers just and equitable having regard to that finding.

(13) If the employer fails, without reasonable justification, to comply with a recommendation made by an employment tribunal under paragraph (7)(c) the tribunal may, if it thinks it just and equitable to do so—

(a) increase the amount of compensation required to be paid to the complainant in respect of the complaint, where an order was made under paragraph (7)(b); or

(b) make an order under paragraph (7)(b).

Successive fixed-term contracts

8.—(1) This regulation applies where—

(a) an employee is employed under a contract purporting to be a fixed-term contract, and

(b) the contract mentioned in sub-paragraph (a) has previously been renewed, or the employee has previously been employed on a fixed-term contract before the start of the contract mentioned in sub-paragraph (a).

(2) Where this regulation applies then, with effect from the date specified in paragraph (3), the provision of the contract mentioned in paragraph (1)(a) that restricts the duration of the contract shall be of no effect, and the employee shall be a permanent employee, if—

(a) the employee has been continuously employed under the contract mentioned in paragraph 1(a), or under that contract taken with a previous fixed-term contract, for a period of four years or more, and

    (b) the employment of the employee under a fixed-term contract was not justified on objective grounds—
       (i) where the contract mentioned in paragraph (1)(a) has been renewed, at the time when it was last renewed;
       (ii) where that contract has not been renewed, at the time when it was entered into.

(3) The date referred to in paragraph (2) is whichever is the later of—
    (a) the date on which the contract mentioned in paragraph (1)(a) was entered into or last renewed, and
    (b) the date on which the employee acquired four years' continuous employment.

(4) For the purposes of this regulation Chapter 1 of Part 14 of the 1996 Act shall apply in determining whether an employee has been continuously employed, and any period of continuous employment falling before the 10th July 2002 shall be disregarded.

(5) A collective agreement or a workforce agreement may modify the application of paragraphs (1) to (3) of this regulation in relation to any employee or specified description of employees, by substituting for the provisions of paragraph (2) or paragraph (3), or for the provisions of both of those paragraphs, one or more different provisions which, in order to prevent abuse arising from the use of successive fixed-term contracts, specify one or more of the following—
    (a) the maximum total period for which the employee or employees of that description may be continuously employed on a fixed-term contract or on successive fixed-term contracts;
    (b) the maximum number of successive fixed-term contracts and renewals of such contracts under which the employee or employees of that description may be employed; or
    (c) objective grounds justifying the renewal of fixed-term contracts, or the engagement of the employee or employees of that description under successive fixed-term contracts,
and those provisions shall have effect in relation to that employee or an employee of that description as if they were contained in paragraphs (2) and (3).

Right to receive written statement of variation

9.—(1) If an employee who considers that, by virtue of regulation 8, he is a permanent employee requests in writing from his employer a written statement confirming that his contract is no longer fixed-term or that he is now a permanent employee, he is entitled to be provided, within twenty-one days of his request, with either—
    (a) such a statement, or
    (b) a statement giving reasons why his contract remains fixed-term.

(2) If the reasons stated under paragraph (1)(b) include an assertion that there were objective grounds for the engagement of the employee under a fixed-term contract, or the renewal of such a contract, the statement shall include a statement of those grounds.

(3) A written statement under this regulation is admissible as evidence in any proceedings before a court, an employment tribunal and the Commissioners of the Inland Revenue.

(4) If it appears to the court or tribunal in any proceedings—
    (a) that the employer deliberately, and without reasonable excuse, omitted to provide a written statement, or
    (b) that the written statement is evasive or equivocal,
it may draw any inference which it considers it just and equitable to draw.

(5) An employee who considers that, by virtue of regulation 8, he is a permanent employee may present an application to an employment tribunal for a declaration to that effect.

(6) No application may be made under paragraph (5) unless—

(a) the employee in question has previously requested a statement under paragraph (1) and the employer has either failed to provide a statement or given a statement of reasons under paragraph (1)(b), and

(b) the employee is at the time the application is made employed by the employer.

PART III   MISCELLANEOUS

Restrictions on contracting out

10. Section 203 of the 1996 Act (restrictions on contracting out) shall apply in relation to these Regulations as if they were contained in that Act.

11. [omitted]

Liability of employers and principals

12.—(1) Anything done by a person in the course of his employment shall be treated for the purposes of these Regulations as also done by his employer, whether or not it was done with the employer's knowledge or approval.

(2) Anything done by a person as agent for the employer with the authority of the employer shall be treated for the purposes of these Regulations as also done by the employer.

(3) In proceedings under these Regulations against any person in respect of an act alleged to have been done by an employee of his, it shall be a defence for that person to prove that he took such steps as were reasonably practicable to prevent the employee from—

(a) doing that act, or

(b) doing, in the course of his employment, acts of that description.

13.–17. [omitted]

PART V   EXCLUSIONS

18. [omitted]

Agency workers

19.—(1) These Regulations shall not have effect in relation to employment under a fixed-term contract where the employee is an agency worker.

(2) In this regulation 'agency worker' means any person who is supplied by an employment business to do work for another person under a contract or other arrangements made between the employment business and the other person.

(3) In this regulation 'employment business' means the business (whether or not carried on with a view to profit and whether or not carried on in conjunction with any other business) of supplying persons in the employment of the person carrying on the business, to act for, and under the control of, other persons in any capacity.

20. [omitted]

Regulations 1 and 8   SCHEDULE I

WORKFORCE AGREEMENTS

1. An agreement is a workforce agreement for the purposes of these Regulations if the following conditions are satisfied—

(a) the agreement is in writing;

(b) it has effect for a specified period not exceeding five years;

(c) it applies either—

(i)   to all of the relevant members of the workforce, or

(ii) to all of the relevant members of the workforce who belong to a particular group;

(d) the agreement is signed—
  (i) in the case of an agreement of the kind referred to in sub-paragraph (c)(i), by the representatives of the workforce, and in the case of an agreement of the kind referred to in sub-paragraph (c)(ii) by the representatives of the group to which the agreement applies (excluding, in either case, any representative not a relevant member of the workforce on the date on which the agreement was first made available for signature), or
  (ii) if the employer employed 20 or fewer employees on the date referred to in sub-paragraph (d)(i), either by the appropriate representatives in accordance with that sub-paragraph or by the majority of the employees employed by him;
(e) before the agreement was made available for signature, the employer provided all the employees to whom it was intended to apply on the date on which it came into effect with copies of the text of the agreement and such guidance as those employees might reasonably require in order to understand it fully.

2. For the purposes of this Schedule—'a particular group' is a group of the relevant members of a workforce who undertake a particular function, work at a particular workplace or belong to a particular department or unit within their employer's business;

'relevant members of the workforce' are all of the employees employed by a particular employer, excluding any employee whose terms and conditions of employment are provided for, wholly or in part, in a collective agreement;

'representatives of the workforce' are employees duly elected to represent the relevant members of the workforce, 'representatives of the group' are employees duly elected to represent the members of a particular group, and representatives are 'duly elected' if the election at which they were elected satisfied the requirements of paragraph 3 of this Schedule.

3. The requirements concerning elections referred to in paragraph 2 are that—
(a) the number of representatives to be elected is determined by the employer;
(b) the candidates for election as representatives of the workforce are relevant members of the workforce, and the candidates for election as representatives of a group are members of that group;
(c) no employee who is eligible to be a candidate is unreasonably excluded from standing for election;
(d) all the relevant members of the workforce are entitled to vote for representatives of the workforce, and all the members of a particular group are entitled to vote for representatives of the group;
(e) the employees entitled to vote may vote for as many candidates as there are representatives to be elected;
(f) the election is conducted so as to secure that—
  (i) so far as is reasonably practicable, those voting do so in secret, and
  (ii) the votes given at the election are fairly and accurately counted.

The Flexible Working (Eligibility, Complaints and Remedies) Regulations 2002
(SI 2002 No. 3236)

Entitlement to request a contract variation

3.—(1) An employee is entitled to make an application to his employer for a contract variation if he—
(a) has been continuously employed for a period of not less than 26 weeks;

(b) is either—
    (i) the mother, father, adopter, guardian or foster parent of the child or;
    (ii) married to, the civil partner or the partner of the child's mother, father, adopter, guardian or foster parent;
(c) has, or expects to have responsibility for the upbringing of the child.

(2) The reference in paragraph (1) to a period of continuous employment is to a period computed in accordance with Chapter 1 of Part 14 of the 1996 Act, as if that paragraph were a provision of that Act.

Compensation

7. The maximum amount of compensation that an employment tribunal may award under section 80I of the 1996 Act where it finds a complaint by an employee under section 80H of the Act well-founded is 8 weeks' pay.

The Paternity and Adoption Leave Regulations 2002
(SI 2002 No. 2788)

PART I GENERAL

1. [omitted]

Interpretation

2.—(1) In these Regulations—
'the 1996 Act' means the Employment Rights Act 1996;
'additional adoption leave' means leave under section 75B of the 1996 Act;
'additional maternity leave' means leave under section 73 of the 1996 Act;
'adopter', in relation to a child, means a person who has been matched with the child for adoption, or, in a case where two people have been matched jointly, whichever of them has elected to be the child's adopter for the purposes of these Regulations;
'adoption agency' has the meaning given, in relation to England and Wales, by section 1(4) of the Adoption Act 1976 and, in relation to Scotland, by section 1(4) of the Adoption (Scotland) Act 1978;
'adoption leave' means ordinary or additional adoption leave;
'child' means a person who is, or when placed with an adopter for adoption was, under the age of 18;
'contract of employment' means a contract of service or apprenticeship, whether express or implied, and (if it is express) whether oral or in writing;
'employee' means an individual who has entered into or works under (or, where the employment has ceased, worked under) a contract of employment;
'employer' means the person by whom an employee is (or, where the employment has ceased, was) employed;
'expected week', in relation to the birth of a child, means the week, beginning with midnight between Saturday and Sunday, in which it is expected that the child will be born;
'ordinary adoption leave' means leave under section 75A of the 1996 Act; 'parental leave' means leave under regulation 13(1) of the Maternity and Parental Leave etc. Regulations 1999;
'partner', in relation to a child's mother or adopter, means a person (whether of a different sex or the same sex) who lives with the mother or adopter and the child in an enduring family relationship but is not a relative of the mother or adopter of a kind specified in paragraph (2);
'paternity leave' means leave under regulation 4 or regulation 8 of these Regulations;
'statutory leave' means leave provided for in Part 8 of the 1996 Act.

(2) The relatives of a child's mother or adopter referred to in the definition of 'partner' in paragraph (1) are the mother's or adopter's parent, grandparent, sister, brother, aunt or uncle.

(3) References to relationships in paragraph (2)—

    (a) are to relationships of the full blood or half blood or, in the case of an adopted person, such of those relationships as would exist but for the adoption, and

    (b) include the relationship of a child with his adoptive, or former adoptive, parents,

but do not include any other adoptive relationships.

(4) For the purposes of these Regulations—

    (a) a person is matched with a child for adoption when an adoption agency decides that that person would be a suitable adoptive parent for the child, either individually or jointly with another person, and

    (b) a person is notified of having been matched with a child on the date on which he receives notification of the agency's decision, under regulation 11(2) of the Adoption Agencies Regulations 1983 or regulation 12(3) of the Adoption Agencies (Scotland) Regulations 1996;

    (c) a person elects to be a child's adopter, in a case where the child is matched with him and another person jointly, if he and that person agree, at the time at which they are matched, that he and not the other person will be the adopter.

(5) A reference in any provision of these Regulations to a period of continuous employment is to a period computed in accordance with Chapter 1 of Part 14 of the 1996 Act, as if that provision were a provision of that Act.

(6) For the purposes of these Regulations, any two employers shall be treated as associated if—

    (a) one is a company of which the other (directly or indirectly) has control; or

    (b) both are companies of which a third person (directly or indirectly) has control;

and 'associated employer' shall be construed accordingly.

    3. [omitted]

PART II   PATERNITY LEAVE

Entitlement to paternity leave: birth

4.—(1) An employee is entitled to be absent from work for the purpose of caring for a child or supporting the child's mother if he—

    (a) satisfies the conditions specified in paragraph (2), and

    (b) has complied with the notice requirements in regulation 6 and, where applicable, the evidential requirements in that regulation.

(2) The conditions referred to in paragraph (1) are that the employee—

    (a) has been continuously employed for a period of not less than 26 weeks ending with the week immediately preceding the 14th week before the expected week of the child's birth;

    (b) is either—

        (i) the father of the child or;

        (ii) married to, the civil partner or the partner of the child's mother, but not the child's father;

    (c) has, or expects to have—

        (i) if he is the child's father, responsibility for the upbringing of the child;

        (ii) if he is the mother's husband, the civil partner or partner but not the child's father, the main responsibility (apart from any responsibility of the mother) for the upbringing of the child.

(3) An employee shall be treated as having satisfied the condition in paragraph (2)(a) on the date of the child's birth notwithstanding the fact that he has not then been continuously employed for a period of not less than 26 weeks, where—

(a) the date on which the child is born is earlier than the 14th week before the week in which its birth is expected, and

(b) the employee would have been continuously employed for such a period if his employment had continued until that 14th week.

(4) An employee shall be treated as having satisfied the condition in paragraph (2)(b)(ii) if he would have satisfied it but for the fact that the child's mother has died.

(5) An employee shall be treated as having satisfied the condition in paragraph (2)(c) if he would have satisfied it but for the fact that the child was stillborn after 24 weeks of pregnancy or has died.

(6) An employee's entitlement to leave under this regulation shall not be affected by the birth, or expected birth, of more than one child as a result of the same pregnancy.

Options in respect of leave under regulation 4

5.—(1) An employee may choose to take either one week's leave or two consecutive weeks' leave in respect of a child under regulation 4.

(2) The leave may only be taken during the period which begins with the date on which the child is born and ends—

(a) except in the case referred to in sub-paragraph (b), 56 days after that date;

(b) in a case where the child is born before the first day of the expected week of its birth, 56 days after that day.

(3) Subject to paragraph (2) and, where applicable, paragraph (4), an employee may choose to begin his period of leave on—

(a) the date on which the child is born;

(b) the date falling such number of days after the date on which the child is born as the employee may specify in a notice under regulation 6, or

(c) a predetermined date, specified in a notice under that regulation, which is later than the first day of the expected week of the child's birth.

(4) In a case where the leave is in respect of a child whose expected week of birth begins before 6th April 2003, an employee may choose to begin a period of leave only on a predetermined date, specified in a notice under regulation 6, which is at least 28 days after the date on which that notice is given.

Notice and evidential requirements for leave under regulation 4

6.—(1) An employee must give his employer notice of his intention to take leave in respect of a child under regulation 4, specifying—

(a) the expected week of the child's birth;

(b) the length of the period of leave that, in accordance with regulation 5(1), the employee has chosen to take, and

(c) the date on which, in accordance with regulation 5(3) or (4), the employee has chosen that his period of leave should begin.

(2)–(8) [omitted]

7. [omitted]

Entitlement to paternity leave: adoption

8.—(1) An employee is entitled to be absent from work for the purpose of caring for a child or supporting the child's adopter if he—

(a) satisfies the conditions specified in paragraph (2), and

(b) has complied with the notice requirements in regulation 10 and, where applicable, the evidential requirements in that regulation.

(2) The conditions referred to in paragraph (1) are that the employee—

(a) has been continously employed for a period of not less than 26 weeks ending with the week in which the child's adopter is notified of having been matched with the child;

  (b) is either married to, the civil partner or the partner of the child's adopter, and
  (c) has, or expects to have, the main responsibility (apart from the responsibility of the adopter) for the upbringing of the child.

(3) In paragraph (2)(a), 'week' means the period of seven days beginning with Sunday.

(4) An employee shall be treated as having satisfied the condition in paragraph (2)(b) if he would have satisfied it but for the fact that the child's adopter died during the child's placement.

(5) An employee shall be treated as having satisfied the condition in paragraph (2)(c) if he would have satisfied it but for the fact that the child's placement with the adopter has ended.

(6) An employee's entitlement to leave under this regulation shall not be affected by the placement for adoption of more than one child as part of the same arrangement.

Options in respect of leave under regulation 8

9.—(1) An employee may choose to take either one week's leave or two consecutive weeks' leave in respect of a child under regulation 8.

(2) The leave may only be taken during the period of 56 days beginning with the date on which the child is placed with the adopter.

(3) Subject to paragraph (2) and, where applicable, paragraph (4), an employee may choose to begin a period of leave under regulation 8 on—
  (a) the date on which the child is placed with the adopter;
  (b) the date falling such number of days after the date on which the child is placed with the adopter as the employee may specify in a notice under regulation 10, or
  (c) a predetermined date, specified in a notice under that regulation, which is later than the date on which the child is expected to be placed with the adopter.

(4) In a case where the adopter was notified of having been matched with the child before 6th April 2003, the employee may choose to begin a period of leave only on a pre-determined date, specified in a notice under regulation 10, which is at least 28 days after the date on which that notice is given.

Notice and evidential requirements for leave under regulation 8

10.—(1) An employee must give his employer notice of his intention to take leave in respect of a child under regulation 8, specifying—
  (a) the date on which the adopter was notified of having been matched with the child;
  (b) the date on which the child is expected to be placed with the adopter;
  (c) the length of the period of leave that, in accordance with regulation 9(1), the employee has chosen to take, and
  (d) the date on which, in accordance with regulation 9(3) or (4), the employee has chosen that his period of leave should begin.

(2)–(8) [omitted]

11. [omitted]

Application of terms and conditions during paternity leave

12.—(1) An employee who takes paternity leave—
  (a) is entitled, during the period of leave, to the benefit of all of the terms and conditions of employment which would have applied if he had not been absent, and
  (b) is bound, during that period, by any obligations arising under those terms and conditions, subject only to the exception in section 80C(1)(b) of the 1996 Act.

(2) In paragraph (1)(a), 'terms and conditions of employment' has the meaning given by section 80C(5) of the 1996 Act, and accordingly does not include terms and conditions about remuneration.

(3) For the purposes of section 80C of the 1996 Act, only sums payable to an employee by way of wages or salary are to be treated as remuneration.

Right to return after paternity leave

13.—(1) An employee who returns to work after a period of paternity leave which was—

(a) an isolated period of leave, or

(b) the last of two or more consecutive periods of statutory leave, which did not include any period of additional maternity leave or additional adoption leave or a period of parental leave of more than four weeks,

is entitled to return from leave to the job in which he was employed before his absence.

(2) An employee who returns to work after a period of paternity leave not falling within the description in paragraph (1)(a) or (b) above is entitled to return from leave to the job in which he was employed before his absence, or, if it is not reasonably practicable for the employer to permit him to return to that job, to another job which is both suitable for him and appropriate for him to do in the circumstances.

(3) The reference in paragraphs (1) and (2) to the job in which an employee was employed before his absence is a reference to the job in which he was employed—

(a) if his return is from an isolated period of paternity leave, immediately before that period began;

(b) if his return is from consecutive periods of statutory leave, immediately before the first such period.

Incidents of the right to return after paternity leave

14.—(1) An employee's right to return under regulation 13 is a right to return—

(a) with his seniority, pension rights and similar rights—

(i)   in a case where the employee is returning from consecutive periods of statutory leave which included a period of additional adoption leave or additional maternity leave, as they would have been if the period or periods of his employment prior to the additional adoption leave or (as the case may be) additional maternity leave were continuous with the period of employment following it;

(ii) in any other case, as they would have been if he had not been absent, and

(b) on terms and conditions not less favourable than those which would have applied if he had not been absent.

(2) The provision in paragraph (1)(a)(i) concerning the treatment of periods of additional maternity leave or additional adoption leave is subject to the requirements of paragraphs 5 and 6 of Schedule 5 to the Social Security Act 1989 (equal treatment under pension schemes: maternity absence and family leave).

(3) The provisions in paragraph (1)(a)(ii) and (b) for an employee to be treated as if he had not been absent refer to his absence—

(a) if his return is from an isolated period of paternity leave, since the beginning of that period;

(b) if his return is from consecutive periods of statutory leave, since the beginning of the first such period.

PART III   ADOPTION LEAVE

Entitlement to ordinary adoption leave

15.—(1) An employee is entitled to ordinary adoption leave in respect of a child if he—

(a) satisfies the conditions specified in paragraph (2), and

(b) has complied with the notice requirements in regulation 17 and, where applicable, the evidential requirements in that regulation.

(2) The conditions referred to in paragraph (1) are that the employee—

(a) is the child's adopter;

(b) has been continuously employed for a period of not less than 26 weeks ending with the week in which he was notified of having been matched with the child, and

(c) has notified the agency that he agrees that the child should be placed with him and on the date of placement.

(3) In paragraph (2)(b), 'week' means the period of seven days beginning with Sunday.

(4) An employee's entitlement to leave under this regulation shall not be affected by the placement for adoption of more than one child as part of the same arrangement.

Options in respect of ordinary adoption leave

16.—(1) Except in the case referred to in paragraph (2), an employee may choose to begin a period of ordinary adoption leave on—

(a) the date on which the child is placed with him for adoption, or

(b) a predetermined date, specified in a notice under regulation 17, which is no more than 14 days before the date on which the child is expected to be placed with the employee and no later than that date.

(2) In a case where the employee was notified of having been matched with the child before 6th April 2003, the employee may choose to begin a period of leave only on a pre-determined date, specified in a notice under regulation 17, which is after 6th April 2003 and at least 28 days after the date on which that notice is given.

Notice and evidential requirements for ordinary adoption leave

17.—(1) An employee must give his employer notice of his intention to take ordinary adoption leave in respect of a child, specifying—

(a) the date on which the child is expected to be placed with him for adoption, and

(b) the date on which, in accordance with regulation 16(1) or (2), the employee has chosen that his period of leave should begin.

(2)–(8) [omitted]

Duration and commencement of ordinary adoption leave

18.—(1) Subject to regulations 22 and 24, an employee's ordinary adoption leave period is a period of 26 weeks.

(2) Except in the case referred to in paragraph (3), an employee's ordinary adoption leave period begins on the date specified in his notice under regulation 17(1), or, where he has varied his choice of date under regulation 17(4), on the date specified in his notice under that provision (or the last such date if he has varied his choice more than once).

(3) In a case where—

(a) the employee has chosen to begin his period of leave on the date on which the child is placed with him, and

(b) he is at work on that date,

the employee's period of leave begins on the day after that date.

Application of terms and conditions during ordinary adoption leave

19.—(1) An employee who takes ordinary adoption leave—

(a) is entitled, during the period of leave, to the benefit of all of the terms and conditions of employment which would have applied if he had not been absent, and

(b) is bound, during that period, by any obligations arising under those terms and conditions, subject only to the exception in section 75A(3)(b) of the 1996 Act.

(2) In paragraph (1)(a), 'terms and conditions of employment' has the meaning given by section 75A(4) of the 1996 Act, and accordingly does not include terms and conditions about remuneration.

(3) For the purposes of section 75A of the 1996 Act, only sums payable to an employee by way of wages or salary are to be treated as remuneration.

Additional adoption leave: entitlement, duration and commencement

20.—(1) An employee is entitled to additional adoption leave in respect of a child if—

(a) the child was placed with him for adoption,

(b) he took ordinary adoption leave in respect of the child, and

(c) his ordinary adoption leave period did not end prematurely under regulation 22(2)(a) or 24.

(2) Subject to regulations 22 and 24, an employee's additional adoption leave period is a period of 26 weeks beginning on the day after the last day of his ordinary adoption leave period.

Application of terms and conditions during additional adoption leave

21. An employee who takes additional adoption leave—

(a) is entitled, during the period of leave, to the benefit of his employer's implied obligation to him of trust and confidence and of any terms and conditions of his employment relating to—

(i) notice of the termination of the employment contract by his employer;

(ii) compensation in the event of redundancy, or

(iii) disciplinary or grievance procedures; and

(b) is bound, during that period, by his implied obligation to his employer of good faith and of any terms and conditions of his employment relating to—

(i) notice of the termination of the employment contract by him,

(ii) the disclosure of confidential information;

(iii) the acceptance of gifts or other benefits, or

(iv) the employee's participation in any other business.

22. [omitted]

Redundancy during adoption leave

23.—(1) This regulation applies where, during an employee's ordinary or additional adoption leave period, it is not practicable by reason of redundancy for his employer to continue to employ him under his existing contract of employment.

(2) Where there is a suitable available vacancy, the employee is entitled to be offered (before the end of his employment under his existing contract) alternative employment with his employer or his employer's successor, or an associated employer, under a new contract of employment which complies with paragraph (3) and takes effect immediately on the ending of his employment under the previous contract.

(3) The new contract of employment must be such that—

(a) the work to be done under it is of a kind which is both suitable in relation to the employee and appropriate for him to do in the circumstances, and

(b) its provisions as to the capacity and place in which he is to be employed, and as to the other terms and conditions of his employment, are not substantially less favourable to him than if he had continued to be employed under the previous contract.

Dismissal during adoption leave

24.—(1) Where an employee is dismissed after an ordinary or additional adoption leave period has begun but before the time when (apart from this regulation) that period would end, the period ends at the time of the dismissal.

25. [omitted]

Right to return after adoption leave

26.—(1) An employee who returns to work after a period of ordinary adoption leave which was—

(a) an isolated period of leave, or

(b) the last of two or more consecutive periods of statutory leave, which did not include any period of additional maternity leave or additional adoption leave or a period of parental leave of more than four weeks,

is entitled to return from leave to the job in which he was employed before his absence.

(2) An employee who returns to work after—

(a) a period of additional adoption leave, whether or not preceded by another period of statutory leave, or

(b) a period of ordinary adoption leave not falling within the description in paragraph (1)(a) or (b) above,

is entitled to return from leave to the job in which he was employed before his absence, or, if it is not reasonably practicable for the employer to permit him to return to that job, to another job which is both suitable for him and appropriate for him to do in the circumstances.

(3) The reference in paragraphs (1) and (2) to the job in which an employee was employed before his absence is a reference to the job in which he was employed—

(a) if his return is from an isolated period of adoption leave, immediately before that period began;

(b) if his return is from consecutive periods of statutory leave, immediately before the first such period.

(4) This regulation does not apply where regulation 23 applies.

Incidents of the right to return from adoption leave

27.—(1) An employee's right to return under regulation 26 is to return—

(a) with his seniority, pension rights and similar rights—

(i) in a case where the employee is returning from additional adoption leave, or consecutive periods of statutory leave which included a period of additional adoption leave or additional maternity leave, as they would have been if the period or periods of his employment prior to his additional adoption leave or (as the case may be) additional maternity leave were continuous with the period of employment following it;

(ii) in any other case, as they would have been if he had not been absent, and

(b) on terms and conditions not less favourable than those which would have been applied to him if he had not been absent.

(2) The provision in paragraph (1)(a)(i) concerning the treatment of periods of additional adoption leave or additional maternity leave is subject to the requirements of paragraphs 5 and 6 of Schedule 5 to the Social Security Act 1989 (equal treatment under pension schemes: maternity absence and family leave).

(3) The provisions in paragraph (1)(a)(ii) and (b) for an employee to be treated as if he had not been absent refer to his absence—

(a) if his return is from an isolated period of ordinary adoption leave, since the beginning of that period;

(b) if his return is from consecutive periods of statutory leave, since the beginning of the first such period.

PART IV   PROVISIONS APPLICABLE IN RELATION TO BOTH PATERNITY AND ADOPTION LEAVE

Protection from detriment

28.—(1) An employee is entitled under section 47C of the 1996 Act not to be subjected to any detriment by any act, or any deliberate failure to act, by his employer because—

(a) the employee took or sought to take paternity leave or ordinary or additional adoption leave;

(b) the employer believed that the employee was likely to take ordinary or additional adoption leave, or

(c) the employee failed to return after a period of additional adoption leave in a case where—

(i) the employer did not notify him, in accordance with regulation 17(7) and (8) or otherwise, of the date on which that period ended, and he reasonably believed that the period had not ended, or

(ii) the employer gave him less than 28 days' notice of the date on which the period would end, and it was not reasonably practicable for him to return on that date.

(2) Paragraph (1) does not apply where the detriment in question amounts to dismissal within the meaning of Part 10 of the 1996 Act.

Unfair dismissal

29.—(1) An employee who is dismissed is entitled under section 99 of the 1996 Act to be regarded for the purpose of Part 10 of that Act as unfairly dismissed if—

(a) the reason or principal reason for the dismissal is of a kind specified in paragraph (3), or

(b) the reason or principal reason for the dismissal is that the employee is redundant, and regulation 23 has not been complied with.

(2) An employee who is dismissed shall also be regarded for the purposes of Part 10 of the 1996 Act as unfairly dismissed if—

(a) the reason (or, if more than one, the principal reason) for the dismissal is that the employee was redundant;

(b) it is shown that the circumstances constituting the redundancy applied equally to one or more employees in the same undertaking who had positions similar to that held by the employee and who have not been dismissed by the employer, and

(c) it is shown that the reason (or, if more than one, the principal reason) for which the employee was selected for dismissal was a reason of a kind specified in paragraph (3).

(3) The kinds of reason referred to in paragraph (1) and (2) are reasons connected with the fact that—

(a) the employee took, or sought to take, paternity or adoption leave;

(b) the employer believed that the employee was likely to take ordinary or additional adoption leave, or

(c) the employee failed to return after a period of additional adoption leave in a case where—

(i) the employer did not notify him, in accordance with regulation 17(7) and (8) or otherwise, of the date on which that period would end, and he reasonably believed that the period had not ended, or

(ii) the employer gave him less than 28 days' notice of the date on which the period would end, and it was not reasonably practicable for him to return on that date.

(4) Paragraph (1) does not apply in relation to an employee who took adoption leave if—

(a) immediately before the end of his additional adoption leave period (or, if it ends by reason of dismissal, immediately before the dismissal) the number of employees employed by his employer, added to the number employed by any associated employer of his employer, did not exceed five, and

(b) it is not reasonably practicable for the employer (who may be the same employer or a successor of his) to permit the employee to return to a job which is both suitable for the employee and appropriate for him to do in the circumstances or for an associated employer to offer the employee a job of that kind.

(5) Paragraph (1) does not apply in relation to an employee if—

(a) it is not reasonably practicable for a reason other than redundancy for the employer (who may be the same employer or a successor of his) to permit the employee to return to a job which is both suitable for the employee and appropriate for him to do in the circumstances;

(b) an associated employer offers the employee a job of that kind, and

(c) the employee accepts or unreasonably refuses that offer.

(6) Where, on a complaint of unfair dismissal, any question arises as to whether the operation of paragraph (1) is excluded by the provisions of paragraph (4) or (5), it is for the employer to show that the provisions in question were satisfied in relation to the complainant.

Contractual rights to paternity or adoption leave

30.—(1) This regulation applies where an employee is entitled to—

(a) paternity leave,

(b) ordinary adoption leave, or

(c) additional adoption leave,

(referred to in paragraph (2) as a 'statutory right') and also to a right which corresponds to that right and which arises under the employee's contract of employment or otherwise.

(2) In a case where this regulation applies—

(a) the employee may not exercise the statutory right and the corresponding right separately but may, in taking the leave for which the two rights provide, take advantage of whichever right is, in any particular respect, the more favourable, and

(b) the provisions of the 1996 Act and of these Regulations relating to the statutory right apply, subject to any modifications necessary to give effect to any more favourable contractual terms, to the exercise of the composite right described in sub-paragraph (a) as they apply to the exercise of the statutory right.

31. [omitted]

The Employment Equality (Religion or Belief) Regulations 2003

(SI 2003 No. 1660)

PART I   GENERAL

Citation, commencement and extent

1.—(1) These regulations may be cited as the Employment equality (Religion or Belief) Regulations 2003, and shall come into force on 2nd December 2003.

(2) These Regulations do not extend to Northern Ireland.

Interpretation

2.—(1) In these regulations—

(a) 'religion' means any religion,

(b) 'belief' means any religious or philosophical belief,

(c) a reference to religion includes a reference to lack of religion, and

(d) a reference to belief includes a reference to lack of belief.

(2) In these Regulations, references to discrimination are to any discrimination falling within regulation 3 (discrimination on grounds of religion or belief) or 4 (discrimination by way of victimisation) and related expressions shall be construed accordingly, and references to harassment shall be construed in accordance with regulation 5 (harassment on grounds of religion or belief).

(3) In these Regulations—

'act' includes a deliberate omission;

'benefits', except in regulation 9A (trustees and managers of occupational pension schemes), includes facilities and services;

'detriment' does not include harassment within the meaning of regulation 5;

references to 'employer', in their application to a person at any time seeking to employ another, include a person who has no employees at that time;

'employment' means employment under a contract of service or of apprenticeship or a contract personally to do any work, and related expressions shall be construed accordingly;

. . .

Discrimination on grounds of religion or belief

3.—(1) For the purposes of these Regulations, a person ('A') discriminates against another person ('B') if—

(a) on the grounds of the religion or belief of B or of any other person except A (whether or not it is also A's religion or belief) A treats B less favourably than he treats or would treat other persons;

(b) A applies to B a provision, criterion or practice which he applies or would apply equally to persons not of the same religion or belief as B, but—

(i) which puts or would put persons of the same religion or belief as B at a particular disadvantage when compared with other persons,

(ii) which puts B at that disadvantage, and

(iii) which A cannot show to be a proportionate means of achieving a legitimate aim.

(2) [revoked]

(3) A comparison of B's case with that of another person under paragraph (1) must be such that the relevant circumstances in the one case are the same, or not materially different, in the other.

Discrimination by way of victimisation

4.—(1) For the purposes of these Regulations, a person ('A') discriminates against another person ('B') if he treats B less favourably than he treats or would treat other persons in the same circumstances, and does so by reason that B has—

(a) brought proceedings against A or any other person under these Regulations;

(b) given evidence or information in connection with proceedings brought by any person against A or any other person under these Regulations;

(c) otherwise done anything under or by reference to these Regulations in relation to A or any other person; or

(d) alleged that A or any other person has committed an act which (whether or not the allegation so states) would amount to a contravention of these Regulations,

or by reason that A knows that B intends to do any of those things, or suspects that B has done or intends to do any of them.

(2) Paragraph (1) does not apply to treatment of B by reason of any allegation made by him, or evidence or information given by him, if the allegation, evidence or information was false and not made (or, as the case may be, given) in good faith.

Harassment on grounds of religion or belief

5.—(1) For the purposes of these Regulations, a person ('A') subjects another person ('B') to harassment where, on grounds of religion or belief, A engages in unwanted conduct which has the purpose or effect of—

(a) violating B's dignity; or

(b) creating an intimidating, hostile, degrading, humiliating or offensive environment for B.

(2) Conduct shall be regarded as having the effect specified in paragraph (1)(a) or (b) only if, having regard to all the circumstances, including in particular the perception of B, it should reasonably be considered as having that effect.

PART II   DISCRIMINATION IN EMPLOYMENT AND
VOCATIONAL TRAINING

Applicants and employees

6.—(1) It is unlawful for an employer, in relation to employment by him at an establishment in Great Britain, to discriminate against a person—

(a) in the arrangements he makes for the purpose of determining to whom he should offer employment;

(b) in the terms on which he offers that person employment; or

(c) by refusing to offer, or deliberately not offering, him employment.

(2) It is unlawful for an employer, in relation to a person whom he employs at an establishment in Great Britain, to discriminate against that person—

(a) in the terms of employment which he affords him;

(b) in the opportunities which he affords him for promotion, a transfer, training, or receiving any other benefit;

(c) by refusing to afford him, or deliberately not affording him, any such opportunity; or

(d) by dismissing him, or subjecting him to any other detriment.

(3) It is unlawful for an employer, in relation to employment by him at an establishment in Great Britain, to subject to harassment a person whom he employs or who has applied to him for employment.

(4) Paragraph (2) does not apply to benefits of any description if the employer is concerned with the provision (for payment or not) of benefits of that description to the public, or to a section of the public which includes the employee in question, unless—

(a) that provision differs in a material respect from the provision of the benefits by the employer to his employees; or

(b) the provision of the benefits to the employee in question is regulated by his contract of employment; or

(c) the benefits relate to training.

(5) In paragraph (2)(d) reference to the dismissal of a person from employment includes reference—

(a) to the termination of that person's employment by the expiration of any period (including a period expiring by reference to an event or circumstance), not being a termination immediately after which the employment is renewed on the same terms; and

(b) to the termination of that person's employment by any act of his (including the giving of notice) in circumstances such that he is entitled to terminate it without notice by reason of the conduct of the employer.

Exception for genuine occupational requirement

7.—(1) In relation to discrimination falling within regulation 3 (discrimination on grounds of religion or belief)—

(a) regulation 6(1)(a) or (c) does not apply to any employment;

(b) regulation 6(2)(b) or (c) does not apply to promotion or transfer to, or training for, any employment; and

(c) regulation 6(2)(d) does not apply to dismissal from any employment, where paragraph (2) or (3) applies.

(2) This paragraph applies where, having regard to the nature of the employment or the context in which it is carried out—

(a) being of a particular religion or belief is a genuine and determining occupational requirement;

(b) it is proportionate to apply that requirement in the particular case; and

(c) either—

(i) the person to whom that requirement is applied does not meet it, or

(ii) the employer is not satisfied, and in all the circumstances it is reasonable for him not to be satisfied, that that person meets it,

and this paragraph applies whether or not the employer has an ethos based on religion or belief.

(3) This paragraph applies where an employer has an ethos based on religion or belief and, having regard to that ethos and to the nature of the employment or the context in which it is carried out—

(a) being of a particular religion or belief is a genuine occupational requirement for the job;

(b) it is proportionate to apply that requirement in the particular case; and

(c) either—

    (i) the person to whom that requirement is applied does not meet it, or

    (ii) the employer is not satisfied, and in all the circumstances it is reasonable for him not to be satisfied, that that person meets it.

Contract workers

8.—(1) It is unlawful for a principal, in relation to contract work at an establishment in Great Britain, to discriminate against a contract worker—

(a) in the terms on which he allows him to do that work;

(b) by not allowing him to do it or continue to do it;

(c) in the way he affords him access to any benefits or by refusing or deliberately not affording him access to them; or

(d) by subjecting him to any other detriment.

(2) It is unlawful for a principal, in relation to contract work at an establishment in Great Britain, to subject a contract worker to harassment.

(3) A principal does not contravene paragraph (1)(b) by doing any act in relation to a contract worker where, if the work were to be done by a person taken into the principal's employment, that act would be lawful by virtue of regulation 7 (exception for genuine occupational requirement).

(4) Paragraph (1) does not apply to benefits of any description if the principal is concerned with the provision (for payment or not) of benefits of that description to the public, or to a section of the public to which the contract worker in question belongs, unless that provision differs in a material respect from the provision of the benefits by the principal to his contract workers.

(5) In this regulation—

'principal' means a person ('A') who makes work available for doing by individuals who are employed by another person who supplies them under a contract made with A;

'contract work' means work so made available; and

'contract worker' means any individual who is supplied to the principal under such a contract.

9.–20. [omitted]

Relationships which have come to an end

21.—(1) In this regulation a 'relevant relationship' is a relationship during the course of which an act of discrimination against, or harassment of, one party to the relationship ('B') by the other party to it ('A') is unlawful by virtue of any preceding provision of this Part.

(2) Where a relevant relationship has come to an end, it is unlawful for A—

(a) to discriminate against B by subjecting him to a detriment; or

(b) to subject B to harassment, where the discrimination or harassment arises out of and is closely connected to that relationship.

(3) In paragraph (1), reference to an act of discrimination or harassment which is unlawful includes, in the case of a relationship which has come to an end before the coming into force of these Regulations, reference to an act of discrimination or harassment which would, after the coming into force of these Regulations, be unlawful.

PART III   OTHER UNLAWFUL ACTS

Liability of employers and principals

22.—(1) Anything done by a person in the course of his employment shall be treated for the purposes of these Regulations as done by his employer as well as by him, whether or not it was done with the employer's knowledge or approval.

(2) Anything done by a person as agent for another person with the authority (whether express or implied, and whether precedent or subsequent) of that other person shall be treated for the purposes of these Regulations as done by that other person as well as by him.

(3) In proceedings brought under these Regulations against any person in respect of an act alleged to have been done by an employee of his it shall be a defence for that person to prove that he took such steps as were reasonably practicable to prevent the employee from doing that act, or from doing in the course of his employment acts of that description.

Aiding unlawful acts

23.—(1) A person who knowingly aids another person to do an act made unlawful by these Regulations shall be treated for the purpose of these Regulations as himself doing an unlawful act of the like description.

(2) For the purposes of paragraph (1) an employee or agent for whose act the employer or principal is liable under regulation 22 (or would be so liable but for regulation 22(3)) shall be deemed to aid the doing of the act by the employer or principal.

(3) A person does not under this regulation knowingly aid another to do an unlawful act if—

    (a) he acts in reliance on a statement made to him by that other person that, by reason of any provision of these Regulations, the act which he aids would not be unlawful; and

    (b) it is reasonable for him to rely on the statement.

(4) A person who knowingly or recklessly makes a statement such as is referred to in paragraph (3)(a) which in a material respect is false or misleading commits an offence, and shall be liable on summary conviction to a fine not exceeding level 5 on the standard scale.

PART IV   GENERAL EXCEPTIONS FROM PARTS II AND III

Exception for national security

24. Nothing in Part II or III shall render unlawful an act done for the purpose of safeguarding national security, if the doing of the act was justified by that purpose.

Exceptions for positive action

25.—(1) Nothing in Part II or III shall render unlawful any act done in or in connection with—

    (a) affording persons of a particular religion or belief access to facilities for training which would help fit them for particular work; or

    (b) encouraging persons of a particular religion or belief to take advantage of opportunities for doing particular work,

where it reasonably appears to the person doing the act that it prevents or compensates for disadvantages linked to religion or belief suffered by persons of that religion or belief doing that work or likely to take up that work.

(2) Nothing in Part II or III shall render unlawful any act done by a trade organisation within the meaning of regulation 15 in or in connection with—

    (a) affording only members of the organisation who are of a particular religion or belief access to facilities for training which would help fit them for holding a post of any kind in the organisation; or

(b) encouraging only members of the organisation who are of a particular religion or belief to take advantage of opportunities for holding such posts in the organisation,

where it reasonably appears to the organisation that the act prevents or compensates for disadvantages linked to religion or belief suffered by those of that religion or belief holding such posts or likely to hold such posts.

(3) Nothing in Part II or III shall render unlawful any act done by a trade organisation within the meaning of regulation 15 in or in connection with encouraging only persons of a particular religion or belief to become members of the organisation where it reasonably appears to the organisation that the act prevents or compensates for disadvantages linked to religion or belief suffered by persons of that religion or belief who are, or are eligible to become, members.

26. [omitted]

PART V   ENFORCEMENT

Restriction of proceedings for breach of Regulations

27.—(1) Except as provided by these Regulations no proceedings, whether civil or criminal, shall lie against any person in respect of an act by reason that the act is unlawful by virtue of a provision of these Regulations.

(2) Paragraph (1) does not prevent the making of an application for judicial review or the investigation or determination of any matter in accordance with Part X (investigations of the Pensions Ombudsman) of the Pension Schemes Act 1993 by the Pensions Ombudsman.

Jurisdiction of employment tribunals

28.—(1) A complaint by any person ('the complainant') that another person ('the respondent')—

(a) has committed against the complainant an act to which this regulation applies; or
(b) is by virtue of regulation 22 (liability of employers and principals) or 23 (aiding unlawful acts) to be treated as having committed against the complainant such an act, may be presented to an employment tribunal.

(2) This regulation applies to any act of discrimination or harassment which is unlawful by virtue of any provision of Part II other than—

(a) where the act is one in respect of which an appeal or proceedings in the nature of an appeal may be brought under any enactment, regulation 16 (qualifications bodies);
(b) regulation 20 (institutions of further and higher education); or
(c) where the act arises out of and is closely connected to a relationship between the complainant and the respondent which has come to an end but during the course of which an act of discrimination against, or harassment of, the complainant by the respondent would have been unlawful by virtue of regulation 20, regulation 21 (relationships which have come to an end).

(3) In paragraph (2)(c), reference to an act of discrimination or harassment which would have been unlawful includes, in the case of a relationship which has come to an end before the coming into force of these Regulations, reference to an act of discrimination or harassment which would, after the coming into force of these Regulations, have been unlawful.

(4) In this regulation, 'enactment' includes an enactment comprised in, or in an instrument made under, an Act of the Scottish Parliament.

Burden of proof: employment tribunals

29.—(1) This regulation applies to any complaint presented under regulation 28 to an employment tribunal.

(2) Where, on the hearing of the complaint, the complainant proves facts from which the tribunal could, apart from this regulation, conclude in the absence of an adequate explanation that the respondent—

(a) has committed against the complainant an act to which regulation 28 applies; or

(b) is by virtue of regulation 22 (liability of employers and principals) or 23 (aiding unlawful acts) to be treated as having committed against the complainant such an act,

the tribunal shall uphold the complaint unless the respondent proves that he did not commit, or as the case may be, is not to be treated as having committed, that act.

Remedies on complaints in employment tribunals

30.—(1) Where an employment tribunal finds that a complaint presented to it under regulation 28 is well-founded, the tribunal shall make such of the following as it considers just and equitable—

(a) an order declaring the rights of the complainant and the respondent in relation to the act to which the complaint relates;

(b) an order requiring the respondent to pay to the complainant compensation of an amount corresponding to any damages he could have been ordered by a county court or by a sheriff court to pay to the complainant if the complaint had fallen to be dealt with under regulation 31 (jurisdiction of county and sheriff courts);

(c) a recommendation that the respondent take within a specified period action appearing to the tribunal to be practicable for the purpose of obviating or reducing the adverse effect on the complainant of any act of discrimination or harassment to which the complaint relates.

(2) As respects an unlawful act of discrimination falling within regulation 3(1)(b), if the respondent proves that the provision, criterion or practice was not applied with the intention of treating the complainant unfavourably on grounds of religion or belief, an order may be made under paragraph (1)(b) only if the employment tribunal—

(a) makes such order under paragraph (1)(a) (if any) and such recommendation under paragraph (1)(c) (if any) as it would have made if it had no power to make an order under paragraph (1)(b); and

(b) (where it makes an order under paragraph (1)(a) or a recommendation under paragraph (1)(c) or both) considers that it is just and equitable to make an order under paragraph (1)(b) as well.

(3) If without reasonable justification the respondent to a complaint fails to comply with a recommendation made by an employment tribunal under paragraph (1)(c), then, if it thinks it just and equitable to do so—

(a) the tribunal may increase the amount of compensation required to be paid to the complainant in respect of the complaint by an order made under paragraph (1)(b); or

(b) if an order under paragraph (1)(b) was not made, the tribunal may make such an order.

(4) Where an amount of compensation falls to be awarded under paragraph (1)(b), the tribunal may include in the award interest on that amount subject to, and in accordance with, the provisions of the Employment Tribunals (Interest on Awards in Discrimination Cases) Regulations 1996.

(5) [omitted]

Jurisdiction of county and sheriff courts

31.—(1) A claim by any person ('the claimant') that another person ('the respondent')—

(a) has committed against the claimant an act to which this regulation applies; or

(b) is by virtue of regulation 22 (liability of employers and principals) or 23 (aiding unlawful acts) to be treated as having committed against the claimant such an act, may be made the subject of civil proceedings in like manner as any other claim in tort or (in Scotland) in reparation for breach of statutory duty.

(2) Proceedings brought under paragraph (1) shall—

(a) in England and Wales, be brought only in a county court; and

(b) in Scotland, be brought only in a sheriff court.

(3) For the avoidance of doubt it is hereby declared that damages in respect of an unlawful act to which this regulation applies may include compensation for injury to feelings whether or not they include compensation under any other head.

(4) This regulation applies to any act of discrimination or harassment which is unlawful by virtue of—

(a) regulation 20 (institutions of further and higher education); or

(b) where the act arises out of and is closely connected to a relationship between the claimant and the respondent which has come to an end but during the course of which an act of discrimination against, or harassment of, the claimant by the respondent would have been unlawful by virtue of regulation 20, regulation 21 (relationships which have come to an end).

(5) In paragraph (4)(b), reference to an act of discrimination or harassment which would have been unlawful includes, in the case of a relationship which has come to an end before the coming into force of these Regulations, reference to an act of discrimination or harassment which would, after the coming into force of these Regulations, have been unlawful.

Burden of proof: county and sheriff courts

32.—(1) This regulation applies to any claim brought under regulation 31 in a county court in England and Wales or a sheriff court in Scotland.

(2) Where, on the hearing of the claim, the claimant proves facts from which the court could, apart from this regulation, conclude in the absence of an adequate explanation that the respondent—

(a) has committed against the claimant an act to which regulation 31 applies; or

(b) is by virtue of regulation 22 (liability of employers and principals) or 23 (aiding unlawful acts) to be treated as having committed against the claimant such an act, the court shall uphold the claim unless the respondent proves that he did not commit, or as the case may be, is not to be treated as having committed, that act.

33. [omitted]

Period within which proceedings to be brought

34.—(1) An employment tribunal shall not consider a complaint under regulation 28 unless it is presented to the tribunal before the end of—

(a) the period of three months beginning when the act complained of was done; or

(b) in a case to which regulation 36(7) (armed forces) applies, the period of six months so beginning.

(1A) Where the period within which a complaint must be presented in accordance with paragraph (1) is extended by regulation 15 of the Employment Act 2002 (Dispute Resolution) Regulations 2004, the period within which the complaint must be presented shall be the extended period rather than the period in paragraph (1).

(2) A county court or a sheriff court shall not consider a claim brought under regulation 31 unless proceedings in respect of the claim are instituted before the end of the period of six months beginning when the act complained of was done.

(3) A court or tribunal may nevertheless consider any such complaint or claim which is out of time if, in all the circumstances of the case, it considers that it is just and equitable to do so.

(4) For the purposes of this regulation and regulation 33 (help for persons in obtaining information etc.)—

(a) when the making of a contract is, by reason of the inclusion of any term, an unlawful act, that act shall be treated as extending throughout the duration of the contract; and

(b) any act extending over a period shall be treated as done at the end of that period; and

(c) a deliberate omission shall be treated as done when the person in question decided upon it,

and in the absence of evidence establishing the contrary a person shall be taken for the purposes of this regulation to decide upon an omission when he does an act inconsistent with doing the omitted act or, if he has done no such inconsistent act, when the period expires within which he might reasonably have been expected to do the omitted act if it was to be done.

35.–39. [omitted]

SCHEDULE 4   VALIDITY OF CONTRACTS, COLLECTIVE AGREEMENT AND RULES OF UNDERTAKINGS

PART I   VALIDITY AND REVISION OF CONTRACTS

1. (1) A term of a contract is void where—
    (a) the making of the contract is, by reason of the inclusion of the term, unlawful by virtue of these Regulations;
    (b) it is included in furtherance of an act which is unlawful by virtue of these Regulations; or
    (c) it provides for the doing of an act which is unlawful by virtue of these Regulations.

    (2) Sub-paragraph (1) does not apply to a term the inclusion of which constitutes, or is in furtherance of, or provides for, unlawful discrimination against, or harassment of, a party to the contract, but the term shall be unenforceable against that party.

    (3) A term in a contract which purports to exclude or limit any provision of these Regulations is unenforceable by any person in whose favour the term would operate apart from this paragraph.

    (4) Sub-paragraphs (1), (2) and (3) shall apply whether the contract was entered into before or after the date on which these Regulations come into force; but in the case of a contract made before that date, those sub-paragraphs do not apply in relation to any period before that date.

2. (1) Paragraph 1(3) does not apply—
    (a) to a contract settling a complaint to which regulation 28(1) (jurisdiction of employment tribunals) applies where the contract is made with the assistance of a conciliation officer within the meaning of section 211 of the Trade Union and Labour Relations (Consolidation) Act 1992;
    (b) to a contract settling a complaint to which regulation 28(1) applies if the conditions regulating compromise contracts under this Schedule are satisfied in relation to the contract; or
    (c) to a contract settling a claim to which regulation 31 (jurisdiction of county or sheriff courts) applies.

    (2) The conditions regulating compromise contracts under this Schedule are that—
    (a) the contract must be in writing;
    (b) the contract must relate to the particular complaint;
    (c) the complainant must have received advice from a relevant independent adviser as to the terms and effect of the proposed contract and in particular its effect on his ability to pursue a complaint before an employment tribunal;

(d) there must be in force, when the adviser gives the advice, a contract of insurance, or an indemnity provided for members of a profession or professional body, covering the risk of a claim by the complainant in respect of loss arising in consequence of the advice;

(e) the contract must identify the adviser; and

(f) the contract must state that the conditions regulating compromise contracts under this Schedule are satisfied.

(3)–(8) [omitted]

3. (1) On the application of a person interested in a contract to which paragraph 1(1) or (2) applies, a county court or a sheriff court may make such order as it thinks fit for—

(a) removing or modifying any term rendered void by paragraph 1(1); or

(b) removing or modifying any term made unenforceable by paragraph 1(2); but such an order shall not be made unless all persons affected have been given notice in writing of the application (except where under rules of court notice may be dispensed with) and have been afforded an opportunity to make representations to the court.

(2) An order under sub-paragraph (1) may include provision as respects any period before the making of the order (but after the coming into force of these Regulations).

PART II   COLLECTIVE AGREEMENTS AND RULES OF UNDERTAKINGS

4. (1) This Part of this Schedule applies to—

(a) any term of a collective agreement, including an agreement which was not intended, or is presumed not to have been intended, to be a legally enforceable contract;

(b) any rule made by an employer for application to all or any of the persons who are employed by him or who apply to be, or are, considered by him for employment;

(c) any rule made by a trade organisation (within the meaning of regulation 15) or a qualifications body (within the meaning of regulation 16) for application to—

(i) all or any of its members or prospective members; or

(ii) all or any of the persons on whom it has conferred professional or trade qualifications (within the meaning of regulation 16) or who are seeking the professional or trade qualifications which it has power to confer.

(2) Any term or rule to which this Part of this Schedule applies is void where—

(a) the making of the collective agreement is, by reason of the inclusion of the term, unlawful by virtue of these Regulations;

(b) the term or rule is included or made in furtherance of an act which is unlawful by virtue of these Regulations; or

(c) the term or rule provides for the doing of an act which is unlawful by virtue of these Regulations.

(3) Sub-paragraph (2) shall apply whether the agreement was entered into, or the rule made, before or after the date on which these Regulations come into force; but in the case of an agreement entered into, or a rule made, before the date on which these Regulations come into force, that sub-paragraph does not apply in relation to any period before that date.

5. A person to whom this paragraph applies may present a complaint to an employment tribunal that a term or rule is void by virtue of paragraph 4 if he has reason to believe—

(a) that the term or rule may at some future time have effect in relation to him; and

(b) where he alleges that it is void by virtue of paragraph 4(2)(c), that—

(i) an act for the doing of which it provides, may at some such time be done in relation to him, and

(ii) the act would be unlawful by virtue of these Regulations if done in relation to him in present circumstances.

6. In the case of a complaint about—
    (a) a term of a collective agreement made by or on behalf of—
        (i) an employer,
        (ii) an organisation of employers of which an employer is a member, or
        (iii) an association of such organisations of one of which an employer is a member, or
    (b) a rule made by an employer within the meaning of paragraph 4(1)(b), paragraph 5 applies to any person who is, or is genuinely and actively seeking to become, one of his employees.

7. In the case of a complaint about a rule made by an organisation or body to which paragraph 4(1)(c) applies, paragraph 5 applies to any person—
    (a) who is, or is genuinely and actively seeking to become, a member of the organisation or body;
    (b) on whom the organisation or body has conferred a professional or trade qualification (within the meaning of regulation 16); or
    (c) who is genuinely and actively seeking such a professional or trade qualification which the organisation or body has power to confer.

8. (1) When an employment tribunal finds that a complaint presented to it under paragraph 5 is well-founded the tribunal shall make an order declaring that the term or rule is void.

(2) An order under sub-paragraph (1) may include provision as respects any period before the making of the order (but after the coming into force of these Regulations).

9. The avoidance by virtue of paragraph 4(2) of any term or rule which provides for any person to be discriminated against shall be without prejudice to the following rights (except in so far as they enable any person to require another person to be treated less favourably than himself), namely—
    (a) such of the rights of the person to be discriminated against; and
    (b) such of the rights of any person who will be treated more favourably in direct or indirect consequence of the discrimination.
as are conferred by or in respect of a contract made or modified wholly or partly in pursuance of, or by reference to, that term or rule.

10. In this Schedule 'collective agreement' means any agreement relating to one or more of the matters mentioned in section 178(2) of the Trade Union and Labour Relations (Consolidation) Act 1992 (meaning of trade dispute), being an agreement made by or on behalf of one or more employers or one or more organisations of employers or associations of such organisations with one or more organisations of workers or associations of such organisations.

The Employment Equality (Sexual Orientation) Regulations 2003
(SI 2003 No. 1661)

PART I   GENERAL

Citation, commencement and extent
    1.—(1) These Regulations may be cited as the Employment Equality (Sexual Orientation) Regulations 2003, and shall come into force on 1st December 2003.
    (2) These Regulations do not extend to Northern Ireland.

Interpretation
    2.—(1) In these Regulations, 'sexual orientation' means a sexual orientation towards—
    (a) persons of the same sex;

(b) persons of the opposite sex; or

(c) persons of the same sex and of the opposite sex.

(2) In these Regulations, references to discrimination are to any discrimination falling within regulation 3 (discrimination on grounds of sexual orientation) or 4 (discrimination by way of victimisation) and related expressions shall be construed accordingly, and references to harassment shall be construed in accordance with regulation 5 (harassment on grounds of sexual orientation).

(3) In these Regulations—

'act' includes a deliberate omission;

'benefits', except in regulation 9A (trustees and managers of occupational pension schemes), includes facilities and services;

'detriment' does not include harassment within the meaning of regulation 5;

references to 'employer', in their application to a person at any time seeking to employ another, include a person who has no employees at that time;

'employment' means employment under a contract of service or of apprenticeship or a contract personally to do any work, and related expressions shall be construed accordingly;

. . .

Discrimination on grounds of sexual orientation

3.—(1) For the purposes of these Regulations, a person ('A') discriminates against another person ('B') if—

(a) on grounds of sexual orientation, A treats B less favourably than he treats or would treat other persons; or

(b) A applies to B a provision, criterion or practice which he applies or would apply equally to persons not of the same sexual orientation as B, but—

(i) which puts or would put persons of the same sexual orientation as B at a particular disadvantage when compared with other persons,

(ii) which puts B at that disadvantage, and

(iii) which A cannot show to be a proportionate means of achieving a legitimate aim.

(2) A comparison of B's case with that of another person under paragraph (1) must be such that the relevant circumstances in the one case are the same, or not materially different, in the other.

(3) For the purposes of paragraph (2), in a comparison of B's case with that of another person the fact that one of the persons (whether or not B) is a civil partner while the other is married shall not be treated as a material difference between their respective circumstances.

Discrimination by way of victimisation

4.—(1) For the purposes of these Regulations, a person ('A') discriminates against another person ('B') if he treats B less favourably than he treats or would treat other persons in the same circumstances, and does so by reason that B has—

(a) brought proceedings against A or any other person under these Regulations;

(b) given evidence or information in connection with proceedings brought by any person against A or any other person under these Regulations;

(c) otherwise done anything under or by reference to these Regulations in relation to A or any other person; or

(d) alleged that A or any other person has committed an act which (whether or not the allegation so states) would amount to a contravention of these Regulations,

or by reason that A knows that B intends to do any of those things, or suspects that B has done or intends to do any of them.

(2) Paragraph (1) does not apply to treatment of B by reason of any allegation made by him, or evidence or information given by him, if the allegation, evidence or information was false and not made (or, as the case may be, given) in good faith.

Harassment on grounds of sexual orientation

5.—(1) For the purposes of these Regulations, a person ('A') subjects another person ('B') to harassment where, on grounds of sexual orientation, A engages in unwanted conduct which has the purpose or effect of—

(a) violating B's dignity; or

(b) creating an intimidating, hostile, degrading, humiliating or offensive environment for B.

(2) Conduct shall be regarded as having the effect specified in paragraph (1)(a) or (b) only if, having regard to all the circumstances, including in particular the perception of B, it should reasonably be considered as having that effect.

PART II   DISCRIMINATION IN EMPLOYMENT AND VOCATIONAL TRAINING

Applicants and employees

6.—(1) It is unlawful for an employer, in relation to employment by him at an establishment in Great Britain, to discriminate against a person—

(a) in the arrangements he makes for the purpose of determining to whom he should offer employment;

(b) in the terms on which he offers that person employment; or

(c) by refusing to offer, or deliberately not offering, him employment.

(2) It is unlawful for an employer, in relation to a person whom he employs at an establishment in Great Britain, to discriminate against that person—

(a) in the terms of employment which he affords him;

(b) in the opportunities which he affords him for promotion, a transfer, training, or receiving any other benefit;

(c) by refusing to afford him, or deliberately not affording him, any such opportunity; or

(d) by dismissing him, or subjecting him to any other detriment.

(3) It is unlawful for an employer, in relation to employment by him at an establishment in Great Britain, to subject to harassment a person whom he employs or who has applied to him for employment.

(4) Paragraph (2) does not apply to benefits of any description if the employer is concerned with the provision (for payment or not) of benefits of that description to the public, or to a section of the public which includes the employee in question, unless—

(a) that provision differs in a material respect from the provision of the benefits by the employer to his employees; or

(b) the provision of the benefits to the employee in question is regulated by his contract of employment; or

(c) the benefits relate to training.

(5) In paragraph (2)(d) reference to the dismissal of a person from employment includes reference—

(a) to the termination of that person's employment by the expiration of any period (including a period expiring by reference to an event or circumstance), not being a termination immediately after which the employment is renewed on the same terms; and

(b) to the termination of that person's employment by any act of his (including the giving of notice) in circumstances such that he is entitled to terminate it without notice by reason of the conduct of the employer.

Exception for genuine occupational requirement etc.

7.—(1) In relation to discrimination falling within regulation 3 (discrimination on grounds of sexual orientation)—

(a) regulation 6(1)(a) or (c) does not apply to any employment;

(b) regulation 6(2)(b) or (c) does not apply to promotion or transfer to, or training for, any employment; and

(c) regulation 6(2)(d) does not apply to dismissal from any employment, where paragraph (2) or (3) applies.

(2) This paragraph applies where, having regard to the nature of the employment or the context in which it is carried out—

(a) being of a particular sexual orientation is a genuine and determining occupational requirement;

(b) it is proportionate to apply that requirement in the particular case; and

(c) either—

    (i) the person to whom that requirement is applied does not meet it, or

    (ii) the employer is not satisfied, and in all the circumstances it is reasonable for him not to be satisfied, that that person meets it,

and this paragraph applies whether or not the employment is for purposes of an organised religion.

(3) This paragraph applies where—

(a) the employment is for purposes of an organised religion;

(b) the employer applies a requirement related to sexual orientation—

    (i) so as to comply with the doctrines of the religion, or

    (ii) because of the nature of the employment and the context in which it is carried out, so as to avoid conflicting with the strongly held religious convictions of a significant number of the religion's followers; and

(c) either—

    (i) the person to whom that requirement is applied does not meet it, or

    (ii) the employer is not satisfied, and in all the circumstances it is reasonable for him not to be satisfied, that that person meets it.

[Note: the remainder of these regulations are in similar form to the Employment Equality (Religion or Belief) Regulations 2003 which are printed above.]

The ACAS Arbitration Scheme (Great Britain) Order 2004
(SI 2004 No. 753)

SCHEDULE

I. INTRODUCTION

1. The ACAS Arbitration Scheme ('the Scheme') is implemented pursuant to section 212A of the Trade Union and Labour Relations (Consolidation) Act 1992 ('the 1992 Act').

2. The Scheme provides a voluntary alternative to the employment tribunal for the resolution of unfair dismissal disputes, in the form of arbitration.

3. Resolution of disputes under the Scheme is intended to be confidential, informal, relatively fast and cost efficient. Procedures under the Scheme are non-legalistic, and far more flexible than the traditional model of the employment tribunal and the courts. For example (as explained in more detail below), the Scheme avoids the use of formal pleadings and formal witness and documentary procedures. Strict rules of evidence will not apply, and, as far as possible, instead of applying strict law or legal precedent, general principles of fairness and good conduct will be taken into account (including, for example, principles referred to in any relevant ACAS 'Disciplinary and Grievance Procedures' Code of Practice or 'Discipline and Grievances at Work' Handbook). Arbitral decisions ('awards') will be final, with very limited opportunities for parties to appeal or otherwise challenge the result.

4. The Scheme also caters for requirements imposed as a matter of law (eg, the Human Rights Act 1998, devolution issues, existing law in the field of arbitration and EC law).

5. The Scheme accommodates certain differences between the law of Scotland and the law of England and Wales relating to arbitrations generally. It does so by providing, to the extent necessary in order to accommodate those differences, separate provisions applicable to Scottish arbitrations on the one hand and to English or Welsh arbitrations on the other. For convenience, paragraphs that apply only to Scottish arbitrations are marked 'S' and paragraphs that apply only to English or Welsh arbitrations are marked 'EW'.

6.–16. [omitted]

V. ARBITRATOR'S TERMS OF REFERENCE

17. Every agreement to refer a dispute to arbitration under this Scheme shall be taken to be an agreement that the arbitrator decide the dispute according to the following Terms of Reference:

In deciding whether the dismissal was fair or unfair, the arbitrator shall:
(i)   have regard to general principles of fairness and good conduct in employment relations (including, for example, principles referred to in any relevant ACAS 'Disciplinary and Grievance Procedures' Code of Practice or 'Discipline and Grievances at Work' Handbook), instead of applying legal tests or rules (eg court decisions or legislation);
(ii) apply EC law.
  The arbitrator shall not decide the case by substituting what he or she would have done for the actions taken by the Employer.
  If the arbitrator finds the dismissal unfair, he or she shall determine the appropriate remedy under the terms of this Scheme.

VI. SCOPE OF THE SCHEME

Cases that are covered by the Scheme

18. This Scheme only applies to cases of alleged unfair dismissal (ie disputes involving proceedings, or claims which could be the subject of proceedings, before an employment tribunal arising out of a contravention, or alleged contravention, of Part X of the Employment Rights Act 1996).

19. The Scheme does not extend to other kinds of claim which are often related to, or raised at the same time as, a claim of unfair dismissal. For example, sex discrimination cases, and claims for unpaid wages are not covered by the Scheme.

20. If a claim of unfair dismissal has been referred for resolution under the Scheme, any other claim, even if part of the same dispute, must be settled separately, or referred to the employment tribunal, or withdrawn. In the event that different aspects of the same dispute are being heard in the employment tribunal as well as under the Scheme, the arbitrator may decide, if appropriate or convenient, to postpone the arbitration proceedings pending a determination by the employment tribunal.

Waiver of Jurisdictional Issues

21. Because of its informal nature, the Scheme is not designed for disputes raising jurisdictional issues, such as for example:
  — whether or not the Employee was employed by the Employer;
  — whether or not the Employee had the necessary period of continuous service to bring the claim;
  — whether or not time limits have expired and/or should be extended.

22. Accordingly, when agreeing to refer a dispute to arbitration under the Scheme, both parties will be taken to have accepted as a condition of the Scheme that no jurisdictional issue is in dispute between them. The arbitrator will not therefore deal with such issues during the arbitration process, even if they are raised by the parties, and the parties will be taken to have waived any rights in that regard.

23. In particular, in agreeing to arbitration under the Scheme, the parties will be treated as having agreed that a dismissal has taken place.

Inappropriate cases

24. The Scheme is not intended for disputes involving complex legal issues. Whilst such cases will be accepted for determination (subject to the Terms of Reference), parties are advised, where appropriate, to consider applying to the employment tribunal or settling their dispute by other means.

VII.   ACCESS TO THE SCHEME

25. The Scheme is an entirely voluntary system of dispute resolution: it will only apply if parties have so agreed.

Requirements for entry into the Scheme

26. Any agreement to submit a dispute to arbitration under the Scheme must satisfy the following requirements (an 'Arbitration Agreement'):

    (i)   the agreement of each party (which may be expressed in the same or in separate documents) must be in writing;

    (ii) the agreement must concern an existing dispute;

    (iii) the agreement must not seek to alter or vary any provision of the Scheme;

    (iv) the agreement must have been reached either:

        (a) where a conciliation officer has taken action under section 18 of the Employment Tribunals Act 1996, or

        (b) through a compromise agreement, where the conditions regulating such agreements under the Employment Rights Act 1996 are satisfied; and

    (v) the agreement must be accompanied by a completed Waiver Form for each party. Parties applying for English/Welsh arbitrations should complete Appendix A; parties applying for Scottish arbitrations should complete Appendix B.

27. Where an agreement fails to satisfy any one of these requirements or where the parties are unable to agree whether the arbitration should be an English/Welsh arbitration or a Scottish arbitration, no valid reference to the Scheme will have been made, and the parties will have to settle their dispute by other means or have recourse to the employment tribunal.

28.–33. [omitted]

VIII.   SETTLEMENT AND WITHDRAWAL FROM THE SCHEME

Withdrawal by the Employee

34. At any stage of the arbitration process, once an Arbitration Agreement has been concluded and the reference has been accepted by ACAS, the party bringing the unfair dismissal claim may withdraw from the Scheme, provided that any such withdrawal is in writing. Such a withdrawal shall constitute a dismissal of the claim and the arbitrator shall upon receipt of such withdrawal in writing issue an award dismissing the claim.

Withdrawal by the Employer

35. Once an Arbitration Agreement has been concluded and the reference has been accepted by ACAS, the party against whom a claim is brought cannot unilaterally withdraw from the Scheme.

36.–62. [omitted]

X.   GENERAL DUTY OF THE ARBITRATOR

63. The arbitrator shall:
  (i)   act fairly and impartially as between the parties, giving each party a reasonable opportunity of putting his or her case and dealing with that of his or her opponent, and
  (ii)   adopt procedures suitable to the circumstances of the particular case, avoiding unnecessary delay or expense, so as to provide a fair means for the resolution of the matters falling to be determined.

64. The arbitrator shall comply with the general duty (see paragraph 63 above) in conducting the arbitral proceedings, in his or her decisions on matters of procedure and evidence and in the exercise of all other powers conferred on him or her.

XI.   GENERAL DUTY OF THE PARTIES

65. The parties shall do all things necessary for the proper and expeditious conduct of the arbitral proceedings. This includes (without limitation) complying without delay with any determination of the arbitrator as to procedural or evidential matters, or with any order or directions of the arbitrator, and co-operating in the arrangement of any hearing.

XII.   CONFIDENTIALITY AND PRIVACY

66. Arbitrations, and all associated procedures under the Scheme, are strictly private and confidential. This rule does not prevent a party to the arbitration taking any step reasonably necessary for the purposes of any application to the court or enforcement of an award.

67. Hearings may only be attended by the arbitrator, the parties, their representatives, any interpreters, signers or communicators, witnesses and a legal adviser, if appointed. If the parties so agree, an ACAS official or arbitrator in training may also attend.

68.–105. [omitted]

XVII.   QUESTIONS OF EC LAW, DEVOLUTION ISSUES AND THE HUMAN RIGHTS ACT 1998

Appointment of legal adviser

106. The arbitrator shall have the power, on the application of any party or of his or her own motion, to require the appointment of a legal adviser to assist with respect to any issue of EC law or the Human Rights Act 1998 or any devolution issue that, in the arbitrator's view and subject to paragraph 17 above (Arbitrator's Terms of Reference), might be involved and relevant to the resolution of the dispute.

107. The legal adviser will be appointed by ACAS, to report to the arbitrator and the parties, and shall be subject to the duty of disclosure set out in paragraphs 44 and 45 above.

108. The arbitrator shall allow the legal adviser to attend the proceedings, and may order an adjournment and/or change in venue to facilitate this.

109. The parties shall be given a reasonable opportunity to comment on any information, opinion or advice offered by the legal adviser, following which the arbitrator shall take such information, opinion or advice into account in determining the dispute.

110.–112S. [omitted]

XVIII.   AUTOMATIC UNFAIRNESS

113. In deciding whether the dismissal was fair or unfair, subject to paragraph 17 above (Arbitrator's Terms of Reference), the arbitrator shall have regard to:
  (i)   any provision of Part X of the Employment Rights Act 1996 (as amended from time to time) requiring a dismissal for a particular reason to be regarded as unfair, and

(ii) any other legislative provision requiring a dismissal for a particular reason to be regarded as unfair for the purpose of Part X of the Employment Rights Act 1996.

114.–122. [omitted]

Remedies

123. In the event that the arbitrator finds that the dismissal was unfair:

(i) if the Employee expresses such a wish, the arbitrator may make, in an award, an order for reinstatement or re-engagement (in accordance with the provisions below); or

(ii) if no such order for reinstatement or re-engagement is made, the arbitrator shall make an award of compensation (calculated in accordance with the provisions below) to be paid by the Employer to the Employee.

124. In cases where the arbitrator finds that the dismissal was unfair by reason of the operation of EC law, the arbitrator shall in an English/Welsh arbitration apply the relevant provisions of English law and shall in a Scottish arbitration apply the relevant provisions of Scots law with respect to remedies for unfair dismissal, in so far as these may differ from Parts XX and XXI of the Scheme.

125.–227S. [omitted]

APPENDIX A

Waiver of Rights

English/Welsh Arbitrations

The ACAS Arbitration Scheme ('the Scheme') is entirely voluntary. In agreeing to refer a dispute to arbitration under the Scheme, both parties agree to waive rights that they would otherwise have if, for example, they had referred their dispute to the employment tribunal. This follows from the informal nature of the Scheme, which is designed to be a confidential, relatively fast, cost-efficient and non-legalistic process.

As required by Part VII of the Scheme, as a confirmation of the parties' agreement to waive their rights, this form must be completed by each party and submitted to ACAS together with the agreement to arbitration.

A detailed description of the informal nature of arbitration under the Scheme, and the important differences between this and the employment tribunal, is contained in the ACAS Guide to the Scheme ('the ACAS Guide'), which should be read by each party before completing this form.

The Scheme is not intended for disputes involving complex legal issues, or questions of EC law. Parties to such disputes are strongly advised to consider applying to the employment tribunal, or settling their dispute by other means.

This form does not list all the differences between the Scheme and the employment tribunal, or all of the features of the Scheme to which each party agrees in referring their dispute to arbitration.

There are differences between the law of England and Wales on the one hand and the law of Scotland on the other. The Scheme accordingly makes separate provision for English/Welsh arbitrations and Scottish arbitrations. This form confirms the parties' agreement that the arbitration between them will be an English/Welsh arbitration.

I,...................., the Applicant / Respondent / Respondent's duly authorised representative [delete as appropriate] confirm my agreement to each of the following points:

1. Unlike proceedings in the employment tribunal, all proceedings under the Scheme, including all hearings, are conducted in private. There are no public hearings, and the final award will be confidential.

2. All arbitrators under the Scheme are appointed by ACAS from the ACAS Arbitration Panel (which is a panel of impartial, mainly non-lawyer, arbitrators appointed by ACAS on fixed, but renewable, terms). The appointment process and the ACAS Arbitration Panel are described in the Scheme and the ACAS Guide. Neither party will have any choice of arbitrator.

3. Proceedings under the Scheme are conducted differently from the employment tribunal. In particular:
   — arbitrators will conduct proceedings in an *informal manner* in all cases;
   — the attendance of witnesses and the production of documents cannot be compelled (although failure to co-operate may be taken into account by the arbitrator);
   — there will be no oaths or affirmations, and no cross-examination of witnesses by parties or their representatives;
   — the arbitrator will take the initiative in asking questions and ascertaining the facts (with the aim of ensuring that all relevant issues are considered), as well as hearing each side's arguments;
   — the arbitrator's decision will only contain the main considerations that have led to the result; it will not contain full or detailed reasons;
   — the arbitrator has no power to order interim relief.

4. Once parties have agreed to refer their dispute to arbitration in accordance with the Scheme, the parties cannot then return to the employment tribunal.

5. In deciding whether or not the dismissal was fair or unfair, the arbitrator shall have regard to general principles of fairness and good conduct in employment relations (including, for example, principles referred to in any relevant ACAS 'Disciplinary and Grievance Procedures' Code of Practice or 'Discipline and Grievances at Work' Handbook). Unlike the employment tribunal, the arbitrator will not apply strict legal tests or rules (eg court decisions or legislation), with certain limited exceptions set out in the Scheme (see eg paragraph 17).
   Similarly, in cases that do not involve EC law, the arbitrator will calculate compensation or award any other remedy in accordance with the terms of the Scheme, instead of applying strict legal tests or rules.

6. Unlike the employment tribunal, there is no right of appeal from awards of arbitrators under the Scheme (except for a limited right to appeal questions of EC law and, aside from procedural matters set out in the Scheme, questions concerning the Human Rights Act 1998 and devolution issues).

7. Unlike the employment tribunal, in agreeing to arbitration under the Scheme, parties agree that there is no jurisdictional argument, ie no reason why the claim cannot be heard and determined by the arbitrator. In particular, the arbitrator will assume that a dismissal has taken place, and will only consider whether or not this was unfair. This is explained further in the Scheme and in the ACAS Guide.

8. The arbitration shall be an English/Welsh arbitration.

SIGNED: . . . .

DATED: . . . .

IN THE PRESENCE OF

Signature: . . . .

Full Name: . . . .

Position: . . . .

Address: . . . .

Appendix B [omitted]

The Employment Act 2002 (Dispute Resolution) Regulations 2004
(SI 2004 No. 752)

1. [omitted]

Interpretation

2.—(1) In these Regulations—

'the 1992 Act' means the Trade Union and Labour Relations (Consolidation) Act 1992;

'the 1996 Act' means the Employment Rights Act 1996;

'the 1999 Act' means the Employment Relations Act 1999;

'the 2002 Act' means the Employment Act 2002;

'action' means any act or omission;

'applicable statutory procedure' means the statutory procedure that applies in relation to a particular case by virtue of these Regulations;

'collective agreement' has the meaning given to it by section 178(1) of the 1992 Act;

'dismissal and disciplinary procedures' means the statutory procedures set out in Part 1 of Schedule 2;

'dismissed' has the meaning given to it in section 95(1)(a) and (b) of the 1996 Act;

'employers' association' has the meaning given to it by section 122 of the 1992 Act;

'grievance' means a complaint by an employee about action which his employer has taken or is contemplating taking in relation to him;

'grievance procedures' means the statutory procedures set out in Part 2 of Schedule 2;

'independent trade union' has the meaning given to it by section 5 of the 1992 Act;

'modified dismissal procedure' means the procedure set out in Chapter 2 of Part 1 of Schedule 2;

'modified grievance procedure' means the procedure set out in Chapter 2 of Part 2 of Schedule 2;

'non-completion' of a statutory procedure includes non-commencement of such a procedure except where the term is used in relation to the non-completion of an identified requirement of a procedure or to circumstances where a procedure has already been commenced;

'party' means the employer or the employee;

'relevant disciplinary action' means action, short of dismissal, which the employer asserts to be based wholly or mainly on the employee's conduct or capability, other than suspension on full pay or the issuing of warnings (whether oral or written);

'standard dismissal and disciplinary procedure' means the procedure set out in Chapter 1 of Part 1 of Schedule 2;

'standard grievance procedure' means the procedure set out in Chapter 1 of Part 2 of Schedule 2;

and a reference to a Schedule is a reference to a Schedule to the 2002 Act.

(2) In determining whether a meeting or written communication fulfils a requirement of Schedule 2, it is irrelevant whether the meeting or communication deals with any other matter (including a different matter required to be dealt with in a meeting or communication intended to fulfil a requirement of Schedule 2).

Application of dismissal and disciplinary procedures

3.—(1) Subject to paragraph (2) and regulation 4, the standard dismissal and disciplinary procedure applies when an employer contemplates dismissing or taking relevant disciplinary action against an employee.

(2) Subject to regulation 4, the modified dismissal procedure applies in relation to a dismissal where—

(a) the employer dismissed the employee by reason of his conduct without notice;

(b) the dismissal occurred at the time the employer became aware of the conduct or immediately thereafter;

(c) the employer was entitled, in the circumstances, to dismiss the employee by reason of his conduct without notice or any payment in lieu of notice; and

(d) it was reasonable for the employer, in the circumstances, to dismiss the employee before enquiring into the circumstances in which the conduct took place,

but neither of the dismissal and disciplinary procedures applies in relation to such a dismissal where the employee presents a complaint relating to the dismissal to an employment tribunal at a time when the employer has not complied with paragraph 4 of Schedule 2.

Dismissals to which the dismissal and disciplinary procedures do not apply

4.—(1) Neither of the dismissal and disciplinary procedures applies in relation to the dismissal of an employee where—

(a) all the employees of a description or in a category to which the employee belongs are dismissed, provided that the employer offers to re-engage all the employees so dismissed either before or upon the termination of their contracts;

(b) the dismissal is one of a number of dismissals in respect of which the duty in section 188 of the 1992 Act (duty of employer to consult representatives when proposing to dismiss as redundant a certain number of employees) applies;

(c) at the time of the employee's dismissal he is taking part in—

(i) an unofficial strike or other unofficial industrial action, or

(ii) a strike or other industrial action (being neither unofficial industrial action nor protected industrial action), unless the circumstances of the dismissal are such that, by virtue of section 238(2) of the 1992 Act, an employment tribunal is entitled to determine whether the dismissal was fair or unfair;

(d) the reason (or, if more than one, the principal reason) for the dismissal is that the employee took protected industrial action and the dismissal would be regarded, by virtue of section 238A(2) of the 1992 Act, as unfair for the purposes of Part 10 of the 1996 Act;

(e) the employer's business suddenly ceases to function, because of an event unforeseen by the employer, with the result that it is impractical for him to employ any employees;

(f) the reason (or, if more than one principal reason) for the dismissal is that the employee could not continue to work in the position which he held without contravention (either on his part or on that of his employer) of a duty or restriction imposed by or under any enactment;

(g) the employee is one to whom a dismissal procedures agreement designated by an order under section 110 of the 1996 Act applies at the date of dismissal, or

(h) the reason (or, if more than one, the principal reason) for the dismissal is retirement of the employee (to be determined in accordance with section 98ZA to 98ZF of the 1996 Act.

(2) For the purposes of paragraph (1)—

'unofficial' shall be construed in accordance with subsections (2) to (4) of section 237 of the 1992 Act;

'strike' has the meaning given to it by section 246 of the 1992 Act;

'protected industrial action' shall be construed in accordance with section 238A(1) of the 1992 Act;

and an employer shall be regarded as offering to re-engage an employee if that employer, a successor of that employer or an associated employer of that employer offers to re-engage the employee, either in the job which he held immediately before the date of dismissal or in a different job which would be suitable in his case.

Circumstances in which parties are treated as complying with the dismissal and disciplinary procedures

5.—(1) Where—

(a) either of the dismissal and disciplinary procedures is the applicable statutory procedure in relation to a dismissal;

(b) the employee presents an application for interim relief to an employment tribunal pursuant to section 128 of the 1996 Act (interim relief pending determination of complaint) in relation to his dismissal; and

(c) at the time the application is presented, the requirements of paragraphs 1 and 2 or, as the case may be, paragraph 4 of Schedule 2 have been complied with but the requirements of paragraph 3 or 5 of Schedule 2 have not,

the parties shall be treated as having complied with the requirements of paragraph 3 or 5 of Schedule 2.

(2) Where either of the dismissal and disciplinary procedures is the applicable statutory procedure in relation to the dismissal of an employee or to relevant disciplinary action taken against an employee but—

(a) at the time of the dismissal or the taking of the action an appropriate procedure exists;

(b) the employee is entitled to appeal under that procedure against his dismissal or the relevant disciplinary action taken against him instead of appealing to his employer; and

(c) the employee has appealed under that procedure,

the parties shall be treated as having complied with the requirements of paragraph 3 or 5 of Schedule 2.

(3) For the purposes of paragraph (2) a procedure is appropriate if it—

(a) gives the employee an effective right of appeal against dismissal or disciplinary action taken against him; and

(b) operates by virtue of a collective agreement made between two or more employers or an employers' association and one or more independent trade unions.

Application of the grievance procedures

6.—(1) The grievance procedures apply, in accordance with the paragraphs (2) to (7) of this regulation, in relation to any grievance about action by the employer that could form the basis of a complaint by an employee to an employment tribunal under a jurisdiction listed in Schedule 3 or 4, or could do so if the action took place.

(2) Subject to paragraphs (3) to (7), the standard grievance procedure applies in relation to any such grievance.

(3) Subject to paragraphs (4) to (7), the modified grievance procedure applies in relation to a grievance where—

    (a) the employee has ceased to be employed by the employer;

    (b) the employer—

        (i) was unaware of the grievance before the employment ceased, or

        (ii) was so aware but the standard grievance procedure was not commenced or was not completed before the last day of the employee's employment; and

    (c) the parties have agreed in writing in relation to the grievance, whether before, on or after that day, but after the employer became aware of the grievance, that the modified procedure should apply.

(4) Neither of the grievance procedures applies where—

    (a) the employee has ceased to be employed by the employer;

    (b) neither procedure has been commenced; and

    (c) since the employee ceased to be employed it has ceased to be reasonably practicable for him to comply with paragraph 6 or 9 of Schedule 2.

(5) Neither of the grievance procedures applies where the grievance is that the employer has dismissed or is contemplating dismissing the employee.

(6) Neither of the grievance procedures applies where the grievance is that the employer has taken or is contemplating taking relevant disciplinary action against the employee unless one of the reasons for the grievance is a reason mentioned in regulation 7(1).

(7) Neither of the grievance procedures applies where regulation 11(1) applies.

Circumstances in which parties are treated as complying with the grievance procedures

7.—(1) Where the grievance is that the employer has taken or is contemplating taking relevant disciplinary action against the employee and one of the reasons for the grievance is—

    (a) that the relevant disciplinary action amounted to or, if it took place, would amount to unlawful discrimination; or

    (b) that the grounds on which the employer took the action or is contemplating taking it were or are unrelated to the grounds on which he asserted that he took the action or is asserting that he is contemplating taking it,

the standard grievance procedure or, as the case may be, modified grievance procedure shall apply but the parties shall be treated as having complied with the applicable procedure if the employee complies with the requirement in paragraph (2).

(2) The requirement is that the employee must set out the grievance in a written statement and send the statement or a copy of it to the employer—

    (a) where either of the dismissal and disciplinary procedures is being followed, before the meeting referred to in paragraph 3 or 5 (appeals under the dismissal and disciplinary procedures) of Schedule 2; or

    (b) where neither of those procedures is being followed, before presenting any complaint arising out of the grievance to an employment tribunal.

(3) In paragraph (1)(a) "unlawful discrimination' means an act or omission in respect of which a right of complaint lies to an employment tribunal under any of the following tribunal jurisdictions (specified in Schedules 3 and 4)—

    section 2 of the Equal Pay Act 1970;

    section 63 of the Sex Discrimination Act 1975;

    section 54 of the Race Relations Act 1976;

    section 17A of the Disability Discrimination Act 1995;

    regulation 28 of the Employment Equality (Religion or Belief) Regulations 2003;

    regulation 28 of the Employment Equality (Sexual Orientation) Regulations 2003.

8.—(1) Where—

    (a) the standard grievance procedure is the applicable statutory procedure;

(b) the employee has ceased to be employed by the employer;

(c) paragraph 6 of Schedule 2 has been complied with (whether before or after the end of his employment); and

(d) since the end of his employment it has ceased to be reasonably practicable for the employee, or his employer, to comply with the requirements of paragraph 7 or 8 of Schedule 2,

the parties shall be treated, subject to paragraph (2), as having complied with such of those paragraphs of Schedule 2 as have not been complied with.

(2) In a case where paragraph (1) applies and the requirements of paragraphs 7(1) to (3) of Schedule 2 have been complied with but the requirement in paragraph 7(4) of Schedule 2 has not, the employer shall be treated as having failed to comply with paragraph 7(4) unless he informs the employee in writing of his decision as to his response to the grievance.

9.—(1) Where either of the grievance procedures is the applicable statutory procedure, the parties shall be treated as having complied with the requirements of the procedure if a person who is an appropriate representative of the employee having the grievance has—

(a) written to the employer setting out the grievance; and

(b) specified in writing to the employer (whether in setting out the grievance or otherwise) the names of at least two employees, of whom one is the employee having the grievance, as being the employees on behalf of whom he is raising the grievance.

(2) For the purposes of paragraph (1), a person is an appropriate representative if, at the time he writes to the employer setting out the grievance, he is—

(a) an official of an independent trade union recognised by the employer for the purposes of collective bargaining in respect of a description of employees that includes the employee having the grievance; or

(b) an employee of the employer who is an employee representative elected or appointed by employees consisting of or including employees of the same description as the employee having the grievance and who, having regard to the purposes for which and method by which he was elected or appointed, has the authority to represent employees of that description under an established procedure for resolving grievances agreed between employee representatives and the employer.

(3) For the purposes of paragraph (2)(a) the terms "official', "recognised' and "collective bargaining' have the meanings given to them by, respectively, sections 119, 178(3) and 178(1) of the 1992 Act.

10. Where either of the grievance procedures is the applicable statutory procedure but—

(a) at the time the employee raises his grievance there is a procedure in operation, under a collective agreement made between two or more employers or an employers' association and one or more independent trade unions, that provides for employees of the employer to raise grievances about the behaviour of the employer and have them considered; and

(b) the employee is entitled to raise his grievance under that procedure and does so, the parties shall be treated as having complied with the applicable statutory procedure.

General circumstances in which the statutory procedures do not apply or are treated as being complied with

11.—(1) Where the circumstances specified in paragraph (3) apply and in consequence the employer or employee does not commence the procedure that would otherwise be the applicable statutory procedure (by complying with paragraph 1, 4, 6 or 9 of Schedule 2), the procedure does not apply.

(2) Where the applicable statutory procedure has been commenced, but the circumstances specified in paragraph (3) apply and in consequence a party does not comply with a

subsequent requirement of the procedure, the parties shall be treated as having complied with the procedure.

(3) The circumstances referred to in paragraphs (1) and (2) are that—

    (a) the party has reasonable grounds to believe that commencing the procedure or complying with the subsequent requirement would result in a significant threat to himself, his property, any other person or the property of any other person;

    (b) the party has been subjected to harassment and has reasonable grounds to believe that commencing the procedure or complying with the subsequent requirement would result in his being subjected to further harassment; or

    (c) it is not practicable for the party to commence the procedure or comply with the subsequent requirement within a reasonable period.

(4) In paragraph (3)(b), "harassment' means conduct which has the purpose or effect of—

    (a) violating the person's dignity; or

    (b) creating an intimidating, hostile, degrading, humiliating or offensive environment for him,

but conduct shall only be regarded as having that purpose or effect if, having regard to all the circumstances, including in particular the perception of the person who was the subject of the conduct, it should reasonably be considered as having that purpose or effect.

Failure to comply with the statutory procedures

12.—(1) If either party fails to comply with a requirement of an applicable statutory procedure, including a general requirement contained in Part 3 of Schedule 2, then, subject to paragraph (2), the non-completion of the procedure shall be attributable to that party and neither party shall be under any obligation to comply with any further requirement of the procedure.

(2) Except as mentioned in paragraph (4), where the parties are to be treated as complying with the applicable statutory procedure, or any requirement of it, there is no failure to comply with the procedure or requirement.

(3) Notwithstanding that if regulation 11(1) applies the procedure that would otherwise be the applicable statutory procedure does not apply, where that regulation applies because the circumstances in sub-paragraph (a) or (b) of regulation 11(3) apply and it was the behaviour of one of the parties that resulted in those circumstances applying, that party shall be treated as if—

    (a) the procedure had applied; and

    (b) there had been a failure to comply with a requirement of the procedure that was attributable to him.

(4) In a case where regulation 11(2) applies in relation to a requirement of the applicable statutory procedure because the circumstances in sub-paragraph (a) or (b) of regulation 11(3) apply, and it was the behaviour of one of the parties that resulted in those circumstances applying, the fact that the requirement was not complied with shall be treated as being a failure, attributable to that party, to comply with a requirement of the procedure.

Failure to attend a meeting

13.—(1) Without prejudice to regulation 11(2) and (3)(c), if it is not reasonably practicable for—

    (a) the employee, or, if he is exercising his right under section 10 of the 1999 Act (right to be accompanied), his companion; or

    (b) the employer,

to attend a meeting organised in accordance with the applicable statutory procedure for a reason which was not foreseeable when the meeting was arranged, the employee or, as the case may be, employer shall not be treated as having failed to comply with that requirement of the procedure.

(2) In the circumstances set out in paragraph (1), the employer shall continue to be under the duty in the applicable statutory procedure to invite the employee to attend a

meeting and, where the employee is exercising his rights under section 10 of the 1999 Act and the employee proposes an alternative time under subsection (4) of that section, the employer shall be under a duty to invite the employee to attend a meeting at that time.

(3) The duty to invite the employee to attend a meeting referred to in paragraph (2) shall cease if the employer has invited the employee to attend two meetings and paragraph (1) applied in relation to each of them.

(4) Where the duty in paragraph (2) has ceased as a result of paragraph (3), the parties shall be treated as having complied with the applicable statutory procedure.

Questions to obtain information not to constitute statement of grievance

14.—(1) Where a person aggrieved questions a respondent under any of the provisions set out in paragraph (2), those questions shall not constitute a statement of grievance under paragraph 6 or 9 of Schedule 2.

(2) The provisions referred to in paragraph (1) are—

section 7B of the Equal Pay Act 1970;

section 74 of the Sex Discrimination Act 1975;

section 65 of the Race Relations Act 1976;

section 56 of the Disability Discrimination Act 1995;

regulation 33 of the Employment Equality (Religion or Belief) Regulations 2003;

regulation 33 of the Employment Equality (Sexual Orientation) Regulations 2003.

Extension of time limits

15.—(1) Where a complaint is presented to an employment tribunal under a jurisdiction listed in Schedule 3 or 4 and—

(a) either of the dismissal and disciplinary procedures is the applicable statutory procedure and the circumstances specified in paragraph (2) apply; or

(b) either of the grievance procedures is the applicable statutory procedure and the circumstances specified in paragraph (3) apply;

the normal time limit for presenting the complaint is extended for a period of three months beginning with the day after the day on which it would otherwise have expired.

(2) The circumstances referred to in paragraph (1)(a) are that the employee presents a complaint to the tribunal after the expiry of the normal time limit for presenting the complaint but had reasonable grounds for believing, when that time limit expired, that a dismissal or disciplinary procedure, whether statutory or otherwise (including an appropriate procedure for the purposes of regulation 5(2)), was being followed in respect of matters that consisted of or included the substance of the tribunal complaint.

(3) The circumstances referred to in paragraph (1)(b) are that the employee presents a complaint to the tribunal—

(a) within the normal time limit for presenting the complaint but in circumstances in which section 32(2) or (3) of the 2002 Act does not permit him to do so; or

(b) after the expiry of the normal time limit for presenting the complaint, having complied with paragraph 6 or 9 of Schedule 2 in relation to his grievance within that normal time limit.

(4) For the purposes of paragraph (3) and section 32 of the 2002 Act the following acts shall be treated, in a case to which the specified regulation applies, as constituting compliance with paragraph 6 or 9 of Schedule 2—

(a) in a case to which regulation 7(1) applies, compliance by the employee with the requirement in regulation 7(2);

(b) in a case to which regulation 9(1) applies, compliance by the appropriate representative with the requirement in sub-paragraph (a) or (b) of that regulation, whichever is the later; and

(c) in a case to which regulation 10 applies, the raising of his grievance by the employee in accordance with the procedure referred to in that regulation.

(5) In this regulation "the normal time limit' means—
  (a) subject to sub-paragraph (b), the period within which a complaint under the relevant jurisdiction must be presented if there is to be no need for the tribunal, in order to be entitled to consider it to—
    (i) exercise any discretion, or
    (ii) make any determination as to whether it is required to consider the complaint, that the tribunal would have to exercise or make in order to consider a complaint presented outside that period; and
  (b) in relation to claims brought under the Equal Pay Act 1970, the period ending on the date on or before which proceedings must be instituted in accordance with section 2(4) of that Act.

National security

16. Where it would not be possible to comply with an applicable statutory procedure without disclosing information the disclosure of which would be contrary to the interests of national security, nothing in these Regulations requires either party to comply with that procedure.

17.–18. [omitted]

The Information and Consultation of Employees Regulations 2004
(SI 2004 No. 3426)

ARRANGEMENT OF REGULATIONS

PART I   GENERAL

PART II   EMPLOYEE NUMBERS AND ENTITLEMENT TO DATA

PART III   NEGOTIATED AGREEMENTS

PART IV   STANDARD INFORMATION AND CONSULTATION PROVISIONS

PART V   DUTY OF CO-OPERATION

PART VI   COMPLIANCE AND ENFORCEMENT

PART VII   CONFIDENTIAL INFORMATION

PART VIII   PROTECTIONS FOR INFORMATION AND CONSULTATION REPRESENTATIVES, ETC.

SCHEDULE 1   APPLICATION OF REGULATIONS

PART 1   GENERAL

1 [omitted]

2 Interpretation
In these Regulations—
  'the 1996 Act' means the Employment Rights Act 1996;
  'Appeal Tribunal' means the Employment Appeal Tribunal;
  'CAC' means the Central Arbitration Committee;
  'consultation' means the exchange of views and establishment of a dialogue between—
    (a) information and consultation representatives and the employer; or
    (b) in the case of a negotiated agreement which provides as mentioned in regulation 16(1)(f)(ii), the employees and the employer;
  'contract of employment' means a contract of service or apprenticeship, whether express or implied, and (if it is express) whether oral or in writing;
  'date of the ballot' means the day or last day on which voting may take place and, where voting in different parts of the ballot is arranged to take place on different days or during periods ending on different days, the last of those days;
  'employee' means an individual who has entered into or works under a contract of employment and in Part VIII and regulation 40 includes, where the employment has ceased, an individual who worked under a contract of employment;
  'employee request' means a request by employees under regulation 7 for the employer to initiate negotiations to reach an agreement under these Regulations;

'employer notification' means a notification by an employer under regulation 11 that he wishes to initiate negotiations to reach an agreement under these Regulations;

'information' means data transmitted by the employer—

(a) to the information and consultation representatives; or

(b) in the case of a negotiated agreement which provides as mentioned in regulation 16(1)(f)(ii), directly to the employees,

in order to enable those representatives or those employees to examine and to acquaint themselves with the subject matter of the data;

'Information and Consultation Directive' means European Parliament and Council Directive 2002/14/EC of 11 March 2002 establishing a general framework for informing and consulting employees in the European Community;

'information and consultation representative' means—

(a) in the case of a negotiated agreement which provides as mentioned in regulation 16(1)(f)(i), a person appointed or elected in accordance with that agreement; or

(b) a person elected in accordance with regulation 19(1);

'negotiated agreement' means—

(a) an agreement between the employer and the negotiating representatives reached through negotiations as provided for in regulation 14 which satisfies the requirements of regulation 16(1); or

(b) an agreement between the employer and the information and consultation representatives referred to in regulation 18(2);

'negotiating representative' means a person elected or appointed pursuant to regulation 14(1)(a);

'parties' means the employer and the negotiating representatives or the information and consultation representatives, as the case may be;

'Pension Schemes Regulations' means the Occupational and Personal Pension Schemes (Consultation by Employers and Miscellaneous Amendment) Regulations 2006;

'pre-existing agreement' means an agreement between an employer and his employees or their representatives which—

(a) is made prior to the making of an employee request; and

(b) satisfies the conditions set out in regulation 8(1)(a) to (d),

but does not include an agreement concluded in accordance with regulations 17 or 42 to 45 of the Transnational Information and Consultation of Employees Regulations 1999 or a negotiated agreement;

'standard information and consultation provisions' means the provisions set out in regulation 20;

'undertaking' means a public or private undertaking carrying out an economic activity, whether or not operating for gain;

'valid employee request' means an employee request made to their employer by the employees of an undertaking to which these Regulations apply (under regulation 3) that satisfies the requirements of regulation 7 and is not prevented from being valid by regulation 12.

3 Application

(1) These Regulations apply to undertakings—

(a) employing in the United Kingdom, in accordance with the calculation in regulation 4, at least the number of employees in column 1 of the table in Schedule 1 to these Regulations on or after the corresponding date in column 2 of that table; and

(b) subject to paragraph (2), whose registered office, head office or principal place of business is situated in Great Britain.

(2) Where the registered office is situated in Great Britain and the head office or principal place of business is situated in Northern Ireland or vice versa, these Regulations shall only apply where the majority of employees are employed to work in Great Britain.

(3) In these Regulations, an undertaking to which these Regulations apply is referred to, in relation to its employees, as 'the employer'.

PART II   EMPLOYEE NUMBERS AND ENTITLEMENT TO DATA

4   Calculation of number of employees

(1) Subject to paragraph (4), the number of employees for the purposes of regulation 3(1) shall be determined by ascertaining the average number of employees employed in the previous twelve months, calculated in accordance with paragraph (2).

(2) Subject to paragraph (3), the average number of employees is to be ascertained by determining the number of employees employed in each month in the previous twelve months (whether they were employed throughout the month or not), adding together those monthly figures and dividing the number by 12.

(3) For the purposes of the calculation in paragraph (2) if, for the whole of a month within the twelve month period, an employee works under a contract by virtue of which he would have worked for 75 hours or less in that month—

    (i)   were the month to have contained 21 working days;

    (ii) were the employee to have had no absences from work; and

    (iii) were the employee to have worked no overtime,

the employee may be counted as representing half of a full-time employee for the month in question, if the employer so decides.

(4) If the undertaking has been in existence for less than twelve months, the references to twelve months in paragraphs (1), (2) and (3), and the divisor of 12 referred to in paragraph (2), shall be replaced by the number of months the undertaking has been in existence.

5–6   [omitted]

PART III   NEGOTIATED AGREEMENTS

7   Employee request to negotiate an agreement in respect of information and consultation

(1) On receipt of a valid employee request, the employer shall, subject to paragraphs (8) and (9), initiate negotiations by taking the steps set out in regulation 14(1).

(2) Subject to paragraph (3), an employee request is not a valid employee request unless it consists of—

    (a) a single request made by at least 10% of the employees in the undertaking; or

    (b) a number of separate requests made on the same or different days by employees which when taken together mean that at least 10% of the employees in that undertaking have made requests, provided that the requests are made within a period of six months.

(3) Where the figure of 10% in paragraph (2) would result in less than 15 or more than 2,500 employees being required in order for a valid employee request to be made, that paragraph shall have effect as if, for the figure of 10%, there were substituted the figure of 15, or as the case may be, 2,500.

(4) An employee request is not a valid employee request unless the single request referred to in paragraph (2)(a) or each separate request referred to in paragraph (2)(b)—

    (a) is in writing;

    (b) is sent to—

        (i) the registered office, head office or principal place of business of the employer; or

        (ii) the CAC; and

    (c) specifies the names of the employees making it and the date on which it is sent.

(5) Where a request is sent to the CAC under paragraph (4)(b)(ii), the CAC shall—

(a) notify the employer that the request has been made as soon as reasonably practicable;

(b) request from the employer such information as it needs to verify the number and names of the employees who have made the request; and

(c) inform the employer and the employees who have made the request how many employees have made the request on the basis of the information provided by the employees and the employer.

(6)–(8) [omitted]

(9) If an application is made to the CAC under regulation 13, the employer shall not be required to initiate negotiations unless and until if the CAC declares that there was a valid employee request or that the employer's notification was valid.

8–10   [omitted]

11   Employer notification of decision to initiate negotiations

(1) The employer may start the negotiation process set out in regulation 14(1) on his own initiative by issuing a written notification satisfying the requirements of paragraph (2), and where the employer issues such a notification regulations 14 to 17 shall apply.

(2) The notification referred to in paragraph (1) must—

(a) state that the employer intends to start the negotiating process and that the notification is given for the purpose of these Regulations;

(b) state the date on which it is issued; and

(c) be published in such a manner as to bring it to the attention of, so far as reasonably practicable, all the employees of the undertaking.

12   Restrictions on employee request and employer notification

(1) Subject to paragraph (2), no employee request or employer notification is valid if it is made or issued, as the case may be,—

(a) where a negotiated agreement applies, within a period of three years from the date of the agreement or, where the agreement is terminated within that period, before the date on which the termination takes effect;

(b) where the standard information and consultation provisions apply within a period of three years from the date on which they started to apply; and

(c) where the employer has held a ballot under regulation 8, or was one of the employers who held a ballot under regulation 9 and the result was that the employees did not endorse the valid employee request referred to in regulation 8(1), within a period of three years from the date of that request.

(2) Paragraph (1) does not apply where there are material changes in the undertaking during the applicable period having the result—

(a) where a ballot held under regulation 8 or 9 had the result that the employees did not endorse the valid employee request, that there is no longer a pre-existing agreement which satisfies paragraph (1)(b) and (c) of regulation 8 or in the case of a ballot held under regulation 9, that there is no longer an agreement satisfying paragraph (1)(b) of that regulation; or

(b) where a negotiated agreement exists, that the agreement no longer complies with the requirement in regulation 16(1) that it must cover all the employees of the undertaking.

13   Dispute about employee request, employer notification or whether obligation in regulation 7(1) applies

(1) If the employer considers that there was no valid employee request—

(a) because the employee request did not satisfy any requirement of regulation 7(2) to (4) or was prevented from being valid by regulation 12, or

(b) because the undertaking was not one to which these Regulations applied (under Regulation 3) on the date on which the employee request was made,

the employer may apply to the CAC for a declaration as to whether there was a valid employee request.

(2) If an employee or an employees' representative considers that an employer notification was not valid because it did not comply with one or more of the requirements in regulation 11(2) or was prevented from being valid by regulation 12, he may apply to the CAC for a declaration as to whether the notification was valid.

(3) The CAC shall only consider an application for a declaration made under paragraph (1) or (2) if the application is made within a one month period beginning on the date of the employee request or the date on which the employer notification is made.

14 Negotiations to reach an agreement

(1) In order to initiate negotiations to reach an agreement under these Regulations the employer must as soon as reasonably practicable—

    (a) make arrangements, satisfying the requirements of paragraph (2), for the employees of the undertaking to elect or appoint negotiating representatives; and thereafter

    (b) inform the employees in writing of the identity of the negotiating representatives; and

    (c) invite the negotiating representatives to enter into negotiations to reach a negotiated agreement.

(2)–(7) [omitted]

15 [omitted]

16 Negotiated agreements

(1) A negotiated agreement must cover all employees of the undertaking and may consist either of a single agreement or of different parts (each being approved in accordance with paragraph (4)) which, taken together, cover all the employees of the undertaking. The single agreement or each part must—

    (a) set out the circumstances in which the employer must inform and consult the employees to which it relates;

    (b) be in writing;

    (c) be dated;

    (d) be approved in accordance with paragraphs (3) to (5);

    (e) be signed by or on behalf of the employer; and

    (f) either—

        (i) provide for the appointment or election of information and consultation representatives to whom the employer must provide the information and whom the employer must consult in the circumstances referred to in sub-paragraph (a); or

        (ii) provide that the employer must provide information directly to the employees to which it relates and consult those employees directly in the circumstances referred to in sub-paragraph (a).

(2) Where a negotiated agreement consist of different parts they may provide differently in relation to the matters referred to in paragraph (1)(a) and (f).

(3) A negotiated agreement consisting of a single agreement shall be treated as being approved for the purpose of paragraph (1)(d) if—

    (a) it has been signed by all the negotiating representatives; or

    (b) it has been signed by a majority of negotiating representatives and either—

        (i) approved in writing by at least 50% of employees employed in the undertaking, or

(ii) approved by a ballot of those employees, the arrangements for which satisfied the requirements set out in paragraph (5), in which at least 50% of the employees voting, voted in favour of approval.

(4) A part shall be treated as being approved for the purpose of paragraph (1)(d) if the part—

(a) has been signed by all the negotiating representatives involved in negotiating the part; or

(b) has been signed by a majority of those negotiating representatives and either—

(i) approved in writing by at least 50% of employees (employed in the undertaking) to which the part relates, or

(ii) approved by a ballot of those employees, the arrangements for which satisfied the requirements set out in paragraph (5), in which at least 50% of the employees voting, voted in favour of approving the part.

(5)–(6) [omitted]

17 and 17A [omitted]

PART IV   STANDARD INFORMATION AND CONSULTATION PROVISIONS

18   Application of standard information and consultation provisions

(1) Subject to paragraph (2)—

(a) where the employer is under a duty, following the making of a valid employee request or issue of a valid employer notification, to initiate negotiations in accordance with regulation 14 but does not do so, the standard information and consultation provisions shall apply from the date—

(i) which is six months from the date on which the valid employee request was made or the valid employer notification was issued, or

(ii) information and consultation representatives are elected under regulation 19, whichever is the sooner; and

(b) if the parties do not reach a negotiated agreement within the time limit referred to in regulation 14(3) (or that period as extended by agreement under paragraph (5) of that regulation) the standard information and consultation provisions shall apply from the date—

(i) which is six months from the date on which that time limit expires; or

(ii) information and consultation representatives are elected under regulation 19, whichever is the sooner.

(2) Where the standard information and consultation provisions apply, the employer and the information and consultation representatives elected pursuant to regulation 19 may, at any time, reach an agreement that provisions other than the standard information and consultation provisions shall apply.

(3) An agreement referred to in paragraph (2) shall only have effect if it covers all the employees of the undertaking, complies with the requirements listed in regulation 16(1)(a) to (c), (e) and (f), and is signed by a majority of the information and consultation representatives.

19   Election of information and consultation representatives

(1) Where the standard information and consultation provisions are to apply, the employer shall, before the standard information and consultation provisions start to apply, arrange for the holding of a ballot of its employees to elect the relevant number of information and consultation representatives.

(2) The provisions in Schedule 2 to these Regulations apply in relation to the arrangements for and conduct of any such ballot.

(3) In this regulation the 'relevant number of information and consultation representatives' means one representative per fifty employees or part thereof, provided that that number is at least 2 and does not exceed 25.

(4) An employee or an employees's representative may complain to the CAC that the employer has not arranged for the holding of a ballot in accordance with paragraph (1).

(5) Where the CAC finds the complaint well-founded, it shall make an order requiring the employer to arrange, or re-arrange, and hold the ballot.

(6) Where the CAC finds a complaint under paragraph (4) well-founded, the employee or the employee's representative may make an application to the Appeal Tribunal under regulation 22(6) and paragraphs (7) and (8) of that regulation shall apply to any such application.

20   Standard information and consultation provisions

(1) Where the standard information and consultation provisions apply pursuant to regulation 18, the employer must provide the information and consultation representatives with information on—

(a) the recent and probable development of the undertaking's activities and economic situation;

(b) the situation, structure and probable development of employment within the undertaking and on any anticipatory measures envisaged, in particular, where there is a threat to employment within the undertaking; and

(c) subject to paragraph (5), decisions likely to lead to substantial changes in work organisation or in contractual relations, including those referred to in—

(i)   sections 188 to 192 of the Trade Union and Labour Relations (Consolidation) Act 1992; and

(ii)   regulations 10 to 12 of the Transfer of Undertakings (Protection of Employment) Regulations 1981.

(2) The information referred to in paragraph (1) must be given at such time, in such fashion and with such content as are appropriate to enable, in particular, the information and consultation representatives to conduct an adequate study and, where necessary, to prepare for consultation.

(3) The employer must consult the information and consultation representatives on the matters referred to in paragraph (1)(b) and (c).

(4) The employer must ensure that the consultation referred to in paragraph (3) is conducted—

(a) in such a way as to ensure that the timing, method and content of the consultation are appropriate;

(b) on the basis of the information supplied by the employer to the information and consultation representatives and of any opinion which those representatives express to the employer;

(c) in such a way as to enable the information and consultation representatives to meet the employer at the relevant level of management depending on the subject under discussion and to obtain a reasoned response from the employer to any such opinion; and

(d) in relation to matters falling within paragraph (1)(c), with a view to reaching agreement on decisions within the scope of the employer's powers.

(5) The duties in this regulation to inform and consult the information and consultation representatives on decisions falling within paragraph (1)(c) cease to apply once the employer is under a duty under—

(a) section 188 of the Act referred to in paragraph (1)(c)(i) (duty of employer to consult representatives);

(b) regulation 10 of the Regulations referred to in paragraph (1)(c)(ii) (duty to inform and consult representatives), or

(c) any of regulations 11 to 13 of the Pension Schemes Regulations, and he has notified the information and consultation representatives in writing that he will be complying with his duty under the legislation referred to in sub-paragraph (a) or (b), or (c) as the case may be, instead of under these Regulations, provided that the notification is given on each occasion on which the employer has become or is about to become subject to the duty.

(6) Where there is an obligation in these Regulations on the employer to inform and consult his employees, a failure on the part of a person who controls the employer (either directly or indirectly) to provide information to the employer shall not constitute a valid reason for the employer failing to inform and consult.

PART V   DUTY OF CO-OPERATION

21   Co-operation

The parties are under a duty, when negotiating or implementing a negotiated agreement or when implementing the standard information and consultation provisions, to work in a spirit of co-operation and with due regard for their reciprocal rights and obligations, taking into account the interests of both the undertaking and the employees.

PART VI   COMPLIANCE AND ENFORCEMENT

22   Disputes about operation of a negotiated agreement or the standard information and consultation provisions

(1) Where—
    (a) a negotiated agreement has been agreed; or
    (b) the standard information and consultation provisions apply,
a complaint may be presented to the CAC by a relevant applicant who considers that the employer has failed to comply with the terms of the negotiated agreement or, as the case may be, one or more of the standard information and consultation provisions.

(2) A complaint brought under paragraph (1) must be brought within a period of three months commencing with the date of the alleged failure.

(3) In this regulation—
'failure' means an act or omission; and
'relevant applicant' means—
    (a) in a case where information and consultation representatives have been elected or appointed, an information and consultation representative, or
    (b) in a case where no information and consultation representatives have been elected or appointed, an employee or an employees' representative.

(4) Where the CAC finds the complaint well-founded it shall make a declaration to that effect and may make an order requiring the employer to take such steps as are necessary to comply with the terms of the negotiated agreement or, as the case may be, the standard information and consultation provisions.

(5) An order made under paragraph (4) shall specify—
    (a) the steps which the employer is required to take; and
    (b) the period within which the order must be complied with.

(6) If the CAC makes a declaration under paragraph (4) the relevant applicant may, within the period of three months beginning with the date on which the declaration is made, make an application to the Appeal Tribunal for a penalty notice to be issued.

(7) Where such an application is made, the Appeal Tribunal shall issue a written penalty notice to the employer requiring him to pay a penalty to the Secretary of State in respect of the failure unless satisfied, on hearing representations from the employer, that the failure

resulted from a reason beyond the employer's control or that he has some other reasonable excuse for his failure.

(8) Regulation 23 shall apply in respect of a penalty notice issued under this regulation.

(9) No order of the CAC under this regulation shall have the effect of suspending or altering the effect of any act done or of any agreement made by the employer or of preventing or delaying any act or agreement which the employer proposes to do or to make.

23   Penalties

(1) A penalty notice issued under regulation 22 shall specify—
   (a) the amount of the penalty which is payable;
   (b) the date before which the penalty must be paid; and
   (c) the failure and period to which the penalty relates.

(2) No penalty set by the Appeal Tribunal under this regulation may exceed £75,000.

(3) Matters to be taken into account by the Appeal Tribunal when setting the amount of the penalty shall include—
   (a) the gravity of the failure;
   (b) the period of time over which the failure occurred;
   (c) the reason for the failure;
   (d) the number of employees affected by the failure; and
   (e) the number of employees employed by the undertaking or, where a negotiated agreement covers employees in more than one undertaking, the number of employees employed by both or all of the undertakings.

(4) The date specified under paragraph (1)(b) must not be earlier than the end of the period within which an appeal against a declaration or order made by the CAC under regulation 22 may be made.

(5) If the specified date in a penalty notice has passed and—
   (a) the period during which an appeal may be made has expired without an appeal having been made; or
   (b) such an appeal has been made and determined,
the Secretary of State may recover from the employer, as a civil debt due to him, any amount payable under the penalty notice which remains outstanding.

(6) The making of an appeal suspends the effect of a penalty notice.

(7) [omitted]

24   Exclusivity of remedy

The remedy for infringement of the rights conferred by Parts I to VI of these Regulations is by way of complaint to the CAC, and not otherwise.

PART VII   CONFIDENTIAL INFORMATION

25   Breach of statutory duty

(1) A person to whom the employer, pursuant to his obligations under these Regulations, entrusts any information or document on terms requiring it to be held in confidence shall not disclose that information or document except, where the terms permit him to do so, in accordance with those terms.

(2) In this regulation a person referred to in paragraph (1) to whom information or a document is entrusted is referred to as a 'recipient'.

(3) The obligation to comply with paragraph (1) is a duty owed to the employer, and a breach of the duty is actionable accordingly (subject to the defences and other incidents applying to actions for breaches of statutory duty).

(4) Paragraph (3) shall not affect any legal liability which any person may incur by disclosing the information or document, or any right which any person may have in relation to such disclosure otherwise than under this regulation.

(5) No action shall lie under paragraph (3) where the recipient reasonably believed the disclosure to be a 'protected disclosure' within the meaning given to that expression by section 43A of the 1996 Act.

(6) A recipient to whom the employer has entrusted any information or document on terms requiring it to be held in confidence may apply to the CAC for a declaration as to whether it was reasonable for the employer to require the recipient to hold the information or document in confidence.

(7) If the CAC considers, on an application under paragraph (6), that the disclosure of the information or document by the recipient would not, or would not be likely to, harm the legitimate interests of the undertaking, it shall make a declaration that it was not reasonable for the employer to require the recipient to hold the information or document in confidence.

(8) If a declaration is made under paragraph (7), the information or document shall not at any time thereafter be regarded as having been entrusted to the recipient who made the application under paragraph (6), or to any other recipient, on terms requiring it to be held in confidence.

26   Withholding of information by the employer

(1) The employer is not required to disclose any information or document to a person for the purposes of these Regulations where the nature of the information or document is such that, according to objective criteria, the disclosure of the information or document would seriously harm the functioning of, or would be prejudicial to, the undertaking.

(2) If there is a dispute between the employer and—
    (a) where information and consultation representatives have been elected or appointed, such a representative; or
    (b) where no information and consultation representatives have been elected or appointed, an employee or an employees' representative,

as to whether the nature of the information or document which the employer has failed to provide is such as is described in paragraph (1), the employer or a person referred to in sub-paragraph (a) or (b) may apply to the CAC for a declaration as to whether the information or document is of such a nature.

(3) If the CAC makes a declaration that the disclosure of the information or document in question would not, according to objective criteria, be seriously harmful or prejudicial as mentioned in paragraph (1), the CAC shall order the employer to disclose the information or document.

(4) An order under paragraph (3) shall specify—
    (a) the information or document to be disclosed;
    (b) the person or persons to whom the information or document is to be disclosed;
    (c) any terms on which the information or document is to be disclosed; and
    (d) the date before which the information or document is to be disclosed.

PART VIII   PROTECTIONS FOR INFORMATION AND CONSULTATION REPRESENTATIVES, ETC.

27   Right to time off for information and consultation representatives, etc.

(1) An employee who is—
    (a) a negotiating representative; or
    (b) an information and consultation representative,

is entitled to be permitted by his employer to take reasonable time off during the employee's working hours in order to perform his functions as such a representative.

(2) For the purposes of this regulation, the working hours of an employee shall be taken to be any time when, in accordance with his contract of employment, the employee is required to be at work.

28   Right to remuneration for time off under regulation 27

(1) An employee who is permitted to take time off under regulation 27 is entitled to be paid remuneration by his employer for the time taken off at the appropriate hourly rate.

(2) Chapter II of Part XIV of the 1996 Act (a week's pay) shall apply in relation to this regulation as it applies in relation to section 62 of the 1996 Act.

(3)–(7) [omitted]

29   Right to time off: complaint to tribunals

(1) An employee may present a complaint to an employment tribunal that his employer—

> (a) has unreasonably refused to permit him to take time off as required by regulation 27; or
>
> (b) has failed to pay the whole or part of any amount to which the employee is entitled under regulation 28.

(2)–(5) [omitted]

30   Unfair dismissal

(1) An employee who is dismissed and to whom paragraph (2) or (5) applies shall be regarded, if the reason (or, if more than one, the principal reason) for the dismissal is a reason specified in, respectively, paragraph (3) or (6), as unfairly dismissed for the purposes of Part 10 of the 1996 Act.

(2) This paragraph applies to an employee who is—

> (a) an employees' representative;
>
> (b) a negotiating representative;
>
> (c) an information and consultation representative; or
>
> (d) a candidate in an election in which any person elected will, on being elected, be such a representative.

(3) The reasons are that—

> (a) the employee performed or proposed to perform any functions or activities as such a representative or candidate;
>
> (b) the employee exercised or proposed to exercise an entitlement conferred on the employee by regulation 27 or 28; or
>
> (c) the employee (or a person acting on his behalf) made or proposed to make a request to exercise such an entitlement.

(4) Paragraph (1) does not apply in the circumstances set out in paragraph (3)(a) where the reason (or principal reason) for the dismissal is that in the performance, or purported performance, of the employee's functions or activities he has disclosed any information or document in breach of the duty in regulation 25, unless the employee reasonably believed the disclosure to be a 'protected disclosure' within the meaning given to that expression by section 43A of the 1996 Act.

(5) This paragraph applies to any employee whether or not he is an employee to whom paragraph (2) applies.

(6) The reasons are that the employee—

> (a) took, or proposed to take, any proceedings before an employment tribunal to enforce a right or secure an entitlement conferred on him by these Regulations;
>
> (b) exercised, or proposed to exercise, any entitlement to apply or complain to the CAC or the Appeal Tribunal conferred by these Regulations or to exercise the right to appeal in connection with any rights conferred by these Regulations;
>
> (c) requested, or proposed to request, data in accordance with regulation 5;
>
> (d) acted with a view to securing that an agreement was or was not negotiated or that the standard information and consultation provisions did or did not become applicable;

(e) indicated that he supported or did not support the coming into existence of a negotiated agreement or the application of the standard information and consultation provisions;

(f) stood as a candidate in an election in which any person elected would, on being elected, be a negotiating representative or an information and consultation representative;

(g) influenced or sought to influence by lawful means the way in which votes were to be cast by other employees in a ballot arranged under these Regulations;

(h) voted in such a ballot;

(i) expressed doubts, whether to a ballot supervisor or otherwise, as to whether such a ballot had been properly conducted; or

(j) proposed to do, failed to do, or proposed to decline to do, any of the things mentioned in sub-paragraphs (d) to (i).

(7) It is immaterial for the purpose of paragraph (6)(a)—

(a) whether or not the employee has the right or entitlement; or

(b) whether or not the right has been infringed;

but for that sub-paragraph to apply, the claim to the right and, if applicable, the claim that it has been infringed must be made in good faith.

31 [omitted]

32 Detriment

(1) An employee to whom paragraph (2) or (5) applies has the right not to be subjected to any detriment by any act, or deliberate failure to act, by his employer, done on a ground specified in, respectively, paragraph (3) or (6).

(2) This paragraph applies to an employee who is—

(a) an employees' representative;

(b) a negotiating representative;

(c) an information and consultation representative; or

(d) a candidate in an election in which any person elected will, on being elected, be such a representative.

(3) The ground is that—

(a) the employee performed or proposed to perform any functions or activities as such a representative or candidate;

(b) the employee exercised or proposed to exercise an entitlement conferred on the employee by regulation 27 or 28; or

(c) the employee (or a person acting on his behalf) made or proposed to make a request to exercise such an entitlement.

(4) Paragraph (1) does not apply in the circumstances set out in paragraph (3)(a) where the ground (or principal ground) for the subjection to detriment is that in the performance, or purported performance, of the employee's functions or activities he has disclosed any information or document in breach of the duty in regulation 25, unless the employee reasonably believed the disclosure to be a 'protected disclosure' within the meaning given to that expression by section 43A of the 1996 Act.

(5) This paragraph applies to any employee whether or not he is an employee to whom paragraph (2) applies.

(6) The grounds are that the employee—

(a) took, or proposed to take, any proceedings before an employment tribunal to enforce a right or secure an entitlement conferred on him by these Regulations;

(b) exercised, or proposed to exercise, any entitlement to apply or complain to the CAC or the Appeal Tribunal conferred by these Regulations or to exercise the right to appeal in connection with any rights conferred by these Regulations;

(c) requested, or proposed to request, data in accordance with regulation 5;

(d) acted with a view to securing that an agreement was or was not negotiated or that the standard information and consultation provisions did or did not become applicable;

(e) indicated that he supported or did not support the coming into existence of a negotiated agreement or the application of the standard information and consultation provisions;

(f) stood as a candidate in an election in which any person elected would, on being elected, be a negotiating representative or an information and consultation representative;

(g) influenced or sought to influence by lawful means the way in which votes were to be cast by other employees in a ballot arranged under these Regulations;

(h) voted in such a ballot;

(i) expressed doubts, whether to a ballot supervisor or otherwise, as to whether such a ballot had been properly conducted; or

(j) proposed to do, failed to do, or proposed to decline to do, any of the things mentioned in sub-paragraphs (d) to (i).

(7) It is immaterial for the purpose of paragraph (6)(a)—

(a) whether or not the employee has the right or entitlement; or

(b) whether or not the right has been infringed,

but for that sub-paragraph to apply, the claim to the right and, if applicable, the claim that it has been infringed must be made in good faith.

(8) This regulation does not apply where the detriment in question amounts to dismissal.

33 Detriment: enforcement and subsidiary provisions

(1) An employee may present a complaint to an employment tribunal that he has been subjected to a detriment in contravention of regulation 32.

(2) The provisions of sections 48(2) to (4) and 49(1) to (5) of the 1996 Act (complaints to employment tribunals and remedies) shall apply in relation to a complaint under this regulation as they apply in relation to a complaint under section 48 of the Act but taking references to the employer as references to the employer within the meaning of regulation 32(1) above.

34–43 [omitted]

SCHEDULE 1   APPLICATION OF REGULATIONS

Number of employees	Date Regulations apply
At least 150	6 April 2005
At least 100	6 April 2007
At least 50	6 April 2008

Schedule 2 [omitted]

The Employment Equality (Age) Regulations 2006
(SI 2006 No. 1031)

PART 1   GENERAL

2. Interpretation
3. Discrimination on grounds of age
4. Discrimination by way of victimisation
5. Instructions to discriminate
6. Harassment on grounds of age

PART 2   DISCRIMINATION IN EMPLOYMENT AND VOCATIONAL TRAINING

PART 3   OTHER UNLAWFUL ACTS

PART 4   GENERAL EXCEPTIONS FROM PARTS 2 AND 3

PART 5   ENFORCEMENT

SCHEDULE 5

Validity of contracts, collective agreements and rules of undertakings

PART 1

Validity and revision of contracts

PART 2

Collective agreements and rules of undertakings

SCHEDULE 6

Duty to consider working beyond retirement

PART 1   GENERAL

1 [omitted]

2   Interpretation
(1) In these Regulations, references to discrimination are to any discrimination falling within regulation 3 (discrimination on grounds of age), regulation 4 (discrimination by way

of victimisation) or regulation 5 (instructions to discriminate) and related expressions shall be construed accordingly, and references to harassment shall be construed in accordance with regulation 6 (harassment on grounds of age).

(2) In these Regulations—

'1996 Act' means the Employment Rights Act 1996;

'act' includes a deliberate omission;

'benefit', except in regulation 11 and Schedule 2 (pension schemes), includes facilities and services;

'commencement date' means 1st October 2006;

'Crown employment' means—

(a) service for purposes of a Minister of the Crown or government department, other than service of a person holding a statutory office; or

(b) service on behalf of the Crown for purposes of a person holding a statutory office or purposes of a statutory body;

'detriment' does not include harassment within the meaning of regulation 6;

'employment' means employment under a contract of service or of apprenticeship or a contract personally to do any work, and related expressions (such as 'employee' and 'employer') shall be construed accordingly, but this definition does not apply in relation to regulation 30 (exception for retirement) or to Schedules 2, 6, 7 and 8;

. . .

'worker' in relation to regulations 32 and 34 and to Schedule 2, means, as the case may be—

(a) an employee;

(b) a person holding an office or post to which regulation 12 (office-holders etc) applies;

(c) a person holding the office of constable;

(d) a partner within the meaning of regulation 17 (partnerships);

(e) a member of a limited liability partnership within the meaning of that regulation;

(f) a person in Crown employment;

(g) a relevant member of the House of Commons staff;

(h) a relevant member of the House of Lords staff.

(3) In these Regulations references to 'employer', in their application to a person at any time seeking to employ another, include a person who has no employees at that time.

3 Discrimination on grounds of age

(1) For the purposes of these Regulations, a person ('A') discriminates against another person ('B') if—

(a) on grounds of B's age, A treats B less favourably than he treats or would treat other persons, or

(b) A applies to B a provision, criterion or practice which he applies or would apply equally to persons not of the same age group as B, but—

(i)   which puts or would put persons of the same age group as B at a particular disadvantage when compared with other persons, and

(ii) which puts B at that disadvantage,

and A cannot show the treatment or, as the case may be, provision, criterion or practice to be a proportionate means of achieving a legitimate aim.

(2) A comparison of B's case with that of another person under paragraph (1) must be such that the relevant circumstances in the one case are the same, or not materially different, in the other.

(3) In this regulation—

(a) 'age group' means a group of persons defined by reference to age, whether by reference to a particular age or a range of ages; and

(b) the reference in paragraph (1)(a) to B's age includes B's apparent age.

4   Discrimination by way of victimisation

(1) For the purposes of these Regulations, a person ('A') discriminates against another person ('B') if he treats B less favourably than he treats or would treat other persons in the same circumstances, and does so by reason that B has—

(a) brought proceedings against A or any other person under or by virtue of these Regulations;

(b) given evidence or information in connection with proceedings brought by any person against A or any other person under or by virtue of these Regulations;

(c) otherwise done anything under or by reference to these Regulations in relation to A or any other person; or

(d) alleged that A or any other person has committed an act which (whether or not the allegation so states) would amount to a contravention of these Regulations,

or by reason that A knows that B intends to do any of those things, or suspects that B has done or intends to do any of them.

(2) Paragraph (1) does not apply to treatment of B by reason of any allegation made by him, or evidence or information given by him, if the allegation, evidence or information was false and not made (or, as the case may be, given) in good faith.

5   Instructions to discriminate

For the purposes of these Regulations, a person ('A') discriminates against another person ('B') if he treats B less favourably than he treats or would treat other persons in the same circumstances, and does so by reason that—

(a) B has not carried out (in whole or in part) an instruction to do an act which is unlawful by virtue of these Regulations, or

(b) B, having been given an instruction to do such an act, complains to A or to any other person about that instruction.

6   Harassment on grounds of age

(1) For the purposes of these Regulations, a person ('A') subjects another person ('B') to harassment where, on grounds of age, A engages in unwanted conduct which has the purpose or effect of—

(a) violating B's dignity; or

(b) creating an intimidating, hostile, degrading, humiliating or offensive environment for B.

(2) Conduct shall be regarded as having the effect specified in paragraph (1)(a) or (b) only if, having regard to all the circumstances, including in particular the perception of B, it should reasonably be considered as having that effect.

PART 2   DISCRIMINATION IN EMPLOYMENT AND VOCATIONAL TRAINING

7   Applicants and employees

(1) It is unlawful for an employer, in relation to employment by him at an establishment in Great Britain, to discriminate against a person—

(a) in the arrangements he makes for the purpose of determining to whom he should offer employment;

(b) in the terms on which he offers that person employment; or

(c) by refusing to offer, or deliberately not offering, him employment.

(2) It is unlawful for an employer, in relation to a person whom he employs at an establishment in Great Britain, to discriminate against that person—

(a) in the terms of employment which he affords him;

(b) in the opportunities which he affords him for promotion, a transfer, training, or receiving any other benefit;

(c) by refusing to afford him, or deliberately not affording him, any such opportunity; or

(d) by dismissing him, or subjecting him to any other detriment.

(3) It is unlawful for an employer, in relation to employment by him at an establishment in Great Britain, to subject to harassment a person whom he employs or who has applied to him for employment.

(4) Subject to paragraph (5), paragraph (1)(a) and (c) does not apply in relation to a person—

(a) whose age is greater than the employer's normal retirement age or, if the employer does not have a normal retirement age, the age of 65; or

(b) who would, within a period of six months from the date of his application to the employer, reach the employer's normal retirement age or, if the employer does not have a normal retirement age, the age of 65.

(5) Paragraph (4) only applies to a person to whom, if he was recruited by the employer, regulation 30 (exception for retirement) could apply.

(6) Paragraph (2) does not apply to benefits of any description if the employer is concerned with the provision (for payment or not) of benefits of that description to the public, or to a section of the public which includes the employee in question, unless—

(a) that provision differs in a material respect from the provision of the benefits by the employer to his employees; or

(b) the provision of the benefits to the employee in question is regulated by his contract of employment; or

(c) the benefits relate to training.

(7) In paragraph (2)(d) reference to the dismissal of a person from employment includes reference—

(a) to the termination of that person's employment by the expiration of any period (including a period expiring by reference to an event or circumstance), not being a termination immediately after which the employment is renewed on the same terms; and

(b) to the termination of that person's employment by any act of his (including the giving of notice) in circumstances such that he is entitled to terminate it without notice by reason of the conduct of the employer.

(8) In paragraph (4) 'normal retirement age' is an age of 65 or more which meets the requirements of section 98ZH of the 1996 Act.

8 Exception for genuine occupational requirement etc

(1) In relation to discrimination falling within regulation 3 (discrimination on grounds of age)—

(a) regulation 7(1)(a) or (c) does not apply to any employment;

(b) regulation 7(2)(b) or (c) does not apply to promotion or transfer to, or training for, any employment; and

(c) regulation 7(2)(d) does not apply to dismissal from any employment,

where paragraph (2) applies.

(2) This paragraph applies where, having regard to the nature of the employment or the context in which it is carried out—

(a) possessing a characteristic related to age is a genuine and determining occupational requirement;

(b) it is proportionate to apply that requirement in the particular case; and

(c) either—

(i) the person to whom that requirement is applied does not meet it, or

(ii) the employer is not satisfied, and in all the circumstances it is reasonable for him not to be satisfied, that that person meets it.

9 Contract workers

(1) It is unlawful for a principal, in relation to contract work at an establishment in Great Britain, to discriminate against a contract worker—

(a) in the terms on which he allows him to do that work;

(b) by not allowing him to do it or continue to do it;

(c) in the way he affords him access to any benefits or by refusing or deliberately not affording him access to them; or

(d) by subjecting him to any other detriment.

(2) It is unlawful for a principal, in relation to contract work at an establishment in Great Britain, to subject a contract worker to harassment.

(3) A principal does not contravene paragraph (1)(b) by doing any act in relation to a contract worker where, if the work were to be done by a person taken into the principal's employment, that act would be lawful by virtue of regulation 8 (exception for genuine occupational requirement etc).

(4) Paragraph (1) does not apply to benefits of any description if the principal is concerned with the provision (for payment or not) of benefits of that description to the public, or to a section of the public to which the contract worker in question belongs, unless that provision differs in a material respect from the provision of the benefits by the principal to his contract workers.

(5) In this regulation—

'principal' means a person ('A') who makes work available for doing by individuals who are employed by another person who supplies them under a contract made with A;

'contract work' means work so made available; and

'contract worker' means any individual who is supplied to the principal under such a contract.

10–17 [omitted]

18 Trade organisations

(1) It is unlawful for a trade organisation to discriminate against a person—

(a) in the terms on which it is prepared to admit him to membership of the organisation; or

(b) by refusing to accept, or deliberately not accepting, his application for membership.

(2) It is unlawful for a trade organisation, in relation to a member of the organisation, to discriminate against him—

(a) in the way it affords him access to any benefits or by refusing or deliberately omitting to afford him access to them;

(b) by depriving him of membership, or varying the terms on which he is a member; or

(c) by subjecting him to any other detriment.

(3) It is unlawful for a trade organisation, in relation to a person's membership or application for membership of that organisation, to subject that person to harassment.

(4) In this regulation—

'trade organisation' means an organisation of workers, an organisation of employers, or any other organisation whose members carry on a particular profession or trade for the purposes of which the organisation exists;

'profession' includes any vocation or occupation; and

'trade' includes any business.

19–23 [omitted]

24 Relationships which have come to an end

(1) In this regulation a 'relevant relationship' is a relationship during the course of which an act of discrimination against, or harassment of, one party to the relationship ('B') by the other party to it ('A') is unlawful by virtue of any preceding provision of this Part.

(2) Where a relevant relationship has come to an end, it is unlawful for A—

    (a) to discriminate against B by subjecting him to a detriment; or

    (b) to subject B to harassment;

where the discrimination or harassment arises out of and is closely connected to that relationship.

(3) In paragraph (1), reference to an act of discrimination or harassment which is unlawful includes, in the case of a relationship which has come to an end before the coming into force of these Regulations, reference to an act of discrimination or harassment which would, after the coming into force of these Regulations, be unlawful.

PART 3   OTHER UNLAWFUL ACTS

25   Liability of employers and principals

(1) Anything done by a person in the course of his employment shall be treated for the purposes of these Regulations as done by his employer as well as by him, whether or not it was done with the employer's knowledge or approval.

(2) Anything done by a person as agent for another person with the authority (whether express or implied, and whether precedent or subsequent) of that other person shall be treated for the purposes of these Regulations as done by that other person as well as by him.

(3) In proceedings brought under these Regulations against any person in respect of an act alleged to have been done by an employee of his it shall be a defence for that person to prove that he took such steps as were reasonably practicable to prevent the employee from doing that act, or from doing in the course of his employment acts of that description.

26   Aiding unlawful acts

(1) A person who knowingly aids another person to do an act made unlawful by these Regulations shall be treated for the purpose of these Regulations as himself doing an unlawful act of the like description.

(2) For the purposes of paragraph (1) an employee or agent for whose act the employer or principal is liable under regulation 25 (or would be so liable but for regulation 25(3)) shall be deemed to aid the doing of the act by the employer or principal.

(3) A person does not under this regulation knowingly aid another to do an unlawful act if—

    (a) he acts in reliance on a statement made to him by that other person that, by reason of any provision of these Regulations, the act which he aids would not be unlawful; and

    (b) it is reasonable for him to rely on the statement.

(4) A person who knowingly or recklessly makes a statement such as is referred to in paragraph (3)(a) which in a material respect is false or misleading commits an offence, and shall be liable on summary conviction to a fine not exceeding level 5 on the standard scale.

PART 4   GENERAL EXCEPTIONS FROM PARTS 2 AND 3

27–28   [omitted]

29   Exceptions for positive action

(1) Nothing in Part 2 or 3 shall render unlawful any act done in or in connection with—

    (a) affording persons of a particular age or age group access to facilities for training which would help fit them for particular work; or

    (b) encouraging persons of a particular age or age group to take advantage of opportunities for doing particular work;

where it reasonably appears to the person doing the act that it prevents or compensates for disadvantages linked to age suffered by persons of that age or age group doing that work or likely to take up that work.

(2) Nothing in Part 2 or 3 shall render unlawful any act done by a trade organisation within the meaning of regulation 18 in or in connection with—

(a) affording only members of the organisation who are of a particular age or age group access to facilities for training which would help fit them for holding a post of any kind in the organisation; or

(b) encouraging only members of the organisation who are of a particular age or age group to take advantage of opportunities for holding such posts in the organisation,

where it reasonably appears to the organisation that the act prevents or compensates for disadvantages linked to age suffered by those of that age or age group holding such posts or likely to hold such posts.

(3) Nothing in Part 2 or 3 shall render unlawful any act done by a trade organisation within the meaning of regulation 18 in or in connection with encouraging only persons of a particular age or age group to become members of the organisation where it reasonably appears to the organisation that the act prevents or compensates for disadvantages linked to age suffered by persons of that age or age group who are, or are eligible to become, members.

30 Exception for retirement

(1) This regulation applies in relation to an employee within the meaning of section 230(1) of the 1996 Act, a person in Crown employment, a relevant member of the House of Commons staff, and a relevant member of the House of Lords staff.

(2) Nothing in Part 2 or 3 shall render unlawful the dismissal of a person to whom this regulation applies at or over the age of 65 where the reason for the dismissal is retirement.

(3) For the purposes of this regulation, whether or not the reason for a dismissal is retirement shall be determined in accordance with sections 98ZA to 98ZF of the 1996 Act.

31 [omitted]

32 Exception for provision of certain benefits based on length of service

(1) Subject to paragraph (2), nothing in Part 2 or 3 shall render it unlawful for a person ('A'), in relation to the award of any benefit by him, to put a worker ('B') at a disadvantage when compared with another worker ('C'), if and to the extent that the disadvantage suffered by B is because B's length of service is less than that of C.

(2) Where B's length of service exceeds 5 years, it must reasonably appear to A that the way in which he uses the criterion of length of service, in relation to the award in respect of which B is put at a disadvantage, fulfils a business need of his undertaking (for example, by encouraging the loyalty or motivation, or rewarding the experience, of some or all of his workers).

(3) In calculating a worker's length of service for these purposes, A shall calculate—

(a) the length of time the worker has been working for him doing work which he reasonably considers to be at or above a particular level (assessed by reference to the demands made on the worker, for example, in terms of effort, skills and decision making); or

(b) the length of time the worker has been working for him in total;

and on each occasion on which he decides to use the criterion of length of service in relation to the award of a benefit to workers, it is for him to decide which of these definitions to use to calculate their lengths of service.

(4) For the purposes of paragraph (3), in calculating the length of time a worker has been working for him—

(a) A shall calculate the length of time in terms of the number of weeks during the whole or part of which the worker was working for him;

(b) A may discount any period during which the worker was absent from work (including any period of absence which at the time it occurred was thought by A or the worker to be permanent) unless in all the circumstances (including the way in which other workers' absences occurring in similar circumstances are treated by A in calculating their lengths of service) it would not be reasonable for him to do so;

(c) A may discount any period of time during which the worker was present at work ("the relevant period") where—

    (i) the relevant period preceded a period during which the worker was absent from work, and

    (ii) in all the circumstances (including the length of the worker's absence, the reason for his absence, the effect his absence has had on his ability to discharge the duties of his work, and the way in which other workers are treated by A in similar circumstances) it is reasonable for A to discount the relevant period.

(5) For the purposes of paragraph (3)(b), a worker shall be treated as having worked for A during any period during which he worked for another if—

(a) that period is treated as a period of employment with A for the purposes of the 1996 Act by virtue of the operation of section 218 of that Act; or

(b) were the worker to be made redundant by A, that period and the period he has worked for A would amount to "relevant service" within the meaning of section 155 of that Act.

(6) In paragraph (5)—

(a) the reference to being made redundant is a reference to being dismissed by reason of redundancy for the purposes of the 1996 Act;

(b) the reference to section 155 of that Act is a reference to that section as modified by the Redundancy Payments (Continuity of Employment in Local Government, etc.) (Modification) Order 1999.

(7) In this regulation—

'benefit' does not include any benefit awarded to a worker by virtue of his ceasing to work for A; and

'year' means a year of 12 calendar months.

33–34 [omitted]

PART 5   ENFORCEMENT

35   Restriction of proceedings for breach of Regulations

(1) Except as provided by these Regulations no proceedings, whether civil or criminal, shall lie against any person in respect of an act by reason that the act is unlawful by virtue of a provision of these Regulations.

(2) [omitted]

36   Jurisdiction of employment tribunals

(1) A complaint by any person ('the complainant') that another person ('the respondent')—

(a) has committed against the complainant an act to which this regulation applies; or

(b) is by virtue of regulation 25 (liability of employers and principals) or 26 (aiding unlawful acts) to be treated as having committed against the complainant such an act;

may be presented to an employment tribunal.

(2) This regulation applies to any act of discrimination or harassment which is unlawful by virtue of any provision of Part 2 other than—

(a) where the act is one in respect of which an appeal or proceedings in the nature of an appeal may be brought under any enactment, regulation 19 (qualifications bodies);

(b) regulation 23 (institutions of further and higher education); or
(c) where the act arises out of and is closely connected to a relationship between the complainant and the respondent which has come to an end but during the course of which an act of discrimination against, or harassment of, the complainant by the respondent would have been unlawful by virtue of regulation 23, regulation 24 (relationships which have come to an end).

(3) In paragraph (2)(c), reference to an act of discrimination or harassment which would have been unlawful includes, in the case of a relationship which has come to an end before the coming into force of these Regulations, reference to an act of discrimination or harassment which would, after the coming into force of these Regulations, have been unlawful.

(4) In this regulation, 'enactment' includes an enactment comprised in, or in an instrument made under, an Act of the Scottish Parliament.

37   Burden of proof: employment tribunals

(1) This regulation applies to any complaint presented under regulation 36 to an employment tribunal.

(2) Where, on the hearing of the complaint, the complainant proves facts from which the tribunal could, apart from this regulation, conclude in the absence of an adequate explanation that the respondent—
(a) has committed against the complainant an act to which regulation 36 applies; or
(b) is by virtue of regulation 25 (liability of employers and principals) or 26 (aiding unlawful acts) to be treated as having committed against the complainant such an act,
the tribunal shall uphold the complaint unless the respondent proves that he did not commit, or as the case may be, is not to be treated as having committed, that act.

38   Remedies on complaints in employment tribunals

(1) Where an employment tribunal finds that a complaint presented to it under regulation 36 is well-founded, the tribunal shall make such of the following as it considers just and equitable—
(a) an order declaring the rights of the complainant and the respondent in relation to the act to which the complaint relates;
(b) an order requiring the respondent to pay to the complainant compensation of an amount corresponding to any damages he could have been ordered by a county court or by a sheriff court to pay to the complainant if the complaint had fallen to be dealt with under regulation 39 (jurisdiction of county and sheriff courts);
(c) a recommendation that the respondent take within a specified period action appearing to the tribunal to be practicable for the purpose of obviating or reducing the adverse effect on the complainant of any act of discrimination or harassment to which the complaint relates.

(2) As respects an unlawful act of discrimination falling within regulation 3(1)(b) (discrimination on the grounds of age), if the respondent proves that the provision, criterion or practice was not applied with the intention of treating the complainant unfavourably on grounds of age, an order may be made under paragraph (1)(b) only if the employment tribunal—
(a) makes such order under paragraph (1)(a) (if any) and such recommendation under paragraph (1)(c) (if any) as it would have made if it had no power to make an order under paragraph (1)(b); and
(b) where it makes an order under paragraph (1)(a) or a recommendation under paragraph (1)(c) or both) considers that it is just and equitable to make an order under paragraph (1)(b) as well.

(3) If without reasonable justification the respondent to a complaint fails to comply with a recommendation made by an employment tribunal under paragraph (1)(c), then, if it thinks it just and equitable to do so—

(a) the tribunal may increase the amount of compensation required to be paid to the complainant in respect of the complaint by an order made under paragraph (1)(b); or

(b) if an order under paragraph (1)(b) was not made, the tribunal may make such an order.

(4) Where an amount of compensation falls to be awarded under paragraph (1)(b), the tribunal may include in the award interest on that amount subject to, and in accordance with, the provisions of the Employment Tribunals (Interest on Awards in Discrimination Cases) Regulations 1996.

(5) This regulation has effect subject to paragraph 6 of Schedule 2 (pension schemes).

39 Jurisdiction of county and sheriff courts

(1) A claim by any person ('the claimant') that another person ('the respondent')—

(a) has committed against the claimant an act to which this regulation applies; or

(b) is by virtue of regulation 25 (liability of employers and principals) or 26 (aiding unlawful acts) to be treated as having committed against the claimant such an act,

may be made the subject of civil proceedings in like manner as any other claim in tort or (in Scotland) in reparation for breach of statutory duty.

(2) Proceedings brought under paragraph (1) shall—

(a) in England and Wales, be brought only in a county court; and

(b) in Scotland, be brought only in a sheriff court.

(3) For the avoidance of doubt it is hereby declared that damages in respect of an unlawful act to which this regulation applies may include compensation for injury to feelings whether or not they include compensation under any other head.

(4) This regulation applies to any act of discrimination or harassment which is unlawful by virtue of—

(a) regulation 23 (institutions of further and higher education); or

(b) where the act arises out of and is closely connected to a relationship between the claimant and the respondent which has come to an end but during the course of which an act of discrimination against, or harassment of, the claimant by the respondent would have been unlawful by virtue of regulation 23, regulation 24 (relationships which have come to an end).

(5) In paragraph (4)(b), reference to an act of discrimination or harassment which would have been unlawful includes, in the case of a relationship which has come to an end before the coming into force of these Regulations, reference to an act of discrimination or harassment which would, after the coming into force of these Regulations, have been unlawful.

40–41 [omitted]

42 Period within which proceedings to be brought

(1) An employment tribunal shall not consider a complaint under regulation 36 unless it is presented to the tribunal before the end of the period of three months beginning when the act complained of was done.

(2) A county court or a sheriff court shall not consider a claim brought under regulation 39 unless proceedings in respect of the claim are instituted before the end of the period of six months beginning when the act complained of was done.

(3) A court or tribunal may nevertheless consider any such complaint or claim which is out of time if, in all the circumstances of the case, it considers that it is just and equitable to do so.

(4) For the purposes of this regulation and regulation 41 (help for persons in obtaining information etc)—

(a) when the making of a contract is, by reason of the inclusion of any term, an unlawful act, that act shall be treated as extending throughout the duration of the contract; and

(b) any act extending over a period shall be treated as done at the end of that period; and

(c) a deliberate omission shall be treated as done when the person in question decided upon it,

and in the absence of evidence establishing the contrary a person shall be taken for the purposes of this regulation to decide upon an omission when he does an act inconsistent with doing the omitted act or, if he has done no such inconsistent act, when the period expires within which he might reasonably have been expected to do the omitted act if it was to be done.

43–49 [omitted]

SCHEDULE 5   VALIDITY OF CONTRACTS, COLLECTIVE AGREEMENTS AND RULES OF UNDERTAKINGS

PART 1   VALIDITY AND REVISION OF CONTRACTS

1.—(1) A term of a contract is void where—
   (a) the making of the contract is, by reason of the inclusion of the term, unlawful by virtue of these Regulations;
   (b) it is included in furtherance of an act which is unlawful by virtue of these Regulations; or
   (c) it provides for the doing of an act which is unlawful by virtue of these Regulations.

(2) Sub-paragraph (1) does not apply to a term the inclusion of which constitutes, or is in furtherance of, or provides for, unlawful discrimination against, or harassment of, a party to the contract, but the term shall be unenforceable against that party.

(3) A term in a contract which purports to exclude or limit any provision of these Regulations is unenforceable by any person in whose favour the term would operate apart from this paragraph.

(4) [omitted]

2.—(1) Paragraph 1(3) does not apply—
   (a) to a contract settling a complaint to which regulation 36(1) (jurisdiction of employment tribunals) applies where the contract is made with the assistance of a conciliation officer within the meaning of section 211 of the Trade Union and Labour Relations (Consolidation) Act 1992;
   (b) to a contract settling a complaint to which regulation 36(1) applies if the conditions regulating compromise contracts under this Schedule are satisfied in relation to the contract; or
   (c) to a contract settling a claim to which regulation 39 (jurisdiction of county or sheriff courts) applies.

(2) The conditions regulating compromise contracts under this Schedule are that—
   (a) the contract must be in writing;
   (b) the contract must relate to the particular complaint;
   (c) the complainant must have received advice from a relevant independent adviser as to the terms and effect of the proposed contract and in particular its effect on his ability to pursue a complaint before an employment tribunal;
   (d) there must be in force, when the adviser gives the advice, a contract of insurance, or an indemnity provided for members of a profession or professional body, covering the risk of a claim by the complainant in respect of loss arising in consequence of the advice;
   (e) the contract must identify the adviser; and

(f) the contract must state that the conditions regulating compromise contracts under this Schedule are satisfied.

(3)–(8) [omitted]

(9) An agreement under which the parties agree to submit a dispute to arbitration—

(a) shall be regarded for the purposes of sub-paragraphs (1)(a) and (b) as being a contract settling a complaint if—

(i) the dispute is covered by a scheme having effect by virtue of an order under section 212A of the Trade Union and Labour Relations (Consolidation) Act 1992, and

(ii) the agreement is to submit it to arbitration in accordance with the scheme, but

(b) shall be regarded as neither being nor including such a contract in any other case.

3.—(1) On the application of a person interested in a contract to which paragraph 1(1) or (2) applies, a county court or a sheriff court may make such order as it thinks fit for—

(a) removing or modifying any term rendered void by paragraph 1(1), or

(b) removing or modifying any term made unenforceable by paragraph 1(2);

but such an order shall not be made unless all persons affected have been given notice in writing of the application (except where under rules of court notice may be dispensed with) and have been afforded an opportunity to make representations to the court.

(2) An order under sub-paragraph (1) may include provision as respects any period before the making of the order (but after the coming into force of these Regulations).

PART 2   COLLECTIVE AGREEMENTS AND RULES OF UNDERTAKINGS

4.—(1) This Part of this Schedule applies to—

(a) any term of a collective agreement, including an agreement which was not intended, or is presumed not to have been intended, to be a legally enforceable contract;

(b) any rule made by an employer for application to all or any of the persons who are employed by him or who apply to be, or are, considered by him for employment;

(c) any rule made by a trade organisation (within the meaning of regulation 18) or a qualifications body (within the meaning of regulation 19) for application to—

(i) all or any of its members or prospective members; or

(ii) all or any of the persons on whom it has conferred professional or trade qualifications (within the meaning of regulation 19) or who are seeking the professional or trade qualifications which it has power to confer.

(2) Any term or rule to which this Part of this Schedule applies is void where—

(a) the making of the collective agreement is, by reason of the inclusion of the term, unlawful by virtue of these Regulations;

(b) the term or rule is included or made in furtherance of an act which is unlawful by virtue of these Regulations; or

(c) the term or rule provides for the doing of an act which is unlawful by virtue of these Regulations.

(3) Sub-paragraph (2) shall apply whether the agreement was entered into, or the rule made, before or after the date on which these Regulations come into force; but in the case of an agreement entered into, or a rule made, before the date on which these Regulations come into force, that sub-paragraph does not apply in relation to any period before that date.

5. A person to whom this paragraph applies may present a complaint to an employment tribunal that a term or rule is void by virtue of paragraph 4 if he has reason to believe—

(a) that the term or rule may at some future time have effect in relation to him; and

(b) where he alleges that it is void by virtue of paragraph 4(2)(c), that—

(i) an act for the doing of which it provides, may at some such time be done in relation to him, and

(ii) the act would be unlawful by virtue of these Regulations if done in relation to him in present circumstances.

6. In the case of a complaint about—

(a) a term of a collective agreement made by or on behalf of—

(i) an employer,

(ii) an organisation of employers of which an employer is a member, or

(iii) an association of such organisations of one of which an employer is a member, or

(b) a rule made by an employer within the meaning of paragraph 4(1)(b),

paragraph 5 applies to any person who is, or is genuinely and actively seeking to become, one of his employees.

7. In the case of a complaint about a rule made by an organisation or body to which paragraph 4(1)(c) applies, paragraph 5 applies to any person—

(a) who is, or is genuinely and actively seeking to become, a member of the organisation or body;

(b) on whom the organisation or body has conferred a professional or trade qualification (within the meaning of regulation 19) which the organisation or body has power to confer; or

(c) who is genuinely and actively seeking such a professional or trade qualification which the organisation or body has power to confer.

8.—(1) When an employment tribunal finds that a complaint presented to it under paragraph 5 is well-founded the tribunal shall make an order declaring that the term or rule is void.

(2) An order under sub-paragraph (1) may include provision as respects any period before the making of the order (but after the coming into force of these Regulations).

9. The avoidance by virtue of paragraph 4(2) of any term or rule which provides for any person to be discriminated against shall be without prejudice to the following rights (except in so far as they enable any person to require another person to be treated less favourably than himself), namely—

(a) such of the rights of the person to be discriminated against; and

(b) such of the rights of any person who will be treated more favourably in direct or indirect consequence of the discrimination,

as are conferred by or in respect of a contract made or modified wholly or partly in pursuance of, or by reference to, that term or rule.

10. In this Schedule "collective agreement" means any agreement relating to one or more of the matters mentioned in section 178(2) of the Trade Union and Labour Relations (Consolidation) Act 1992 (collective agreements and collective bargaining), being an agreement made by or on behalf of one or more employers or one or more organisations of employers or associations of such organisations with one or more organisations of workers or associations of such organisations.

Regulation 47   SCHEDULE 6

DUTY TO CONSIDER WORKING BEYOND RETIREMENT

Interpretation

1—(1) In this Schedule—

'dismissal' means a dismissal within the meaning of section 95 of the 1996 Act;

'employee' means a person to whom regulation 30 (exception for retirement) applies and references to 'employer' shall be construed accordingly;

'intended date of retirement' has the meaning given by sub-paragraph (2);

'operative date of termination' means (subject to paragraph 10(3))—

    (a) where the employer terminates the employee's contract of employment by notice, the date on which the notice expires, or

    (b) where the employer terminates the contract of employment without notice, the date on which the termination takes effect;

'request' means a request made under paragraph 5; and

'worker' has the same meaning as in section 230(3) of the 1996 Act.

    (2) In this Schedule 'intended date of retirement' means—

    (a) where the employer notifies a date in accordance with paragraph 2, that date;

    (b) where the employer notifies a date in accordance with paragraph 4 and either no request is made or a request is made after the notification, that date;

    (c) where,

        (i)   the employer has not notified a date in accordance with paragraph 2,

        (ii) a request is made before the employer has notified a date in accordance with paragraph 4 (including where no notification in accordance with that paragraph is given),

        (iii) the request is made by an employee who has reasonable grounds for believing that the employer intends to retire him on a certain date, and,

        (iv) the request identifies that date,

      the date so identified;

    (d) in a case to which paragraph 3 has applied, any earlier or later date that has superseded the date mentioned in paragraph (a), (b) or (c) as the intended date of retirement by virtue of paragraph 3(3);

    (e) in a case to which paragraph 10 has applied, the later date that has superseded the date mentioned in paragraph (a), (b) or (c) as the intended date of retirement by virtue of paragraph 10(3)(b).

Duty of employer to inform employee

2—(1) An employer who intends to retire an employee has a duty to notify the employee in writing of—

    (a) the employee's right to make a request; and

    (b) the date on which he intends the employee to retire,

not more than one year and not less than six months before that date.

    (2) The duty to notify applies regardless of—

    (a) whether there is any term in the employee's contract of employment indicating when his retirement is expected to take place,

    (b) any other notification of, or information about, the employee's date of retirement given to him by the employer at any time, and

    (c) any other information about the employee's right to make a request given to him by the employer at any time.

3 and 4   [omitted]

Statutory right to request not to retire

5—(1) An employee may make a request to his employer not to retire on the intended date of retirement.

    (2) In his request the employee must propose that his employment should continue, following the intended date of retirement—

    (a) indefinitely,

    (b) for a stated period, or

    (c) until a stated date;

and, if the request is made at a time when it is no longer possible for the employer to notify in accordance with paragraph 2 and the employer has not yet notified in accordance with paragraph 4, must identify the date on which he believes that the employer intends to retire him.

(3) A request must be in writing and state that it is made under this paragraph.

(4) An employee may only make one request under this paragraph in relation to any one intended date of retirement and may not make a request in relation to a date that supersedes a different date as the intended date of retirement by virtue of paragraph 3(3) or 10(3)(b).

(5) A request is only a request made under this paragraph if it is made—

(a) in a case where the employer has complied with paragraph 2, more than three months but not more than six months before the intended date of retirement, or

(b) in a case where the employer has not complied with paragraph 2, before, but not more than six months before, the intended date of retirement.

An employer's duty to consider a request

6   An employer to whom a request is made is under a duty to consider the request in accordance with paragraphs 7 to 9.

7–9 [omitted]

Dismissal before request considered

10—(1) This paragraph applies where—

(a) by virtue of paragraph 6 an employer is under a duty to consider a request;

(b) the employer dismisses the employee;

(c) that dismissal is the contemplated dismissal to which the request relates; and

(d) the operative date of termination would, but for sub-paragraph (3), fall on or before the day on which the employer gives notice in accordance with paragraph 7(6).

(2) Subject to paragraph (4), the contract of employment shall continue in force for all purposes, including the purpose of determining for any purpose the period for which the employee has been continuously employed, until the day following that on which the notice under paragraph 7(6) is given.

(3) The day following the day on which that notice is given shall supersede—

(a) the date mentioned in sub-paragraph (1)(d) as the operative date of termination; and

(b) the date defined as the intended date of retirement in paragraph (a), (b) or (c) of paragraph 1(2) as the intended date of retirement.

(4) Any continuation of the contract of employment under sub-paragraph (2) shall be disregarded when determining the operative date of termination for the purposes of sections 98ZA to 98ZH of the 1996 Act.

Complaint to employment tribunal: failure to comply with paragraph 2

11—(1) An employee may present a complaint to an employment tribunal that his employer has failed to comply with the duty to notify him in paragraph 2.

(2) A tribunal shall not consider a complaint under this paragraph unless the complaint is presented—

(a) before the end of the period of three months beginning with—

(i)   the last day permitted to the employer by paragraph 2 for complying with the duty to notify, or

(ii) if the employee did not then know the date that would be the intended date of retirement, the first day on which he knew or should have known that date; or

(b) within such further period as the tribunal considers reasonable in a case where it is satisfied that it was not reasonably practicable for the complaint to be presented before the end of that period of three months.

(3) Where a tribunal finds that a complaint under this paragraph is well-founded it shall order the employer to pay compensation to the employee of such amount, not exceeding 8 weeks' pay, as the tribunal considers just and equitable in all the circumstances.

(4) Chapter 2 of Part 14 of the 1996 Act (calculation of a week's pay) shall apply for the purposes of sub-paragraph (3); and in applying that Chapter the calculation date shall be taken to be the date on which the complaint was presented or, if earlier, the operative date of termination.

(5) The limit in section 227(1) of the 1996 Act (maximum amount of a week's pay) shall apply for the purposes of sub-paragraph (3).

12–13 [omitted]

The Transfer of Undertakings (Protection of Employment) Regulations 2006
(SI 2006, No. 246)

1. [omitted]

Interpretation

2.—(1) In these Regulations—

'assigned' means assigned other than on a temporary basis;

'collective agreement', 'collective bargaining' and 'trade union' have the same meanings respectively as in the 1992 Act;

'contract of employment' means any agreement between an employee and his employer determining the terms and conditions of his employment;

references to 'contractor' in regulation 3 shall include a sub-contractor;

'employee' means any individual who works for another person whether under a contract of service or apprenticeship or otherwise but does not include anyone who provides services under a contract for services and references to a person's employer shall be construed accordingly;

'insolvency practitioner' has the meaning given to the expression by Part XIII of the Insolvency Act 1986;

references to 'organised grouping of employees' shall include a single employee;

'recognised' has the meaning given to the expression by section 178(3) of the 1992 Act;

'relevant transfer' means a transfer or a service provision change to which these Regulations apply in accordance with regulation 3 and 'transferor' and 'transferee' shall be construed accordingly and in the case of a service provision change falling within regulation 3(1)(b), 'the transferor' means the person who carried out the activities prior to the service provision change and "the transferee" means the person who carries out the activities as a result of the service provision change;

'the 1992 Act' means the Trade Union and Labour Relations (Consolidation) Act 1992;

'the 1996 Act' means the Employment Rights Act 1996;

'the 1996 Tribunals Act' means the Employment Tribunals Act 1996;

'the 1981 Regulations' means the Transfer of Undertakings (Protection of Employment) Regulations 1981.

(2) For the purposes of these Regulations the representative of a trade union recognised by an employer is an official or other person authorised to carry on collective bargaining with that employer by that trade union.

(3) [omitted]

A relevant transfer

3.—(1) These Regulations apply to—

    (a) a transfer of an undertaking, business or part of an undertaking or business situated immediately before the transfer in the United Kingdom to another person where there is a transfer of an economic entity which retains its identity;

(b) a service provision change, that is a situation in which—

    (i) activities cease to be carried out by a person ('a client') on his own behalf and are carried out instead by another person on the client's behalf ('a contractor');

    (ii) activities cease to be carried out by a contractor on a client's behalf (whether or not those activities had previously been carried out by the client on his own behalf) and are carried out instead by another person ('a subsequent contractor') on the client's behalf; or

    (iii) activities cease to be carried out by a contractor or a subsequent contractor on a client's behalf (whether or not those activities had previously been carried out by the client on his own behalf) and are carried out instead by the client on his own behalf,

and in which the conditions set out in paragraph (3) are satisfied.

(2) In this regulation 'economic entity' means an organised grouping of resources which has the objective of pursuing an economic activity, whether or not that activity is central or ancillary.

(3) The conditions referred to in paragraph (1)(b) are that—

(a) immediately before the service provision change—

    (i) there is an organised grouping of employees situated in Great Britain which has as its principal purpose the carrying out of the activities concerned on behalf of the client;

    (ii) the client intends that the activities will, following the service provision change, be carried out by the transferee other than in connection with a single specific event or task of short-term duration; and

(b) the activities concerned do not consist wholly or mainly of the supply of goods for the client's use.

(4) Subject to paragraph (1), these Regulations apply to—

(a) public and private undertakings engaged in economic activities whether or not they are operating for gain;

(b) a transfer or service provision change howsoever effected notwithstanding—

    (i) that the transfer of an undertaking, business or part of an undertaking or business is governed or effected by the law of a country or territory outside the United Kingdom or that the service provision change is governed or effected by the law of a country or territory outside Great Britain;

    (ii) that the employment of persons employed in the undertaking, business or part transferred or, in the case of a service provision change, persons employed in the organised grouping of employees, is governed by any such law;

(c) a transfer of an undertaking, business or part of an undertaking or business (which may also be a service provision change) where persons employed in the undertaking, business or part transferred ordinarily work outside the United Kingdom.

(5) An administrative reorganisation of public administrative authorities or the transfer of administrative functions between public administrative authorities is not a relevant transfer.

(6) A relevant transfer—

(a) may be effected by a series of two or more transactions; and

(b) may take place whether or not any property is transferred to the transferee by the transferor.

(7) [omitted]

Effect of relevant transfer on contracts of employment

4.—(1) Except where objection is made under paragraph (7), a relevant transfer shall not operate so as to terminate the contract of employment of any person employed by the transferor and assigned to the organised grouping of resources or employees that is subject to the relevant transfer, which would otherwise be terminated by the transfer, but any such contract shall have effect after the transfer as if originally made between the person so employed and the transferee.

(2) Without prejudice to paragraph (1), but subject to paragraph (6), and regulations 8 and 15(9), on the completion of a relevant transfer—

(a) all the transferor's rights, powers, duties and liabilities under or in connection with any such contract shall be transferred by virtue of this regulation to the transferee; and

(b) any act or omission before the transfer is completed, of or in relation to the transferor in respect of that contract or a person assigned to that organised grouping of resources or employees, shall be deemed to have been an act or omission of or in relation to the transferee.

(3) Any reference in paragraph (1) to a person employed by the transferor and assigned to the organised grouping of resources or employees that is subject to a relevant transfer, is a reference to a person so employed immediately before the transfer, or who would have been so employed if he had not been dismissed in the circumstances described in regulation 7(1), including, where the transfer is effected by a series of two or more transactions, a person so employed and assigned or who would have been so employed and assigned immediately before any of those transactions.

(4) Subject to regulation 9, in respect of a contract of employment that is, or will be, transferred by paragraph (1), any purported variation of the contract shall be void if the sole or principal reason for the variation is—

(a) the transfer itself; or

(b) a reason connected with the transfer that is not an economic, technical or organisational reason entailing changes in the workforce.

(5) Paragraph (4) shall not prevent the employer and his employee, whose contract of employment is, or will be, transferred by paragraph (1), from agreeing a variation of that contract if the sole or principal reason for the variation is—

(a) a reason connected with the transfer that is an economic, technical or organisational reason entailing changes in the workforce; or

(b) a reason unconnected with the transfer.

(6) Paragraph (2) shall not transfer or otherwise affect the liability of any person to be prosecuted for, convicted of and sentenced for any offence.

(7) Paragraphs (1) and (2) shall not operate to transfer the contract of employment and the rights, powers, duties and liabilities under or in connection with it of an employee who informs the transferor or the transferee that he objects to becoming employed by the transferee.

(8) Subject to paragraphs (9) and (11), where an employee so objects, the relevant transfer shall operate so as to terminate his contract of employment with the transferor but he shall not be treated, for any purpose, as having been dismissed by the transferor.

(9) Subject to regulation 9, where a relevant transfer involves or would involve a substantial change in working conditions to the material detriment of a person whose contract of employment is or would be transferred under paragraph (1), such an employee may treat the contract of employment as having been terminated, and the employee shall be treated for any purpose as having been dismissed by the employer.

(10) No damages shall be payable by an employer as a result of a dismissal falling within paragraph (9) in respect of any failure by the employer to pay wages to an employee in respect of a notice period which the employee has failed to work.

(11) Paragraphs (1), (7), (8) and (9) are without prejudice to any right of an employee arising apart from these Regulations to terminate his contract of employment without notice in acceptance of a repudiatory breach of contract by his employer.

Effect of relevant transfer on collective agreements

5. Where at the time of a relevant transfer there exists a collective agreement made by or on behalf of the transferor with a trade union recognised by the transferor in respect of any employee whose contract of employment is preserved by regulation 4(1) above, then—

    (a) without prejudice to sections 179 and 180 of the 1992 Act (collective agreements presumed to be unenforceable in specified circumstances) that agreement, in its application in relation to the employee, shall, after the transfer, have effect as if made by or on behalf of the transferee with that trade union, and accordingly anything done under or in connection with it, in its application in relation to the employee, by or in relation to the transferor before the transfer, shall, after the transfer, be deemed to have been done by or in relation to the transferee; and

    (b) any order made in respect of that agreement, in its application in relation to the employee, shall, after the transfer, have effect as if the transferee were a party to the agreement.

Effect of relevant transfer on trade union recognition

6.—(1) This regulation applies where after a relevant transfer the transferred organised grouping of resources or employees maintains an identity distinct from the remainder of the transferee's undertaking.

(2) Where before such a transfer an independent trade union is recognised to any extent by the transferor in respect of employees of any description who in consequence of the transfer become employees of the transferee, then, after the transfer—

    (a) the trade union shall be deemed to have been recognised by the transferee to the same extent in respect of employees of that description so employed; and

    (b) any agreement for recognition may be varied or rescinded accordingly.

Dismissal of employee because of relevant transfer

7.—(1) Where either before or after a relevant transfer, any employee of the transferor or transferee is dismissed, that employee shall be treated for the purposes of Part X of the 1996 Act (unfair dismissal) as unfairly dismissed if the sole or principal reason for his dismissal is—

    (a) the transfer itself; or

    (b) a reason connected with the transfer that is not an economic, technical or organisational reason entailing changes in the workforce.

(2) This paragraph applies where the sole or principal reason for the dismissal is a reason connected with the transfer that is an economic, technical or organisational reason entailing changes in the workforce of either the transferor or the transferee before or after a relevant transfer.

(3) Where paragraph (2) applies—

    (a) paragraph (1) shall not apply;

    (b) without prejudice to the application of section 98(4) of the 1996 Act (test of fair dismissal), the dismissal shall, for the purposes of sections 98(1) and 135 of that Act (reason for dismissal), be regarded as having been for redundancy where section 98(2)(c) of that Act applies, or otherwise for a substantial reason of a kind such as to justify the dismissal of an employee holding the position which that employee held.

(4) The provisions of this regulation apply irrespective of whether the employee in question is assigned to the organised grouping of resources or employees that is, or will be, transferred.

(5) Paragraph (1) shall not apply in relation to the dismissal of any employee which was required by reason of the application of section 5 of the Aliens Restriction (Amendment) Act 1919 to his employment.

(6) Paragraph (1) shall not apply in relation to a dismissal of an employee if the application of section 94 of the 1996 Act to the dismissal of the employee is excluded by or under any provision of the 1996 Act, the 1996 Tribunals Act or the 1992 Act.

Insolvency

8.—(1) If at the time of a relevant transfer the transferor is subject to relevant insolvency proceedings paragraphs (2) to (6) apply.

(2) In this regulation 'relevant employee' means an employee of the transferor—

(a) whose contract of employment transfers to the transferee by virtue of the operation of these Regulations; or

(b) whose employment with the transferor is terminated before the time of the relevant transfer in the circumstances described in regulation 7(1).

(3) The relevant statutory scheme specified in paragraph (4)(b) (including that sub-paragraph as applied by paragraph 5 of Schedule 1) shall apply in the case of a relevant employee irrespective of the fact that the qualifying requirement that the employee's employment has been terminated is not met and for those purposes the date of the transfer shall be treated as the date of the termination and the transferor shall be treated as the employer.

(4) In this regulation the 'relevant statutory schemes' are—

(a) Chapter VI of Part XI of the 1996 Act;

(b) Part XII of the 1996 Act.

(5) Regulation 4 shall not operate to transfer liability for the sums payable to the relevant employee under the relevant statutory schemes.

(6) In this regulation 'relevant insolvency proceedings' means insolvency proceedings which have been opened in relation to the transferor not with a view to the liquidation of the assets of the transferor and which are under the supervision of an insolvency practitioner.

(7) Regulations 4 and 7 do not apply to any relevant transfer where the transferor is the subject of bankruptcy proceedings or any analogous insolvency proceedings which have been instituted with a view to the liquidation of the assets of the transferor and are under the supervision of an insolvency practitioner.

Variations of contract where transferors are subject to relevant insolvency proceedings

9.—(1) If at the time of a relevant transfer the transferor is subject to relevant insolvency proceedings these Regulations shall not prevent the transferor or transferee (or an insolvency practitioner) and appropriate representatives of assigned employees agreeing to permitted variations.

(2) For the purposes of this regulation 'appropriate representatives' are—

(a) if the employees are of a description in respect of which an independent trade union is recognised by their employer, representatives of the trade union; or

(b) in any other case, whichever of the following employee representatives the employer chooses—

(i) employee representatives appointed or elected by the assigned employees (whether they make the appointment or election alone or with others) otherwise than for the purposes of this regulation, who (having regard to the purposes for, and the method by which they were appointed or elected) have authority from those employees to agree permitted variations to contracts of employment on their behalf;

(ii) employee representatives elected by assigned employees (whether they make the appointment or election alone or with others) for these particular pur-poses, in an election satisfying requirements identical to those contained in regulation 14 except those in regulation 14(1)(d).

(3) An individual may be an appropriate representative for the purposes of both this regulation and regulation 13 provided that where the representative is not a trade union representative he is either elected by or has authority from assigned employees (within the meaning of this regulation) and affected employees (as described in regulation 13(1)).

(4) [omitted]

(5) Where assigned employees are represented by non-trade union representatives—

    (a) the agreement recording a permitted variation must be in writing and signed by each of the representatives who have made it or, where that is not reasonably practicable, by a duly authorised agent of that representative; and

    (b) the employer must, before the agreement is made available for signature, provide all employees to whom it is intended to apply on the date on which it is to come into effect with copies of the text of the agreement and such guidance as those employees might reasonably require in order to understand it fully.

(6) A permitted variation shall take effect as a term or condition of the assigned employee's contract of employment in place, where relevant, of any term or condition which it varies.

(7) In this regulation—

'assigned employees' means those employees assigned to the organised grouping of resources or employees that is the subject of a relevant transfer;

'permitted variation' is a variation to the contract of employment of an assigned employee where—

    (a) the sole or principal reason for it is the transfer itself or a reason connected with the transfer that is not an economic, technical or organisational reason entailing changes in the workforce; and

    (b) it is designed to safeguard employment opportunities by ensuring the survival of the undertaking, business or part of the undertaking or business that is the subject of the relevant transfer;

'relevant insolvency proceedings' has the meaning given to the expression by regulation 8(6).

Pensions

10.—(1) Regulations 4 and 5 shall not apply—

    (a) to so much of a contract of employment or collective agreement as relates to an occupational pension scheme within the meaning of the Pension Schemes Act 1993; or

    (b) to any rights, powers, duties or liabilities under or in connection with any such contract or subsisting by virtue of any such agreement and relating to such a scheme or otherwise arising in connection with that person's employment and relating to such a scheme.

(2) For the purposes of paragraphs (1) and (3), any provisions of an occupational pension scheme which do not relate to benefits for old age, invalidity or survivors shall not be treated as being part of the scheme.

(3) An employee whose contract of employment is transferred in the circumstances described in regulation 4(1) shall not be entitled to bring a claim against the transferor for—

    (a) breach of contract; or

    (b) constructive unfair dismissal under section 95(1)(c) of the 1996 Act,

arising out of a loss or reduction in his rights under an occupational pension scheme in consequence of the transfer, save insofar as the alleged breach of contract or dismissal (as the case may be) occurred prior to the date on which these Regulations took effect.

Notification of Employee Liability Information

11.—(1) The transferor shall notify to the transferee the employee liability information of any person employed by him who is assigned to the organised grouping of resources or employees that is the subject of a relevant transfer—

    (a) in writing; or

    (b) by making it available to him in a readily accessible form.

(2) In this regulation and in regulation 12 'employee liability information' means—

    (a) the identity and age of the employee;

(b) those particulars of employment that an employer is obliged to give to an employee pursuant to section 1 of the 1996 Act;

(c) information of any—

(i) disciplinary procedure taken against an employee;

(ii) grievance procedure taken by an employee,

within the previous two years, in circumstances where the Employment Act 2002 (Dispute Resolution) Regulations 2004 apply;

(d) information of any court or tribunal case, claim or action—

(i) brought by an employee against the transferor, within the previous two years;

(ii) that the transferor has reasonable grounds to believe that an employee may bring against the transferee, arising out of the employee's employment with the transferor; and

(e) information of any collective agreement which will have effect after the transfer, in its application in relation to the employee, pursuant to regulation 5(a).

(3) Employee liability information shall contain information as at a specified date not more than fourteen days before the date on which the information is notified to the transferee.

(4) The duty to provide employee liability information in paragraph (1) shall include a duty to provide employee liability information of any person who would have been employed by the transferor and assigned to the organised grouping of resources or employees that is the subject of a relevant transfer immediately before the transfer if he had not been dismissed in the circumstances described in regulation 7(1), including, where the transfer is effected by a series of two or more transactions, a person so employed and assigned or who would have been so employed and assigned immediately before any of those transactions.

(5) Following notification of the employee liability information in accordance with this regulation, the transferor shall notify the transferee in writing of any change in the employee liability information.

(6) A notification under this regulation shall be given not less than fourteen days before the relevant transfer or, if special circumstances make this not reasonably practicable, as soon as reasonably practicable thereafter.

(7) A notification under this regulation may be given—

(a) in more than one instalment;

(b) indirectly, through a third party.

Remedy for failure to notify employee liability information

12.—(1) On or after a relevant transfer, the transferee may present a complaint to an employment tribunal that the transferor has failed to comply with any provision of regulation 11.

(2) An employment tribunal shall not consider a complaint under this regulation unless it is presented—

(a) before the end of the period of three months beginning with the date of the relevant transfer;

(b) within such further period as the tribunal considers reasonable in a case where it is satisfied that it was not reasonably practicable for the complaint to be presented before the end of that period of three months.

(3) Where an employment tribunal finds a complaint under paragraph (1) well-founded, the tribunal—

(a) shall make a declaration to that effect; and

(b) may make an award of compensation to be paid by the transferor to the transferee.

(4) The amount of the compensation shall be such as the tribunal considers just and equitable in all the circumstances, subject to paragraph (5), having particular regard to—

(a) any loss sustained by the transferee which is attributable to the matters complained of; and

(b) the terms of any contract between the transferor and the transferee relating to the transfer under which the transferor may be liable to pay any sum to the transferee in respect of a failure to notify the transferee of employee liability information.

(5) Subject to paragraph (6), the amount of compensation awarded under paragraph (3) shall be not less than £500 per employee in respect of whom the transferor has failed to comply with a provision of regulation 11, unless the tribunal considers it just and equitable, in all the circumstances, to award a lesser sum.

(6) In ascertaining the loss referred to in paragraph (4)(a) the tribunal shall apply the same rule concerning the duty of a person to mitigate his loss as applies to any damages recoverable under the common law of England and Wales, Northern Ireland or Scotland, as applicable.

(7) Section 18 of the 1996 Tribunals Act (conciliation) shall apply to the right conferred by this regulation and to proceedings under this regulation as it applies to the rights conferred by that Act and the employment tribunal proceedings mentioned in that Act.

Duty to inform and consult representatives

13.—(1) In this regulation and regulations 14 and 15 references to affected employees, in relation to a relevant transfer, are to any employees of the transferor or the transferee (whether or not assigned to the organised grouping of resources or employees that is the subject of a relevant transfer) who may be affected by the transfer or may be affected by measures taken in connection with it; and references to the employer shall be construed accordingly.

(2) Long enough before a relevant transfer to enable the employer of any affected employees to consult the appropriate representatives of any affected employees, the employer shall inform those representatives of—

(a) the fact that the transfer is to take place, the date or proposed date of the transfer and the reasons for it;

(b) the legal, economic and social implications of the transfer for any affected employees;

(c) the measures which he envisages he will, in connection with the transfer, take in relation to any affected employees or, if he envisages that no measures will be so taken, that fact; and

(d) if the employer is the transferor, the measures, in connection with the transfer, which he envisages the transferee will take in relation to any affected employees who will become employees of the transferee after the transfer by virtue of regulation 4 or, if he envisages that no measures will be so taken, that fact.

(3) For the purposes of this regulation the appropriate representatives of any affected employees are—

(a) if the employees are of a description in respect of which an independent trade union is recognised by their employer, representatives of the trade union; or

(b) in any other case, whichever of the following employee representatives the employer chooses—

(i) employee representatives appointed or elected by the affected employees otherwise than for the purposes of this regulation, who (having regard to the purposes for, and the method by which they were appointed or elected) have authority from those employees to receive information and to be consulted about the transfer on their behalf;

(ii) employee representatives elected by any affected employees, for the purposes of this regulation, in an election satisfying the requirements of regulation 14(1).

(4) The transferee shall give the transferor such information at such a time as will enable the transferor to perform the duty imposed on him by virtue of paragraph (2)(d).

(5) The information which is to be given to the appropriate representatives shall be given to each of them by being delivered to them, or sent by post to an address notified by them to the employer, or (in the case of representatives of a trade union) sent by post to the trade union at the address of its head or main office.

(6) An employer of an affected employee who envisages that he will take measures in relation to an affected employee, in connection with the relevant transfer, shall consult the appropriate representatives of that employee with a view to seeking their agreement to the intended measures.

(7) In the course of those consultations the employer shall—

(a) consider any representations made by the appropriate representatives; and

(b) reply to those representations and, if he rejects any of those representations, state his reasons.

(8) The employer shall allow the appropriate representatives access to any affected employees and shall afford to those representatives such accommodation and other facilities as may be appropriate.

(9) If in any case there are special circumstances which render it not reasonably practicable for an employer to perform a duty imposed on him by any of paragraphs (2) to (7), he shall take all such steps towards performing that duty as are reasonably practicable in the circumstances.

(10) Where—

(a) the employer has invited any of the affected employee to elect employee representatives; and

(b) the invitation was issued long enough before the time when the employer is required to give information under paragraph (2) to allow them to elect representatives by that time,

the employer shall be treated as complying with the requirements of this regulation in relation to those employees if he complies with those requirements as soon as is reasonably practicable after the election of the representatives.

(11) If, after the employer has invited any affected employees to elect representatives, they fail to do so within a reasonable time, he shall give to any affected employees the information set out in paragraph (2).

(12) The duties imposed on an employer by this regulation shall apply irrespective of whether the decision resulting in the relevant transfer is taken by the employer or a person controlling the employer.

Election of employee representatives

14.—(1) The requirements for the election of employee representatives under regulation 13(3) are that—

(a) the employer shall make such arrangements as are reasonably practicable to ensure that the election is fair;

(b) the employer shall determine the number of representatives to be elected so that there are sufficient representatives to represent the interests of all affected employees having regard to the number and classes of those employees;

(c) the employer shall determine whether the affected employees should be represented either by representatives of all the affected employees or by representatives of particular classes of those employees;

(d) before the election the employer shall determine the term of office as employee representatives so that it is of sufficient length to enable information to be given and consultations under regulation 13 to be completed;

(e) the candidates for election as employee representatives are affected employees on the date of the election;

(f) no affected employee is unreasonably excluded from standing for election;

(g) all affected employees on the date of the election are entitled to vote for employee representatives;

(h) the employees entitled to vote may vote for as many candidates as there are representatives to be elected to represent them or, if there are to be representatives for particular classes of employees, may vote for as many candidates as there are representatives to be elected to represent their particular class of employee;

(i) the election is conducted so as to secure that—

(i) so far as is reasonably practicable, those voting do so in secret; and

(ii) the votes given at the election are accurately counted.

(2) Where, after an election of employee representatives satisfying the requirements of paragraph (1) has been held, one of those elected ceases to act as an employee representative and as a result any affected employees are no longer represented, those employees shall elect another representative by an election satisfying the requirements of paragraph (1)(a), (e), (f) and (i).

Failure to inform or consult

15.—(1) Where an employer has failed to comply with a requirement of regulation 13 or regulation 14, a complaint may be presented to an employment tribunal on that ground—

(a) in the case of a failure relating to the election of employee representatives, by any of his employees who are affected employees;

(b) in the case of any other failure relating to employee representatives, by any of the employee representatives to whom the failure related;

(c) in the case of failure relating to representatives of a trade union, by the trade union; and

(d) in any other case, by any of his employees who are affected employees.

(2) If on a complaint under paragraph (1) a question arises whether or not it was reasonably practicable for an employer to perform a particular duty or as to what steps he took towards performing it, it shall be for him to show—

(a) that there were special circumstances which rendered it not reasonably practicable for him to perform the duty; and

(b) that he took all such steps towards its performance as were reasonably practicable in those circumstances.

(3) If on a complaint under paragraph (1) a question arises as to whether or not an employee representative was an appropriate representative for the purposes of regulation 13, it shall be for the employer to show that the employee representative had the necessary authority to represent the affected employees.

(4) On a complaint under paragraph (1)(a) it shall be for the employer to show that the requirements in regulation 14 have been satisfied.

(5) On a complaint against a transferor that he had failed to perform the duty imposed upon him by virtue of regulation 13(2)(d) or, so far as relating thereto, regulation 13(9), he may not show that it was not reasonably practicable for him to perform the duty in question for the reason that the transferee had failed to give him the requisite information at the requisite time in accordance with regulation 13(4) unless he gives the transferee notice of his intention to show that fact; and the giving of the notice shall make the transferee a party to the proceedings.

(6) In relation to any complaint under paragraph (1), a failure on the part of a person controlling (directly or indirectly) the employer to provide information to the employer shall not constitute special circumstances rendering it not reasonably practicable for the employer to comply with such a requirement.

(7) Where the tribunal finds a complaint against a transferee under paragraph (1) well-founded it shall make a declaration to that effect and may order the transferee to pay appropriate compensation to such descriptions of affected employees as may be specified in the award.

(8) Where the tribunal finds a complaint against a transferor under paragraph (1) well-founded it shall make a declaration to that effect and may—

(a) order the transferor, subject to paragraph (9), to pay appropriate compensation to such descriptions of affected employees as may be specified in the award; or

(b) if the complaint is that the transferor did not perform the duty mentioned in paragraph (5) and the transferor (after giving due notice) shows the facts so mentioned, order the transferee to pay appropriate compensation to such descriptions of affected employees as may be specified in the award.

(9) The transferee shall be jointly and severally liable with the transferor in respect of compensation payable under sub-paragraph (8)(a) or paragraph (11).

(10) An employee may present a complaint to an employment tribunal on the ground that he is an employee of a description to which an order under paragraph (7) or (8) relates and that—

(a) in respect of an order under paragraph (7), the transferee has failed, wholly or in part, to pay him compensation in pursuance of the order;

(b) in respect of an order under paragraph (8), the transferor or transferee, as applicable, has failed, wholly or in part, to pay him compensation in pursuance of the order.

(11) Where the tribunal finds a complaint under paragraph (10) well-founded it shall order the transferor or transferee as applicable to pay the complainant the amount of compensation which it finds is due to him.

(12) An employment tribunal shall not consider a complaint under paragraph (1) or (10) unless it is presented to the tribunal before the end of the period of three months beginning with—

(a) in respect of a complaint under paragraph (1), the date on which the relevant transfer is completed; or

(b) in respect of a complaint under paragraph (10), the date of the tribunal's order under paragraph (7) or (8),

or within such further period as the tribunal considers reasonable in a case where it is satisfied that it was not reasonably practicable for the complaint to be presented before the end of the period of three months.

Failure to inform or consult: supplemental

16.—(1) Section 205(1) of the 1996 Act (complaint to be sole remedy for breach of relevant rights) and section 18 of the 1996 Tribunals Act (conciliation) shall apply to the rights conferred by regulation 15 and to proceedings under this regulation as they apply to the rights conferred by those Acts and the employment tribunal proceedings mentioned in those Acts.

(2) An appeal shall lie and shall lie only to the Employment Appeal Tribunal on a question of law arising from any decision of, or arising in any proceedings before, an employment tribunal under or by virtue of these Regulations; and section 11(1) of the Tribunals and Inquiries Act 1992 (appeals from certain tribunals to the High Court) shall not apply in relation to any such proceedings.

(3) 'Appropriate compensation' in regulation 15 means such sum not exceeding thirteen weeks' pay for the employee in question as the tribunal considers just and equitable having regard to the seriousness of the failure of the employer to comply with his duty.

(4) Sections 220 to 228 of the 1996 Act shall apply for calculating the amount of a week's pay for any employee for the purposes of paragraph (3) and, for the purposes of that calculation, the calculation date shall be—

(a) in the case of an employee who is dismissed by reason of redundancy (within the meaning of sections 139 and 155 of the 1996 Act) the date which is the calculation date for the purposes of any entitlement of his to a redundancy payment (within the meaning of those sections) or which would be that calculation date if he were so entitled;

(b) in the case of an employee who is dismissed for any other reason, the effective date of termination (within the meaning of sections 95(1) and (2) and 97 of the 1996 Act) of his contract of employment;

(c) in any other case, the date of the relevant transfer.

17. [omitted]

Restriction on contracting out

18. Section 203 of the 1996 Act (restrictions on contracting out) shall apply in relation to these Regulations as if they were contained in that Act, save for that section shall not apply in so far as these Regulations provide for an agreement (whether a contract of employment or not) to exclude or limit the operation of these Regulations.

19–21 [omitted]

PART III

....

Non-Statutory Materials

ACAS Code of Practice 1 Disciplinary and Grievance Procedures
(Revised 2004)

SECTION 1   DISCIPLINARY RULES AND PROCEDURES

5. ...

Core principles of reasonable behaviour

- Use procedures primarily to help and encourage employees to improve rather than just as a way of imposing a punishment.
- Inform the employee of the complaint against them, and provide them with an opportunity to state their case before decisions are reached.
- Allow employees to be accompanied at disciplinary meetings.
- Make sure that disciplinary action is not taken until the facts of the case have been established and that the action is reasonable in the circumstances.
- Never dismiss an employee for a first disciplinary offence, unless it is a case of gross misconduct.
- Give the employee a written explanation for any disciplinary action taken and make sure they know what improvement is expected.
- Give the employee an opportunity to appeal.
- Deal with issues as thoroughly and promptly as possible.
- Act consistently.

Dealing with disciplinary issues in the workplace

8. When a potential disciplinary matter arises, the employer should make necessary investigations to establish the facts promptly before memories of events fade. It is important to keep a written record for later reference. Having established the facts, the employer should decide whether to drop the matter, deal with it informally or arrange for it to be handled formally. Where an investigatory meeting is held solely to establish the facts of a case, it should be made clear to the employee involved that it is not a disciplinary meeting.

9. In certain cases, for example in cases involving gross misconduct, where relationships have broken down or there are risks to an employer's property or responsibilities to other parties, consideration should be given to a brief period of suspension with full pay whilst unhindered investigation is conducted. Such a suspension should only be imposed after careful consideration and should be reviewed to ensure it is not unnecessarily protracted. It should be made clear that the suspension is not considered a disciplinary action.

10. When dealing with disciplinary issues in the workplace employers should bear in mind that they are required under the Disability Discrimination Act 1995 to make reasonable adjustments to cater for employees who have a disability, for example providing for wheel-chair access if necessary.

Informal action

11. Cases of minor misconduct or unsatisfactory performance are usually best dealt with informally. A quiet word is often all that is required to improve an employee's conduct or performance. The informal approach may be particularly helpful in small firms, where problems can be dealt with quickly and confidentially. There will, however, be situations where matters are more serious or where an informal approach has been tried but is not working.

12. If informal action does not bring about an improvement, or the misconduct or unsatisfactory performance is considered to be too serious to be classed as minor, employers should provide employees with a clear signal of their dissatisfaction by taking formal action.

Formal action

Inform the employee of the problem

13. The first step in any formal process is to let the employee know in writing what it is they are alleged to have done wrong. The letter or note should contain enough information for the individual to be able to understand both what it is they are alleged to have done wrong and the reasons why this is not acceptable. If the employee has difficulty reading, or if English is not their first language, the employer should explain the content of the letter or note to them orally. The letter or note should also invite the individual to a meeting at which the problem can be discussed, and it should inform the individual of their right to be accompanied at the meeting (see section 3). The employee should be given copies of any documents that will be produced at the meeting.

Hold a meeting to discuss the problem

14. Where possible, the timing and location of the meeting should be agreed with the employee. The length of time between the written notification and the meeting should be long enough to allow the employee to prepare but not so long that memories fade. The employer should hold the meeting in a private location and ensure there will be no interruptions.

15. At the meeting, the employer should explain the complaint against the employee and go through the evidence that has been gathered. The employee should be allowed to set out their case and answer any allegations that have been made. The employee should also be allowed to ask questions, present evidence, call witnesses and be given an opportunity to raise points about any information provided by witnesses.

16. An employee who cannot attend a meeting should inform the employer in advance whenever possible. If the employee fails to attend through circumstances outside their control and unforeseeable at the time the meeting was arranged (eg illness) the employer should arrange another meeting. A decision may be taken in the employee's absence if they fail to attend the re-arranged meeting without good reason. If an employee's companion cannot attend on a proposed date, the employee can suggest another date so long as it is reasonable and is not more than five working days after the date originally proposed by the employer. This five day time limit may be extended by mutual agreement.

Decide on outcome and action

17. Following the meeting the employer must decide whether disciplinary action is justified or not. Where it is decided that no action is justified the employee should be informed. Where it is decided that disciplinary action is justified the employer will need to consider what form this should take. Before making any decision the employer should take account of the employee's disciplinary and general record, length of service, actions taken in any previous similar case, the explanations given by the employee and—most important of all—whether the intended disciplinary action is reasonable under the circumstances.

18. Examples of actions the employer might choose to take are set out in paragraphs 19–25. It is normally good practice to give employees at least one chance to improve their conduct or performance before they are issued with a final written warning. However, if an

employee's misconduct or unsatisfactory performance—or its continuance—is sufficiently serious, for example because it is having, or is likely to have, a serious harmful effect on the organisation, it may be appropriate to move directly to a final written warning. In cases of gross misconduct, the employer may decide to dismiss even though the employee has not previously received a warning for misconduct. (Further guidance on dealing with gross misconduct is set out at paragraphs 35–36.)

First formal action—unsatisfactory performance

19. Following the meeting, an employee who is found to be performing unsatisfactorily should be given a written note setting out:
   - the performance problem;
   - the improvement that is required;
   - the timescale for achieving this improvement;
   - a review date; and
   - any support the employer will provide to assist the employee.

20. The employee should be informed that the note represents the first stage of a formal procedure and that failure to improve could lead to a final written warning and, ultimately, dismissal. A copy of the note should be kept and used as the basis for monitoring and reviewing performance over a specified period (eg six months).

First formal action—misconduct

21. Where, following a disciplinary meeting, an employee is found guilty of misconduct, the usual first step would be to give them a written warning setting out the nature of the misconduct and the change in behaviour required.

22. The employee should be informed that the warning is part of the formal disciplinary process and what the consequences will be of a failure to change behaviour. The consequences could be a final written warning and ultimately, dismissal. The employee should also be informed that they may appeal against the decision. A record of the warning should be kept, but it should be disregarded for disciplinary purposes after a specified period (eg six months).

23. Guidance on dealing with cases of gross misconduct is provided in paragraphs 35–36.

Final written warning

24. Where there is a failure to improve or change behaviour in the timescale set at the first formal stage, or where the offence is sufficiently serious, the employee should normally be issued with a final written warning—but only after they have been given a chance to present their case at a meeting. The final written warning should give details of, and grounds for, the complaint. It should warn the employee that failure to improve or modify behaviour may lead to dismissal or to some other penalty, and refer to the right of appeal. The final written warning should normally be disregarded for disciplinary purposes after a specified period (for example 12 months).

Dismissal or other penalty

25. If the employee's conduct or performance still fails to improve, the final stage in the disciplinary process might be dismissal or (if the employee's contract allows it or it is mutually agreed) some other penalty such as demotion, disciplinary transfer, or loss of seniority/pay. A decision to dismiss should only be taken by a manager who has the authority to do so. The employee should be informed as soon as possible of the reasons for the dismissal, the date on which the employment contract will terminate, the appropriate period of notice and their right of appeal.

26. It is important for employers to bear in mind that before they dismiss an employee or impose a sanction such as demotion, loss of seniority or loss of pay, they must as a minimum

have followed the statutory dismissal and disciplinary procedures. The standard statutory procedure to be used in almost all cases requires the employer to:

Step 1

Write to the employee notifying them of the allegations against them and the basis of the allegations and invite them to a meeting to discuss the matter.

Step 2

Hold a meeting to discuss the allegations—at which the employee has the right to be accompanied—and notify the employee of the decision.

Step 3

If the employee wishes to appeal, hold an appeal meeting at which the employee has the right to be accompanied—and inform the employee of the final decision.

27. More detail on the statutory standard procedure is set out at Annex A. There is a modified two-step procedure for use in special circumstances involving gross misconduct and details of this are set out at Annex B. Guidance on the modified procedure is contained in paragraph 36. There are a number of situations in which it is not necessary for employers to use the statutory procedures or where they will have been deemed to be completed and these are described in Annex E.

28. If the employer fails to follow this statutory procedure (where it applies), and an employee who is qualified to do so makes a claim for unfair dismissal, the employment tribunal will automatically find the dismissal unfair. The tribunal will normally increase the compensation awarded by 10 per cent, or, where it feels it is just and equitable to do so, up to 50 per cent. Equally, if the employment tribunal finds that an employee has been dismissed unfairly but has failed to follow the procedure (for instance they have failed to attend the disciplinary meeting without good cause), compensation will be reduced by, normally, 10 per cent, or, if the tribunal considers it just and equitable to do so, up to 50 per cent.

29. If the tribunal considers there are exceptional circumstances, compensation may be adjusted (up or down) by less than 10 per cent or not at all.

30. Employers and employees will normally be expected to go through the statutory dismissal and disciplinary procedure unless they have reasonable grounds to believe that by doing so they might be exposed to a significant threat, such as violent, abusive or intimidating behaviour, or they will be harassed. There will always be a certain amount of stress and anxiety for both parties when dealing with any disciplinary case, but this exemption will only apply where the employer or employee reasonably believes that they would come to some serious physical or mental harm; their property or some third party is threatened or the other party has harassed them and this may continue.

31. Equally, the statutory procedure does not need to be followed if circumstances beyond the control of either party prevent one or more steps being followed within a reasonable period. This will sometimes be the case where there is a long-term illness or a long period of absence abroad but, in the case of employers, wherever possible they should consider appointing another manager to deal with the procedure.

32. Where an employee fails to attend a meeting held as part of the statutory discipline procedure without good reason the statutory procedure comes to an end. In those circumstances the employee's compensation may be reduced if they bring a successful complaint before an employment tribunal. If the employee does have a good reason for non-attendance, the employer must re-arrange the meeting. If the employee does not attend the second meeting for good reason the employer need not arrange a third meeting but there will be no adjustment of compensation.

What if a grievance is raised during a disciplinary case?

33. In the course of a disciplinary process, an employee might raise a grievance that is related to the case. If this happens, the employer should consider suspending the disciplinary procedure for a short period while the grievance is dealt with. Depending on the nature of the grievance, the employer may need to consider bringing in another manager to deal with the

disciplinary process. In small organisations this may not be possible, and the existing manager should deal with the case as impartially as possible.

34. Where the action taken or contemplated by the employer is dismissal the statutory grievance procedure does not apply. Where the action taken or contemplated is paid suspension or a warning the statutory grievance procedure and not the dismissal and disciplinary procedure applies to any grievance. However, where the employer takes, or is contemplating other action short of dismissal and asserts that the reason for the action is conduct or capability related, the statutory grievance procedure does not apply unless the grievance is that the action amounts, or would amount, to unlawful discrimination, or that the true reason for the action is not the reason given by the employer. In those cases the employee must have raised a written grievance in accordance with the statutory grievance procedure before presenting any complaint to an employment tribunal about the issue raised by the grievance. However, if the written grievance is raised before any disciplinary appeal meeting, the rest of the grievance procedure does not have to be followed, although the employer may use the appeal meeting to discuss the grievance.

Dealing with gross misconduct

35. If an employer considers an employee guilty of gross misconduct, and thus potentially liable for summary dismissal, it is still important to establish the facts before taking any action. A short period of suspension with full pay may be helpful or necessary, although it should only be imposed after careful consideration and should be kept under review. It should be made clear to the employee that the suspension is not a disciplinary action and does not involve any prejudgement.

36. It is a core principle of reasonable behaviour that employers should give employees the opportunity of putting their case at a disciplinary meeting before deciding whether to take action. This principle applies as much to cases of gross misconduct as it does to ordinary cases of misconduct or unsatisfactory performance. There may however be some very limited cases where despite the fact that an employer has dismissed an employee immediately without a meeting an employment tribunal will, very exceptionally, find the dismissal to be fair. To allow for these cases there is a statutory modified procedure under which the employer is required to write to the employee after the dismissal setting out the reasons for the dismissal and to hold an appeal meeting, if the employee wants one. The statutory procedure that must be followed by employers in such cases is set out in Annex B. If an employer fails to follow this procedure and the case goes to tribunal, the dismissal will be found to be automatically unfair.

Dealing with absence from work

37. When dealing with absence from work, it is important to determine the reasons why the employee has not been at work. If there is no acceptable reason, the matter should be treated as a conduct issue and dealt with as a disciplinary matter.

38. If the absence is due to genuine (including medically certified) illness, the issue becomes one of capability, and the employer should take a sympathetic and considerate approach. When thinking about how to handle these cases, it is helpful to consider:

- how soon the employee's health and attendance will improve;
- whether alternative work is available;
- the effect of the absence on the organisation;
- how similar situations have been handled in the past; and
- whether the illness is a result of disability in which case the provisions of the Disability Discrimination Act 1995 will apply.

39. The impact of long-term absences will nearly always be greater on small organisations, and they may be entitled to act at an earlier stage than large organisations.

40. In cases of extended sick leave both statutory and contractual issues will need to be addressed and specialist advice may be necessary.

Dealing with special situations

If the full procedure is not immediately available

41. Special arrangements might be required for handling disciplinary matters among nightshift employees, employees in isolated locations or depots, or others who may be difficult to reach. Nevertheless the appropriate statutory procedure must be followed where it applies.

Trade union representatives

42. Disciplinary action against a trade union representative can lead to a serious dispute if it is seen as an attack on the union's functions. Normal standards apply but, if disciplinary action is considered, the case should be discussed, after obtaining the employee's agreement, with a senior trade union representative or permanent union official.

Criminal charges or convictions not related to employment

43. If an employee is charged with, or convicted of, a criminal offence not related to work, this is not in itself reason for disciplinary action. The employer should establish the facts of the case and consider whether the matter is serious enough to warrant starting the disciplinary procedure. The main consideration should be whether the offence, or alleged offence, is one that makes the employee unsuitable for their type of work. Similarly, an employee should not be dismissed solely because they are absent from work as a result of being remanded in custody.

Appeals

44. Employees who have had disciplinary action taken against them should be given the opportunity to appeal. It is useful to set a time limit for asking for an appeal—five working days is usually enough.

45. An employee may choose to appeal for example because:
   • they think a finding or penalty is unfair;
   • new evidence comes to light; or
   • they think the disciplinary procedure was not used correctly.

It should be noted that the appeal stage is part of the statutory procedure and if the employee pursues an employment tribunal claim the tribunal may reduce any award of compensation if the employee did not exercise the right of appeal.

46. As far as is reasonably practicable a more senior manager not involved with the case should hear the appeal. In small organisations, even if a more senior manager is not available, another manager should hear the appeal, if possible. If that is not an option, the person overseeing the case should act as impartially as possible. Records and notes of the original disciplinary meeting should be made available to the person hearing the appeal.

47. The employers should contact the employee with appeal arrangements as soon as possible, and inform them of their statutory right to be accompanied at the appeal meeting.

48. The manager must inform the employee about the appeal decision, and the reasons for it, as soon as possible. They should also confirm the decision in writing. If the decision is the final stage of the organisation's appeals procedure, the manager should make this clear to the employee.

Keeping records

49. It is important, and in the interests of both employers and employees, to keep written records during the disciplinary process. Records should include:
   • the complaint against the employee;
   • the employee's defence;
   • findings made and actions taken;
   • the reason for actions taken;
   • whether an appeal was lodged;
   • the outcome of the appeal;
   • any grievances raised during the disciplinary procedure; and
   • subsequent developments.

50. Records should be treated as confidential and be kept no longer than necessary in accordance with the Data Protection Act 1998. This Act gives individuals the right to request and have access to certain personal data.

51. Copies of meeting records should be given to the employee including copies of any formal minutes that may have been taken. In certain circumstances (for example to protect a witness) the employer might withhold some information.

Drawing up disciplinary rules and procedures

52. Management is responsible for maintaining and setting standards of performance in an organisation and for ensuring that disciplinary rules and procedures are in place. Employers are legally required to have disciplinary procedures. It is good practice to involve employees (and, where appropriate, their representatives) when making or changing rules and procedures, so that everyone affected by them understands them.

Rules

53. When making rules, the aim should be to specify those that are necessary for ensuring a safe and efficient workplace and for maintaining good employment relations.

54. It is unlikely that any set of rules will cover all possible disciplinary issues, but rules normally cover:
- bad behaviour, such as fighting or drunkenness;
- unsatisfactory work performance;
- harassment or victimisation;
- misuse of company facilities (for example email and internet);
- poor timekeeping;
- unauthorised absences; and
- repeated or serious failure to follow instructions.

55. Rules should be specific, clear and recorded in writing. They also need to be readily available to employees, for instance on a noticeboard or, in larger organisations, in a staff handbook or on the intranet. Management should do all they can to ensure that every employee knows and understands the rules, including those employees whose first language is not English or who have trouble reading. This is often best done as part of an induction process.

56. Employers should inform employees of the likely consequences of breaking disciplinary rules. In particular, they should list examples of acts of gross misconduct that may warrant summary dismissal.

57. Acts which constitute gross misconduct are those resulting in a serious breach of contractual terms and are best decided by organisations in the light of their own particular circumstances. However, examples of gross misconduct might include:
- theft or fraud;
- physical violence or bullying;
- deliberate and serious damage to property;
- serious misuse of an organisation's property or name;
- deliberately accessing internet sites containing pornographic, offensive or obscene material;
- serious insubordination;
- unlawful discrimination or harassment;
- bringing the organisation into serious disrepute;
- serious incapability at work brought on by alcohol or illegal drugs;
- causing loss, damage or injury through serious negligence;
- a serious breach of health and safety rules; and
- a serious breach of confidence.

Procedures

58. Disciplinary procedures should not be seen primarily as a means of imposing sanctions but rather as a way of encouraging improvement amongst employees whose conduct or

performance is unsatisfactory. Some organisations may prefer to have separate procedures for dealing with issues of conduct and capability. Large organisations may also have separate procedures to deal with other issues such as harassment and bullying.

59. When drawing up and applying procedures employers should always bear in mind the requirements of natural justice. This means that employees should be given the opportunity of a meeting with someone who has not been involved in the matter. They should be informed of the allegations against them, together with the supporting evidence, in advance of the meeting. Employees should be given the opportunity to challenge the allegations before decisions are reached and should be provided with a right of appeal.

60. Good disciplinary procedures should:
- be put in writing;
- say to whom they apply;
- be non-discriminatory;
- allow for matters to be dealt without undue delay;
- allow for information to be kept confidential;
- tell employees what disciplinary action might be taken;
- say what levels of management have the authority to take disciplinary action;
- require employees to be informed of the complaints against them and supporting evidence, before a meeting;
- give employees a chance to have their say before management reaches a decision;
- provide employees with the right to be accompanied;
- provide that no employee is dismissed for a first breach of discipline, except in cases of gross misconduct;
- require management to investigate fully before any disciplinary action is taken;
- ensure that employees are given an explanation for any sanction; and
- allow employees to appeal against a decision.

61. It is important to ensure that everyone in an organisation understands the disciplinary procedures including the statutory requirements. In small firms this is best done by making sure all employees have access to a copy of the procedures, for instance on a noticeboard, and by taking a few moments to run through the procedures with the employee. In large organisations formal training for those who use and operate the procedures may be appropriate.

Further action

62. It is sensible to keep rules and procedures under review to make sure they are always relevant and effective. New or additional rules should only be introduced after reasonable notice has been given to all employees and any employee representatives have been consulted.

Section 2 (Grievance procedures) and Section 3 (the right to be accompanied) [omitted]

ACAS Code of Practice 2 Disclosure of Information to Trade Unions for Collective Bargaining Purposes
(Revised 1997)

Providing information

9. The absence of relevant information about an employer's undertaking may to a material extent impede trade unions in collective bargaining; particularly if the information would influence the formulation, presentation or pursuance of a claim, or the conclusion of an agreement. The provision of relevant information in such circumstances would be in accordance with good industrial relations practice.

10. To determine what information will be relevant negotiators should take account of the subject-matter of the negotiations and the issues raised during them; the level at which

negotiations take place (department, plant, division, or company level); the size of the company; and the type of business the company is engaged in.

11. Collective bargaining within an undertaking can range from negotiations on specific matters arising daily at the work place affecting particular sections of the workforce, to extensive periodic negotiations on terms and conditions of employment affecting the whole work-force in multiplant companies. The relevant information and the depth, detail and form in which it could be presented to negotiators will vary accordingly. Consequently, it is not possible to compile a list of items that should be disclosed in all circumstances. Some examples of information relating to the undertaking which could be relevant in certain collective bargaining situations are given below:

    (i) **Pay and benefits:** principles and structure of payment systems; job evaluation systems and grading criteria; earnings and hours analysed according to work-group, grade, plant, sex, out-workers and homeworkers, department or division, giving, where appropriate, distributions and make-up of pay showing any additions to basic rate or salary; total pay bill; details of fringe benefits and non-wage labour costs.

    (ii) **Conditions of service:** policies on recruitment, redeployment, redundancy, training, equal opportunity, and promotion; appraisal systems; health, welfare and safety matters.

    (iii) **Manpower:** numbers employed analysed according to grade, department, location, age and sex; labour turnover; absenteeism; overtime and short-time; manning standards; planned changes in work methods, materials, equipment or organisation; available manpower plans; investment plans.

    (iv) **Performance:** productivity and efficiency data; savings from increased productivity and output; return on capital invested; sales and state of order book.

    (v) **Financial:** cost structures; gross and net profits; sources of earnings; assets; liabilities; allocation of profits; details of government financial assistance; transfer prices; loans to parent or subsidiary companies and interest charged.

12. These examples are not intended to represent a check list of information that should be provided for all negotiations. Nor are they meant to be an exhaustive list of types of information as other items may be relevant in particular negotiations.

Restrictions on the duty to disclose

13. Trade unions and employers should be aware of the restrictions on the general duty to disclose information for collective bargaining.

14. Some examples of information which if disclosed in particular circumstances might cause substantial injury are: cost information on individual products; detailed analysis of proposed investment, marketing or pricing policies; and price quotas or the make-up of tender prices. Information which has to be made available publicly, for example under the Companies Acts, would not fall into this category.

15. Substantial injury may occur if, for example, certain customers would be lost to competitors, or suppliers would refuse to supply necessary materials, or the ability to raise funds to finance the company would be seriously impaired as a result of disclosing certain information. The burden of establishing a claim that disclosure of certain information would cause substantial injury lies with the employer.

Trade union responsibilities

16. Trade unions should identify and request the information they require for collective bargaining in advance of negotiations whenever practicable. Misunderstandings can be avoided, costs reduced, and time saved, if requests state as precisely as possible all the information required, and the reasons why the information is considered relevant. Requests should conform to an agreed procedure. A reasonable period of time should be allowed for employers to consider a request and to reply.

17. Trade unions should keep employers informed of the names of the representatives authorised to carry on collective bargaining on their behalf.

18. Where two or more trade unions are recognised by an employer for collective bargaining purposes they should co-ordinate their requests for information whenever possible.

19. Trade unions should review existing training programmes or establish new ones to ensure negotiators are equipped to understand and use information effectively.

Employers' responsibilities

20. Employers should aim to be as open and helpful as possible in meeting trade union requests for information. Where a request is refused, the reasons for the refusal should be explained as far as possible to the trade union representatives concerned and be capable of being substantiated should the matter be taken to the Central Arbitration Committee.

21. Information agreed as relevant to collective bargaining should be made avaialble as soon as possible once a request for the information has been made by an authorised trade union representative. Employers should present information in a form and style which recipients can reasonably be expected to understand.

Joint arrangements for disclosure of information

22. Employers and trade unions should endeavour to arrive at a joint understanding on how the provisions on the disclosure of information can be implemented most effectively. They should consider what information is likely to be required, what is available, and what could reasonably be made available. Consideration should also be given to the form in which the information will be presented, when it should be presented and to whom. In particular, the parties should endeavour to reach an understanding on what information could most appropriately be provided on a regular basis.

23. Procedures for resolving possible disputes concerning any issues associated with the disclosure of information should be agreed. Where possible such procedures should normally be related to any existing arrangements within the undertaking or industry and the complaint, conciliation and arbitration procedure described in the Act.

Department of Employment Code of Practice on Picketing
(Revised 1992)

SECTION D   ROLE OF THE POLICE

45. It is not the function of the police to take a view of the merits of a particular trade dispute. They have a general duty to uphold the law and keep the peace, whether on the picket line or elsewhere. The lawgives the police discretion to take whatever measures may reasonably be considered necessary to ensure that picketing remains peaceful and orderly.

46. The police have no responsibility for enforcing the civil law. An employer cannot require the police to help in identifying the pickets against whom he wishes to seek an order from the civil court. Nor is it the job of the police to enforce the terms of an order. Enforcement of an order on the application of a plaintiff is a matter for the court and its officer. The police may, however, decide to assist the officer of the court if they think there may be a breach of the peace.

47. As regards the criminal law the police have considerable discretionary powers to limit the number of pickets at any one place where they have reasonable cause to fear disorder. The law does not impose a specific limit on the number of people who may picket at any one place; nor does this Code affect in any way the discretion of the police to limit the number of people on a particular picket line. It is for the police to decide, taking into account all the circumstances, whether the number of pickets at any particular place provides reasonable

grounds for the belief that a breach of the peace is likely to occur. If a picket does not leave the picket line when asked to do so by the police, he is liable to be arrested for obstruction either of the highway or of a police officer in the execution of his duty if the obstruction is such as to cause, or be likely to cause, a breach of the peace.

SECTION E   LIMITING NUMBERS OF PICKETS

48. Violence and disorder on the picket line is more likely to occur if there are excessive numbers of pickets. Wherever large numbers of people with strong feelings are involved there is danger that the situation will get out of control, and that those concerned will run the risk of committing an offence, with consequent arrest and prosecution, or of committing a civil wrong which exposes them, or anyone organising them, to civil proceedings.

49. This is particularly so whenever people seek by sheer weight of numbers to stop others going into work or delivering or collecting goods. In such cases, what is intended is not peaceful persuasion, but obstruction or harassment—if not intimidation. Such a situation is often described as 'mass picketing'. In fact, it is not picketing in its lawful sense of an attempt at peaceful persuasion, and may well result in a breach of the peace or other criminal offences.

50. Moreover, anyone seeking to demonstrate support for those in dispute should keep well away from any picket line so as not to create a risk of a breach of the peace or other criminal offence being committed on that picket line. Just as with a picket itself, the numbers involved in any such demonstration should not be excessive, and the demonstration should be conducted lawfully. Section 14 of the Public Order Act 1986 provides the police with the power to impose conditions (for example, as to numbers, location and duration) on public assemblies of 20 or more people where the assembly is likely to result in serious public disorder; or serious damage to property; or serious disruption to the life of the community; or if its purpose is to coerce.

51. Large numbers on a picket line are also likely to give rise to fear and resentment amongst those seeking to cross that picket line, even where no criminal offence is committed. They exacerbate disputes and sour relations not only between management and employees but between the pickets and their fellow employees. Accordingly pickets and their organisers should ensure that in general the number of pickets does not exceed six at any entrance to, or exit from, a workplace; frequently a smaller number will be appropriate.

SECTION F   ORGANISATION OF PICKETING

52. Sections B and C of this Code outline aspects of the civil law and the criminal law, as they may apply to pickets, and to anyone, including a trade union, who organises a picket. While it is possible that a picket may be entirely 'spontaneous', it is much more likely that it will be organised by an identifiable individual or group.

53. Paragraphs 36–38 in Section B of this Code describe how to identify whether a trade union is, in fact, responsible in terms of civil law liability, for certain acts. As explained in these paragraphs, the law means, for example, that if such an act takes place in the course of picketing, and if a trade union official has done, authorised or endorsed the act, then the official's union will be responsible in law unless the act is 'effectively repudiated' by the union's national leadership.

Functions of the picket organiser

54. Wherever picketing is 'official' (i.e., organised by a trade union), an experienced person, preferably a trade union official who represents those picketing, should always be in charge of the picket line. He should have a letter of authority from his union which he can show to the police officers or to people who want to cross the picket line. Even when he is not on the picket line himself he should be available to give the pickets advice if a problem arises.

55. A picket should not be designated as an 'official' picket unless it is actually organised by a trade union. Nor should pickets claim the authority and support of a union unless the

union is prepared to accept the consequent responsibility. In particular, union authority and support should not be claimed by the pickets if the union has, in fact, repudiated calls to take industrial action made, or being made, in the course of the picketing.

56. Whether a picket is 'official' or 'unofficial', an organiser of pickets should maintain close contact with the police. Advance consultation with the police is always in the best interests of all concerned. In particular the organiser and the pickets should seek directions from the police on the number of people who should be present on the picket line at any one time and on where they should stand in order to avoid obstructing the highway.

57. The other main functions of the picket organiser should include ensuring that:
* the pickets understand the law and are aware of the provisions of this Code, and that the picketing is conducted peacefully and lawfully;
* badges or armbands, which authorised pickets should wear so that they are clearly identified, are distributed to such pickets and are worn while they are picketing;
* workers from other places of work do not join the picket line, and that any offers of support on the picket line from outsiders are refused;
* the number of pickets at any entrance to, or exit from, a place of work is not so great as to give rise to fear and resentment amongst those seeking to cross that picket line (see paragraph 51 in Section E of this Code);
* close contact with his own union office (if any), and with the offices of other unions if they are involved in the picketing, is established and maintained;
* such special arrangements as may be necessary for essential supplies, services or operations (see paragraphs 62–64 in Section G of this Code) are understood and observed by the pickets.

Consultation with other trade unions

58. Where several unions are involved in a dispute, they should consult each other about the organisation of any picketing. It is important that they should agree how the picketing is to be carried out, how many pickets there should be from each union, and who should have overall responsibility for organising them.

Right to cross picket lines

59. Everyone has the right to decide for himself whether he will cross a picket line. Disciplinary action should not be taken or threatened by a union against a member on the grounds that he has crossed a picket line.

60. If a union disciplines any member for crossing a picket line, the member will have been 'unjustifiably disciplined'. In such a case, the individual can make a complaint to an employment tribunal. If the tribunal finds the complaint well-founded, it will make a declaration to that effect.

61. If the union has not lifted the penalty imposed on the member, or if it has not taken all necessary steps to reverse anything done in giving effect to the penalty, an application for compensation should be made to the Employment Appeal Tribunal (EAT). In any other case, the individual can apply to an employment tribunal for compensation. The EAT or tribunal will award whatever compensation it considers just and equitable in all the circumstances, subject to a specified maximum amount. Where the application is made to the EAT, there will normally be a specified minimum award.

SECTION G   ESSENTIAL SUPPLIES, SERVICES AND OPERATIONS

62. Pickets, and anyone organising a picket should take very great care to ensure that their activities do not cause distress, hardship or inconvenience to members of the public who are not involved in the dispute. Particular care should be taken to ensure that the movement of essential goods and supplies, the carrying out of essential maintenance of plant and equipment, and the provision of services essential to the life of the community are not impeded, still less prevented.

63. The following list of essential supplies and services is provided as an illustration of the kind of activity which requires special protection to comply with the recommendations in paragraph 62 above. However, the list is not intended to be comprehensive. The supplies and services which may need to be protected in accordance with these recommendations could cover different activities in different circumstances. Subject to this *caveat*, 'essential supplies, services and operations' include:
* the production, packaging, marketing and/or distribution of medical and pharmaceutical products;
* the provision of supplies and services essential to health and welfare institutions, e.g., hospitals, old peoples' homes;
* the provision of heating fuel for schools, residential institutions, medical institutions and private residential accommodation;
* the production and provision of other supplies for which there is a crucial need during a crisis in the interests of public health and safety (e.g., chlorine, lime and other agents for water purification; industrial and medical gases; sand and salt for road gritting purposes);
* activities necessary to the maintenance of plant and machinery;
* the proper care of livestock;
* necessary safety procedures (including such procedures as are necessary to maintain plant and machinery);
* the production, packaging, marketing and/or distribution of food and animal feeding stuffs;
* the operation of essential services, such as police, fire, ambulance, medical and nursing services, air safety, coastguard and air sea rescue services, and services provided by voluntary bodies (e.g., Red Cross and St John's ambulance, meals on wheels, hospital car service), and mortuaries, burial and cremation services.

64. Arrangements to ensure these safeguards for essential supplies, services and operations should be agreed in advance between the pickets, or anyone organising the picket, and the employer, or employers, concerned.

Equal Opportunities Commission Code of Practice for the Elimination of Discrimination on the Grounds of Sex and Marriage and the Promotion of Equal Opportunity in Employment

PART 1   RECRUITMENT

12. It is unlawful: unless the job is covered by an exception: to discriminate directly or indirectly on the grounds of sex or marriage:
— in the arrangements made for deciding who should be offered a job
— in any terms of employment
— by refusing or omitting to offer a person employment
13. It is therefore recommended that:
(a) each individual should be assessed according to his or her personal capability to carry out a given job. It should not be assumed that men only or women only will be able to perform certain kinds of work;
(b) any qualifications or requirements applied to a job which effectively inhibit applications from one sex or from married people should be retained only if they are justifiable in terms of the job to be done;

(c) any age limits should be retained only if they are necessary for the job. An unjustifiable age limit could constitute unlawful indirect discrimination, for example, against women who have taken time out of employment for child-rearing;

(d) where trade unions uphold such qualifications or requirements as union policy, they should amend that policy in the light of any potentially unlawful effect.

GENUINE OCCUPATIONAL QUALIFICATIONS (GOQs)

14. It is unlawful: except for certain jobs when a person's sex is a genuine occupational qualification (GOQ) for that job to select candidates on the ground of sex.

15. There are very few instances in which a job will qualify for a GOQ on the ground of sex. However, exceptions may arise, for example, where considerations of privacy and decency or authenticity are involved. The SDA expressly states that the need of the job for strength and stamina does not justify restricting it to men. When a GOQ exists for a job, it applies also to promotion, transfer, or training for that job, but cannot be used to justify a dismissal.

16. In some instances, the GOQ will apply to some of the duties only. A GOQ will not be valid, however, where members of the appropriate sex are already employed in sufficient numbers to meet the employer's likely requirements without undue inconvenience. For example, in a job where sales assistants may be required to undertake changing room duties, it might not be lawful to claim a GOQ in respect of *all* the assistants on the grounds that any of them might be required to undertake changing room duties from time to time.

17. It is therefore recommended that:
   — A job for which a GOQ was used in the past should be re-examined if the post falls vacant to see whether the GOQ still applies. Circumstances may well have changed, rendering the GOQ inapplicable.

SOURCES OF RECRUITMENT

18. It is unlawful: unless the job is covered by an exception:
   — to discriminate on grounds of sex or marriage in the arrangements made for determining who should be offered employment whether recruiting by advertisements, through employment agencies, jobcentres, or career offices.
   — to imply that applications from one sex or from married people will not be considered.
   — to instruct or put pressure on others to omit to refer for employment people of one sex or married people unless the job is covered by an exception. It is also unlawful when advertising job vacancies,
   — to publish or cause to be published an advertisement which indicates or might reasonably be understood as indicating an intention to discriminate unlawfully on grounds of sex or marriage.

19. It is therefore recommended that:

Advertising
   (a) job advertising should be carried out in such a way as to encourage applications from suitable candidates of both sexes. This can be achieved both by wording of the advertisements and, for example, by placing advertisements in publications likely to reach both sexes. All advertising material and accompanying literature relating to employment or training issues should be reviewed to ensure that it avoids presenting men and women in stereotyped roles. Such sterotyping tends to perpetuate sex segregation in jobs and can also lead people of the opposite sex to believe that they would be unsuccessful in applying for particular jobs;
   (b) where vacancies are filled by promotion or transfer, they should be published to all eligible employees in such a way that they do not restrict applications from either sex;

(c) recruitment solely or primarily by word of mouth may unnecessarily restrict the choice of applicants available. The method should be avoided in a workforce predominantly of one sex, if in practice it prevents members of the opposite sex from applying;

(d) where applicants are supplied through trade unions and members of one sex only come forward, this should be discussed with the unions and an alternative approach adopted.

Careers Service/Schools

20. When notifying vacancies to the Careers Service, employers should specify that these are open to both boys and girls. This is especially important when a job has traditionally been done exclusively or mainly by one sex. If dealing with single sex schools, they should ensure, where possible, that both boys' and girls' schools are approached; it is also a good idea to remind mixed schools that jobs are open to boys and girls.

SELECTION METHODS

Tests

21. (a) If selection tests are used, they should be specifically related to job and/or career requirements and should measure an individual's actual or inherent ability to do or train for the work or career.

(b) Tests should be reviewed regularly to ensure that they remain relevant and free from any unjustifiable basis, either in contents or in scoring mechanism.

Applications and Interviewing

22. It is unlawful: unless the job is covered by an exception: To discriminate on grounds of sex or marriage by refusing or deliberately omitting to offer employment.

23. It is therefore recommended that:

(a) employers should ensure that personnel staff, line managers and all other employees who may come into contact with job applicants, should be trained in the provisions of the SDA, including the fact that it is unlawful to instruct or put pressure on others to discriminate;

(b) applications from men and women should be processed in exactly the same way. For example, there should not be separate lists of male and female or married and single applicants. All those handling applications and conducting interviews should be trained in the avoidance of unlawful discrimination and records of interviews kept, where practicable, showing why applicants were or were not appointed;

(c) questions should relate to the requirements of the job. Where it is necessary to assess whether personal circumstances will affect performance of the job (for example, where it involves unsocial hours or extensive travel) this should be discussed objectively without detailed questions based on assumptions about marital status, children and domestic obligations. Questions about marriage plans or family intentions should not be asked, as they could be construed as showing bias against women. Information necessary for personnel records can be collected after a job offer has been made.

PROMOTION, TRANSFER AND TRAINING

24. It is unlawful: unless the job is covered by an exception, for employers to discriminate directly or indirectly on the grounds of sex or marriage in the way they afford access to opportunities for promotion, transfer or training.

25. It is therefore recommended that:

(a) where an appraisal system is in operation, the assessment criteria should be examined to ensure that they are not unlawfully discriminatory and the scheme monitored to assess how it is working in practice;

(b) when a group of workers predominantly of one sex is excluded from an appraisal scheme, access to promotion, transfer and training and to other benefits should be reviewed, to ensure that there is no unlawful indirect discrimination;

(c) promotion and career development patterns are reviewed to ensure that the traditional qualifications are justifiable requirements for the job to be done. In some circumstances, for example, promotion on the basis of length of service could amount to unlawful indirect discrimination, as it may unjustifiably affect more women than men;

(d) when general ability and personal qualities are the main requirements for promotion to a post, care should be taken to consider favourably candidates of both sexes with differing career patterns and general experience;

(e) rules which restrict or preclude transfer between certain jobs should be questioned and changed if they are found to be unlawfuly discriminatory. Employees of one sex may be concentrated in sections from which transfers are traditionally restricted without real justification;

(f) policies and practices regarding selection for training, day release and personal development should be examined for unlawful direct and indirect discrimination. Where there is found to be an imbalance in training as between sexes, the cause should be identified to ensure that it is not discriminatory;

(g) age limits for access to training and promotion should be questioned.

HEALTH AND SAFETY LEGISLATION

26. Equal treatment of men and women may be limited by statutory provisions which require men and women to be treated differently. For example, the Factories Act 1961 places restrictions on the hours of work of female manual employees, although the Health and Safety Executive can exempt employers from these restrictions, subject to certain conditions. The Mines and Quarries Act 1954 imposes limitations on women's work and there are restrictions where there is special concern for the unborn child (e.g., lead and ionising radiation). However the broad duties placed on employers by the Health and Safety at Work, etc., Act, 1974 makes no distinctions between men and women. Section 2(1) requires employers to ensure, so far as is reasonably practicable, the health and safety and welfare at work of *all* employees.
Specific health and safety requirements under earlier legislation are unaffected by the Act.
It is therefore recommended that:

— company policy should be reviewed and serious consideration given to any significant differences in treatment between men and women, and there should be well-founded reasons if such differences are maintained or introduced.

TERMS OF EMPLOYMENT, BENEFITS, FACILITIES AND SERVICES

27. It is unlawful: unless the job is covered by an exception: to discriminate on the grounds of sex or marriage, directly or indirectly, in the terms on which employment is offered or in affording access to any benefits, facilities or services.

28. It is therefore recommended that:

(a) all terms of employment, benefits, facilities and services are reviewed to ensure that there is no unlawful discrimination on grounds of sex or marriage. For example, part-time work, domestic leave, company cars and benefits for dependants should be available to both male and female employees in the same or not materially different circumstances.

29. In an establishment where part-timers are solely or mainly women, unlawful indirect discrimination may arise if, as a group, they are treated less favourably than other employees without justification.

It is therefore recommended that:

(b) where part-time workers do not enjoy pro-rata pay or benefits with full-time workers, the arrangements should be reviewed to ensure that they are justified without regard to sex.

GRIEVANCES, DISCIPLINARY PROCEDURES AND VICTIMISATION

30. It is unlawful: to victimise an individual for a complaint made in good faith about sex or marriage discrimination or for giving evidence about such a complaint.

31. It is therefore recommended that:

(a) particular care is taken to ensure that an employee who has in good faith taken action under the Sex Discrimination Act or the Equal Pay Act does not receive less favourable treatment than other employees, for example by being disciplined or dismissed;

(b) employees should be advised to use the internal procedures, where appropriate, but this is without prejudice to the individual's right to apply to an employment tribunal within the statutory time limit, i.e., before the end of the period of three months beginning when the act complained of was done (There is no time limit if the victimisation is continuing.);

(c) particular care is taken to deal effectively with all complaints of discrimination, victimisation or harassment. It should not be assumed that they are made by those who are over-sensitive.

DISMISSALS, REDUNDANCIES AND OTHER UNFAVOURABLE TREATMENT OF EMPLOYEES

32. It is unlawful: to discriminate directly or indirectly on grounds of sex or marriage in dismissals or by treating an employee unfavourably in any other way.

It is therefore recommended that:

(a) care is taken that members of one sex are not disciplined or dismissed for performance or behaviour which would be overlooked or condoned in the other sex;

(b) redundancy procedures affecting a group of employees predominantly of one sex should be reviewed, so as to remove any effects which could be disproportionate and unjustifiable;

(c) conditions of access to voluntary redundancy benefit should be made available on equal terms to male and female employees in the same or not materially different circumstances;

(d) where there is down-grading or short-time working (for example, owing to a change in the nature or volume of an employer's business) the arrangements should not unlawfully discriminate on the ground of sex;

(e) all reasonably practical steps should be taken to ensure that a standard of conduct or behaviour is observed which prevents members of either sex from being intimidated, harassed or otherwise subjected to unfavourable treatment on the ground of their sex.

PART 2   THE ROLE OF GOOD EMPLOYMENT PRACTICES IN PROMOTING EQUALITY OF OPPORTUNITY

33. This section of the Code describes those employment practices which help to promote equality of opportunity. It gives information about the formulation and implementation of equal opportunities policies. While such policies are not required by law, their value has been recognised by a number of employers who have voluntarily adopted them. Others may wish to follow this example.

FORMULATING AN EQUAL OPPORTUNITIES POLICY

34. An equal opportunities policy will ensure the effective use of human resources in the best interests of both the organisation and its employees. It is a commitment by an employer to the development and use of employment procedures and practices which do not discriminate on grounds of sex or marriage and which provide genuine equality of opportunity for all employees. The detail of the policy will vary according to size of the organisation.

IMPLEMENTING THE POLICY

35. An equal opportunities policy must be seen to have the active support of management at the highest level. To ensure that the policy is fully effective, the following procedure is recommended:
   (a) the policy should be clearly stated and, where appropriate, included in a collective agreement;
   (b) overall responsibility for implementing the policy should rest with senior management;
   (c) the policy should be made known to all employees and, where reasonably practicable, to all job applicants.
36. Trade unions have a very important part to play in implementing genuine equality of opportunity and they will obviously be involved in the review of established procedures to ensure that these are consistent with the law.

MONITORING

37. It is recommended that the policy is monitored regularly to ensure that it is working in practice. Consideration could be given to setting up a joint Management/ Trade Union Review Committee.
38. In a small firm with a simple structure it may be quite adequate to assess the distribution and payment of employees from personal knowledge.
39. In a large and complex organisation a more formal analysis will be necessary, for example, by sex, grade and payment in each unit. This may need to be introduced by stages as resources permit. Any formal analysis should be regularly updated and available to Management and Trade Unions to enable any necessary action to be taken.
40. Sensible monitoring will show, for example, whether members of one sex:
   (a) do not apply for employment or promotion, or that fewer apply than might be expected;
   (b) are not recruited, promoted or selected for training and development or are appointed/selected in a significantly lower proportion than their rate of application;
   (c) are concentrated in certain jobs, sections or departments.

POSITIVE ACTION

Recruitment, Training and Promotion

41. Selection for recruitment or promotion must be on merit, irrespective of sex. However, the Sex Discrimination Act does allow certain steps to redress the effects of previous unequal opportunities. Where there have been few or no members of one sex in particular work in their employment for the previous 12 months, the Act allows employers to give special encouragement to, and provide specific training for, the minority sex. Such measures are usually described as Positive Action.

42. Employers may wish to consider positive measures such as:
    (a) training their own employees (male or female) for work which is traditionally the preserve of the other sex, for example, training women for skilled manual or technical work;
    (b) positive encouragement to women to apply for management posts—special courses may be needed;
    (c) advertisements which encourage applications from the minority sex, but make it clear that selection will be on merit without reference to sex;
    (d) notifying job agencies, as part of a Positive Action Programme that they wish to encourage members of one sex to apply for vacancies, where few or no members of that sex are doing the work in question. In these circumstances, job agencies should tell both men and women about the posts and, in addition, let the under-represented sex know that applications from them are particularly welcome. Withholding information from one sex in an attempt to encourage applications from the opposite sex would be unlawful.

Other working arrangements

43. There are other forms of action which could assist both employer and employee by helping to provide continuity of employment to working parents, many of whom will have valuable experience or skills.

Employers may wish to consider with their employees whether:
    (a) certain jobs can be carried out on a part-time or flexi-time basis;
    (b) personal leave arrangements are adequate and available to both sexes. It should not be assumed that men may not need to undertake domestic responsibilities on occasion, especially at the time of childbirth;
    (c) child-care facilities are available locally or whether it would be feasible to establish nursery facilities on the premises or combine with other employers to provide them;
    (d) residential training could be facilitated for employees with young children. For example, where this type of training is necessary, by informing staff who are selected well in advance to enable them to make child-care and other personal arrangements; employers with their own residential training centres could also consider whether childcare facilities might be provided;
    (e) the statutory maternity leave provisions could be enhanced, for example, by reducing the qualifying service period, extending the leave period, or giving access to part-time arrangements on return.

These arrangements, and others, are helpful to both sexes but are of particular benefit to women in helping them to remain in gainful employment during the years of child-rearing.

Equal Opportunities Commission Code of Practice on Equal Pay
(Revised 2003)

SECTION TWO   GOOD EQUAL PAY PRACTICE

Introduction

68. The loss to women arising out of the gender pay gap is well documented, but organisations also lose out by failing to properly reward the range of skills and experience that women bring to the workforce. The most commonly recognised risk of failing to ensure that pay is determined without sex discrimination is equal pay cases being taken against the organisation.

The direct costs of a claim can include not only any eventual equal pay award to the woman bringing the claim (see paragraph 67) but also the costs of time spent at a hearing, and the costs of legal representation. The indirect costs are harder to quantify, but include lower productivity on the part of those employees who consider that they are not getting equal pay and on the part of managers whose time is taken up in dealing with the claim.

69. Tackling the gender pay gap reduces the risk of litigation. It can also increase efficiency by attracting the best employees, reducing staff turnover, increasing commitment, and reducing absenteeism. Pay is one of the key factors affecting motivation and relationships at work. It is therefore important to develop pay arrangements that are right for the organisation and that reward employees fairly. Providing equal pay for equal work is central to the concept of rewarding people fairly for what they do.

The essential features of an equal pay review

70. Employers are responsible for providing equal pay and for ensuring that pay systems are transparent. Pay arrangements are frequently complicated and the features that can give rise to sex discrimination are not always obvious. A structured pay system is more likely to provide equal pay and is easier to check than a system that relies primarily on managerial discretion. Acas, the employment relations' experts, provide basic advice on the various different types of pay systems and on job evaluation.

71. The advice given in paragraphs 39–46 on striking a balance between transparency and confidentiality are also relevant to equal pay reviews. The EOC has produced a guidance note that explains an employer's legal obligations when carrying out an equal pay review.

72. While employers are not required, by law, to carry out an equal pay review, this Code recommends equal pay reviews as the most appropriate method of ensuring that a pay system delivers equal pay free from sex bias. Whatever kind of equal pay review process is used, it should include:

- Comparing the pay of men and women doing equal work. Here employers need to check for one or more of the following: like work; work rated as equivalent; work of equal value. *These checks are the foundation of an equal pay review*.
- Identifying any equal pay gaps
- Eliminating those pay gaps that cannot satisfactorily be explained on grounds other than sex.

These features are the same whatever the size of the organisation and they are essential. **A pay review process that does not include these features cannot claim to be an equal pay review**. Moreover, an equal pay review is not simply a data collection exercise. It entails a commitment to put right any sex based pay inequalities and this means that the review must have the involvement and support of managers with the authority to deliver the necessary changes.

73. The validity of the review and success of subsequent action taken will be enhanced if the pay system is understood and accepted by the managers who operate the system, by the employees and by their unions. Employers should therefore aim to secure the involvement of employees and, where possible, trade union representatives, when carrying out an equal pay review.

VOLUNTARY EQUAL PAY REVIEWS

A model for carrying out an equal pay review

74. The EOC recommends a five-step equal pay review model:

STEP 1: Deciding the scope of the review and identifying the data required

STEP 2: Determining where men and women are doing equal work

STEP 3: Collecting pay data to identify equal pay gaps

STEP 4: Establishing the causes of any significant pay gaps and assessing the reasons for these

STEP 5: Developing an equal pay action plan and/or reviewing and monitoring.

The EOC Equal Pay Review Kit sets out the detail of the model recommended here and provides supporting guidance notes.

STEP 1: Deciding the scope of the review and identifying the data required

75. In scoping the review employers need to decide:
    - Which employees are going to be included? It is advisable to include all employees who are deemed to be in the same establishment or service (see paragraph 21).
    - What information will be needed? Employers will need to collect and compare broad types of information about:
    - All the various elements of pay, including pensions and other benefits
    - The personal characteristics of each employee, that is, gender; full-time or part-time; qualifications relevant to the job; hours worked and when and where they work these; length of service; role and time in grade and performance related pay ratings
    - It is particularly important to ensure that information is collected about part-time employees.

The information will vary depending upon the type of organisation, its pay policies and practices and the scope of the review.

    - Who should be involved in carrying out the review? An equal pay review requires different types of input from people with different perspectives. There will be a need for knowledge and understanding of the pay and grading arrangements; of any job evaluation schemes; and of the payroll and human resource systems. It can also be helpful to have someone with an understanding of equality issues, particularly the effects of indirect discrimination in pay systems.
    - When to involve the workforce? Employers need to consider when to involve the trade unions or other employee representatives.
    - Whether expert advice is needed? Employers may also wish to consider whether to bring in outside expertise. Acas can provide practical, independent and impartial advice on the employee relations aspects of equal pay reviews.

The scope of the Equal Pay Review

In nearly three quarters of organisations, the review applied (or applies) to the whole workforce. In over half of all the cases it involved an examination of a job evaluation system to ensure that it was free of sex bias. Moreover, just under half of organisations had extended the review beyond pay and gender, to include other processes such as recruitment and selection; two-fifths had covered pay differences by ethnicity; more than a third had covered age and nearly a third had covered disability.

The scope of the Equal Pay Review	Percentage of organisations covering
Whole workforce	73
Examination of job evaluation system	55
Other HR processes	49
Pay differences by ethnic origin	40
Pay differences by age	36
Pay differences by disability	31
N = number of organisations	67

Include ethnicity and disability in the review

76. This Code is concerned with an important, but narrow, aspect of sex discrimination in employment—the pay of women compared to men doing equal work, (or vice versa). It does not deal with comparisons on the grounds of ethnicity or disability. However, as a matter of good practice employers may also want to look at ethnicity and disability, or age. Before deciding to do so it may be helpful to consider the quality of the information available to the employer, and whether it is adequate for the purposes of carrying out a wider review. To ensure the relevant provisions of race and disability legislation are taken into account, it

would be appropriate to seek advice from the Commission for Racial Equality and/or the Disability Rights Commission.

77. Public Sector organisations obliged by the Race Relations (Amendment) Act 2000 to adopt an Equality Scheme should ensure that their pay review deals with any pay gaps between workers from different ethnic groups as well as the gaps between men's and women's pay. Here too, advice can be obtained from the Commission for Racial Equality.

STEP 2: Determining where men and women are doing equal work

78. In Step 2 employers need to do one or more of the following checks:
- Like work.
- Work rated as equivalent.
- Work of equal value.

These checks determine where men and women are doing equal work. They are the foundation of an equal pay review.

Example—determining where men and women are doing equal work
Human Resources and the unions met to agree which areas to examine. According to the HR manager, 'we already had an idea of where the discrepancies were'. Data collection was on the basis of figures from: the personnel database, the pay database, the performance pay database and the starters and leavers database. A small local consultancy had helped to introduce a new job evaluation scheme; however, the basis for making equal work comparisons was predominantly by existing grade. The organisation looked at global differences, differences by grade and differences by components of pay (basic pay, overtime and allowances).

---

79. Employers who do not have analytical job evaluation schemes designed with equal value in mind will need to find an alternative means of estimating whether men and women are doing equal work. The EOC Equal Pay Review Kit includes suggestions as to how this can be done. Employers who do use analytical job evaluation schemes need to check that their scheme has been designed and implemented in such a way and at all times so as not to discriminate on grounds of sex.

STEP 3: Collecting pay data to identify equal pay gaps

80. In Step 3 employers need to collect and compare pay information for men and women doing equal work by:
- Calculating average basic pay and total earnings.
- Comparing access to and amounts received of each element of the pay package.

To ensure comparisons are consistent, when calculating average basic pay and average total earnings for men and women separately, employers should do this either on an hourly basis or on a full-time salary basis (grossing up or down for those who work fewer, or more, hours—excluding overtime—per week than the norm).

81. Employers then need to review the pay comparisons to identify any gender pay gaps and decide if any are significant enough to warrant further investigation. It is advisable to record all the significant or patterned pay gaps that have been identified.

Example—data collection and analysis
The organisation had a well-established process for undertaking equal pay audits. Data were brought together and presented in tabular form by the data analysis section of the human resources department. The data were then reviewed, analysed and commented on by the head of employee relations, who shared the data with trade union representatives. Union and management worked together to develop action points arising from the data.

STEP 4: Establishing the causes of any significant pay gaps and assessing the reasons for these

82. In Step 4 employers need to:
- Find out if there is a genuine and material reason for the difference in pay that has nothing to do with the sex of the jobholders.
- Examine their pay systems to find out which pay policies and practices are contributing to any gender pay gaps.

Example—finding out which policies and practices are contributing to the gender pay gap

The review showed a 23 per cent gap in the average basic pay of men and women across the organisation. In grades with a large enough number of staff to make a comparison, 50 per cent had variances of five per cent or greater in favour of either men or women. Starting pay was not found to be an issue, nor was performance pay. The key factor in grade inequalities was identified as long pay ranges and the impact of past restructuring. There was a body of staff (largely male), who had reached the upper quartile of their current pay range prior to the most recent restructuring. However, new appointees, who were increasingly female, and those who had taken career breaks, had little chance of progressing to this level.

The other area of concern identified by the review was premium payments for working unsocial hours. These were paid at the rate of 20 per cent of basic salary to some grades. However, in 1998 these payments were restricted to existing staff. The period since 1998 had seen an increase in the number of female recruits into what were traditionally male areas. Due to the change in the rules they were not eligible for the premium payments. The result was that overall in the eligible grades, men received on average two and a half times the amount of earnings from premium pay that women received.

---

83. Pay systems vary considerably. Pay systems that group jobs into pay grades or bands have traditionally treated jobs in the same grade or band as being of broadly equal value, either because they have been evaluated with similar scores under a job evaluation scheme, or because they are simply regarded as equivalent. However, recent years have seen a trend towards structures with fewer, broader grades or bands and greater use of performance pay and market factors. A single broad band or grade may contain jobs or roles of significantly different value because it encompasses a wide range of job evaluation scores. This, coupled with a wider use of other determinants of pay and more complex methods of pay progression, means that it is important for employers to check all aspects of the pay system from a variety of standpoints: design, implementation, and impact on men and women.

STEP 5: Developing an equal pay action plan and/or reviewing and monitoring

84. Where the reason for the pay difference is connected with sex, employers will need to provide equal pay for current and future employees.

85. Employers who find no gaps between men's and women's pay, or who find gaps for which there are genuinely non-discriminatory reasons, should nevertheless keep their pay systems under review by introducing regular monitoring undertaken jointly with trade unions. This will ensure that the pay system remains free of sex bias.

Example—developing an action plan

Following the review, an Action Plan looking at internal processes was developed. This is ongoing and is reviewed through partnership processes. The aim is to integrate equal pay issues into employee relations' work.

Early action has been in relation to internal recruitment processes. This included looking at whether people were encouraged (or not) to apply for particular jobs. This lack of recognition of potential opportunities was closing off progression routes to some groups, and impacting on the organisational gender pay gap. The organisation also found that it had a body of staff (mainly women) that did not seek promotion. A challenge for the organisation was to encourage more women to aim for promotion, especially once they had fewer family responsibilities. The remuneration manager anticipated that the gender pay gap in the main staff would fall from the 13 per cent identified in the pay review to under five per cent over the following five years. A recent repeat of the review had already shown a fall, however, the decline in the gap might not always be maintained. This is because the company's pay system is highly market sensitive and a tightening of the labour market in areas in which men are in the majority (such as Information Technology) would have a negative impact on the downward trend.

SECTION THREE   AN EQUAL PAY POLICY

The organisation's intentions in respect of equal pay

86. It is good equal pay practice to provide employees with a clear statement of the organisation's intentions in respect of equal pay. Evidence of an equal pay policy may assist an employer's defence against an equal pay claim

87. It is recommended that an equal pay policy should:
- Commit the organisation to carry out an equal pay review and to monitor pay regularly in partnership with trade union/employee representatives.
- Set objectives.
- Identify the action to be taken.
- Implement that action in a planned programme in partnership with the workforce.
- Assign responsibility and accountability for the policy to a senior manager.
- Commit the organisation to set aside the resources necessary to achieve equal pay.

88. Everyone involved in setting the pay of staff should be committed to and, if possible, trained in the identification of sex discrimination in the pay process.

A model equal pay policy

We are committed to the principle of equal pay for all our employees. We aim to eliminate any sex bias in our pay systems.

We understand that equal pay between men and women is a legal right under both domestic and European law.

It is in the interest of the organisation to ensure that we have a fair and just pay system. It is important that employees have confidence in the process of eliminating sex bias and we are therefore committed to working in partnership with the recognised trade unions. As good business practice we are committed to working with trade union/employee representatives to take action to ensure that we provide equal pay.

We believe that in eliminating sex bias in our pay system we are sending a positive message to our staff and customers. It makes good business sense to have a fair, transparent reward system and it helps us to control costs. We recognise that avoiding unfair discrimination will improve morale and enhance efficiency.

Our objectives are to:
- Eliminate any unfair, unjust or unlawful practices that impact on pay.
- Take appropriate remedial action.

We will:
- Implement an equal pay review in line with EOC guidance for all current staff and starting pay for new staff (including those on maternity leave, career breaks, or non-standard contracts).

- Plan and implement actions in partnership with trade union/employee representatives.
- Provide training and guidance for those involved in determining pay.
- Inform employees of how these practices work and how their own pay is determined.
- Respond to grievances on equal pay as a priority.
- In conjunction with trade union/employee representatives, monitor pay statistics annually.

Commission for Racial Equality Code of Practice on Racial Equality in Employment
(2005)

THE RESPONSIBILITIES OF EMPLOYERS: EQUALITY OF OPPORTUNITY AND GOOD EMPLOYMENT PRACTICE

RECRUITMENT

PRINCIPLES OF GOOD PRACTICE

4.4 The following principles apply to all aspects of recruitment for employment, including promotion, and training.
- a. Recruitment policies, procedures and practices should meet all the terms and objectives of the organisation's equal opportunities policy and action plan.
- b. All staff responsible for recruitment should receive training in the equal opportunities policy.
- c. Opportunities for employment, including promotion, and training should be equally open to all eligible candidates, and selection should be based solely on merit (except where the positive action exception applies to training; see Appendix 1).
- d. No applicant or worker should be placed at a disadvantage by rules, requirements, conditions or practices that have a disproportionately adverse effect on his or her racial group.

PLANNING

Person specifications
4.8 A person specification describes the skills, knowledge, abilities, qualifications, experience and qualities that are considered necessary or desirable in a candidate, in order to perform all the duties in the job description satisfactorily. It is recommended that employers prepare a written person specification to accompany the job description.

4.9 To avoid claims that a person specification includes potentially discriminatory requirements, criteria or conditions, employers need to make sure of the following.
- a. The person specification includes only the criteria needed to perform the duties in the job description satisfactorily.
- b. The person specification does not overstate the requirements; for example, by calling for 'excellent knowledge of English' (or Welsh in Wales) when 'good

understanding' is more appropriate, or by asking for higher qualifications than are actually needed to do the job satisfactorily.

c. The person specification makes clear the relative importance placed on each criterion, and whether it is necessary or desirable.

d. As far as possible, all the criteria are capable of being tested objectively. This means avoiding vague or subjective qualities. Attributes such as 'leadership', which are widely used in the selection process, need to be precisely and objectively defined in terms of the measurable skills and qualities that contribute to it; for example, fairness, knowledge, diplomacy, imagination and decisiveness.

e. The person specification makes clear that degrees or diplomas obtained abroad are acceptable, if they are of an equivalent standard to UK qualifications (see Appendix 5 for details of UK National Academic Recognition Information Centre).

f. To reduce the risk of including criteria that reflect personal preferences rather than justifiable requirements, as far as possible, the manager responsible for the post obtains approval of the person specification from the person responsible for equal opportunities in the organisation (in smaller organisations, this might be the director or proprietor).

4.10 Employers should consider reviewing the person specifications they have used over a period of time, or a representative sample of them, as part of their equal opportunities review of the recruitment process, to make sure the requirements and criteria applied do not contribute to any significant disparities between the success rates for different racial groups.

THE SELECTION PROCESS

4.16 Employers are responsible for making sure their selection procedures are fair, and operate consistently, to ensure the appointment of the best person for the job, irrespective of race, colour, nationality (including citizenship) or ethnic or national origins.

Terms and conditions

4.37 It is unlawful for employers to discriminate, on racial grounds, in the terms and conditions of work they offer, including pay, hours of work, overtime, bonuses, holiday entitlement, sickness leave, and maternity and paternity leave.

4.38 It is recommended that employers make sure their rules and requirements on access to any benefits, facilities or services, such as luncheon vouchers, discount travel services or membership of a gym, do not unlawfully discriminate against a particular racial group (or groups) (see paras 2.9–2.13).

4.39 When employees' cultural or religious practices, such as those expressed in dress codes, conflict with an employer's policies or workplace requirements, it is recommended that the employer consider whether it is practicable to vary or adapt these requirements. Employers should consult staff, trades unions and other workplace representatives on practical ways in which they can accommodate workers' needs. Discrimination in the field of employment on grounds of religion or belief is unlawful under the Employment Equality (Religion or Belief) Regulations 2003. If the policy or requirement affects people from a particular racial group (or groups), it might also amount to unlawful indirect racial discrimination (see paras 2.9–2.13).

IN THE COURSE OF EMPLOYMENT

Language in the workplace

4.46 There is a clear business interest in having a common language in the workplace, to avoid misunderstandings, with all the risks these can entail, whether legal, financial or in relation to health and safety. It is also a matter of courtesy, conducive to good working relations, not to exclude people from conversations that might concern them, when they are present. In the main, English is the language of business in Britain and is likely to be the preferred language of communication in most workplaces (see Example 15 on p 57), unless other languages are specifically required.

4.48 However, employers should make sure that any rules, requirements, conditions, policies or practices involving the use of a particular language during or outside working hours, for example during work breaks, do not amount to unlawful racial discrimination or harassment against a worker or job applicant (see Example 7, p 22). Employers should be able to justify these as being a reasonable means of achieving a legitimate business end. Blanket rules, requirements or practices involving the use of a particular language are often unlikely to be justifiable. Even during working hours, most types of work permit casual conversation at the same time, for example while picking fruit, or filing papers. An employer who prohibits workers from talking casually to each other in a language they do not share with all colleagues, or uses occasions when this happens to trigger disciplinary or capability procedures or impede progress, may be considered to be acting unreasonably.

4.49 Employers should always consult workers, trade unions and other workplace representatives before drawing up any proposals on the use of language in the workplace.

4.50 Where the workforce includes people who are not proficient in the language of the workplace, employers should consider taking reasonable steps to improve communication (see Example I at para 4.58). These might include providing:

Example 15: Language

Shah v George Grassic t/a The Suite Factory [1995] DCLD 24

An Asian worker in a furniture factory (where there were eight Asians in a workforce of 40) came out of a disciplinary meeting onto the shop floor and, in the owner's presence, began to speak to other Asian workers in their own language. The owner instructed him to speak English, so that he knew what was being said. The worker refused and was warned that if he did not do as he had been instructed he would be dismissed immediately. The worker said he could speak in any language he wished and continued to ignore the instruction. He was then summarily dismissed. The tribunal dismissed the worker's complaint that he had been discriminated against on racial grounds, and ruled that, whether or not it is discriminatory to forbid people to speak in their native language depends on the circumstances: 'If the worker had been told not to speak in his native tongue at all on any occasion at work, in any circumstances, then that, in our view, would clearly be a discriminatory instruction. . . . [but in these circumstances] It was not unreasonable for [the owner] to expect the common courtesy of being spoken to, or about, in a way in which he could understand.'

---

a. interpreting and translation facilities; for example, multilingual safety signs and notices, to make sure workers understand health and safety requirements;
b. training in language and communication skills; and
c. training for managers and supervisors on the various populations and cultures that make up Britain today.

Performance assessment

4.53 It is unlawful to discriminate against, or harass, a worker, on racial grounds in assessing his or her performance.

4.54 To strengthen their legal defence in any proceedings alleging unlawful racial discrimination, employers need to make sure that performance assessments are not used to pass judgements about the person, based on assumptions about their capabilities as members of certain racial groups. Employers will find it helpful to base all assessments on actual performance of specific tasks, measured by impartial and objective standards. This is particularly important when performance is linked to promotion or a benefit, such as pay or bonuses (see Example 16, p 59).

4.55 It is recommended that training courses for managers on the equal opportunities policy (see para 3.20) should include guidance on objective performance assessment. Equally, any training on assessment methods should take the organisation's equal opportunities policy fully into account.

4.56 To be sure workers are being assessed fairly, and consistently, employers will find it helpful to monitor the results of performance assessments, by racial group (see paras 3.25–3.31), and use the data to inform their review of the organisation's policies, procedures and practices in this area. Any significant disparities in assessment marks between racial groups should be investigated, and steps taken to deal with possible causes.

Example 16: Performance assessment
Nasr v Salisbury Health Care NHS Trust, Case No. 3102492/99
A consultant of Egyptian origin was not awarded a discretionary point to take his salary above the standard, whereas his 12 colleagues, who were white and of British origin, had each been awarded at least one point. The tribunal upheld his claim of unlawful direct discrimination. It found that the members of the discretionary points committee did not independently record their assessment of each of the candidates against the appropriate criteria and guidelines. Nor were any notes kept of the discussions or the assessment process. The tribunal concluded that 'such a high level of subjectivity is anathema to the successful application of equal opportunity guidelines, since it works to the disadvantage of ethnic minorities, both in operation and perception'. The complainant was awarded £18,000 in exemplary damages.

Example H. A large-scale study of appraisal in 13 civil service departments in 2000 found that staff from white racial groups were consistently awarded higher marks than staff from other racial groups. This was true across grades, age groups, and length-of-service bands. The researchers found no evidence of significant differences in education or training between the groups that were likely to affect performance. Interviews with staff from all racial groups revealed common concerns about the appraisal system itself. Staff from 'non-white' groups were concerned that their performance reviews and appraisal markings reflected stereotyped attitudes about their racial groups. The researchers produced reports and made recommendations for each department. Departments are now acting on these and are themselves monitoring appraisal results and carrying out further investigations and analyses, for example of the language used in appraisal reports, depending on the racial groups concerned.

Promotion

4.60 It is unlawful for employers to discriminate against, or harass, workers on racial grounds in the way they make opportunities for promotion available, or by refusing or deliberately failing to make them available (see Example 18 below).

4.61 It is recommended that all promotion opportunities, including development opportunities that could lead to permanent promotion, should be advertised widely throughout the organisation, and filled in line with the organisation's equal opportunities and recruitment policies and procedures. This would mean using the organisation's standard job application form (if it has one) to fill all promotion and development opportunities, and making sure that selection is based strictly on demonstrable merit.

Example 18: Promotion
Dr Halim v Moray College, Case No. S/200267/02
The complainant, who was a lecturer at a college in Scotland, was twice overlooked for promotion, even though he was better qualified than those who were promoted. He believed this was because he had complained to the college principal that his line manager was racist and that he had given him unfair appraisals. The principal had advised the complainant to raise the matter directly with his line manager. There were nine applicants for the first post, including the complainant and his line manager, and the panel included the principal. The principal's sole comment on the complainant was 'This man's not for shortlisting'. At the tribunal hearing, he said he did not consider the application to be 'a serious one' and thought it was all 'part of a sad ruse'. The complainant's line manager was appointed to the post. The panel for the second promotion included the complainant's line manager and the principal and deputy principal. This time he was rejected because the panel said he did not meet some of the essential criteria. The principal also told the tribunal that the complainant 'did not understand what the job was about'.

The tribunal found the college's explanations unconvincing. In upholding the complainant's claim, it took into account the following: unlike the shortlisted candidates, the complainant had met some of the essential criteria; the panel members had been aware of the complainant's grievance; and the person who was the subject of the grievance had been a member of the panel. The tribunal awarded £14,000 in damages.

4.62 Employers should avoid by-passing their recruitment procedures, unless a temporary promotion is absolutely necessary. In this case, the promotion should last no longer than the time needed to fill the post permanently, and openly, through the organisation's recruitment procedures.

4.63 Employers will find it helpful to build the following guidelines into their policies and procedures for promotion and career development.

    a. Where posts are advertised internally and externally, the same selection procedures and criteria should apply to both internal and external candidates. Discussions about candidates, particularly internal candidates, should not be based on rumours or unsubstantiated opinions.

    b. As far as possible, selection decisions based on performance assessments should be endorsed by the organisation's personnel department (if it has one).

    c. No assumptions should be made about the eligibility of staff, based on their grade, current post or racial group, and information about all promotion and other development opportunities that could lead to permanent promotion, such as deputising and secondments, should be communicated to all staff; restricting applications for promotion and other development opportunities to staff at a particular grade or level could indirectly discriminate against some racial groups.

    d. Records should be kept, by racial group, of who is taking up different types of opportunities, and who is not (see paras 3.25–3.31); who is successful, and who is not.

4.64 As part of their equal opportunities review of the recruitment process, employers should use the monitoring data on promotions to see if there are significant disparities between racial groups in the take-up of promotion and other development opportunities, success rates and length of time spent at a particular grade. If disparities are found, employers should investigate the possible causes in each case and take steps to remove any barriers.

Discipline and grievance

4.65 Employers must not discriminate on racial grounds in the way they respond to grievances, or invoke disciplinary measures. Disciplinary action is an extreme measure and should be taken fairly and consistently, regardless of the worker's racial group. Equally, allegations of racial discrimination or harassment must always be taken seriously and investigated promptly, not dismissed as 'oversensitivity' on a worker's part.

4.66 All employers (irrespective of their size) must now have minimum statutory procedures in place for dealing with dismissal, disciplinary action and grievances in the workplace (section 3 of the Employment Rights Act 1996, as amended by the Employment Act 2002) (see 'disciplinary procedure' and 'grievance procedure' in the glossary at Appendix 7, and ACAS in Appendix 5). These provisions apply only to employees (see the glossary at Appendix 7).

4.67 It is in the interests of employers to attempt, wherever possible, to resolve grievances as they arise, and before they become major problems, through mediation. Grievance procedures can provide an open and fair way for complainants to make their concerns known, and for their grievances to be resolved quickly, without having to bring legal proceedings.

4.68 It is recommended that employers monitor, by racial group, the number of workers who have brought grievances or been subjected to disciplinary action (public authorities with at least 150 full-time-equivalent workers have a legal duty to do this; see paras 3.32–3.34), and the outcomes of each case. It will also be useful to be able to match the data with information about the workers' grades, their managers and the areas of the organisation where they work.

4.69 If an investigation into a grievance or disciplinary matter finds evidence that the grievance was brought in bad faith, for example, to get another worker into trouble, the employer should take steps to make sure this does not happen again, either by recommending training or taking disciplinary action against the worker in question, as appropriate. However, employers must be careful not to punish someone for having made a complaint that proves to have been unfounded, but that was made in good faith, as that could amount to unlawful victimisation (see paras 2.14–2.15).

4.70 It is recommended that, before taking disciplinary action, employers should consider the possible effect on a worker's behaviour of the following:
    a. racist abuse or other provocation on racial grounds;
    b. difficulty in communicating with, or understanding, colleagues; and
    c. different cultural norms.

4.71 As part of their equal opportunities review, employers should use the monitoring data on grievances and disciplinary action to see if there are significant disparities between racial groups, investigate the possible causes in each case, and take steps to deal with them.

Harassment

4.72 It is unlawful for employers to engage in, or condone, unwanted conduct that will violate the dignity of workers or job applicants, or create an intimidating, hostile,

---

Example 19: Harassment
Milovanovic v Hebden Dyeing and Finishing Co Ltd, Case No. 29691/94 [1995] DCLD No. 24
A Serbian worker, who had lived in Britain for over 40 years, was one of 25 workers in a dyeing company. He complained in vain of persistent harassment based on his ethnic background, especially after the war in Bosnia began. He faced comments such as 'Go back to Bosnia or wherever you belong, and fight and die like a dog instead of our lads'; and 'If all foreigners and blacks go back to their own country, we will have a better environment in this country'. He handed in his notice and brought a successful claim of direct racial discrimination against the company (see para 2.16). The complainant was awarded around £4,000 in damages.

Example 20: Harassment
Mohammed Wahid Zia v Killermont Polo Club (Scotland) Ltd, Case No. S/105430/ 2001
A Muslim of Pakistani origin, who was employed as a part-time waiter in Glasgow, claimed that his employers, who were Indian Sikhs, harassed, humiliated and demeaned him on racial grounds, and that they also made derogatory remarks about his religion. The tribunal upheld his claims of direct racial discrimination (see para 2.16), victimisation and unfair dismissal. The application was made before 19 July 2003, when it became unlawful to treat a worker or a job applicant less favourably on grounds of religion or belief. Since then, in similar circumstances, the case could have been brought on religious as well as racial grounds. The complainant was awarded a total of around £33,000 in compensation, including £22,000 for injury to feelings.

---

degrading, offensive or humiliating atmosphere for that person (see Example 7, p 22, and Examples 19 and 20 above).

4.73 It is recommended that employers introduce a policy for dealing with racial harassment. The policy could be part of a wider anti-harassment policy or the organisation's policies on discipline and grievance, or a policy covering dignity in the workplace. Whatever form the policy takes, it should make clear what is and what is not acceptable behaviour in the organisation (see the sample policy at Appendix 3).

4.74 To make sure the policy is effective, it is recommended that employers:
   a. publicise the policy through the organisation's websites, notice boards and other forms of communication, so that all staff know about it and understand why it has been adopted, how it will work and how it affects them;
   b. make both the policy for dealing with racial harassment and the equal opportunities policy standard components of all training, including induction and specialist courses; and
   c. offer an informal route to resolving a grievance as well as the formal one of an investigation.

4.75 If an allegation of racial harassment or discrimination is upheld, it is in the interest of good workplace relations for the employer to make sure that:
   a. the harassment has actually stopped, particularly if the parties continue to work together, and
   b. the complainant is not victimised for having brought the grievance.

Dismissal and termination of employment

4.76 It is unlawful for employers to discriminate against, or harass, workers on racial grounds, by dismissing them or subjecting them to any other detriment (see Example 21 below and Example 22, p 66). Dismissal includes termination of a contract by the employer (with or without notice), and non-renewal or expiry of a fixed-term contract, unless a genuine occupational requirement applies (see para 2.36 and Appendix 1).

4.77 It is recommended that employers make sure the criteria they use for dismissal (including redundancies) are not indirectly discriminatory, and that their procedures are fair and objective, and are followed consistently.

4.78 Dismissal, or any other detriment—such as demotion or compulsory transfer—must always be fair and reasonable. Employers should make sure such decisions are based on a worker's actual performance or conduct during his or her employment, as reflected in any

---

Example 21: Dismissal
Birdi v Waites (1) and Waites Architecture (2), Case No. 37708/95 [1996] DCLD 30
A tribunal found that a firm of architects had a record of dismissing black and Asian professional staff after short service, and that this amounted to unlawful racial

discrimination. It found that an Asian architect had been criticised without reason during his employment with the firm, marginalised and then dismissed after nine months, for poor performance. He was the third consecutive ethnic minority worker to be dismissed in under 12 months.

Example 22: Redundancy
Sahota and ORS v Shareporter Ltd, [1983] COIT 1414/148
Three sewing machinists, each with less than a year's service, claimed compensation for their selection for redundancy. Two were of Indian origin and the third was an Italian. The machine room supervisor, whose views of black and Asian workers were known to be both strong and derogatory, had made the selection.

The tribunal did not accept the company's claim that the machinists had been selected objectively, on the grounds of skill, as one of the machinists was a high bonus earner of some speed and reliability. The tribunal ruled that all three complainants had been dismissed in a redundancy situation because of their race.

---

performance assessments. Any aptitude tests designed to select people for redundancy should be objective, and fairly and consistently administered (see paras 4.23–4.26). Wherever possible, employers should consult their workers, and trade unions and other workplace representatives, about proposed redundancies, and the criteria for selection.

4.79 Staff responsible for selecting workers for dismissal should be instructed not to discriminate on racial grounds, and trained in the organisation's equal opportunities policy, and how it might apply to dismissal and redundancy.

4.80 Workers who are eligible for redeployment should be given the chance to show they have the skills or abilities required in alternative jobs. Employers should use their normal recruitment policy to fill these jobs.

4.81 It is recommended that employers monitor all dismissals, by racial group (see also paras 3.25 and 3.31). They will find it useful to be able to match this data with information about the workers' grades, the areas of the organisation where they work, and their managers.

4.82 As well as the guidelines proposed in relation to disciplinary action (see paras 4.65–4.71), employers will find it helpful to:
   a. make sure the decision to dismiss is not made by one individual, but, as far as possible, in discussion with a senior member of staff in the personnel department (if the organisation has one);
   b. keep written records of all decisions to dismiss; and
   c. encourage leavers to give feedback about their employment.

4.83 Employers should use the monitoring data to see if policies, procedures or practices that might have been criticised in the feedback could be contributing to any significant disparities between racial groups, for example in performance ratings or promotion.

The Disability Rights Commission Code of Practice on Employment and Occupation
(Issued 2004)

When is direct discrimination likely to occur?

4.7 Treatment of a disabled person is 'on the ground of' his disability if it is caused by the fact that he is disabled or has the disability in question. In general, this means that treatment is on the ground of disability if a disabled person would not have received it but for his disability. However, disability does not have to be the only (or even the main) cause of the treatment complained of—provided that it is an effective cause, determined objectively from all the circumstances.

4.8 Consequently, if the less favourable treatment occurs because of the employer's generalised, or stereotypical, assumptions about the disability or its effects, it is likely to be direct discrimination. This is because an employer would not normally make such assumptions about a non-disabled person, but would instead consider his individual abilities.

> A blind woman is not short-listed for a job involving computers because the employer wrongly assumes that blind people cannot use them. The employer makes no attempt to look at the individual circumstances. The employer has treated the woman less favourably than other people by not short-listing her for the job. The treatment was on the ground of the woman's disability (because assumptions would not have been made about a non-disabled person).

4.9 In addition, less favourable treatment which is disability-specific, or which arises out of prejudice about disability (or about a particular type of disability), is also likely to amount to direct discrimination.

> An employer seeking a shop assistant turns down a disabled applicant with a severe facial disfigurement solely on the ground that other employees would be uncomfortable working alongside him. This would amount to direct discrimination and would be unlawful.

> A disabled woman who uses a wheelchair applies for a job. She can do the job just as well as any other applicant, but the employer wrongly assumes that the wheelchair will cause an obstruction in the office. He therefore gives the job to a person who is no more suitable for the job but who is not a wheelchair-user. This would amount to direct discrimination and would be unlawful.

4.10 In some cases, an apparently neutral reason for less favourable treatment of a disabled person may, on investigation, turn out to be a pretext for direct discrimination.

4.11 Direct discrimination will often occur where the employer is aware that the disabled person has a disability, and this is the reason for the employer's treatment of him. Direct discrimination need not be conscious—people may hold prejudices that they do not admit, even to themselves. Thus, a person may behave in a discriminatory way while believing that he would never do so. Moreover, direct discrimination may sometimes occur even though the employer is unaware of a person's disability.

> An employer advertises a promotion internally to its workforce. The job description states that people with a history of mental illness would not be suitable for the post. An employee who would otherwise be eligible for the promotion has a history of schizophrenia, but the employer is unaware of this. The employee would, nevertheless, have a good claim for unlawful direct discrimination in relation to the promotion opportunities afforded to him by his employer. The act of direct discrimination in this case is the blanket ban on anyone who has had a mental illness, effectively rejecting whole categories of people with no consideration of their individual abilities.

4.12 In situations such as those described in the above examples, it will often be readily apparent that the disabled person concerned has been treated less favourably on the ground of his disability. In other cases, however, this may be less obvious. Whether or not the basis for the treatment in question appears to be clear, a useful way of telling whether or not it is discriminatory, (and of establishing what kind of discrimination it is), is to focus on the person with whom the disabled person should be compared. That person may be real or hypothetical (see paragraph 4.18).

Identifying comparators in respect of direct discrimination

4.13 In determining whether a disabled person has been treated less favourably in the context of direct discrimination, his treatment must be compared with that of an appropriate comparator. This must be someone who does not have the same disability. It could be a non-disabled person or a person with other disabilities.

A person who becomes disabled takes six months' sick leave because of his disability, and is dismissed by his employer. A non-disabled fellow employee also takes six months' sick leave (because he has broken his leg) but is not dismissed. The difference in treatment is attributable to the employer's unwillingness to employ disabled staff and the treatment is therefore on the ground of disability. The non-disabled employee is an appropriate comparator in the context of direct discrimination because his relevant circumstances are the same as those of the disabled person. It is the fact of having taken six months' sick leave which is relevant in these circumstances. As the disabled person has been treated less favourably than the comparator, this is direct discrimination.

4.14 It follows that, in the great majority of cases, some difference will exist between the circumstances (including the abilities) of the comparator and those of the disabled person—there is no need to find a comparator whose circumstances are the same as those of the disabled person in every respect. What matters is that the comparator's **relevant** circumstances (including his abilities) must be the same as, or not materially different from, those of the disabled person.

In the previous example, the position would be different if it were the employer's policy to dismiss any member of staff who has been off sick for six months, and that policy were applied equally to disabled and non-disabled staff. In this case there would be no direct discrimination because the disabled person would not have been treated less favourably than the comparator—both would have been dismissed. Nevertheless, there may be a claim for failure to make reasonable adjustments to the policy, for example by allowing disability leave (see paragraph 4.25). In addition, the employer's policy may give rise to a claim for disability-related discrimination (see paragraph 4.27).

4.15 Once an appropriate comparator is identified, it is clear that the situation described in the example at paragraph 4.8 amounts to direct discrimination:

In the example about the blind woman who is not short-listed for a job involving computers, there is direct discrimination because the woman was treated less favourably on the ground of her disability than an appropriate comparator (that is, a person who is not blind but who has the same abilities to do the job as the blind applicant): such a person would not have been rejected out of hand without consideration of her individual abilities.

4.16 The examples of direct discrimination in paragraph 4.9 also become clearer when the appropriate comparator is identified in each case:

> In the example about the disabled person with a severe facial disfigurement who applies to be a shop assistant, there is direct discrimination because the man was treated less favourably on the ground of his disability than an appropriate comparator (that is, a person who does not have such a disfigurement but who does have the same abilities to do the job): such a person would not have been rejected in the same way.

> In the example about the disabled woman who is not offered a job because she uses a wheelchair, there is direct discrimination because the woman was treated less favourably on the ground of her disability than an appropriate comparator (that is, a person who does not use a wheelchair but who does have the same abilities to do the job): such a person would not have been rejected in the same way.

4.17 The comparator used in relation to direct discrimination under the Act is the same as it is for other types of direct discrimination—such as direct sex discrimination. It is, however, made explicit in the Act that the comparator must have the same relevant abilities as the disabled person.

4.18 It may not be possible to identify an actual comparator whose relevant circumstances are the same as (or not materially different from) those of the disabled person in question. In such cases a hypothetical comparator may be used. Evidence which helps to establish how a hypothetical comparator would have been treated is likely to include details of how other people (not satisfying the statutory comparison test) were treated in circumstances which were broadly similar.

> A disabled person works in a restaurant. She makes a mistake on the till and this results in a small financial loss to her employer. She is dismissed because of this. The situation has not arisen before, and so there is no actual comparator. Nevertheless, six months earlier a non-disabled fellow employee was disciplined for taking home items of food without permission and received a written warning. The treatment of that person might be used as evidence that a hypothetical non-disabled member of staff who makes an error on the till would not have been dismissed for that reason.

4.19 It should be noted that the type of comparator described in the preceding paragraphs is only relevant to disability discrimination when assessing whether there has been **direct** discrimination. A different comparison falls to be made when assessing whether there has been a failure to comply with a duty to make reasonable adjustments (see paragraphs 5.3 and 5.4) or when considering disability-related discrimination (see paragraph 4.30).

Focusing on relevant circumstances

4.20 As stated in paragraph 4.14, direct discrimination only occurs where the **relevant** circumstances of the comparator, including his abilities, are the same as, or not materially different from, those of the disabled person himself. It is therefore important to focus on those circumstances which are, in fact, relevant to the matter to which the less favourable treatment relates. Although, in some cases, the effects of the disability may be relevant, the fact of the disability itself is not a relevant circumstance for these purposes. This is because the comparison must be with a person **not** having that particular disability.

A disabled person with arthritis who can type at 30 words per minute (wpm) applies for an administrative job which includes typing, but is rejected on the ground that her typing speed is too slow. The correct comparator in a claim for direct discrimination would be a person not having arthritis who also has a typing speed of 30 wpm (with the same accuracy rate).

A disabled person with a severe visual impairment applies for a job as a bus driver and is refused the job because he fails to meet the minimum level of visual acuity which is essential to the safe performance of the job. The correct comparator is a person not having that particular disability (for example, a person who merely has poorer than average eyesight) also failing to meet that minimum standard.

A disabled person with schizophrenia applies for a job as an administrative assistant with his local authority, and declares his history of mental illness. The local authority refuses him employment, relying on a negative medical report from the authority's occupational health adviser which is based on assumptions about the effects of schizophrenia, without adequate consideration of the individual's abilities and the impact of the impairment in his particular case. This is likely to amount to direct discrimination and to be unlawful. The comparator here is a person who does not have schizophrenia, but who has the same abilities to do the job (including relevant qualifications and experience) as the disabled applicant: such a person would not have been rejected without adequate consideration of his individual abilities.

4.21 If (as in the above examples) a disabled person alleges that he has been refused the offer of a job on the ground of his disability, it is only appropriate to compare those of his circumstances which are relevant to his ability to do the job. It is not appropriate to compare other circumstances which are not relevant to this issue. The need to focus on relevant circumstances applies not only to recruitment cases of this kind, but also to any other situation where direct discrimination may have occurred.

A disabled man with arthritis applies for an administrative job which includes typing, but is rejected in favour of a non-disabled candidate. Because of his arthritis, the man has a slow typing speed and has difficulty walking. The job is entirely desk-based, and does not require the person doing it to be able to walk further than a few metres within the office. The comparator in a claim of direct discrimination would be a non-disabled applicant with the same slow typing speed (and with the same abilities to do the job— e.g., the same typing accuracy rate, and the same knowledge of word-processing packages)—but it would not be necessary for the comparator to have mobility problems (because the ability to walk further than a few metres is not relevant to the candidates' ability to do the job).

Relevance of reasonable adjustments to comparison

4.22 In making the comparison in respect of a claim of direct discrimination, the disabled person's abilities must be considered **as they in fact are**. In some cases, there will be particular reasonable adjustments which an employer was required by the Act to make, but in fact failed to make. It may be that those adjustments would have had an effect on the disabled person's abilities to do the job. But in making the comparison, the disabled person's abilities should be considered as they **in fact** were, and not as they would or might have been had those adjustments been made. On the other hand, if adjustments have **in fact** been made which have had the effect of enhancing the disabled person's abilities, then it is those enhanced abilities which should be considered. The disabled person's abilities are being considered as they in fact are (and not as they might have been if the adjustments had not been made).

A disabled person who applies for an administrative job which includes typing is not allowed to use her own adapted keyboard (even though it would have been reasonable for the employer to allow this) and types a test document at 30 wpm. Her speed with the adapted keyboard would have been 50 wpm. A non-disabled candidate is given the job because her typing speed on the test was 45 wpm with the same accuracy rate. This is not direct discrimination, as the comparator is a non-disabled person typing at 30 wpm. (But the disabled person would be likely to have good claims in respect of two other forms of discrimination—failure to make reasonable adjustments and disability-related dis-crimination—see paragraph 4.37.)

A disabled person with arthritis who applies for a similar job is allowed to use an adapted keyboard and types a test document at 50 wpm. A non-disabled candidate types at 30 wpm with the same accuracy rate. However, the disabled candidate is rejected because of prejudice and the other candidate is offered the job instead. This is direct discrimination, as the comparator would be a person not having arthritis who could type at 50 wpm.

Can direct discrimination be justified?

4.23 [s 3A(4)] Treatment of a disabled person which amounts to direct discrimination under the Act's provisions on employment and occupation is unlawful. It can never be justified.

Failure to make reasonable adjustments—relationship to discrimination

4.24 [s 3A(2)] For the reason given in paragraph 4.3, it may be necessary to consider whether an employer has failed to comply with a duty to make a reasonable adjustment in order to determine whether disability-related discrimination has occurred.

4.25 Irrespective of its relevance to disability-related discrimination, however, a failure to comply with a duty to make a reasonable adjustment in respect of a disabled person amounts to discrimination in its own right. Such a failure is therefore unlawful. Chapter 5 explains the circumstances in which an employer has such a duty, and gives guidance as to what employers need to do when the duty arises.

4.26 As with direct discrimination, the Act does not permit an employer to justify a failure to comply with a duty to make a reasonable adjustment (see paragraphs 5.43 and 5.44).

What is disability-related discrimination?

What does the Act say?

4.27 [s 3A(1)] The Act says that an employer's treatment of a disabled person amounts to discrimination if:
- it is for a reason related to his disability
- the treatment is less favourable than the way in which the employer treats (or would treat) others to whom that reason does not (or would not) apply, and
- the employer cannot show that the treatment is justified.

4.28 Although the Act itself does not use the term 'disability-related discrimination', this expression is used in the Code when referring to treatment of a disabled person which:

- is unlawful because each of the conditions listed in paragraph 4.27 is satisfied, but
- does not amount to direct discrimination under the Act.

4.29 In general, direct discrimination occurs when the reason for the less favourable treatment in question is the disability, while disability-related discrimination occurs when the reason relates to the disability but is not the disability itself. The expression 'disability-related discrimination' therefore distinguishes less favourable treatment which amounts to direct discrimination from a wider class of less favourable treatment which, although not amounting to direct discrimination, is nevertheless unlawful.

When does disability-related discrimination occur?

4.30 In determining whether disability-related discrimination has occurred, the employer's treatment of the disabled person must be compared with that of a person **to whom the disability-related reason does not apply**. This contrasts with direct discrimination, which requires a comparison to be made with a person without the disability in question but whose relevant circumstances are the same. The comparator may be non-disabled or disabled—but the key point is that the disability-related reason for the less favourable treatment must not apply to him.

> A disabled man is dismissed for taking six months' sick leave which is disability-related. The employer's policy, which has been applied equally to all staff (whether disabled or not) is to dismiss all employees who have taken this amount of sick leave. The disability-related reason for the less favourable treatment of the disabled person is the fact of having taken six months' sick leave, and the correct comparator is a person to whom that reason does not apply—that is, someone who has not taken six months' sick leave. Consequently, unless the employer can show that the treatment is justified, it will amount to disability-related discrimination because the comparator would not have been dismissed. However, the reason for the treatment is not the disability itself (it is only a matter related thereto, namely the amount of sick leave taken). So there is no direct discrimination.

> A disabled woman is refused an administrative job because she cannot type. She cannot type because she has arthritis. A non-disabled person who was unable to type would also have been turned down. The disability-related reason for the less favourable treatment is the woman's inability to type, and the correct comparator is a person to whom that reason does not apply—that is, someone who can type. Such a person would not have been refused the job. Nevertheless, the disabled woman has been treated less favourably for a disability-related reason and this will be unlawful unless it can be justified. There is no direct discrimination, however, because the comparator for direct discrimination is a person who does not have arthritis, but who is also unable to type.

4.31 The relationship between a disabled person's disability and the employer's treatment of him must be judged objectively. The reason for any less favourable treatment may well relate to the disability even if the employer does not have knowledge of the disability as such, or of whether its salient features are such that it meets the definition of disability in the Act. Less favourable treatment which is not itself direct discrimination will still be unlawful (subject to justification) if, in fact, the reason for it relates to the person's disability.

> A woman takes three periods of sickness absence in a two month period because of her disability, which is multiple sclerosis (MS). Her employer is unaware that she has MS and

dismisses her, in the same way that it would dismiss any employee for a similar attendance record. Nevertheless, this is less favourable treatment for a disability-related reason (namely, the woman's record of sickness absence) and would be unlawful unless it can be justified.

4.32–4.37 [omitted]

What does the Act say about harassment?

4.38 [s 3B(1)] The Act says that harassment occurs where, for a reason which relates to a person's disability, another person engages in unwanted conduct which has the purpose or effect of:

- violating the disabled person's dignity, or
- creating an intimidating, hostile, degrading, humiliating or offensive environment for him.

4.39 [s 3B(2)] If the conduct in question was engaged in with the intention that it should have either of these effects, then it amounts to harassment irrespective of its actual effect on the disabled person. In the absence of such intention, however, the conduct will only amount to harassment if it should reasonably be considered as having either of these effects. Regard must be had to all the circumstances in order to determine whether this is the case. Those circumstances include, in particular, the perception of the disabled person.

A man with a learning disability is often called 'stupid' and 'slow' by a colleague at work. This is harassment, whether or not the disabled man was present when these comments were made, because they were said with the intention of humiliating him.

A man with a stammer feels he is being harassed because his manager makes constant jokes about people with speech impairments. He asks his manager to stop doing this, but the manager says he is being 'oversensitive' as he habitually makes jokes in the office about many different sorts of people. This is likely to amount to harassment because making remarks of this kind should reasonably be considered as having either of the effects mentioned above.

An employee with HIV uses a colleague's mug. The colleague then makes a point of being seen washing the mug with bleach, which is not something she would do if anyone else used her mug. She also makes offensive comments about having her mug used by someone with HIV. This is likely to amount to harassment.

An employee circulates by email a joke about people with autism. A colleague with autism receives the email and finds the joke offensive. This is likely to amount to harassment.

A woman with depression considers that she is being harassed by her manager who constantly asks her if she is feeling all right, despite the fact that she has asked him not to do so in front of the rest of the team. This could amount to harassment.

4.40–5.44 [omitted]

6 Justification

6.1 [omitted]

When does the Act permit justification?

6.2 Paragraph 4.27 explains that one of the forms of discrimination which is unlawful under Part 2 is disability-related discrimination. However, an employer's conduct towards a disabled person does not amount to disability-related discrimination if it can be justified. This chapter explains the limited circumstances in which this may happen.

6.3 **[s 3A(3) & (4)]** Where less favourable treatment of a disabled person is capable of being justified (that is, where it is **not** direct discrimination), the Act says that it will, in fact, be justified if, but only if, the reason for the treatment is both material to the circumstances of the particular case and substantial. This is an objective test. 'Material' means that there must be a reasonably strong connection between the reason given for the treatment and the circumstances of the particular case. 'Substantial' means, in the context of justification, that the reason must carry real weight and be of substance.

> A man who has severe back pain and is unable to bend is rejected for a job as a carpet fitter as he cannot carry out the essential requirement of the job, which is to fit carpets. This would be lawful as the reason he is rejected is a substantial one and is clearly material to the circumstances.

6.4 In certain circumstances, the existence of a material and substantial reason for disability-related less favourable treatment is not enough to justify that treatment. This is the case where an employer is also under a duty to make reasonable adjustments in relation to the disabled person but fails to comply with that duty.

6.5 **[s 3A(6)]** In those circumstances, it is necessary to consider not only whether there is a material and substantial reason for the less favourable treatment, but also whether the treatment would still have been justified even if the employer had complied with its duty to make reasonable adjustments. In effect, it is necessary to ask the question 'would a reasonable adjustment have made any difference?' If a reasonable adjustment would have made a difference to the reason that is being used to justify the treatment, then the less favourable treatment cannot be justified.

> An applicant for an administrative job appears not to be the best person for the job, but only because her typing speed is too slow as a result of arthritis in her hands. If a reasonable adjustment—perhaps an adapted keyboard—would overcome this, her typing speed would not in itself be a substantial reason for not employing her. Therefore the employer would be unlawfully discriminating if, on account of her typing speed, he did not employ her or provide that adjustment.

6.6 In relation to disability-related discrimination, the fact that an employer has failed to comply with a duty to make a reasonable adjustment means that the sequence of events for justifying disability-related less favourable treatment is as follows:

- The disabled person proves facts from which it could be inferred in the absence of an adequate explanation that:
   a. for a reason related to his disability, he has been treated less favourably than a person to whom that reason does not apply has been, or would be, treated, and
   b. a duty to make a reasonable adjustment has arisen in respect of him and the employer has failed to comply with it.
- The employer will be found to have discriminated unless it proves that:
   a. the reason for the treatment is both material to the circumstances of the particular case and substantial, and

b. the reason would still have applied if the reasonable adjustment had been made.

Can health and safety concerns justify less favourable treatment?

6.7 Stereotypical assumptions about the health and safety implications of disability should be avoided, both in general terms and in relation to particular types of disability. Indeed, less favourable treatment which is based on such assumptions may itself amount to direct discrimination—which is incapable of justification (see paragraph 4.5). The fact that a person has a disability does not necessarily mean that he represents an additional risk to health and safety.

An employer has a policy of not employing anyone with diabetes because it believes that people with this condition are a health and safety risk. A person with diabetes applies to work for this employer and is turned down on the basis of her disability, without regard to her personal circumstances. A stereotypical assumption has been made which is likely to amount to direct discrimination and is therefore unlawful.

6.8 Under health and safety law it is the duty of every employer to ensure, so far as is reasonably practicable, the health, safety and welfare at work of all employees. Part of this duty is a requirement for all employers to assess the risks to the health and safety of all employees in the workplace and then to put in place measures that reduce the risks to as low a level as can reasonably be achieved. Genuine concerns about the health and safety of anybody (including a disabled employee) may be relevant when seeking to establish that disability-related less favourable treatment of a disabled person is justified. However, it is important to remember that health and safety law does not require employers to remove all conceivable risk, but to ensure that risk is properly appreciated, understood and managed. Further information can be obtained from the Health and Safety Executive (see Appendix C for details).

6.9 It is the employer who must decide what action to take in response to concerns about health and safety. However, when an employer has reason to think that the effects of a person's disability may give rise to an issue about health and safety, it is prudent for it to have a new risk assessment carried out by a suitably qualified person. This is because:

- If an employer treats a disabled person less favourably merely on the basis of generalised assumptions about the health and safety implications of having a disability, such treatment may itself amount to direct discrimination—which is incapable of justification.
- Even where there is no direct discrimination, an employer which treats a disabled person less favourably without having a suitable and sufficient risk assessment carried out is unlikely to be able to show that its concerns about health and safety justify the less favourable treatment.

A pilot develops a heart condition, and his employer asks him to undertake a risk assessment to be carried out by an appropriate consultant. This is likely to be justifiable.

6.10 Nevertheless, an employer should not subject a disabled person to a risk assessment if this is not merited by the particular circumstances of the case. A person with a learning disability has been working in a shop for many years, stocking shelves without any problems. A new manager is appointed who insists that a risk assessment is carried out for her but not for all the other shelf stackers. This is unlikely to be warranted—and indeed it is likely to amount to direct discrimination.

6.11 A risk assessment must be suitable and sufficient. It should identify the risks associated with a work activity, taking account of any reasonable adjustments put in place for the disabled person, and should be specific for the individual carrying out a particular task. It is therefore unlikely that an employer which has a **general** policy of treating people with certain disabilities (such as epilepsy, diabetes or mental health problems) less favourably than other people will be able to justify doing so—even if that policy is in accordance with the advice of an occupational health adviser.

6.12 A 'blanket' policy of this nature will usually be unlawful. This is because it is likely to amount to direct discrimination (which cannot ever be justified) or to disability-related less favourable treatment which is not justifiable in the circumstances—ie disability-related discrimination (see paragraphs 7.8 and 7.9).

6.13 Reasonable adjustments made by an employer may remove or reduce health and safety risks related to a person's disability. A suitable and sufficient assessment of such risks therefore needs to take account of the impact which making any reasonable adjustments would have. If a risk assessment is not conducted on this basis, then an employer is unlikely to be able to show that its concerns about health and safety justify less favourable treatment of the disabled person.

Can medical information justify less favourable treatment?

6.14 Consideration of medical information (such as a doctor's report or the answers to a medical questionnaire) is likely to form part of an assessment of health and safety risks. In most cases, however, having a disability does not adversely affect a person's general health. In other cases, its effect on a person's health may fluctuate. Although medical information about a disability may justify an adverse employment decision (such as a decision to dismiss or not to promote), it will not do so if there is no effect on the person's ability to do the job (or if any effect is less than substantial), no matter how great the effects of the disability are in other ways. Indeed, less favourable treatment of a disabled person in a case where his disability has no effect on his ability to do the job may well amount to direct discrimination— which is incapable of being justified.

> An employer requires all candidates for a job as a technician in a chemical plant to complete a medical questionnaire. Medical information about one candidate shows that she has a degenerative condition which is likely to affect her ability to walk. This is not relevant to her ability to do the sedentary job in question. It would be unlawful for the employer to reject her on the ground of her disability as her disability is irrelevant to her ability to do the job. This would amount to direct discrimination.

> The same employer is looking for a technician to work on a specific project for two years. A medical questionnaire shows that a candidate has a degenerative condition which could mean that he would not be able to work for that long. Because of this, further medical evidence is requested from his doctor and this confirms that he would not be able to work for two years. It is likely to be lawful to reject this candidate if the two-year requirement is justified in terms of the work and if there are no reasonable adjustments that could be made.

6.15 In addition, where medical information is available, employers must weigh it up in the context of the actual job, and the capabilities of the individual. An employer should also consider whether reasonable adjustments could be made in order to overcome any problems which may have been identified as a result of the medical information. It should not be taken for granted that the person who provides the medical information will be aware that employers have a duty to make reasonable adjustments, what these adjustments might be, or of the relevant working arrangements. It is good practice, therefore, to ensure that medical advisers are made aware of these matters. Information provided by a medical adviser should only be relied on if the adviser has the appropriate knowledge and expertise.

> An occupational health adviser recommends that an administrative assistant cannot carry on in her current job because she has been diagnosed with Repetitive Strain Injury. The employer has another member of staff who uses voice recognition software, and considers this technology may be of relevance. The employer asks the adviser to review his conclusion taking this into account. The adviser revises his opinion and concludes that, with appropriate software, she can continue in her role.

6.16 In any event, although medical evidence may generally be considered as an 'expert contribution', it should not ordinarily be the sole factor influencing an employer's decision on employment related matters. The views of the disabled person (about his own capabilities and possible adjustments) should also be sought. In addition, and subject to the considerations about confidentiality explained in paragraphs 8.21 and 8.22, other contributions could come from the disabled person's line manager (about the nature of the job and possible adjustments). It may also be possible to seek help from disability organisations or from Jobcentre Plus, who have staff trained to advise about disability issues in the workplace. Ultimately, it is for the employer—and not the medical adviser—to take decisions as to whether, for example, to reject a job applicant or to maintain a disabled person's employment.

> An employer receives advice from an occupational health adviser stating simply that an employee is 'unfit for work'. In spite of this the employer must consider whether there are reasonable adjustments which should be made.

7   Discrimination in the recruitment of employees
7.1–7.6 [omitted]

Specifying the job

How does the Act affect the way in which a job description or person specification should be prepared?

7.7 The inclusion of unnecessary or marginal requirements in a job description or person specification can lead to discrimination.

> An employer stipulates that employees must be 'active and energetic', when in fact the job in question is largely sedentary in nature. This requirement could unjustifiably exclude some people whose disabilities result in them getting tired more easily than others.

> An employer specifies that a driving licence is required for a job which involves limited travel. An applicant for the job has no driving licence because of the particular effects in his case of cerebral palsy. He is otherwise the best candidate for that job, he could easily and cheaply do the travelling involved other than by driving and it is likely to be a reasonable adjustment for the employer to let him do so. It would be discriminatory to insist on the specification and reject his application solely because he has no driving licence.

> An employer stipulates that employees must be 'good team players', when in fact the job in question does not involve working in a team. This requirement could unjustifiably

exclude some people who have difficulty communicating, such as some people with autism.

7.8 Blanket exclusions (i.e. exclusions which do not take account of individual circumstances) can also lead to discrimination. Indeed, such exclusions are likely to amount to direct discrimination, and so be incapable of justification (see paragraph 4.5).

An employer excludes people with epilepsy from all driving jobs. One of the jobs, in practice, only requires a standard licence and standard insurance cover. If, as a result, someone with epilepsy, who has such a licence and can obtain such insurance cover, is turned down for the job, the employer will have discriminated unlawfully in excluding her from consideration.

An employer stipulates that candidates for a job must not have a history of mental illness, believing that such candidates will have poor attendance. The employer rejects an applicant solely because he has had a mental illness, without checking the individual's actual attendance record. This will amount to discrimination—and will be unlawful.

An employer stipulates that anyone with an infectious disease cannot work in the food preparation area. It refuses to employ someone with AIDS in this area, believing him to be a health and safety risk. Whether or not the employer has a written policy to this effect, this action will amount to discrimination, as the employer has not considered the actual circumstances of the case.

7.9 In addition, stating that a certain personal, medical or health-related characteristic is essential or desirable can lead to discrimination if the characteristic is not necessary for the performance of the job. An employer would therefore need to ensure that any such requirements were genuinely essential to the job, and that it would not be reasonable to waive them in any individual case.

A television company requires all television engineers to have a high standard of hearing and vision. A woman with a hearing impairment is turned down for a job in the graphic design department because she does not pass a hearing test. If this standard of hearing is not necessary in order to do the particular job she applied for, the employer will have unlawfully discriminated against her by failing to make a reasonable adjustment to its policy of requiring job applicants to pass the test.

7.10 Likewise, although an employer is entitled to specify that applicants for a job must have certain qualifications, it will have to justify rejecting a disabled person for lacking a qualification if the reason why the disabled person lacks it is related to his disability. Justification will involve showing that the qualification is relevant and significant in terms of the particular job and the particular applicant, and that there is no reasonable adjustment which would change this. In some circumstances it might be feasible to reassign the duties to which the qualification relates, or to waive the requirement for the qualification if this particular applicant has alternative evidence of the necessary level of competence.

An employer seeking someone to work in an administrative post specifies that candidates must have the relevant NVQ Level 4 qualification. If Level 4 fairly reflects the complex and varied nature and substantial personal responsibility of the work, and these aspects of the job cannot reasonably be altered, the employer will be able to justify rejecting a disabled applicant who has only been able to reach Level 3 because of his disability and who cannot show the relevant level of competence by other means.

An employer specifies that two GCSEs are required for a certain post. This is to show that a candidate has the general level of ability required. No particular subjects are specified. An applicant whose dyslexia prevented her from passing written examinations cannot meet this requirement. The employer would be unable to justify rejecting her on this account alone if she could show in some other way that she had the expertise called for in the post.

7.11–7.31 [omitted]

Offers of employment

7.32 Terms and conditions of service should not discriminate against a disabled person. In general, an employer should not offer a job to a disabled person on terms which are less favourable than those which would be offered to other people.

A person with a history of depression is offered employment with a six month probationary period, even though other employees are only required to serve a three month probationary period. This will amount to direct discrimination and will be unlawful.

8   Discrimination against employees
8.1–8.3 [omitted]

Terms and conditions of service

8.4 As stated at paragraph 7.32, terms and conditions of service should not discriminate against a disabled person. The employer should consider whether any reasonable adjustments need to be made to the terms and conditions which would otherwise apply.

An employer's terms and conditions state the hours an employee has to be in work. It might be a reasonable adjustment to change these hours for someone whose disability means that she has difficulty using public transport during rush hours.

8.5 Where the terms and conditions of employment include an element of performance-related pay, the employer must ensure that the way such pay arrangements operate does not discriminate against a disabled employee. If, on the ground of disability, an employee is denied the opportunity to receive performance-related pay, this is likely to be direct discrimination. Even if less favourable treatment of an employee in relation to performance-related pay is not directly discriminatory, it will amount to disability-related discrimination unless the employer can show that it is justified.

8.6 If an employee has a disability which adversely affects his rate of output, the effect may be that he receives less under a performance-related pay scheme than other employees. The employer must consider whether there are reasonable adjustments which would overcome this substantial disadvantage.

A disabled man with arthritis works in telephone sales and is paid commission on the value of his sales. Because of a worsening of his impairment he is advised to switch to new computer equipment. This equipment slows his work down for a period of time while he gets used to it and consequently the value of his sales falls. It is likely to be a reasonable adjustment for his employer to continue to pay him his previous level of commission for the period in which he adjusts to the new equipment.

A disabled home-worker, who is paid a fixed rate for each item he produces, has a reduced output rate because he does not have the right equipment to do the job to the best of his ability. It is likely to be a reasonable adjustment for the employer to provide that equipment, possibly with funding or advice from the Access to Work scheme, to improve the disabled worker's output and consequently his pay.

A woman who has recently become disabled because of diabetes works for an employer that operates a performance related bonus scheme. When she has her annual appraisal, the woman is unable to demonstrate that she has met all her objectives for the year, unlike in previous years when she had in fact exceeded her objectives. The reason why the woman has not met her objectives this year is that she has been adjusting to her disability (attending hospital appointments, paying careful attention to her diet, taking regular breaks etc.). The disabled woman's employer is likely to be discriminating against her if, because she has not met her objectives for the year, it refuses to pay her a bonus.

8.7–8.20 [omitted]

Confidential information

8.21 The extent to which an employer is entitled to let other staff know about an employee's disability will depend partly on the terms of employment. An employer could be discriminating against the employee by revealing such information if the employer would not reveal similar information about another person for an equally legitimate management purpose; or if the employer revealed such information without consulting the individual, instead of adopting the usual practice of talking to an employee before revealing personal information about him. Employers also need to be aware that they have obligations under the Data Protection Act in respect of personal data.

8.22 However, as noted at paragraph 5.22, sometimes a reasonable adjustment will not work without the co-operation of other employees. In order to secure such co-operation, it may be necessary for the employer to tell one or more of a disabled person's colleagues (in confidence) about a disability which is not obvious. This may be limited to the disabled person's supervisor, or it may be appropriate to involve other colleagues, depending on the nature of the disability and the reason they need to know about it. In any event, an employer must not disclose confidential details about an employee without his consent. A disabled person's refusal to give such consent may impact upon the effectiveness of the adjustments which the employer is able to make or its ability to make adjustments at all.

In order for a person with epilepsy to work safely in a particular factory, it may be necessary to advise fellow workers about how they can assist the disabled worker to manage her condition.

An office worker with cancer says that he does not want colleagues to know of his condition. As an adjustment he needs extra time away from work to receive treatment and to rest. Neither his colleagues nor the line manager need to be told the precise

> reasons for the extra leave but the latter will need to know that the adjustment is required in order to implement it effectively.

8.23 The Act does not prevent a disabled person keeping a disability confidential from an employer. But keeping a disability confidential is likely to mean that unless the employer could reasonably be expected to know about it anyway, the employer will not be under a duty to make a reasonable adjustment. If a disabled person expects an employer to make a reasonable adjustment, he will need to provide the employer—or someone acting on its behalf—with sufficient information to carry out that adjustment.

> An employee has symptomatic HIV. He prefers not to tell his employer of the condition. However, as the condition progresses, he finds it increasingly difficult to work the required number of hours in a week. Until he tells his employer of his condition—or the employer becomes aware of it (or could reasonably be expected to be aware of it)—the employer does not have to make a reasonable adjustment by changing his working hours to overcome the difficulty. However, once the employer is informed he may then have to make a reasonable adjustment.

Termination of employment

8.24 Where a disabled person is dismissed or is selected for redundancy or for compulsory early retirement (including compulsory ill-health retirement), the employer must ensure that the disabled person is not being discriminated against. It is likely to be direct discrimination if the dismissal or selection is made on the ground of disability (see paragraph 4.5). If the dismissal or selection is not directly discriminatory, but is made for a reason related to the disability, it will amount to disability-related discrimination unless the employer can show that it is justified. The reason would also have to be one which could not be removed by any reasonable adjustment.

> It would be justifiable to terminate the employment of an employee whose disability makes it impossible for him to perform the main functions of his job any longer, if an adjustment such as a move to a vacant post elsewhere in the business is not practicable or otherwise not reasonable for the employer to have to make.

8.25 When setting criteria for redundancy selection, employers should consider whether any proposed criterion would adversely impact upon a disabled employee. If so, it may be necessary for the employer to make reasonable adjustments. For example, it is likely to be a reasonable adjustment to discount disability-related sickness absence when assessing attendance as part of a redundancy selection scheme. Some employers use 'flexibility' as a selection criterion for redundancy (for example, willingness to re-locate or to work unpopular hours, or ability to carry out a wide variety of tasks). An employer should carefully consider how to apply this criterion to a disabled employee as it might be discriminatory.

8.26 Where the dismissal of a disabled person is being considered for a reason relating to that person's conduct, the employer should consider whether any reasonable adjustments need to be made to the disciplinary or dismissal process. In addition, if the conduct in question is related to the employee's disability, that may be relevant in determining the sanction which it is appropriate to impose.

> A young man with learning disabilities asks if he can bring a friend to a disciplinary hearing, rather than a work colleague. It is likely to be a reasonable adjustment for his employer to allow this.

A woman shouts at her line manager in front of work colleagues and uses inappropriate language. The employer would usually consider dismissal as a sanction for such behaviour, but takes into account the fact that she was in great pain on the day in question because of her disability and instead issues a warning. This is likely to be a reasonable adjustment to make.

8.27–13.31 [omitted]

PART IV

European Community Materials

Treaty of Rome

Note: the following Articles are as amended and re-numbered by the Treaty of Amsterdam.

Article 12 (ex Article 6)
Within the scope of application of this Treaty, and without prejudice to any special provisions contained therein, any discrimination on grounds of nationality shall be prohibited. The Council, acting in accordance with the procedure referred to in Article 251, may adopt rules designed to prohibit such discrimination.

Article 39 (ex Article 48)
  1. Freedom of movement for workers shall be secured within the Community.
  2. Such freedom of movement shall entail the abolition of any discrimination based on nationality between workers of the Member States as regards employment, remuneration and other conditions of work and employment.
  3. It shall entail the right, subject to limitations justified on grounds of public policy, public security or public health:
  (a) to accept offers of employment actually made;
  (b) to move freely within the territory of Member States for this purpose;
  (c) to stay in a Member State for the purpose of employment in accordance with the provisions governing the employment of nationals of that State laid down by law, regulation or administrative action;
  (d) to remain in the territory of a Member State after having been employed in that State, subject to conditions which shall be embodied in implementing regulations to be drawn up by the Commission.
  4. The provisions of this Article shall not apply to employment in the public service.

Article 40 (ex Article 49)
The Council shall, acting in accordance with the procedure referred to in Article 251 and after consulting the Economic and Social Committee, issue directives or make regulations setting out the measures required to bring about freedom of movement for workers, as defined in Article 39, in particular:
  (a) by ensuring close co-operation between national employment services;
  (b) by abolishing those administrative procedures and practices and those qualifying periods in respect of eligibility for available employment, whether resulting from national legislation or from agreements previously concluded between Member States, the maintenance of which would form an obstacle to liberalisation of the movement of workers;
  (c) by abolishing all such qualifying periods and other restrictions provided for either under national legislation or under agreements previously concluded between Member States as impose on workers of other Member States conditions regarding the free choice of employment other than those imposed on workers of the State concerned;

(d) by setting up appropriate machinery to bring offers of employment into touch with applications for employment and to facilitate the achievement of a balance between supply and demand in the employment market in such a way as to avoid serious threats to the standard of living and level of employment in the various regions and industries.

Article 136   (ex Article 117)

The Community and the Member States, having in mind fundamental social rights such as those set out in the European Social Charter signed at Turin on 18 October 1961 and in the 1989 CommunityCharter of the Fundamental Social Rights of Workers, shall have as their objectives the promotion of employment, improved living and working conditions, so as to make possible their harmonisation while the improvement is being maintained, proper social protection, dialogue between management and labour, the development of human resources with a view to lasting high employmentand the combating of exclusion.

To this end the Community and the Member States shall implement measures which take account of the diverse forms of national practices, in particular in the field of contractual relations, and the need to maintain the competitiveness of the Community economy.

They believe that such a development will ensue not only from the functioning of the common market, which will favour the harmonisation of social systems, but also from the procedures provided for in this Treaty and from the approximation of provisions laid down by law, regulation or administrative action.

Article 137   (ex Article 118)

1. With a view to achieving the objectives of Article 136, the Community shall support and complement the activities of the Member States in the following fields:
   — improvement in particular of the working environment to protect workers' health and safety;
   — working conditions;
   — the information and consultation of workers;
   — the integration of persons excluded from the labour market, with prejudice to Article 150;
   — equality between men and women with regard to labout market opportunities and treatment at work.

2. To this end, the Council may adopt, by means of directives, minimum requirements for gradual implementation, having regard to the conditions and technical rules obtaining in each of the Member States. Such directives shall avoid imposing administrative, financial and legal constraints in a way which would hold back the creation and development of small and medium-sized undertakings.

The Council shall act in accordance with the procedure referred to in Article 251 after consulting the Economic and Social Committee and the Committee of the Regions.

The Council, acting in accordance with the same procedure, may adopt measures designed to encourage cooperation between Member States through initiatives aimed at improving knowledge, developing exchanges of information and best practices, promoting innovative approaches and evaluating experiences in order to combat social exclusion.

3. However, the Council shall act unanimously on a proposal from the Commission, after consulting the European Parliament, the Economic and Social Committee and the Committee of the Regions in the following areas:
   — social security and social protection of workers;
   — protection of workers where their employment contract is terminated;
   — representation and collective defence of the interests of workers and employers, including co-determination, subject to paragraph 6;
   — conditions of employment for third-country nationals legally residing in Community territory;

— financial contributions for promotion of employment and job-creation, without prejudice to the provisions relating to the Social Fund.

4. A Member State may entrust management and labour, at their joint request, with the implementation of directives adopted pursuant to paragraphs 2 and 3.

In this case, it shall ensure that, no later than the date on which a directive must be transposed in accordance with Article 249, management and labour have introduced the necessary measures by agreement, the Member State concerned being required to take any necessary measure enabling it at any time to be in a position to guarantee the results imposed by that directive.

5. The provisions adopted pursuant to this Article shall not prevent any Member State from maintaining or introducing more stringent protective measures compatible with this Treaty.

6. The provisions of this Article shall not apply to pay, the right of association, the right to strike or the right to impose lock-outs.

Article 138   (ex Article 118a)

1. The Commission shall have the task of promoting the consultation of management and labour at Community level and shall take any relevant measure to facilitate their dialogue by ensuring balanced support for the parties.

2. To this end, before submitting proposals in the social policy field, the Commission shall consult management and labour on the possible direction of Community action.

3. If, after such consultation, the Commission considers Community action advisable, it shall consult management and labour on the content of the envisaged proposal. Management and labour shall forward to the Commission an opinion or, where appropriate, a recommendation.

4. On the occasion of such consultation, management and labour may inform the Commission of their wish to initiate the process provided for in Article 139. The duration of the procedure shall not exceed nine months, unless the management and labour concerned and the Commission decide jointly to extend it.

Article 139   (ex Article 118b)

1. Should management and labour so desire, the dialogue between them at Community level may lead to contractual relations, including agreements.

2. Agreements concluded at Community level shall be implemented either in accordance with the procedures and practices specific to management and labour and the Member States or, in matters covered by Article 137, at the joint request of the signatory parties, by a Council decision on a proposal from the Commission.

The Council shall act by qualified majority, except where the agreement in question contains one or more provisions relating to one of the areas referred to in Article 137(3), in which case it shall act unanimously.

Article 140   (ex Article 118c)

With a view to achieving the objectives of Article 136 and without prejudice to the other provisions of this Treaty, the Commission shall encourage cooperation between the Member States and facilitate the coordination of their action in all social policy fields under this chapter, particularly in matters relating to

— employment;

— labour law and working conditions;

— basic and advanced vocational training;

— social security;

— prevention of occupational accidents and diseases;

— occupational hygiene;

— the right of association and collective bargaining between employers and workers.

To this end, the Commission shall act in close contact with Member States by making studies, delivering opinions and arranging consultations both on problems arising at national level and on those of concern to international organisations.

Before delivering the opinions provided for in this Article, the Commission shall consult the Economic and Social Committee.

Article 141   (ex Article 119)

1. Each Member State shall ensure that the principle of equal pay for male and female workers for equal work or work of equal value is applied.

2. For the purpose of this Article 'pay' means the ordinary basic or minimum wage or salary and any other consideration, whether in cash or in kind, which the worker receives directly or indirectly, in respect of his employment, from his employer.

Equal pay without discrimination based on sex means:

> (a) that pay for the same work at piece rates shall be calculated on the basis of the same unit of measurement;
>
> (b) that pay for work at time rates shall be the same for the same job.

3. The Council, acting in accordance with the procedure referred to in Article 251, and after consulting the Economic and Social Committee, shall adopt measures to ensure the application of the principle of equal opportunities and equal treatment of men and women in matters of employment and occupation, including the principle of equal pay for equal work or work of equal value.

4. With a view to ensuring full equality in practice between men and women in working life, the principle of equal treatment shall not prevent any Member State from maintaining or adopting measures providing for specific advantages in order to make it easier for the under-represented sex to pursue a vocational activity or to prevent or compensate for disadvantages in professional careers.

Article 142   (ex Article 119a)

Member States shall endeavour to maintain the existing equivalence between paid holiday schemes.

Treaty on European Union (The Maastricht Treaty)
(O.J. 1992, C/224)

on social policy concluded between the Member States of the European Community

Article 1

The Community and the Member States shall have as their objectives the promotion of employment, improved living and working conditions, proper social protection, dialogue between management and labour, the development of human resources with a view to lasting high employment and the combatting of exclusion. To this end the Community and the Member States shall implement measures which take account of the diverse forms of national practices, in particular in the field of contractual relations, and the need to maintain the competitiveness of the Community economy.

Article 2

1. With a view to achieving the objectives of Article 1, the Community shall support and complement the activities of the Member States in the following fields:

> — improvement in particular of the working environment to protect workers' health and safety;
>
> — working conditions;
>
> — the information and consultation of workers;
>
> — equality between men and women with regard to labour market opportunities and treatment at work;
>
> — the integration of persons excluded from the labour market, without prejudice to Article 127 of the Treaty establishing the European Community (hereinafter referred to as 'the Treaty').

2. To this end, the Council may adopt, by means of directives, minimum requirements for gradual implementation, having regard to the conditions and technical rules obtaining in each of the Member States. Such directives shall avoid imposing administrative, financial and legal constraints in a way which would hold back the creation and development of small and medium-sized undertakings.

The Council shall act in accordance with the procedure referred to in Article 189c of the Treaty after consulting the Economic and Social Committee.

3. However, the Council shall act unanimously on a proposal from the Commission, after consulting the European Parliament and the Economic and Social Committee, in the following areas:

— social security and social protection of workers;
— protection of workers where their employment contract is terminated;
— representation and collective defence of the interests of workers and employers, including co-determination, subject to paragraph 6;
— conditions of employment for third-country nationals legally residing in Community territory;
— financial contributions for promotion of employment and job-creation, without prejudice to the provisions relating to the Social Fund.

4. A Member State may entrust management and labour, at their joint request, with the implementation of directives adopted pursuant to paragraphs 2 and 3.

In this case, it shall ensure that, no later than the date on which a directive must be transposed in accordance with Article 189, management and labour have introduced the necessary measures by agreement, the Member State concerned being required to take any necessary measure enabling it at any time to be in a position to guarantee the results imposed by that directive.

5. The provisions adopted pursuant to this Article shall not prevent any Member State from maintaining or introducing more stringent protective measures compatible with the Treaty.

6. The provisions of this Article shall not apply to pay, the right of association, the right to strike or the right to impose lock-outs.

Article 3

1. The Commission shall have the task of promoting the consultation of management and labour at Community level and shall take any relevant measure to facilitate their dialogue by ensuring balanced support for the parties.

2. To this end, before submitting proposals in the social policy field, the Commission shall consult management and labour on the possible direction of Community action.

3. If, after such consultation, the Commission considers Community action advisable, it shall consult management and labour on the content of the envisaged proposal. Management and labour shall forward to the Commission an opinion or, where appropriate, a recommendation.

4. On the occasion of such consultation, management and labour may inform the Commission of their wish to initiate the process provided for in Article 4. The duration of the procedure shall not exceed nine months, unless the management and labour concerned and the Commission decide jointly to extend it.

Article 4

1. Should management and labour so desire, the dialogue between them at Community level may lead to contractual relations, including agreements.

2. Agreements concluded at Community level shall be implemented either in accordance with the procedures and practices specific to management and labour and the Member

States or, in matters covered by Article 2, at the joint request of the signatory parties, by a Council decision on a proposal from the Commission.

The Council shall act by qualified majority, except where the agreement in question contains one or more provisions relating to one of the areas referred to in Article 2(3), in which case it shall act unanimously.

Article 5

With a view to achieving the objectives of Article 1 and without prejudice to the other provisions of the Treaty, the Commission shall encourage cooperation between the Member States and facilitate the coordination of their action in all social policy fields under this Agreement.

Article 6

1. Each Member State shall ensure that the principle of equal pay for male and female workers for equal work is applied.

2. For the purpose of this Article, 'pay' means the ordinary basic or minimum wage or salary and any other consideration, whether in cash or in kind, which the worker receives directly or indirectly, in respect of his employment, from his employer.

Equal pay without discrimination based on sex means:

(a) that pay for the same work at piece rates shall be calculated on the basis of the same unit of measurement;

(b) that pay for work at time rates shall be the same for the same job.

3. This Article shall not prevent any Member State from maintaining or adopting measures providing for specific advantages in order to make it easier for women to pursue a vocational activity or to prevent or compensate for disadvantages in their professional careers.

Article 7

The Commission shall draw up a report each year on progress in achieving the objectives of Article 1, including the demographic situation in the Community. It shall forward the report to the European Parliament, the Council and the Economic and Social Committee.

The European Parliament may invite the Commission to draw up reports on particular problems concerning the social situation.

Declarations

1. Declaration on Article 2(2)

The eleven High Contracting Parties note that in the discussions on Article 2(2) of the Agreement it was agreed that the Community does not intend, in laying down minimum requirements for the protection of the safety and health of employees, to discriminate in a manner unjustified by the circumstances against employees in small and medium-sized undertakings.

2. Declaration on Article 4(2)

The eleven High Contracting Parties declare that the first of the arrangements for application of the agreements between management and labour at Community level—referred to in Article 4(2)—will consist in developing, by collective bargaining according to the rules of each Member State, the content of the agreements, and that consequently this arrangement implies no obligation on the Member States to apply the agreements directly or to work out rules for their transposition, nor any obligation to amend national legislation in force to facilitate their implementation.

Charter of Fundamental Rights of the European Union
(O.J. 2000, C/364/1, 18 December 2000)

Note: This charter is not legally binding

CHAPTER II FREEDOMS

Article 12 Freedom of assembly and of association

1. Everyone has the right to freedom of peaceful assembly and to freedom of association at all levels, in particular in political, trade union and civic matters, which implies the right of everyone to form and to join trade unions for the protection of his or her interests.

2. Political parties at Union level contribute to expressing the political will of the citizens of the Union.

Article 15 Freedom to choose an occupation and right to engage in work

1. Everyone has the right to engage in work and to pursue a freely chosen or accepted occupation.

2. Every citizen of the Union has the freedom to seek employment, to work, to exercise the right of establishment and to provide services in any Member State.

3. Nationals of third countries who are authorised to work in the territories of the Member States are entitled to working conditions equivalent to those of citizens of the Union.

CHAPTER III EQUALITY

Article 21 Non-discrimination

1. Any discrimination based on any ground such as sex, race, colour, ethnic or social origin, genetic features, language, religion or belief, political or any other opinion, membership of a national minority, property, birth, disability, age or sexual orientation shall be prohibited.

2. Within the scope of application of the Treaty establishing the European Community and of the Treaty on European Union, and without prejudice to the special provisions of those Treaties, any discrimination on grounds of nationality shall be prohibited.

Article 23 Equality between men and women

Equality between men and women must be ensured in all areas, including employment, work and pay.

The principle of equality shall not prevent the maintenance or adoption of measures providing for specific advantages in favour of the under-represented sex.

CHAPTER IV SOLIDARITY

Article 27 Workers' right to information and consultation within the undertaking

Workers or their representatives must, at the appropriate levels, be guaranteed information and consultation in good time in the cases and under the conditions provided for by Community law and national laws and practices.

Article 28 Right of collective bargaining and action

Workers and employers, or their respective organisations, have, in accordance with Community law and national laws and practices, the right to negotiate and conclude collective agreements at the appropriate levels and, in cases of conflicts of interest, to take collective action to defend their interests, including strike action.

Article 30 Protection in the event of unjustified dismissal

Every worker has the right to protection against unjustified dismissal, in accordance with Community law and national laws and practices.

Article 31   **Fair and just working conditions**

1. Every worker has the right to working conditions which respect his or her health, safety and dignity.

2. Every worker has the right to limitation of maximum working hours, to daily and weekly rest periods and to an annual period of paid leave.

Article 32   **Prohibition of child labour and protection of young people at work**

The employment of children is prohibited. The minimum age of admission to employment may not be lower than the minimum school-leaving age, without prejudice to such rules as may be more favourable to young people and except for limited derogations.

Young people admitted to work must have working conditions appropriate to their age and be protected against economic exploitation and any work likely to harm their safety, health or physical, mental, moral or social development or to interfere with their education.

Article 33   **Family and professional life**

1. The family shall enjoy legal, economic and social protection.

2. To reconcile family and professional life, everyone shall have the right to protection from dismissal for a reason connected with maternity and the right to paid maternity leave and to parental leave following the birth or adoption of a child.

Council Regulation No. 1612/68
(O.J. 1968/475)

on Freedom of Movement for Workers within the Community

PART I   EMPLOYMENT AND WORKERS' FAMILIES

Title I—Eligibility for Employment

Article 1

1. Any national of a Member State, shall irrespective of his place of residence, have the right to take up an activity as an employed person, and to pursue such activity, within the territory of another Member State in accordance with the provisions laid down by law, regulation or administrative action governing the employment of nationals of that State.

2. He shall, in particular, have the right to take up available employment in the territory of another Member State with the same priority as nationals of that State.

Article 2

Any national of a Member State and any employer pursuing an activity in the territory of a Member State may exchange their applications for and offers of employment, and may conclude and perform contracts of employment in accordance with the provisions in force laid down by law, regulation or administrative action, without any discrimination resulting therefrom.

Article 3

1. Under this Regulation, provisions laid down by law, regulation or administrative action or administrative practices of a Member State shall not apply:
  — where they limit application for and offers of employment, or the right of foreign nationals to take up and pursue employment or subject these to conditions not applicable in respect of their own nationals; or
  — where, though applicable irrespective of nationality, their exclusive or principal aim or effect is to keep nationals of other Member States away from the employment offered.

This provision shall not apply to conditions relating to linguistic knowledge required by reason of the nature of the post to be filled.

2. There shall be included in particular among the provisions or practices of a Member State referred to in the first subparagraph of paragraph 1 those which:

(a) prescribe a special recruitment procedure for foreign nationals;

(b) limit or restrict the advertising of vacancies in the press or through any other medium or subject it to conditions other than those applicable in respect of employers pursuing their activities in the territory of that Member State;

(c) subject eligibility for employment to conditions of registration with employment offices or impede recruitment of individual workers, where persons who do not reside in the territory of that State are concerned.

Article 4

1. Provisions laid down by law, regulation or administrative action of the Member States which restrict by number or percentage the employment of foreign nationals in any undertaking, branch of activity or region, or at a national level, shall not apply to nationals of the other Member States.

2. When in a Member State the granting of any benefit to undertakings is subject to a minimum percentage of national workers being employed, nationals of the other Member States shall be counted as national workers, subject to the provisions of the Council Directive of October 15, 1963 (J.O. 1963, 2661).

Article 5

A national of a Member State who seeks employment in the territory of another Member State shall receive the same assistance there as that afforded by the employment offices in that State to their own nationals seeking employment.

Article 6

1. The engagement and recruitment of a national of one Member State for a post in another Member State shall not depend on medical, vocational or other criteria which are discriminatory on grounds of nationality by comparison with those applied to nationals of the other Member State who wish to pursue the same activity.

2. Nevertheless, a national who holds an offer in his name from an employer in a Member State other than that of which he is a national may have to undergo a vocational test, if the employer expressly requests this when making his offer of employment.

Title II—Employment and Equality of Treatment

Article 7

1. A worker who is a national of a Member State may not, in the territory of another Member State, be treated differently from national workers by reason of his nationality in respect of any conditions of employment and work, in particular as regards remuneration, dismissal, and should he become unemployed, reinstatement or re-employment.

2. He shall enjoy the same social and tax advantages as national workers.

3. He shall also, by virtue of the same right and under the same conditions as national workers, have access to training in vocational schools and retraining centres.

4. Any clause of a collective or individual agreement or of any other collective regulation concerning eligibility for employment, remuneration and other conditions of work or dismissal shall be null and void in so far as it lays down or authorises discriminatory conditions in respect of workers who are nationals of the other Member States.

Article 8

1. A worker who is a national of a Member State and who is employed in the territory of another Member State shall enjoy equality of treatment as regards membership of trade unions and the exercise of rights attaching thereto, including the right to vote and to be eligible for the administrative or management posts of a trade union; he may be excluded from taking part in the management of bodies governed by public law and from holding an

office governed by public law. Furthermore, he shall have the right of eligibility for workers' representative bodies in the undertaking. The provisions of this Article shall not affect laws or regulations in certain Member States which grant more extensive rights to workers coming from the other Member States.

Article 9

1. A worker who is a national of a Member State and who is employed in the territory of another Member State shall enjoy all the rights and benefits accorded to national workers in matters of housing, including ownership of the housing he needs.

2. Such worker may, with the same right as nationals, put his name down on the housing lists in the region in which he is employed, where such lists exist; he shall enjoy the resultant benefits and priorities.

If his family has remained in the country whence he came, they shall be considered for this purpose as residing in the said region, where national workers benefit from a similar presumption.

Council Directive No. 75/117
(O.J. 1975, L45/19)

**on the approximation of the laws of the Member States relating to the application
of the principle of equal pay for men and women**

Article 1

The principle of equal pay for men and women outlined in Article 119 of the Treaty, hereinafter called 'principle of equal pay', means, for the same work or for work to which equal value is attributed, the elimination of all discrimination on grounds of sex with regard to all aspects and conditions of remuneration.

In particular, where a job classification system is used for determining pay, it must be based on the same criteria for both men and women and so drawn up as to exclude any discrimination on grounds of sex.

Article 2

Member States shall introduce into their national legal system such measures as are necessary to enable all employees who consider themselves wronged by failure to apply the principle of equal pay to pursue their claims by judicial process after possible recourse to other competent authorities.

Article 3

Member States shall abolish all discrimination between men and women arising from laws, regulations or administrative provisions which is contrary to the principle of equal pay.

Article 4

Member States shall take the necessary measures to ensure that provisions appearing in collective agreements, wage scales, wage agreements or individual contracts of employment which are contrary to the principle of equal pay shall be, or may be declared, null and void or may be amended.

Article 5

Member States shall take the necessary measures to protect employees against dismissal by the employer as a reaction to a complaint within the undertaking or to any legal proceedings aimed at enforcing compliance with the principle of equal pay.

Article 6

Member States shall, in accordance with their national circumstances and legal systems, take the measures necessary to ensure that the principle of equal pay is applied. They shall see that effective means are available to take care that this principle is observed.

Council Directive No. 76/207
(O.J. 1976, L39/40 as amended by Directive 2002/73)

on the implementation of the principle of equal treatment for men and women as regards access to employment, vocational training and promotion, and working conditions

Article 1

1. The purpose of this Directive is to put into effect in the Member States the principle of equal treatment for men and women as regards access to employment, including promotion, and to vocational training and as regards working conditions and, on the conditions referred to in paragraph 2, social security. This principle is hereinafter referred to as 'the principle of equal treatment'.

1a. Member States shall actively take into account the objective of equality between men and women when formulating and implementing laws, regulations, administrative provisions, policies and activities in the areas referred to in paragraph 1.

2. With a view to ensuring the progressive implementation of the principle of equal treatment in matters of social security, the Council, acting on a proposal from the Commission, will adopt provisions defining its substance, its scope and the arrangements for its application.

Article 2

1. For the purposes of the following provisions, the principle of equal treatment shall mean that there shall be no discrimination whatsoever on grounds of sex either directly or indirectly by reference in particular to marital or family status.

2. For the purposes of this Directive, the following definitions shall apply:
   — direct discrimination: where one person is treated less favourably on grounds of sex than another is, has been or would be treated in a comparable situation,
   — indirect discrimination: where an apparently neutral provision, criterion or practice would put persons of one sex at a particular disadvantage compared with persons of the other sex, unless that provision, criterion or practice is objectively justified by a legitimate aim, and the means of achieving that aim are appropriate and necessary,
   — harassment: where an unwanted conduct related to the sex of a person occurs with the purpose or effect of violating the dignity of a person, and of creating an intimidating, hostile, degrading, humiliating or offensive environment,
   — sexual harassment: where any form of unwanted verbal, non-verbal or physical conduct of a sexual nature occurs, with the purpose or effect of violating the dignity of a person, in particular when creating an intimidating, hostile, degrading, humiliating or offensive environment.

3. Harassment and sexual harassment within the meaning of this Directive shall be deemed to be discrimination on the grounds of sex and therefore prohibited. A person's rejection of, or submission to, such conduct may not be used as a basis for a decision affecting that person.

4. An instruction to discriminate against persons on grounds of sex shall be deemed to be discrimination within the meaning of this Directive.

5. Member States shall encourage, in accordance with national law, collective agreements or practice, employers and those responsible for access to vocational training to take measures to prevent all forms of discrimination on grounds of sex, in particular harassment and sexual harassment at the workplace.

6. Member States may provide, as regards access to employment including the training leading thereto, that a difference of treatment which is based on a characteristic related to sex shall not constitute discrimination where, by reason of the nature of the particular occupational activities concerned or of the context in which they are carried out, such a characteristic constitutes a genuine and determining occupational requirement, provided that the objective is legitimate and the requirement is proportionate.

7. This Directive shall be without prejudice to provisions concerning the protection of women, particularly as regards pregnancy and maternity.

A woman on maternity leave shall be entitled, after the end of her period of maternity leave, to return to her job or to an equivalent post on terms and conditions which are no less favourable to her and to benefit from any improvement in working conditions to which she would be entitled during her absence.

Less favourable treatment of a woman related to pregnancy or maternity leave within the meaning of Directive 92/85/EEC shall constitute discrimination within the meaning of this Directive.

This Directive shall also be without prejudice to the provisions of Council Directive 96/34/EC of 3 June 1996 on the framework agreement on parental leave concluded by UNICE, CEEP and the ETUC(14) and of Council Directive 92/85/EEC of 19 October 1992 on the introduction of measures to encourage improvements in the safety and health at work of pregnant workers and workers who have recently given birth or are breastfeeding (tenth individual Directive within the meaning of Article 16(1) of Directive 89/391/EEC)(15). It is also without prejudice to the right of Member States to recognise distinct rights to paternity and/or adoption leave. Those Member States which recognise such rights shall take the necessary measures to protect working men and women against dismissal due to exercising those rights and ensure that, at the end of such leave, they shall be entitled to return to their jobs or to equivalent posts on terms and conditions which are no less favourable to them, and to benefit from any improvement in working conditions to which they would have been entitled during their absence.

8. Member States may maintain or adopt measures within the meaning of Article 141(4) of the Treaty with a view to ensuring full equality in practice between men and women.

Article 3

1. Application of the principle of equal treatment means that there shall be no direct or indirect discrimination on the grounds of sex in the public or private sectors, including public bodies, in relation to:

(a) conditions for access to employment, to self-employment or to occupation, including selection criteria and recruitment conditions, whatever the branch of activity and at all levels of the professional hierarchy, including promotion;

(b) access to all types and to all levels of vocational guidance, vocational training, advanced vocational training and retraining, including practical work experience;

(c) employment and working conditions, including dismissals, as well as pay as provided for in Directive 75/117/EEC;

(d) membership of, and involvement in, an organisation of workers or employers, or any organisation whose members carry on a particular profession, including the benefits provided for by such organisations.

2. To that end, Member States shall take the necessary measures to ensure that:

(a) any laws, regulations and administrative provisions contrary to the principle of equal treatment are abolished;

(b) any provisions contrary to the principle of equal treatment which are included in contracts or collective agreements, internal rules of undertakings or rules governing the independent occupations and professions and workers' and employers' organisations shall be, or may be declared, null and void or are amended.

Articles 4–5   [revoked]

Article 6

1. Member States shall ensure that judicial and/or administrative procedures, including where they deem it appropriate conciliation procedures, for the enforcement of obligations under this Directive are available to all persons who consider themselves wronged by failure

to apply the principle of equal treatment to them, even after the relationship in which the discrimination is alleged to have occurred has ended.

2. Member States shall introduce into their national legal systems such measures as are necessary to ensure real and effective compensation or reparation as the Member States so determine for the loss and damage sustained by a person injured as a result of discrimination contrary to Article 3, in a way which is dissuasive and proportionate to the damage suffered; such compensation or reparation may not be restricted by the fixing of a prior upper limit, except in cases where the employer can prove that the only damage suffered by an applicant as a result of discrimination within the meaning of this Directive is the refusal to take his/her job application into consideration.

3. Member States shall ensure that associations, organisations or other legal entities which have, in accordance with the criteria laid down by their national law, a legitimate interest in ensuring that the provisions of this Directive are complied with, may engage, either on behalf or in support of the complainants, with his or her approval, in any judicial and/or administrative procedure provided for the enforcement of obligations under this Directive.

4. Paragraphs 1 and 3 are without prejudice to national rules relating to time limits for bringing actions as regards the principle of equal treatment.';

Article 7
Member States shall introduce into their national legal systems such measures as are necessary to protect employees, including those who are employees' representatives provided for by national laws and/or practices, against dismissal or other adverse treatment by the employer as a reaction to a complaint within the undertaking or to any legal proceedings aimed at enforcing compliance with the principle of equal treatment.

Articles 8–11   [omitted]

Council Directive No. 97/81
(O.J. 1998, L14/9)

concerning the framework agreement on part-time work concluded by
UNICE, CEEP and the ETUC

FRAMEWORK AGREEMENT ON PART-TIME WORK

Clause 1:   Purpose
The purpose of this Framework Agreement is:
> (a) to provide for the removal of discrimination against part-time workers and to improve the quality of part-time work;
> (b) to facilitate the development of part-time work on a voluntary basis and to contribute to the flexible organisation of working time in a manner which takes into account the needs of employers and workers.

Clause 2:   Scope
1. This Agreement applies to part-time workers who have an employment contract or employment relationship as defined by the law, collective agreement or practice in force in each Member State.

2. Member States, after consultation with the social partners in accordance with national law, collective agreements or practice, and/or the social partners at the appropriate level in conformity with national industrial relations practice may, for objective reasons, exclude wholly or partly from the terms of this Agreement part-time workers who work on a casual

basis. Such exclusions should be reviewed periodically to establish if the objective reasons for making them remain valid.

Clause 3: Definitions
For the purpose of this agreement:
1. The term 'part-time worker' refers to an employee whose normal hours of work, calculated on a weekly basis or on average over a period of employment of up to one year, are less than the normal hours of work of a comparable full-time worker.
2. The term 'comparable full-time worker' means a full-time worker in the same establishment having the same type of employment contract or relationship, who is engaged in the same or a similar work/occupation, due regard being given to other considerations which may include seniority and qualification/skills.

Where there is no comparable full-time worker in the same establishment, the comparison shall be made by reference to the applicable collective agreement or, where there is no applicable collective agreement, in accordance with national law, collective agreements or practice.

Clause 4: Principle of non-discrimination
1. In respect of employment conditions, part-time workers shall not be treated in a less favourable manner than comparable full-time workers solely because they work part time unless different treatment is justified on objective grounds.
2. Where appropriate, the principle of *pro rata temporis* shall apply.
3. The arrangements for the application of this clause shall be defined by the Member States and/or social partners, having regard to European legislation, national law, collective agreements and practice.
4. Where justified by objective reasons, Member States after consultation of the social partners in accordance with national law, collective agreements or practice and/or social partners may, where appropriate, make access to particular conditions of employment subject to a period of service, time worked or earnings qualification. Qualifications relating to access by part-time workers to particular conditions of employment should be reviewed periodically having regard to the principle of non-discrimination as expressed in Clause 4.1.

Clause 5: Opportunities for part-time work
1. In the context of Clause 1 of this Agreement and of the principle of non-discrimination between part-time and full-time workers:
   (a) Member States, following consultations with the social partners in accordance with national law or practice, should identify and review obstacles of a legal or administrative nature which may limit the opportunities for part-time work and, where appropriate, eliminate them;
   (b) the social partners, acting within their sphere of competence and through the procedures set out in collective agreements, should identify and review obstacles which may limit opportunities for part-time work and, where appropriate, eliminate them.
2. A worker's refusal to transfer from full-time to part-time work or vice-versa should not in itself constitute a valid reason for termination of employment, without prejudice to termination in accordance with national law, collective agreements and practice, for other reasons such as may arise from the operational requirements of the establishment concerned.
3. As far as possible, employers should give consideration to:
   (a) requests by workers to transfer from full-time to part-time work that becomes available in the establishment;
   (b) requests by workers to transfer from part-time to full-time work or to increase their working time should the opportunity arise;
   (c) the provision of timely information on the availability of part-time and full-time positions in the establishment in order to facilitate transfers from full-time to part-time or vice versa;

(d) measures to facilitate access to part-time work at all levels of the enterprise, including skilled and managerial positions, and where appropriate, to facilitate access by part-time workers to vocational training to enhance career opportunities and occupational mobility;

(e) the provision of appropriate information to existing bodies representing workers about part-time working in the enterprise.

Council Directive No. 98/59
(O.J. 1998, L225/16)

on the approximation of the laws of the Member States relating to collective redundancies

SECTION 1   DEFINITIONS AND SCOPE

Article 1

1. For the purposes of this Directive:
   (a) 'collective redundancies' means dismissals effected by an employer for one or more reasons not related to the individual workers concerned where, according to the choice of the member states, the number of redundancies is:
      (i) either, over a period of 30 days:
         — at least 10 in establishments normally employing more than 20 and less than 100 workers,
         — at least 10% of the number of workers in establishments normally employing at least 100 but less than 300 workers,
         — at least 30 in establishments normally employing 300 workers or more,
      (ii) or, over a period of 90 days, at least 20, whatever the number of workers normally employed in the establishments in question;
   (b) 'workers' representatives' means the workers' representatives provided for by the laws or practices of the member states.

For the purpose of calculating the number of redundancies provided for in the first subparagraph of point (a), terminations of an employment contract which occur on the employer's initiative for one or more reasons not related to the individual workers concerned shall be assimilated to redundancies, provided that there are at least five redundancies.

2. This Directive shall not apply to:
   (a) collective redundancies affected under contracts of employment concluded for limited periods of time or for specific tasks except where such redundancies take place prior to the date of expiry or the completion of such contracts;
   (b) workers employed by public administrative bodies or by establishments governed by public law (or, in member states where this concept is unknown, by equivalent bodies);
   (c) the crews of sea-going vessels.

SECTION II   INFORMATION AND CONSULTATION

Article 2

1. Where an employer is contemplating collective redundancies, he shall begin consultations with the workers' representatives in good time with a view to reaching an agreement.

2. These consultations shall, at least, cover ways and means of avoiding collective redundancies or reducing the number of workers affected, and of mitigating the consequences by recourse to accompanying social measures aimed, inter alia, at aid for redeploying or retraining workers made redundant.

Member States may provide that the workers' representatives may call upon the services of experts in accordance with national legislation and/or practice.

3. To enable workers' representatives to make constructive proposals, the employers shall in good time during the course of the consultations:

(a) supply them with all relevant information and
(b) in any event notify them in writing of:
    (i)   the reasons for the projected redundancies;
    (ii) the number of categories of workers to be made redundant;
    (iii) the number and categories of workers normally employed;
    (iv) the period over which the projected redundancies are to be effected;
    (v) the criteria proposed for the selection of the workers to be made redundant in so far as national legislation and/or practice confers the power therefor upon the employer;
    (vi) the method for calculating any redundancy payments other than those arising out of national legislation and/or practice.

The employer shall forward to the competent public authority a copy of, at least, the elements of the written communication which are provided for in the first subparagraph, point (b), subpoints (i) to (v).

4. The obligations laid down in paragraphs 1, 2 and 3 shall apply irrespective of whether the decision regarding collective redundancies is being taken by the employer or by an undertaking controlling the employer. In considering alleged breaches of the information, consultation and notification requirements laid down by this Directive, account shall not be taken of any defence on the part of the employer on the ground that the necessary information has not been provided to the employer by the undertaking which took the decision leading to collective redundancies.

SECTION III   PROCEDURE FOR COLLECTIVE REDUNDANCIES

Article 3

1. Employers shall notify the competent public authority in writing of any projected collective redundancies.

However, Member States may provide that in the case of planned collective redundancies arising from termination of the establishment's activities as the result of a judicial decision, the employer shall be obliged to notify the competent public authority in writing only if the latter so requests.

This notification shall contain all relevant information concerning the projected collective redundancies and the consultations with workers' representatives provided for in Article 2, and particularly the reasons for the redundancies, the number of workers to be made redundant, the number of workers normally employed and the period over which the redundancies are to be effected.

2. Employers shall forward to the workers' representatives a copy of the notification provided for in paragraph 1.

The workers' representatives may send any comments they may have to the competent public authority.

Article 4

1. Projected collective redundancies notified to the competent public authority shall take effect not earlier than 30 days after the notification referred to in Article 3(1) without prejudice to any provisions governing individual rights with regard to notice of dismissal.

Member States may grant the competent public authority the power to reduce the period provided for in the preceding subparagraph.

2. The period provided for in paragraph 1 shall be used by the competent public authority to seek solutions in the problems raised by the projected collective redundancies.

3. Where the initial period provided for in paragraph 1 is shorter than 60 days, member states may grant the competent public authority the power to extend the initial period to 60 days following notification where the problems raised by the projected collective redundancies are not likely to be solved within the initial period.

Member States may grant the competent public authority wider powers of extension. The employer must be informed of the extension and the grounds for it before expiry of the initial period provided for in paragraph 1.

4. Member States need not apply this Article to collective redundancies arising from termination of the establishment's activities where this is the result of a judicial decision.

SECTION IV   FINAL PROVISIONS

Article 5
This Directive shall not affect the right of member states to apply or to introduce laws, regulations or administrative provisions which are more favourable to workers or to promote or to allow the application of collective agreements more favourable to workers.

Article 6
Member States shall ensure that judicial and/or administrative procedures for the enforcement of obligations under this directive are available to the workers' representatives and/or workers.

Council Directive No. 99/70
(O.J. 1999, L175/43)

concerning the framework agreement on fixed-term work

[Articles 1–4 omitted]

ANNEX

(Clause 1) Purpose
The purpose of this framework agreement is to:
> (a) improve the quality of fixed-term work by ensuring the application of the principle of non-discrimination;
> (b) establish a framework to prevent abuse arising from the use of successive fixed-term employment contracts or relationships.

(Clause 2) Scope
1. This agreement applies to fixed-term workers who have an employment contract or employment relationship as defined in law, collective agreements or practice in each Member State.

2. Member States after consultation with the social partners and/or the social partners may provide that this agreement does not apply to:
> (a) initial vocational training relationships and apprenticeship schemes;
> (b) employment contracts and relationships which have been concluded within the framework of a specific public or publicly-supported training, integration and vocational retraining programme.

(Clause 3) Definitions
1. For the purpose of this agreement the term 'fixed-term worker' means a person having an employment contract or relationship entered into directly between an employer and a worker where the end of the employment contract or relationship is determined by objective conditions such as reaching a specific date, completing a specific task, or the occurrence of a specific event.

2. For the purpose of this agreement, the term 'comparable permanent worker' means a worker with an employment contract or relationship of indefinite duration, in the same establishment, engaged in the same or similar work/occupation, due regard being given to qualifications/skills.

Where there is no comparable permanent worker in the same establishment, the comparison shall be made by reference to the applicable collective agreement, or where there is no applicable collective agreement, in accordance with national law, collective agreements or practice.

(Clause 4) Principles of non-discrimination

1. In respect of employment conditions, fixed-term workers shall not be treated in a less favourable manner than comparable permanent workers solely because they have a fixed-term contract or relation unless different treatment is justified on objective grounds.

2. Where appropriate, the principle of pro rata temporis shall apply.

3. The arrangements for the application of this clause shall be defined by the Member States after consultation with the social partners and/or the social partners, having regard to Community law and national law, collective agreements and practice.

4. Period-of-service qualifications relating to particular conditions of employment shall be the same for fixed-term workers as for permanent workers except where different length-of-service qualifications are justified on objective grounds.

(Clause 5) Measures to prevent abuse

1. To prevent abuse arising from the use of successive fixed-term employment contracts or relationships, Member States, after consultation with social partners in accordance with national law, collective agreements or practice, and/or the social partners, shall, where there are no equivalent legal measures to prevent abuse, introduce in a manner which takes account of the needs of specific sectors and/or categories of workers, one or more of the following measures:

    (a) objective reasons justifying the renewal of such contracts or relationships;
    (b) the maximum total duration of successive fixed-term employment contracts or relationships;
    (c) the number of renewals of such contracts or relationships.

2. Member States after consultation with the social partners and/or the social partners shall, where appropriate, determine under what conditions fixed-term employment contracts or relationships:

    (a) shall be regarded as 'successive'
    (b) shall be deemed to be contracts or relationships of indefinite duration.

(Clause 6) Information and employment opportunities

1. Employers shall inform fixed-term workers about vacancies which become available in the undertaking or establishment to ensure that they have the same opportunity to secure permanent positions as other workers. Such information may be provided by way of a general announcement at a suitable place in the undertaking or establishment.

2. As far as possible, employers should facilitate access by fixed-term workers to appropriate training opportunities to enhance their skills, career development and occupational mobility.

(Clause 7) Information and consultation

1. Fixed-term workers shall be taken into consideration in calculating the threshold above which workers' representative bodies provided for in national and Community law may be constituted in the undertaking as required by national provisions.

2. The arrangements for the application of clause 7.1 shall be defined by Member States after consultation with the social partners and/or the social partners in accordance with national law, collective agreements or practice and having regard to clause 4.1.

3. As far as possible, employers should give consideration to the provision of appropriate information to existing workers' representative bodies about fixed-term work in the undertaking.

Council Directive No. 2000/43
(O.J. 2000, L180/22)

implementing the principle of equal treatment between persons irrespective of racial or ethnic origin

CHAPTER I   GENERAL PROVISIONS

Article 1   **Purpose**
The purpose of this Directive is to lay down a framework for combating discrimination on the grounds of racial or ethnic origin, with a view to putting into effect in the Member States the principle of equal treatment.

Article 2   **Concept of discrimination**
1. For the purposes of this Directive, the principle of equal treatment shall mean that there shall be no direct or indirect discrimination based on racial or ethnic origin.
2. For the purposes of paragraph 1:
  (a) direct discrimination shall be taken to occur where one person is treated less favourably than another is, has been or would be treated in a comparable situation on grounds of racial or ethnic origin;
  (b) indirect discrimination shall be taken to occur where an apparently neutral provision, criterion or practice would put persons of a racial or ethnic origin at a particular disadvantage compared with other persons, unless that provision, criterion or practice is objectively justified by a legitimate aim and the means of achieving that aim are appropriate and necessary.
3. Harassment shall be deemed to be discrimination within the meaning of paragraph 1, when an unwanted conduct related to racial or ethnic origin takes place with the purpose or effect of violating the dignity of a person and of creating an intimidating, hostile, degrading, humiliating or offensive environment. In this context, the concept of harassment may be defined in accordance with the national laws and practice of the Member States.
4. An instruction to discriminate against persons on grounds of racial or ethnic origin shall be deemed to be discrimination within the meaning of paragraph 1.

Article 3   **Scope**
1. Within the limits of the powers conferred upon the Community, this Directive shall apply to all persons, as regards both the public and private sectors, including public bodies, in relation to:
  (a) conditions for access to employment, to self-employment and to occupation, including selection criteria and recruitment conditions, whatever the branch of activity and at all levels of the professional hierarchy, including promotion;
  (b) access to all types and to all levels of vocational guidance, vocational training, advanced vocational training and retraining, including practical work experience;
  (c) employment and working conditions, including dismissals and pay;
  (d) membership of and involvement in an organisation of workers or employers, or any organisation whose members carry on a particular profession, including the benefits provided for by such organisations;

(e) social protection, including social security and healthcare;

(f) social advantages;

(g) education;

(h) access to and supply of goods and services which are available to the public, including housing.

2. This Directive does not cover difference of treatment based on nationality and is without prejudice to provisions and conditions relating to the entry into and residence of third-country nationals and stateless persons on the territory of Member States, and to any treatment which arises from the legal status of the third-country nationals and stateless persons concerned.

Article 4 Genuine and determining occupational requirements

Notwithstanding Article 2(1) and (2), Member States may provide that a difference of treatment which is based on a characteristic related to racial or ethnic origin shall not constitute discrimination where, by reason of the nature of the particular occupational activities concerned or of the context in which they are carried out, such a characteristic constitutes a genuine and determining occupational requirement, provided that the objective is legitimate and the requirement is proportionate.

Article 5 Positive action

With a view to ensuring full equality in practice, the principle of equal treatment shall not prevent any Member State from maintaining or adopting specific measures to prevent or compensate for disadvantages linked to racial or ethnic origin.

Article 6 [omitted]

CHAPTER II   REMEDIES AND ENFORCEMENT

Article 7 Defence of rights

1. Member States shall ensure that judicial and/or administrative procedures, including where they deem it appropriate conciliation procedures, for the enforcement of obligations under this Directive are available to all persons who consider themselves wronged by failure to apply the principle of equal treatment to them, even after the relationship in which the discrimination is alleged to have occurred has ended.

2. Member States shall ensure that associations, organisations or other legal entities, which have, in accordance with the criteria laid down by their national law, a legitimate interest in ensuring that the provisions of this Directive are complied with, may engage, either on behalf or in support of the complainant, with his or her approval, in any judicial and/or administrative procedure provided for the enforcement of obligations under this Directive.

3. Paragraphs 1 and 2 are without prejudice to national rules relating to time limits for bringing actions as regards the principle of equality of treatment.

Article 8 Burden of proof

1. Member States shall take such measures as are necessary, in accordance with their national judicial systems, to ensure that, when persons who consider themselves wronged because the principle of equal treatment has not been applied to them establish, before a court or other competent authority, facts from which it may be presumed that there has been direct or indirect discrimination, it shall be for the respondent to prove that there has been no breach of the principle of equal treatment.

2. Paragraph 1 shall not prevent Member States from introducing rules of evidence which are more favourable to plaintiffs.

3. Paragraph 1 shall not apply to criminal procedures.

4. Paragraphs 1, 2 and 3 shall also apply to any proceedings brought in accordance with Article 7(2).

5. Member States need not apply paragraph 1 to proceedings in which it is for the court or competent body to investigate the facts of the case.

Article 9 Victimisation

Member States shall introduce into their national legal systems such measures as are necessary to protect individuals from any adverse treatment or adverse consequence as a reaction to a complaint or to proceedings aimed at enforcing compliance with the principle of equal treatment.

Articles 10–12 [omitted]

CHAPTER III   BODIES FOR THE PROMOTION OF EQUAL TREATMENT

Article 13

1. Member States shall designate a body or bodies for the promotion of equal treatment of all persons without discrimination on the grounds of racial or ethnic origin. These bodies may form part of agencies charged at national level with the defence of human rights or the safeguard of individuals' rights.

2. Member States shall ensure that the competences of these bodies include:
   — without prejudice to the right of victims and of associations, organisations or other legal entities referred to in Article 7(2), providing independent assistance to victims of discrimination in pursuing their complaints about discrimination,
   — conducting independent surveys concerning discrimination,
   — publishing independent reports and making recommendations on any issue relating to such discrimination.

Articles 14–19 [omitted]

Council Directive 2000/78
(O.J. 2000, L303/16)

**establishing a general framework for equal treatment in
employment and occupation**

CHAPTER I   GENERAL PROVISIONS

Article 1 Purpose

The purpose of this Directive is to lay down a general framework for combating discrimination on the grounds of religion or belief, disability, age or sexual orientation as regards employment and occupation, with a view to putting into effect in the Member States the principle of equal treatment.

Article 2 Concept of discrimination

1. For the purposes of this Directive, the 'principle of equal treatment' shall mean that there shall be no direct or indirect discrimination whatsoever on any of the grounds referred to in Article 1.

2. For the purposes of paragraph 1:
   (a) direct discrimination shall be taken to occur where one person is treated less favourably than another is, has been or would be treated in a comparable situation, on any of the grounds referred to in Article 1;
   (b) indirect discrimination shall be taken to occur where an apparently neutral provision, criterion or practice would put persons having a particular religion or belief, a particular disability, a particular age, or a particular sexual orientation at a particular disadvantage compared with other persons unless:
      (i) that provision, criterion or practice is objectively justified by a legitimate aim and the means of achieving that aim are appropriate and necessary, or

(ii) as regards persons with a particular disability, the employer or any person or organisation to whom this Directive applies, is obliged, under national legislation, to take appropriate measures in line with the principles contained in Article 5 in order to eliminate disadvantages entailed by such provision, criterion or practice.

3. Harassment shall be deemed to be a form of discrimination within the meaning of paragraph 1, when unwanted conduct related to any of the grounds referred to in Article 1 takes place with the purpose or effect of violating the dignity of a person and of creating an intimidating, hostile, degrading, humiliating or offensive environment. In this context, the concept of harassment may be defined in accordance with the national laws and practice of the Member States.

4. An instruction to discriminate against persons on any of the grounds referred to in Article 1 shall be deemed to be discrimination within the meaning of paragraph 1.

5. This Directive shall be without prejudice to measures laid down by national law which, in a democratic society, are necessary for public security, for the maintenance of public order and the prevention of criminal offences, for the protection of health and for the protection of the rights and freedoms of others.

Article 3 Scope

1. Within the limits of the areas of competence conferred on the Community, this Directive shall apply to all persons, as regards both the public and private sectors, including public bodies, in relation to:

(a) conditions for access to employment, to self-employment or to occupation, including selection criteria and recruitment conditions, whatever the branch of activity and at all levels of the professional hierarchy, including promotion;

(b) access to all types and to all levels of vocational guidance, vocational training, advanced vocational training and retraining, including practical work experience;

(c) employment and working conditions, including dismissals and pay;

(d) membership of, and involvement in, an organisation of workers or employers, or any organisation whose members carry on a particular profession, including the benefits provided for by such organisations.

2. This Directive does not cover differences of treatment based on nationality and is without prejudice to provisions and conditions relating to the entry into and residence of third-country nationals and stateless persons in the territory of Member States, and to any treatment which arises from the legal status of the third-country nationals and stateless persons concerned.

3. This Directive does not apply to payments of any kind made by state schemes or similar, including state social security or social protection schemes.

4. Member States may provide that this Directive, in so far as it relates to discrimination on the grounds of disability and age, shall not apply to the armed forces.

Article 4 Occupational requirements

1. Notwithstanding Article 2(1) and (2), Member States may provide that a difference of treatment which is based on a characteristic related to any of the grounds referred to in Article 1 shall not constitute discrimination where, by reason of the nature of the particular occupational activities concerned or of the context in which they are carried out, such a characteristic constitutes a genuine and determining occupational requirement, provided that the objective is legitimate and the requirement is proportionate.

2. Member States may maintain national legislation in force at the date of adoption of this Directive or provide for future legislation incorporating national practices existing at the date of adoption of this Directive pursuant to which, in the case of occupational activities within churches and other public or private organisations the ethos of which is based on religion or belief, a difference of treatment based on a person's religion or belief shall not constitute discrimination where, by reason of the nature of these activities or of the context

in which they are carried out, a person's religion or belief constitute a genuine, legitimate and justified occupational requirement, having regard to the organisation's ethos. This difference of treatment shall be implemented taking account of Member States' constitutional provisions and principles, as well as the general principles of Community law, and should not justify discrimination on another ground.

Provided that its provisions are otherwise complied with, this Directive shall thus not prejudice the right of churches and other public or private organisations, the ethos of which is based on religion or belief, acting in conformity with national constitutions and laws, to require individuals working for them to act in good faith and with loyalty to the organisation's ethos.

Article 5   Reasonable accommodation for disabled persons
In order to guarantee compliance with the principle of equal treatment in relation to persons with disabilities, reasonable accommodation shall be provided. This means that employers shall take appropriate measures, where needed in a particular case, to enable a person with a disability to have access to, participate in, or advance in employment, or to undergo training, unless such measures would impose a disproportionate burden on the employer. This burden shall not be disproportionate when it is sufficiently remedied by measures existing within the framework of the disability policy of the Member State concerned.

Article 6   Justification of differences of treatment on grounds of age
1. Notwithstanding Article 2(2), Member States may provide that differences of treatment on grounds of age shall not constitute discrimination, if, within the context of national law, they are objectively and reasonably justified by a legitimate aim, including legitimate employment policy, labour market and vocational training objectives, and if the means of achieving that aim are appropriate and necessary.
Such differences of treatment may include, among others:
   (a) the setting of special conditions on access to employment and vocational training, employment and occupation, including dismissal and remuneration conditions, for young people, older workers and persons with caring responsibilities in order to promote their vocational integration or ensure their protection;
   (b) the fixing of minimum conditions of age, professional experience or seniority in service for access to employment or to certain advantages linked to employment;
   (c) the fixing of a maximum age for recruitment which is based on the training requirements of the post in question or the need for a reasonable period of employment before retirement.
2. Notwithstanding Article 2(2), Member States may provide that the fixing for occupational social security schemes of ages for admission or entitlement to retirement or invalidity benefits, including the fixing under those schemes of different ages for employees or groups or categories of employees, and the use, in the context of such schemes, of age criteria in actuarial calculations, does not constitute discrimination on the grounds of age, provided this does not result in discrimination on the grounds of sex.

Article 7   Positive action
1. With a view to ensuring full equality in practice, the principle of equal treatment shall not prevent any Member State from maintaining or adopting specific measures to prevent or compensate for disadvantages linked to any of the grounds referred to in Article 1.
2. With regard to disabled persons, the principle of equal treatment shall be without prejudice to the right of Member States to maintain or adopt provisions on the protection of health and safety at work or to measures aimed at creating or maintaining provisions or facilities for safeguarding or promoting their integration into the working environment.

Article 8   [omitted]

CHAPTER II   REMEDIES AND ENFORCEMENT

Article 9   **Defence of rights**

1. Member States shall ensure that judicial and/or administrative procedures, including where they deem it appropriate conciliation procedures, for the enforcement of obligations under this Directive are available to all persons who consider themselves wronged by failure to apply the principle of equal treatment to them, even after the relationship in which the discrimination is alleged to have occurred has ended.

2. Member States shall ensure that associations, organisations or other legal entities which have, in accordance with the criteria laid down by their national law, a legitimate interest in ensuring that the provisions of this Directive are complied with, may engage, either on behalf or in support of the complainant, with his or her approval, in any judicial and/or administrative procedure provided for the enforcement of obligations under this Directive.

3. Paragraphs 1 and 2 are without prejudice to national rules relating to time limits for bringing actions as regards the principle of equality of treatment.

Article 10   **Burden of proof**

1. Member States shall take such measures as are necessary, in accordance with their national judicial systems, to ensure that, when persons who consider themselves wronged because the principle of equal treatment has not been applied to them establish, before a court or other competent authority, facts from which it may be presumed that there has been direct or indirect discrimination, it shall be for the respondent to prove that there has been no breach of the principle of equal treatment.

2. Paragraph 1 shall not prevent Member States from introducing rules of evidence which are more favourable to plaintiffs.

3. Paragraph 1 shall not apply to criminal procedures.

4. Paragraphs 1, 2 and 3 shall also apply to any legal proceedings commenced in accordance with Article 9(2).

5. Member States need not apply paragraph 1 to proceedings in which it is for the court or competent body to investigate the facts of the case.

Article 11   **Victimisation**

Member States shall introduce into their national legal systems such measures as are necessary to protect employees against dismissal or other adverse treatment by the employer as a reaction to a complaint within the undertaking or to any legal proceedings aimed at enforcing compliance with the principle of equal treatment.

Articles 12–20   [omitted]

Council Directive No. 2001/23

(O.J. 2001, L82/16)

on the approximation of the laws of the Member States relating to the safeguarding of employees' rights in the event of transfers of undertakings, businesses or parts of undertakings or businesses

Article 1

1. (a) This Directive shall apply to the transfer of an undertaking, business or part of an undertaking or business to another employer as a result of a legal transfer or merger.

   (b) Subject to subparagraph (a) and the following provisions of this Article, there is a transfer within the meaning of this Directive where there is a transfer of an economic entity which retains its identity, meaning an organised grouping of resources which has the objective of pursuing an economic activity, whether or not that activity is central or ancillary.

(c) This Directive shall apply to public and private undertakings engaged in economic activities whether or not they are operating for gain. An administrative reorganisation of public administrative authorities, or the transfer of administrative functions between public administrative authorities is not a transfer within the meaning of this Directive.

2. This Directive shall apply where and in so far as the undertaking, business or part of the undertaking or business to be transferred is situated within the territorial scope of the Treaty.

3. This Directive shall not apply to sea-going vessels.

Article 2

1. For the purposes of this Directive:

(a) 'transferor' means any natural or legal person who, by reason of a transfer within the meaning of Article 1(1), ceases to be the employer in respect of the undertaking, business or part of the undertaking or business;

(b) 'transferee' means any natural or legal person who, by reason of a transfer within the meaning of Article 1(1), becomes the employer in respect of the undertaking, business or part of the undertaking or business;

(c) 'representatives of employees' and related expressions shall mean the representatives of the employees provided for by the laws or practices of the Member States;

(d) 'employee' shall mean any person who, in the Member State concerned, is protected as an employee under national employment law.

2. This Directive shall be without prejudice to national law as regards the definition of contract of employment or employment relationship.

However, Member States shall not exclude from the scope of this Directive contracts of employment or employment relationships solely because:

(a) of the number of working hours performed or to be performed,

(b) they are employment relationships governed by a fixed-duration contract of employment within the meaning of Article 1(1) of Council Directive 91/383/EEC of 25 June 1991 supplementing the measures to encourage improvements in the safety and health at work of workers with a fixed-duration employment relationship or a temporary employment relationship, or

(c) they are temporary employment relationships within the meaning of Article 1(2) of Directive 91/383/EEC, and the undertaking, business or part of the undertaking or business transferred is, or is part of, the temporary employment business which is the employer.

Article 3

1. The transferor's rights and obligations arising from a contract of employment or from an employment relationship existing on the date of a transfer shall, by reason of such transfer, be transferred to the transferee.

Member States may provide that, after the date of transfer the transferor and the transferee shall be jointly and severally liable in respect of obligations which arose before the date of transfer from a contract of employment or an employment relationship existing on the date of the transfer.

2. Member States may adopt appropriate measures to ensure that the transferor notifies the transferee of all the rights and obligations which will be transferred to the transferee under this Article, so far as those rights and obligations are or ought to have been known to the transferor at the time of the transfer. A failure by the transferor to notify the transferee of

any such right or obligation shall not affect the transfer of that right or obligation and the rights of any employees against the transferee and/or transferor in respect of that right or obligation.

3. Following the transfer, the transferee shall continue to observe the terms and conditions agreed in any collective agreement on the same terms applicable to the transferor under that agreement, until the date of termination or expiry of the collective agreement or the entry into force or application of another collective agreement.

Member States may limit the period for observing such terms and conditions, with the proviso that it shall not be less than one year.

4.   (a) Unless Member States provide otherwise, paragraphs 1 and 3 shall not apply in relation to employees' rights to old-age, invalidity or survivors' benefits under supplementary company or inter-company pension schemes outside the statutory social security schemes in Member States.

    (b) Even where they do not provide in accordance with subparagraph (a) that paragraphs 1 and 3 apply in relation to such rights, Member States shall adopt the measures necessary to protect the interests of employees and of persons no longer employed in the transferor's business at the time of the transfer in respect of rights conferring on them immediate or prospective entitlement to old age benefits, including survivors' benefits, under supplementary schemes referred to in sub-paragraph (a).

Article 4

1. The transfer of an undertaking, business or part of the undertaking or business shall not in itself constitute grounds for dismissal by the transferor or the transferee. This provision shall not stand in the way of dismissals that may take place for economic, technical or organisational reasons entailing changes in the workforce.

Member States may provide that the first subparagraph shall not apply to certain specific categories of employees who are not covered by the laws or practice of the Member States in respect of protection against dismissal.

2. If the contract of employment or the employment relationship is terminated because the transfer involves a substantial change in working conditions to the detriment of the employee, the employer shall be regarded as having been responsible for termination of the contract of employment or of the employment relationship.

Article 5

1. Unless Member States provide otherwise, Articles 3 and 4 shall not apply to any transfer of an undertaking, business or part of an undertaking or business where the transferor is the subject of bankruptcy proceedings or any analogous insolvency proceedings which have been instituted with a view to the liquidation of the assets of the transferor and are under the supervision of a competent public authority (which may be an insolvency practitioner authorised by a competent public authority).

2. Where Articles 3 and 4 apply to a transfer during insolvency proceedings which have been opened in relation to a transferor (whether or not those proceedings have been instituted with a view to the liquidation of the assets of the transferor) and provided that such proceedings are under the supervision of a competent public authority (which may be an insolvency practitioner determined by national law) a Member State may provide that:

    (a) notwithstanding Article 3(1), the transferor's debts arising from any contracts of employment or employment relationships and payable before the transfer or before the opening of the insolvency proceedings shall not be transferred to the transferee, provided that such proceedings give rise, under the law of the Member State, to protection at least equivalent to that provided for in situations covered by Council Directive 80/987/EEC of 20 October 1980 on the approximation of the laws of the Member States relating to the protection of employees in the event of the insolvency of their employer;

and, or alternatively, that

(b) the transferee, transferor, or person or persons exercising the transferor's functions, on the one hand, and the representatives of the employees on the other hand may agree alterations, insofar as current law or practice permits, to the employees' terms and conditions of employment designed to safeguard employment opportunities by ensuring the survival of the undertaking, business or part of the undertaking or business.

3. A Member state may apply paragraph 2(b) to any transfers where the transferor is in a situation of serious economic crisis, as defined by national law, provided that the situation is declared by a competent public authority and open to judicial supervision, on condition that such provisions already exist in national law by 17 July 1998.

The Commission shall present a report on the effects of this provision before 17 July 2003 and shall submit any appropriate proposals to the Council.

4. Member States shall take appropriate measures with a view to preventing misuse of insolvency proceedings in such a way as to deprive employees of the rights provided for in this Directive.

Article 6

1. If the undertaking, business or part of an undertaking or business preserves its autonomy, the status and function of the representatives or of the representation of the employees affected by the transfer shall be preserved on the same terms and subject to the same conditions as existed before the date of the transfer by virtue of law, regulation, administrative provision or agreement, provided that the conditions necessary for the constitution of the employees' representation are fulfilled.

The first subparagraph shall not apply if, under the laws, regulations, administrative provisions or practice in the Member States, or by agreement with the representatives of the employees, the conditions necessary for the reappointment of the representatives of the employees or for the reconstitution of the representation of the employees are fulfilled.

Where the transferor is the subject of bankruptcy proceedings or any analogous insolvency proceedings which have been instituted with a view to the liquidation of the assets of the transferor and are under the supervision of a competent public authority (which may be an insolvency practitioner authorised by a competent public authority), Member States may take the necessary measures to ensure that the transferred employees are properly represented until the new election or designation or representatives of the employees.

If the undertaking, business or part of an undertaking or business does not preserve its autonomy, the Member States shall take the necessary measures to ensure that the employees transferred who were represented before the transfer continue to be properly represented during the period necessary for the reconstitution or reappointment of the representation of employees in accordance with national law or practice.

2. If the term of office of the representatives of the employees affected by the transfer expires as a result of the transfer, the representatives shall continue to enjoy the protection provided by the laws, regulations, administrative provisions or practice of the Member States.

Article 7

1. The transferor and the transferee shall be required to inform the representatives of their respective employees affected by a transfer of the following:

— the date or proposed date of the transfer,
— the reasons for the transfer,
— the legal, economic and social implications of the transfer for the employees,
— any measures envisaged in relation to the employees.

The transferor must give such information to the representatives of his employees in good time before the transfer is carried out.

The transferee must give such information to the representatives of his employees in good time, and in any event before his employees are directly affected by the transfer as regards their conditions of work and employment.

2. Where the transferor or the transferee envisages measures in relation to his employees, he shall consult the representatives of his employees in good time on such measures with a view to seeking agreement.

3. Member States whose laws, regulations or administrative provisions provide that representatives of the employees may have recourse to an arbitration board to obtain a decision on the measures to be taken in relation to employees may limit the obligations laid down in paragraphs 1 and 2 to cases where the transfer carried out gives rise to a change in the business likely to entail serious disadvantages for a considerable number of the employees.

The information and consultations shall cover at least the measures envisaged in relation to the employees.

The information must be provided and consultations take place in good time before the change in the business as referred to in the first subparagraph is effected.

4. The obligations laid down in this Article shall apply irrespective of whether the decision resulting in the transfer is taken by the employer or an undertaking controlling the employer.

In considering alleged breaches of the information and consultation requirements laid down by this Directive, the argument that such a breach occurred because the information was not provided by an undertaking controlling the employer shall not be accepted as an excuse.

5. Member States may limit the obligations laid down in paragraphs 1, 2 and 3 to undertakings or businesses which, in terms of the number of employees, meet the conditions for the election or nomination of a collegiate body representing the employees.

6. Member States shall provide that, where there are no representatives of the employees in an undertaking or business through no fault of their own, the employees concerned must be informed in advance of:
— the date or proposed date of the transfer,
— the reason for the transfer,
— the legal, economic and social implications of the transfer for the employees,
— any measures envisaged in relation to the employees.

Council Directive No. 2003/88
(O.J. 2003, L299/9)

concerning certain aspects of the organisation of working time

CHAPTER 1   SCOPE AND DEFINITIONS

Article 1 Purpose and scope
1. This Directive lays down minimum safety and health requirements for the organisation of working time.

2. This Directive applies to:
    (a) minimum periods of daily rest, weekly rest and annual leave, to breaks and maximum weekly working time; and
    (b) certain aspects of night work, shift work and patterns of work.

3. This Directive shall apply to all sectors of activity, both public and private, within the meaning of Article 2 of Directive 89/391/EEC, without prejudice to Articles 14, 17, 18 and 19 of this Directive.

This Directive shall not apply to seafarers, as defined in Directive 1999/63/EC without prejudice to Article 2(8) of this Directive.

4. The provisions of Directive 89/391/EEC are fully applicable to the matters referred to in paragraph 2, without prejudice to more stringent and/or specific provisions contained in this Directive.

Article 2   Definitions

For the purposes of this Directive, the following definitions shall apply:

1. 'working time' means any period during which the worker is working, at the employer's disposal and carrying out his activity or duties, in accordance with national laws and/or practice;

2. 'rest period' means any period which is not working time;

3. 'night time' means any period of not less than seven hours, as defined by national law, and which must include, in any case, the period between midnight and 5.00;

4. 'night worker' means:

   (a) on the one hand, any worker, who, during night time, works at least three hours of his daily working time as a normal course; and

   (b) on the other hand, any worker who is likely during night time to work a certain proportion of his annual working time, as defined at the choice of the Member State concerned:

      (i) by national legislation, following consultation with the two sides of industry; or

      (ii) by collective agreements or agreements concluded between the two sides of industry at national or regional level;

5. 'shift work' means any method of organising work in shifts whereby workers succeed each other at the same work stations according to a certain pattern, including a rotating pattern, and which may be continuous or discontinuous, entailing the need for workers to work at different times over a given period of days or weeks;

6. 'shift worker' means any worker whose work schedule is part of shift work;

7. 'mobile worker' means any worker employed as a member of travelling or flying personnel by an undertaking which operates transport services for passengers or goods by road, air or inland waterway;

8. 'offshore work' means work performed mainly on or from offshore installations (including drilling rigs), directly or indirectly in connection with the exploration, extraction or exploitation of mineral resources, including hydrocarbons, and diving in connection with such activities, whether performed from an offshore installation or a vessel;

9. 'adequate rest' means that workers have regular rest periods, the duration of which is expressed in units of time and which are sufficiently long and continuous to ensure that, as a result of fatigue or other irregular working patterns, they do not cause injury to themselves, to fellow workers or to others and that they do not damage their health, either in the short term or in the longer term.

CHAPTER 2   MINIMUM REST PERIODS—OTHER ASPECTS OF THE
ORGANISATION OF WORKING TIME

Article 3   Daily rest

Member States shall take the measures necessary to ensure that every worker is entitled to a minimum daily rest period of 11 consecutive hours per 24-hour period.

Article 4   Breaks

Member States shall take the measures necessary to ensure that, where the working day is longer than six hours, every worker is entitled to a rest break, the details of which, including duration and the terms on which it is granted, shall be laid down in collective agreements or agreements between the two sides of industry or, failing that, by national legislation.

Article 5   Weekly rest period

Member States shall take the measures necessary to ensure that, per each seven-day period, every worker is entitled to a minimum uninterrupted rest period of 24 hours plus the 11 hours' daily rest referred to in Article 3.

If objective, technical or work organisation conditions so justify, a minimum rest period of 24 hours may be applied.

Article 6   Maximum weekly working time

Member States shall take the measures necessary to ensure that, in keeping with the need to protect the safety and health of workers:

(a) the period of weekly working time is limited by means of laws, regulations or administrative provisions or by collective agreements or agreements between the two sides of industry;

(b) the average working time for each seven-day period, including overtime, does not exceed 48 hours.

Article 7   Annual leave

1. Member States shall take the measures necessary to ensure that every worker is entitled to paid annual leave of at least four weeks in accordance with the conditions for entitlement to, and granting of, such leave laid down by national legislation and/or practice.

2. The minimum period of paid annual leave may not be replaced by an allowance in lieu, except where the employment relationship is terminated.

CHAPTER 3   NIGHT WORK—SHIFT WORK—PATTERNS OF WORK

Article 8   Length of night work

Member States shall take the measures necessary to ensure that:

(a) normal hours of work for night workers do not exceed an average of eight hours in any 24-hour period;

(b) night workers whose work involves special hazards or heavy physical or mental strain do not work more than eight hours in any period of 24 hours during which they perform night work.

For the purposes of point (b), work involving special hazards or heavy physical or mental strain shall be defined by national legislation and/or practice or by collective agreements or agreements concluded between the two sides of industry, taking account of the specific effects and hazards of night work.

Article 9   Health assessment and transfer of night workers to day work

1. Member States shall take the measures necessary to ensure that:

(a) night workers are entitled to a free health assessment before their assignment and thereafter at regular intervals;

(b) night workers suffering from health problems recognised as being connected with the fact that they perform night work are transferred whenever possible to day work to which they are suited.

2. The free health assessment referred to in paragraph 1(a) must comply with medical confidentiality.

3. The free health assessment referred to in paragraph 1(a) may be conducted within the national health system.

Article 10   Guarantees for night-time working

Member States may make the work of certain categories of night workers subject to certain guarantees, under conditions laid down by national legislation and/or practice, in the case of workers who incur risks to their safety or health linked to night-time working.

Article 11   Notification of regular use of night workers

Member States shall take the measures necessary to ensure that an employer who regularly uses night workers brings this information to the attention of the competent authorities if they so request.

Article 12   Safety and health protection
Member States shall take the measures necessary to ensure that:
    (a) night workers and shift workers have safety and health protection appropriate to the nature of their work;
    (b) appropriate protection and prevention services or facilities with regard to the safety and health of night workers and shift workers are equivalent to those applicable to other workers and are available at all times.

Article 13   Pattern of work
Member States shall take the measures necessary to ensure that an employer who intends to organise work according to a certain pattern takes account of the general principle of adapting work to the worker, with a view, in particular, to alleviating monotonous work and work at a predetermined work-rate, depending on the type of activity, and of safety and health requirements, especially as regards breaks during working time.

CHAPTER 4   MISCELLANEOUS PROVISIONS

Article 14   More specific Community provisions
This Directive shall not apply where other Community instruments contain more specific requirements relating to the organisation of working time for certain occupations or occupational activities.

Article 15   More favourable provisions
This Directive shall not affect Member States' right to apply or introduce laws, regulations or administrative provisions more favourable to the protection of the safety and health of workers or to facilitate or permit the application of collective agreements or agreements concluded between the two sides of industry which are more favourable to the protection of the safety and health of workers.

Article 16   Reference periods
Member States may lay down:
    (a) for the application of Article 5 (weekly rest period), a reference period not exceeding 14 days;
    (b) for the application of Article 6 (maximum weekly working time), a reference period not exceeding four months.
The periods of paid annual leave, granted in accordance with Article 7, and the periods of sick leave shall not be included or shall be neutral in the calculation of the average;
    (c) for the application of Article 8 (length of night work), a reference period defined after consultation of the two sides of industry or by collective agreements or agreements concluded between the two sides of industry at national or regional level.
If the minimum weekly rest period of 24 hours required by Article 5 falls within that reference period, it shall not be included in the calculation of the average.

CHAPTER 5   DEROGATIONS AND EXCEPTIONS

Article 17   Derogations
    1. With due regard for the general principles of the protection of the safety and health of workers, Member States may derogate from Articles 3 to 6, 8 and 16 when, on account of the specific characteristics of the activity concerned, the duration of the working time is not measured and/or predetermined or can be determined by the workers themselves, and particularly in the case of:
    (a) managing executives or other persons with autonomous decision-taking powers;
    (b) family workers; or
    (c) workers officiating at religious ceremonies in churches and religious communities.

2. Derogations provided for in paragraphs 3, 4 and 5 may be adopted by means of laws, regulations or administrative provisions or by means of collective agreements or agreements between the two sides of industry provided that the workers concerned are afforded equivalent periods of compensatory rest or that, in exceptional cases in which it is not possible, for objective reasons, to grant such equivalent periods of compensatory rest, the workers concerned are afforded appropriate protection.

3. In accordance with paragraph 2 of this Article derogations may be made from Articles 3, 4, 5, 8 and 16:

(a) in the case of activities where the worker's place of work and his place of residence are distant from one another, including offshore work, or where the worker's different places of work are distant from one another;

(b) in the case of security and surveillance activities requiring a permanent presence in order to protect property and persons, particularly security guards and caretakers or security firms;

(c) in the case of activities involving the need for continuity of service or production, particularly:

(i) services relating to the reception, treatment and/or care provided by hospitals or similar establishments, including the activities of doctors in training, residential institutions and prisons;

(ii) dock or airport workers;

(iii) press, radio, television, cinematographic production, postal and telecommunications services, ambulance, fire and civil protection services;

(iv) gas, water and electricity production, transmission and distribution, household refuse collection and incineration plants;

(v) industries in which work cannot be interrupted on technical grounds;

(vi) research and development activities;

(vii) agriculture;

(viii) workers concerned with the carriage of passengers on regular urban transport services;

(d) where there is a foreseeable surge of activity, particularly in:

(i) agriculture;

(ii) tourism;

(iii) postal services;

(e) in the case of persons working in railway transport:

(i) whose activities are intermittent;

(ii) who spend their working time on board trains; or

(iii) whose activities are linked to transport timetables and to ensuring the continuity and regularity of traffic;

(f) in the circumstances described in Article 5(4) of Directive 89/391/EEC;

(g) in cases of accident or imminent risk of accident.

4. In accordance with paragraph 2 of this Article derogations may be made from Articles 3 and 5:

(a) in the case of shift work activities, each time the worker changes shift and cannot take daily and/or weekly rest periods between the end of one shift and the start of the next one;

(b) in the case of activities involving periods of work split up over the day, particularly those of cleaning staff.

5. In accordance with paragraph 2 of this Article, derogations may be made from Article 6 and Article 16(b), in the case of doctors in training, in accordance with the provisions set out in the second to the seventh subparagraphs of this paragraph.

With respect to Article 6 derogations referred to in the first subparagraph shall be permitted for a transitional period of five years from 1 August 2004.

Member States may have up to two more years, if necessary, to take account of difficulties in meeting the working time provisions with respect to their responsibilities for the organisation and delivery of health services and medical care. At least six months before the end of the transitional period, the Member State concerned shall inform the Commission giving its reasons, so that the Commission can give an opinion, after appropriate consultations, within the three months following receipt of such information. If the Member State does not follow the opinion of the Commission, it will justify its decision. The notification and justification of the Member State and the opinion of the Commission shall be published in the Official Journal of the European Union and forwarded to the European Parliament.

Member States may have an additional period of up to one year, if necessary, to take account of special difficulties in meeting the responsibilities referred to in the third subparagraph. They shall follow the procedure set out in that subparagraph.

Member States shall ensure that in no case will the number of weekly working hours exceed an average of 58 during the first three years of the transitional period, an average of 56 for the following two years and an average of 52 for any remaining period.

The employer shall consult the representatives of the employees in good time with a view to reaching an agreement, wherever possible, on the arrangements applying to the transitional period. Within the limits set out in the fifth subparagraph, such an agreement may cover:

(a) the average number of weekly hours of work during the transitional period; and

(b) the measures to be adopted to reduce weekly working hours to an average of 48 by the end of the transitional period.

With respect to Article 16(b) derogations referred to in the first subparagraph shall be permitted provided that the reference period does not exceed 12 months, during the first part of the transitional period specified in the fifth subparagraph, and six months thereafter.

Article 18   Derogations by collective agreements

Derogations may be made from Articles 3, 4, 5, 8 and 16 by means of collective agreements or agreements concluded between the two sides of industry at national or regional level or, in conformity with the rules laid down by them, by means of collective agreements or agreements concluded between the two sides of industry at a lower level.

Member States in which there is no statutory system ensuring the conclusion of collective agreements or agreements concluded between the two sides of industry at national or regional level, on the matters covered by this Directive, or those Member States in which there is a specific legislative framework for this purpose and within the limits thereof, may, in accordance with national legislation and/or practice, allow derogations from Articles 3, 4, 5, 8 and 16 by way of collective agreements or agreements concluded between the two sides of industry at the appropriate collective level.

The derogations provided for in the first and second subparagraphs shall be allowed on condition that equivalent compensating rest periods are granted to the workers concerned or, in exceptional cases where it is not possible for objective reasons to grant such periods, the workers concerned are afforded appropriate protection.

Member States may lay down rules:

(a) for the application of this Article by the two sides of industry; and

(b) for the extension of the provisions of collective agreements or agreements concluded in conformity with this Article to other workers in accordance with national legislation and/or practice.

Article 19   Limitations to derogations from reference periods

The option to derogate from Article 16(b), provided for in Article 17(3) and in Article 18, may not result in the establishment of a reference period exceeding six months.

However, Member States shall have the option, subject to compliance with the general principles relating to the protection of the safety and health of workers, of allowing, for objective or technical reasons or reasons concerning the organisation of work, collective agreements or agreements concluded between the two sides of industry to set reference periods in no event exceeding 12 months.

Before 23 November 2003, the Council shall, on the basis of a Commission proposal accompanied by an appraisal report, re-examine the provisions of this Article and decide what action to take.

Article 20   Mobile workers and offshore work

1. Articles 3, 4, 5 and 8 shall not apply to mobile workers.

Member States shall, however, take the necessary measures to ensure that such mobile workers are entitled to adequate rest, except in the circumstances laid down in Article 17(3)(f) and (g).

2. Subject to compliance with the general principles relating to the protection of the safety and health of workers, and provided that there is consultation of representatives of the employer and employees concerned and efforts to encourage all relevant forms of social dialogue, including negotiation if the parties so wish, Member States may, for objective or technical reasons or reasons concerning the organisation of work, extend the reference period referred to in Article 16(b) to 12 months in respect of workers who mainly perform offshore work.

3. Not later than 1 August 2005 the Commission shall, after consulting the Member States and management and labour at European level, review the operation of the provisions with regard to offshore workers from a health and safety perspective with a view to pre-senting, if need be, the appropriate modifications.

Article 21   [omitted]

Article 22   Miscellaneous provisions

1. A Member State shall have the option not to apply Article 6, while respecting the general principles of the protection of the safety and health of workers, and provided it takes the necessary measures to ensure that:

(a) no employer requires a worker to work more than 48 hours over a seven-day period, calculated as an average for the reference period referred to in Article 16(b), unless he has first obtained the worker's agreement to perform such work;

(b) no worker is subjected to any detriment by his employer because he is not willing to give his agreement to perform such work;

(c) the employer keeps up-to-date records of all workers who carry out such work;

(d) the records are placed at the disposal of the competent authorities, which may, for reasons connected with the safety and/or health of workers, prohibit or restrict the possibility of exceeding the maximum weekly working hours;

(e) the employer provides the competent authorities at their request with informa-tion on cases in which agreement has been given by workers to perform work exceeding 48 hours over a period of seven days, calculated as an average for the reference period referred to in Article 16(b).

Before 23 November 2003, the Council shall, on the basis of a Commission proposal accompanied by an appraisal report, re-examine the provisions of this paragraph and decide on what action to take.

2 and 3 [omitted]

PART V

International Obligations

European Convention for the Protection of Human Rights and Fundamental Freedoms

Article 9   Freedom of thought, conscience and religion

1. Everyone has the right to freedom of thought, conscience and religion; this right includes freedom to change his religion or belief and freedom, either alone or in community with others and in public or private, to manifest his religion or belief, in worship, teaching, practice and observance.

2. Freedom to manifest one's religion or beliefs shall be subject only to such limitations as are prescribed by law and are necessary in a democratic society in the interests of public safety, for the protection of public order, health or morals, or for the protection of the rights and freedoms of others.

Article 10   Freedom of expression

1. Everyone has the right to freedom of expression. This right shall include freedom to hold opinions and to receive and impart information and ideas without interference by public authority and regardless of frontiers. This Article shall not prevent States from requiring the licensing of broadcasting, television or cinema enterprises.

2. The exercise of these freedoms, since it carries with it duties and responsibilities, may be subject to such formalities, conditions, restrictions or penalties as are prescribed by law and are necessary in a democratic society, in the interests of national security, territorial integrity or public safety, for the prevention of disorder or crime, for the protection of health or morals, for the protection of the reputation or rights of others, for preventing the disclosure of information received in confidence, or for maintaining the authority and impartiality of the judiciary.

Article 11   Freedom of Assembly and Association

1. Everyone has the right to freedom of peaceful assembly and to freedom of association with others, including the right to form and to join trade unions for the protection of his interests.

2. No restrictions shall be placed on the exercise of these rights other than such as are prescribed by law and are necessary in a democratic society in the interests of national security or public safety, for the prevention of disorder or crime, for the protection of health or morals or for the protection of the rights and freedoms of others. This Article shall not prevent the imposition of lawful restrictions on the exercise of these rights by members of the armed forces, of the police or of the administration of the State.

Article 14   Prohibition of Discrimination

The enjoyment of the rights and freedoms set forth in this Convention shall be secured without discrimination on any ground such as sex, race, colour, language, religion, political or other opinion, national or social origin, association with a national minority, property, birth or other status.

European Social Charter
(Revised 1996)

[Note: the United Kingdom has not yet ratified the revised version]

Article 1   The right to work

With a view to ensuring the effective exercise of the right to work, the Contracting Parties undertake:

1. to accept as one of their primary aims and responsibilities the achievement and maintenance of as high and stable a level of employment as possible, with a view to the attainment of full employment;

2. to protect effectively the right of the worker to earn his living in an occupation freely entered upon;

3. to establish or maintain free employment services for all workers;

4. to provide or promote appropriate vocational guidance, training and rehabilitation.

Article 2   The right to just conditions of work

With a view to ensuring the effective exercise of the right to just conditions of work, the Parties undertake:

1. to provide for reasonable daily and weekly working hours, the working week to be progressively reduced to the extent that the increase of productivity and other relevant factors permit;

2. to provide for public holidays with pay;

3. to provide for a minimum of four weeks annual holiday with pay;

4. to eliminate risks in inherently dangerous or unhealthy occupations, and where it has not yet been possible to eliminate or reduce sufficiently these risks, to provide for either a reduction of working hours or additional paid holidays for workers engaged in such occupations;

5. to ensure a weekly rest period which shall, as far as possible, coincide with the day recognised by tradition or custom in the country or region concerned as a day of rest.

6. to ensure that workers are informed in written form, as soon as possible, and in any event not later than two months after the date of commencing their employment, of the essential aspects of the contract or employment relationship;

7. to ensure that workers performing night work benefit from measures which take account of the special nature of the work.

Article 3   The right to safe and healthy working conditions

With a view to ensuring the effective exercise of the right to safe and healthy working conditions, the Parties undertake, in consultation with employers' and workers' organisations:

1. to formulate, implement and periodically review a coherent national policy on occupational safety, occupational health and the working environment. The primary aim of this policy shall be to improve occupational safety and health and to prevent accidents and injury to health arising out of, linked with or occurring in the course of work, particularly by minimising the causes of hazards inherent in the working environment;

2. to issue safety and health regulations;

3. to provide for the enforcement of such regulations by measures of supervision;

4. to promote the progressive development of occupational health services for all workers with essentially preventive and advisory functions.

Article 4   The right to a fair remuneration

With a view to ensuring the effective exercise of the right to a fair remuneration, the Parties undertake:

1. to recognise the right of workers to a remuneration such as will give them and their families a decent standard of living;

2. to recognise the right of workers to an increased rate of remuneration for overtime work, subject to exceptions in particular cases;

3. to recognise the right of men and women workers to equal pay for work of equal value;

4. to recognise the right of all workers to a reasonable period of notice for termination of employment;

5. to permit deductions from wages only under conditions and to the extent prescribed by national laws or regulations or fixed by collective agreements or arbitration awards.

The exercise of these rights shall be achieved by freely concluded collective agreements, by statutory wage-fixing machinery, or by other means appropriate to national conditions.

Article 5 The right to organise

With a view to ensuring or promoting the freedom of workers and employers to form local, national or international organisations for the protection of their economic and social interests and to join those organisations, the Parties undertake that national law shall not be such as to impair, nor shall it be so applied as to impair, this freedom. The extent to which the guarantees provided for in this Article shall apply to the police shall be determined by national laws or regulations. The principle governing the application to the members of the armed forces of these guarantees and the extent to which they shall apply to persons in this category shall equally be determined by national laws or regulations.

Article 6 The right to bargain collectively

With a view to ensuring the effective exercise of the right to bargain collectively, the Parties undertake:

1. to promote joint consultation between workers and employers;

2. to promote, where necessary and appropriate, machinery for voluntary negotiations between employers or employers' organisations and workers' organisations, with a view to the regulation of terms and conditions of employment by means of collective agreements;

3. to promote the establishment and use of appropriate machinery for conciliation and voluntary arbitration for the settlement of labour disputes; and recognise:

4. the right of workers and employers to collective action in cases of conflicts of interest, including the right to strike, subject to obligations that might arise out of collective agreements previously entered into.

Article 7 The right of children and young persons to protection

With a view to ensuring the effective exercise of the right of children and young persons to protection, the Contracting Parties undertake:

1. to provide that the minimum age of admission to employment shall be 15 years, subject to exceptions for children employed in prescribed light work without harm to their health, morals or education;

2. to provide that a higher minimum age of admission to employment shall be 18 with respect to prescribed occupations regarded as dangerous or unhealthy;

3. to provide that persons who are still subject to compulsory education shall not be employed in such work as would deprive them of the full benefit of their education;

4. to provide that the working hours of persons under 18 years of age shall be limited in accordance with the needs of their development, and particularly with their need for vocational training;

5. to recognise the right of young workers and apprentices to a fair wage or other appropriate allowances;

6. to provide that the time spent by young persons in vocational training during the normal working hours with the consent of the employer shall be treated as forming part of the working day;

7. to provide that employed persons of under 18 years of age shall be entitled to a minimum of four weeks' annual holiday with pay;

8. to provide that persons under 18 years of age shall not be employed in night work with the exception of certain occupations provided for by national laws or regulations;

9. to provide that persons under 18 years of age employed in occupations prescribed by national laws or regulations shall be subject to regular medical control;

10. to ensure special protection against physical and moral dangers to which children and young persons are exposed, and particularly against those resulting directly or indirectly from their work.

Article 8   The right of employed women to protection of maternity
With a view to ensuring the effective exercise of the right of employed women to the protection of maternity, the Contracting Parties undertake:

1. to provide either by paid leave, by adequate social security benefits or by benefits from public funds for women to take leave before and after childbirth up to a total of at least fourteen weeks;

2. to consider it as unlawful for an employer to give a woman notice of dismissal during the period from the time when she notifies her employer that she is pregnant until the end of her maternity leave or to give her notice of dismissal at such a time that the notice would expire during such absence;

3. to provide that mothers who are nursing their infants shall be entitled to sufficient time off for this purpose;

4. to regulate the employment in night work of pregnant women, women who have recently given birth and women nursing their infants;

5. to prohibit the employment of pregnant women, women who have recently given birth or who are nursing their infants in underground mining and all other work which is unsuitable by reason of its dangerous, unhealthy or arduous nature and to take appropriate measures to protect the employment rights of these women.

Article 20   The right to equal opportunities and equal treatment in matters of employment and occupation without discrimination on the grounds of sex
1. With a view to ensuring the effective exercise of the right to equal opportunities and equal treatment in matters of employment and occupation without discrimination on the grounds of sex, the Parties undertake to recognise that right and to take appropriate measures to ensure or promote its application in the following fields:
   — access to employment, protection against dismissal and occupational resettlement;
   — vocational guidance, training, retraining and rehabilitation;
   — terms of employment and working conditions including remuneration;
   — career development including promotion.

Article 21   The right to information and consultation
1. With a view to ensuring the effective exercise of the right of workers to be informed and consulted within the undertaking, the Parties undertake to adopt or encourage measures enabling workers or their representatives, in accordance with national legislation and practice:
   (a) to be informed regularly or at the appropriate time and in a comprehensible way about the economic and financial situation of the undertaking employing them, on the understanding that the disclosure of certain information which could be prejudicial to the undertaking may be refused or subject to confidentiality; and
   (b) to be consulted in good time on proposed decisions which could substantially affect the interests of workers, particularly on those decisions which could have an important impact on the employment situation in the undertaking.

Article 22   The right to take part in the determination and improvement of the working conditions and working environment
1. With a view to ensuring the effective exercise of the right of workers to take part in the determination and improvement of the working conditions and working environment in the

undertaking, the Parties undertake to adopt or encourage measures enabling workers or their representatives, in accordance with national legislation and practice, to contribute:

(a) to the determination and the improvement of the working conditions, work organisation and working environment;

(b) to the protection of health and safety within the undertaking;

(c) to the organisation of social and socio-cultural services and facilities within the undertaking;

(d) to the supervision of the observance of regulations on these matters.

International Labour Organisation
Convention (No. 87) concerning Freedom of Association and Protection of the Right to Organise

PART I   FREEDOM OF ASSOCIATION

Article 1
Each Member of the International Labour Organisation for which this Convention is in force undertakes to give effect to the following provisions.

Article 2
Workers and employers, without distinction whatsoever, shall have the right to establish and, subject only to the rules of the organisation concerned, to join organisations of their own choosing without previous authorisation.

Article 3
1. Workers' and employers' organisations shall have the right to draw up their constitutions and rules, to elect their representatives in full freedom, to organise their administration and activities and to formulate their programmes.

2. The public authorities shall refrain from any interference which would restrict this right or impede the lawful exercise thereof.

Article 4
Workers' and employers' organisations shall not be liable to be dissolved or suspended by administrative authority.

Article 5
Workers' and employers' organisations shall have the right to establish and join federations and confederations and any such organisation, federation or confederation shall have the right to affiliate with international organisations of workers and employers.

Article 6
The provisions of Articles 2, 3 and 4 hereof apply to federations and confederations of workers' and employers' organisations.

Article 7
The acquisition of legal personality by workers' and employers' organisations, federations and confederations shall not be made subject to conditions of such a character as to restrict the application of the provisions of Articles 2, 3 and 4 hereof.

Article 8
1. In exercising the rights provided for in this Convention workers and employers and their respective organisations, like other persons or organised collectivities, shall respect the law of the land.

2. The law of the land shall not be such as to impair, nor shall it be so applied as to impair, the guarantees provided for in this Convention.

Article 9

1. The extent to which the guarantees provided for in this Convention shall apply to the armed forces and the police shall be determined by national laws or regulations.

2. In accordance with the principle set forth in paragraph 8 of Article 19 of the Constitution of the International Labour Organisation the ratification of this Convention by any Member shall not be deemed to affect any existing law, award, custom or agreement in virtue of which members of the armed forces or the police enjoy any right guaranteed by this Convention.

Article 10

In this Convention the term 'organisation' means any organisation of workers or of employers for furthering and defending the interests of workers or of employers.

PART II   PROTECTION OF THE RIGHT TO ORGANISE

Article 11

Each Member of the International Labour Organisation for which this Convention is in force undertakes to take all necessary and appropriate measures to ensure that workers and employers may exercise freely the right to organise.

International Labour Organisation
Convention (No. 98) concerning the Application of the Principles of the Right to Organise and to Bargain Collectively

Article 1

1. Workers shall enjoy adequate protection against acts of anti-union discrimination in respect of their employment.

2. Such protection shall apply more particularly in respect of acts calculated to—
   (a) make the employment of a worker subject to the condition that he shall not join a union or shall relinquish trade union membership;
   (b) cause the dismissal of or otherwise prejudice a worker by reason of union membership or because of participation in union activities outside working hours or, with the consent of the employer, within working hours.

Article 2

1. Workers' and employers' organisations shall enjoy adequate protection against any acts of interference by each other or each other's agents or members in their establishment, functioning or administration.

2. In particular, acts which are designed to promote the establishment of workers' organisations under the domination of employers or employers' organisations, or to support workers' organisations by financial or other means, with the object of placing such organisations under the control of employers or employers' organisations, shall be deemed to constitute acts of interference within the meaning of this Article.

Article 3

Machinery appropriate to national conditions shall be established, where necessary, for the purpose of ensuring respect for the right to organise as defined in the preceding Articles.

Article 4

Measures appropriate to national conditions shall be taken, where necessary, to encourage and promote the full development and utilisation of machinery for voluntary negotiation between employers or employers' organisations and workers' organisations, with a view to the regulation of terms and conditions of employment by means of collective agreements.

Article 5

1. The extent to which the guarantees provided for in this Convention shall apply to the armed forces and the police shall be determined by national laws or regulations.

2. In accordance with the principle set forth in paragraph 8 of Article 19 of the Constitution of the International Labour Organisation the ratification of this Convention by any Member shall not be deemed to affect any existing law, award, custom or agreement in virtue of which members of the armed forces or the police enjoy any right guaranteed by this Convention.

Article 6

This Convention does not deal with the position of public servants engaged in the administration of the State, nor shall it be construed as prejudicing their rights or status in any way.

INDEX

T